THE
PERSONALITY
PUZZLE

W · W · NORTON & COMPANY

NEW YORK · LONDON

THE
PERSONALITY
PUZZLE

David C. Funder
UNIVERSITY OF CALIFORNIA, RIVERSIDE

For my father

Copyright © 1997 by W. W. Norton & Company, Inc.

The text of this book is composed in Minion
with the display set in Matrix
Composition by University Graphics, Inc.
Manufacturing by Courier
Cover design by Andrew Newman
Cover illustration: *Icarus*, 1943, from "Jazz," by Henri Matisse, © 1996 Succession H. Matisse, Paris/Artists Rights Society (ARS), New York.

Photo credits: page 8, H. Armstrong Roberts, Inc.; page 56, © Kathryn McLaughlin Abbe and Frances McLaughlin Gill, 1980, from *Twins on Twins* (New York: Clarkson N. Potter, Inc., 1980); page 148, *Primal Source* © 1993 James Balog; page 198, adapted from Bem, *Psychological Review* 103 (1996): 321. Copyright 1996 by the American Psychological Association; page 202, courtesy Wide World Photos; page 282, © John Chiasson/Liaison International; page 334, *Untitled* © Carrie Mae Weems/P.P.O.W. Gallery.

Library of Congress Cataloging-in-Publication Data
Funder, David Charles.
    The personality puzzle / David C. Funder.
      p. cm.
    Includes bibliographical references and index.
    1. Personality. I. Title.
  BF698.F84   1996
  155.2—dc20   96-2140

ISBN 0-393-96993-2

W. W. Norton & Company, Inc., 500 Fifth Avenue, New York, N.Y. 10110
http://web.wwnorton.com
W. W. Norton & Company Ltd., 10 Coptic Street, London WC1A 1PU

1 2 3 4 5 6 7 8 9 0

Anybody in science, if there are enough anybodies, can find the answer—it's an Easter-egg hunt. That isn't the idea. The idea is: Can you ask the question in such a way as to facilitate the answer?
—Gerald Edelman

The first step is to measure whatever can easily be measured. That's OK as far as it goes. The second step is to pretend that whatever cannot easily be measured isn't very important. That's dangerous. The third step is to pretend that whatever cannot easily be measured doesn't exist. That's suicide.
—Daniel Yankelovich

There once was an entomologist who found a bug he couldn't classify—so he stepped on it.
—Ernest R. Hilgard

Interpretation is the revenge of the intellect upon art.
—Susan Sontag

CONTENTS IN BRIEF

PREFACE **xxiii**

1 THE STUDY OF THE PERSON 1

PART I

Research Methods 9

2 CLUES TO PERSONALITY: THE BASIC SOURCES OF DATA 11

3 PERSONALITY PSYCHOLOGY AS SCIENCE: RESEARCH METHODS 34

PART II

How People Differ: The Trait Approach 57

4 PERSONALITY TRAITS AND BEHAVIOR 59

5 PERSONALITY ASSESSMENT I: PERSONALITY TESTING AND ITS CONSEQUENCES 76

6 PERSONALITY ASSESSMENT II: PERSONALITY JUDGMENT IN DAILY LIFE 98

7 USING PERSONALITY TRAITS TO UNDERSTAND BEHAVIOR 118

PART III

Biological Approaches to Personality 149

8 ANATOMY, BIOCHEMISTRY, AND PERSONALITY 151

9 THE INHERITANCE OF PERSONALITY: BEHAVIORAL GENETICS AND EVOLUTIONARY THEORY 179

PART IV

The Hidden World of the Mind: The Psychoanalytic Approach 203

10 INTRODUCTION TO THE PSYCHOANALYTIC APPROACH 205
11 STRUCTURE AND DEVELOPMENT 216
12 DEFENSES AND SLIPS 240
13 PSYCHOANALYSIS AFTER FREUD 261

PART V

Experience and Awareness: Humanistic and Cross-Cultural Psychology 283

14 EXISTENCE, EXPERIENCE, AND FREE WILL: THE PHENOMENOLOGICAL APPROACH 285
15 CULTURAL VARIATION IN EXPERIENCE, BEHAVIOR, AND PERSONALITY 308

PART VI

Behavior and Thought: Behaviorist, Social Learning, and Cognitive Approaches 335

16 HOW THE WORLD CREATES WHO YOU ARE: BEHAVIORISM AND THE VIEW FROM OUTSIDE 337
17 MOTIVATION, THOUGHT, AND BEHAVIOR: THE SOCIAL LEARNING THEORIES 362
18 COGNITION AND PERSONALITY 382

19 LOOKING BACK AND LOOKING AHEAD 411

CONTENTS

PREFACE   xxiii

1 | THE STUDY OF THE PERSON   1

The Goal of Personality Psychology   1

Mission: Impossible   2
On Advantages as Disadvantages, and Vice Versa   3

The Plan of This Book   5

Pigeonholing vs. Appreciation of Individual
Differences   6

Summary   7

Part I

Research Methods 9

2 | CLUES TO PERSONALITY: THE BASIC SOURCES
OF DATA   11

Data Are Clues   11

Four Kinds of Clues   12

Life Outcomes: L Data   13
Ask Somebody Who Knows: I Data   15
Ask the Person Directly: S Data   21
Watch What the Person Does: T Data   25

Conclusion   32

Summary   33

3 | PERSONALITY PSYCHOLOGY AS SCIENCE:
RESEARCH METHODS   34

Psychology's Emphasis on Method   34

Scientific Education and Technical
Training   35

Quality of Data   36
Reliability   36
Validity   39
Generalizability   40

Correlational and Experimental Designs   44

Effect Sizes   46
Significance vs. Importance   46
Correlations   47
The Binomial Effect Size Display   49

Ethics   51
The Uses of Psychological Research   51
Truthfulness   52
Deception   52

Summary   54

Suggested Readings: Research Methods   55

Part II

How People Differ:
The Trait Approach   57

4 | PERSONALITY TRAITS AND BEHAVIOR   59

The Measurement of Individual
Differences   60

People Are Inconsistent   61

The Person-Situation Debate   62

Predictability   64
Situationism   69
Are Person Perceptions Erroneous?   73

The Bottom Line   74

Summary   74

5 | PERSONALITY ASSESSMENT I: PERSONALITY
TESTING AND ITS CONSEQUENCES 76

The Nature of Personality Assessment   76

The Business of Testing   78

Personality Tests   79

Projective Tests   80
Objective Tests   82

Methods of Objective Test
Construction   83

The Rational Method   83
The Factor Analytic Method   86
The Empirical Method   89
A Combination of Methods   93

Purposes of Personality Testing   93

Testing to Categorize People   93
Other Uses of Testing   96

Summary   97

6 | PERSONALITY ASSESSMENT II: PERSONALITY
JUDGMENT IN DAILY LIFE 98

Consequences of Lay Judgments of Personality 98

Everybody Who Knows You   99
Self-Judgments   103

The Accuracy of Lay Judgments of Personality 105

Criteria for Accuracy   106
Moderators of Accuracy   106
The Process of Accurate Judgment   114

Conclusion   116

Summary   116

7 | USING PERSONALITY TRAITS TO UNDERSTAND BEHAVIOR 118

The Many-Trait Approach   119

The California Q-Set   119
Delay of Gratification   121
Other Behaviors   125

The Single-Trait Approach   129

Authoritarianism   129
Conscientiousness   137
Self-Monitoring   138

The Essential-Trait Approach   143

Reducing the Many to a Few   143
The Big Five   144

Conclusion   146

Summary   146

Suggested Readings: The Trait Approach   147

Part III

Biological Approaches to Personality 149

8 | ANATOMY, BIOCHEMISTRY, AND
   PERSONALITY 151

The Anatomy and Function of the
Brain 151
The Reptilian Brain 151
The Paleomammalian Brain 152
The Neomammalian Brain 153
The Human Brain 155
Functions of the Brain 160
The Brain and Personality 167

The Biochemistry of Personality 167
Galen's Ancient Theory 167
Modern Research Complications 168
Neurotransmitters 169
Hormones 173

A Synthesis 176

Summary 177

9 | THE INHERITANCE OF PERSONALITY:
   BEHAVIORAL GENETICS AND EVOLUTIONARY
   THEORY 179

Behavioral Genetics 179
Calculating Heritabilities 180
Gene-Environment Interactions 186

Evolutionary Theory 187
Sex Differences in Mating Behavior 188

Objections and Responses   191

Will Biology Replace Psychology?   195

Putting It All Together: Sexual
Orientation   197

Summary   200

Suggested Readings: Biological
Approaches   201

Part IV

The Hidden World of the Mind:
The Psychoanalytic Approach   203

10 | INTRODUCTION TO THE PSYCHOANALYTIC
APPROACH   205

Psychic Determinism   205

Internal Structure   206

Mental Energy   206

Psychic Conflict   207

Unique Aspects of Psychoanalytic
Theory   207

Controversy   207
Distinct from Other Approaches   209
A Beautiful Theory   210
Psychoanalysis and Western Culture   211

Freud Himself   212

Freud and the English Department   214

Summary   215

II | STRUCTURE AND DEVELOPMENT 216

Life and Death 216

Psychological Development: "Follow the Money" 218

Oral Stage 219
Anal Stage 222
Phallic Stage 225
Genital Stage 227
Moving through Stages 229

The Structure of the Mind 231

The Id 231
The Ego 232
The Superego 233

Primary and Secondary Process Thinking 234

Consciousness 236

Psychoanalytic Therapy 237

Summary 238

12 | DEFENSES AND SLIPS 240

Anxiety and Defense 240

Sources of Anxiety 240
Defense Mechanisms 242

The Expression of Impulse 250

Parapraxes 251
Wit 254
Parapraxes vs. Wit 257

Psychoanalytic Theory: An Evaluation 257

Lack of Parsimony 258
Case Study Method 258

Poor Definitions 258
Untestability 259
Sexism 259
The Theory Is Valuable Anyway 260

Summary 260

13 | PSYCHOANALYSIS AFTER FREUD 261

Modern Reactions to Freud 261

Maintaining the Theory Inviolate 262
Interpreting Freud 262
Replacing Freud 263

Neo-Freudian Issues and Theorists 264

Inferiority and Compensation: Adler 266
The Collective Unconscious, Persona, and Personality: Jung 267
Feminine Psychology and Basic Anxiety: Horney 268
Psychosocial Development: Erikson 269
Where Have All the Neo-Freudian Theorists Gone? 272

Modern Psychoanalytic Research 272

Testing Psychoanalytic Hypotheses 273
Attachment and Romantic Love 275

The Future of Psychoanalysis 279

Summary 280

Suggested Readings: Psychoanalysis 281

Part V

Experience and Awareness: Humanistic and Cross-Cultural Psychology 283

14 | EXISTENCE, EXPERIENCE, AND FREE WILL: THE PHENOMENOLOGICAL APPROACH 285

A Humanistic Psychology 285

A Diverse Approach 286
Awareness Is Everything 287
Free Will 288
Understanding Others 288

Existentialism 289

Three Parts of Experience 289
"Thrown-ness" and Angst 290
Bad Faith 291
Authentic Existence 293

The Modern and More Cheerful Humanists 293

Existential Optimism: Rogers and Maslow 294
Personal Constructs: Kelly 297
Flow: Csikszentmihalyi 301

Humanistic Psychology Today 302

Conclusion 304

On Happiness 304
The Mystery of Experience 305
The Influence of the Phenomenological Approach 306

Summary 306

15 | CULTURAL VARIATION IN EXPERIENCE, BEHAVIOR, AND PERSONALITY 308

The Importance of Cross-Cultural Differences 308

Possible Limits on Generalizability 308
Cross-Cultural Conflict 309
Varieties of Human Experience 310

Difficulties of Cross-Cultural Research   311

Ethnocentrism   312

Outgroup Bias   313

Going Native, and Other Hazards   313

Three Approaches to Cross-Cultural Psychology   314

Ignoring Cross-Cultural Issues   314

Deconstructionism   315

The Comparative Cultural Approach   320

The Question of Origin   327

The Deconstructionist Dodge   327

The Ecological Approach   327

Implications of Cultural Psychology   329

The Culture and the Individual   329

Cultures and Values   329

Process and Content   330

The Universal Human Condition   331

Summary   332

Suggested Readings: Experience and Awareness   333

Part VI

Behavior and Thought: Behaviorist, Social Learning, and Cognitive Approaches   335

16 | HOW THE WORLD CREATES WHO YOU ARE: BEHAVIORISM AND THE VIEW FROM OUTSIDE   337

Functional Analysis   338

The Philosophical Roots of Behaviorism 339

Empiricism 339
Associationism 339
Hedonism and Utilitarianism 341

Three Kinds of Learning 343

Habituation 343
Classical Conditioning 344
Operant Conditioning 349
Classical and Operant Conditioning Compared 354

Punishment 355

How to Punish 357
Dangers of Punishment 358
The Bottom Line 360

Contributions and Shortcomings of Behaviorism 360

Summary 361

17 | MOTIVATION, THOUGHT, AND BEHAVIOR: THE SOCIAL LEARNING THEORIES 362

What Behaviorism Leaves Out 362

Dollard and Miller's Social Learning Theory 363

Motivation and Drives 365
Frustration and Aggression 366
Psychological Conflict 367
Defense Mechanisms 369

Rotter's Social Learning Theory 370

The Expectancy Value Theory of Decision Making 370
Adjustment and Maladjustment 374
Psychotherapy 376

Bandura's Social Learning Theory   376

Efficacy Expectations   377
Observational Learning   378
Reciprocal Determinism and the Self   379

Summary   380

18 | COGNITION AND PERSONALITY   382

The Roots of the Cognitive Approach   382

A General Cognitive Model   383

The Sensory/Perceptual Buffer   384
Short-Term Memory   387
Working Memory   389
The Movement from Short-Term to Long-Term Memory   390
Long-Term Memory   391

Cognitive Social Learning Theory: Mischel   396

Cognitive Person Variables   397
The Personality System   398
Cognitive vs. Trait Approaches   399

Social Intelligence: Cantor and Kihlstrom   401

Schemas   402
Goals   403
Strategies   404

A Cognitive Approach to Motivation: Dweck   405

Performance and Learning Goals   405
Entity and Incremental Theories   406
Research and Measurement   406
Entity and Incremental Theories Reconsidered   407

The Cognitive Approach and Its Intersections   408

Summary   409

Suggested Readings: Behavior and
Thought   410

---

19 | LOOKING BACK AND LOOKING AHEAD   411

The Different Approaches   411

Which One Is Right?   412
The Order of Approaches   412

Conclusions   414

No Single Perspective Accounts for Everything   414
You Probably Must Choose   415

The Future of Personality Psychology   416

Further Development of the Cognitive Approach   417
Renewed Attention to Emotion and Experience   417
Biology   418
Cross-Cultural Psychology   418
Integration of Personality, Social, and Cognitive Psychology   419

The Quest for Understanding   420

Summary   420

REFERENCES   421
GLOSSARY   441
NAME INDEX   451
SUBJECT INDEX   455

PREFACE

The way a personality course should be taught—and the way its textbook should be written—depends on its purpose. Therefore, any instructor or author needs to ask at the outset, what do I hope to accomplish? Several different answers are possible, all of them legitimate. Each implies a different approach to teaching and to textbook writing.

GOALS FOR A PERSONALITY COURSE

First, one might wish to ensure that one's students become deeply familiar with the classic theories of personality and learn to appreciate the history of and the intellectual connections between these theories. The course in personality is often treated as part of a liberal education, and sometimes even fits into a "great books" curriculum. This goal is well served by any of the hefty theoretical tomes that have been on the market for many years. But students sometimes end such a course with very little idea of what modern personality psychology is really all about.

A second, very different goal is to make sure one's students know all about the current activities of modern personality psychologists and the very latest research findings. The classic theories of personality are neglected, sometimes on the grounds that they are all false and only modern empirical research has any validity. (I have actually heard psychology professors say this.) Several recent books seem to have been written with this goal in mind.

But of course, the modern empirical literature is not an infallible source of eternal truths. Moreover, a field of personality that focuses exclusively on what modern personality psychologists do is limited to whatever topics current research happens to emphasize. I do not know that any of the answers psychology has provided are eternal, but some of the questions are. And some of these questions are neglected in modern research.

This book serves both of the goals just listed. It covers the main theories of personality and traces some relevant intellectual history. It also includes a fair amount of current research, including recent work on person perception, biology, and cross-cultural psychology.

But the ultimate goal of this book is very different. The goal that has driven the selection of its topics and its writing, above all others, is to convince the reader that personality psychology is worthwhile and exciting. Theory *and* research in personality contain much that is of intellectual interest, as well as many useful insights into real-life concerns. Moreover, it is important for personality psychology to continue to make progress. To the extent that, on the final page, the reader of this text ends up believing these things, this book will have accomplished what it set out to do.

PERSONALITY AND LIFE

To convince somebody new to the field that personality psychology is important, each basic approach must be taught in a form that is relevant not just to its historical antecedents or to current research, but to everyday life. Establishing this relevance is one thing I have tried to do more distinctively than anything else in this book. The result is a presentation that strays from the conventional versions of the basic approaches to personality in favor of a new and modern rendition of each.

This strategy is most obvious in the Freud chapters, where I present a psychoanalytic approach to personality that certainly stems from Freud but departs from orthodoxy in numerous ways and, in the end, may not really be Freud any more. Someone who wants to learn what Freud really said should read a different book. But someone who wants to see how some derivations from Freud's basic ideas can be presented in what I think is a fairly convincing contemporary context might find this book illuminating. Parallel comments could be made about the presentations of the other approaches.

One goal of this writing strategy is to make the book a little more interesting to read than some others in the same genre. The humorist Dave Barry once wrote a history of the United States that he touted as more interesting than any other because, he said, he left out all the boring parts. While I have not gone that far, I have freed myself of the obligation to cover topics just because they are there, or are traditional, or are covered in every other book. Instead of emphasizing precise historical documentation or exactly tracing the empirical origins of some ideas, I have focused on the meaning and relevance of those ideas.

TOPICS VS. THEORIES

In broadest outline, this book follows the traditional organization according to "theories" or "paradigms" (I call them "approaches"). It begins with a treatment of research methods, then considers the five basic approaches to personality: trait, biological, psychoanalytic, phenomenological, and behaviorist (in which I include social learning theory and cognitive approaches as important variants).

I am well aware that some of my colleagues believe this organization is outdated and should be replaced by a scheme that instead focuses on "topics" like aggression, or development, or the self. The differing ideas of the differing basic approaches presumably would be scattered across these topical chapters. The suggested model seems to be that of social psychology, which in its courses and textbooks almost always follows such a topical organization.

There are several reasons why a topical organization is a mistake for a personality text, however. A pragmatic reason is that the basic approaches are complex theoretical systems, and breaking all of them up across topics seems unlikely to yield a clear understanding of any of them. A more substantive reason is that, in my opinion, the topical approach of social psychology represents an intellectual deficit of that field, as compared with personality psychology, rather than any sort of advantage. Social psychology lacks even one organizing, theoretical approach with any scope, as far as I am aware; it organizes itself by topic because it must. Personality psychology, by contrast, has at least five approaches, each of which offers an organized way to cover a wide range of data and theory about human psychology.

A further reason became clearer as I worked on this book. In personality, a "topics" organization and a "basic approaches" organization are not, at a deep level, truly different. A consistent theme throughout this book is that the five basic approaches to personality are not different answers to the same question—they are different questions! To put this point another way, each of the basic approaches to personality has a few topics it addresses most centrally, and many others it ignores. The basic topics ignored by each tend to be central concerns of one or more of the others. As a result, a basic approaches organization *is* a topics organization, to a considerable degree, because each basic approach can be associated with a different basic topic:

individual differences = trait approach
biological influences = biological approach
psychodynamics and the unconscious = psychoanalytic approach
experience and awareness = phenomenological approach
(I include cross-cultural psychology here)
learning and behavior change = behavioral approach

I hope this organizational scheme makes this volume easy to use as a textbook in a personality course. It matches in broad outline the way in which most courses are now taught. Beyond that, it should not be hard for an instructor using this text to find places where she or he wishes to amplify, supplement, or disagree. For example, an instructor wishing to go beyond this text in her or his own lectures could talk in detail about any of the personality tests that are only mentioned here; or consider some of the neo-Freudians who in this book make a relatively brief appearance; or provide further detail on the cognitive approaches to personality that are so prominent in the modern literature.

The reader will also find that I present opinions in this book. An instructor who disagrees with some of these opinions—and surely nobody will agree with me on everything—will be able to put together compelling lectures about those disagreements. The result of this intellectual give-and-take between instructor and author could be, for the student, an exciting introduction to a facinating subject.

ACKNOWLEDGMENTS

It is with pleasure that I acknowledge some of the help I received with this project. First of all, my wife, Patti, has been a source of emotional support, clever ideas, and critical comments throughout the writing of this book. Her insights and her continued belief that psychology is not really a science (she was trained as a biologist) has helped to keep me on my toes.

Tiffany Wright, a graduate student at the University of California, Riverside, Chris Langston, a colleague, and Cathy Wick, my editor at Norton, read the entire second draft of this book and made many comments and suggestions, nearly all of which I followed. Paul Rozin read both the first and the second drafts, and his insights and ideas affected many parts of the presentation. His encouragement and consistent support have been even more important. Henry Gleitman provided helpful ideas and encouragement. Traci Nagle carefully, thoughtfully, and gracefully copyedited the final draft. Don Fusting, a former Norton editor, used the softest sell in the history of publishing to convince me to undertake this project in the first place. If not for him, this book would not exist.

I am also grateful for the useful comments provided by Diane S. Berry, Southern Methodist University; William K. Gabrenya, Florida Institute of Technology; D. Brett King, the University of Colorado, Boulder; Christopher Langston, Purdue University; Aaron L. Pincus, Pennsylvania State University; Joseph F. Rychlak, Loyola University of Chicago; Drew Westen, Harvard University; and Marvin Zuckerman, the University of Delaware.

Finally, I want to acknowledge the first person to read the first draft of this book all the way through. He made comments on nearly every page. Usually, they were notations like "what does this mean?" or "what are you talking about?" These invariably identified places where I had lapsed into incomprehensible jargon or otherwise failed to make sense. Sometimes his comments were just strong expressions of agreement or disagreement. Over the several years this project took to be completed, I never once had a conversation with him that did not include the question "how is the book coming along?" and some sort of suggestion that I really ought to be working faster. He looked forward to seeing this book in print, and didn't miss it by much. My father, Elvin Funder, died in August 1995, just as I was putting the finishing touches on the last chapters. I dedicate this book to him.

David C. Funder

Riverside, California
October 1995

CHAPTER I

THE STUDY OF THE PERSON

You may already have been told that psychology is not what you think it is. Some psychology professors delight in conveying this surprising news to their students on the first day of the term. Maybe you expect psychology to be about what people are thinking and feeling under the surface, these professors expound, maybe you think it's about sexuality, and dreams, and creativity, and aggression, and consciousness, and how people are different from one another, and interesting things like that. Wrong, they say. Psychology is about the precise manipulation of independent variables for the furtherance of compelling theoretical accounts of well-specified phenomena, such as how many milliseconds it takes to find a circle in a field of squares. If that makes psychology boring, well, that's just too bad. Science does not have to be interesting to be valuable.

Fortunately, most personality psychologists do not talk that way. This is because the study of *personality* comes pretty close to being what nonpsychologists intuitively expect psychology to be. The most common image that people have of psychologists, of course, is as clinical practitioners. Most personality psychologists are not practitioners, but their field of research comes closer to clinical concerns than any of the other areas of research in psychology. More important, personality psychologists have no excuse for being boring, because their field of study includes everything that makes psychology interesting.[1]

THE GOAL OF PERSONALITY PSYCHOLOGY

Personality refers to an individual's characteristic patterns of thought, emotion, and behavior, together with the psychological mechanisms—hidden or not—

---

[1]Thus, if you end up finding this book boring, it is all my fault. There is no reason it should be, given its subject matter.

behind those patterns. This definition means that among their colleagues in other subfields of psychology, those psychologists who study personality have a unique mandate: to explain *whole persons*. I am not claiming that personality psychologists always succeed at this job. But that *is* what they are supposed to be doing—putting the pieces of the puzzle contributed by the various other subfields of psychology, as well as by their own research, back into an integrated view of whole, functioning individuals in their social context.

Mission: Impossible

There is only one problem with this mission. It is impossible. In fact, this interesting mission is the source of personality psychology's biggest difficulty. If you try to understand everything about a person all at once you will immediately find yourself completely overwhelmed and your mind, instead of broadening, will be in danger of going blank.

The only way out, perhaps ironically, is to choose to limit what you look at. Rather than trying to account for everything at once, you must search for *patterns*—ways of tying together different kinds of observations. This search will require you to limit yourself to certain kinds of observations, certain kinds of patterns, and certain ways of thinking about these patterns. A systematic, self-imposed limitation of this sort is what I will call a **basic approach** (another commonly used term is "paradigm").

Some personality psychologists focus their efforts on the ways that people differ psychologically from one another and how these differences might be conceptualized and measured. They adhere to the **trait approach** (the reference here is to personality traits). Other psychologists try to understand personality in terms of basic biological mechanisms, such as anatomy, physiology, inheritance, and even evolutionary theory. They adhere to the **biological approach**. Another group of psychologists is primarily concerned with psychic energy, the workings of the unconscious mind, and the nature and resolution of internal mental conflict. These psychologists adhere to the **psychoanalytic approach**. Another group of psychologists is primarily concerned with our conscious experience of the world, the ways in which we might have free will, and the consequences of having free will. These psychologists adhere to the **phenomenological approach** (also called the humanistic approach).

Three other groups of psychologists see themselves as the experimental scientists of personality. They all follow variants of the **behavioristic approach**. Classical behaviorists focus tightly upon overt behavior and the ways in which it can be affected by rewards and punishments. A second and later subgroup of scientists attempts to draw inferences about mental processes, such as observation and self-evaluation, that determine how behaviors are learned and performed. This group adheres to the social learning approach, a direct outgrowth of classical behaviorism. A third and even more recent group uses behavioral observations to build rigorous theoretical models of how people process information. These theories, which grew directly out of social learning theory, focus on how the basic cognitive processes of perception, memory, and thought affect behavior and personality. These psychologists adhere to the cognitive approach.

These five approaches[2] do not really compete with one another; they address different questions about human psychology. An employer trying to decide who to hire, for instance, must compare different individuals. The employer's problem is addressed by the trait assessment approach. When a televangelist is arrested for soliciting prostitutes, questions might be raised about what is going on in his mind, both consciously and unconsciously. A psychoanalytic approach seems called for here. And a parent who is worried about aspects of a teenage child's behavior and how the parent's actions might make a difference probably needs a behavioral approach.

While each of the several approaches to personality psychology is quite good at handling its own key concerns, each also and rather disconcertingly tends to ignore the key concerns of all the other approaches. For example, the behaviorist approach has almost nothing to say about the unconscious processes of the mind; the psychoanalytic approach is notoriously ineffective at changing behavior, and so on. Doing one thing well, it seems, entails doing many other things poorly. (This has long been a basic principle of engineering.) For that reason, personality psychology needs to look at people from *all* of these directions and utilize *all* of these basic approaches.

On Advantages as Disadvantages, and Vice Versa

In the introduction to his novel, *Mother Night*, Kurt Vonnegut does his readers the unusual service of telling them the moral of the book they are about to read. "I don't think it's a marvelous moral," he writes, "I just happen to know what it is" (Vonnegut, 1966, p. v). My guess is that he hoped to save thousands of

---

[2]To reiterate and clarify where this number comes from, I am treating the social learning and cognitive approaches as subtypes of the behavioral approach. As will be apparent in Chapters 17 and 18, the social learning theories have obvious and direct ties to behaviorism, and cognitive approaches grew directly out of the social learning theories. This latter call was a close one, however: the cognitive approach comes close to meriting its own major category. As cognitive research continues to develop, this classification might eventually change. For now, however, I think the five basic approaches to personality are best categorized as trait, biological, psychoanalytic, phenomenological, and behavioral.

English classes thousands of hours of trying to figure out what the author "meant to say." (I doubt he succeeded.)[3]

As a writer I do not much resemble Vonnegut but I, too, think I know what the moral of my book is, or at least what one of its major themes will turn out to be: In life and in psychology, advantages and disadvantages have a way of being so tightly interconnected as to be inseparable. *Great strengths are usually great weaknesses, and surprisingly often the opposite is true as well.* Sometimes I enjoy calling this observation **Funder's First Law** (there will be several other such "laws" in this book). This first law applies to fields of research, to theories, and also to individual people.

Personality psychology provides an excellent example of Funder's First Law. As has been noted already, personality psychology's biggest advantage over other areas of psychology is that it has a broad mandate to account for the psychology of whole persons and to be relevant to real-life concerns. This mandate makes the study of personality more inclusive, interesting, important, and even more fun than it would be otherwise. But guess what? This mandate is also personality psychology's biggest problem. In the wrong hands it can lead research to be *over*inclusive, unfocused, or vague. Even in the best of hands, personality psychology can seem to fall far short of what it ought to accomplish. The challenge for a personality psychologist, then, is to maximize the advantages of the field's mandate for breadth, and to try to minimize the disadvantages, even though the two are related and therefore may be inseparable.

The same is true about the various approaches within personality psychology. Each is quite good at addressing certain topics, and extremely poor at addressing others. (Actually, each basic approach usually just ignores the topics it is not good at explaining.) But these two aspects of each approach go hand-in-hand; for example, behaviorism is so effective at changing behavior in part *because* it ignores everything else, whereas the reason the phenomenological approach gives such a nice account of free will is because it ignores how schedules of reinforcement can be shown to shape behavior. The good points come with—and are even sometimes a consequence of—the bad, and vice versa.

Think about your own strongest point as an individual. How is it a problem to you? Now think about your own weakest point. What are its benefits for you? Given the necessary tradeoffs, would you *really* like to lose all your "weaknesses," and keep all your "strengths"? Given the way your strengths and weaknesses are connected to and even grow out of each other, is this even possible?

Personality psychology is perpetually faced with a similar dilemma. If its scope were narrowed, the field would be more manageable and research would

---

[3]For the record, Vonnegut wrote that the moral of *Mother Night* is this: "We are what we pretend to be, so we must be careful about what we pretend to be" (p. v). Come to think of it, this would not be a bad moral for a psychology textbook.

become easier to do. But then the study of personality would lose much of what makes it distinctive, important, and interesting. Similarly, each basic approach to personality has made a more-or-less deliberate decision to ignore some aspects of human psychology; this is a heavy cost to pay, but it seems to be necessary in order for each approach to make progress in its chosen area.

THE PLAN OF THIS BOOK

This book begins at the beginning, with a brief introduction to and overview of personality psychology that you have almost finished reading. The next two chapters of this introductory section concern how personality psychologists do their research, and will be useful for understanding the material in the chapters that follow. Chapter 2 describes the different kinds of data, or information, that psychologists use to better understand personality, and discusses some of the advantages and disadvantages of each. The chapter's goal will be to burn the following sentence into your psyche: "There are no perfect indicators of personality, there are only clues, and clues are always ambiguous." Chapter 3 describes some of the ways these data can be analyzed and considers some issues particular to the analysis of personality data.

The second section of the book comprises four chapters that address how people are different from one another, the central concern of the trait assessment approach. Chapter 4 discusses the basic issue of whether differences between people are really important (hint: the answer is "yes"). Chapter 5 describes several ways in which such differences are measured by psychologists, the topic of "personality assessment." Chapter 6 carries that topic further by describing some research on how we all do personality assessment in our daily lives. Chapter 7 describes some examples of how personality traits have been used to understand behavior.

An exciting new direction in psychological research is emerging from rapid, modern advances in biology. These discoveries are beginning to be applied to the study of personality traits and human nature, and some of that research is surveyed in Chapters 8 and 9. Chapter 8 reviews current knowledge about how the architecture and physiology of the nervous system affect behavior and personality. Chapter 9 considers the possibility that personality is to some degree inherited, by looking at two branches of biology: behavioral genetics, which studies how parents might pass on personality traits to their offspring, and evolutionary biology, which tries to find the origins of human nature in the evolutionary history of the species.

The next four chapters consider the psychoanalytic approach closely identified with Sigmund Freud. Chapter 10 is a basic introduction to the psychoanalytic approach. Chapter 11 describes the elements of the structure of the mind and of psychological development, according to psychoanalytic theory. Chapter

12 describes how psychoanalytic theory addresses defense mechanisms, mistakes, and humor, and offers an evaluation of this perspective. Chapter 13 concludes the story of psychoanalysis by bringing it into the present day, with some consideration of the "neo-Freudians" (psychoanalysts who came after Freud himself) and modern research that is relevant to psychoanalytic ideas.

The next pair of chapters considers the topics of thought, experience, and existence. Chapter 14 describes how existential philosophy developed into an approach to psychology called "phenomenological" or "humanistic." The basic theme here is that the particular worldview or set of lenses through which you view reality is the central aspect of your personality. Chapter 15 takes this point one step further, by considering how individuals' personalities and worldviews—and maybe the whole notion of personality itself—may vary significantly across cultures. Like many people in our society, personality psychologists are becoming increasingly sensitive to cross-cultural issues; some of those are considered in Chapter 15.

The last three substantive chapters describe behaviorism and its modern-day descendants. About seventy years ago, several influential psychologists decided to focus upon what people (and animals) actually did rather than upon what was going on in the hidden recesses of their minds. The original psychologists who took this approach were the classical behaviorists, such as John Watson and B. F. Skinner. Behaviorism and some of its applications are described in Chapter 16. Over the latter decades of the twentieth century, three different derivative theories grew out of behaviorism—theories that were increasingly focused on social interaction and, even more, upon mental (cognitive) processes. Interestingly, all three were called "social learning theory." The social learning theories of Dollard and Miller, Rotter, and Bandura are described in Chapter 17. Over time, these theories became increasingly influenced by the rapidly developing separate field of cognitive psychology. The eventual result was a distinctively cognitive approach to personality psychology, which is an extremely active research area today. A basic approach to cognition and its application to personality is described in Chapter 18. Also surveyed in that chapter is some of the modern cognitive research on personality.

The final chapter in this book, Chapter 19, offers an overall evaluation of the different perspectives of personality psychology and does some crystal ball–gazing about the future of the field.

PIGEONHOLING VS. APPRECIATION OF INDIVIDUAL DIFFERENCES

Personality psychology tends to emphasize how individuals are different from one another. If one wanted to be pejorative, one could even say that personality psychology tends to categorize, or "pigeonhole," human beings. Some people are uncomfortable with this emphasis, perhaps because they find it implausible, undignified, or both.[4]

Other areas of psychology, by contrast, are more likely to treat all people as if they were the same, or nearly the same. Not only do the various experimental subfields of psychology, such as cognitive and social psychology, tend to ignore differences between people, but the statistical analyses that are central to their experimental research literally put individual differences into their "error" terms (see Chapter 3).

But here is yet another example of a potential disadvantage working to one's advantage (remember this process can work in either direction, according to Funder's First Law). Although the emphasis of personality psychology indeed often entails categorizing and labeling people, it also leads the field to be extraordinarily sensitive to the fact that people really *are* different from each other. We do not all like the same things, we are not all attracted to the same people (fortunately), nor do we all desire to enter the same occupation or pursue the same goals in life. This fact of individual differences is the starting place for all of personality psychology, and gives the field a distinctive and humanistic mission of appreciating the uniqueness of each individual.[5] People are different, and it is necessary as well as natural to wonder how and why.

Summary

Personality psychology's unique mission is to try to explain the psychological functioning of whole individuals. This is an impossible mission, however, so different approaches to personality must limit themselves in various ways. Personality psychology can be organized into five basic approaches: trait, biological, psychoanalytic, phenomenological, and behavioral. Each addresses certain aspects of human psychology quite well, and ignores others. The advantages and disadvantages of each approach seem inseparable. The book is grouped into five sections that survey each basic approach. Sometimes regarded as a demeaning attempt to pigeonhole people, personality psychology's real implication is an appreciation of the ways in which each individual is unique.

---

[4]I cannot help recalling here an old saw that there are two kinds of people in the world: those who think there are two kinds of people in the world, and those who don't.

[5]This is obviously true about the trait and psychoanalytic approaches to personality, which concentrate, respectively, on the quantitative measurement of individual differences and on individual psychological case studies. But, less obviously, it is also true (one could argue that it is especially true) of behaviorist approaches. The behaviorist approach sees the person as being the sum total of everything he or she has learned. For each individual, this learning history is unique. See Chapter 16.

PART I

Research Methods

A colleague of mine once was selecting the material to include in a psychology course she was about to teach. She decided to poll her students to find out what they wanted to learn. She listed all the standard topics in psychology she could think of. One topic scored so low in the poll it wasn't even funny. The all-time least favorite topic in psychology is . . . research methods.

This finding helps explain why students so often think their psychology professors are strange. Almost without exception, the people who are trained to do psychological research and who teach most college courses seem obsessed with the topic. Methods of research, including statistics, are emphasized, sometimes seemingly above all else, in course after course. As a result, students sometimes feel the real purpose of teaching research methods is to take a topic, psychology, that should be fun, and make it boring.

I think students are turned off by research methods in part because their teaching tends to be overly technical from the outset. Rules, procedures, and formulas sometimes are thrown at the student with wild abandon, and it is easy to lose sight of the whole point. So I hope to emphasize in the next two chapters that "research methods" is really not an obscure topic at all, and it is only natural that somebody who wants to learn more about psychology *should* be interested.

Let's imagine an acquaintance tells you he knows how to read minds—he has ESP. Would you be curious to find out whether he was telling the truth? Maybe not (what *does* it take to pique your interest?). But if you are, then the next question is, how would you find out? Maybe you can imagine a few procedures that might put his claim to the test. Maybe you would have him guess what playing card you are thinking of, for example. You might even keep track of the number of right and wrong answers he gives.

Suddenly, you are in the realm of research design. You have designed experiments and even (by writing down the number of right and wrong answers) ventured into the world of statistics! And all you are doing is applying common sense.

That is what research methods are really all about: the application of good sense to learn more about questions of interest. When we want to know something about behavior or about the mind that is not yet known, we need some procedures to follow. These procedures all begin with observation—we look at what we want to know about—and end with "data analysis," which just means we try to understand the observations we have recorded.

Chapter 2 presents a detailed account of the kinds of observations you can make to understand personality. These observations are all "data," and I will categorize them into four basic kinds, called L, I, S, and T data. Chapter 3 will summarize some concerns about the quality of data—their reliability, validity, and generalizability. Chapter 3 also addresses "research design," which is simply the plan for how one will go about gathering data. Finally, Chapter 3 will consider the issue of data analysis I believe to be the most important: how to interpret the "size" or strength of the results that your research has obtained.

CHAPTER

CLUES TO PERSONALITY: THE BASIC SOURCES OF DATA

An individual's personality is manifested by the characteristic way in which he or she thinks, feels, and behaves. An individual might be deeply afraid of certain things, or attracted to particular kinds of people, or obsessed with accomplishing some highly personal and idiosyncratic goals. Patterns of thought, emotion, and behavior such as these typically are complex, and may be revealed in many different areas of behavior and life. Therefore, when we try to learn about or measure personality we cannot base this endeavor on just one kind of information. We need many kinds.

This brings us to **Funder's Second Law**: *There are no perfect indicators of personality; there are only clues, and clues are always ambiguous.*

DATA ARE CLUES

The information that can be gathered about personality is best characterized as a set of clues. These clues are always ambiguous because an individual's personality is something that resides inside that individual. We can can never see it directly. We must *infer* both its existence and its nature, and inference is always uncertain.

Inferences about personality must be based upon its outward manifestations. These can include what a person does in daily life, how that person answers questions, or how he or she responds to certain situations set up in a laboratory. The clues can be almost anything, but the important thing to remember is that any one of them alone will *always* be ambiguous. The psychologist's task is to piece these clues together, much like pieces of a puzzle, into a convincing and useful portrait of the individual's personality.

In that sense, a psychologist trying to understand an individual's personality is a bit like a detective trying to solve a mystery: clues may abound, but the trick is to understand correctly what they mean. For example, a detective comes on the scene of a burglary and finds fingerprints on the windowsill and footprints in the flower bed outside the window. These are clues. The detective would be foolish not to pay attention to them. But, it might turn out that the fingerprints belong to the careless police officer who first arrived at the scene and the foot-prints belong to an innocent gardener. These possibilities are not reasons for the detective to ignore the clues, but they are reasons to be wary about their meaning.

The situation is similar for a personality psychologist. The psychologist might look at an individual's test scores, or his or her degree of success in daily living, or his or her responses to a laboratory assessment procedure. These are all clues about personality. The psychologist, like the detective, would be foolish not to gather as many of them as possible. Also like the detective, the psychologist should maintain a healthy skepticism about the possibility that some or all of them might be misleading.

But this skepticism should not go too far. It can sometimes be tempting to conclude that because one kind of clue might be uninformative or misleading, the clue should not be gathered at all. At different times, various psychologists have argued that self-report questionnaires, demographic data, peer's descrip-tions of personality, "projective" personality tests, summaries of clinical cases, or laboratory assessment procedures should never be used. The reason given? The method can produce misleading results.

No competent detective would think this way. You gather all the clues you can. Any of them might be misleading; on a bad day, they all might be. This is no excuse to not gather them. The only alternative to gathering information that might be misleading is to gather no information. That is not progress.

Funder's Third Law, then, is this: *Something beats nothing, two times out of three.*

FOUR KINDS OF CLUES

There are four general kinds of clues one can use to try to understand person-ality. Each can provide important information but, equally important, each has shortcomings, as well. The advantages and shortcomings are probably insepa-rable (which is no surprise, if you remember Funder's First Law). Before we begin, it is worth emphasizing once again that all of these clues are important and useful, but none is perfect. The imperfections are inevitable and are not a reason to ignore any of these sources of information. Instead, they are the reason you need all of them.

The principle behind the four clues is this: To find out what a person is like, you can do any of four different things: (1) You can see how the person is faring in life, (2) you can ask his or her acquaintances for their opinions, (3) you can ask the person in question for his or her *own* opinions, or (4) you can watch, as directly as you can, what the person actually does. Clues of these four types can be called L, I , S, and T data (notice the acronym, LIST).[1] As we shall see, each of them is potentially informative about personality, and each is potentially misleading.

Life Outcomes: L Data

Have you ever been arrested? Have you graduated from high school? Are you married? How many times have you been hospitalized? Are you employed? What is your annual income? The answers to questions like these constitute L or "life" data. **L data** are more or less easily verifiable, concrete, real-life outcomes of possible psychological significance. This type of data can be obtained from archival records such as a police blotter, a medical file, or a tax return, or by asking the subject directly. As information about human personality, L data have two advantages and one big disadvantage.

ADVANTAGE: INTRINSIC IMPORTANCE

The first reason L data are important is that often they constitute exactly what the psychologist needs to know. To an applied psychologist working as a parole officer, a social worker, a school counselor, or a medical researcher, L data are the justification for his or her professional existence. These professionals are supposed to predict and even influence someone's criminal behavior, employment status, success in school, or health. The goal of every applied psychologist is to have a positive effect on the real-life outcomes of his or her clients. Those real-life outcomes are L data.

ADVANTAGE: PSYCHOLOGICAL RELEVANCE

The second reason L data are important is that they are in many cases strongly affected by and uniquely informative about psychological variables. Some people have a psychological makeup that makes them more likely than others to engage in criminal behavior. Other psychological attributes, such as a certain amount of conscientiousness, are necessary to hold a job for any length of time or to graduate from school. An increasing amount of research is showing that a person's personality can have an important effect on his or her health (e.g., Friedman, Hall, & Harris, 1985).

---

[1] The definitions I shall give for these kinds of data are based upon but do not exactly follow a scheme developed by Block and Block (1980), which is itself an adaptation of another, still earlier formulation by Cattell (1957).

Clinical psychologists have long believed that a simple bit of L data, being never-married at age forty, is a fairly reliable marker of psychopathology. That is to say, people who reach the age of 40 having never married are more likely to exhibit one or more forms of mental illness than are those that have been married at least once by then. However, one must be careful with this little nugget of psychological lore. Lots of people who are unmarried at age forty are *not* mentally ill. It is also important to realize that mental illness is quite rare among both married and unmarried forty-year-olds. It just seems to be *less* rare among the unmarried ones. Moreover, there are many reasons besides mental illness why one might be unmarried at forty, such as working all day in a single-sex workplace, being economically unable to support a family, or simply having given other goals a higher priority than that given to finding a spouse.

This observation is true about the other varieties of L data as well; they are often affected by many factors that are *not* psychological. A person's criminal behavior is affected to an important degree by his or her neighborhood and degree of economic opportunity. During a recession, many people lose their jobs for reasons that have nothing to do with their degree of conscientiousness or any other psychological attribute. Whether one graduates from school may depend upon finances rather than dedication. Your health might be affected by your mental outlook, but it is also a function of sanitation, exposure to toxins, and the availability of vaccines, among other things.

DISADVANTAGE: MULTI-DETERMINATION

These observations bring us directly to the biggest disadvantage of L data: they are sometimes not even slightly informative about psychological attributes. Frequently, L data are affected by too many other things to tell us much, by themselves, about a person's psychology.

This disadvantage has an important implication: If your business is to predict L data from an understanding of a person's psychology, no matter how good you are at your job, your chances of success are severely limited. No matter how well you understand an individual's psychological makeup, your ability to predict his or her criminal behavior, employment status, school graduation, health, marriage, or anything else will be constrained by the degree to which any of these outcomes is affected by the individual's personality in the first place.

This fact needs to be kept in mind more often. Psychologists who have the difficult job of trying to predict L data are often criticized severely for their limited success, and they are sometimes even more severe in their criticism of themselves. But even in the absolute best case, a psychologist can only predict something to the degree it is psychologically caused, and L data often are psychologically caused only to a small degree. A psychologist who attains *any* degree of success at predicting criminality, employment, school performance, health, or marriage has accomplished something rather remarkable.

Ask Somebody Who Knows: I Data

A second way to learn about an individual's personality is to gather the opinions of the people who know that person well in daily life. *I* stands for "informant"; **I data** are judgments, by knowledgeable human informants, of general attributes of the individual's personality, such as traits. My own research usually focuses on college students. To gather information about the personalities of these students, I ask each to provide the names and phone numbers of the two people on campus who know him or her the best. These people are then called and asked to come to the lab to describe the student's personality. These informants are asked questions such as "On a nine-point scale, how dominant, sociable, aggressive, or shy is your acquaintance?" The numbers yielded by judgments like these constitute I data.

When I say that these informants are knowledgeable, I mean that they know well the person they are judging. The informants might be the individual's acquaintances from daily life (as in my own research) or they might be clinical psychologists who have worked with the individual for an extended period of time. The key aspect of the informants' knowledgeableness is that they know the person well, not that they have a great deal of formal knowledge about psychology—usually they do not. Moreover, they do not need it; usually close acquaintanceship paired with common sense is enough to allow people to make judgments of each other with impressive accuracy (Funder, 1993).

Another important element of the definition is that I data are **judgments**; they derive from somebody watching somebody else in whatever contexts they happen to have encountered them, and then rendering a general opinion—e.g., how dominant the person is—on the basis of such observation. In that sense, I data are judgmental and irreducibly human.[2]

As a source of information for understanding personality, I data have four advantages and three disadvantages.

ADVANTAGE: LARGE AMOUNT OF INFORMATION

An acquaintance who is providing a description of someone else's personality has the ability, in principle, to base that description upon hundreds of behaviors in dozens of situations. The typical informant in my own research is a college roommate. This person would have observed the "target" of his or her judgment working, relaxing, interacting with a boyfriend or girlfriend, reacting to an "A"

---

[2]In other accounts this type of data is often called *O* for "observer" data. To avoid confusing this type of data with T data (which are direct observations of behavior), and to highlight that it comprises an informant's judgments, I have changed the label to *I* or "informants'" data.

grade, receiving medical school rejection letters, and so on. Such behaviors-in-context are not only commonly observed by acquaintances of a subject, they are also very important. A clinical psychologist providing I data may have many fewer observations to go on—that is why, in my own work, I generally prefer the judgments of well-acquainted lay persons to less-acquainted professionals. That is not to say that clinical psychologists can never provide good I data; they may have more behavioral observations on which to base their judgments than could reasonably be included in any other form of data. For example, a clinician might have observed the individual during hundreds of hours of therapy.

The first good thing about I data, therefore, is that they can be based on an extraordinarily large amount of behavioral observation.

ADVANTAGE: REAL-WORLD BASIS

The second advantage of I data is that they are derived from the observation of behavior in real life. Much of the other information about people that psychologists use is not; psychologists often base their conclusions on information that comes from contrived tests of one kind or another, or on the observation of behavior in carefully constructed and controlled environments. The fact that I data ultimately derive from behaviors performed in real contexts may give I data a better chance of being relevant to aspects of personality that affect important outcomes in life.

ADVANTAGE: COMMON SENSE

Recall that I data are not simply counts or mechanical combinations of the behaviors the informant has seen; they comprise the informant's judgments about what the behaviors mean, in general, about the individual's personality. A third advantage of I data derives from this basis in human judgment. In the final analysis, I data are distillations of behavioral observations that are filtered through the informant's common sense. This fact allows I data to take account of the context and the intention of behavior to a degree that no other source of information about people can equal.

An informant with ordinary common sense will take into account two contexts when turning an observation of behavior into a judgment of personality (Funder, 1991). The first kind of context is the immediate situation. The psychological meaning of an aggressive behavior, for example, can change radically as a function of the situation that prompted it. It makes a difference whether you screamed and yelled at somebody who accidentally bumped you in a crowded elevator, or at somebody who deliberately rammed your car in a parking lot. And, if you see an acquaintance crying, you will—appropriately—draw different conclusions about his or her personality depending on whether the crying was caused by the death of a close friend or by the fact that it is raining and your acquaintance was hoping to play Ultimate Frisbee today.

A second kind of context is provided by the *prior* behaviors an informant may know the individual in question to have performed. Imagine that you see an acquaintance give a lavish gift to his or her worst enemy. Your interpretation of the meaning of this behavior may (and should) vary depending upon whether this acquaintance is someone who, in the past, has been consistently generous, or someone who has been consistently sneaky, manipulative, and Machiavellian. In the first case, the gift may be a sincere peace offering. In the second case, there are grounds for suspecting that the gift may be part of some sinister, manipulative scheme.

Or say your acquaintance is upset after an argument with a friend. Your interpretation of this reaction, and even your conclusion about how serious the argument was, depends upon whether you know this acquaintance to be some-one who is easily upset, as opposed to someone who tends to be disturbed only under extreme circumstances.

It is a complex matter to apply information about these two kinds of con-texts to the judgment of personality. The science of psychology has not even come close to developing a formal set of rules, procedures, or computer pro-grams for interpreting behavioral observations in this manner, and is unlikely to do so anytime soon. The considerations are just too complex; too many possible situational and contextual variations interact with the implications of too many different kinds of behavior. And no catalog of these variations exists. Yet it is not as difficult for a human judge. The intuitions provided by ordinary common sense perform this kind of adjustment easily, naturally, and almost automatically.

ADVANTAGE: CAUSAL FORCE

The fourth consideration that makes I data important for understanding per-sonality is quite different from the other three. Because I data are, in a sense, a reflection of the social world of the individual being described—they represent opinions of people who interact with him or her daily—they have an importance that goes beyond their value as a description of the person. They are the person's reputation and, as the cliché goes, your reputation is your most important pos-session (Hogan, 1992).

The opinions that others have of your personality greatly affect both your opportunities and expectancies. If a person who is considering hiring you be-lieves you to be competent and conscientious, you are much more likely to enjoy the opportunity of getting the job than you would be if that person thought you did not have those qualities. This will be true quite aside from how competent and conscientious you really are. Similarly, if someone believes you to be honest he or she will be more likely to lend you money than if he or she believes otherwise. Your actual honesty is a separate matter. And, if you strike people who meet you as warm and friendly, you will develop more friendships than you would if you appeared cold and aloof. Again, these appearances may be false and unfair, but their consequences will nonetheless be important.

Moreover, there is evidence—considered in Chapter 6—that to some degree we become the people others expect us to be. If others for some reason expect us to be sociable, aloof, or even intelligent, we may tend to become just that! This is called the **expectancy effect**, and it provides another reason to care what others think of you.

Now consider some disadvantages of I data as sources of information about personality.

DISADVANTAGE: LIMITED AMOUNT OF INFORMATION

The first disadvantage of I data is the reciprocal of the first advantage considered above. Although the acquaintance who might be a source for I data has seen your behavior in a large number and variety of situations, he or she still has not been with you *all* of the time. There is a good deal about you that even your closest friends do not know. Their knowledge is limited in two ways.

The first limitation is that there is a sense in which each of us lives inside a series of separate compartments, and each of those compartments contains different people. For instance, much of your life is probably spent at work or at school, and within each of those environments are numerous individuals whom you might see quite frequently there, but no place else. When you go home you see a different group of people, at church or in a club still another group, and so forth. The interesting psychological fact is that you may be a very different person in each of these different environments. The stern and disciplined boss might act entirely differently with her children, the demure churchgoer on Sunday morning might be a party animal on Friday night, and so forth.

One telling example concerns an experience that is typical of college students. When you go away from your parents' home to attend college, a drastic change occurs in your social environment. The essence of the change is not so much that college towns are unique places, though they are to some extent, but that nearly everybody in this new environment is a stranger. You are suddenly surrounded by a large number of people of about the same age who have no pre-existing knowledge of you; they do not know (yet) whether you are the class clown or a workaholic or a jock or a preppy or an artist. (Joining the military can result in a similar situation.)

This can be a disorienting but also extremely liberating experience, especially if you have lived for a long time in a small town with the same group of people. You are free of the expectations of others and you have an opportunity to design a whole new personality for yourself. Many students do just that, trying out new identities that have long been latent within their characters, in front of a new audience of peers who do not know that they are seeing something new. The students who avail themselves of this opportunity learn at least as much from the experience as from any of their classes.

Now consider the first visit home. In many cases, the person who comes home for winter break seems very different from the one who left in August. The parents and perhaps even the student's hometown friends become frustrated and angry when they try to deal in their accustomed way with someone who no longer fits their image of him or her; the student is equally frustrated and perhaps also anxious about the stability of his or her new identity among people with old expectations. Although this experience can be traumatic, the personality experimentation and growth that causes it is probably a good thing. If parents, friends, and the student are all patient, they can eventually get used to the "new you." For our purposes, the point to be aware of is that neither a description of the student's personality provided by hometown friends and parents nor the description drawn by college friends will tell the whole story of what that student is really like.

Another example of the complexities introduced by the compartmentalization of our lives concerns what happens when people who have adjusted to one identity, developed in and adapted to one life environment, confront the same person in a different environment where he or she may have developed a very different identity. You may be a conscientious and reliable employee much appreciated by your boss, but you will probably be upset if you suddenly encounter this boss at a wild, Friday night party where you are dancing with a lampshade on your head. At work seeing your boss is not a problem, but at that party, what do you do? In general, we are more comfortable if the people who inhabit the compartments of our lives stay put and do not cross over into compartments in which they do not belong.

Occasionally, I am with my seven- and nine-year-old daughters at the supermarket, contemplating the current sale on breakfast cereal, when I realize I am standing next to one of my university students. Although in general I like my students, I think this kind of encounter is mildly upsetting for us both. At best we will exchange awkward greetings; more often we will simply pretend not to have seen each other.

Why? Is either of us really so ashamed to be seen in the supermarket? No, but at the university both of us have well-defined roles that we know how to perform. I know how to relate to a student; most students know how to act with a professor. At the supermarket these roles are irrelevant, so neither of us knows quite how to act.

In some cases boundary violation can be upsetting. Once my wife and I hired a babysitter and set out for a romantic dinner. When we arrived at the restaurant, the hostess who seated us was one of my wife's students, who happened to have failed one of her quizzes that very afternoon. Another of my wife's students was sitting at the next table. The evening amounted to less than we had hoped. On another occasion, I was at the university gym, taking a shower. At the next spigot, similarly soaped up, was one of my students. "Dr. Funder," he said, "would it be a problem if I handed in my paper a week late?"

The point here is that we are to a certain degree different people in different environments. I am not exactly the same person in the classroom as I am at the gym—though surely there is some resemblance—nor are students always as studious as they appear in the lecture hall. Any acquaintance who might provide I data is likely to know you in one or, at best, a few of your different environmental compartments. To the extent that you are a different person in these different compartments, the I data provided by any one person will have limited validity as a description of what you are like in general.

The second limitation in even a close acquaintance's knowledge of you is that some of your life is private in a deep sense. We all have an inner mental life that most of us share sparingly if at all. We all have private fantasies, fears, hopes, and dreams. These are important facts about our personality, but can be reflected in I data only to the extent that we have chosen to share them with somebody. I data provide a view of personality from the outside; information about the inner psychology of thoughts, emotions, and experience must be obtained in some other manner (McCrae, 1994).

DISADVANTAGE: BIAS

Because I data consist of acquaintances' and other informants' judgments of your personality, they can be profoundly affected by whatever biases these informants may have about the person they are judging. In my own research, as I mentioned, I try to find the two available people who know the person best. But there are potential pitfalls in this practice. Perhaps the person I call, unbeknownst to me and to the subject, does not like or even detests the person he or she is being recruited to describe. On the other hand, perhaps he or she is in love with the subject! Perhaps the informant is in competition with the subject for some prize or job—in college this is quite common. Detesting, loving, or competing with someone can do great damage to your ability to judge him or her accurately. For this reason, one should always get at least two informants whenever possible. This practice does not solve the problem of potential bias, but it does help.

Biases of a more general type are also potentially important. Perhaps the subject is a member of a minority racial group and the informant is a racist. Perhaps the informant is a sexist who has strong ideas about what all women are like. If you are a psychology student, you may have experienced another kind of bias. Your acquaintances might have ideas about your personality, based on their knowledge that you are a "psych major." If you are from an area where few people go to college, you may find that people have an image of you largely based on the fact that you are in college.

All of these sources of bias, both personal and more general, can affect the judgments that constitute I data and make them less than a royal road to truth about personality.

DISADVANTAGE: ERROR

Judgments of personality by informants not only might be biased, they might simply be mistaken. The previous section proposed that I data provided by a close acquaintance can be based, in principle, on the observation of hundreds of behaviors in dozens of situational contexts. But that is *in principle*. What happens in practice may be a different matter, because no informant can remember everything. The capacity of human memory is remarkable but it is neither infinite nor perfect. Therefore, an informant's judgment is based on what he or she happens to remember about the person being described, and that will necessarily be less than everything that might be relevant.

Behaviors that are extreme, unusual, or emotionally arousing are particularly likely to stick in memory (Tversky & Kahneman, 1973). This fact could have important consequences for I data. An informant judging an acquaintance might have a tendency to remember more clearly the fistfight his or her acquaintance got involved in (once in four years), or the time he or she got drunk (for the first and only time), or how he or she accidentally knocked a bowl of guacamole dip onto white carpeting (perhaps an unusual act by a normally graceful person). If the behaviors that one performs consistently, day in and day out, are those that are most informative about personality, then this tendency by informants to remember the unusual or dramatic is likely to lead to judgments that are less accurate than they could be.

Ask the Person Directly: S Data

Another way you can find out what somebody is like is simply to ask him or her. **S data** are self-judgments. Using the same kinds of trait terms that constitute I data, people can be asked to provide judgments of their own personalities. The person simply tells you the degree to which he or she is dominant, or friendly, or conscientious. This might be done on a nine-point scale, where the person indicates a number from 1 (I am not at all dominant) to 9 (I am very dominant). Or, the procedure might be even simpler: The person might be read a statement such as "I usually dominate the discussions I have with others" and then respond "true" or "false." The principle behind the use of S data is that the world's best expert about your personality is very probably *you*.

It is important to understand that, like I data, there is nothing complicated about S data. S data are simple because the psychologist does not interpret what the subject says about himself or herself, or ask about one thing in order to find out about something else. The questionnaires typically used to gather S data are

face valid—they are intended to measure what they actually seem to measure, on their face.

For instance, right here and now you could make up an S data personality questionnaire. How about a new "friendliness" scale? You might include items such as "I really like most people" (to be answered true or false, a true answer assumed to reflect friendliness), "I go to many parties," and "I think people are horrible and mean" (here answering "false" would raise one's friendliness score). There is nothing tricky about a scale like this; the more ways in which the subject describes himself or herself as friendly, the higher a friendliness score that person earns. In essence, all this questionnaire really asks, over and over, in various phrasings, is, "are you a friendly person?"

Another kind of S data can be obtained by asking subjects more open-ended questions. For example, one current research project asks subjects to list, on a blank sheet of paper, their "personal strivings." These are defined as "objectives you are typically trying to accomplish or attain." Some of the strivings college students have reported include "make my mother proud of me," "be honest in my speech and behavior," and "enjoy life." These responses all constitute S data because they are the subject's own direct, undisguised descriptions of goals he or she trying to accomplish (Emmons & King, 1988; Emmons & McAdams, 1991).

By far, S data are the most frequently used basis for personality assessment. Not only are the questionnaires in *Self* magazine and *Cosmopolitan* (such as "Rate your love potential!") S data, but so are most of the questionnaires used by personality researchers, although the latter are usually more careful in their methods of test construction and validation. The reason for the widespread use of S data is obvious: there is no easier and less expensive way to gather so much information about people. If you want S data on five hundred people, all you have to do is print five hundred questionnaires, pass them out to an Introductory Psychology class, and then collect them.

As a source of information for understanding personality, S data have three advantages and three disadvantages.

ADVANTAGE: BEST EXPERT

Recall that an important advantage of I data was that the close acquaintances who often provide such data have wide experience with the individual they are judging, and perhaps have observed him or her performing thousands of different behaviors in real life. With S data this advantage is even greater, in two ways.

First, while a close acquaintance might be with you in *many* situations in your life, you are present in *all* of them. In the 1960s, many young adults owned a book called the *Whole Earth Catalog*, throughout the margins of which were sprinkled small aphorisms. My favorite read, "Wherever you go, there you are."

This aphorism describes an important advantage of S data. We live our lives in compartments and most of our acquaintances see us only within one or at most a few of these compartments. The only person on earth in a position to know how you act at home, and at school, and at work, and with your enemies, and with your friends, and with your parents, is you. This means that you have a unique perspective on the general nature of your personality and that the S data you can provide can reflect complex, general aspects of character that no other data source could access.

A second possible informational advantage of S data over I data is that much, though perhaps not all, of your inner mental life that is invisible to anyone else *is* visible to you. You know your own fantasies, hopes, dreams, and fears; you directly experience your emotions. Other people can know about these things only if you reveal them. To the extent that these aspects of inner, mental life are important to an understanding of personality, therefore, S data would seem to provide an indispensable route for finding out about them.

ADVANTAGE: CAUSAL FORCE

Recall what was said about expectancy effects related to I data. The same point holds, even more strongly, for S data. Because S data reflect what a person thinks of himself or herself, they have a way of making themselves come true. What you will attempt depends upon what you think you are capable of, and your view of the kind of person you are has important effects on the goals that you set for yourself. This idea is considered more fully in Chapter 6. For now, it is sufficient to note that part of the reason S data are important is that they can make themselves come true.

ADVANTAGE: SIMPLE AND EASY

As mentioned previously, S data cannot be beat for cost-effectiveness. Other kinds of data require the psychologist to look up information in public records, recruit informants, or (for T data, upcoming) find some way to observe the subject directly. These are all time-consuming and therefore expensive procedures. But to obtain S data all the psychologist has to do is write up a questionnaire that asks about what he or she wants to know—e.g., how friendly or how conscientious are you? Then he or she prints copies of the questionnaire and hands them out to everybody around. The psychologist will have an awful lot of interesting, important information about a lot of people, very quickly and at relatively little cost.

Psychological research is done on a very low budget compared to research in any of the other sciences; the research of many psychologists is "funded" essentially by office-supply allowances and whatever they can spare from their own salaries. Even those psychologists who do have research grants from the government usually have grants much smaller than their counterparts in fields such as biology, chemistry, or physics.[3] The importance of the inexpensive nature of S data, therefore, is difficult to exaggerate. Sometimes, for very concrete and compelling reasons, no other kind of data is possible.

DISADVANTAGE: MAYBE THEY WON'T TELL YOU

As discussed above, an important advantage of S data is that oneself is the only person who knows how one acts in all of the situations of one's life, and the only person who knows about the nature of one's private experience. However, this knowledge only translates into S data if one is willing to tell about it. There is no way to force a person to provide an accurate account of his or her own personality if he or she does not want to.

Perhaps the person the psychologist is asking for S data is ashamed of some aspect of his or her personality or behavior. Perhaps the person wishes to brag, to claim some virtue that he or she does not actually possess. Perhaps the person prefers to keep some aspects of his or her personality private. There is no way to prevent a subject from withholding information for any of these reasons—in fact one can sympathize with these reasons—but if the person does choose to withhold information, the accuracy of the S data he or she provides will be compromised. There is nothing the psychologist can do about it, and he or she probably won't even know.

DISADVANTAGE: MAYBE THEY CAN'T TELL YOU

Even if an individual is, for some reason, entirely willing to tell a psychologist everything he or she knows about him or herself, the individual may not be able to do so. Like the memory of informants, one's memory for one's own behavior is finite and imperfect; what you happen to remember about yourself is not necessarily the most important information that is needed to understand your personality. The Freudians would point out that some important memories of our selves may be actively *repressed*; they might be so painful to remember that our ego prevents them from emerging into consciousness (see Chapter 12).

Another factor is simple lack of insight. Some people—maybe all people—lack the perspicacity to see accurately all aspects of their own personality. The self-judgment of personality, like the judgment of personality more generally, can be a complex undertaking that is unlikely to be 100 percent successful. For

---

[3]This discrepancy might make sense if either (a) people were easier to understand than cells, chemicals, or particles, or (b) if it were less important to understand people than cells, chemicals, or particles. Both of these presumptions—if indeed anybody holds them—are of course highly doubtful. Write your senator.

most if not all people, there are important aspects of our own personalities that we are simply the last to know about, even though they might be obvious to everyone else.

For example, research has identified a certain kind of person, called the *narcissist*, who characteristically exaggerates his or her own abilities and accomplishments (John & Robins, 1994). As a result, anything he or she says about himself or herself must be taken with a large grain of salt. Do you know anybody like this?

Another, even more common failing of self-judgment stems from what could be called the "fish-and-water" effect (Kolar, Funder, & Colvin, in press). We are so used to the way we characteristically react and behave that our own actions stop seeming remarkable. For example, you might have been frugal for so long that you no longer even think about spending money, and frugality is one of the last terms that would occur to you to characterize yourself. But when your acquaintances describe you, one of the first things they may mention is what a cheapskate you are. Over time, therefore, the aspects of our behavior that are the most characteristic of us might become invisible, for roughly the same reason that it is said fish have difficulty perceiving water.

Failure of memory, active repression, and lack of insight can all cause S data to provide less accurate renditions of personality than we might wish.

DISADVANTAGE: TOO SIMPLE AND TOO EASY

We have already seen that the single biggest advantage of S data, the one that makes them the most widely used form of data in personality psychology, is that they are so cheap and easy to get. If you remember Funder's First Law (about advantages being disadvantages), you can guess what is coming next: S data are so cheap and easy that they are probably overused.

The issue is not that there is anything especially problematic about S data; they have their advantages and disadvantages, just like all the other types of data. Moreover, Funder's Third Law (about something usually beating nothing) also comes into play here; you definitely should gather S data if that is all you can get. The problem is that S data have been used by so many investigators, to the exclusion of other kinds of data, that some seem to have forgotten that other kinds of data even exist. We should try to remember to gather L, I, and T data whenever we can.

Watch What the Person Does: T Data

A final tactic you might use to learn about someone's personality is to observe, as directly as possible, what he or she actually does. You might watch the person's behavior in a laboratory experiment, or you might watch what the person does in a setting in real life. Either way, the information you record from such direct observation constitutes T data.

But the *T* in T data is potentially very misleading. To avoid misunderstandings, I sometimes tell my students that *T* stands for "The." Perhaps this type of data should be renamed, but then we would lose the acronym (LIST) and, besides, no one has yet come up with a better (or worse) label for this data type.

Now that you have been suitably warned, I can tell you that T data is "Test" data. The label is confusing, because although some kinds of personality tests are T data, most are not. The idea of T data is that subjects are found or put in a "testing" situation, and then their behavior is directly observed. The testing situation might be a context in the person's real life (e.g., a classroom) or a situation that a psychologist sets up in an experimental laboratory. T data can also be derived from certain kinds of personality tests. What all these cases have in common, as we shall see, is that the **T data** derive from the researcher's *direct* observation of what the subject does in some predefined context.

T data are gathered in two kinds of testing contexts, natural and contrived.

NATURAL T DATA

T data can, with some difficulty, be gathered from direct observations of the subject's behavior in one or more real-life contexts. The unrealistic ultimate in T data would be to hire a private detective, armed with state-of-the-art surveillance devices and a complete lack of respect for anybody's privacy, to follow the subject around night and day. The detective's report would specify in exact detail everything the subject said and did, in all of the contexts of the subject's life.

Ultimate, but impossible and unethical, too. Therefore, psychologists who try to gather natural T data must in some manner compromise from this ideal. One compromise is to watch what subjects do in the not-quite-natural contexts to which a psychologist can gain access. Years ago, I did a study in a nursery school that was operated by a university psychology department. From the children's point of view this place was simply their nursery school. But from a psychologist's point of view it was a gold mine of data. Each classroom was equipped with one-way mirrors and listening devices, and one could observe any of the children unobtrusively, all day long, as they went about their nursery-school business. One could gather data that reflected these direct behavioral observations, such as the number of times a child asked a teacher for help, or disagreed with another child, or played with magic markers. These data reflected directly and in quantifiable terms what the child had been observed doing in a specific context, which is the hallmark of T data.

Another compromise form of T data can be provided by diary and beeper methods. My own current research uses both. Subjects fill out daily diaries that detail what they did that day: how many people they talked to, how many times they told a joke, how much time they spent studying or sleeping, and so on. In a sense these are S data, of course—I said it was a compromise. But they are not self-judgments as S data are; they are are reasonably direct indications of what the subject did each day, described in specific terms. Diary methods are best thought of as a marriage of T data and S data, because the subject rather than the psychologist is the one who actually makes the behavioral observations (Spain, 1994).

Another kind of compromised T data is the beeper method (Csikszentmihalyi & Larson, 1992; Spain, 1994). Subjects wear radio-controlled pagers (of the sort that can be rented from a commercial service) that beep at several randomly selected times during the day. The subjects then write down exactly what they were doing (and with whom) when the beeper sounded. One might suspect that subjects would edit what they report, producing a sanitized version of their life events. Based on the beeper reports I have read, I think this is unlikely. At least I hope so. A colleague of mine once did a beeper study at his university just after sending his own eighteen-year-old twin daughters to college in another state. After reading the beeper reports from his own university students, he was tempted to bring his daughters back home!

Still another kind of hybrid T data are reports of specific behaviors offered by the subject or by one of his or her acquaintances. A person might tell you how many phone calls he or she made in a day or parties he or she went to in a week, or a close acquaintance might provide the same information. Such reports are not S data or I data because they are not judgments of personality. But admittedly, data like these are not pure T data either. They obviously contain elements of both self and informant reporting. Still, counts of specific behaviors, provided by the self or by others, are the kind of approximation to T data for which we usually must settle.

The great thing about T data gathered from real life is that they are realistic; they describe what the subjects actually do in their daily activities. The disadvantages of naturalistic T data are their considerable expense—even the compromises described above are difficult and expensive—and the fact that some contexts in which you might wish to observe your subject may occur seldom in the subject's daily life. For both of these reasons, T data derived from contrived testing contexts are more common than those from natural contexts.

Contrived T Data

Experiments Contrived testing comes in two varieties. The first is the psychological experiment. A subject is put into a room, something happens in the room, and the psychologist directly observes what the subject then does.[4] The something that happens can be dramatic or mundane. The subject might be put in a room and given a form to fill out, when suddenly smoke begins pouring under the door. The psychologist, sitting just outside holding a stopwatch, intends to measure how long it will take before the subject goes for help, if he or she ever does (some sit there until they can no longer see a hand in front of their face). If one wanted to know this information about a subject from naturalistic T data, one would have to wait a long time for the appropriate situation to come along. In an experiment, the psychologist can make it happen.

The situation also might be fairly mundane, but intended to be representative of real-life contexts that are difficult to observe directly. In my own research, I have subjects meet subjects of the opposite sex and simply engage in a conversation. I assume this is not a completely bizarre situation compared to those of daily life, although it is unusual because the subjects know it is an experiment and know it is being videotaped. My purpose is to directly observe aspects of my subjects' interpersonal behavior and style. In other videotaped situations, my subjects compete with each other, cooperate in building a Tinkertoy, or engage in a group discussion. All of these settings are artificial, but are designed to allow direct observation of various aspects of the subjects' interpersonal behavior, which would be difficult if not impossible to access otherwise. I put my subjects in these situations because I want to see what they will do. My observations become T data (Funder & Colvin, 1991).

(Certain) Personality Tests Certain kinds of personality tests also yield T data. As was discussed above, many and probably most personality questionnaires produce S data—they simply ask the subjects what they are like and the psychologist, in essence, chooses to believe whatever the subjects say. T data personality tests are different.

For example, the most widely used personality test, the **Minnesota Multiphasic Personality Inventory**, or MMPI, is an example of T data (Dahlstrom & Welsh, 1960). The original version of this test (it was recently revised) included this true/false item: "I am a special messenger of the Lord." The presence of an item like this usually signals that the test is looking for T data and not S data. Why? Because the psychologist is not really seeking bearers of heavenly messages. This item was included because people who answer it "true" tend to be a little unusual. It appeared on the MMPI's schizophrenia scale, because schizophrenics are more likely to answer it "true" than are nonschizophrenics. A person who

---

[4]By this definition, nearly all data gathered by social and cognitive psychologists are T data, even though those psychologists are not ordinarily accustomed to classifying their data as such and do not usually devote much thought to the fact that their technique of data gathering is limited to just one of four possible types.

answered the item "true" was not believed; instead he or she was suspected of being mentally ill.

Another kind of T data personality test is the **projective test**, such as the **Thematic Apperception Test** (or TAT; Murray, 1943), or the famous **Rorschach Test** (Rorschach, 1921). In the TAT, you are shown a picture of some people doing something. In the Rorschach, you are shown a blob of ink. In both cases, you are asked to describe what you see. The situation here is much like that in any other sort of contrived psychological experiment; the psychologist puts you in a situation in which you are confronted with a stimulus that you might not otherwise ever have confronted, and then watches you closely to see what you will say and do. Your responses to the TAT or to the Rorschach are carefully recorded and, eventually, interpreted.

In my experience, students find the distinction between S data personality tests and T data personality tests rather confusing. Indeed, the distinction *is* confusing, but it is also important. One way to clarify the distinction may be to look at it in the following way: If, on a personality test, a psychologist asks you a question because he or she wants to *know* the answer, the test constitutes S data. If, however, the psychologist asks the question because he or she wants to see *what* you will answer, the test constitutes T data.

In an S-data test, when the psychologist wants to know something about you, he or she simply asks you about it. To diagnose sociability, the psychologist asks you how friendly you are. In a T-data test, by contrast, the psychologist gives you a stimulus—perhaps a question, perhaps a picture—to see how you will respond. Your behavior is directly observed and precisely measured—which makes it T data—but your answer is not necessarily believed. Instead, it is interpreted; your claim that you are a special messenger of the Lord means not that you are such a messenger, but that you may be a schizophrenic.

T data have two advantages and one big disadvantage.

ADVANTAGE: RANGE OF CONTEXTS

Some aspects of personality are regularly manifest in people's ordinary, daily lives. Your degree of sociability, for instance, is probably manifest during many hours every day. But other aspects are hidden or, in a sense, latent. How do you know how you would respond to being in a room, alone, with smoke pouring under the door, unless you are actually confronted with that situation? One important advantage of contrived T data is that the psychologist does not have to sit around waiting for the latter situation to happen; if you can be enticed to be in an experiment, the psychologist can make it happen. Similarly, a psychologist might believe that the way people interpret certain pictures or inkblots can provide important information about aspects of their personalities that are ordinarily hidden. In an assessment or research context, this psychologist can present these stimuli to the subjects and see how they react. The variety of

T data that can be gathered are limited only by the psychologist's resources and imagination.

ADVANTAGE: OBJECTIVE AND QUANTIFIABLE

Probably the most important advantage of T data, and the basis of most of their appeal to scientifically minded psychologists, is this: T data are based upon the *direct* observation of behavior; they are not filtered through the judgments of nonpsychologists nor are they based on life outcomes that are produced by uncertain and perhaps unknown causes. Because T-data observations are direct, the psychologist can devise techniques to assess them with precision.

Often the measurement of behavior seems so direct that it is possible to forget that it is an observation. For example, when a cognitive psychologist measures how long it takes, in milliseconds, for a subject to respond to a visual stimulus flashed on a tachistoscope, this measurement is simply a behavioral observation: How long did it take the subject to respond? Similarly, when a social psychologist measures a subject's "conformity" or "aggression," the measurement is essentially an observation of behavior. In my own laboratory, I can derive from the videotapes taken of my subjects' conversations measurements of how long each one talked, how much each one dominated the interaction, how nervous each one seemed, and so forth. All of these measurements, from cognitive, social, or personality psychology, are expressed in numerical form and, when appropriate care is employed, can be gathered with high reliability (see Chapter 3 for more on reliability).

The combination of direct assessment, numerical expression, and high reliability is irresistible to some psychologists. It seems like a direct pipeline to behavioral truth. But occasionally a psychologist can get carried away. One writer has gone so far as to refer to T data as "actual behavior," in contrast with I data, which he called "rated behavior" (Shweder, 1975). The intended pejorative connotation was that direct behavioral observation is real, whereas everything else is just "ratings." Of course, this view is naive. T data have a disadvantage too— a big one.

DISADVANTAGE: UNCERTAIN INTERPRETATION

Whether it be a response to an MMPI item, a description of a Rorschach inkblot, a phone call to a friend, or a moment of social behavior in the laboratory, a bit of T data is just that: a bit of data. It is usually a number, and a number does not interpret itself. Worse, when it comes to T data, appearances are often ambiguous or even misleading, and so it is impossible to be entirely certain what they mean.

For example, how do we know what it means when someone claims that he or she is a special messenger of the Lord? There is certainly nothing in the content of the item that tells us; we need further information, such as the empirical fact that schizophrenics respond "true" to this item more often than nonschizophrenics. With that fact in hand, we might conclude that it is a rather crazy thing to say. But the point is, we *cannot* conclude that the subject is schizophrenic without further information.

The same thing is true of any kind of behavior seen in the laboratory. The person may say he is a messenger of the Lord, or may say an inkblot looks like some favorite relative, or may sit and wait a long time for a small reward. These are all behaviors, and can be measured with great precision. We can see directly which box the person checked next to the question about being a holy messenger, or write down exactly what he said about the ink blot, or time his waiting behavior with a stopwatch. But what these behaviors might *mean*, psychologically, is another question entirely.

A particular example from a study I did some years ago concerned delayed gratification. A large number of laboratory procedures have been developed for measuring this behavior in children (e.g., Mischel & Ebbesen, 1970). One procedure is to show the child two treats, ask the child which she prefers, and then say, "Okay, I am going to leave the room now, but you can bring me back at any time by ringing this bell. If you do, you can have the [less preferred treat]. But if you don't ring the bell, and wait for me to come back by myself, you can have the [more preferred treat]." The measure of the child's "delay of gratification" is how long, in minutes and seconds, the child waits before ringing the bell. This measure is a prototypical example of contrived T data.

It is easy to see why this measure of behavior is called "delay of gratification." That is certainly what it looks like, and seems even to be built into the experimental procedure. If the child waits, she gets something better, if she does not wait, she gets something worse; the test is how long she can wait. What could be more obvious?

However, the measure here is simple only if one is content to regard it *nonpsychologically*, that is, as a measure of time. To label this minutes-and-seconds measurement "delay of gratification" is to make a deeper, *psychological* claim: that what the child is experiencing during that time is a psychological tension between desiring the better treat and not wanting to wait, a tension that is mediated according to the child's ability to delay gratification. What if the child doesn't mind waiting? Or, what if the child doesn't really like the "better" treat all that much? Then it would seem misguided to call this behavioral measure of waiting time "delay of gratification."

Some years ago, Daryl Bem and I did a study in which we put a group of children through the procedure described above, and also gathered personality descriptions of the children (I data) from their parents. We then analyzed our data to see how the children who waited the longest in our laboratory were described by their parents as acting at home (Bem & Funder, 1978).

The results surprised us: The most notable attribute of our longest-delaying children was not their ability to delay gratification in other contexts—this ability was a correlate, but a relatively minor one. The longest-delaying children were more likely to be described as helpful, cooperative, obedient, and *not* particularly interesting or intelligent. Our interpretation of these correlates was that the minutes and seconds of waiting that this study measured were not so much a measure of the children's ability to delay gratification, but of their tendency to cooperate with adults. Because these children were offered something better if they waited, they thought we wanted them to wait. (After all, isn't that how life usually works?) The ones inclined to be obedient and cooperative did what they thought we wanted.

This study demonstrates that the meaning of a behavioral measurement is known for certain only at the most trivial, operational level. Minutes and seconds measure waiting time; that is is trivially obvious. It is as a measure of "delay of gratification" that minutes and seconds become ambiguous.

The bottom line is that one cannot know what a bit of T data means and measures, psychologically, just by looking it, nor even by designing it. (This caution is true of the other kinds of data as well, but it is more frequently forgotten with regard to T data because T data can *seem* so objective.) All too often, T data do *not* measure what they would appear superficially to measure. This is true with all direct measures of behavior, whether the behavior measured is the length of time someone will wait, the number of phone calls he or she makes in a day, or his or her description of an inkblot. To find out what a T-data behavioral measurement means, other information is necessary. The most important information is how the T data correlate with L, I, and S data.

CONCLUSION

There are no infallible indicators of personality, there are only clues, and clues are always ambiguous. All four kinds of clues and data for personality psychology are valuable and important. But all four have major disadvantages that cause each to fall far short of being a perfect source of information about personality. Occasionally I meet someone who reaches the depressing conclusion that this implies we might as well just give up—all psychological data are flawed, so why bother?

This is not my conclusion, however. The fact that all possible sources of data about personality are incomplete, ambiguous, and even potentially misleading means, paradoxically, that we can spare none of them. The investigation of personality, and of psychology in general, requires that *all* of these sources of data be employed. Only then can the different advantages and disadvantages of each type of data begin to compensate for each other. And when all four sources of data begin to point in the same direction, you are probably on to something.

All of which brings us to **Funder's Fourth Law**: *There are only two kinds of* *data.* The first kind is Terrible Data: data that are ambiguous, potentially misleading, incomplete, and imprecise. The second kind is No Data. Unfortunately, there is no third kind, anywhere in the world.

Which of these two kinds of data do you think offers a more promising route toward beginning to understand personality? Some people really seem to prefer the second; unless the data are unambiguous and precise, they would rather do without. My own preference is derived from Funder's Third Law, already expounded: Something beats nothing, two times out of three.

Summary

All science begins with observation. The observations a scientist makes are called data. For the scientific study of personality, four kinds of data are available, summarized by the acronym LIST. Each kind has advantages and disadvantages. L data comprise observable life outcomes such as being arrested, getting sick, or graduating from college. L data have the advantage of being intrinsically important and of being psychologically relevant at least sometimes, but have the disadvantage of not always being psychologically relevant. I data comprise the judgments of knowledgable informants about the personality traits of the person being studied. The advantages of I data include the large amount of information on which informants' judgments typically are based, that this information comes from real life, that informants can use common sense, and that the judgments of people who know the person are important because they have a causal force all their own. The disadvantages of I data are that no informant knows everything about another person, that informants' judgments can be biased or subject to errors such as forgetting, and that a few informants may not have common sense. S data comprise the person's own self-judgments of his or her own personality. The advantages of S data are that each individual is the best expert about herself or himself, that S data also have a causal force all their own, and that S data are simple and easy to gather. The disadvantages are that people sometimes will not or cannot tell you about themselves, and that S data may be so easy to obtain that psychologists use them too much. T data comprise direct observations of a person doing something in a testing situation. This situation may be a personality test such as the Rorschach ink blot, a social setting constructed in a psychological laboratory, or the person's real-life environment. The advantages of T data are that they can look at many different kinds of behaviors, including those that might not occur in normal life, and that because T data are obtained through direct observation they are in a sense objective. The disadvantage of T data is that for all their superficial objectivity, it is still not always clear what they mean, psychologically. Because each kind of data for personality research is potentially valuable *and* potentially misleading, researchers should gather and compare all of them.

CHAPTER

PERSONALITY PSYCHOLOGY AS SCIENCE: RESEARCH METHODS

It is sometimes said that the main thing psychologists know is not content, but method. This statement is not usually meant as a compliment. When all is said and done psychologists often do not seem to have final answers to many of the questions they and others ask about the mind and behavior. What they have instead are methods for generating research aimed at these questions. Indeed, psychologists sometimes seem more interested in the research process itself than in the answers their research is supposed to be seeking.

PSYCHOLOGY'S EMPHASIS ON METHOD

Such characterizations are not entirely fair, but they do have a kernel of truth. Like other scientists, psychologists never really expect to reach a final answer to any question. Their research is aimed more at improving upon the tentative answers (hypotheses) constantly being developed, than at settling anything once and for all.

Another kernel of truth in the caricature above is that more than any other kind of scientist, psychologists are sensitive and even somewhat self-conscious about research methodology, about the way they use statistics, and even about the basic procedures by which they draw theoretical inferences from empirical data. Biologists and chemists, it seems, don't worry about these matters as much. For example, introductory biology or chemistry textbooks usually do not contain an introspective chapter—like this one—on research methods, whereas no psychology text seems complete without one.

This emphasis on methods and process is sometimes seen as a weakness of psychology, even by psychologists themselves. One might say that many psychologists suffer from what is sometimes called "physics envy." But this self-consciousness about method is one of my favorite things about psychology. I remember being almost immediately turned off to the study of chemistry when one of my first assignments was to memorize the periodic table of elements. Where did this table come from, I immediately wanted to know, and why should I believe it? But the answers to these questions were not part of the introductory curriculum in chemistry. Certain things, at least early in one's study of the subject, were just to be accepted—and memorized.

When I first took a psychology course, however, I found the approach to be drastically different. Although I was somewhat disappointed that the professor did not immediately teach me how to read people's minds (even though I was sure he was reading mine), I was engaged by the approach to knowledge he employed. Everything was open to question and no "fact" was presented without both a description of the experiment that found it and a discussion of whether or not the experiment's evidence was actually persuasive. Some students did not like this approach, of course: Why not just tell us the facts, they complained, like the professor does in chemistry class? But I loved it. It allowed me to think for myself. Early in the semester, I decided that some of the facts of psychology did not seem solidly based. Later on, I even began to imagine some ways in which I could find out more myself. I was hooked.

SCIENTIFIC EDUCATION AND TECHNICAL TRAINING

Psychology seems unscientific to some people because all of its conclusions are so tentative. It seems constantly to be seeking answers but never quite reaching them. Real science has real facts, according to a commonly held stereotype, so psychology—especially its "softer" subfields such as personality psychology—is not quite a real science.[1]

This view is ironic because it has things precisely backward. True science is the *seeking* of knowledge, not the cataloging of facts known for certain. This distinction is the fundamental difference between scientific education and technical training. Technical training conveys what is already known about a subject, so that that knowledge can be applied. Scientific education, by contrast, teaches not only what is known but (much more importantly) how to find out what is not yet known.

---

[1] By a long-standing tradition, biological and cognitive psychology are referred to as "hard" psychology, and social, developmental, and personality psychology are referred to as "soft" psychology. Most social, developmental, and personality psychologists find this tradition irritating—it seems to imply their fields of research are less scientific and even easier—but it seems in no danger of dying out.

By this definition, medical education is technical rather than scientific—it focuses on teaching what is known and how to use it. Education in human biology might cover much of the same material but focus instead on how to learn more about how the body works. Similar contrasts can be drawn between pharmacists and pharmacologists, gardeners and botanists, or computer operators and computer scientists. The issue is not whether one of these is "better" than the other. They are both necessary, and each depends upon the other. The biologist goes to a physician when sick; most of what the physician knows was discovered by biologists.

When we get to the substantive parts of this book (beginning with the very next chapter) it will quickly become obvious that, by the terms we are now using, its approach is scientific rather than technical. This book will convey rather few facts, and offer even fewer lessons on how to close that big deal or how to read your spouse's mind. Instead, it will focus on several basic approaches to understanding personality and how each is being developed in an effort to learn more. The invitation this book proffers is not to learn to read minds, but to join this quest yourself.

Research methods are the tools of the scientific quest. There are many excellent books devoted entirely to this subject (e.g., Rosenthal & Rosnow, 1991, and Hammond, Householder, & Castellan, 1970) and this chapter is not the place for a detailed treatment. But it may be useful, before proceeding any further, to review a few fundamental points of methodology that help illuminate the possibilities and difficulties of research in personality.

QUALITY OF DATA

All science begins with observation. The observations you make, in whatever form you record them, are data. In Chapter 2 we considered the four basic types of data for personality research: L, I, S, and T data. For any type of data, in any field, two aspects of their quality are paramount: (1) Are the data reliable? and (2) Are the data valid?

Reliability

In science, the term "reliability" has a technical meaning that is narrower than its everyday usage. The question of scientific reliability asks whether your measurement is free of irrelevant influences that might tend to lessen your ability to see the trait or state you are trying to measure. The effects of such extraneous influences are called **measurement error**, and the less there is of such error the more reliable the measurement is.

The influences that are considered extraneous depend on what you are measuring. If you are trying to measure a person's current mood—his or her **state**—

then the fact that he or she won the lottery ten minutes ago is highly relevant and not at all extraneous. But if you are trying to measure the person's general, or "trait," level of emotional experience, then this sudden event *is* extraneous, and you might want to wait for a more ordinary day to take your measurement.

When one is trying to measure a stable attribute of personality—a **trait** rather than a state—the question of **reliability** reduces to this: Can you can get the same result more than once? A method or an instrument that provides the same comparative information repeatedly is reliable; one that does not is un-reliable. For example, a personality test that over a long period of time repeatedly picks out the same individuals as the friendliest in the class, and others as the least friendly, would be a reliable test (although not necessarily valid—that's another matter). A personality test that on one occasion picked out one student as the most friendly and on another occasion identified a different student as the most friendly, however, would be unreliable. A test that is unreliable in this way could not be a valid measure of a stable trait of friendliness. It might instead be a measure of a state or momentary level of friendliness, or (more likely in this case) it might be a measure of nothing at all.

Reliability is something that must be assessed with any scientific measure-ment, whether the measurement be a personality test, a thermometer reading, the output of a brain-wave scanner, or a blood count. This point is not always appreciated. For example, an acquaintance of mine, a research psychologist, once had a vasectomy. As part of the procedure, a sperm count was taken before and after the operation. He asked the doctor a question that is natural for a psy-chologist to ask: How reliable is a sperm count? What he wanted to know was, does a man's sperm count vary widely according to time of day, or what he has eaten lately, or his mood? Moreover, does it matter which technician does the count, or does the same result occur regardless of who the counter is? The physician failed to understand the question and even seemed insulted. "We count very carefully," he replied. My acquaintance, trying to clarify matters, asked a follow-up question: "What I mean is, what's the error variance of a sperm count?" ("Error variance" refers to the fluctuation of a number around its mean upon repeated measurements, due to uncontrolled influences such as those just listed.) The physician really was insulted now. "We don't make er-rors," he replied in a huff.

Several methods can be used to enhance the reliability of a measurement and to minimize its error variance. One way, of course, is simply to be careful. Another way is to measure something that is important, rather than something that is trivial. The most important and generally useful way to enhance reliability, however, is **aggregation**, or averaging.

When I was in high school, a science teacher whom I now believe to have been brilliant (I failed to be as impressed at the time) provided our class with the best demonstration of aggregation that I have ever seen. He gave each of us a meter stick, a piece of wood cut to the length of one meter. We then went outside and measured the distance to the elementary school down the street, about a kilometer (1,000 meters) away. We did this by laying our sticks down, then laying them down again against the end of where they were before, and counting how many times we had to do this to get to the other school.

In each class the counts varied widely—from about 750 to over 1200, as I recall. The next day, the teacher wrote on the blackboard all the different results. It seemed that the elementary school just would not hold still! To put this observation another way, our individual measurements were quite unreliable. It is hard to keep laying the stick down over and over with precision, and it is also hard to keep from losing count of how many times you have done it.

But then, the teacher did an amazing thing. He took the 35 measurements from the 9:00 class and averaged them. He got 957. Then he averaged the 35 measurements from the 10:00 class. He got 959. The 35 measurements from the 11:00 class averaged 956. Almost by magic, the error variance had almost disappeared and we suddenly had what looked like an extremely stable estimate of the distance to the elementary school.

What had happened? The teacher had taken advantage of the power of aggregation. Each of the mistakes we made in laying our sticks down and forgetting what number we were on were essentially random. And over the long haul, random influences tend to cancel one another out (By definition in psychometrics, random influences sum to zero—if they didn't, they wouldn't be random!). While I may have been laying my sticks too close together, one of my classmates was surely laying them too far apart. When my measurement was averaged with hers, our errors cancelled each other out. With 35 measurements being averaged, the result was highly stable.

This is a basic and powerful principle of measurement. If you have doubts about the stability of what you are measuring, take as many measurements as you can, and average them. The Spearman-Brown formula in psychometrics[2] describes exactly how this works, but the principle is simple: Random errors tend to cancel one another out. So the more error-filled your measurements, the more of them you need. The "truth" will be in there someplace, near the average. (For further illustrations and discussion of applications of the Spearman-Brown formula to personality measurement, see Burnett, 1974; Epstein, 1980; and Rosenthal, 1973.)

An important application of this principle in personality psychology is to the prediction of behavior. The "consistency controversy" (see Chapter 4) developed, in part, from a realization that single behaviors are very difficult to predict accurately from personality measurements. However, the principle of aggregation tells you that the *average* of a person's behavior should be much easier to predict. Maybe a friendly person is sometimes more friendly at some

---

[2]Psychometrics is the technology of psychological measurement.

times than at other times—we all have bad days. But the average of the person's behavior across both good and bad days should be *reliably* more friendly than that of an unfriendly person (Epstein, 1979).

Validity

Validity, as I said above, is another matter. It is also a slippier concept. **Validity** is the degree to which a measurement actually reflects what you think or hope it does. The concept of validity is slippery for a couple of reasons.

One complication is that for a measure to be valid, it must be reliable. But a reliable measure is not necessarily valid. Should I say this again? A measure that is reliable gives you the same answer time after time. If the answer changes, how can it be the right answer? So for a measure to be valid, it must first be reliable. But even if a measure is the same time after time, that does not necessarily mean it is *correct*. Maybe it reliably gives the wrong answer (like the clock in my old Toyota, which was correct only twice each day). Reliability is what the logicians call a "necessary but not sufficient condition" for validity.

A second and even more difficult complication to the idea of validity is that the concept seems to invoke a notion of ultimate truth. On the one hand, you have ultimate, true reality. On the other hand, you have a measurement. If the measurement matches ultimate, true reality, it is valid. Thus, an IQ measure is valid if it really measures intelligence. A sociability score is valid if it really measures sociability. But here is the problem: How do we know what intelligence or sociability "really" are?

Some psychologists believe we never do know what these concepts really are, so we never know whether a measure of them is valid or not. However, many psychologists are not quite as willing to give up. They use a strategy called **construct validation** (Cronbach & Meehl, 1955). This is a research strategy that amounts to gathering as many different measurements as you can of a construct you are interested in—such as intelligence or sociability. Those that start to hang together—to consistently pick out the same people as intelligent or sociable—begin to validate each other. Even though you never reach an ultimate truth, you start to believe you are measuring something real when you can develop a battery of tests, all quite different, that all yield more or less the same result.

For example, you might give subjects a sociability test, and ask their acquaintances how sociable they are, and count how many phone calls they make in a week, and how many parties they go to. If these four measures all correlate—if they all tend to pick out the same individuals as highly sociable—then you might start to believe that each of them has some degree of validity as a measure of sociability. Furthermore, you might believe this even though you never gathered a "real" measure of "true" sociability (for what would that be?).

At its essence, construct validation is theory testing. You have an idea of what you are trying to measure, and this idea generates hypotheses about the traits or behaviors to which your measurement should and should not be related. If my measure of X is *really* a measure of X, then it ought to correlate positively with Y and Z, negatively with K, and not at all with A or B. You then test these hypotheses. Such a theory is never really proven, of course, but as more supportive evidence is found it is reasonable to start to believe it. Similarly, a measurement can never be *proven* valid, but as more evidence accumulates it is reasonable to start to believe that it is.

Generalizability

Classic treatments of psychometrics regarded reliability and validity as quite distinct from each other. When two tests that were "the same" were compared with each other, their correlation indicated the degree of reliability. For example, the correlation between a test given at one time and the same test given again, a week later, would be considered a measurement of reliability. The correlation between scores on one form of a test and scores on another form of the same test (maybe consisting of the same items only slightly rephrased) would also be considered a gauge of reliability. But when two tests that were "different" were compared with each other, their correlation indicated the degree of validity. For example, the correlation between one form of a test and a different test (perhaps in which the items have entirely different content) would be considered a measure of validity. But when you begin to look at it closely, the distinction between which tests one should consider "the same" or "different" turns out to be rather fuzzy.

In recent years, therefore, psychometricians have started to regard the distinction between reliability and validity as also being rather fuzzy. Instead, they have begun to view both concepts as aspects of a broader concept called **generalizability** (Cronbach et al., 1972). The question of generalizability, applied to a measurement or to the results of an experiment, asks the following: To what else does your measurement or your result generalize? That is, is the result you get with one test equivalent, or generalizable, to the result you would get using a different test? Does your result also apply to other kinds of people than the ones you assessed, or does it apply to the same people at other times, or would you find the same result using different research assistants? These are all questions regarding different *facets* of generalizability.

GENERALIZABILITY OVER SUBJECTS

One important type of generalizability is generalizability over subjects. For example, you might do a case study of one individual, but then wonder about whether what you have found applies to people in general or just to this one person. Or, it is often pointed out that because most psychological research is done by university professors, most subjects in research are college students.

There tend to be a lot of students near professors, and gathering data from anybody else—such as randomly selected members of the community—is much more difficult and expensive, even if it is possible.

This latter fact raises a basic question of generalizability over subjects: To what degree do you learn about people in general by studying only college students? After all, college students are not representative of the broader population. They are somewhat more affluent, more liberal, and less likely to belong to ethnic minorities, for example. These facts call into question the degree to which research results found with such students will prove to be true about the wider population of this country, let alone the world (Sears, 1986).

Gender Bias   An even more egregious example of conclusions being based on a limited sample of humanity comes from the fact that until well into the 1960s it was fairly routine for American psychological research to gather data only from male subjects. Some of the classic empirical investigations of personality, such as those by Henry Murray (1938) and Gordon Allport (1937), examined only men. I once had a conversation with one of the major contributors to personality research during the 1940s and 1950s, who is still very active and who admitted frankly that he was embarrassed to have used only male subjects in his research during that period. "It is hard to recall why we did that," he said in 1986. "As best as I can remember, it simply never occurred to any of us to do anything different—to include women in the groups we studied."

There is some indication that in recent years the problem may have reversed, in an ironic way. There is one particular fact about recruiting subjects that nearly all psychologists have known for years: Females are more likely to sign up to be in experiments than are males, and once signed up are more likely to actually appear at the scheduled time. The difference is not small—it has never been systematically studied as far as I know, although it certainly should be—but it is on the order of two to one or more. From my desk in the psychology department I look directly across the hallway to a sign-up sheet for my own research project, which uses paid, volunteer subjects. Because my work needs an exactly equal number of males and females, the sign-up sheet has two columns, one for each. At any hour of any day, there typically will be more than twice as many names in the "women" column as in the "men" column. As I write this, there are about five times as many women.

This big difference raises a couple of issues. One is theoretical: Why this difference? One hypothesis could be that college-age women are generally more conscientious and cooperative than men in that age range, or the difference might go deeper than that. A second issue is that this difference raises a worry about the subjects we do recruit. It is not so much that samples are unbalanced. You can keep them balanced; in our lab, we simply call *all* of the men who sign up and about one in three of the women. Rather the problem is that because men are less likely to volunteer than women, the men who are in our studies are unusual men. I wish I knew in what specific way they are unusual, but it is awfully difficult to do an empirical study comparing "shows" with "no-shows."

Cohort Effects   Another possible failure of generalizability stems from the fact that research results may be *historically* limited. It has been argued that much of psychology is really "history," meaning it is the study of a particular group of people in a particular place and time (Gergen, 1973). The research that fills psychological journals today may be interesting as a historical artifact concerning what late-twentieth-century, North American college students are like, according to this argument, but says little about what people are like in general or, more particularly, what they may have been like across the years and centuries.

Some evidence does indicate that aspects of personality can be affected by the specific historical period in which one lives. One study of Americans who grew up during the Great Depression of the 1930s found that they took from that experience certain attitudes toward work and financial security that were quite distinct from the outlooks of those who grew up earlier or later (Elder, 1974). The tendency of a group of people who lived at a particular time to be different in some way from those who lived earlier or later is called by psychologists a **cohort effect**.

Despite the existence of few such investigations, psychologists more often worry about cohort effects than deal with them directly. The reason is that the necessary research is prohibitively expensive, insofar as it is possible. The only real way to find out which of our research results are true across time, and which are just characteristics of the cohort we happen to be studying, is to study other subjects from other eras. This is nearly impossible. To some degree one can use old data archives and try to go back a little way in time. For the future, one must begin new studies, or just wait. None of these tactics is terribly practical, and all of them are very expensive.

Ethnic Diversity   A generalizability issue that is beginning to receive more attention concerns the fact that most modern empirical research in psychology is based on a limited subset of the modern population—specifically, the largely white, middle-class college sophomores referred to earlier. This is becoming a particular issue in the United States, where ethnic diversity has always been wide and where various minority groups are becoming more assertive in their insistence upon being included in all aspects of society—including psychological research. The pressure to include minority subjects is as much political as it is scientific. One place to see the result of such political pressure is in the latest grant application guidelines published by one branch of the federal government:

Applications for grants . . . that involve human subjects are required to include minorities and both genders in study populations. . . . This policy applies to *all* research involving human subjects and human materials, and applies to males and females of all ages. If one gender and/or minorities are excluded or are inadequately represented in this research . . . a clear, compelling rationale for exclusion or inadequate respresentation should be provided. . . . Assess carefully the feasibility of including the broadest possible representation of minority groups (Public Health Service, 1991, p. 21).

This set of guidelines addresses the representation of *American* ethnic minorities in research funded by the United States government. As the tone of this governmental directive hints, accomplishing such representation is difficult. But notice that even if every goal this directive espouses were to be accomplished, the American researchers subject to its edict would still be restricted to studying residents of a modern, Western, capitalist, post-industrial society. This may be an interesting society to study, but its denizens are a minority, since 70 percent of the world's population does not live in Europe or North America (Triandis, 1994).

The Burden of Proof

It is easy to get carried away with these kinds of worries. The concern with generalizability, the degree to which one's research results apply to all people around the world and at all times, is a fundamental issue for any psychological research. But two points are worth bearing in mind.

First, getting the facts straight about members of our own culture at our own time seems to be difficult enough, so we should resist making facile and simplistic generalizations about members of other cultures—including jumping to conclusions about ways they might be different from us. To really understand the degree to which and ways in which cultures differ psychologically from one another will require a vast amount of further research more equally spread across cultures and less concentrated in Europe and North America. Such research is beginning to appear, but it is coming slowly and is proving to be both difficult and expensive. In the meantime, we simply do not know very much about these differences, or even how wide they really are.

Second, it is one thing to worry, in a general way, that our results or theories might not generalize, and quite another to propose just *how* and *why* a particular result or a particular theory might not apply to another culture. Not all of the burden of proof should be put on those who are trying to do research that is generalizable. Some should be put on those who claim it is not, to show when, how, and why it is not. Simply to observe that our data base is limited, and then to conclude that all of our research and theory is therefore worthless is—as the old saying goes—to throw the baby out with the bathwater.

Representative Design

A great psychologist who studied perception and judgment in the 1940s and 1950s, Egon Brunswik, pointed out that subjects are not the only place where one must generalize in research (1956). Equally pressing, though less often addressed, are concerns about generalizability across **stimuli** and **responses**. That is, you might use one particular method to induce a state of "anxiety" in your subjects. You get good results, but what if you had used a different method? Your research cannot say. Or, maybe you measure one particular behavior (perhaps test performance) to detect whether your experimental manipulation has affected how well people perform. Again, you get good results, but what if you had used a different method or a different kind of performance test? Your research cannot say.

Brunswik said that the solution to this dilemma should be the use of "representative design"—that is, research should be designed to sample across *all* of the domains to which the investigator will wish to generalize the results. If you want to generalize to all people subject for jury duty, for example, your subjects should be drawn randomly from a sample of those who are subject for jury duty. It also means that if you wish to generalize your experimental manipulation to all methods of producing cognitive dissonance, your research should employ a sample of possible methods (you do not need to use *all* methods any more than you need to recruit every subject on earth, but the ones you use should be representative). Representative design also means that if you wish to generalize your results to all ways of showing attitude change, your research needs to sample from those as well; it should try to change attitudes in several different ways that reflect the range of tactics that you think exist in real life.

Perhaps you will be surprised to learn that up to and including the present day, Brunswik's advice is seldom followed. Researchers do tend to sample a group of subjects—they usually do not study just one—although they do not often worry about the fact that their college students are not really representative of people in the real world. But at least they use more than one subject. In the other domains of generalizability, sampling is almost nonexistent. The typical experimental study uses *one* kind of experimental manipulation, and measures just *one* behavior. This makes the research less generalizable—less broadly relevant—than it might otherwise be.

Brunswik's notion of representative design, though it strikes me as elementary good sense about research, has yet to affect the practice of psychological research in a significant way. But a small group of psychologists, who call themselves "Brunswikians," is working to make his ideas more widely accepted and utilized (e.g., Hammond, et al., 1992).

CORRELATIONAL AND EXPERIMENTAL DESIGNS

The really big schism over research methods in psychology is between advocates of the experimental and correlational methods. Suppose you wish to examine the relationship between anxiety and test performance. You could do this in either of two ways.

The experimental way would be to divide your subjects into two groups. Do something you assume will make one of the groups anxious, such as telling them, "your life depends upon your performance on this test" (but see the discussion on ethics and deception later in this chapter). Presumably this will make your subjects anxious. Then give them a math test. If anxiety hurts performance, then you would expect the subjects in your "life depends" group to do worse on the test than the subjects who did not hear this dire message. (Ideally, all your subjects should have close to the same ability in math, or you should have a separate measure of their mathematical aptitudes to allow you to adjust your results accordingly.)

The correlational way to examine the same hypothesis would be to measure the amount of anxiety that your subjects already have. Give all of them a questionnaire asking such questions as "how anxious do you feel right now?" on a scale of 1 to 7. Then give them the math test. Now the hypothesis would be that if anxiety hurts performance, then those who scored higher on your anxiety measure will score worse on the math test than will those who received lower anxiety scores. (Again, it would be necessary to adjust the scores for the subjects' overall abilities in math.)

The experimental and correlational methods are often discussed as if they were utterly different and diametrically opposed. But I hope this example makes clear that they are neither. Both methods attempt to assess the relation between two variables; in the case above they were "anxiety" and "performance." The only difference is that in the experimental method the presumably causal variable—anxiety—is *manipulated,* whereas in the correlational method the same variable is *measured.*

Each method has advantages and disadvantages. The most touted advantage of the experimental method is that it allows the assessment of **causality**. You may have heard the statement "correlation is not causality"—it's true. Just because high anxiety is correlated with poor performance does not mean that anxiety causes poor performance. It might be the reverse—maybe poor performance causes anxiety—or there might be another, unmeasured variable, such as being sick that day, that is causing both anxiety *and* poor performance. In the experimental method, by contrast, the only difference between the two groups was that one of them was told something (your life depends on it) and the other was not. Any difference in performance between the groups must therefore be a result of what they were told, and therefore legitimately can be said to have been "caused" by it.

The experimental method is not without its own disadvantages, however. One problem with the experimental method is that you can never be sure exactly what you are manipulating and, therefore, of where the causality was actually located. In one of the examples above, I presumed that telling subjects "your life depends on how you do" would make them anxious. The results then confirm the hypothesis: anxiety hurts performance. But how do I know my statement made them anxious? Maybe it made them angry, or disgusted at such an obvious lie, for instance. I only know what I manipulated at the most trivial level—I know what I said to the subjects. The *psychological* variable that I manipulated, however, the one that actually affected behavior, can only be inferred. (This difficulty is related to the problem with T data that was discussed in Chapter 2.)

A second problem with the experimental method is that it can create levels of a variable that are unlikely or even impossible in real life. Assuming the experimental manipulation worked as intended, how often is your life literally hanging in the balance when you take a math test? Any extrapolation from the results of this experiment to the levels of anxiety that ordinarily exist during exams could be highly misleading. Moreover, maybe in real life most people are medium-anxious. But in the experiment, two groups were artificially created: One was highly anxious, the other (again, presumably) was not anxious at all. In real life, both groups may be rare. Therefore, the effect of anxiety on performance may be exaggerated in this experiment, with respect to the degree of importance it has in real life; differences in anxiety level are typically less extreme. The correlational method, by contrast, assesses levels of anxiety that *already* exist in the subjects. Thus, these levels are not artificial and they are more likely to represent anxiety as it really exists in average people. The results of the correlational study are therefore more likely to reflect the degree to which anxiety affects performance in "nature" (i.e., real life).

A third disadvantage particular to the experimental method as opposed to the correlational method is that the experimental method often requires deception. I will discuss deception later, but for now just note that psychological experiments often require experimenters to lie to subjects. Correlational studies rarely do.

EFFECT SIZES
Significance vs. Importance

Psychologists, being human, like to brag about their results. Often—maybe too often—they describe the effects they have discovered as being "large," "important," or even "dramatic." Nearly always, they will describe their results as "significant." These descriptions can be very confusing because there are no rules about how the first three terms can be employed. "Large," "important," and even "dramatic" are just adjectives and unfortunately can be used at will. However, there are rather strict rules about how the term "significant" can be employed.

A "significant" result, in research parlance, is not necessarily large or important, let alone dramatic. But it is a result that *probably* did not occur by chance. An experimental result, or a correlation, that is said to be significant at the "5 percent" level is one that, by chance alone, would be expected about 5 percent of the time. One significant at the 1 percent level is to be expected by chance about 1 percent of the time, and so is often considered a better result. Various statistical formulas, some quite complex, are employed to calculate the likelihood of experimental or correlational results. The more unlikely, the better.

I am not sure I can recommend that you think about all this too closely. In fact, this kind of analysis does not bear close philosophical analysis very well, because it is far from clear what statements like "would be expected 5 percent of the time" really mean (Gigerenzer et al., 1991). Five percent of *what* time? Five percent of experiments exactly like the one just conducted? (In that case the same result should be obtained every time, unless the universe is nondeterminist.) Or five percent of experiments that vary in unspecified ways? What ways? Moreover, how can a single event—an experimental result—that has already occurred have a probability? (The real probability of something that has already happened is 1.0!) As I said, thinking about this in detail in hazardous. But if you sense (as I did when I first took a statistics course) that there is something rather fishy about assessing significance against a chance model, I (and Gigerenzer) think you are on to something. (For further discussion of the question of significance, see Cohen, 1994.)

Correlations

Sometimes on the basis of doubts like these and sometimes not, those psychologists who are the better data analysts do not just stop with significance. They move on to calculate a number that will reflect the size, as opposed to the likelihood, of their result. This number is called an **effect size**, and it is much more meaningful than a significance level. It tells you how much of one variable is contained within or even caused by another variable.

The most commonly used measure of effect size is the **correlation coefficient**. Of course, correlational studies such as those discussed above always yield a correlation coefficient that tells you, for example, that the correlation between anxiety and performance is .40. But it is less often recognized that experimental studies can also yield correlation coefficients, because the statistics used to analyze experiments are derived from the same basic statistical model as the correlation. The conversion of an experimental statistic to a correlational effect size, for example, is a matter of simple algebra (e.g., Funder & Ozer, 1983).[3]

A correlation coefficient is a number between -1 and $+1$ that indexes the association between any two variables. This number is calculated by arranging the two variables in columns (traditionally, the columns are labeled X and Y) and applying a common statistical formula found in any methods or statistics textbook. If the variables are positively associated—as one goes up the other tends to go up too, like height and weight—then the correlation coefficient will be greater than zero, or a positive number. If the variables are negatively associated—as one goes up the other tends to go down, like anxiety and test performance—then the correlation coefficient will be less than zero, or a negative number. Essentially, if two variables are correlated, one of them can be predicted from a knowledge of the other. If I know how anxious you are, then I can predict (to a degree) how well you will do on a math test. If two variables are unrelated, the correlation between them will be near zero.

How does one interpret a correlation coefficient? You cannot just use statistical significance. A correlation becomes "significant" in a statistical sense merely by *probably* not being zero, which depends as much on how many subjects you managed to recruit as on how strong the effect really is. Instead you need to look at the actual size of the correlation. Some textbooks provide rules of thumb: One that I happen to own says that a correlation (positive or negative) of .6 to .8 is "quite strong," one from .3 to .5 is "weaker but still important," and one from .3 to .2 is "rather weak." I have no idea what this is supposed to mean. Do you?

Another commonly taught way to evaluate effect sizes is to square them, which will tell you "what percent of the variance the correlation explains." This certainly sounds like what you need to know, and the calculation is wonderfully easy. A correlation of .30 means that "only" 9 percent of the variance is explained by the correlation (.30 squared being .09). A correlation of .40 means that "only" 16 percent of the variance is explained. These correlations are often viewed as small, however, perhaps because a further calculation tells you that in the case

---

[3]As you may have learned in a statistics course, the most commonly used statistic that reflects a difference between two experimental groups is the t (the outcome of a t-test). The standard symbol for the Pearson correlation coefficient is r. The experimental t can be converted to the correlational r through the following formula:

$$r = \sqrt{\frac{t^2}{t^2 + (n_1 + n_2 - 2)}}$$

where n_1 and n_2 are the sizes of the two samples being compared (Rosenthal & Rosnow, 1991).

of a correlation of .30, 91 percent of the variance is *un*explained, and in the case of a correlation of .40, 84 percent is unexplained.

Despite the wide popularity of this squaring method (if you have taken a statistics course you were probably taught it), I think it is a poor method for evaluating effect size. It is statistically confusing and substantively misleading. The variance being "accounted for" is the sum of the *squared* deviations of each observation from the mean of that variable across all the observations in the sample. That is why you square the correlation. These deviations are usually squared in statistics for reasons of convenience (it removes negative numbers) and mathematical elegance. But they have nothing to do with evaluating the size of an effect. Of more interest, I would think, is the *absolute*, unsquared deviation of each score from its mean. The sum of these terms is sometimes called the variation—as opposed to "variance"—and to find out how much of the *variation* the correlation between two variables accounts for you do not have to do any calculation at all. A correlation of .30 accounts for 30 percent of the variation; a correlation of .40 accounts for 40 percent of the variation (Ozer, 1985).

This may all be exceedingly technical for present purposes, but my larger point is not: The practice of squaring correlations to yield the "percent of variance explained" is misleading in two ways. The first is that the terminology sounds like more is being accomplished than is actually the case. Words like "variance" and, especially, "explained" *sound* like they get at just what anybody would want to know, but they really do not.

Second, the real result of this pseudo-sophisticated calculation is to make correlations seem very small. It is the case that both in correlational research in personality and in experimental research in social psychology, the effect sizes expressed in correlations rarely exceed .40 (Funder & Ozer, 1983). If this result is to be considered to "explain" (whatever that means) "16 percent of the variance" (whatever that means) leaving "84 percent unexplained," then we are left with the vague but somehow convincing conclusion that neither sort of research has accomplished much. Yet this conclusion is not correct, either.

The Binomial Effect Size Display

What is needed is a method, beyond squaring correlations, to demonstrate in some concrete manner how big these effect size correlations really are. A brilliant technique for doing just that has been provided by Rosenthal and Rubin (1982). They invented a technique called the **Binomial Effect Size Display**, or BESD. Let's use Rosenthal and Rubin's favorite example to illustrate how to use the BESD technique.

Assume you are studying 200 subjects, all of whom are sick. An experimental drug is given to 100 of them; the other 100 are given nothing. At the end of the study, 100 are alive and 100 are dead. The question is, how much difference did the drug make?

TABLE 3.1

THE BINOMIAL EFFECT SIZE DISPLAY[1]

	Alive	Dead	Total
Drug	70	30	100
No drug	30	70	100
Total	100	100	200

[1]This table shows how a correlation of .40 would translate into frequencies of living and dying in a hypothetical, 200-subject drug trial.

(After Rosenthal & Rubin, 1982)

Sometimes the answer to this question may be reported in the form of a correlation coefficient that is calculated from the data on how many subjects lived and died. For example, you may be told that the data show that the correlation between taking the drug or not, and living or dying, is .40. If the report stops here (as it usually does), you are left with the question: What does this mean? Was the effect big or little? If you were to follow the common practice of squaring correlations to yield "variance explained," you might conclude that "only 16 percent of the variance is explained" (which does not sound like much) and decide the drug is nearly worthless.

But the BESD provides another way to think about the size of a correlation coefficient. Through some further, simple calculations, you can move from a report that "the correlation is .40" to a concrete display of what that correlation means in terms of specific outcomes. For example, as shown in Table 3.1, a correlation of .40 means that 70 percent of those who got the drug are still alive, whereas only 30 percent of those who did not get the drug are still with us. If the correlation is .30, those figures would be 65 percent and 35 percent, respectively. As Rosenthal and Rubin point out, these effects might only explain 16 percent or even 9 percent of the variance, but in either case if you got sick, would you want this drug?

The computational method begins by assuming a correlation of 0, which gives each of the four cells in the table an entry of 50 (if there is no effect, then it does not matter whether you get the treatment or not). Then take the actual correlation (in our example, .40), remove the decimal (.40 becomes 40), divide by two (in this case yielding 20), and add it to the 50 in the upper left-hand cell (yielding 70). Then adjust the other three cells by subtraction: Because each row and column must total 100, the four cells, reading clockwise, become 70, 30, 70, and 30.

This technique works with any kind of data. Alive and dead can be replaced with any kind of dichotomized outcomes—"better-than-average school success" and "worse-than-average school success," for example. The drug variable could become "taught with new method" and "taught with old method." Or, the variable could be "scores above average on school motivation," and "scores below average on school motivation," or any other personality variable.

The fundamental message of the BESD is that correlational effects need to be more carefully interpreted than they usually are. It is both facile and misleading to use the frequently taught method of squaring correlations if your intention is to evaluate effect size (squaring *is* useful for other, more technical purposes). The BESD, by contrast, shows vividly both how much of an effect an experimental intervention is likely to have, and how well you can predict an outcome from an individual measurement of difference. So, when you read—later in this book or in a psychological research article—that one variable is related to another with a correlation of .30, or .40, or whatever, you should construct a BESD in your mind and evaluate the size of the correlation accordingly.

ETHICS
The Uses of Psychological Research

Like any other human activity, research involves ethical issues. Some of those issues are common to all research. One is the concern that one's results may be used for harmful purposes. Just as physicists who build H-bombs should worry about what H-bombs can do to people, so too should psychologists be aware of the consequences of what their research might discover.

For example, one part of psychology—behaviorism—has long aimed to develop a technology to control behavior. The technology is not quite here yet, but if it ever comes it will obviously raise ethical questions about who decides what behaviors to create and whose behavior should be controlled. The main figure in behaviorism, B. F. Skinner, wrote extensively about these issues (e.g., Skinner, 1948, 1971).

Other psychologists study racial differences and sex differences. Putting aside whatever purely scientific merits this work might have, there is a fundamental question about whether its findings are likely to do more harm than good. If some racial group really is lower in intelligence, or if men really are better (or worse) at math than women, would these findings have constructive uses? The arguments in favor of exploring these issues are that science should study everything and (on a more applied level) that knowing the basic abilities of a group might help in tailoring educational programs specifically to members of the group. The arguments against this research are that such findings are bound to be misused by racists and sexists and can therefore become tools of oppression themselves, and that knowledge of group characteristics is not really very useful for tailoring programs to individual needs.

Truthfulness

Truthfulness is another ethical issue common to all research. The past few years have seen a number of scandals in which researchers have either plagiarized the work of others or have even fabricated their own data. Lies cause difficulty in all sectors of life, but they are particularly worrisome in research because science is based upon truth and trust. Scientific research is the attempt to seek truth in as unbiased a way as one can manage. Scientific lies, when they happen, undermine the very foundation of the field. Science without truthfulness is completely meaningless.

All scientists *must* trust each other for the process to work. If I report to you some data that I have found, you might disagree with my interpretation—that is fine. But if you cannot be sure that I really did find those data, then there is no basis for further discussion. Even scientists who vehemently disagree with each other on fundamental issues must take each other's truthfulness for granted (contrast this with the situation in politics). If they cannot, then science stops dead in its tracks.

Deception

The fundamental reliance of science upon truth is what makes the use of deception in research so worrisome to me. Quite frequently, psychologists tell their research subjects something that is not true.[4] The purpose of such deception is to make the research "realistic." A subject might be told—falsely—that a test he or she is taking is a valid IQ or personality test, for example, so that the subject's reaction can be studied when he or she receives a poor score. Or a subject might be told that another person was described by a "trained psychologist" as "friendly" and "unsociable," to see how the subject resolves this sort of inconsistency. One of the most famous deception experiments was the one in which Stanley Milgram led subjects to believe they were administering fatal electric shocks to an innocent, screaming victim. (The "victim" was actually an actor; Milgram, 1975.)

The American Psychological Association has developed a detailed set of ethical guidelines that psychological researchers are supposed to follow. These

---

[4]This is not the same thing as simply withholding information, as in a double-blind drug trial, where neither the patient nor doctor knows whether the drug or the placebo is being administered. Deception involves knowingly telling a lie.

guidelines do allow deception, although the limits are narrower than they used to be. The Milgram experiment probably would not be allowed today, although studies like the other two described above are still conducted frequently.

Two arguments are usually given for why deception should be allowed. The first is that subjects have given their "informed consent" to be deceived. The second is that the little white lies told to subjects usually do no harm. I think these arguments are inadequate, however (see also Baumrind, 1985).

First of all, I do not see how one can give "informed" consent to be deceived; the situation seems oxymoronic. But more important, I think that excuses for deception that focus on the supposed lack of harm to the subject miss the point. The real victim of a deception experiment, in my opinion, is the psychologist. The problem with lying is that once it begins you never know when it has stopped. In a deception experiment, one person (a psychologist) has told a lie to another person (the subject). When the experimenter says, "I lied to you, but the experiment is now over," is it really over? (In at least one experiment I know of, it wasn't! Ross, Lepper, & Hubbard, 1975). And, on a broader scale, the psychologist has been exposed as somebody who, if for a "right" end, will lie to you. What does this do to the credibility of psychology as a science (Greenberg & Folger, 1988)?

One small way in which I see this harm is in my own research. Although I no longer do deception experiments (and since I made that decision I have never really felt the lack), often my subjects do not believe me! They spend the experimental hour wondering what I am *really* studying. Being sophisticated about psychologists and what they do, my subjects find it hard to believe that I am actually studying what I have said I am studying. And I cannot blame them one bit. Until psychologists stop employing deception as a matter of routine, why should anybody believe a word they say? (For a contrary view on this matter, see Sharpe, Adair, & Roese, 1992.)

Eschewing deception might have another interesting effect, besides making psychologists more credible: It might make research more realistic. The usual reason deception is employed in research is to create an artificial reality—a fake "failure" experience, for example, or a fake stimulus person who would never exist in real life (such as the "friendly/unsociable" fiction described above). Without lying, such artificial realities cannot be constructed. Defenders of deception say, "How else can I see how people will respond to such situations?"

One possible way is by going into the real world. Instead of showing your subjects hypothetical stimulus persons who not only do not exist but who probably never could, let your subjects watch and judge somebody who is real. Instead of constructing artificial situations where people are led to think they have succeeded or failed (assuming they believe you), follow them into their real lives where success and failure happen all the time. This is my final argument against the use of deception in psychology. When we stop lying to our subjects, we will no longer be able to view them in artificial environments that might create misleading results. Studying people as they really are, in my opinion, ought to be the fundamental purpose of all the methods of psychology.

This issue has a lot of room for reasonable disagreement, and my own opinion is surely a minority point of view within the field. Most psychologists believe that with proper controls the use of deception in research is perfectly safe and ethical. They further believe that deception is necessary to allow psychological research to address certain important issues. If you are reading this book as part of a personality course, your instructor probably has a strong opinion about the permissibility of deception. Why not ask him or her what that opinion is, and why? Then, draw your own conclusions.

SUMMARY

Psychology puts a great deal of emphasis on the methods by which knowledge can be obtained and in general is more concerned with improving our understanding of human nature than with practical applications. Personality psychology particularly emphasizes the reliability, validity, and generalizability of the measurements that it gathers. Reliability refers to the stability or repeatability of measurements. Validity refers to the degree to which a measurement actually measures what it is trying to measure. Generalizability is a broader concept that subsumes both reliability and validity, and refers to the class of other measurements to which a given measurement is related. "Representative design" is a technique used to maximize the generalizability of one's research results. Psychological data are gathered through experimental and correlational designs. Experimental designs manipulate the variable of interest, whereas correlational designs measure a variable as it already exists in the subjects being studied. Both approaches have advantages and disadvantages. The best way to summarize research results is in terms of effect size, which describes numerically the degree to which one variable is related to another. One good measure of effect size is the correlation coefficient, which can be evaluated with the Binomial Effect Size Display. Ethical issues relevant to psychology include the way research results are used, truthfulness in science, and the use of deception in research with human participants.

SUGGESTED READINGS: RESEARCH METHODS

Rosenthal, R., & Rosnow, R. L. (1991). *Essentials of behavioral research: Methods and data analysis* (2nd ed.). New York: McGraw-Hill.

> *One of the best primers for a beginning researcher, this book includes many topics (such as effect size) not handled well in other methods/statistics texts. You will have to read this book to see what its authors mean by the advice, "Think Yiddish, write British."*

Block, J. (1993). Studying personality the long way. In D. C. Funder, R. D. Parke, C. Tomlinson-Keasey, & K. Widaman (Eds.), *Studying lives through time: Personality and development* (pp. 9–41). Washington, DC: American Psychological Association.

> *A survey of his own approach to research by one of the most respected modern personality psychologists. Jack Block describes his approach to data gathering and research design, including longitudinal research (which follows individuals over long spans of time to see how they develop).*

Cronbach, L. J., & Meehl, P. E. (1955). Construct validity in psychological tests. *Psychological Bulletin, 52*, 281–302.

> *A difficult article, but the classic presentation of how personality psychologists think about the validity of their measurements. One of the most influential methodological articles of this century.*

Cronbach, L. J., Gleser, G. C., Nanda, H., & Rajaratnam, N. (1972). *The dependability of behavioral measurements: Theory of generalizability for scores and profiles.* New York: Wiley.

> *If anything, this book is even more difficult than Cronbach & Meehl, but it is nearly as important. This is the definitive treatment of generalizability theory, which has fundamentally changed the way psychologists think about reliability and validity.*

Gigerenzer, G., Swijtink, Z. G., Porter, T. M., & Daston, L. (1989). *The empire of chance: How probability changed science and everyday life.* Cambridge, England: Cambridge University Press.

> *A fascinating and surprising intellectual history of how statistical reasoning and probability testing entered science. It may lead you to wonder, was it all a mistake?*

PART II

How People Differ: The Trait Approach

People are psychologically different from each other, or it certainly seems that way. Everyday language contains many words to describe these differences. Some years ago, two psychologists named Allport and Odbert (1936) went through an unabridged English dictionary and reported finding 17,953 such words. The list included "arrogant," "shy," "trustworthy," and "conscientious," as well as more obscure terms such as "delitescent," "vulnific," and "earthbred." All these words describe personality traits, and the development of such a vast number and variety of them suggests that traits are an important part of how people talk and think about each other.

The trait approach to personality psychology attempts to build upon this suggestion by translating the informal language of personality traits into a formal psychology that measures traits and uses them to predict and explain human behavior. The measurement and use of personality traits is the topic of the following four chapters.

Chapter 4 will consider a first, basic question about the approach: Do personality traits exist? If they didn't, of course, a trait approach wouldn't make much sense. A debate over this very issue occupied many psychologists for several years, as you will learn in Chapter 4. Chapter 5 will describe how psychologists construct and use tests for personality assessment. Chapter 6 will describe how "laypeople"—nonpsychologists—also assess personalities in their daily lives, and will consider the circumstances under which such lay assessments are and are not likely to be accurate. Chapter 7 will describe how personality traits have been used to understand several different important kinds of human behavior, including self-control, drug abuse, and racial prejudice, and will also consider this question: Are all 17,953 personality traits necessary? Can we reduce this list to just a few, essential traits?

The overall goal of the next four chapters is to provide an introduction to the way personality psychologists try to measure and understand the ways in which people are psychologically different from one another.

CHAPTER 4

PERSONALITY TRAITS AND BEHAVIOR

The trait approach sometimes describes the psychological differences between individuals in terms of special dimensions invented by psychologists. These dimensions may have names like "neuroticism," "ego control," or even "parmia." More often, however, the trait approach is based on ordinary language (e.g., Gough, 1995). The trait approach then provides a theoretical and empirical basis for the scientific measurement of the degree to which individuals differ in sociability, reliability, dominance, nervousness, cheerfulness, and so forth (Funder, 1991). This accomplishment, in turn, opens the possibility of evaluating the accuracy of lay judgments of personality: When your acquaintance says you are sociable and reliable, is she correct? Perhaps even more important, if *you* claim you are sociable and reliable, are *you* correct?

Two things are important to note as we begin to consider the trait approach. The first is that this approach is based on empirical research, mostly correlational in nature (see Chapter 3). Trait psychologists put a great deal of effort into the careful construction of methods, often in the form of personality tests, for the accurate measurement of the ways that people differ. As we will see, some of these methods have become complex and statistically sophisticated. Whether the method is beguilingly simple or fearsomely complex, however, an ultimate criterion for any measurement of a personality trait is whether it can be used to predict behavior (Wiggins, 1973). If a person scores high on a measure of "dominance," can we accurately predict that he or she will act in a dominant manner in one or more of the situations of life? The answer to this question will be indexed, statistically, by the correlation between the score obtained on the measure of dominance and some separate indication of the person's dominant behavior in daily life.

The second notable aspect of the trait approach is that it focuses exclusively on individual differences. It does not attempt to measure how dominant, sociable, or nervous anybody is in any absolute sense; there is no zero point on any dominance scale or on any measure of any other trait. The trait approach does try to measure the degree to which you might be more or less dominant, sociable, or nervous than someone else. (Technically, therefore, trait measurements are made on ordinal rather than ratio scales.)

This focus on comparisons is one of the great strengths of the trait approach. It is important to understand and to be able to assess how people are different from one another, as they always are. But as so often happens (remember Funder's First Law), it must also be considered a weakness: The trait approach, by its very nature, is prone to neglect those aspects of human psychology that are common to all people, as well as the ways in which each person is unique. (Other approaches to personality, considered later in this book, do focus on those aspects of human nature.)

The Measurement of Individual Differences

One of my favorite quotes from the personality literature comes from an article by Clyde Kluckhohn and Henry Murray (1961; please pardon the sexist phrasing, which in some way contributes to its elegance):

Every man is in certain respects (a) like all other men, (b) like some other men, (c) like no other man. (p. 53).

What Kluckhohn and Murray meant, first, is that *certain* psychological properties and processes are universal. We all have similar, basic needs for food, water, and sex, for example. Their second point is that *other* properties of people differ, but in ways that allow individuals to be grouped. People who are highly dominant, for instance, might be essentially alike in a way that allows them to be meaningfully distinguished from those who are more submissive (although they might still differ among themselves in other respects). And third, in still other ways each individual is unique, and cannot be meaningfully compared to anyone else. Your genetic makeup, your past experience, and your view of the world are all different from those of anyone who ever has lived or ever will live (Allport, 1937).

The trait approach comes in at the second, middle level of this analysis; it neglects the other two levels. Because the trait approach is based on the ideas that "all men are like *some* other men" and that it is meaningful and useful to assess broad categories of individual difference, it assumes that in some real sense people *are* their traits. Theorists differ on whether this means that traits simply describe how you act, are the sum of everything you have learned, come from your underlying biology, or some combination of all of these. But for all trait theorists, these dimensions of individual difference are the building blocks of which personality is constructed.

Which raises a fundamental problem.

PEOPLE ARE INCONSISTENT

You can judge or you can measure how shy, conscientious, or dominant someone is, but even minimal experience will show that whatever you conclude the truth to be, there will be numerous exceptions. The individual may be shy with strangers but warm, open, and friendly with family members. The individual may be conscientious at work but sloppy and disorganized at home. The individual may be dominant with people of the same sex but deferential to people of the opposite sex, or vice versa. This kind of inconsistency is seen all the time.

Casual observation, therefore, is sufficient to confirm that personality traits are not the only thing that controls an individual's behavior; situations are important, as well. Some situations will make you more or less shy, more or less careful, more or less friendly, and more or less dominant. This is because situations vary according to what people are present and what the implicit rules are (Price & Bouffard, 1974). You act differently at home than you do at work partly because your home is inhabited by your family members, while your workplace is inhabited by your co-workers (and, perhaps, competitors). You act differently at a party than at a church because some pretty specific, albeit usually implicit, rules of decorum limit what is acceptable behavior at a church. There are implicit rules for parties, too, but they provide more leeway (Snyder & Ickes, 1985).

If situations are so important, then what role does personality play? Some people might answer, not much. Perhaps the behavior of individuals is so inconsistent and apt to change according to the given situation that there is no use characterizing them in terms of broad or global personality traits. If correct, this answer would imply not only that the personality assessments that many professional psychologists do are a colossal waste of time, but also that much of our everyday thinking and talking about people is fundamentally wrong. We should consider the possibility, therefore, that traits do not exist, that people change who they are according to the situation they are in, and that everybody is basically the same.

Do you find this idea outrageous? The answer you give may depend upon your age and stage in life. When I teach personality psychology to undergraduates, who are typically 18 to 22 years old, I find most students nod and calmly accept the possibility raised in the preceding paragraph. The suggestion that people have few consistent attributes to their personality and change who they are from moment to moment depending on the immediate situation sounds about right to them—or at least it does not strike them immediately as a ridiculous proposition.

Thus I was somewhat taken aback the first time I presented this same possibility to a night-school class. The course was ostensibly the same as the one I was teaching during the daytime that semester, but the night-school students were for the most part adult, working professionals from the metropolitan area, rather than dorm-dwelling 18- to 22-year-olds. These older students had the opposite reaction to the idea that individual differences are not important and that who you are depends upon the situation you are in: "Are you crazy?"

I wish I could document this developmental trend more formally, but I cannot, because the relevant study has not yet been done. But it is my strong impression that students who are still financially dependent upon their parents, have not yet found spouses or started a family, and have not yet selected a career goal find the idea that people are the same and that how you act depends upon the situation to be quite reasonable—indeed, they wonder why anybody would make a fuss about it. After all, their own personalities are still in the design stage. Older students who are on a career track, have started families, and otherwise have undertaken adult roles and responsibilities, by contrast, find the idea outrageous and even somewhat ridiculous.

What I am proposing, therefore, is that people differ from each other in the degree to which they have developed a consistent personality for themselves (Baumeister & Tice, 1988; Bem & Allen, 1974; Snyder & Monson, 1975). This might be related to age and life experience—older people and those with greater and broader experience may have more consistent personalities. If I am right about this, then the degree to which one finds acceptable the idea that personality does not exist might depend upon whether one has yet developed a consistent personality oneself!

THE PERSON-SITUATION DEBATE

Whether or not it violates your intuition to claim that behavior is so inconsistent that, for all intents and purposes, personality traits do not exist, an argument about just this point occupied a good deal of the attention of a large number of personality psychologists for more than two decades (and continues to occupy the attention of some—see Ross & Nisbett, 1991; Kenrick & Funder, 1988). These psychologists were and are the protagonists in the "person-situation debate," which focuses on this very question: Which is more important for determining what people do, the person or the situation?

To a considerable degree, the debate was triggered by the publication in 1968 of a book by Walter Mischel entitled *Personality and Assessment*.[1] Mischel

---

[1] Ironically, given its title, the book is often interpreted as arguing that personality does not exist and that assessment is impossible.

argued in his book that behavior is too inconsistent from one situation to the next to allow individual differences to be characterized accurately in terms of broad personality traits. Others—including, not surprisingly, psychologists who were heavily invested in the technology and practice of personality assessment—emphatically disagreed. Thus was the person-situation debate joined.

The rest of this chapter will review the basis and resolution of this debate. Ordinarily, arguments among psychologists are one of the things I am trying to spare you in this book. I would rather teach you about psychology itself than about what psychologists do or what they argue about. At the risk of sounding defensive, I hope to convince you that this particular argument is different. It is not just a tempest in a teapot, as arguments among specialists so often are. Rather, the consistency controversy goes to the heart of how we think about people.

There are two issues here. The first is, Does the personality of an individual transcend the immediate situation and moment and provide a consistent guide to his or her actions, or is what a person does utterly dependent upon the situation he or she is in at the time? Because our intuitions tell us that people do have consistent personalities (we certainly use personality trait terms all the time), this question leads to a second: Are our ordinary intuitions about people fundamentally flawed, or basically correct?

When I talk about the debate that was, to some extent, triggered by Mischel's book, I want to avoid falling into the trap of focusing too much on Mischel and his book, and not enough on the issues that make the debate they triggered both interesting and important. A small cottage industry sprang up within personality psychology during the 1970s, the main activity of which seemed to be to figure out what Mischel did and did not actually say. I was briefly a member of this enterprise myself (Funder, 1983).

But figuring out what Mischel did and did not say is a frustrating way to spend your time, both because the original book contained many qualifying phrases and escape clauses, and because Mischel seems to have changed his position on some fundamental issues during the intervening years (e.g., Mischel & Shoda, 1995). Mischel has frequently disavowed some of the more extreme renderings of his views. He often protests, for example, that he never meant to say that personality does not exist. At one psychologists' meeting chaired by Mischel himself, years ago, the chairman looked up and down the table and then intoned, ironically, "we don't seem to have a Mischelian here with us today" (E. R. Hilgard, personal communication, October 1975).

Nevertheless, the situationist arguments are important, despite what Mischel or others say about them today, because they attack the foundations of the trait approach. In the discussion that follows I believe that my presentation of the situationist position is faithful to its basic tenets.

Stripped to its essentials, the situationist argument as argued in Mischel's book has three parts:

1. (a) A thorough review of the personality research literature reveals that there is a limit to how well one can predict what a person will do based upon any measurement of any aspect of that person's personality; and (b) this upper limit is a small upper limit.

2. Therefore, situations are more important than personality traits in determining behavior. (This is the origin of the term "situationism"; Bowers, 1973.)

3. Therefore, not only is the professional practice of personality assessment a waste of time, but our everyday intuitions about people are fundamentally flawed. The trait words we use to describe people are not legitimately descriptive and, more generally, we tend to see people as being more consistent across situations than they really are.

Let us consider each of these three parts separately.

Predictability

THE SITUATIONIST ARGUMENT

The definitive test of the usefulness of a personality trait is its ability to predict behavior. If you know somebody's level or score on a trait, you should be able to forecast what that person will do in the future. Situationists argue that this ability is severely limited. There is no trait that you can use to predict someone's behavior with very much accuracy.

Mischel's book surveys some of the research concerning the relationships between self-descriptions of personality and direct measurements of behavior, between others' descriptions of personality and direct measurements of behavior, and between one measurement of behavior and another. Or, to use the terms introduced in Chapter 2, Mischel looked at the relationships between S data and T data, between I data and T data, and between T data and other T data. The first two comparisons address the ability of personality trait judgments to predict behavior—for example, can an acquaintance's judgment of your sociability predict how sociable you will be at Friday's party? The third comparison addresses the consistency of behavior across situations—for instance, if you are sociable at Friday's party, will you also be sociable at Tuesday's work meeting?

The data reported in the studies that Mischel reviewed were not, for the most part, taken from real life. The behavioral measurements—the T data—were nearly all gathered in laboratory settings. Some studies measured "attitude toward authority" by asking subjects for their opinions of photographs of older men, some measured "self-control" by seeing how long children could wait for candy treats provided by the experimenters, and so forth. Only rarely was behavior assessed in more-or-less natural situations, such as measures taken of cheating on games at a summer camp. Such studies were (and remain) rare, primarily because they are so difficult and expensive (see the discussion of T data in Chapter 2). Either way, the critical result is how well a person's behavior in one situation can be predicted, either from his or her behavior in another situation, or from his or her personality trait scores.

In the research literature, both sorts of predictability or consistency are indexed by a statistic called a **correlation coefficient**. As you will recall from Chapter 3, a correlation is a number that ranges between -1 and $+1$ and that indexes the association or relation between two variables, such as a personality score and a behavioral measurement. If the correlation is positive, it means that as one variable increases so does the other; the higher someone's sociability score, for example, the more parties he or she is likely to attend. If the correlation is negative, it means that as one variable increases the other decreases; the higher someone's shyness score, for example, the fewer parties he or she is likely to attend. Both positive *and* negative correlations imply that one variable can be predicted from a knowledge of the other. But if the correlation is near zero, it means the two variables are unrelated; perhaps sociability scores have nothing to do with how many parties one attends.

Mischel's original argument was that correlations between personality and behavior, or between behavior in one situation and behavior in another, seldom exceed .30. Another prominent situationist, Richard Nisbett, later revised this estimate upward, to .40 (Nisbett, 1980). The implication in both cases, of course, was that such correlations are small. The rhetoric of the situationists even belittled correlations in the .30 (or .40) range, calling them "personality coefficients" (Mischel, 1968). The term sounds and was meant to be insulting to the importance of personality in the shaping of behavior.

This claim concerning the (un)predictability of behavior hit the field of personality psychology in the early 1970s with surprisingly devastating force. Some personality psychologists, and even more psychologists outside the field of personality, concluded that a predictive limit corresponding to a correlation of .40 meant that personality did not exist. This conclusion was based upon two premises. The first was that situationists are right and .40 is the upper limit for the predictability of behavior from personality variables or behavior in other situations. The other, implicit but necessary premise was that this upper limit is a small upper limit.

THE RESPONSE

It took the representatives of the pro-personality side of this debate a few years to get their rebuttals in line, but when they finally did, they came up with three.

Unfair Literature Review   The first counterargument was that Mischel's review of the personality literature, which kicked off the whole controversy, was selective and unfair. After all, the relevant research literature goes back more than sixty years and contains literally thousands of studies. Mischel's review, by contrast, is quite short (only sixteen pages [pp. 20–36] of his book, about the length of a typical undergraduate term paper), and concentrates on a few studies that obtained disappointing results rather than on those—perhaps more numerous—studies that obtained more impressive results.

This is a very difficult ponit to prove or disprove, however. On the one hand, it is obvious that Mischel's review is selective because it is so short. Moreover, it is obvious that he did not go out of his way to find the best studies in the literature; the very first empirical study that Mischel cites (Burwen & Campbell, 1957) was hardly exemplary. The study was full of methodological and empirical flaws (e.g., a number of the authors' subjects deliberately sabotaged the research questionnaires) yet still managed to find a bit of evidence in favor of the trait it examined, which was "attitude toward authority." Many of the other studies Mischel cites were no better; moreover, even some of those managed, despite everything, to find evidence for the consistency of personality and behavior (see Block, 1977).

On the other hand, some studies are bound to find positive results on the basis of chance alone. And although it would be easy to put together a short literature review that looks much more positive than Mischel's, it is not clear how one would prove that such a review were any more fair or less selective. It is extremely difficult to characterize the general findings of entire research literatures (see Rosenthal, 1980), and the literature on behavioral consistency is no exception.

I frankly do not know how to establish whether the literature in general supports consistency, with a few exceptions, or whether it supports *in*consistency, with a few exceptions. So, to move the argument along, let us just "stipulate" (as lawyers say) the Mischel-Nisbett figure: Assume that a correlation of about .40 is the upper limit for how well personality traits can predict behavior, as well as for how consistent behavior is from one situation to another.

We Can Do Better   A second counterargument to the situationist critique essentially grants the .40 upper limit, as I just did, but claims that this upper limit is a result of poor or less-than-optimal research methodology. The weak findings summarized by Mischel do not imply that personality is unimportant, therefore; they merely imply that we can and must do better research.

One way in which research could be done better, according to this counterargument, is for research to take place out of the laboratory a bit more often. As I mentioned above, the behavioral measurements that formed the basis for the situationist critique were nearly all made in laboratory situations. Some of these situations were probably dull and uninvolving for the subjects. How about behavior in real life? Personality is much more likely to appear, it has been argued, in situations that are real, vivid, and important to the individual in question (Allport, 1961). For example, when a person is asked in the laboratory to respond to a picture of an older person, his or her personality may or may not become involved (Burwen & Campbell, 1957). But when a person is about to make his or her first parachute jump, personality seems likely to play a more important role (Epstein, 1980; Fenz & Epstein, 1967).

A second kind of research improvement that frequently has been advocated takes account of the fact that some people might be more consistent than others. "Moderator variables" could be used to identify those people.[2] For example, one study asked subjects how consistent they were on the trait of sociability, and found that the behavior of those who said they were consistent was easier to predict accurately than the behavior of those who said they were inconsistent (Bem & Allen, 1974).[3] Research on the trait of self-monitoring suggests that some people, called high self-monitors, quickly change their behavior according to the situation they are in, whereas low self-monitors are more likely to express their personality consistently from one situation to the next (Snyder, 1987; see also Chapter 7). Finally, some *behaviors* might be more consistent than others. Elements of expressive behavior, such as how much you gesture or how loudly you talk, are likely to be consistent across situations, whereas more goal-directed behaviors, such as trying to impress someone, are more likely to depend on the situation you are in at the moment (Funder & Colvin, 1991; see also Allport & Vernon, 1933).

A third research improvement that has been advocated proposes focusing efforts to predict behavior upon general behavioral *trends*, instead of actions at particular moments. Thus, rather than try to predict whether somebody will act in a friendly fashion next Tuesday at 3:00 PM, we might be better off trying to predict how friendly that person will behave on average over the next year. Elementary psychometric principles of reliability, which you will recall from Chapter 3, establish that the predictability of such an average will be much better than the predictability of a single act at a single time (Fishbein & Ajzen, 1974; Epstein, 1979).

But the issue here is more than just a matter of psychometric reliability. It concerns the meaning and purpose of personality trait judgments. When you say that somebody is friendly, or conscientious, or shy, are you trying to predict what he or she will do at a specific time and place, or are you expressing a

---

[2]A moderator variable is one that affects, or "moderates," the relationship between two other variables.

[3]Although this was an influential finding and an important idea, Chaplin and Goldberg (1985) have provided evidence that the finding is difficult to replicate. More recently, Zuckerman et al. (1988) have surveyed a broad range of research literature and concluded that this effect of self-rated consistency on the behavioral predictability is small but probably real.

prediction of how that person will generally act, over the long haul? In most cases, I think, the answer is the latter. When we wish to understand someone, or wish to select a roommate or an employee, it is not as critical to know what the person will do at a specific place and time, because that will always depend upon the exact situation at the moment. Rather, we need to know how the person will act *in general* across the various relevant situations of life. We understand that somebody might be late on rare occasions because their car will not start; we know that everybody can have a bad day and be grouchy. But when choosing an employee or a roommate what we really need to know is how reliable will the person be in general? Or, how friendly is the person, usually?

These three suggestions—measure behavior in real life, check for moderator variables, and predict behavioral trends rather than single acts—are all good ideas for improving personality research. However, it must be admitted that they represent potential more than reality. To follow any of these suggestions is difficult. Real-life behaviors are not easy to assess (see Chapter 2), moderator variables may be subtle and difficult to measure themselves (Chaplin, 1991), and the prediction of behavioral trends requires, by definition, that many, not just a few, direct behavioral measurements be taken. So, although these suggestions provide good reasons to think that the situationist critique may underestimate the levels of consistency in people's behavior, there is not yet enough research to prove that behavioral consistency can regularly get much higher than the .40 correlational range that the situationists now concede.

Besides, both of the first two responses to the situationist critique miss a more basic point:

.40 Is Not Small   Remember that to be impressed (or depressed) by the situationist critique of personality traits, you must believe *two* things: (1) A correlation of .40 represents the true, upper limit to which one can predict behavior from personality, or see consistency in behavior from one situation to another; and (2) That upper limit is a small upper limit. The discussion so far has concentrated on responses to point 1. But if for some reason you were to conclude that a correlation of .40 was not small in the first place (point 2), then that limit really would not be worrisome, and the force of the situationist critique would largely dissipate.

Thus it is critical to evaluate how much predictability a correlation in the range granted by the situationist critiques really represents. But to evaluate whether .40 is big or little, or to assess any other statistic, you need a standard of comparison.

Two kinds of standard are possible, absolute and relative. To evaluate this correlation against an absolute standard, we would calculate how many correct and incorrect decisions a trait measurement with this degree of validity would yield in a hypothetical context. To evaluate this correlation against a relative standard, we can compare this degree of predictability conceded for personality traits with the ability of other methods to predict behavior. We will do both.

An absolute evaluation of a .40 correlation can be obtained from Rosenthal and Rubin's (1982) Binomial Effect Size Display (BESD), which was described in Chapter 3. I won't repeat the description here but will go straight to the bottom line: According to the BESD, a correlation of .40 means that a prediction of behavior based on a personality trait score is likely to be accurate 70 percent of the time (assuming a chance accuracy rate of 50 percent). (This figure should not be confused with the "percentages of variance explained" discussed in Chapter 3, which are computed in a different way and have a far different—and far more difficult—interpretation). 70 percent is far from perfect, of course, but it is enough to be useful for many purposes. For instance, an employer choosing who to put through an expensive training program could save large amounts of money by being able to predict with 70 percent accuracy who will or will not be a successful employee at the conclusion of the program.

Let's work through an example. Say a company has 200 employees it is considering for further training, but can only afford to train 100 of them. Let's further assume that, overall, 50 percent of the company's employees could successfully complete the program. The company picks 100 employees at random, and spends $10,000 to train each one. But, as we said, only half of them are successful. So the company has spent a total of $1 million to get 50 successfully trained employees, or $20,000 each.

But consider what happens if the company uses a selection test to decide who to train—a test that has been shown to correlate at .40 with training success. By selecting the top half of the scorers on this test for training, the company will get 70 successful trainees (instead of 50) out of the 100 who are trained, still at a total cost of $1 million but now at only about $14,300 per successful trainee. In other words, using a test with a .40 validity could save the company $5,700 per successful trainee, or about $400,000. That will pay for a lot of testing.

What about a relative standard? Well, what is the most appropriate basis of comparison when trying to evaluate the predictive ability of personality traits? Situationists, you will recall, believe that it is the *situation*, not the person, that is all-important in the determination of behavior. To evaluate the ability of personality traits to predict behavior, therefore, the appropriate comparison to draw would seem to be with the ability of situational variables to predict behavior. That is the topic of the next section.

Situationism

A key tenet of the situationist position is that personality does not determine behavior—situations do. To evaluate the degree to which a behavior is affected by a personality variable, the routine practice is to correlate a measure of behavior with a measure of personality. But how does one evaluate the degree to which behavior is affected by a situational variable?

This question has received surprisingly little attention over the years. When it has been addressed, the usual practice was rather strange: the power of situations was determined by subtraction. Thus, if it was found that a personality variable correlated .40 with a behavioral measurement and that it therefore "explained 16 percent of the variance," the other 84 percent was assigned, by default, to the situation (e.g., Mischel, 1968).

Of course, this is not a legitimate practice, even if it used to be common. We have already considered the needlessly misleading obscurity of the whole "percent of variance" language (see Chapter 3). But even if one accepts this terminology, it would be just as reasonable to attribute the "missing" variance to other personality variables that you did not measure as it would be to attribute it to situational variables that you also did not measure (Ahadi & Diener, 1989). Moreover, to assign variance by subtraction in this way does not allow you to say anything about *which* aspects of the situation might be important, in a way parallel to how trait measures tell you which aspects of personality are important.

It has long seemed remarkable to me that the situationists have been willing to claim that situations are important, yet have been seemingly unconcerned with measuring situational variables in a way that indicates precisely how or how much situations affect behavior. When situationists claim that situations are important but do not specify what about them is important or to what extent, then, as one trait psychologist pointed out,

. . . situations turn out to be "powerful" in the same sense as Scud missiles [the erratic weapons used by Iraq during the Persian Gulf war] are powerful: They may have huge effects, or no effects, and such effects may occur virtually anywhere, all over the map (Goldberg, 1992, p. 90).

Moreover, there is no need for the situationists to sell themselves so short—to be so vague about what specific aspects of situations can affect behavior. There is a large and impressive body of psychological research that *does* specify the effects of situations. The evidence comprises nearly every study in experimental social-psychology (e.g., Aronson, 1972).

In the typical social-psychological experiment, two (or more) separate groups of subjects are placed, randomly and usually one at a time, into one or another of two (or more) different situations. The social psychologist measures what the subjects do. If the average behavior of the subjects who are placed in one situation or "condition" turns out to be significantly different (statistically speaking—see Chapter 3) from the average behavior of the subjects placed in the other condition, then the experiment is deemed successful.

For example, one might be interested in the effect of incentives on attitude change. In an experiment, you could ask subjects to make a statement they do not believe, such as that a dull game was really interesting. Then, you could test to see if they come to believe these statements—that the game was not dull after all. Some of your subjects could be offered a large incentive (say, $20) to make the counter-attitudinal statement, while the rest are offered a smaller incentive (say, 50¢). If the two groups of subjects change their attitudes about the game to different degrees, then one can conclude that the difference in incentive between the two conditions had some effect on this difference in attitude. The way the two situations were constructed to be different must have been the reason that the subjects responded differently, and therefore the experiment has demonstrated an effect of a situational variable on behavior (Festinger & Carlsmith, 1959).

The vast literature of experimental social psychology provides a treasure trove of specific examples of situational effects. For our present topic, we need to ask how large those effects are, compared to the effects of personality variables on behavior. Perhaps surprisingly, social psychologists historically have paid very little attention to the size of the situational effects they study. They have concentrated on statistical significance, or the degree to which their results would not have been expected by chance. As was discussed in Chapter 3, this is a separate matter from effect size or what one might consider "actual" significance, because even a small effect can be highly significant statistically, if one has studied a large enough number of subjects.

Personality psychologists, by contrast, have always focused on the size of the effects they study. The key statistic in personality research, the correlation coefficient, is a measure of effect size and not statistical significance. The "personality coefficient" of .40 is ordinarily not comparable with the effects found in social-psychological studies of situational variables, therefore, because the two styles of research do not employ a common metric.

Fortunately, this difficulty can easily be remedied. As was mentioned in Chapter 3, the experimental statistics used by social psychologists can be converted algebraically into correlations of the sort used by personality psychologists. A few years back, Dan Ozer and I did just that (Funder & Ozer, 1983). From the social psychological literature we chose three prominent examples of the power of situations to shape behavior. We then converted the results of those studies to effect-size correlations.

The first classic study that we chose concerned the "forced compliance" effect observed by Festinger and Carlsmith (1959) in a study similar to the one I described above. Subjects were induced to tell innocent, new subjects that a dull experiment was actually interesting. The subjects were offered either twenty dollars or fifty cents for doing this. The counterintuitive result was that the subjects paid fifty cents actually changed their attitudes, after telling the lie, to believe that the experiment was more interesting than they had originally thought. The subjects paid twenty dollars, in contrast, did not change their attitudes—they still thought the experiment had been boring.

This study was one of the early, important demonstrations of the workings of **cognitive dissonance**. The explanation given by Festinger and Carlsmith was that subjects felt dissonance as a result of saying something they did not believe, but that a payment of twenty dollars was sufficient to reduce their uneasy feelings. Fifty cents was not enough to ease these feelings, however, so those subjects had to change their own attitudes in order for their words not to be so out of line with their beliefs.

This effect is a classic of the social-psychological literature, and perhaps one of the most important and interesting findings in the field. Yet the size of this effect had seldom been calculated or reported. Ozer and I performed the simple calculation: the effect of incentive on attitude change following counter-attitudinal advocacy turns out to correspond to a correlation of .36. This is a direct, statistical measure of how strongly rewards can affect attitude change.

A second important program of research in social psychology has concerned bystander intervention. Darley and his colleagues staged several faked, but dramatic, incidents in which subjects came upon apparently distressed individuals lying helplessly in their path (Darley & Batson, 1967; Darley & Latane, 1968). The research was intended to find out if the subjects would help the distressed person.

The answer turned out to depend, among other things, on whether other people were present and on whether the subject was in a hurry. The more people that were present the less likely the subject was to stop and help; the correlation indexing the size of this effect was −.38. Also, the greater the subject's hurry, the less likely the subject was to help; the correlation indexing the size of this effect was −.39.

The third program of research we examined was Stanley Milgram's classic investigation of obedience. In a famous series of studies, Milgram's research assistants ordered subjects to give apparently painful and dangerous (but fortunately bogus) electric shocks to an innocent "victim" (Milgram, 1975). If the subjects objected, the assistant said "the experiment requires that you continue."

Milgram identified two variables as particularly important in determining whether the subjects would obey this command. The first was the isolation of the victim: if the victim was in the next room and could not be heard protesting, or could be heard only weakly, obedience was more likely than if the victim was right in front of the subject. The correlation that reflects the size of the effect of victim isolation is .42. The second important variable was the proximity of the experimenter: obedience was more likely if the research assistant giving the orders was physically present than if he gave orders over the phone or on a tape recorder. The correlation that reflects the size of the effect of experimenter proximity turned out to be .36.

Recall that the size of the personality coefficient that was supposed to reflect the maximum relationship that can be obtained between personality variables and behavior is about .40. Now, compare that to the effects of situational variables on behavior, as just surveyed: .36, .38, 39., .42, and .36.

One can draw two different conclusions from these results. A number of writers have concluded from these analyses that neither personality variables nor situational variables have much of an effect on behavior. That was hardly our point! We re-analyzed these particular experiments precisely because, as far as we knew, nobody doubted that each of them demonstrated a powerful, important influence of a situational variable on behavior. The experiments we chose are among the truly classic studies of social psychology—they will be found in any textbook on the subject and have contributed important insights into the bases of social behavior.

We prefer a second conclusion, therefore: that the situational variables are important determinants of behavior, but that many personality variables are important as well. When put on a common scale for comparison, the size of the effects of the person and of the situation are much more similar than had been previously realized. In this light, calling a correlation of .40 a "personality coefficient" seems to lose a little of its pejorative edge.

With some sort of perspective on the issue, we are ready to consider the third part of the situationist argument.

Are Person Perceptions Erroneous?

Recall that the situationists argue that the ability of personality variables to predict behavior is limited if not nonexistent, that situations are much more important, and that our everyday perceptions of one another, which consist to a large degree of judgments of personality traits, are therefore largely erroneous. Now that we have carefully dealt with the first two parts of this argument, the third falls apart largely of its own weight. The effects of personality on behavior *do* seem sufficient to be perceived accurately. Despite the situationist critique, our intuitions probably were not that far off base after all.

Both everyday experience and any fair reading of the research literature make one thing abundantly clear: We do not just make up differences between the personalities of the different people we know. People really do act differently from each other. When it comes to personality, one size does not fit all. Even when they are all in the same situation, some individuals will be more sociable, or nervous, or talkative, or active than others. And when the situation changes, those differences will still be there (e.g., Funder & Colvin, 1991).

The 17,953 trait terms in the English language did not just appear out of thin air. Ideas about personality traits are an important part of our culture and overall view of the world. Consider Eskimos and snow: It has long been noted that the Eskimo languages have many more words to describe snow than do the languages of those who live farther south (Whorf, 1956; Clark & Clark, 1977). This is assumed to be because snow is important to Eskimos; they build shelters from it, they travel across it, and so forth. (Skiers also have a specialized vocabulary that contains many different words for snow.) The need to discriminate between many different kinds of snow has led Eskimos to develop words to describe each kind, in order to communicate better with one another about this important topic.

The same thing seems to have happened with the language of personality. People are psychologically different and it is both important and interesting to note just how. Words arose to describe these differences, words that make us more sensitive to the differences and that make it possible to talk about them. The proliferation of trait words is not over yet; consider the relatively "new" words jock, geek, preppie, and Val.[4] Personality psychologists are not leaving the language alone either. They have introduced the terms self-monitoring, private self-consciousness, public self-consciousness, and even parmia and threctia to delineate aspects of personality that they did not believe were described precisely enough by the existing English language (Cattell, 1965).

THE BOTTOM LINE

There is a consumer-affairs television reporter in Los Angeles who likes to conclude his reports by saying, "Here's the bottom line for your money." I think I can give you a bottom line here, too. The person-situation debate raged for some years but is basically over (Kenrick & Funder, 1988). The bottom line is this: personality trait words are important, and refer to real aspects of human psychology that can be meaningfully assessed and used to predict and, more important, to understand behavior.

SUMMARY

The trait approach to personality begins by assuming that individuals differ in their characteristic patterns of thought, feeling, and behavior. These patterns are called personality traits. Classifying people in this way raises an important problem, however: people are inconsistent. Indeed, it has been suggested by some psychologists that people are so inconsistent in their behavior from one situation to the next that it is not worthwhile try to characterize them in terms of personality traits. The debate among psychologists over this issue was called the consistency controversy. Opponents of traits argue that a review of the personality literature reveals that the ability of traits to predict behavior is extremely limited; that situations are therefore more important than personality traits for

---

[4]In a bit of regional (California) slang that is probably already passé, a "Val" (short for "Valley Girl") is a teenage girl from the San Fernando Valley (just north of Los Angeles) who is stereotyped as being empty-headed, materialistic, and boy-crazy.

determining what people do; and that not only is personality assessment (the measurement of traits) a waste of time, but many of our intuitions about each other are fundamentally wrong. The responses to the first of these arguments are that a fair review of the literature reveals that the predictability of behavior from traits is better than is sometimes acknowledged; that better research methods can make this predictability even higher; and that the upper limit for predictability (a correlation of about .40) is bigger than sometimes recognized. The response to the second of these arguments is that many important effects of situations on behavior are no bigger, statistically, than the documented size of the effects of personality traits on behavior. If the responses to the first two criticisms are valid, then the third, that assessment and our intuitions are both fundamentally flawed, falls apart of its own weight. The many personality trait terms in our language give support to the importance of traits, which provide a useful way to predict behavior and understand personality.

CHAPTER

PERSONALITY ASSESSMENT I: PERSONALITY TESTING AND ITS CONSEQUENCES

Once it is determined that you have a particular personality trait—dominance, or nervousness, or conscientiousness, for example—the next question is *how* dominant, nervous, or conscientious you are. Specifically, do you manifest more or less of this trait than the next person? For personality traits to be useful for the scientific understanding of the mind, for the prediction of behavior, or for any other purpose, they must be measured in some way. The next two chapters will explore how personality traits are measured, or assessed.

THE NATURE OF PERSONALITY ASSESSMENT

Personality assessment is a professional activity of numerous research, clinical, and industrial psychologists, and it is a prosperous business. Clinicians may measure how depressed you are in order to plan treatment, whereas potential employers would probably be more interested in measuring your conscientiousness in order to decide whether to offer you a job. But there is more to personality assessment than just measuring traits.

An individual's **personality** consists of *any* characteristic pattern of behavior, thought, or emotional experience that exhibits relative consistency across time and situations (Allport, 1937). These patterns include the terms commonly thought of as personality traits that were discussed in the preceding chapter and illustrated above, and personality psychology has a long, still active, and still fruitful tradition of conceptualizing and assessing such traits.

But these patterns also include other kinds of variables, including motives, intentions, goals, strategies, and subjective representations (the ways in which people perceive and construct their worlds). These variables would indicate the degree to which a person desires one goal as opposed to another, or thinks the world is changeable as opposed to fixed, or is generally happy, or is optimistic as opposed to pessimistic, or is sexually attracted to members of the same or the opposite sex. All of these variables, and many others, are relatively stable attributes of the psychological makeup of individuals, and any attempt to measure them necessarily entails personality assessment. As a result, assessment is relevant to an extremely broad range of research, including nearly every topic of interest to personality, developmental, and social psychologists.

And personality assessment is not an activity only of psychologists. Of course, most assessments we usually hear of are done by psychologists in research, in clinics, or in private industry; their results sometimes have important consequences for the individuals involved. But assessments by *non*psychologists are even more widespread, and some would argue that they are even more important.

These personality assessments are done by you, your friends, your family—and by me, in my off-duty hours—all day long, every day. As was mentioned at the beginning of Chapter 4, personality traits are a fundamental part of how we think about ourselves and each other. We base our feelings about ourselves partly on our beliefs about our personalities—are we competent, or kind, or tough? We choose who to befriend and who to avoid on the basis of our assessments of them—will this person be reliable, or helpful, or honest—and they make the same judgments and choices concerning us. The judgments we make of the personalities of ourselves and each other are at least as consequential as those that any psychologist will ever make.

Regardless of the source of a judgment of someone's personality, whether that source be a psychologist, an acquaintance, or a psychological test, the most important thing to know about that judgment is the degree to which it is right or wrong. And, regardless of the sources of various judgments, they all must be evaluated according to the same criteria. When professional personality judgments or personality tests are evaluated, it is typically said that we are evaluating their *validity*. When amateur judgments are evaluated, what we are usually evaluating is their *accuracy*.

Despite the difference in terms, the evaluation is the same. For evaluating validity or accuracy, two basic criteria are used: agreement and prediction. The agreement criterion asks, Does this judgment agree with other judgments obtained through other techniques or from other judges (whether professional or amateur)? The prediction criterion asks, Can this judgment of personality be used to predict behavior? (see Funder, 1987, 1995).

The topic of this chapter and the next is personality assessment—by professionals and by amateurs. The remainder of this chapter considers the business of personality assessment and how psychologists construct and use personality tests, as well as some of the consequences of testing. Chapter 6 will consider personality assessment by amateurs—people who are not trained or paid to be psychologists, but who nonetheless practice psychology every day.

THE BUSINESS OF TESTING

Each year the American Psychological Association (APA) holds an annual convention. It's quite an event. Thousands of psychologists take over most of the downtown hotels in a city such as San Francisco, Boston, or Washington, D.C., for a week of meetings, symposia, and cocktail parties. One of the biggest attractions is always the exhibit hall, where dozens of high-tech, artistically designed booths fill a room that seems to go on for acres. Most of these booths are set up, at great expense, by one of two kinds of company. One group is textbook publishers; all the tools of advertising are applied to the task of convincing college professors like me to assign their students to read (and buy) books such as the one you now hold in your hand. The second group is psychological testers. Their booths are usually larger and fancier than the publishers' booths. Free samples are generously distributed, including not only personality and ability tests, but shopping bags, notebooks, and even beach umbrellas. These freebies prominently display the logo of their corporate sponsor: the Psychological Corporation, Consulting Psychologists Press, the Institute for Personality and Ability Testing, and so on. These goodies are, of course, paid for by what they are intended to sell: personality tests.

You can get a free "personality test" even without going to the APA convention. On North Michigan Avenue in Chicago, on the Boston Common, at Fisherman's Wharf in San Francisco, and in Westwood in Los Angeles, I have seen people distribute brightly colored brochures on which are printed these words: ARE YOU CURIOUS ABOUT YOURSELF? FREE PERSONALITY TEST ENCLOSED. Inside the brochure is something that in many ways looks like a conventional personality test—two hundred questions to be answered true or false (one item reads "Having settled an argument out do you continue to feel disgruntled for a while?"). But as it turns out, it is really a recruitment pitch. If you take the test and go for your "free evaluation"—which I do not recommend—you will be told (a) that you are all messed up, and (b) that the people who gave you the test have the cure: you need to join a certain "church" that will provide the therapy you desperately need.

The personality testers who distribute free samples at the APA convention and those who hand out free "personality tests" on North Michigan Avenue have a surprising amount in common. They both hope to make some money. They both use all the usual techniques of advertising, including free samples.

The tests they distribute look superficially alike. And they both trade off what seems to be a nearly universal desire to know more about personality. The brochure labelled "Are you curious about yourself" is asking a pretty irresistible question. The more staid tests distributed at the APA convention likewise offer an intriguing promise of finding out something about your own or somebody else's personality that might be interesting, important, or useful.

But below the surface they are not the same. The tests peddled at the APA convention are, for the most part, well-validated instruments that are useful for many purposes. The ones being pushed at tourist destinations from coast to coast are potentially dangerous frauds. But you cannot tell which is which just by looking at them. To tell a valid test from an invalid one you need to know something about how personality tests and assessments are constructed, how they work, and how they can fail. Read on.

PERSONALITY TESTS

The personality testing companies that are so well represented at APA meetings do a good business. They sell their product to clinical psychologists, to the personnel departments of large corporations, and to the military, for example. You have most likely taken at least one personality test at some point in your life, and you are likely to take more.

One of the most widely used personality tests is the Minnesota Multiphasic Personality Inventory, or MMPI.[1] This test was designed for use in the clinical assessment of individuals with psychological difficulties, but it has also been widely used for purposes such as employment screening. Another widely used test is the California Psychological Inventory, or CPI; it is similar to the MMPI in many ways, but is designed for use with *non*disturbed individuals. Others include the Sixteen Personality Factor Questionnaire, or 16PF, the Strong Vocational Interest Blank, or SVIB (often used for vocational guidance in school settings), and on and on.

Many personality tests, including those just listed, are "omnibus" inventories. Omnibus inventories are several tests in one; they are designed to measure a wide range of personality traits. A personality test called the NEO, for instance, measures five broad traits but also includes a large number of sub-scales (Costa & McCrae, 1985).

Other personality tests are designed to measure just one trait. These special-purpose tests are mostly used in psychological research on individual differences

---

[1]By a tradition of mysterious origin, nearly all personality tests are referred to by their initials—all capital letters, no periods.

that researchers wish to study. There are tests to measure shyness, self-consciousness, self-monitoring, empathy, attributional complexity, non-verbal sensitivity, something called "Type A" (a hostile personality pattern that makes you vulnerable to heart attack), something else called "Type C" (a passive personality pattern that supposedly makes you vulnerable to cancer), and so on.

To use the terms introduced in Chapter 2, some personality tests—probably most—are S data. They ask you about what you are like, and the score you receive directly reflects how you describe yourself. The shyness scale consists of a bunch of questions that ask how shy you are, the attributional complexity scale asks you how complexly you think about the causes of people's behavior, and so forth.

Other personality tests are T data. The MMPI is a good example. It presents items—such as "I prefer a shower to a bath"—not because the tester is interested in the literal answer, but because answers to this item have been found to be informative about some aspect of personality (in this case, empathy—preferring the shower is the empathic response, for some reason; Hogan, 1969).

Psychologists have differing opinions about whether or not intelligence should be considered to be a personality trait. But it can be noted that "IQ tests" also yield T data. If we were to assess IQ with an S-data test, we would ask our subjects "are you an intelligent person?" or "are you good at math?" But instead, IQ tests ask people questions of varying difficulty that they might get right or wrong, such as reasoning or math problems. The more of those you get right, the higher your (tested) IQ. These right or wrong answers comprise T data. You cannot get a high IQ score just by claiming to be intelligent; you have to perform.

In my opinion, the distinction between S-data tests and T-data tests is important, but in the conventional literature on personality testing this distinction is rarely drawn. Distinctions are more commonly made between objective and projective tests.

Projective Tests

Projective tests are designed on the basis of a particular theory of how to see into someone's mind. The theory is that if you ask somebody to describe or to interpret a meaningless, ambiguous stimulus—such as an inkblot—the answer he or she gives *cannot* come from the stimulus itself, because the stimulus does not, in truth, mean anything. The answer he or she gives must instead come from (be a "projection" of) the inner workings of the person's mind (Murray, 1943). The answer may even tell you something the person does not know about him or herself.

This is the theory behind the famous Rorschach ink blot test, for instance (Rorschach, 1921; Exner, 1993). The Swiss psychiatrist Hermann Rorschach dropped blots of india ink onto notecards, folded the cards in half, and then unfolded them. The result was a set of symmetric blots.[2] Over the years, numerous psychiatrists and clinical psychologists have shown these blots to their clients and asked them what they saw.

Of course, the only literally correct answer is "an ink blot," but that is not considered a cooperative response. Instead, the examiner is interested in whether the patient will report seeing a cloud, or a devil, or her mother, or whatever. The idea is that whatever the client sees, precisely because it is *not* in the card, must tell you something about the contents of the client's mind.

Numerous other projective tests are based on the same logic. The "draw-a-person" test requires the client to draw (you guessed it!) a person, and the drawing is interpreted according to what kind of person is drawn, which body parts are exaggerated or omitted, and so forth (Machover, 1949). Various versions of the Thematic Apperception Test (TAT) ask clients to tell stories about pictures they are shown (Morgan & Murray, 1935; Murray, 1943). The themes of these stories are held to be informative about the client's motivational state (e.g., McClelland, 1975). If a person looks at a picture of two people and thinks they are fighting, for example, this might reveal a desire for aggression; if the two people are described as in love, this might reflect a need for intimacy; if one is seen as giving orders to the other, this might reflect a need for power, and so on.

The idea common to all these tests is interesting and reasonable, and interpretations of actual responses can be fascinating. A large number of practicing clinicians swear by their efficacy. Objective research data on their validity—the degree to which they actually measure what they are supposed to measure—is surprisingly thin, however (Wiggins, 1973). It is probably fair to say that only two projective tests have a background of evidence that comes even close to establishing validity according to the standards by which other tests are evaluated. One of them is the TAT (McClelland, 1984); the other is the Rorschach, when it is scored according to one particular technique (Exner, 1993).

To again use the terminology introduced in Chapter 2, projective tests all provide T data. They are specific, directly observed responses to particular stimuli, whether ink blots, pictures, or instructions to draw somebody. The greatest disadvantage of T data therefore applies to projective tests: You cannot be sure what they mean. What does it mean when somebody thinks an ink blot looks like genitalia, or imagines that an ambiguous picture portrays a murder, or draws a person with no ears? The answer, and the validity of the answer, critically depend upon the test interpreter (Sundberg, 1977). Two different interpreters of the same response might come to different conclusions (of projective tests,

---

[2]According to legend, Rorschach made many blots in this way but kept only the "best" ones. It would be fascinating—and perhaps revealing—to know how he decided what a good blot was.

only the TAT is well standardized in its scoring). A system has also been developed for scoring the Rorschach test (Exner, 1993), but not everybody uses it.

The survival of projective tests into the late twentieth century is something of a mystery. They certainly have not survived because of overwhelming scientific evidence as to their validity. Perhaps their endurance comes from the fact that they are so interesting to work with. Perhaps, as some have suggested, these tests serve a useful, if nonpsychometric, function of "breaking the ice" between client and therapist by giving them something to do during the first visit. Or, just possibly, there *is* a real validity to these instruments in actual clinical application, and in the hands of certain skilled clinicians, that has not been successfully repeated by controlled research studies.

Objective Tests

The tests that psychologists call "objective" can be detected at a glance. If a test consists of a list of questions, answered yes/no or true/false, and especially if it uses a computer-scorable answer sheet, then it is an **objective test**. The term comes from the idea that the questions that make up the test seem more objective than the pictures and blots of projective tests.

It is not clear that the term "objective" is really justified, however. Consider the first item of the famous MMPI: "I like mechanics magazines," which is to be answered true or false (Wiggins, 1973). The item may seem objective, compared to a question like "what do you see in this ink blot?" But the appearance of objectivity may be misleading. For instance, does "like" mean interest, fondness, admiration, or tolerance? Does liking such magazines require that you actually read them? Are *Popular Mechanics* and *High Fidelity* both mechanics magazines? How about *Computer World*? Are only popular magazines included in the classification, or does the item also refer to trade journals of professional mechanics, or the research literature produced by professors of mechanical engineering? This example is not a particularly problematic objective item. Instead, it is rather typical. And it illustrates how objectivity is harder to attain than it might seem at first.

It is hard to escape the conclusion that the items on "objective" tests, while perhaps not as ambiguous as those that constitute projective tests, are still not truly objective. Writing truly objective items might be impossible, and even if it were possible, such items might not work for personality assessment. Think about it for a moment: If everybody read and interpreted an item in exactly the same way, then might not everybody tend also to *answer* the item in the same way? If so, the item would not be very useful for the assessment of individual differences. In some cases, the ambiguity of "objective" items might *not* be a flaw; items may have to be somewhat ambiguous to be informative for personality assessment.

Harrison Gough, the inventor of the CPI, included on his test a scale called "commonality," which consists solely of items that are answered in the same way by at least 95 percent of *all* people. Such a scale is of small value for detecting individual differences, since the items are selected to be ones on which few people differ. He included it to detect illiterates who are pretending to know how to read, and individuals who are deliberately trying to sabotage the test. The average score on this scale is about 95 percent, but an illiterate answering at random will score about 50 percent (since it is a true-false scale) and will therefore be immediately identifiable, as will someone who (like one of my former students) answered the CPI by flipping a coin—heads true, tails false.

This is an interesting and clever use for a commonality scale, but it is included here to make a different point. Gough reports that when individuals encounter a commonality item—one being "I would fight if someone tried to take my rights away" (keyed true)—they do *not* say to themselves, "What a dumb, obvious item. I bet everybody answers it the same way." Instead, they say, "At last! A non-ambiguous item I can really understand!" People like the commonality items because they are not ambiguous. Unfortunately, such items are not as useful for personality measurement as are scales containing more ambiguous items (Gough, 1968).[3]

METHODS OF OBJECTIVE TEST CONSTRUCTION

Though useful in many situations, personality tests are not magic. Good personality tests must be constructed very carefully. Understanding how good tests are designed and constructed can make you a more discerning consumer and, in certain cases, a less likely victim.

There are three basic methods for constructing objective personality tests: the rational method, the factor analytic method, and the empirical method. Sometimes, a mixture of methods is employed, but let's begin by considering the pure application of each.

The Rational Method

Calling one method of test construction "rational" does not mean the others are irrational. It simply means that the basis of this approach is to come up with items that seem directly, obviously, and rationally related to what it is you wish to measure. Sometimes this is done through careful derivation from a theory of the trait in which the researcher is interested. Thus the test developer Douglas

---

[3]Another item from the commonality scale reads, "Education is more important than most people think." Paradoxically, almost everybody responds "true."

Jackson wrote items to capture the "needs" postulated years earlier by Henry Murray (Jackson, 1971). Other times, the process of writing the items is less systematic, reflecting whatever comes to mind as something relevant to ask. The data that are gathered are S data (Chapter 2), or direct and undisguised self-reports.

An early example of a test constructed by the rational method is drawn from World War I. The U.S. Army discovered, not surprisingly, that inducting soldiers who were mentally ill, housing them in crowded barracks, and giving them loaded weapons could cause certain problems. To avoid these problems, the Army developed a structured interview consisting of a list of questions that a psychiatrist could ask each potential recruit. As the number of inductees increased, however, this long interview process became impractical—there were not enough psychiatrists nor was there enough time available to interview everybody.

To get around these limitations, a psychologist named Woodworth (1917) proposed that the questions typically asked in such an interview could be printed on a sheet that would be given to recruits. The recruits could check off their answers with a pencil. Woodworth's list, which became known as the Woodworth Personality Data Sheet (or, inevitably, the WPDS), consisted of 116 questions, all of which were deemed relevant to potential psychiatric problems. The questions included "Do you wet your bed?", "Have you ever had fits of dizziness?", and "Are you troubled with dreams about your work?" A recruit who responded "yes" to more than a small number of these questions was referred for more direct psychiatric examination. Recruits who answered "no" to all the questions were inducted forthwith into the Army.

Woodworth's idea of listing all the commonly-asked questions was not unreasonable, yet his technique raises a variety of problems that can be identified rather easily. For the WPDS to be a valid indicator of psychiatric disturbance, and for *any* rationally constructed, S data personality test to work, four conditions must *all* hold (Wiggins, 1973).

First, each item must mean the same thing to the person who fills out the form as it did to the psychologist who wrote it. For example, in the case of the example given above from the WPDS, how is "dizziness" defined?

Second, the person who completes the form must be *able* to make an accurate self-assessment for each item. He (or she, but only men were being recruited in the case of the WPDS) must have a good enough understanding of what the item is asking about, as well as the ability to observe the item in himself. He must not be so ignorant or so psychologically disorganized that he cannot accurately report on these psychological symptoms.

Third, the person who completes the form must be *willing* to report his self-assessment on each item accurately and without distortion. He must not try to deny his symptoms (for example, in order to get into the Army), or to exaggerate them (perhaps in order to stay out of the Army).

Fourth and finally, the items on the form must all be valid indicators of what the tester is trying to measure—in this case, mental disturbance. Does dizziness really indicate mental illness? What about dreams about your work?

For a rationally constructed test to measure accurately an attribute of personality, all four of these conditions must be fulfilled. In the case of the WPDS, all four were probably not fulfilled (although given how inexpensive administering the WPDS was, and how expensive the time of psychiatrists was, it may have been cost-effective anyway). In fact, most rationally constructed personality tests fail one or more of these criteria. One might think, therefore, that they are hardly ever used any more.

Wrong. Up to and including the present day, self-report questionnaires that are little different, in principle, from the WPDS remain the most common form of psychological measurement device. Self-tests in popular magazines are always constructed by the rational method— somebody thought of some questions that seemed relevant—and they almost always fail at least two or three of the crucial criteria for validity listed above.

Rationally constructed personality tests appear in psychological journals, too. Such journals present a steady stream of new testing instruments, all of which are developed by the simple technique of thinking up a list of questions that seem relevant. These questions might include measures of health status (how healthy are you?), self-esteem (how good do you feel about yourself?), or goals (what do you want in life?).

For example, some recent research has addressed the differences between college students who follow optimistic or pessimistic strategies in order to motivate themselves to perform academic tasks (such as preparing for an exam). Optimists, as described by this research, motivate themselves to work hard by expecting the best outcome, whereas pessimists motivate themselves by expecting the very worst to happen *unless* they work hard. Both strategies seem to be effective, although optimists may have a more pleasant life (Norem & Cantor, 1986; these strategies will be considered in more detail in Chapter 18).

For purposes of this chapter, the question is, how are optimists and pessimists identified? The researchers in this study used an eight-item questionnaire, on which subjects were asked to respond using an eleven-point scale ranging from "not at all true of me" (1) to "very true of me" (11). The questions used include

- I go into academic situations expecting the worst, even though I will probably do OK.
- I generally go into academic situations with positive expectations about how I will do.
- I often think about how likely it is that I will do very well in an academic situation.

The first and third items listed are "pessimism" items (higher scores reflecting a pessimistic strategy) and the second is an "optimism" item (a higher score reflecting an optimistic strategy; Norem & Cantor, 1986, p. 1211).

By the definitions we have been using, this is a rationally constructed, S-data personality test. And in fact, it seems to work fairly well at identifying students who approach academic life in different ways. So clearly tests like this can be valid, even though the four cautions raised earlier should always be kept in mind.

A slightly different case is presented by the technique used in some recent research to measure "personal strivings." In this research, subjects are asked to list the "objective[s] you are typically trying to accomplish or attain" (Emmons & King, 1988, p. 1042). This measure is rational in the sense that it directly asks about what the researchers are trying to find out. But unlike the rational method considered previously, this measure is open-ended. Instead of answering a set of printed questions by marking "true" or "false," or by choosing a point on an eleven-point scale, the subject writes his or her strivings on a blank piece of paper. This assessment technique, like other rational approaches, will only work to the degree a subject can and will accurately report what he or she is trying to accomplish. (Research indicates that most subjects can and do accurately report the strivings that guide much of their lives; Emmons & McAdams, 1991). This technique does get around some of the problems found in other rationally constructed questionnaires, which ask subjects to answer questions that may be ambiguous or of dubious relevance. Yet it poses a different problem: that of figuring out the relevance and decoding the ambiguity of what the *subject* has written.

The Factor Analytic Method

The factor analytic method of test construction is an example of a psychological tool based on statistics. **Factor analysis** is a statistical method that uses a mathematical technique for finding order amid seeming chaos. The factor analytic technique is designed to identify groups of things—such as test items—that seem to be alike. The property that makes these things alike is called a factor (e.g., Cattell, 1952).

This technique might seem esoteric, but it is not much different from the way most people intuitively think about things. Consider the rides at Disneyland. Some are fast, scary, and are enjoyed the most by teenagers—the Matterhorn ride, for example. Others are slow, include sweet songs, and are enjoyed the most by young children—the "It's A Small World" ride. Because certain properties seem to occur together (e.g., slow rides are usually accompanied by sweet songs) and others rarely occur together (e.g., few rides include sweet songs *and* are scary), the groupings of properties can be seen to constitute factors. The properties of being fast, scary, and appealing to teenagers all go together and form a factor that we might call "excitement." Likewise, the properties of being slow, having sweet music, and appealing to young children form a factor that we might call "comfort." We could now go out and measure *all* the rides at Disneyland—or even a new ride—according to both of these factors.

To use this technique in constructing a personality test, you start with a long list of objective items of the sort we discussed earlier. The items can be drawn from anywhere; the test-writer's own imagination is one common source. If the test-writer has a theory about what he or she wants to measure, that theory might suggest items to include. Another, surprisingly common way to get items is to mine them from *old* tests. The goal is to end up with a large number of items; thousands are not too many.

The next step is to administer these items to a large number of subjects. You get these subjects however you can, which is why they are often college students. Sometimes, for other kinds of tests, the subjects are mental patients. Ideally, they should represent well the kind of people with whom you hope, eventually, to use this test.

After your large group of subjects has taken the initial test that consists of these (maybe) thousands of items, you and your computer can do the factor analysis. In short, the analysis consists of calculating correlation coefficients (see Chapter 3) between every item and every other item. Many items—probably most items—will not correlate highly with much of anything and can be dropped. But those items that do correlate highly (or even somewhat) with each other will begin to group together. For example, if a person answers "true" to the item "I trust strangers," you might find that he or she is also likely to answer true to "I am careful to turn up when someone expects me," and to answer false to "I could stand being a hermit." Such a pattern of likelihood or co-occurence means that these three items are correlated. The next steps are to read the items, decide what they have in common, and then name the factor.

The three correlated items just listed, according to Cattell (1965), are all related to the dimension *cool vs. warm*, with a true, true, false pattern of responses indicating a "warm" personality. (Cattell decided this simply by reading them, as you just did). The factor represented by these items, therefore, is "warm-cool" or, if you prefer to name it by just one pole, "warmth." These three items now can be said to form a warmth scale; to measure this dimension in a new subject, you would administer these three items, as well as whatever other items in your original list correlated highly with them, eliminating most of the thousands you started with.

Factor analysis has been used not only to construct tests, but to decide how many fundamental traits exist—how many out of the thousands in the dictionary are truly essential. Various analysts have come up with different answers. Cattell (1957) thought there were sixteen. Eysenck (1976) believes there are just three. More recently, McCrae and Costa (e.g., 1987) have claimed five; theirs is perhaps the most widely accepted answer at present. These five traits—sometimes called the Big Five—are extraversion, neuroticism, conscientiousness, agreeableness, and openness (see Chapter 7).

At one point some psychologists hoped that factor analysis would provide an infallible mathematical tool for objectively locating the most important dimensions of personality and the best questions with which to measure these dimensions. They were wrong, however. Over the years, it has become clear that the factor analytic technique for constructing personality tests and for identifying important dimensions of personality is limited in at least three important ways (Block, 1995).

The first limitation is that the quality of the solution you get from a factor analysis will be limited by the quality of the items you put into it in the first place. Or as they say in computer science, GIGO (garbage in, garbage out). Ideally, a factor analysis requires an initial set of items that are fairly representative of the universe of all possible items. But how do you get that? Although most investigators do the best they can, it is always possible that some types of item are overrepresented in the initial sample of items and that other, important types were left out. If either of these things happens—and there is no way to ensure that both do not—then the results will provide a distorted view of which factors of personality are really important.

A second limitation of the factor analytic approach is that once a cluster of items has been identified as being statistically related, a human psychologist must then decide how they are related *conceptually*. This is obviously a highly subjective process and so the seeming mathematical rigor and certainty of factor analysis is to some extent an illusion. The items above, for example, could be named "warmth," but they could just as easily be called "sociability" or "interpersonal positivity." These other labels are just as good as the first. Any choice between them is a matter of taste as much as of mathematics or science. And disagreements over labels are common. For example, the very same factor called "agreeableness" by some psychologists has been called "conformity," "likeability," "friendliness," or "friendly compliance" by others. Another factor has been called, variously, "conscientiousness," "dependability," "super-ego strength," "constraint," "self control," and even "will to achieve." It is difficult to choose which label is best (Bergeman et al., 1993).

A third limitation of the factor analytic approach is that sometimes the factors that emerge do not make sense, sometimes not even to the psychologist who did the analysis. Years ago, the psychologist Gordon Allport complained about one such failure to make sense of a factor analysis:

Guilford and Zimmerman (1956) report an "unidentified" factor, called C_2, that represents some baffling blend of impulsiveness, absentmindedness, emotional fluctuation, nervousness, loneliness, ease of emotional expression, and feelings of guilt. When units of this sort appear [from factor analyses]—and I submit that it happens not infrequently—one wonders what to say about them. To me they resemble sausage meat that has failed to pass the pure food and health inspection (Allport, 1958, p. 251).

Matters are not frequently as bad as this. But it is not uncommon for the personality dimensions uncovered by factor analysis to be difficult to name precisely (Block, 1995). It is important to remember that factor analysis is a statistical rather than a psychological tool. It can identify traits or items that go together. As in the example just described, however, figuring out the psychological meaning of this grouping requires psychological thinking.

Factor analysis continues to have important uses. One, which will be described in Chapter 7, is to help reduce the many different personality traits in the dictionary down to an essential few. Another important use is in the refinement of personality tests, in conjuction with the other techniques of test construction. It is useful to know how many different clusters of items are in a new personality test, because some tests turn out to measure more than one trait at the same time. A routine step in modern test development, therefore, is to factor analyze the items (Briggs & Cheek, 1986).

The Empirical Method

The empirical strategy of test construction is an attempt to allow reality to speak for itself. In its pure form, the empirical approach has sometimes been called "dust bowl" empiricism, to denote how "dry" or atheoretical the approach is. Like the factor analytic approach described earlier, the first step of the empirical approach is to gather lots of items. The methods for doing this can be just as eclectic—or haphazard—as described earlier.

The second step, however, is quite different. For this step, you need to have a group of subjects who have *already* been divided into the groups you wish to detect with your test. Occupational groups and diagnostic categories are often used for this purpose. For example, if you wish to measure the aspect of people that makes them good and happy religious ministers, then you need at least two groups of subjects—happy, successful ministers, and a comparison group. (Ideally the comparison group would be miserable and incompetent ministers, but more typically the researcher will settle for people who are not ministers at all). Or, you might want a test to detect different kinds of psychopathology. For this purpose, you would need groups of people who had been diagnosed as suffering from schizophrenia, depression, hysteria, and so forth. A group of normal people—if you can find them—would also be useful for comparison purposes. Whatever groups you wish to include, their members must be identified *before* you develop your test.

Then you are ready for the second step: administering your test items to all of your subjects. The third step is to compare the answers given by the different groups of subjects. If schizophrenics answer a certain group of questions differently from the way everybody else does, those items might form a schizophrenia scale. Thereafter, new subjects who answer questions the same way diagnosed schizophrenics did would score high on your schizophrenia scale. Thus you might suspect them of being schizophrenic, too. (The MMPI, which is the prototypical example of the empirical method of test construction, was built using this strategy.) Or, if successful ministers answer some items in a distinctive way, these items might be combined into a minister scale. New subjects who score high on this scale, because they answer the way successful ministers do, might be guided to become ministers themselves. (The Strong Vocational Interest Blank, or SVIB, was constructed according to this strategy.)

The basic philosophy of the empirical approach, then, is that certain kinds of people have distinctive ways of answering certain questions on personality inventories. If you answer questions the same way that members of some occupational or diagnostic group did in the original derivation study, then you might belong to that group, too. This philosophy can be used even at the individual level. The developers of the MMPI published an atlas, or casebook, of hundreds of individuals who took this test over the years (Hathaway & Meehl, 1951). For each case, the atlas gives the person's scoring pattern and describes his or her clinical case history. The idea is that a clinical psychologist confronted with a new patient can ask the patient to take the MMPI, and then look up those individuals in the atlas who scored similarly in the past. This might provide the clinician with insights or ideas that he or she might not otherwise have gotten.

The sole basis by which items are selected for empirically derived personality scales is whether they are answered differently by different kinds of people. The actual *content* of the items is not important. No matter what the item says, if it successfully identifies the people you want it to identify, it goes on the test. In fact, empirical test-constructors of the old school sometimes prided themselves on never actually reading the items on the tests they developed!

This lack of concern with item content, or with what is sometimes called face validity, has four implications. The first is that empirically derived tests, unlike other kinds, can include items that seem contrary or even absurd. As I mentioned a few pages back, the item "I prefer a shower to a bath," answered true, is correlated with empathy. Similarly, the item "I like tall women" tends to be answered true by impulsive males. Why? According to the empirical approach to test construction, the reason does not matter in the slightest.

Consider some other examples. People with psychopathic personalities (who have little regard for moral or societal rules and lack "conscience") tend to answer false to the item "I have been quite independent and free from family rule." Paranoids answer false to "I tend to be on my guard with people who are somewhat more friendly than expected." One might surmise they do this because they are paranoid about the question itself, but paranoids answer true to "I believe I am being plotted against." Even though the relationship between item content and meaning seems counterintuitive, a true adherent to the empirical strategy of test construction does not really care.

Here are a few other examples (all taken from the excellent discussion in Wiggins, 1973): "I sometimes tease animals" is answered false by depressives; "I enjoy detective or mystery stories" is answered false by hospitalized hysterics; "My daily life is full of things to keep me interested" is answered true by dermatitis patients; "I gossip a little at times" is answered true by people with high IQs; "I do not have a great fear of snakes" is answered false by prejudiced individuals. Again, in each case the indicated people are *more likely* to answer in the indicated direction; they do not always do so.

A second implication of this lack of concern with item content is that responses to empirically derived tests are difficult to fake. With a personality test of the straightforward, S-data variety, you can describe yourself the way you want to be seen and that is indeed the score you will get. But because the items on empirically derived scales sometimes seen backward or absurd, it is difficult to know how to answer in such a way as to guarantee the score you want. This is often held up as one of the great advantages of the empirical approach.

The psychologist interpreting a person's responses to an empirically derived personality test does not really care whether the person told the truth in his or her responses. The literal truth does not matter, because the purpose of the questions on such a test is not to find out the answer, but to see what the answer will be. Thus empirically derived personality tests are T data instead of S data.

The third implication of the lack of concern with item content is that, even more than tests derived through other methods, empirically derived tests are only as good as the criteria by which they are developed. If the distinction between the different kinds of subjects in the derivation sample was drawn incorrectly, the empirically derived test will be fatally and forever flawed. For example, the original MMPI was derived by comparing the responses of patients who had been diagnosed by psychiatrists at the University of Minnesota mental hospitals. If those diagnoses were incorrect in any way, then diagnostic use of the MMPI will only perpetuate those errors. The theory behind the SVIB is that if you answer questions the way a successful minister (or member of any other occupation) does, you too will make a successful minister (or whatever; Strong, 1959). But perhaps the theory is false—perhaps new ministers who are too much like the old ministers will not be successful. Or perhaps some of the "successful" ministers in the derivation sample were not really successful. Such difficulties would make the SVIB a problematic source of vocational advice.

A more general problem here is that the empirical correlates of item response by which these tests are assembled are those found in one place, at one time, with one group of subjects. If no attention is paid to item content, then there is really no valid reason to expect that the test will work in a similar manner at another time, in another place, with different subjects. A particular concern is that the empirical correlates of item response might change over time. The MMPI was developed decades ago, and was revised only recently. Unfortunately, it has yet to be revalidated.

The fourth and final implication of the empirical approach's lack of concern with item content is that it can cause serious public relations and even legal problems—it can be difficult to explain to a layperson why certain questions are being asked. The original MMPI, for example, contained questions about religious preference and health status (including bowel habits). According to some readings of antidiscrimination laws, such questions can be illegal in applied contexts. For example, in 1993 Target Stores had to pay a $2 million judgment to job applicants to whom it had (illegally, the court ruled) asked questions such as "I am very strongly attracted to members of my own sex," "I have never indulged in unusual sex practices," "I have had no difficulty starting or holding my urine," and "I feel sure there is only one true religion." (These items all came from a test called the Rodgers Condensed CPI-MMPI Test, which included items from both the MMPI and the CPI; Silverstein, 1993).

As Target Stores found to its dismay, it can be difficult for users of the MMPI, CPI, or similar tests to explain to judges or congressional investigating committees that they are not actually manifesting an unconstitutional curiosity about religious beliefs or bowel habits, and that they are merely interested in the *correlates* of the answers to these items. Target may have asked these questions not because its management cared about sexual or bathroom habits, but because the scale scores built from these items (and many others—the test they used had 704 items) had shown validity in predicting job performance, in this case as a security guard. Indeed, reports from tests like these typically include only total scores and predictions of job performance, so the responses to the individual items might not have even been available to Target's personnel department. Nevertheless, it must be admitted that in many cases it would not be difficult for an interested test conductor to extract applicants' responses to individual questions, and then to discriminate illegally on the basis of religious or sexual orientation, bowel habits, or health status. For this reason, developers of new tests such as the MMPI-2 are attempting to leave out items of this sort, while still trying to maintain validity.

Developers and users of empirically derived tests have come almost full circle over the last fifty years or so. They began with an explicit and sometimes vehement philosophy that item content does not matter; all that mattered was the external validity, or what the test items could predict. As the social and legal climate has changed over time, however, empirical tests have been forced, to some degree against their will, to acknowledge that item content does matter after all. Regardless of how their responses are used, individuals completing any kind of personality test are telling you things about themselves. And there are certain questions that you are not supposed to ask.

A Combination of Methods

In modern test development, a surprisingly large number of investigators still use a pure form of the rational method: they ask their subjects the questions that seem relevant, and hope for the best. The factor analytic approach still has a few adherents. Pure applications of the empirical approach are rare today.

The best modern test developers use a combination of all three approaches. A good example is the way Douglas Jackson developed the Personality Research Form (the PRF, of course). He came up with items based on their apparent relevance to the theoretical constructs he wished to measure (the rational approach), administered them to large samples of subjects and factor analyzed their responses (the factor analytic approach), and then correlated the factor scores with empirical criteria (the empirical approach; see Jackson, 1967, 1971). Jackson's approach is probably close to the ideal way to proceed. The best way to get items for a personality scale is not haphazardly, but with the intent to sample a particular domain of interest (the rational approach). Factor analysis should then be used to confirm that items that seem similar to each other actually elicit similar responses from real subjects (Briggs & Cheek, 1986). Finally, any personality measure is only as good as the other things with which it correlates or can predict (the empirical approach). To be worth its salt, any personality scale must show that it can predict how people will be seen by others and how they will fare in real life.

PURPOSES OF PERSONALITY TESTING

If we can assume that a personality test has a modicum of validity, then a further question must be considered: How will this test be used? This is an important question that some psychologists, engrossed in the techniques and details of test construction, may forget to ask. The answer one reaches has practical and ethical implications (Hanson, 1993).

Testing to Categorize People

The most obvious uses for personality tests are those to which they are put by the professional personality testers—the ones who set up the booths at APA conventions—and their customers. The customers are typically organizations such as schools, clinics, corporations, or government agencies that wish to know something about the people they encounter. Sometimes this information is desired so that, regardless of the score obtained, the person who is measured can be helped. For example, schools frequently use tests to measure vocational interests in order to help their students choose careers. A clinician might administer a test to get an indication of how serious a client's problem is, or to suggest a therapeutic direction.

Sometimes the motivation for testing is a little more selfish. An employer may test your "integrity" to find out whether you are trustworthy enough to be hired (or even to be retained), or may test to find out about other personality traits deemed relevant to your future job performance. The Central Intelligence Agency (CIA), for example, uses personality testing when selecting its agents (Waller, 1993).

Reasonable arguments can be made for or against any of these uses. By telling people what kind of occupational group they most resemble, vocational interest tests provide potentially valuable information to individuals who may not know what they want to do. On the other hand, these tests are based on the theory that any given field should continue to be populated by individuals like those already in it. For example, if your response profile resembles that obtained from successful mechanics or jet pilots, then perhaps you *should* consider being a mechanic or a jet pilot. But this approach, although it seems reasonable, also could keep occupational fields from evolving and keep certain individuals (e.g., women or members of minority groups) from joining fields from which they may traditionally have been excluded. For example, an ordinarily socialized American woman may have outlooks or responses that are very different from those of the "typical" garage mechanic or jet pilot. Does this mean these women should never become mechanics or jet pilots?

Similarly, many "integrity" tests administered in pre-employment screenings seem to yield valuable information. In particular, they often provide good measures not so much of integrity, but of the broader trait of conscientiousness. That is, people who score high on "integrity" scales often also score high on the trait of conscientiousness, which is highly correlated with learning on the job and with performance in many fields (Ones, Viswesvaran, & Schmidt, 1993; see Chapter 7 for a more detailed discussion).

Still, many of these integrity tests ask questions about minor past offenses (e.g., Have you ever taken office supplies from an employer?), which would seem not only to violate the U.S. Constitution's protection from self-incrimination, but also to put nonliars into the interesting dilemma of whether they should admit past offenses, thereby earning a lower integrity score for being honest, or deny them, and thereby earn a higher integrity score for having lied. Liars, by contrast, experience no such dilemma; they can deny everything, and yet earn a nice, high integrity score.

A more general class of objections is aimed at the wide array of personality tests used by many large organizations, including the CIA, major automobile manufacturers, the phone company, and the military. According to one critic, almost any kind of testing can be objected to on two grounds. First, tests are unfair mechanisms through which institutions can control individuals—by rewarding those with the institutionally determined "correct" traits (such as high conscientiousness), and punishing those with the "wrong" traits (such as low conscientiousness). Second, tests can serve to *invent* the trait being measured (Hanson, 1993). That is, perhaps your degree of conscientiousness or even intelligence is something that comes to exist only *after* and *as a result of* being tested, and in that sense is "constructed." Underlying these two objections seems to be a more general sense, which I think many people share, that there is something undignified or even humiliating about submitting oneself to a test and having one's personality described by a set of scores.

These objections all make sense. Personality tests—along with other kinds of tests such as intelligence, honesty, and even drug tests—do function as a part of society's mechanism for controlling people, by rewarding the "right" kind of people (those who are intelligent and honest and don't do drugs) and punishing the "wrong" kind. It is also correct to note the interesting way in which a trait can seem to spring into existence as soon as a test is invented to measure it. Finally, it is undeniably true that many individuals have had the deeply humiliating experience of "voluntarily" (in order to get a badly needed job) subjecting themselves to testing, only to find out that they somehow failed to measure up. The result is a blow not only to one's employability, which is bad enough, but to one's self-esteem.

On the other hand, these criticisms are also overstated. A relatively minor point to bear in mind is that, as we have seen in the preceding sections of this chapter, personality traits are not merely *invented* or *constructed* by the process of test construction, they are also to an important degree *discovered.* That is, the correlates and nature of a trait measured by a new test cannot be presumed, they must be discovered empirically by examining what life outcomes or other attributes of personality the test can predict. For example, psychologists did not know until *after* doing research that integrity tests are better measures of conscientiousness than of integrity, and this finding forced them to change their conception of what they had incorrectly assumed were honesty tests. The fact that the interpretation of psychological tests depends critically upon the gathering of independent data undermines the argument that personality traits, or any other psychological measurements, are mere social constructions.

A more basic and important point is that the criticisms that view personality testing as undignified or unethical are criticisms that, when considered, appear rather naive. These criticisms seem to object to the idea of determining the degree to which somebody is conscientious, or intelligent, or sociable, and then using that determination as the basis of an important decision (e.g., employment). But if you accept the fact that an employer is not obligated to hire randomly anybody who walks through the door, and that the employer only uses good sense in deciding who would be the best person to hire (if you were an employer, wouldn't you do that?), then you also must accept that traits like conscientiousness, intelligence, and sociability *are* going to be judged. The only real question is *how* these traits are to be judged.

Personality tests are imperfect instruments, as we have seen. But what are the alternatives? One alternative seems to be for the employer to talk with the prospective employee and try to gauge his or her conscientiousness by how well his or her shoes are shined, or hair is cut, or some other such clue. (Employers frequently do exactly that.) Is this method an improvement?

You may argue that you would rather be judged by a person than by a computer scanning a form, regardless of the demonstrated invalidity of the former and validity of the latter (Ones et al., 1993). Although that is a legitimate choice, it is important to be clear about the choice being made. The choice *cannot* be for personality never to be judged—that is going to happen even if all formal tests are burned tomorrow. The only real choice here is this: *How* would you prefer to have your personality judged?

Other Uses of Testing

The argument that tests assess personality more accurately than intuitive judgments do is convincing, but it is not what motivates me to use personality tests (and other assessment techniques) in my own research. My reason for being interested in personality measurement is similar to that of many others in the field: scientific curiosity.

It seems obvious that people differ from one other; psychologically speaking, one size does *not* fit all. Personality testing is one of the ways to measure this fact (others were discussed in Chapter 2). Moreover, nearly every interesting and important psychological question concerning individuals boils down to a concern with personality variables, and thus requires a technology for measuring them. For example, the "optimally adjusted person," as studied by several investigators, is someone who is flexible, tolerant of stress and ambiguity, insightful, cheerful, and conscientious, among other attributes. These are all personality traits, and they are the desired, healthy outcome of psychological development and of positive interventions to improve mental health. An assessment of mental health, therefore, requires that we find some way to measure such attributes.

Assessment is important in measuring many negative mental health outcomes, too. For example, recent research suggests that the usual effects of sexual abuse on young girls include lowered self-esteem, an impaired sense of control and competence, and an increase in negative emotions. These outcomes are all personality attributes, and they can be detected and measured only if somebody does a personality assessment.

The broader implication of the importance of personality assessment is that assessments of *individuals,* such as in the research just described, can sometimes produce important insights about the structure of *society* and how society affects individuals. It is this possibility, of using individual personality assessments to address wider psychological and social issues, that motivates the activity of many and perhaps most personality psychologists (for more examples, see Chapter 7).

Summary

Any characteristic pattern of behavior, thought, and emotional experience that exhibits relative consistency across time and situations is part of an individual's personality. These patterns include personality traits as well as such psychological attributes as goals, moods, and strategies. Personality assessment is a frequent activity of industrial and clinical psychologists and researchers. Everybody also performs personality assessments of the people they know in daily life. An important issue for assessments, whether by psychologists or by laypersons, is the degree to which those assessments are correct. This chapter examined how psychologists' personality tests are constructed and validated. Some personality tests comprise S data and others comprise T data, but a more commonly drawn distinction is between projective tests and objective tests. Projective tests try to gain insight into personality by presenting subjects with ambiguous stimuli, and recording how the subjects respond. Objective tests ask subjects specific questions, and assess personality on the basis of how the subjects answer. Objective tests can be constructed by rational, factor analytic, or empirical methods, and the modern practice is to use a combination of all three methods. Some people are uncomfortable with the practice of personality assessment because they see it as an unfair invasion of privacy. However, because people inevitably judge each others' personalities, the real issue is how personality assessment should be done—through informal intuitions or more formalized techniques.

CHAPTER

PERSONALITY ASSESSMENT II: PERSONALITY JUDGMENT IN DAILY LIFE

Personality assessment is not restricted to psychologists. It is among the most common and important of human activities. With luck, one might go years without being assessed by a psychologist. But there is absolutely no chance that you can long avoid being assessed by your friends, enemies, romantic partners—and yourself.

The topic of this chapter is two-fold. First we will consider how and why the assessments others make of your personality and the assessments you make of yourself are important. The second part of this chapter will consider the validity—or, in the synonomous term traditionally used when considering non-professional judgments, the accuracy—of these assessments. To what degree and under what circumstances do lay judgments of personality agree with each other? And to what degree and under what circumstances can they accurately predict behavior?

CONSEQUENCES OF LAY JUDGMENTS OF PERSONALITY

The people who practice daily, informal assessment of your personality fall into two categories: the first category is everybody you know, or everybody who knows you; the second category has only one person in it—you. The opinions of both are important.

Everybody Who Knows You

The judgments other people make of your personality reflect a significant part of your social world. They represent opinions of people who interact with you daily, and so their importance goes beyond their value as accurate (or inaccurate) descriptions. Furthermore, your reputation among those who know you matters because it greatly affects both opportunities and expectancies.

OPPORTUNITIES

Let's first consider your reputation's effect on your opportunities. If a person who is considering hiring you believes you to be competent and conscientious, you are much more likely to enjoy the opportunity of getting the job than if that person thinks you do not have those qualities. This will be true regardless of how competent and conscientious you really are. Similarly, if someone believes you to be honest, he or she will be more likely to lend you money than if that person believes you to be dishonest. Your *actual* honesty is immaterial. If you impress people who meet you as being warm and friendly, you will develop more friendships than if you seem cold and aloof. These appearances may be false and unfair, but their consequences will be important nonetheless.

Consider the case of shyness. Shy people seem to be quite common in our society; one estimate is that about one person in four considers himself or herself to be chronically shy (Zimbardo, 1977). Shy people are often lonely and may deeply wish to have friends and normal social interaction, but they are so fearful of the process of making friends and of involving themselves socially that they become isolated instead. A frequent consequence is that shy people deny themselves the opportunity to develop normal social skills—they never get any practice. So when they do venture into the world, they may not know how to act; this may cause other people to respond to them negatively, which will only reinforce the shyness that started this whole cycle in the first place (Cheek, 1990b).

A particular problem for shy people is that typically they are *not* perceived by others as shy. Instead, to most observers they seem cold and aloof. This is understandable when you consider how shy people behave. A shy person who lives in your dormitory sees you coming across campus, and you see her. She would actually like to talk to you and perhaps even try to develop a friendship, but she is extremely fearful of rejection or even of not knowing quite what to say. (This apprehension may be realistic, given her lack of social skills.) So, she may very well pretend not to see you, or may suddenly reverse course and dodge behind a building. This kind of behavior, if you detect it (and often you will), is unlikely to give you a warm, fuzzy feeling. There is a good chance that instead you will feel insulted and even angry. You may be inclined thereafter to avoid *her.*

Thus shy people are not cold and aloof, or at least they do not mean to be. But that is how they are frequently perceived. That perception, in turn, affects the lives of shy people in important, negative ways, and is part of a cycle that perpetuates shyness. This is just one example of how the judgments of others— the I data considered in Chapter 2—are an important part of your social world, and can have a significant effect on your personality and your life.

EXPECTANCIES

Judgments of others can also affect you through "self-fulfilling prophecies," more technically known as **expectancy effects**, or just expectancies. These seem to work in both the intellectual and the social domain.

The classic demonstration of expectancy effects in the intellectual domain is the series of studies by Rosenthal and Jacobson (1968). These investigators gave a group of school children a battery of tests, and then told their teachers, falsely, that the tests had identified some of the children as "late bloomers," as being likely to show a sharp increase in IQ in the near future. The children who were described to the teachers in this way were actually selected at random. But when the actual IQ of the "bloomers" was compared to the other children at the end of the school year, the bloomers had actually bloomed! That is, the first-grade children who were expected by their teachers to increase their IQ actually did so by about fifteen points, and the second-graders increased by about ten points, even though these expectations were introduced randomly.

To this day no one has determined how this effect happens. The presumption is that the teachers treat the students about whom they have positive expectancies differently from those about whom they have negative or no expectancies. This difference in treatment, it is further presumed, is what causes the actual changes in IQ. It is certainly difficult to think of any other way this effect could occur.

Still, no one has identified exactly what it is that the teachers do differently to the two groups of students. Various studies have examined whether the teachers pay more attention to the bloomers, or more *contingent* attention (i.e., varying their attention according to the child's performance), or are more positive, or more negative. Preliminary evidence suggests that one or all of these factors might contribute to expectancy effects, but no strong evidence has been found that any one of them is particularly important (Jussim, 1991). At present, therefore, the basis of the expectancy effect remains one of the minor mysteries of social psychology.

A related kind of expectancy effect has been demonstrated in the social rather than the intellectual realm. Mark Snyder and his colleagues (Snyder, Tanke, & Berscheid, 1977) performed the following remarkable experiment. Two previously unacquainted college students of opposite sexes were brought to two different locations in the psychology building. The experimenter approached the female subject with a Polaroid camera and took her picture, saying, "You are about to meet someone on the telephone, but before you do this I need to give him a picture of you so he can visualize who he is talking to." The male subject was not photographed.

The female's real photograph, just taken, was thrown away. Instead, the experimenter gave the male subject one of two photographs of *other* female undergraduates who had previously been identifed as either highly attractive or less attractive. "This is who you will be meeting on the phone," the male subject was told. The telephone connection was then established, and the two students chatted for several minutes as a tape recorder whirred.

Later, the researchers took the tape recording of this chat and erased everything that the *male* student had said. (Remember, he is the one who saw the bogus photograph.) They then played the edited tape, which contained only the female's voice, for a new group of students, and asked them to rate, among other things, how warm, humorous, and poised she seemed.

The result: If the male had seen an attractive photograph, the female was more likely to have behaved in a manner rated as warmer, more humorous, and more poised than when the male student saw an unattractive photograph. This finding means that the male student had somehow acted toward a woman he *thought* to be attractive in such a way as to cause her to respond in a more warm and friendly manner than she would have if he had thought her to be unattractive. Snyder interpreted this effect as another form of self-fulfilling prophecy: Attractive females are expected to be warm and friendly, and those thought to be attractive are treated in such a manner that they indeed respond that way.[1]

---

[1]Two complications are worth brief mention. The first is that a slightly different process may lie behind the result. Rather than males directly inducing the females to confirm their expectancies, it may be the case that males are more friendly to attractive females because they are hoping for a date, and more cold and aloof with unattractive females for whom they do not have such hopes. The women then respond in kind. Such a process would technically not be an expectancy effect, although the final result would be the same.

A related complication concerns the question of whether this effect works the other way around, when female students see the male's picture and the effects on his behavior are examined. A study by Andersen & Bem (1981) addressed this issue. The conclusions were not completely clear, but it did seem to some degree that male and female perceivers could, through what they expected of the other, affect the behavior of both male and female targets.

In some ways this is an even more disturbing finding than Rosenthal's results concerning IQ. This study suggests that to some degree our behavior with other people might be determined by how these other people *expect* us to act, perhaps based on such superficial cues as our physical appearance. Snyder's results imply that to some degree we will actually *become* what other people perceive, or even misperceive, us to be.

Research on expectancy effects is interesting and important and the two studies just described are classics of the genre. However, there recently has been another important development in this area of research. The psychologist Lee Jussim (1991) asked an important question about expectancy effects that, surprisingly, had seldom been considered previously: Where do expectancies generally come from in real life?

The usual experiments do not address this question because the expectancies they study are induced experimentally; Rosenthal's teachers believed that some kids would improve academically because that is what he had told them they would do. Snyder's male students thought some females would be warm and friendly because they were led to develop that expectation based on the common stereotypes they held about attractiveness.

Jussim suggests that the situation in real life is usually quite different. A teacher who expects a child to do well might base that expectation on the child's *actual* test results, rather than bogus ones, as well as on his or her observation of the child's performance in previous classes, what he or she has been told about the child by other teachers, and so forth. A male student who expects a female to be warm and charming might base this on how he has seen her act with other people, what he has been told about her by mutual friends, and so forth. Moreover, research has shown that physically attractive women really *are* more socially skillful and likable on the telephone (Goldman & Lewis, 1977). Therefore, these expectancies, although false in the lab, might sometimes or often in real life be correct. When this is the case, the self-fulfilling prophecies just described might have the effect of slightly magnifying behavioral tendencies that the subject has had all along.

This observation challenges the traditional interpretation of expectancy effects. It implies that rather than restrict themselves to introducing expectancies in the lab, researchers should study expectancies in real life in order to assess how powerful these effects really are. Research is also needed to learn how strong these effects can be under realistic circumstances. The studies to date show that expectancy effects are greater than zero, but are they strong enough to change a low-IQ child into a high-IQ child, or a cold, aloof person into a warm and friendly one, or vice versa? The research suggests that the answer is probably no (e.g., Jussim & Eccles, 1992), but it is difficult to be sure of this conclusion, because research so far has been concerned more with discovering whether expectancy effects exist at all than with assessing how important the effects are in relation to other factors that also influence behavior.

Although what can be said about expectancy effects is less tidy than it would have been a few years ago, such effects remain interesting and important. To some degree, the judgments of personality rendered of you by the people who know you not only reflect what you are like, but can *lead* you to be what you are like.

Self-Judgments

The judgments you inevitably make about your own personality are, if anything, even more important than those others make of you. You very likely have opinions about how sociable you are, how reliable you are, and even how intelligent you are. In psychological parlance, the assembly of all the opinions of this sort that you hold is called your **self-concept**, or just self. Psychologists who study the self are interested in the opinions and judgments individuals have and make about their own personalities and abilities.

Self-judgments matter because they affect how you evaluate yourself and therefore affect your mood, and because they affect what you are willing to attempt to accomplish in life. Your self-esteem plays an important role in how happy or sad you feel. Feelings of worthlessness—extremely low self-esteem—are a classic element of depression. And in interpersonal relations, perhaps the oldest, truest cliche is this: If you don't like yourself first, you won't be able to like anybody else (Shaver & Clark, 1994). Substitute "love" for "like" in that cliche, and the implications become even deeper.

Your self-judgments affect your life in other ways as well. They often determine what you will do, or attempt to do. For example, perhaps you had a friend, just as smart and hard-working as you, with whom you went to high school. But for whatever reason, your friend thought that he or she could not possibly be a successful college student. If you were a true friend, you might have tried to argue otherwise: 'Of course you can do it—if I can, you can too!" But in the face of a negative self-attitude, such arguments are usually ineffective. So you went to college and your friend did not. In a year or two you will graduate, and your friend will still be pumping gas or flipping burgers.[2] The difference was not one of ability or drive—it was in the self. You believed you could do it, while your friend did not have such a positive self-view.

---

[2] I am presuming that with your college education you will attempt to find a better job than those.

This example shows how important and sometimes devastating one's self-concept can be. It also shows the dangers in persuading people that they cannot do certain things. For example, many young girls pick up the message from society that girls can not—or should not—be good at math (Hilton & Berglund, 1974; Stipek & Gralinski, 1991). The result? Here's a personal example: I used to teach at prestigious engineering college, the student body of which was more than 90 percent male—hardly a result of chance. Similarly, members of certain racial groups and economic classes are taught, usually implicitly but powerfully by the media and other sources, that "their kind" do not go to college or otherwise better themselves. So sometimes these individuals give up, or find other ways—not necessarily constructive—to succeed in life.

Beliefs about oneself and what one can do transcend specific domains. People who have the trait called "internal locus of control" believe that the important forces in their lives come from within or inside themselves, and that they can affect what happens to themselves. Those with "external locus of control," by contrast, believe that most of what happens to them is up to others, or is a product of impersonal outside forces. Not surprisingly, "internals" take a much more active role in determining their life outcomes than do "externals," and therefore are more likely to succeed at most things (Rotter, 1954). A related concept, **self-efficacy**, refers to your beliefs about what you will and will not be able to accomplish (Bandura, 1977; Rotter's and Bandura's theories are considered in more detail in Chapter 17). For example, you might have the efficacy expectation that you will someday be able to finish reading this book. I myself, as I am writing these words, am trying to maintain the efficacy expectation that I can finish writing this book. In either case, the belief about what one can do is likely to affect whether one persists at that activity. Since you are reading this book, we can presume that my efficacy expectations held up. How are yours doing?

Efficacy expectations can interact with or be determined by other kinds of self-judgments. For example, if you think you are extremely attractive to the opposite sex, you are more likely to attempt to date someone in whom you are interested than you would be if you saw yourself as unattractive. To use the terms we developed above, your self-concept affects your efficacy expectation in this domain. Of course, both of these concepts—self-concept and efficacy expectation—can be independent of how attractive you really are. A person's actual physical attractiveness might matter less than we sometimes believe; people who merely *think* they are attractive often do surprisingly well, right?

Thus the judgments other people make of your personality matter a good deal, and the judgments you make of yourself probably matter even more. That conclusion leads to the next question: To what degree, and under what circumstances, are these ever-so-consequential judgments accurate?

The Accuracy of Lay Judgments of Personality

Because people constantly make judgments of their own and each others' personalities, and because these judgments are consequential, then it would seem important to know when and to what degree these judgments are accurate. It might surprise you, therefore, to learn that for an extended period of time (about thirty years) psychologists went out of their way to *avoid* doing research on accuracy. Although research on the accuracy of lay judgments of personality was fairly active from about 1940 to 1955, after that the field fell into inactivity, from which it began to emerge only in the mid-1980s (Funder & West, 1993).

There are several reasons why research on accuracy experienced this lengthy hiatus (Funder & West, 1993; Funder, 1995). The most basic reason was that researchers were stymied by a fundamental problem: By what criteria can the personality judgments made by somebody else be judged to be right or wrong (Hastie & Rasinski, 1988; Kruglanski, 1989)? Some psychologists believe this question to be unanswerable, because any attempt to answer it would simply amount to pitting one person's set of criteria for accuracy against another's. Who is to say which is right?

This point of view is bolstered by the attitude called **constructivism**, which is widespread throughout modern intellectual life (Stanovich, 1991). This attitude, slightly simplified—is that reality, as a concrete entity, does not exist. All that does exist is human ideas or *constructions* of reality. This view does provide an answer to the age-old question, "If a tree falls in the forest with no one to hear, does it make a noise?" The constructivist answer is, "No." But an important consequence of this view is that it implies that there is no way to regard one interpretation of reality as accurate and another interpretation as inaccurate, because all interpretations are mere "social constructions" (Kruglanski, 1989).

This point of view—that since there is no reality, judgmental accuracy cannot be meaningfully assessed—is quite fashionable today. Nevertheless, I reject it (Funder, 1995). To regard independent reality as nonexistent and accuracy as meaningless is a nihilistic point of view that cannot withstand serious scrutiny. I find another philosophical school, called **critical realism**, more compatible. Critical realism holds that the absence of perfect, infallible criteria for truth should not force us to conclude that all interpretations of reality are equally likely to be correct (Rorer, 1990). Indeed, even psychological researchers who argue that accuracy issues are not meaningful (constructivists) still choose between research conclusions they regard as more or less valid—even though their choices might sometimes be wrong. As researchers, they implicitly recognize that the only option is to make such choices as reasonably as possible, based on whatever information is at hand or can be gathered. The only alternative is to cease doing research altogether.

Evaluating a personality judgment is no different. We must gather all the information possible that might help us determine whether or not the judgment is valid, and then make the best determination we can. The task remains perfectly reasonable even though the outcome will always be uncertain (Cook & Campbell, 1979; Cronbach & Meehl, 1955).

Criteria for Accuracy

Setting all of these philosophical considerations aside, there is a simpler way to think of this issue. A personality judgment, rendered by an acquaintance, a stranger, or the self, can be thought of as a kind of personality assessment or even a personality test. If you think of it as a test, then the same considerations discussed in the previous two chapters immediately come into play, and the assessment of the *accuracy* of a personality judgment becomes exactly equivalent to the assessment of the *validity* of a personality test. And there is a well-developed and widely accepted method for assessing test validity.

The method is called **convergent validation**. It can be illustrated by the duck test: If it looks like a duck, and walks like a duck, and swims like a duck, and quacks like a duck, it is very probably (but still not absolutely positively) a duck. (Maybe it's a Disney audio-animatronic machine built to resemble a duck. But probably not.) Convergent validation is arrived at by assembling diverse pieces of information—such as appearance, walking and swimming style, and quackiness—that all "converge" on a common conclusion, in this case that it must be a duck. The more items of diverse information that converge, the more confident you are in your conclusion (Block, 1989, pp. 236–37).

For personality judgments, the two primary converging criteria are **interjudge agreement** and **behavioral prediction**. If I judge you to be conscientious, and so do your parents, and so do your friends, and so do you, it is likely that you *are* conscientious. Moreover, if my judgment of you as conscientious converges with the subsequent empirical fact that you will arrive on time for all your class meetings for the next three semesters, and thereby demonstrates **predictive validity**, then my judgment of you is even more certainly correct (although 100 percent certainty is never attained).

In sum, psychological research can evaluate the accuracy of personality judgments, in two ways: (1) Do the judgments agree with one another? and (2) Can they predict behavior? (Funder, 1987, 1995).

Moderators of Accuracy

In psychological parlance, a **moderator** variable is one that affects the relationship between two other variables. A moderator of accuracy, therefore, is a variable that makes the correlation between a judgment and its criterion higher or lower. Research on accuracy has focused primarily on four such potential moderators: (1) properties of the judge, (2) properties of the target (the person who is judged), (3) properties of the trait that is judged, and (4) properties of the information on which the judgment is based.

THE GOOD JUDGE

The oldest question in accuracy research is this: Who is the best judge of personality? Clinical psychologists have long postulated that some people are better at judging personality than are others, and numerous studies tackled this question during the old, pre-1955 wave of research on accuracy (Taft, 1955).

Unfortunately, no satisfying answer was ever reached. It seemed that a good judge in one context, or of one trait, was not always a good judge in other contexts or with other traits. The only somewhat consistent finding seemed to be that highly intelligent and conscientious individuals rendered better judgments—but then again such individuals are good at nearly any task you give them, so it was not clear that these traits were a functional part of any *specific* ability to judge people. Disappointment with this result may be one reason why the first wave of accuracy research waned in the mid-1950s (Funder & West, 1993).

Nevertheless, the topic is not dead. The original research was conducted using inadequate methods (Cronbach, 1955) and therefore the topic is ripe for renewal using modern approaches. One example is a recent study that examines the phenomenon of narcissism (John & Robins, 1994). Narcissists are individuals with grandly inflated opinions of themselves. Such people are particularly likely to render inaccurate assessments of their own contributions to a group discussion, believing their contributions to have been better and greater than is judged by the other participants and by neutral psychologists. On the other hand, any group usually also contains a small number of self-diminishers, who view their contributions as *less* valuable than they appeared to others. Either person—the narcissist or the self-diminisher—is prone to render inaccurate judgments, as determined by the criterion of convergence with the judgments of others (John & Robins, 1994). The ideal self-judge is somewhere between these two extremes.

Another recent study of judgmental ability used behavioral prediction instead of inter-judge convergence as its criterion (Kolar, Funder, & Colvin, in press). In this study, personality judgments were obtained from the subjects' close acquaintances as well as from the subjects themselves. Somewhat surprisingly, in nearly every comparison the acquaintances' judgments had better predictive validity than did the self-judgments. For example, acquaintances' judgments of assertiveness correlated more highly with later assertive behavior observed in the laboratory than did self-judgments of assertiveness. The same was true for talkativeness, initiation of humor, physical attractiveness, feelings of being cheated and victimized by life, and several other traits of personality and behavior. The differences were sometimes small, but the overall pattern was quite consistent.

The conclusion implied by these results is that ordinarily it might be difficult to judge one's own personality traits. From the "inside" we are preoccupied with planning our next move in response to the situation with which we are confronted. But when viewing somebody else from the "outside" we may actually be in a better position to compare what he or she does with what others do, and therefore be better able to evaluate his or her personality traits, which as you will recall from Chapter 4 are *relative* constructs. Their very essence entails comparing one person with another.

Occasionally, however, we can take an "outside" perspective on our own behavior. Reviewing one's *past* behaviors might be one such occasion, when we can see retrospectively how our actions fit into a pattern that was invisible to us at the time of the action. For example, alchoholics asked for the causes of their recent drinking relapses tend to attribute them to a stressful day at work, a fight with a spouse, and so on. But the more time that passes, the more likely the alchoholic is to view the relapse as part of the chronic pattern of being an alcoholic (McKay et al., 1989).

This phenomenon is probably not limited to alchoholism. One of the great misperceptions many of us seem to have about our own behavior is that it is the logical or natural response to the situation at the moment—that it is what anyone would have done (Ross, Greene, & House, 1977). "What else could I do," you may often hear people ask. Such explanations are somewhat like those of the alcoholic who, after a stressful argument, goes on a bender. The alcoholic might say, "The stress caused me to drink," but of course what he or she forgets is that nonalchoholics find other ways to respond to stress. We probably all know people who are hostile, or deceitful, or unpleasant in some way, who similarly believe they are just doing what they must. As outside observers, however, we are in a position to see a chronic *pattern* of behavior, not just momentary pressures, and that other people respond to similar situations differently (Kolar, Funder, & Colvin, in press).

This phenomenon is probably not limited to negative behaviors, although the positive end of the effect has not yet been documented by research. We probably all know people who are consistently kind, or diligent, or brave. When asked about their behavior they seem just as surprised as the alcoholic or hostile person described above: "What else could I do?" they respond. To them, acting in a kind, diligent, or brave manner is simply the obvious response to the situations they experience, and they find it hard to imagine themselves or anyone else acting differently. It takes an outsider's perspective to recognize their behavior as consistent across situations, unusual, and even admirable.

Perhaps this tendency is more pronounced when negative traits like alchoholism are involved. But I think in many cases we can be equally blind to our good qualities.[3]

When people experience consistent problems in living, they often seek psychotherapeutic help. One purpose of many psychotherapies is to induce the client to review his or her past behavior and identify chronic patterns, rather than continuing to see his or her maladaptive behavior merely as responses to momentary pressures. The alchoholic, for example, must realize that his or her drinking is a chronic and characteristic behavior pattern, and not just a normal response to situational stress, in order to change and overcome alcoholism.

THE GOOD TARGET

Another potential moderator of accuracy is the flip side of the good judge: the good target. Some people seem to be as readable as an open book, whereas others seem more closed and enigmatic. Perhaps some individuals are more easily judged than others. As the pioneering personality psychologist Gordon Allport asked in this context, "Who are these people?" (Allport, 1937, p. 443; Colvin, 1993b).

"Judgeable" people are those about whom others reach agreement most easily. Naturally, these tend to be the same people whose behavior is most predictable from judgments of their personalities. As follows from this definition, judgeable people are those for whom "what you see is what you get." Their behavior is organized coherently, in such a way that even different people who know them in different settings describe essentially the same person. Furthermore, the behavior of such people is so consistent that by observing what they have done in the past one can predict what they will do in the future. We could

---

[3]Social psychological research on the "false consensus" effect has studied in detail the tendency of people to see their own behavior as common (see Ross, Greene, & House, 1977). This discussion can also be compared to research on the "actor-observer effect" (e.g., Jones & Nisbett, 1971), which found that people often see their own behavior as a response to momentary, situational pressures, whereas they see the behavior of others as consistent and as a product of their personality attributes. The present discussion differs from earlier presentations of the effect, however, in that it does not follow the traditional assumption that the subject is correct in thinking his or her behavior is caused by the situation, and the observer is wrong. I think that, more often, the subject is blind to consistencies in his or her own behavior, and that those consistencies are better observed from the external perspective of another person (see Funder, 1982; Kolar, Funder, & Colvin, in press).

say that these individuals are stable and well organized, or even that they are psychologically well adjusted (Colvin, 1993b).[4]

Theorists have long postulated that the most psychologically healthy style you can have is to conceal very little from those around you, or to exhibit what is sometimes called a "transparent self" (Jourard, 1971). To the extent that you exhibit any kind of psychological facade and that there are large discrepancies between the person "inside" and the person you display "outside," you are likely to experience excessive isolation from the people around you, which can lead to unhappiness, hostility, and depression.

Recent research builds on this theory by pointing out that judgeability itself—the "what you see is what you get" syndrome—is a part of psychological adjustment, because it consists of behavioral coherence and consistency. Inhibiting the expression of emotion also seems to be harmful to one's physical health (Berry & Pennebaker, 1993; Pennebaker, 1992). Moreover, another recent study indicates that the roots of this kind of adjustment and judgeability reach into early childhood, and that the association between judgeability and psychological adjustment is particularly strong among males (Colvin, 1993a).

THE GOOD TRAIT

All traits are not created equal—some are much easier to judge accurately than others. For example, more-visible traits, such as talkativeness, sociability, and other traits related to extraversion—are judged with much higher levels of interjudge agreement than less-visible traits, such as cognitive and ruminative styles and habits (Funder & Dobroth, 1987). For example, you are more likely to agree with your acquaintances, and they are more likely to agree with each other, about whether you are talkative than about whether you "tend to worry and ruminate." This finding holds true even when the people who judge you are strangers who have looked at you only for a few minutes (Funder & Colvin, 1988; see also Watson, 1989).

This finding might seem rather obvious. I once admitted that the main finding of the study by Funder and Dobroth is that "more visible traits are easier to see." We needed federal funding to learn that? (Don't worry—our grant was very small.) But the finding does have some interesting implications. One concerns the basis of personality judgments by acquaintances. Some psychologists, reluctant to concede that peer judgments of personality can have some accuracy, have proposed that interjudge agreement is a result of conversations judges have had with one another, or with the subjects. Thus, these psychologists conclude,

---

[4]It is reasonable to wonder whether this can go too far. For example, a person who is rigid and inflexible might be easily judged but would not be well adjusted. However, research has not yet identified such judgeable-but-maladjusted individuals.

peer judgments are based not on the subjects' personalities, but only on their socially constructed reputations (McClelland, 1972; Kenny, 1991).

This idea seems plausible, but I doubt it is true. If peers based their personality judgments only on reputation and not on observation, then there would be no reason for observable traits to yield any better agreement than unobservable ones. Other people can manufacture a reputation about your ruminativeness just as well as they can about your talkativeness. But while all traits are equally susceptible to being talked about, certain traits are much harder to observe. Therefore, the finding that more-observable traits yield better interjudge agreement implies quite strongly that peer judgment is based more on direct behavioral observation than on mere reputation (Clark & Paivio, 1989).

Another investigation of the visibility of traits addressed a trait the researchers called "sociosexuality," or the willingness to engage in sexual relations with minimal acquaintanceship with or commitment to and from one's partner (Gangestad, Simpson, DiGeronimo, & Biek, 1992). It is reasonable to postulate that the accurate perception of this trait has been important across the history of our species. According to evolutionary theory, those traits and abilities that make individuals more likely to reproduce are more likely to be present in later generations (for a more detailed discussion of this issue, see Chapter 9). A crucial part of reproduction, of course, is figuring out who might be willing to mate with you. The hypothesis of this study, therefore, was that for evolutionary reasons people should be particularly good at judging this trait as opposed to other traits presumably less important for reproduction of the species.

The study indeed found that individual differences in this trait, as measured by self-report, were more accurately detected by observers than were traits such as social potency and social closeness. And, in an interesting corollary, although this finding held true regardless of the sexes of the perceiver and the person perceived, females judging the sociosexuality of males were especially accurate, and males judging the sociosexuality of other males were even more accurate! This last finding presents a mild problem for the evolutionary explanation of the perception of sociosexuality: What would be the reproductive advantage for a male to know the mating availability of another male? (In case you were wondering, males, probably to their eternal regret, were *not* particularly good at judging the sociosexuality of females.)

GOOD INFORMATION

The final moderator of judgmental accuracy is the amount and kind of information on which the personality judgment is based.

Amount of Information   When it comes to amount of information, it seems clear that more is usually better. In one study, for example, subjects were judged both by close acquaintances (who had known the subjects for at least a year) and also by strangers (who had viewed the subjects only for about five minutes on a videotape). Personality judgments by the close acquaintances agreed much better with each other and with self-judgments than did judgments by strangers (Funder & Colvin, 1988).

But this advantage of longer acquaintanceship did not hold under all circumstances. The videotapes watched by the strangers were of a five-minute conversation that the subject held with a peer of the opposite sex. This observation was the sole basis for their personality judgments. The acquaintances, by contrast, never saw the videotape. Their judgments were based, instead, on their own knowledge of the subject obtained through observations and interactions in daily life over an extended period of time. Interestingly, when the judgments by the strangers and those by the acquaintances were used to try to predict what the subject would do in a further videotaped interaction, with a different opposite-sex peer, the two sets of judgments performed about the same. That is, the advantage of acquaintances over strangers vanishes when the criterion is the ability to predict behavior in a situation similar to one that the strangers have seen, but that the acquaintances have not (Colvin & Funder, 1991).

Let me clarify this finding with a personal example. During most academic quarters, I lecture before 150 or more undergraduates two or three times a week. As a result, there are a lot of people who have seen me lecture but who have no way of knowing what kind of person I am in other settings. My wife, on the other hand, has known me well for more than a dozen years, but has never seen me deliver a lecture (this is not uncommon among college professors and their spouses). If one of my students and my wife are both asked to predict how I will behave in lecture next week, whose predictions will be more accurate? According to Colvin and Funder (1991), the two predictions will be about equally valid. On the other hand, according to Funder and Colvin (1988), if you ask these two people to predict what I might do in any *other* context, my wife will have a clear advantage.

In our 1991 article, Colvin and I called this phenomenon a "boundary" on the acquaintanceship effect, because we seemed to have found the one circumstance under which strangers could provide personality judgments with a predictive validity equal to those offered by close acquaintances. But through a reversed perspective this finding may be even more remarkable. Even though a close acquaintance—such as a spouse—has never seen you in a particular situation, he or she will be able to generalize from observations of you in *other* situations with accuracy sufficient to predict your behavior in that situation as well as someone who has actually seen you in it. From casual observation in daily life, for example, the acquaintances were able to extract information about the subjects' personalities that was just as useful in predicting how they would behave under the gaze of a video camera as was strangers' direct observation of behavior in a highly similar situation. This ability of acquaintances to generalize judgments may be the real news of this research.

Quality of Information An important topic for future research will be how different *kinds* of information, including that gathered through different types of acquaintanceship (e.g., as friend, co-worker, lover) contribute to judgmental accuracy. Little such research has been done so far. Acquaintanceship has typically been measured by asking the judge, "How long have you known the subject" (as in Funder & Colvin, 1988), or in other studies, having the judge rate his or her knowledge of the subject on a simple seven- or nine-point scale (e.g., Jackson, Neill, & Bevan, 1973).

An interesting lead toward evaluating the quality of information was provided by a study in which lay judges of personality listened to interviews in which subjects were asked either about their thoughts and feelings or about their overt behaviors. The judges then tried to describe the subjects' personalities using a set of one hundred different traits. The researchers found that listening to the thoughts-and-feelings interview "produced more 'accurate' social impressions, or at least impressions that were more in accord with speakers' self-assessments prior to the interviews *and* with the assessments made by their close friends, than did [listening to] the behavioral . . . interviews" (Andersen, 1984, p. 294).

This experimental finding suggests that, in real life, knowing someone in a context where you get to know their thoughts and feelings—as a close friend or lover might, for example—is likely to lead to more accurate overall impressions of that person's personality than knowing someone in a setting where you see only what they do—as a co-worker would, for example. This implication has never been empirically tested, however, as far as I know; it deserves future research.

Another way to evaluate the quality of the information on which a judgment is based is to consider how specific observations of behavior are linked to the judgment of specific traits. For example, when a subject is seen to speak in a very loud voice, judges are apt to infer that he or she is extraverted, and that inference is generally correct. However, the loudness of someone's voice has little to do with his or her other traits, such as conscientiousness or agreeableness (Funder & Sneed, 1993; Scherer, 1978).

Other research has shown that just a glance at someone's face can be good enough information for lay perceivers to make surprisingly accurate judgments of his or her dominance and submissiveness (Berry & Finch Wero, 1993). Similarly, the degree to which someone dresses fashionably and has a stylish haircut can lead lay perceivers to infer, with a surprising degree of validity, that he or she is extraverted (Borkenau & Liebler, 1993).

The accurate judgment of personality, then, depends upon both the quantity and quality of the information on which it is based. More information is generally better, but it is just as important for the information to be specifically relevant to the traits that one is trying to judge.

The Process of Accurate Judgment

As renewed research accumulates more knowledge about *when* accurate judgments are made, it will begin to teach us new things about *how* accurate judgments are made. As we have seen, work already completed on judgeable traits, judgeable people, and the amount and kind of information that leads to accurate judgments provides hints about how such judgments are made and even about how accuracy might be improved. But we can go further by specifically focusing upon the process of judgment.

One way to think about how accurate judgments are made is in terms of the "lens model" of perception and judgment introduced some years ago by Egon Brunswik (1956). Brunswik's model is intended to explain how people use the information available in their environment, or "ecology," to reach judgments. For example, consider the diagram in Figure 6.1, which is an adaptation of the classic Brunswikian lens (notice how the diagram looks a bit like light coming into a lens and then coming out again to a focal point). The circle T, on the left, represents the "target" of judgment or, in the case of personality judgment, the attributes of the person being judged. For example, assume our subject person is an extravert; his or her extraversion would be represented by T. The C terms, in the middle of the figure, refer to the behaviors that this person performs as a function of his or her personality attributes (T); these behaviors serve as "cues" that allow the attribute T to be detected. For example

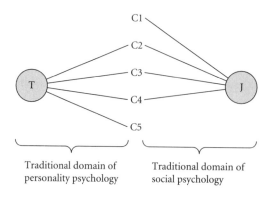

Traditional domain of personality psychology

Traditional domain of social psychology

FIGURE 6.1 A "LENS" MODEL OF PERCEPTION AND JUDGMENT This "lens" model describes how visible attributes of a person—or "cues"—are used to judge his or her personality. Some attributes are valid indicators of personality; others are not (Funder & Sneed, 1993).

our extravert might speak in a loud voice, use vigorous hand gestures, and attend many social gatherings. The circle *J*, on the right, refers to the judgment of personality that the observer makes: ideally, that our subject is extraverted.

A recent study demonstrated that, in real life, judges of personality seem able to perceive which cues are valid (Funder & Sneed, 1993). For example, the behavior "expressive in face, voice or gesture" was significantly correlated with targets' extraversion *and* was correctly used by lay judges as a sign of extraversion; thus it is a valid, useful cue like *C2*, *C3*, or *C4* in the figure. That is the ideal. But a couple of other aspects of Figure 6.1 illustrate what can go awry in personality judgment. For example, the target of judgment might emit informative behaviors that the judge fails to use; this possibility is shown on the figure by *C5*. The behavior "seems to like partner" was actually correlated with targets' extraversion, but was not attended to by lay judges when they judged this trait. The judges did, however, tend to interpret a different behavior, "expresses self-pity," as relevant to introversion, but that cue is not correlated with the dimension; this possibility is represented by *C1*.

In general, the path to accuracy leads through four aspects of the process of personality judgment. First, in some context, a trait produces a behavioral effect; this behavior is therefore relevant to that trait. Second, this behavior must be available to the judge. For example, a "behavior" that comprises an action of the hypothalamus is not ordinarily available to an observer; neither is a behavior that occurs in a context where the observer is not present. Third, this relevant and available behavior must be detected by the judge. This is a hazardous step, because the judge may be inattentive, unperceptive, or distracted, or the behavior itself (e.g., a momentary facial expression), although available in principle, might be extremely difficult to see. Fourth, the relevant, available, detected behavior must be correctly used by the judge. This step is hazardous as well, because as we have seen the judge might believe a behavior to be diagnostic of one trait when it is actually diagnostic of a different one, or of nothing at all (Funder, 1995).

Thinking about personality judgment according to this model offers not only a way to conceptualize the process of accurate personality judgment, but also the potential basis for a technology to improve judgmental accuracy. If we could identify which behavioral cues are and are not associated with various personality traits, and learn to use the valid ones and to ignore the invalid ones, then our judgments of personality would improve even beyond the pretty good degree of accuracy they achieve already.

Traditionally, social psychologists interested in interpersonal perception examine how people combine cues, or stimuli when making judgments of each other, but social psychologists seldom show any interest in the traits with which these cues are actually correlated. Personality psychologists, on the other hand, traditionally look at the behaviors that are correlated with various personality traits, but are seldom interested in how or whether these behavioral cues are used in everyday interpersonal judgment. On Figure 6.1, then, social psychologists occupy the right-hand side, while personality psychologists occupy the left-hand side. In order for a Brunswikian approach to allow us to better understand and improve the accuracy of personality judgment, however, both sides and both approaches are required. The study of personality judgment is an ideal place to begin integrating personality psychology more closely with social psychology (Funder & Sneed, 1993; Funder, 1995).

CONCLUSION

There is no escape from personality assessment. If you manage to evade having your personality judged by tests or by psychologists, you still will find that your personality is judged every day by your acquaintances, co-workers, and friends. Furthermore, these judgments will matter just as much and probably more than any that will ever be rendered by tests or psychologists.

Whether the assessment of your personality comes from a test or from an acquaintance, many of the same considerations apply. The paramount question in both cases is whether the assessment is correct. The degree to which a personality test is correct is called its validity. The degree to which an acquaintance's judgment of your personality is correct is called its accuracy. But these terms refer to exactly the same thing, and are (or should be) evaluated in exactly the same way. In either case, the two key questions remain these: Do assessments from various methods (or various acquaintances) agree with each other? And can they predict behavior? To the degree that the answers to both of these questions are "yes," we can reasonably begin to conclude that the personality test, or the personality judgment, is valid or accurate.

SUMMARY

People judge the personalities of each other and of themselves all the time, and these judgments often have important consequences. The judgments of others can affect your opportunities and can create self-fulfilling prophecies, or expectancy effects. Your judgments of yourself influence what you are likely to attempt to accomplish in life. Therefore, it is important to examine when and how judgments of the self and of others are accurate. Recent research evaluates the accuracy of personality judgment in terms of agreement and predictive validity. That is, judgments that agree with judgments from other sources (such as other people) or that are able to predict the people judged are deemed more likely to be accurate than judgments that do not agree with each other or that cannot predict behavior. Research has examined four kinds of variables that seem to affect the likelihood of accurate personality judgment: (1) the good judge, or the possibility that some judges are more accurate than others; (2) the good target, or the possibility that some individuals are easier to judge than others; (3) the good trait, or the possibility that some traits are easier to judge accurately than others; and (4) good information, or the possiblity that more or better information about the target makes accurate judgment more likely. This research has led recently to a model of the process of accurate personality judgment that describes it as a function of the relevance, availability, detection, and utilization of behavioral cues.

CHAPTER 7

USING PERSONALITY TRAITS TO UNDERSTAND BEHAVIOR

To this point we have considered whether traits exist (Chapter 4) and have reviewed how traits are assessed by psychologists (Chapter 5) and by everybody in daily life (Chapter 6). It is now time to turn to a somewhat different but related topic, the *scientific* use of personality traits. From a scientific perspective, the central question about traits asks how personality traits can be used to understand behavior. Personality psychologists have tried to answer this question in three ways, which I will call the many-trait approach, the single-trait approach, and the essential-trait approach.

First, some researchers approach the investigation of behavior with long lists of traits that are intended to cover comprehensively the domain of personality. These researchers next try to find out which of these traits are correlated with the specific behavior in which the researchers are interested. Then they try to explain these correlations, with the goal of improving our understanding of both the underpinnings of the behavior and the more general workings of personality.

For example, one might measure how long each of a group of children can wait for a reward (a behavior technically called "delay of gratification") and also measure up to one hundred traits in each child. You could then see which of these traits tended to characterize the children who delayed the longest and the shortest lengths of time. As we will see later in this chapter, the results from such an experiment can tell you much about how and why the longest-delaying children were able to do so, as well as something important about the psychological mechanisms that underlie the tendency to delay.

The second approach is to focus on one particular trait and build a research program around that trait. For example, important research programs have examined in detail the traits of authoritarianism, conscientiousness, and self-monitoring, to name only three. In each case, the research question concerns not so much the broader functioning of personality or even the basis of specific behaviors, but how wide-ranging the implications might be of a particular, arguably central, attribute of personality.

A third approach, which has made considerable headway in recent years, is to try to narrow the list of thousands of trait terms that have been used by psychologists and laypersons over the years into a much shorter list comprising only the ones that really matter. Various psychologists have proposed such lists; the most prominent list at present is called the "Big Five," and includes the traits called extraversion, neuroticism, conscientiousness, agreeableness, and openness. There is some debate about whether such a short list is sufficient for characterizing personality, and further questions are being raised about whether the number and nature of essential traits varies from one culture to another.

This chapter will review examples of each of these three approaches to the scientific use of personality traits.

THE MANY-TRAIT APPROACH

A number of personality psychologists—including me—enjoy looking at many traits at once when examining the correlates of behavior. Several more or less comprehensive lists of traits have been developed for this purpose (including Allport and Odbert's list of 17,953, which is a bit long for practical purposes; Allport & Odbert, 1936), but my own favorite is the list of one hundred traits called the **California Q-set** (Bem & Funder, 1978; Block, 1978).

The California Q-Set

Maybe "trait" is not quite the right word for the items of the Q-set. The set consists of one hundred phrases, each of which describes an aspect of personality that might or might not be important for characterizing a particular individual. Each item is printed on a separate card. For example, item 1 reads, "Is critical, skeptical, not easily impressed"; item 2 reads, "Is a genuinely dependable and responsible person"; item 3 reads, "Has a wide range of interests"; and so forth for the remaining ninety-seven items. These phrases are more complex than simple traits, which are usually thought of as single words, but each item does describe a potentially important characteristic of personality (see Table 7.1 for more examples).

The way this list of items is used and the way it originated are both rather unusual. The items are used to express judgments of personality by having the judge sort them into nine categories ranging from "highly uncharacteristic" of the person being described (category 1) to "highly characteristic" (category 9). Items neither characteristic nor uncharacteristic are placed in or near category 5. The distribution is forced, which means that a predetermined number of items must go into each category. The usual distribution is peaked or "normal," mean-

---

TABLE 7.1

SAMPLE ITEMS FROM THE CALIFORNIA Q-SET

1. Is critical, skeptical, not easily impressed.
2. Is a genuinely dependable and responsible person
3. Has a wide range of interests
11. Is protective of those close to him or her
13. Is thin-skinned; sensitive to criticism or insult
18. Initiates humor
24. Prides self on being "objective," rational
26. Is productive; gets things done
28. Tends to arouse liking and acceptance
29. Is turned to for advice and reassurance
43. Is facially and/or gesturally expressive
51. Genuinely values intellectual and cognitive matters
54. Emphasizes being with others; gregarious
58. Enjoys sensuous experiences—including touch, taste, smell, physical contact
71. Has high aspiration level for self
75. Has a clear-cut, internally consistent personality
84. Is cheerful
98. Is verbally fluent
100. Does not vary roles; relates to everyone in the same way

ing that most items are placed near the center and just a few (often just 5 of the 100) can be placed on either end (see Figure 7.1).

The judge who does this sorting might be a friend, or a researcher, or a psychotherapist; in these cases the item placements constitute I data. Alternatively, a person might provide judgments of his or her own personality, in which case the item placements constitute S data. The most important advantage of Q-sorting is that it forces the judge to compare all the items directly against each other within one individual, rather than just relatively across individuals. Furthermore, the judge is permitted to identify only a few items as important for characterizing a particular person. Nobody can be described as "all good" or "all bad," for example; there is simply not enough room to put all the good traits—or all the bad traits—into categories 9 or 1. Finer and more subtle discriminations must be made.

The items of the California Q-set were not derived through factor analysis or any formal, empirical procedure. Rather, they were the result of the efforts of a team of clinical practitioners and investigators to come up with a comprehensive set of terms sufficient to describe the diverse, real-life cases they were seeing every day (Block, 1978). An initial list was formulated, and then these

FIGURE 7.1 THE CALIFORNIA Q-SORT   To describe an individual, one places the items of the Q-set into a symmetric, forced distribution ranging from "not characteristic" (category 1) to "highly characteristic" (category 9). These Q-sorters are in the process of laying the Q-set cards into the prescribed categories.
Photos by author.

investigators would meet regularly to try to use the items to describe the people they were seeing. If an item proved useless or vague, it was revised or eliminated. When the set could be "embarrassed" by lacking an item that was necessary to describe a particular case, a new item was written and added. The resulting set of one hundred items was the product of numerous revisions and refinements of this kind. Later, another pair of investigators revised the set slightly so that its sometimes-technical phrasings could be understood and used by laypersons (Bem & Funder, 1978); it is this slightly revised list that is excerpted in Table 7.1.

Delay of Gratification

One behavior that has been investigated frequently through the multi-trait, Q-sort approach is delay of gratification. Delay has been a classic topic for psychological investigation because denying oneself immediate pleasure for long-term gain seems to be opposed to basic human nature, yet it is also necessary. To hold a job so as to be paid later, to stay in school so as to graduate later, and to invest rather than spend money so as to gain more later are all useful and even necessary abilities to have in our society.

SEX DIFFERENCES

One line of research has focused on sex differences in the ability to delay behavior. It has long been known that males in our society are less prone to delay gratification than are females (J. H. Block, 1973; Maccoby, 1966). Why is this?

One study used the multi-trait approach to try to answer this question (Funder, Block, & Block, 1983). In this study, 116 children (59 boys and 57 girls) were tested in two delay of gratification experiments when they were four years old. In one experiment, each child was shown a festively wrapped gift and told that he or she would receive it after completing a puzzle. The gift was then set down within reach of the child. The researchers then measured how long the child was able to resist reaching out and grabbing the gift.

In the other experiment, each child was told that he or she was forbidden to play with an attractive toy, and then his or her tendency to try to play with it anyway was measured (the more the child tried to play with the toy, the lower his or her delay of gratification score). Each child's two delay scores were then averaged and correlated with Q-sort personality descriptions obtained when the children were three years old (a year before the delay experiments were conducted), four years old (about the time the delay experiments were conducted),

TABLE 7.2

CHILD Q-SORT CORRELATES OF DELAY OF GRATIFICATION: GIRLS

Q-Set Item	Age at Personality Assessment			
	3	4	7	11
Positive Correlates				
Appears to have high intellectual capacity	.27	.51	.27	.24
Is competent, skillful	.37	.28	.39	.19
Is planful; thinks ahead	.38	.28	.32	.16
Is attentive and able to concentrate	.19	.41	.43	.07
Develops genuine and close relationships	.18	.32	.35	.24
Is reflective; thinks before acting	.22	.30	.22	.29
Is resourceful	.37	.23	.18	.18
Uses and responds to reason	.13	.37	.28	.14
Negative Correlates				
Has transient interpersonal relationships	−.24	−.30	−.31	−.41
Is emotionally labile	−.39	−.24	−.43	−.07
Is victimized by other children	−.19	−.17	−.35	−.39
Tries to take advantage of others	−.04	−.23	−.33	−.44
Goes to pieces under stress	−.25	−.25	−.30	−.14
Seeks reassurance from others	−.02	−.39	−.12	−.29
Is easily offended	−.32	−.25	−.11	−.01
Tends to be sulky or whiny	−.30	−.26	−.02	−.09

Source: Funder, Block, & Block, 1983

TABLE 7.3

CHILD Q-SORT CORRELATES OF DELAY OF GRATIFICATION: BOYS

Q-Set Item	Age at Personality Assessment			
	3	4	7	11
Positive Correlates				
Is shy and reserved	.40	.36	.42	.51
Keeps thoughts and feelings to self	.41	.32	.35	.51
Is obedient and compliant	.24	.25	.53	.34
Prefers nonverbal communication	.26	.08	.47	.53
Is reflective; thinks before acting	.32	.34	.36	.30
Is inhibited and constricted	.38	.23	.25	.46
Withdraws under stress	.31	.41	.18	.42
Is indecisive and vacillating	.14	.35	.32	.45
Is physically cautious	.37	.21	.18	.39
Uses and responds to reason	.20	.22	.36	.19
Is fearful and anxious	.32	.02	.21	.35
Is planful; thinks ahead	.30	.26	.03	.22
Negative Correlates				
Is vital, energetic, lively	−.39	−.32	−.44	−.40
Tries to be the center of attention	−.37	−.23	−.39	−.46
Is physically active	−.34	−.15	−.51	−.29
Is self-assertive	−.25	−.21	−.36	−.45
Has rapid personal tempo	−.41	−.28	−.22	−.38
Characteristically stretches limits	−.28	−.16	−.43	−.31
Is emotionally expressive	−.34	−.20	−.36	−.29
Is talkative	−.23	−.10	−.35	−.47
Is curious and exploring	−.21	−.22	−.21	−.39
Is emotionally labile	−.38	−.07	−.39	−.12
Is unable to delay gratification	−.31	−.30	−.17	−.16
Is restless and fidgety	−.27	−.20	−.34	−.16

Source: Funder, Block, & Block, 1983

and years later, when the children were seven and eleven years old. The results are shown in Tables 7.2 and 7.3.

These two tables might appear overwhelming at first glance, but I hope you will bear with me and take a few minutes to examine them closely. The perusal of tables of correlates like these is a crucial part of the work of many personality psychologists. The most important thing such tables show is *not* the exact correlations or the exact items that are present. Instead, we need to look most closely at the general patterns that are shown. Which items are stable over time? What do those items mean? When Tables 7.2 and 7.3 are examined in this way, they show a couple of clear patterns.

One interesting phenomenon revealed by both tables is that the personality correlates of a behavior measured when the children were four years old could be detected through personality assessments provided even seven years later. This evidence, which some psychologists find surprising, indicates that many aspects of personality remain fairly consistent even across the rapid development and changes that occur during childhood.

Another interesting facet of the information in these tables is the similarities and differences in the correlates of delay of gratification between girls and boys. Both girls and boys who are planful, reflective and reasonable, and who are *not* emotionally unstable ("labile" is the term on the tables) are likely to manifest the most delay in the experimental tests. However, girls who delay the most are also intelligent, competent, attentive, and resourceful—correlates missing among the boys. Boys who delay the most are also shy, quiet, compliant, and anxious—all correlates missing among the girls. This finding can be interpreted in terms of two broader personality attributes called "ego control" (which is also sometimes called self-control or inhibition) and "ego resiliency" (which is much like healthy psychological adjustment). In both sexes one finds a higher level of ego control in those children who were able to delay longer, just as one would expect. But in the girls—and only in the girls—one finds that ego resiliency, or adjustment, is also related to delay. The boys who delay the most, by contrast, manifest varying levels of psychological adjustment.

This difference may arise because in our society girls are taught that self-control and delay of gratification is something they *must* learn, whereas boys do not receive this lesson. The result is that those girls most able to absorb society's lessons—the well-adjusted, resilient ones—best absorb the lesson about delay and therefore manifest the behavior more. No such lesson is aimed at boys, however, so their adjustment and resiliency end up being irrelevant or even (especially by age eleven) negatively relevant to their tendency to delay gratification (Funder, Block, & Block, 1983).

THE NATURE OF DELAY

Another study investigated the basic psychological mechanisms behind delay of gratification behavior in adolescents (Funder & Block, 1989). Two different views were compared. The first regards delay behavior as one among many byproducts of a general psychological tendency to inhibit one's impulses, sometimes called ego control (Block & Block, 1980). The other view regards delay of gratification as a cognitive or intellectual skill, through which one has the *ability* to control one's impulses when necessary (Mischel, Shoda, & Peake, 1988). The difference is important, because from the ego-control perspective, delay of gratification might sometimes be a byproduct of an unfortunate tendency toward overcontrol and inhibition, and sometimes you might delay more than is good for you. From the ability perspective, by contrast, delay of gratification is a flexible and adaptive skill of which you cannot have too much—just as you cannot have too much intelligence.

In one experiment, fourteen-year-old subjects were offered the choice between a small monetary payment at each of several sessions, and a single, larger payment at the end of all the sessions (Funder & Block, 1989). The results of this experiment supported elements of *both* views of delay of gratification. Take a close look at Tables 7.4 and 7.5. As you study them a bit, you will begin to see that those adolescents who opted for the larger, delayed payment seemed to be smarter, more ambitious, *and* somewhat inhibited and overcontrolled.

When a study uses rewards that are strongly desired—such as money in this study—*and* gives the subjects something to gain by waiting—also as in this study—then both ego control and intelligence will be related to delay (Funder & Block, 1989). But other studies by other investigators show that when rewards are small and unexciting, delay is simply a matter of following instructions, and only intelligence will matter. Intelligent kids, who are good at following instructions, will delay. But when rewards are great, a powerful impulse must be kept in check, thus ego control will matter more. Only those able—or prone—to control their feelings will be able to delay. The extrapolation of this conclusion into daily life, where the rewards and punishments attached to waiting and acting are much larger than can be simulated in any lab, is that intellect alone will never be sufficient to explain delay of gratification. Deeper tendencies to control or express one's impulses will also prove important.

Other Behaviors

Many other important behaviors have been examined through the multi-trait approach using the Q-sort, including personality correlates of drug use, depression, and even political ideology.

Drug Abuse

One study looked at adolescents who by the age of fourteen were using illegal drugs. These adolescents had all been described with Q-sort items nearly a decade earlier, when they were small children, as being restless and fidgety, emotionally unstable, disobedient, nervous, domineering, immature, aggressive, teasing, and susceptible to stress. These correlates imply that whatever the immediate effects of peer pressure and other external influences might be, the adolescents most likely to use drugs seemed already to be having significant problems years earlier. They further imply that some of the effort to prevent drug abuse should be redirected, away from campaigns such as "just say no" and other immediate, short-term interventions, and toward identifying and remedying the longer-term

TABLE 7.4

Q-SORT CORRELATES OF PAYMENT DELAY IN FOURTEEN-YEAR-OLD
FEMALE SUBJECTS

Q-set Item	r
Positive Correlates	
Genuinely values intellectual and cognitive matters	.49
Is a genuinely dependable and responsible person	.48
Is able to see to the heart of important matters	.48
Is socially perceptive of interpersonal cues	.45
Behaves in an ethically consistent manner	.44
Has insight into own motives and behavior	.43
Has high aspiration level for self	.43
Is productive; gets things done	.40
Tends to arouse liking and acceptance	.40
Has a clear-cut, internally consistent personality	.40
Favors conservative values in a variety of areas	.36
Behaves in a sympathetic or considerate manner	.32
Tends toward over-control of needs and impulses	.32
Has warmth, capacity for close relationships	.32
Appears straightforward, candid	.32
Prides self on being "objective," rational	.31
Is verbally fluent	.31
Appears to have high intellectual capacity	.30
Negative Correlates	
Is unable to delay gratification	−.65
Feels a lack of personal meaning in life	−.50
Is self-indulgent	−.46
Characteristically pushes limits	−.42
Tends to be rebellious and non-conforming	−.41
Is extrapunitive; tends to transfer or project blame	−.41
Has hostility toward others	−.40
Interprets simple situations in complicated ways	−.40
Thinks and associates ideas in unusual ways	−.39
Is over-reactive to minor frustrations, irritable	−.38
Has unpredictable and changeable behavior, attitudes	−.38
Creates and exploits dependency in people	−.38
Is subtly negativistic; undermines and obstructs	−.37
Perceives many contexts in sexual terms	−.37
Is guileful and deceitful; manipulative	−.35
Is basically distrustful	−.35
Expresses hostile feelings directly	−.34
Is sensitive to demands	−.32
Gives up and withdraws from frustration, adversity	−.31
Feels cheated and victimized by life	−.31
Enjoys sensuous experiences	−.30

Note: Correlations smaller than .30 have been omitted.

Source: Funder and Block, 1989

TABLE 7.5

Q-SORT CORRELATES OF PAYMENT DELAY IN FOURTEEN-YEAR-OLD
MALE SUBJECTS

Q-set Item	r
Positive Correlates	
Favors conservative values in a variety of areas	.63
Is a genuinely dependable and responsible person	.60
Is productive; gets things done	.59
Has high aspiration level for self	.57
Has a clear-cut, internally consistent personality	.54
Tends toward over-control of needs and impulses	.52
Behaves in an ethically consistent manner	.52
Genuinely values intellectual and cognitive matters	.49
Is fastidious (perfectionist)	.46
Appears to have high intellectual capacity	.44
Prides self on being "objective," rational	.41
Is moralistic	.39
Judges self and others in conventional terms	.39
Behaves in a sympathetic or considerate manner	.37
Is turned to for advice or reassurance	.35
Appears straightforward, candid	.32
Is able to see to the heart of important problems	.32
Tends to arouse liking and acceptance	.31
Genuinely submissive; accepts domination comfortably	.30
Has a readiness to feel guilt	.29
Negative Correlates	
Is unable to delay gratification	−.69
Has unpredictable and changeable behavior, attitudes	−.62
Tends to be rebellious and non-conforming	−.59
Is self-indulgent	−.58
Characteristically pushes limits	−.50
Has fluctuating moods	−.50
Is guileful and deceitful; manipulative	−.48
Is subtly negativistic; undermines and obstructs	−.44
Is basically distrustful	−.43
Expresses hostile feelings directly	−.42
Has hostility toward others	−.41
Is sensitive to demands	−.38
Feels a lack of personal meaning in life	−.34
Gives up and withdraws from frustration, adversity	−.34
Is self-defeating	−.34
Feels cheated and victimized by life	−.34
Tends to be self-defensive	−.31
Denies unpleasant thoughts and experiences	−.29
Is power oriented	−.29
Perceives many contexts in sexual terms	−.28

Source: Funder and Block, 1989

problems and the susceptibility to stress that seem to underlie drug abuse (Block, Block, & Keyes, 1988; Shedler & Block, 1990).

DEPRESSION

Depression is another common problem of young adults that turns out to have deep roots (Block, Gjerde, & Block, 1991). Young women who were seriously depressed at age eighteen had been described as early as age seven by Q-sort items such as shy and reserved, oversocialized, self-punishing, and over-controlled. Young men who experienced depression at age eighteen had been identified at age seven and even at age three as being unsocialized, aggressive, and undercontrolled. This pattern implies that the risk factors for depression differ between young women and young men. The young women most at risk are those who are oversocialized, overcontrolled, and subsequently inhibited; perhaps they do not get out enough or do enough in life. The young men most at risk, however, show the opposite pattern: they are undersocialized, undercontrolled, and unable to organize their lives. They may be constantly in trouble, and may have difficulty finding a useful or comfortable niche in life. These findings show how the different expectations our society has of men and women affect their psychological development and their psychological health.

POLITICAL ORIENTATION

The last set of findings we will consider in this section compares personality to political orientation. The psychologist Jack Block assessed a group of subjects around the ages of three and four. Years later, when his subjects were twenty-three years old, Block had them complete a questionnaire about their political orientation; it included questions about abortion, expenditures for welfare, national health insurance, rights of criminal suspects, and so forth. From their responses to these questions he assigned each subject a score along a dimension from "liberal" to "conservative," and found a remarkable set of personality correlates dating to early childhood. Children who grew into political conservatives, by Block's definition, were likely to have been described at age three or four as easily victimized, easily offended, indecisive, vacillating, fearful, anxious, rigid, and inhibited. Those who grew into liberals, by contrast, were more likely to have been described as developing close relationships, self-reliant, energetic, and dominant. Interestingly, Block has so far refrained from interpreting these correlations, calling them only "food for thought regarding the underpinnings of political values" (Block, 1993, p. 32). What do you think they mean? (For one possibility, see the discussion of the trait of authoritarianism in the next section.)

THE SINGLE-TRAIT APPROACH

The research summarized in the previous section aimed a shotgun at personality, as it tried to consider as many as one hundred attributes at once. The approach to be considered in this section employs a rifle instead. Some of the most important and influential research in personality has focused on the nature, origins, and consequences of *single* traits that their investigators have deemed important.

In this section, we will consider research on three particular traits. The reasons for deeming these traits important have varied. The first, authoritarianism, has been deemed important because of societal reasons—it has been theorized to be a basis of racial prejudice and even Fascism. The second, conscientiousness, has been deemed important for practical reasons—it has seemed useful for predicting who will be productive employees. The third, self-monitoring, has been deemed important for theoretical reasons—it seems to address important questions concerning the relationship between inner reality and the private self, and external reality and the self as presented to others.

Authoritarianism

Racial prejudice and mindless obedience to corrupt government have been persistent problems throughout human history. These phenomena reached particularly horrifying dimensions in Europe in the 1930s and 1940s. The rise of Adolf Hitler and Nazism in Germany produced not only a repressive, dictatorial state bent on conquering its neighbors, but a massive wave of ethnic oppression that led to the extermination of millions of Jews and members of other disfavored minority groups, such as Gypsies and homosexuals. For this to happen, the German people had to cooperate with or at least accede to atrocities committed by their own government.

While all this was still going on, the philosopher and psychologist Erich Fromm began to wonder how any supposedly civilized people could allow such activities to occur. Fromm formulated an explanation in terms of the influence of history and society. He theorized that the demise of Catholicism and the rise of Protestantism in Germany, combined with the rise of capitalism, gave individuals unprecedented freedom to conceive of God as they wished and to direct their economic activity in any way they chose. But with this freedom came a frightening degree of responsibility, to conceive of God without the comforting certainty of religious dogma, and to choose an occupation or trade in which to thrive rather than starve. Many individuals, according to Fromm, fear this degree of freedom and seek to escape it—hence the title of his book, *Escape from Freedom* (1941). To avoid these frightening personal choices, some people turn their will over to external authority, such as a government or church, and take the comforting attitude that "I am just following orders." In turn, such individuals enjoy the experience of *giving* orders—which they expect to be unquestioned— to those who are below them in the hierarchy. Fromm coined the term "authoritarian character" to describe these personalities. It was the widespread presence of such individuals in Germany, Fromm guessed, that explained how Nazism could arise there.

Fromm's analysis concentrated on societal influences that affect people in general. He also acknowledged, however, that not everybody becomes an authoritarian, not even in 1930s Germany. A decade later, an attempt to understand the difference between authoritarians and nonauthoritarians was reported by the "Berkeley group" of psychologists (Adorno, Frenkel-Brunwik, Levinson, & Sanford, 1950; see also Dillehay, 1978, for an excellent review). These psychologists had been specifically commissioned (by the American Jewish Committee) to search for the root psychological causes of the anti-Semitism that had produced so much death and suffering during the 1930s and 1940s. Their efforts were detailed in a book called the *Authoritarian Personality*, widely considered to be a classic of psychological research.

The Berkeley group began its effort by constructing a questionnaire to measure anti-Semitism. This questionnaire was called the A-S scale, and included items such as "Jews seem to prefer the most luxurious, extravagant, and sensual way of living," "In order to maintain a nice residential neighborhood it is best to prevent Jews from living in it," and "The Jews should give up their un-Christian religion with all its strange customs (Kosher diet, special holidays, etc.) and participate actively and sincerely in the Christian religion" (Adorno et al., pp. 68–69). The people who scored highest and lowest on this scale were singled out for extensive clinical interviews, and were also given other tests.

The first conclusion the psychologists reached was that individuals prejudiced against Jews also tend to be prejudiced against other minority groups. So the next step in the research was to construct a more broadly worded ethnocentrism scale, called the E scale. It contained items such as "Negroes have their rights, but it is best to keep them in their own districts and schools to prevent too much contact with whites," and "The worst danger to real Americanism during the last 50 years has come from foreign ideas and agitators" (p. 142). The researchers found that scores on the E scale were correlated very highly, in the range from .63 to .75, with scores on the A-S scale.

The psychologists of the Berkeley group also believed that a more general political outlook was associated with both anti-Semitism and ethnocentrism, and in an attempt to tap it they developed the politico-economic conservatism (PEC) scale. It was a short step from the PEC to the development of the California F (or "F" meaning Fascism) scale, which an attempt to measure the basic anti-democratic psychological orientation that these researchers believed to be the common foundation of anti-Semitism, racial prejudice, and political (pseudo-) conservatism.[1]

The California F scale, one of the most widely researched personality questionnaires ever developed, appears in Table 7.6. (The method for scoring the scale is explained in a note at the bottom of the table.) Theoretically, the F scale measures the nine different facets that the Berkeley group believed comprised the essence of authoritarianism (pp. 255–257):

1. *Conventionalism:* an unthinking, inflexible tendency to follow mainstream values.
2. *Authoritarian submission:* a tendency to be submissive to and uncritical of societally endorsed moral authorities.
3. *Authoritarian aggression:* a tendency to want to punish severely those who do not obey authority.
4. *Anti-"intraception":* an active aversion to looking within the self and a general suspiciousness of anything philosophical, humanistic, or subjective.
5. *Superstition and stereotypy:* a belief that fate is determined by mysterious, supernatural forces combined with a tendency to think in rigid categories.
6. *Power and toughness:* a fascination with the idea of bosses, power, and domination, and an awe of powerful individuals and institutions.
7. *Destructiveness and cynicism:* a lack of faith in the value of people and a general hostility toward most people.
8. *Projectivity:* the belief that wild and dangerous things are going on in the world, which is interpreted as an outward projection of the authoritarian's own repressed impulses.
9. *Sexual repression:* a disproportionate concern with sexual issues, especially concerning what supposedly immoral things other people might be doing (recall that the Nazis intended to exterminate not only Jews but also homosexuals).

Taken together, these characteristics make up the syndrome of authoritarianism. Their combination can help explain some patterns of behavior and belief that might otherwise seem perplexing or even paradoxical. For example, authoritarians are extremely deferential to and respectful of people with higher rank than their own. Such "superiors" are often surprised when they find a person who treats *them* so respectfully acts contemptuously toward those who rank lower. When I was in graduate school, a departmental administrator was

---

[1]*Pseudo*conservatism is a pattern of radical beliefs that, although right-wing in orientation, are anything but conservative (e.g., the beliefs that criminals should be punished without trials, that the military should be put in charge of the government, and so forth). More will be said about beliefs like these later in this section.

TABLE 7.6

ITEMS OF CALIFORNIA F SCALE

	Disagree	Agree
1. Obedience and respect for authority are the most important virtues children should learn.	−3 −2 −1	+1 +2 +3
2. No weakness or difficulty can hold us back if we have enough will power.	−3 −2 −1	+1 +2 +3
3. Science has its place, but there are many important things that can never possibly be understood by the human mind.	−3 −2 −1	+1 +2 +3
4. Human nature being what it is, there will always be war and conflict.	−3 −2 −1	+1 +2 +3
5. Every person should have complete faith in some supernatural power whose decisions he obeys without question.	−3 −2 −1	+1 +2 +3
6. When a person has a problem or a worry, it is best for him not to think about it, but to keep busy with more cheerful things.	−3 −2 −1	+1 +2 +3
7. A person who has bad manners, habits, and breeding can hardly expect to get along with decent people.	−3 −2 −1	+1 +2 +3
8. What the youth needs most is strict discipline, rugged determination, and the will to work and fight for family and country.	−3 −2 −1	+1 +2 +3
9. Some people are born with an urge to jump from high places.	−3 −2 −1	+1 +2 +3
10. Nowadays when so many different kinds of people move around and mix together so much, a person has to protect himself especially carefully against catching an infection or disease from them.	−3 −2 −1	+1 +2 +3
11. An insult to our honor should always be punished.	−3 −2 −1	+1 +2 +3
12. Young people sometimes get rebellious ideas, but as they grow up they ought to get over them and settle down.	−3 −2 −1	+1 +2 +3
13. It is best to use some prewar authorities in Germany to keep order and prevent chaos.	−3 −2 −1	+1 +2 +3
14. What this country needs most, more than laws and political programs, is a few courageous, tireless, devoted leaders in whom the people can put their faith.	−3 −2 −1	+1 +2 +3
15. Sex crimes, such as rape and attacks on children, deserve more than mere imprisonment; such criminals ought to be publicly whipped, or worse.	−3 −2 −1	+1 +2 +3
16. People can be divided into two distinct classes: the weak and the strong.	−3 −2 −1	+1 +2 +3
17. There is hardly anything lower than a person who does not feel a great love, gratitude, and respect for his parents.	−3 −2 −1	+1 +2 +3

TABLE 7.6

ITEMS OF CALIFORNIA F SCALE (continued)

	Disagree	Agree
18. Some day it will probably be shown that astrology can explain a lot of things.	−3 −2 −1	+1 +2 +3
19. Nowadays more and more people are prying into matters that should remain personal and private.	−3 −2 −1	+1 +2 +3
20. Wars and social troubles may someday be ended by an earthquake or flood that will destroy the whole world.	−3 −2 −1	+1 +2 +3
21. Most of our social problems would be solved if we could somehow get rid of the immoral, crooked, and feebleminded people.	−3 −2 −1	+1 +2 +3
22. The wild sex life of the old Greeks and Romans was tame compared to some of the goings-on in this country, even in places where people might least expect it.	−3 −2 −1	+1 +2 +3
23. If people would talk less and work more, everybody would be better off.	−3 −2 −1	+1 +2 +3
24. Most people don't realize how much of our lives are controlled by plots hatched in secret places.	−3 −2 −1	+1 +2 +3
25. Homosexuals are hardly better than criminals and ought to be severely punished.	−3 −2 −1	+1 +2 +3
26. The businessman and the manufacturer are much more important to society than the artist and the professor.	−3 −2 −1	+1 +2 +3
27. No sane, normal, decent person could ever think of hurting a close friend or relative.	−3 −2 −1	+1 +2 +3
28. Familiarity breeds contempt.	−3 −2 −1	+1 +2 +3
29. Nobody ever learned anything really important except through suffering.	−3 −2 −1	+1 +2 +3

Note: Instructions for scoring:
Assign a point value for each item, as follows:
  −3 = 1 point
  −2 = 2 points
  −1 = 3 points
  +1 = 5 points
  +2 = 6 points
  +3 = 7 points
Then add up the total score.

As of 1950, the average score for American women was approximately 3.5; the average for American men was approximately 4.0.

Source: Adorno et al., 1950, pp. 255–58

extremely hostile and belittling toward graduate students. Yet we had a hard time convincing the faculty of this, because this same administrator was quite respectful toward *them*. Her behavior seemed highly inconsistent and even paradoxical, until it was pointed out (by my own faculty adviser at the time, Daryl Bem) that the administrator was a "classic authoritarian"—worshipful up, contemptuous down. In that sense, her behavior was perfectly consistent.

Consider another example. Some people believe that abortion should be outlawed because, they say, fetuses are alive and human life is absolutely sacred. Yet some of these same people also support the death penalty! They also frequently own guns, not necessarily for purposes of historical interest or target shooting.[2] When challenged about their conflicting beliefs, these individuals are likely to resist the question, show little interest and less insight into the paradoxical structure of their own beliefs, and generally get mad (Meehl, 1992).

The list of authoritarian characteristics listed above can resolve the seeming paradox. The anti-abortion stance—despite claims to the contrary—often comes from characteristic 9 (sexual misbehavior must be punished) and, if the individual's church or other moral authority opposes abortion, also from characteristic 2. Support for the death penalty derives from characteristics 3 (criminals have broken the rules and must pay) and 6 (the big, powerful nation of which I am a part cannot be pushed around by these vermin). Gun ownership, when not just for historical interest or clay-pigeon shooting, often derives from characteristics 8 (there are a lot of dangerous people out there) and 7 (if I shoot one of them it serves them right). Authoritarian individuals do not want to think about these contradictory motivations because of characteristic 4 (Dillehay, 1978).

It is rather impressive that the idea of authoritarianism can account for an individual's holding a collection of otherwise unrelated or even paradoxical beliefs. This feat is even more impressive when you consider that the concept of authoritarianism was first developed in the early 1940s, when anti-Semitism and destructive nationalism were the major issues instead of today's battles over abortion, gun control, and the death penalty. A psychological concept demonstrates power when it is formulated to account for one set of phenomena, then proves itself able to account for another, unforeseen set of phenomena. Authoritarianism is a concept that has proven itself remarkably able to do just that.

Scores on the F scale correlate with a large number of other measures of prejudice and conservatism, and also of particular styles of behavior (Dillehay,

---

[2]I do not want to engage in simplistic stereotyping here. So let me emphasize that many people who hold beliefs against abortion do not support the death penalty and do not own guns and so are logically consistent (the Pope is one well-known example). The present discussion, however, concerns those who do hold seemingly paradoxical patterns of belief.

1978). For example, authoritarians tend to be uncooperative and inflexible when playing experimental games with other individuals, and are relatively likely to obey an authority figure's commands to harm another person (Elms & Milgram, 1966). They also watch more television (Shanahan, 1995)! On the other hand, there seems (perhaps surprisingly) to be no relation between authoritarianism and partisan self-identification; Democrats are nearly as likely to be authoritarian as are Republicans—or at least they were forty years ago, when the most recent data available were produced (Campbell, Converse, Miller, & Stokes, 1960).

In this regard, the authors of *The Authoritarian Personality* tried carefully to distinguish *pseudo*conservativism from genuine conservatism. They did not want to characterize a genuine and viable political ideology, much less a major American political party, as a pathology. Genuine conservatives, according to Adorno (1950), hold an internally consistent set of political beliefs, all of which support institutions and the traditional social order while seeking to protect individual rights, property, and initiative. There is no necessary connection between these beliefs and racism or psychopathology. Pseudoconservatives, by contrast, "show blatant contradictions between their acceptance of all kinds of conventional and traditional values—by no means only in the political sphere—and their simultaneous acceptance of the more destructive [attitudes] ... such as cynicism, punitiveness, and violent anti-Semitism" (Adorno, 1950, p. 683). They also often hold radical positions that are anything but truly conservative—that the Supreme Court should be abolished, for example, or that all taxes should be eliminated or all politicians impeached. This is the sense in which Adorno claims authoritarians are pseudoconservative rather than genuinely conservative.

Where does authoritarianism come from? The original group of investigators theorized that the explanation lies in child-rearing practices. Children who are severely punished on a regular basis end up fearing, obeying, and being unwilling to question authority figures in their adult lives. They also develop the desire to wield power themselves, and thereby become ripe to grow into full-fledged authoritarians (Adorno et al., 1950).

This theory of the development of authoritarianism has never been proved correct or incorrect, however. The necessary research is extraordinarily difficult to conduct. One major difficulty is that it is hard to get accurate information about the early childhood environments of adult authoritarians. Another difficulty is that children typically take on the values of their parents, and authoritarian parents tend to have punitive parental styles. So even if you could show an association between parental style and later authoritarianism, determining which of these factors actually caused the authoritarianism—the parental style itself, or simply the parents' own attitudes being passed on to their children—is nearly impossible (Sabini, 1995). Still another difficulty stems from the common observation that siblings may differ widely in their authoritarianism, among other traits. To this day, therefore, the question of where authoritarianism comes from remains unresolved.

Recent research suggests one possibility that was not considered by the Berkeley group: to some degree, authoritarianism might be directly inherited. The authoritarianism scores of parents and their biological children turn out to be correlated about about .40, and biological siblings' scores are correlated about .36 (Scarr, 1981). The authoritarianism scores of adoptive parents and siblings, however, are correlated with each other between .00 and .14, a difference that implies some degree of genetic basis for authoritarianism (for more on the heritability of personality traits, see Chapter 9).

It is easy to see why authoritarianism has received so much attention. It is a concept focused on an obviously important social problem as well as a significant historical event, and it can be measured easily with a simple, self-report scale. It has also come in for its share of criticism, however.

One frequent criticism points out that all of the items on the authoritarianism scale contribute to a higher score if answered "true." This fact led some psychologists to propose that authoritarians are simply people who will answer "true" to *any* statement, no matter how ludicrous (Peabody, 1966). The tendency to agree with any statement is called the **acquiescence response set**. Other investigators have pointed out, however, that acquiescence is unlikely to be the sole basis of authoritarianism scores, because authoritarianism *has* been found to be related to so many other measures of prejudice and social behavior (Rorer, 1965).

Beyond psychometric issues, another, perhaps more telling criticism of authoritarianism is that it seems to tap not only basic psychological *processes*, but also overt political *content*. In other words, authoritarians are not just hostile, projective, superstitious, and so forth; they are also pseudoconservative "right-wingers." It has been pointed out, cogently, that pseudoliberal left-wingers can be authoritarian, too (Shils, 1954). Just look at Stalin, for example. Although Stalin's followers were communists, and supposedly left-wingers, and Hitler's followers were Nazis, and supposedly right-wingers, psychologically they do not seem to have been very different (and both groups were anti-Semitic). In response to this criticism, scales have been developed to measure dogmatism, which is a dimension said to encompass the "close-minded" aspect of authoritarianism, but without the specific political content (e.g., Rokeach, 1960).

Three conclusions can be reached about authoritarianism. The first is that it is not as broad a construct as its title implies; it is really a measure of right-wing or pseudoconservative authoritarianism, as discussed above. Of course, that does not make it unimportant. We must remember that the original concept was developed to explain the rise of Hitler, not Stalin. Thus the criticism that authoritarianism does not encompass left-wing dogmatism might be to some extent unfair.

A second point is that authoritarianism is an individual-difference construct, and thus it cannot and is not supposed to explain why Nazism arose in Germany rather than in America, or why it arose in 1932 rather than 1882 or 1982 (Sabini,

1995). Instead, it tries to explain which *individuals* within any society—whether Germany or even America—would be most likely to follow a leader like Hitler.

A final observation is that authoritarianism provides an example of how a personality trait can be used to try to understand a complex and important social phenomenon. After all, as I noted above, not *all* Germans became Nazis in the 1930s. An examination of the differences between those who did and those who did not might help us understand who is most and least susceptible, and could also help us understand the psychological mechanisms that make it possible for any person to become—or to avoid becoming—a Nazi.

Conscientiousness

When employers are selecting their employees, what are they looking for? According to one survey, out of eighty-six possible employee qualities ranked in their importance by over three thousand employers, seven out of the top eight involved conscientiousness, integrity, trustworthiness, and similar qualities (the eighth was general mental ability; Michigan Department of Education, 1989). When trying to decide whether to hire you, therefore, almost any prospective employer will try to gauge these traits. As job interview workshops will repeatedly tell you, employers will examine your haircut, your neatness of dress, and your punctuality. (Showing up late or in ragged jeans for a job interview is therefore not recommended.)

Sometimes employers go beyond these casual observations in their attempt to assess conscientiousness in prospective employees, by administering formal personality tests. As a broad category, these are sometimes called "integrity tests," but they are actually purported by their publishers to measure a wide range of qualities, including responsibility, long-term job commitment, consistency, moral reasoning, hostility, work ethics, dependability, depression, energy level, and proneness to violence (O'Bannon, Goldinger, & Appleby, 1989). According to Ones et al. (1993), all these attributes may boil down to what could simply be called conscientiousness.

What is the validity of these various tests of conscientiousness? Ones et al. reviewed over 700 studies that used a total of 576,460 subjects in assessing the validity of 43 different tests of integrity. The best estimate they calculated of the mean true validity of these tests for predicting supervisors' ratings of job performance was equivalent to a correlation of .41. This finding means (recall the discussion in Chapter 3, and the example in Chapter 4) that if a potential employer's prediction of future job performance *without* using the test would be accurate 50 percent of the time, his or her prediction *using* the test would have a more than 70 percent accuracy rate. As we saw in Chapter 4, given the costs of training (and, when necessary, firing) employees, this difference could prove financially quite significant. Of course, all of this assumes that supervisors' ratings are a reasonable measure of job performance.

These tests do less well at predicting employee theft, with a mean validity of .13 (or about 58 percent accuracy as defined above). This may be an underestimate, however, because employee theft is difficult to detect and accurately measure, so the criterion used in these studies may have been flawed. Still, Ones et al. conclude that so-called integrity tests are better viewed more broadly as measures of conscientiousness, rather than more narrowly as tests of honesty, and in that light they are impressively valid predictors of job performance.

This finding not only gives employers a potentially useful tool, but has other implications as well. One rather surprising implication is that measuring conscientiousness could help alleviate the effects of bias in testing. It is well known that African Americans, as a group, score lower than white Americans on many "aptitude" tests used by businesses to select employees. (Although a few psychologists believe this difference to be genetic, more believe it to be a byproduct of the educational and social environments experienced by many African Americans; see Sternberg, 1995.) The results of such tests can damage employment prospects and financial well-being. Tests of conscientiousness (and most other personality tests), however, typically do *not* show racial or ethnic differences (Sackett, Burris, & Callahan, 1989). Thus, if more employers could be persuaded to use personality tests instead of or at least in addition to ability tests, racial imbalance in hiring could be eliminated, or at least lessened, without affecting productivity (Ones et al., 1993).

For many years, employers and organizational psychologists have tried to find and measure the elusive "motivation variable" that distinguishes good workers from poor ones. The findings of Ones et al. suggest that perhaps it has been found. General conscientiousness might not only be a good *predictor* of job performance, but as a trait might also serve as a *cause* of excellence on the job (cf. Schmidt & Hunter, 1992). If true, this conclusion implies that future research should seek to understand how conscientiousness motivates behavior, and what kinds of child-rearing practices and environments promote the development of conscientiousness. Another goad to research on conscientiousness should be the recent finding that more-conscientious people seem to live longer (Friedman et al., 1993).

Self-Monitoring

Authoritarianism was studied to try to understand a social issue and a historical event, and conscientiousness has been studied to a large degree to try to improve corporate productivity. The final trait to be considered in this section, self-monitoring, has been studied for a more philosophical reason.

Mark Snyder, the developer of the concept and test of self-monitoring, has long been interested in the relations and discrepancies between the inner and outer selves. For example, one might drink beer at a fraternity party because being a beer drinker is what that situation calls for, but the same person might be studious, serious, and intelligent in a research seminar because that is the kind of person this academic situation calls for. And yet inside, in his or her heart of hearts, this individual might be another kind of person.

Snyder theorized that the degree to which this is true varies across individuals. Some really do vary in their inner and outer selves and in how they perform in different settings of their lives. Snyder calls these individuals "high self-monitors." Others are largely the same outside as they are inside, and do not vary much from one setting to another. Snyder calls these individuals "low self-monitors" (Snyder, 1974, 1987).

Consider Table 7.7, which lists twenty-five questions of a personality test that has been used widely for research purposes. Before reading beyond this paragraph, take a moment to answer these questions and then score them according to the key at the bottom of the table.

The list of questions you have just answered is the standard measure of self-monitoring (and its standard title, when it is administered, is indeed "Personal Reaction Inventory" and *not* "Self-Monitoring Scale"). In samples of college students, the average score is between 12 and 14. A score above 14 is interpreted as implying high self-monitoring; below 12 implies low self-monitoring.

High self-monitors, according to Snyder, monitor every situation they are in extremely carefully, looking for cues as to the appropriate way to act, and they adjust their behavior accordingly. Low self-monitors, by contrast, tend to be more consistent regardless of the situation they are in, because their behavior is guided more by their personality than by specific elements of specific situations. As a result, you would expect a low self-monitor to be more judgeable, in the sense discussed in Chapter 6, and a high self-monitor to be much less judgeable (Colvin, 1993b).

Snyder has always been careful not to apply value judgments to high or low self-monitoring. One can say good or bad things about either. High self-monitors can be described as adaptable, flexible, popular, sensitive, and able to fit in wherever they go. They can also be described, just as accurately, as wishy-washy, two-faced, utterly without integrity, and slick. Low self-monitors, for their part, can be regarded as self-directed, as having integrity, and as being consistent and honest. Or they can be described as insensitive, inflexible, and stubborn.

One nice thing about the self-monitoring scale is that you probably got the score you would have wanted. If the description of high self-monitors just listed sounded better to you than the description of low self-monitors, the odds are very good that you are in fact a high self-monitor. If you preferred the description of low self-monitors, you are probably one yourself.

Research has demonstrated how high and low self-monitors differ in a number of ways. Some studies have gathered descriptions of these people from those who know them well in daily life. In my own research (Funder & Harris, 1986), high self-monitors were more likely than low self-monitors to be described by those who knew them with Q-sort items such as

TABLE 7.7

PERSONAL REACTION INVENTORY

The statements on this page concern your personal reactions to a number of different situations. No two statements are exactly alike, so consider each statement carefully before answering. If a statement is **true** or **mostly true** as applied to you, circle the **T** next to the statement. If a statement is **false** or **usually not true** as applied to you, circle the **F** next to the statement.

T F **1.** I find it hard to imitate the behavior of other people.

T F **2.** My attitude is usually an expression of my true inner feelings, attitudes, and beliefs.

T F **3.** At parties and social gatherings, I do not attempt to do or say things that others will like.

T F **4.** I can only argue for ideas which I already believe.

T F **5.** I can make impromptu speeches even on topics about which I have almost no information.

T F **6.** I guess I put on a show to impress or entertain people.

T F **7.** When I am uncertain how to act in a social situation, I look to the behavior of others for cues.

T F **8.** I would probably make a good actor.

T F **9.** I rarely seek the advice of my friends to choose movies, books, or music.

T F **10.** I sometimes appear to others to be experiencing deeper emotions than I actually am.

T F **11.** I laugh more when I watch a comedy with others than when I am alone.

T F **12.** In a group of people I am rarely the center of attention.

T F **13.** In different situations and with different people, I often act like very different persons.

T F **14.** I am not particularly good at making other people like me.

T F **15.** Even if I am not enjoying myself, I often pretend to be having a good time.

T F **16.** I'm not always the person I appear to be.

T F **17.** I would not change my opinions (or the way I do things) in order to please someone else or win their favor.

T F **18.** I have considered being an entertainer.

T F **19.** In order to get along and be liked, I tend to be what people expect me to be rather than anything else.

T F **20.** I have never actually been good at games like charades or improvisational acting.

T F **21.** I have trouble changing my behavior to suit different people and different situations.

T F **22.** At a party I let others keep the jokes and stories going.

T F **23.** I feel a bit awkward in company and do not show up quite as well as I should.

TABLE 7.7

PERSONAL REACTION INVENTORY (**continued**)

T   F   **24.** I can look anyone in the eye and tell a lie with a straight face (if for a right end).
T   F   **25.** I may deceive people by being friendly when I really dislike them.

Key: 1-f, 2-f, 3-f, 4-f, 5-t, 6-t, 7-t, 8-t, 9-f, 10-t, 11-t, 12-f, 13-t, 14-f, 15-t, 16-t, 17-f, 18-t, 19-t, 20-f, 21-f, 22-f, 23-f, 24-t, 25-t.

Source: Snyder (1974)

- skilled in social techniques of imaginative play, pretending, and humor (e.g., is good at charades)
- talkative
- self-dramatizing, histrionic (exaggerates emotion)
- initiates humor
- verbally fluent
- expressive in face and gestures
- having social poise and presence.

Low self-monitors, by contrast, were more likely to be described as

- distrustful
- perfectionist
- touchy and irritable
- anxious
- introspective
- independent
- feeling cheated and victimized by life.

It is clear from these lists that the high self-monitors are regarded more positively and are more popular than low self-monitors. However, according to the construct, that discrepancy arises because being positively regarded and popular is more important to high self-monitors, and so, although the description of low self-monitors might seem more negative, it is possible that a low self-monitor may not care—other things, such as independence, may be more important to him or her.

A second kind of research, to borrow a leaf from the empiricists' book (recall Chapter 5), is to compare the self-monitoring scores of members of different criterion groups—groups that, if the theory of self-monitoring were correct, you would expect to score differently. Snyder, for instance, has administered his scale to professional stage actors (Snyder, 1974). Their profession involves putting on the persona that a specific, scripted situation calls for; he expected them to score high on his scale—and they did. He also examined hospitalized mental patients, who typically get hospitalized by acting highly inappropriately in some setting. Snyder expected them to get low scores on self-monitoring—and they did. (Please note: this does not mean that low self-monitor are mentally ill!)

Snyder has also done some interesting experiments with subjects already judged to be high or low self-monitors. For instance, he asked his subject to read the following passage into a tape recorder: "I'm going out now, I won't be back all day. If anyone comes by, just tell them I'm not here." Each subject had to read this passage six times, while trying to project one of a number of emotions—happiness, sadness, anger, fear, disgust, and remorse—by using tone of voice, pitch, speed of talking, and so forth. (Try it yourself, right now.) Other people who listened to these tapes found it easier to discern which emotion was being projected if the reader was a high self-monitor (Snyder, 1974).

In another experiment, Snyder had high and Low self-monitors engage in a group discussion (Snyder & Monson, 1975). In one instance, the group simply discussed a controversial issue in privacy; in another instance, the discussion was videotaped, supposedly so the tape could be shown as a demonstration to large psychology classes. Snyder found that in the "private" discussion, high self-monitors tended to agree with other group members, whereas when the discussion was taped for "public" observation, the high self-monitors were more likely to be assertive and aggressive in expressing their opinions. The low self-monitors, by contrast, did not act differently across the two settings. Snyder interpreted this finding to mean that the high self-monitors in the two scenarios were playing to two different audiences; in the private setting they wished to impress their fellow group members, but in the public setting they played for the camera. The low self-monitors acted the same regardless of the audience. At a more general level, Snyder saw this experiment as helping to confirm that High self-monitors are particularly sensitive to details of the situation when deciding how to act, whereas low self-monitors are more likely to be "themselves" in all settings of life.

Self-monitoring has become a controversial topic in recent years. Critics have factor analyzed (see Chapter 5) the self-monitoring scale and found that its items break apart into three separate scales (Briggs, Cheek, & Buss, 1980). One measures acting ability, one measures extraversion, and one measures "other-directedness," or a tendency to worry about what other people think. The appearance of the latter two factors could be viewed as a serious problem for the self-monitoring construct, because extraverts tend to use an aggressive, assertive style of getting along with others, whereas "other-directed" people try to get along by going along. These are opposite and perhaps mutually exclusive styles, yet either kind of person could get an equally high score on self-monitoring. As a result, the "high self-monitor" could be more than one kind of person, a fact that makes scores on self-monitoring difficult to interpret. The scale has since undergone further refinement (Gangestad & Snyder, 1985). This controversy over self-monitoring provides an illustration of the important role that factor analysis plays in the development and interpretation of personality scales (Briggs & Cheek, 1986).

THE ESSENTIAL-TRAIT APPROACH

If you were to thoroughly survey the literature of personality and clinical psychology, you would find thousands of different traits being measured. Recall Allport and Odbert's famous number: 17,953. It has long seemed to many psychologists that this list needs to be reduced, or at least organized in some fashion. As the first part of this chapter discussed, some psychologists have been happy to work with a still-lengthy list of one hundred traits. But several important psychologists over the years have tried to dismantle the Tower of Babel of traits by reducing them to a much smaller number—those deemed to be truly essential.

Reducing the Many to a Few

For example, more than half a century ago the psychologist Henry Murray (the inventor of the Thematic Apperception Test described in Chapter 5) theorized that twenty trait terms—he called them "needs"—were essential for understanding personality (Murray, 1938). His list included needs for aggression, autonomy, exhibition, order, play, sex, and so on. Murray came up with this list theoretically—that is, by thinking about it.

Later psychologists turned to factor analysis (discussed in Chapter 5) as an empirical method to reduce the many traits in the English language down to an essential few. One of the pioneers in this use of factor analysis, Raymond Cattell, concluded that sixteen traits were essential. These included friendliness, intelligence, stability, sensitivity, and dominance, among others (Cattell & Eber, 1961). Another pioneer, Hans Eysenck, reached a more drastic conclusion. Eysenck concluded that most of what was essential to know about an individual's personality could be reduced to just three traits: extraversion; neuroticism, or unstable emotionality; and a trait he (rather misleadingly) called psychoticism, a blend of aggressiveness, creativity, and impulsiveness (Eysenck, 1947; Eysenck & Long, 1986; as discussed in Chapter 8, he believes these traits have biological bases).

The Big Five

At present, the most widely accepted solution to the problem of reducing the many traits in the language down to the few that are essential has been offered by Robert McCrae and Paul Costa (e.g., 1987). Drawing on earlier work by Warren Norman (1963) and others, McCrae and Costa factor analyzed numerous broad personality-measurement instruments and the English language itself, and concluded that five broad traits summarize a large part of the trait domain.

The traits that make up the so-called Big Five are neuroticism, extraversion, openness, agreeableness, and conscientiousness (re-arranged, these trait terms form the acronym OCEAN; John, 1990). The crux of the argument is that these five traits are "orthogonal," which means that getting a high or low score on any one of these traits implies nothing about your chances of getting a high or low score on any of the others. The further claim is that these five terms are sufficient as a summary of most, if not all, that anybody can say and that any test can measure about personality. For example, as we saw earlier in this chapter, Ones et al. were able to reduce numerous, widely varying tests of "integrity" into the single, Big Five trait of conscientiousness, and thereby brought an important degree of order to a previously confusing field of research.

Another Big Five trait with important implications is neuroticism. It turns out that on various questionnaires that are supposed to assess happiness, well-being, and even physical health, one of the biggest (negative) correlates of the total score turns out to be the individuals' levels of neuroticism (also called negative emotionality). The higher your level of neuroticism, the lower your score on happiness, well-being, health, and a large number of related attributes (McCrae & Costa, 1991; Watson & Clark, 1984). This finding implies that many of these instruments, despite their different intentions and titles, are to some degree measuring the same thing: some people (those high on neuroticism) complain a lot, about a lot; others (those low on neuroticism) complain little.

Although the Big Five have already shown their usefulness, they also remain controversial (Block, 1995). One objection that has been raised is that that the Big Five *do* seem to correlate with each other to some degree; in many samples people who score high on extraversion tend to score low on neuroticism, for example. So it is not clear that the Big Five are, as advertised, five entirely separate and independent traits.

A more important objection is that a good deal of important information about personality cannot be reduced to these five traits. For example, one could summarize authoritarianism, discussed earlier in this chapter, as a combination of high neuroticism, high conscientiousness, low openness, and low agreeableness, but that summary seems to miss the essence of the construct. In particular, it does not account for authoritarians' being deferential and agreeable with those of higher rank but mean and nasty to those of lower rank, and it says nothing about their psychodynamic motivations. Similarly, self-monitoring could be recast as a combination of high extraversion and high agreeableness, but that summary also seems to miss much.

Costa and McCrae do not deny that reducing all of personality to a few factors provides a limited view of human psychology. However, they do argue that their five factors are key, because these five seem to crop up again and again, while other aspects of personality are found more sporadically. Other psychologists debate this point, too (e.g., Briggs, 1989; McAdams, 1992).

One persistent question is, Why five? Is there something magical about these particular five dimensions of personality? Why are there not six, or four? Proponents of the Big Five have responded:

Why [are there] ... five factors, what rationale remains? We believe it is simply an empirical fact, like the fact that there are seven continents on earth or eight American presidents from Virginia. Biologists recognize eight classes of vertebrates (mammals, birds, reptiles, amphibians, and four classes of fishes, one extinct), and the theory of evolution helps to explain the development of these classes. It does not, however, explain why *eight* classes evolved, rather than four or eleven, and no one considers this a defect in the theory. There are, of course, reasons why human beings differ along each of the five personality dimensions—reasons to be found somewhere in evolution, neurobiology, socialization, or the existential human condition. But it is probably not meaningful or profitable to ask why there happen to be just five such dimensions" (McCrae & John, 1992, p. 194)

Another advocate of the Big Five believes they may correspond to five essential, universal questions people need to ask about a stranger they are about to meet:

(1) Is X active and dominant or passive and submissive (Can I bully X or will X try to bully me)? [This question corresponds to extraversion, sometimes also called surgency.] (2) Is X agreeable (warm and pleasant) or disagreeable (cold and distant)? [agreeableness] (3) Can I count on X (Is X responsible and conscientious or undependable and negligent)? [conscientiousness] (4) Is X crazy (unpredictable) or sane (stable)?]neuroticism] (5) Is X smart or dumb (How easy will it be for me to teach X)? [openness, also sometimes called intellect]

Are these universal questions? (Goldberg, 1981, p. 161)

Maybe they are. Several attempts have been made to see whether the Big Five can be found in cultures other than American or European, and in languages other than English. Personality questionnaires translated from English into native languages have been found to yield at least four of the five factors (all except openness) in the Philippines (Guthrie & Bennett, 1971), Japan (Bond, Nakazato, & Shiraishi, 1975), and Hong Kong (Bond, 1979). An even more ambitious study *began* with an analysis of the Chinese language to find the terms commonly used to describe personality, rather than simply employing a Chinese translation of terms commonly used in English (which is what the the other studies did; Yang

& Bond, 1990). A factor analysis of personality descriptions by residents of Taiwan using these terms yielded a somewhat different set of five factors, which were labelled social orientation, competence, expressiveness, self-control, and optimism. The conclusion was that while the Chinese Five seemed to overlap to some degree with the English Five (e.g., expressiveness in the Chinese solution is somewhat similar to extraversion in the English solution), there was not a one-to-one correspondence across the entire list. The broader conclusion that was reached by these investigators—which might seem wishy-washy but which is probably the only reasonable conclusion possible—is that the central attributes of personality are similar to an important degree, yet are also to an important degree different from one culture to another (see Chapter 15 for a more extended discussion of cross-cultural issues).

CONCLUSION

This chapter has tried to show by specific examples that the usefulness of personality assessment goes beyond its ability to predict behavior and performance. When one learns which personality traits are associated with certain behaviors, one can learn much about why people do what they do. We have seen how personality assessment can shed light on how children delay gratification, why some people are prejudiced, use drugs, or are depressed, and other important psychological phenomena. This kind of increase in understanding is the most important goal of science.

SUMMARY

Traits are useful not just for predicting behavior, but for increasing our understanding of the basis of what people do. This chapter examined three basic approaches to the study of traits. The many-trait approach looks at the relationship between a particular behavior and as many different traits as possible. One technique used in this approach, the California Q-sort, assesses one hundred different traits at once. The Q-sort has been used to explore the basis of delay of gratification, drug use, depression, and political ideology. The single-trait approach zeros in on one particular trait deemed to be of special interest and its consequences for behavior; it has been used to study the traits of authoritarianism, conscientiousness, and self-monitoring, among other things. The essential-trait approach attempts to identify those few traits, out of the thousands of possibilities, that are truly central to understanding all of the others. The most widely accepted essential-trait approach is the Big Five, which lists as the essential traits to understand personality extraversion, neuroticism, conscientiousness, agreeableness, and openness.

Suggested Readings:
The Trait Approach

Allport, G. W. (1937). *Personality: A psychological interpretation.* New York: Holt, Rine-hart, & Winston.

> *The classic and perhaps still best presentation of how trait psychologists think about personality. This book is often cited by individuals who underestimate its complexity and subtlety; I recommend a personal reading.*

Wiggins, J. S. (1973). *Personality and prediction: Principles of personality assessment.* Read-ing, MA: Addison-Wesley.

> *The classic basic textbook for personality psychologists, including much of method-ological as well as substantive interest. The book is now slightly out-of-date, but like a true classic has lost little of its interest or value with age. To be competent, a personality psychologist must know what is in this book.*

Mischel, W. (1968). *Personality and assessment.* New York: Wiley.

> *The book that launched a thousand rebuttals—this is the volume that touched off the person-situation debate. It is well-written and, in its key sections, surprisingly brief.*

Kenrick, D. T., & Funder, D. C. (1988). Profiting from controversy: Lessons from the person-situation debate. *American Psychologist, 43,* 23–34.

> *A review of the person-situation debate written for a general audience of psychologists (not just for specialists in personality). This was an attempt to declare the person-situation debate finished.*

Ross, L., & Nisbett, R. E. (1991). *The person and the situation: Perspectives of social psy-chology.* New York: McGraw-Hill.

> *A clearly written exposition of the modern situationist position.*

Adorno, T. W., Frenkel-Brunwik, E., Levinson, D., & Sanford, N. (1950). *The authori-tarian personality.* New York: Harper.

> *A classic work, describing the activities of the Berkeley group to understand the psychological underpinnings of Nazism. An important part of this project was the development of the California F scale, which is described in detail.*

Snyder, M. (1987). *Public appearances, private realities: The psychology of self-monitoring.* New York: Freeman.

> *A summary, by the test's originator, of the research stimulated by the self-monitoring scale. The book goes beyond test-relevant issues and has much of interest to say about basic topics in social psychology, notably self-presentation.*

Megargee, E. I. (1972). *The California Psychological Inventory handbook.* San Francisco: Jossey-Bass.

> *A summary of the research (to that date) on the California Psychological Inventory. This book is at once perhaps the clearest and most thorough presentation of any of the major omnibus psychological tests. It teaches about much more than just the CPI; it serves as an excellent primer in the philosophy and technology of personality test construction.*

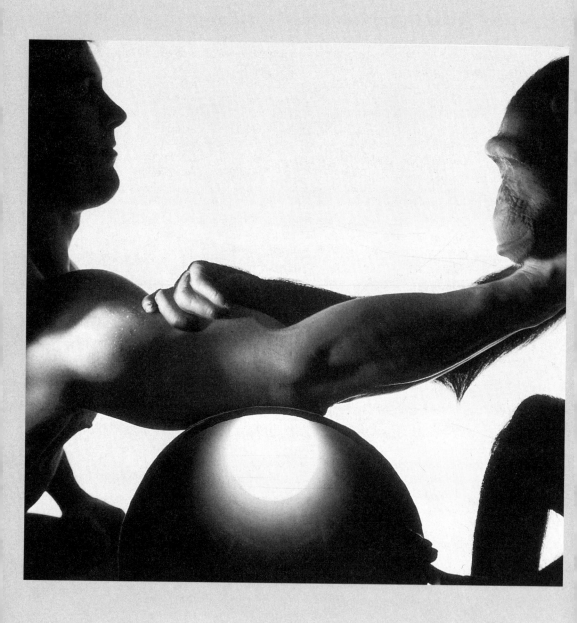

PART III

Biological Approaches to Personality

Every person has a body and a brain. Indeed, in a "reductionist" sense, every person *is* a body and a brain. It is reasonable to assume that the way a person's biological mechanisms function, and the way their functioning differs from one person to another, would have some effect on personality. During the past decade, biological research has made some impressive discoveries, and the increased application of biology to various areas of psychology has made some significant progress.

To appreciate the plight of somebody trying to understand the biological bases of the mind, it might be helpful to picture the following scenario: Imagine giving a portable cassette player equipped with batteries and a prerecorded music tape to Aristotle, a very smart person who lived about 3,000 years ago. Aristotle would have been amazed, and then perplexed. Then, being a curious person, he might have tried to figure out how this remarkable device worked.

What would he do? He could try taking it apart, but of course it is unlikely he would recognize anything he saw inside, and once he took it apart it is unlikely he would ever get it back in working order again. But if he were too cautious to open it up, his only solution would be to observe it, listen to it, and play with its various controls. Only after the battery wore out might he dare open it up to see what is inside (new batteries being unavailable in ancient Greece). Unfortunately, he would only see the inner workings of a mechanism that no longer functions.

In many respects, a psychologist seeking to understand the workings of a human brain faces a similar situation. The psychologist can watch how the person responds to various inputs, such as what she responds or does when you say certain things to her. A researcher cannot easily open up a person's brain, especially while that person is alive. And even when a brain is opened, all one can see is squishy, juicy tissue the function of which is far from obvious at first glance.

Given these limits on biological research, it is remarkable that researchers have managed to discover anything at all about the workings of the brain and nervous system. It is also not surprising that so much remains to be understood. After all, the mind is much more complicated than any cassette player.

Biology has been used to try to help understand personality in four basic ways. The first two ways, which are presented in Chapter 8, explore how the workings of the nervous system might affect personality. The anatomical approach focuses on the functions of various structures of the brain, and the biochemical approach focuses on the effects of chemicals called neurotransmitters and hormones. The other two biological approaches to personality, presented in Chapter 9, examine how personality might be biologically inherited from one's parents and ancestors. Research in behavioral genetics tries to understand how individual differences in personality are transmitted from parent to child and shared by people who are genetically related. Evolutionary biology explores the possibility that the ultimate roots of personality might be found in the early history of the human species.

These next two chapters will guide us through the study of personality via four different branches of biology: anatomy, physiology, genetics, and evolutionary theory.

CHAPTER

ANATOMY, BIOCHEMISTRY, AND PERSONALITY

The biological approach begins with the suggestion that some of the roots of personality might be found in the brain and the system of nerves, attached to the brain, that reaches into every part of the body. The study of the physical basis of personality can be divided into two approaches: anatomical and biochemical. The first part of this chapter describes some of what has been learned about how the brain, and specifically its anatomy, affects behavior. The second part of this chapter describes some of what has been learned about the biochemical basis of personality, or how neurotransmitters and hormones affect behavior by influencing the entire nervous system.

THE ANATOMY AND FUNCTION OF THE BRAIN

If you want to understand the human brain, a reasonable place to begin is with an examination of the brains of animals. The overall function of animal and human brains seems to be about the same—they both control perception and behavior— and their basic anatomy shows some striking consistency of design across widely diverse species.

Indeed, to an observer who is familiar with the brains of many different species, the human brain appears to be three brains in one (MacLean, 1982). It seems to contain the brain of a reptile, one of an ordinary mammal, and a third part that is uniquely human. These three brains are physically wrapped around each other.

The Reptilian Brain

The "reptilian" brain is the core of the human brain, the basic structure around which the rest of the organ is built. It is called the reptilian brain because its

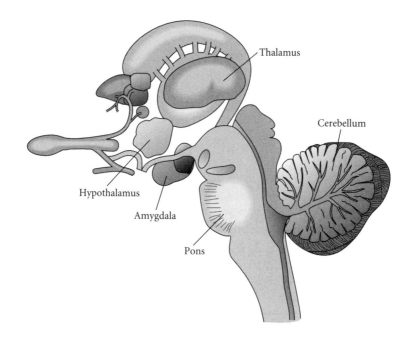

FIGURE 8.1 THE "REPTILIAN" BRAIN The "reptilian" brain is the basic structure around which the rest of the human brain is built. It is called reptilian because its structure resembles the brain of a lizard.

structure is not much different from that of the brain of a lizard. It includes the thalamus, hypothalamus, amygdala, pons, cerebellum, and other organs (see Figure 8.1).

It is worth pausing a moment here and considering what lizards and other reptiles can do. Not only can they walk and run and seek food, they can also engage in complex behaviors such as defending territory, establishing dominance over other reptiles, greeting one another, courting mates, and migrating. So the reptilian brain is far from simple; it's an organ that has impressive capabilities.

However, complex behaviors in reptiles are generally made up of instincts or "fixed action patterns" that are inborn rather than learned. These patterns are rigid and inflexible, in contrast with the more plastic and adaptable behaviors of mammals. Reptiles do not consider their options, plan what they are going to do, or think about what they are doing. They just do it.

The Paleomammalian Brain

In humans, a second, "paleomammalian" brain is wrapped around the outside of the reptilian brain (see Figure 8.2). Its structures are newer, evolutionarily speaking, and are made of extra **cortex**, or outer tissue. This cortical tissue is

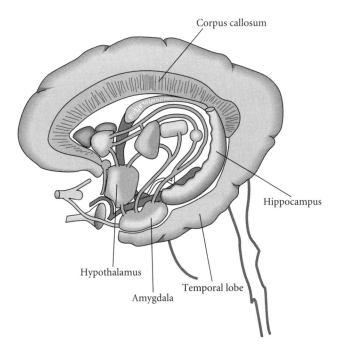

FIGURE 8.2 THE "PALEOMAMMALIAN" (LIMBIC) BRAIN The paleomammalian brain is wrapped around the outside of the reptilian brain. Taken together, the
paleomammalian and reptilian brains resemble the brains of nonhuman mammals
such as dogs, cats, or rats.

believed to provide mammals with their greater flexibility and ability to learn,
compared to reptiles.

When these first two brains, the reptilian and paleomammalian, are taken
together, they look much like the brain of a typical nonhuman mammal, such
as a cat, dog, or rat. In humans, these two portions of the brain make up most
of a structure called the **limbic system**. The limbic system is believed to be the
basis of emotion, motivation, appetite, fear, curiosity, learning, memory, and
other functions that humans share with other animals.

The Neomammalian Brain

The third part of the brain is uniquely human. This "neomammalian" brain,
which is wrapped around the other two parts, is the **cerebral cortex**. This thick
outer layer of tissue is held to be the seat of those cognitive activities, such as
planning, self-awareness, and language, of which only humans are capable. The
neomammalian brain is shown in Figure 8.3.

The cerebral cortex includes large areas of tissue that do not seem to be
necessary to receive inputs from the sensory organs, but do seem to be necessary

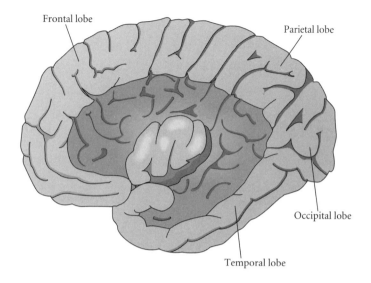

Frontal lobe

Parietal lobe

Occipital lobe

Temporal lobe

FIGURE 8.3 THE "NEOMAMMALIAN" BRAIN   The neomammalian brain is the uniquely human part of the brain. Wrapped around the outside of the reptilian and neomammalian brains, it forms the cerebral cortex, the area of the brain that interprets inputs from senses and other parts of the brain in order to act upon them.

for a person to interpret those inputs. These areas are called the **association cortex**; their function is assumed to involve combining inputs from the various senses and parts of the brain in order to interpret those inputs and act upon them. The association cortex may also be what makes it possible for humans to project consciousness back into the past, so as to profit from experience, and forward into the future, so as to anticipate and make plans (Zuckerman, 1991).

The existence of reptilian and paleomammalian brains inside of the human brain suggests that there might be a considerable degree of overlap between the ways humans and animals feel and think. Humans may appear to differ from animals, but on an anatomical level they are not all that different. Furthermore, the animal-like structures within the human brain are almost certainly important for personality. Some basic functions such as emotion and motivation seem to have their roots in these structures.

Some psychologists have proposed that the existence of these animal-like structures inside every human brain can explain why people sometimes "act like animals." For example, one psychologist has suggested that psychopathic and sadistic human behavior might result when the reptilian brain temporarily dominates the other brains (Bailey, 1987). This seems to some to be an unfair suggestion, however, because animals—even reptiles—are neither psychopathic nor sadistic. If there is some behavior that is specifically characteristic of reptiles, it is probably their propensity to follow fixed action patterns, or repetitive sequences of behavior. On this basis, another psychologist has speculated that the reptilian brain might be the basis of the human attraction to repetitive rituals, such as saying the Pledge of Allegiance (Zuckerman, 1991)!

The Human Brain

As useful as it is, the study of animal brains takes us only part of the way to understanding the human brain. Animals are adapted to different environments than humans are. Sometimes animals manifest specific patterns of behavior that are not shared even by other, seemingly similar, animals—much less by humans (Zuckerman, 1991). Thus, it is necessary to consider the whole, human brain directly.

Knowledge about the human brain comes from two principal sources. The first is the study of people who have suffered accidental brain damage. If enough such cases are observed, it becomes possible to draw conclusions by keeping track of the specific problems that are caused by damage to different parts of the brain. The second source of knowledge is brain surgery, which until recently was performed frequently to treat certain kinds of mental disorders. Attempts have been made to catalog the behavioral results of surgery performed on different parts of the brain.

Recently, a third approach to studying the brain has been invented: Positron Emission Tomography (PET), which can create pictures of the metabolic activity of living human brains. The technology of PET scans is quite new and quite expensive, however, and although its initial results are promising, not much about personality has been learned with it yet.

The structure of the human brain is shown in Figure 8.4.

THE FRONTAL LOBES AND PSYCHOSURGERY

For many years scientists have known that injuries to the brain can affect personality and behavior. One famous case began in 1848, when a railroad construction supervisor named Phineas Gage stood in the wrong place at the wrong time. A dynamite explosion nearby sent a three-and-a-half foot iron rod through his left cheek, into the frontal lobes of his brain, and out the other side. Remarkably, he survived, and lived another fifteen years. According to accounts that were heard and believed by many people at the time, he was fine afterward in all respects, except that he was perhaps a little less emotional than before.

It is unfortunate that this account of normalcy gained such wide currency, because it was incorrect. Gage's physician, who seems to have been an astute observer, recorded in his journal that although Gage did retain some reasonable degree of mental functioning, his personality was noticeably changed, and not

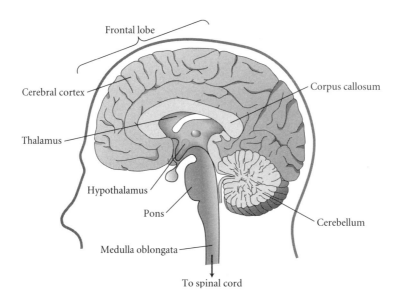

Frontal lobe

Cerebral cortex

Corpus callosum

Thalamus

Hypothalamus

Pons

Cerebellum

Medulla oblongata

To spinal cord

FIGURE 8.4 THE HUMAN BRAIN Although it shows some similarities to the brains of other animals, the human brain is uniquely large and complex. Psychologists are making slow but steady progress in understanding how the human brain functions.

for the better. According to this physician, Gage's behavior became "fitful, irreverent, indulging at times in the grossest profanity (which was not previously his custom), manifesting but little deference for his fellows, impatient of restraint or advice, . . . at times pertinaciously obstinate, yet capricious and facillating [*sic*]. . . ." Overall, Gage had become "a child in his intellectual capacity and manifestations . . . [yet had] the animal passions of a strong man" (Harlow, as quoted in Valenstein, 1986, p. 90).

Phineas Gage was not the only person in history to suffer accidental brain injury, although his case was surely one of the more notable ones. Gunshot wounds to the head and other injuries have shown that people can live despite remarkable amounts of brain tissue having been removed or severed from the rest of the brain. According to some accounts, when these accidents involved the frontal lobes, the victim could still function but perhaps was less excitable and emotional than he or she had been prior to the injury.

Such accounts led some surgeons in the early twentieth century to surmise that removing or severing the frontal lobes from the rest of the brain—procedures called the lobectomy and the lobotomy, respectively—might alleviate certain kinds of severe mental illness. These operations were performed on people with chronic aggressive or violent behavior and (as the procedure became popular) a surprisingly wide range of other disorders. The vague justifications given were usually based on a combination of observations: (a) perhaps the frontal lobes are necessary to maintain the complex mental functions that create mental illness, (b) patients (usually) do not die or become completely nonfunctional after lobotomies, and (c) many of the patients were pretty desperate already— a little brain alteration probably would not do them much harm. Based on such reasoning, dressed up with some (apparently irrelevant) citation of the leading neuropsychologists of the day, the Portugese surgeon Antonio Moniz performed the first recorded lobotomy in Lisbon, Portugal, in 1936 (Valenstein, 1986).

The operation quickly became popular around the world, especially in the United States. For example, Rosemary Kennedy, the mentally retarded elder sister of John, Robert and Edward Kennedy, was given a lobotomy in 1941 in an attempt to control her "mood swings" (Thompson, 1995).[1] The lobotomy procedure received the ultimate scientific seal of approval when Antonio Moniz was awarded the Nobel Prize in 1949 for inventing it.

Often psychosurgery (as it was called) was performed with an astonishing disregard for what the long-term results really were. Zuckerman summarizes many of the early medical articles on psychosurgery this way:

> The neurosurgeons' reports provide a remarkable contrast between accounts of the precise surgical techniques and the imprecise or totally absent methods of [subsequent behavioral] evaluation. Control groups were virtually nonexistent and, with the exception of an occasional use of the MMPI [Minnesota Multiphasic Personality Inventory—see Chapter 5], observations of change were based on the crudest kind of clinical observations, with no tests of reliabilities of ratings or single-blind controls (Zuckerman, 1991, p. 147).

Such studies as were done suggested that the usual results of a lobotomy include

- a lessened tendency to worry and be anxious
- a behavioral pattern called **perseveration**, in which the subject is unable to stop doing one thing in order to begin doing another
- heightened sociability and assertiveness, and sometimes more hostility and less inhibition (as was seen after Phineas Gage's accidental lobotomy)
- in some cases, apathy combined with erratic, inappropriate euphoria.

Even the leading American advocates of the lobotomy described typical results of the procedure in this way:

It is almost impossible to call upon a person who has undergone [an] operation on the frontal lobes for advice on any important matter. His reaction to situations are

---

[1]As of 1995, Rosemary Kennedy was still living in the Wisconsin convent school that had been her home since the lobotomy was performed forty-four years earlier.

direct, hasty, and dependent upon his emotional set at the moment (Freeman & Watts, 1950, p. 549).

Taken as a whole, these findings are consistent with the traditional view that the frontal lobes are centers of cognitive control, serving to anticipate the future and plan for it. The results also suggest that a *particular* function of the frontal lobes might be to anticipate future *negative* outcomes, and to respond emotionally to their possibility—in other words, worrying. One conclusion from these results might be that the frontal lobes are the location in the brain where excessive worrying and neuroticism is located, and therefore that their removal can alleviate such problems.

This conclusion was reached by some psychologists, but it is surely misguided; given what is known about brain function, it is highly unlikely that there is a simple, one-to-one correspondence between psychological problems and brain anatomy. A more reasonable and more subtle interpretation of these findings would be that the frontal lobes include among their functions the regulation of emotional responses to anticipated events. When the frontal lobes are damaged, severed or removed, this regulatory function is disrupted. Although the result may seem to be "less worry," the evidence indicates that emotional responsiveness and future anticipation have in fact become erratic and disorganized. As a result, lobotomized people do not worry when they should, and sometimes worry when they should not. The system has not been adjusted, it has been disrupted.

Recent literature reviews have concluded that the only people whose personalities *may* have been changed for the better by lobotomies were those suffering from extreme anxiety, depression, or obsessiveness, but even those cases often experienced severe side effects from the operation (Valenstein, 1986; Zuckerman, 1991). Attempts to use the operation in the treatment of schizophrenia were a complete failure. Attempts to lesion or surgically excise other portions of the brain for behavioral control were also tried over the years, with equally unimpressive results (Valenstein, 1973).

Tens of thousands of lobotomies and other psychosurgeries were performed over a span of more than four decades, but such operations are rarely performed today. The main reason seems to be that chemical therapies (drugs) were developed that made mentally ill patients manageable, if not cured. Someone like Rosemary Kennedy, who troubled her family with mood swings, would today be tranquilized rather than lobotomized. Another factor behind the decline in lobotomies was the accumulation of a history of poor results, combined with such bad publicity as *One Flew over the Cuckoo's Nest*.[2]

---

[2] *One Flew over the Cuckoo's Nest* is a popular novel, which was made into a play and a movie, about life in a mental hospital and the disastrous effect of a lobotomy on the main character.

One lesson that can be drawn from the history of psychosurgery is that trying to map behavioral patterns directly onto specific brain sites is usually a mistake (Valenstein, 1986). And, of course, trying to cure maladaptive behavioral patterns by surgically removing specific brain sites is a much worse mistake. Modern biopsychology seems to be moving away from trying to locate causes of behavior or other psychological functions in specific structures, and toward trying to identify more diffuse biological systems or neural pathways that influence behavior. Nevertheless, some general conclusions can be drawn from years of psychosurgery, one of which is that the frontal lobes are important for many higher thought processes, including those that involve anticipating and planning for the future.

THE AMYGDALA

The **amygdala** is a part of the limbic system located near the base of the brain in the temporal lobe. It is a structure found both in humans and in many other animals. When the amygdala is surgically removed from rhesus monkeys, they become less aggressive and less fearful, they sometimes try to eat inedible things (even feces and urine), and they may exhibit increased and unusual sexual behavior. Research with humans and other animals indicates that the amygdala has important effects on negative emotions such as anger and fear, as well as on positive emotions such as social attraction and sexual responsiveness. Some psychologists have suggested that the amygdala might therefore be the physical basis of human personality traits such as chronic anxiety, fearfulness, sociability, and sexuality (Zuckerman, 1991).

So, just as the frontal lobes generally have been viewed as the seat of uniquely human cognitive functions such as thinking and planning, the amygdala and associated limbic structures have become widely accepted as the seat of some basic emotions. Furthermore, the fact that many animals, including reptiles, have amygdalas suggests that emotional processes are ancient, evolutionarily speaking, and are more similar across species than we might think.

THE CEREBRAL HEMISPHERES

One attribute of the brain that is evident from simple observation is that it is divided into two parts. The two frontal lobes fold down into the middle of the brain, creating two separate, almost symmetrical **cerebral hemispheres**. Observations of the effects of brain damage have indicated that, in most persons, the left hemisphere is where language is understood and speech is produced. It took scientists a bit longer to discover that the right hemisphere has its own important functions, including visual perception and spatial orientation. Another distinction between the hemispheres that has become more prominent over the years is that between two kinds of thinking. Based on the results of "split-brain" operations that were used, for a time, to control epileptic seizures, researchers have concluded that analytic, verbally mediated, rational thinking is the province of the left hemisphere. More holistic, image-oriented, intuitive thinking appears to be the province of the right hemisphere (Ornstein, 1977).

There is a small amount of evidence that the two hemispheres may be associated with different personality traits (e.g., Flor-Henry, 1969). People who have suffered damage to the right hemispheres of their brains have manifested manic-depressive psychoses, characterized by wide swings in mood and energy level. This finding suggests that the right hemisphere is important for regulating emotional response; when the right hemisphere is damaged, emotions fluctuate more widely and wildly. Likewise, people who have suffered damage to the left hemispheres of their brains may develop forms of schizophrenia, characterized by disorganized and illogical thinking. This finding suggests that the left hemisphere is important for the organization of logical thought; if the left hemisphere becomes damaged, the thought process loses its shape and direction.

Functions of the Brain

A second approach to examining the relationship between the brain and behavior has tried to connect personality traits not with specific anatomical locations, but with brain functions or *mechanisms*. Suprisingly often, these mechanisms have been hypothetical—that is, they have been hypothesized or conjectured to exist, on the basis of a theory, rather than specifically located or demonstrated. A number of psychologists have formulated theories about the basic mechanisms of the brain, and then have tried to determine the anatomical location of those mechanisms.

INHIBITION AND EXCITATION: EYSENCK

One of the pioneers in attempting to relate personality to biology is the British psychologist Hans Eysenck (e.g., 1967, 1987). Eysenck's theory is complex and has evolved somewhat over the years, but one of its basic assumptions is that the human brain has excitatory and inhibitory neural mechanisms, and that important aspects of one's personality are determined by the balance between those mechanisms. Excitatory mechanisms cause an individual to be awake, aroused, and alert. Inhibitory mechanisms have the reverse effect. The balance between the excitatory and inhibitory mechanisms produces the level of psychological arousal at any given moment.

Eysenck has hypothesized that this balance is regulated by the Ascending Reticulocortical Activating System (ARAS), a structure in the brain stem. Research has suggested that the function of this system is to regulate the amount of information or stimulation that goes into the brain. Sometimes the information channels are opened wide (leading to much sensory stimulation of the brain) and sometimes they are closed down (cutting the brain off from sensory stimulation).

Eysenck's conjecture is that each individual's ARAS functions differently. Some people's systems let in a great deal of information and stimulation nearly all the time. Other people's systems tend to cut the brain off from most sensory stimulation. Eysenck theorizes that this difference is the basis of the difference between introverts and extraverts, although the way this works might seem counterintuitive at first: A person whose ARAS cause him or her to be chronically overaroused is an introvert, whereas one whose ARAS cause him or her to be chronically underaroused is an extravert. The reason for this is that when your ARAS opens you up to a large amount of sensory input, you end up getting more stimulation than you need—perhaps more than you can stand. As a result, you will seek to *avoid* stimulation, since you already have more than you need. You will avoid exciting situations, loud noises, and social stimulation. You may turn down invitations to noisy parties, finding it stimulating enough to stay home with a good book (and perhaps an unexciting book at that).

On the other hand, when your ARAS closes off much of the sensory stimulation your brain would otherwise receive, you find yourself craving more. So you seek out stimulation, perhaps going to as many loud parties as you can find. You might more generally become what is called a "sensation seeker," not only going to parties but taking up activities such as race-car driving or parachute jumping (see Zuckerman, 1984). According to Eysenck, you seek out such activities just to keep yourself at the level of arousal that makes you feel good—a level that is higher for extraverts than for introverts.

A second dimension of personality along which people differ for physiological reasons, according to Eysenck, is emotional stability versus neuroticism. A person's position on this dimension is hypothesized to be a function of the way the limbic system responds to emotional stimuli. When a person's limbic system is resilient in response to emotional stress and is able to regulate and modulate extreme emotions, he or she is emotionally stable. But when that person's system breaks down under stress and produces more widely varying emotional extremes, he or she becomes what Eysenck calls "neurotic." (Eysenck's definition of this term is different from its usual usage, which covers almost any kind of mild mental disturbance or maladaptive behavior pattern.)

The combination of these two dimensions of personality—introversion vs. extraversion and emotional stability vs. neuroticism—leads to the "Eysenckian" system diagrammed in Figure 8.5. Any individual's personality can be located on this figure as a function of the degree to which he or she is introverted as opposed to extraverted, and emotionally stable as opposed to unstable or neurotic.

More recently, Eysenck has added a third dimension, which he calls "psychoticism." This dimension is indicated by the dotted line in Figure 8.5. This term "psychoticism" is quite controversial, because the dimension does not seem

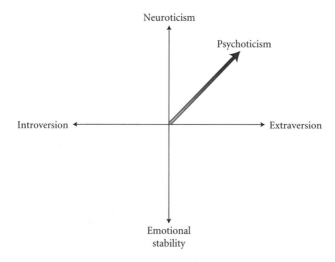

FIGURE 8.5 EYSENCK'S THREE-DIMENSIONAL DESCRIPTION OF PERSONALITY   The psychologist Hans Eysenck theorizes that the three major, biologically based dimensions of personality are extraversion, neuroticism, and psychoticism. According to his theory, any individual can be described by his or her location in this three-dimensional space.

to have much if anything to do with actually being psychotic (a term that usually refers to severe, delusional mental illness). Somebody high on Eysenck's psychoticism scale is described as aggressive, cold, egocentric, impersonal, impulsive, antisocial, and creative (see Eysenck & Eysenck, 1976; Eysenck, Eysenck, & Barrett, 1985). These aspects of personality are thought to be related to the functioning of the amygdala and to the lessening of inhibition that at a more basic level is associated with fighting or fleeing danger.

Empirically, Eysenck's conjectures remain unproven. The best-known study supporting his ideas may be the famous "lemon juice test," in which small amounts of lemon juice were dropped on the tongues of introverts and extraverts (as assessed by Eysenck's personality questionnaire) and the resulting amount of salivation was measured. Introverts salivated more than did extraverts (Eysenck & Eysenck, 1967; Wilson, 1978). This result is consistent with Eysenck's theory, which would expect that introverts, because of their wide-open ARAS, would experience the sour taste more strongly and therefore would react more strongly to it.

Other studies have used brain-wave amplitude, cardiovascular reactivity, and other more sophisticated measures to indicate arousal. The results, taken as a whole, are far from clear. Sometimes they support Eysenck's theory, and sometimes they do not (Zuckerman, 1991).

One recent study does tend to support Eysenck's scheme, however (Bullock

& Gilliland, 1993). In this study, researchers identified introverts and extraverts using the Eysenck Personality Questionnaire and then tried to arouse them psychologically by giving them caffeine and making them do demanding tasks (such as completing complex puzzles under pressure of time). Then they measured each person's neurological arousal through "brainstem auditory evoked responses"—how quickly and strongly the electrical activity of his or her brain, or brainwaves, responded to noises. Their basic findings were that the people who had been given caffeine reported feeling more aroused, but that introverts did not report feeling any more aroused than did extraverts. Their third finding, however, was that across all conditions introverts showed faster neural transmission (via their auditory evoked responses) than did extraverts, and the researchers concluded that this complex pattern of findings was consistent with Eysenck's arousal theory.

Investigations into Eysenck's theory continue, and as psychophysiological measures of arousal and emotionality become more sophisticated, these studies will probably become increasingly interesting. Already, however, it seems apparent that the theory is an oversimplification of an extraordinarily complex system. One important complication is that the ARAS is not as general a system as was first believed; it does not just turn neural stimulation to the entire brain on and off like a faucet (Zuckerman, 1991). Studies have shown that one part of the brain can be stimulated, aroused, and active while another part of the same brain is almost quiescent. In fact, differing levels of arousal across different parts of the brain are more typical than not. This newly developed evidence about the functioning of the brain poses serious problems for any theory that begins with the idea that some people are just chronically "more aroused" than others.

Nevertheless, this might be a good time to recall Funder's Second Law, that something beats nothing two times out of three. Eysenck remains an audacious pioneer in the history of personality psychology. He was the first modern psychologist to attempt seriously to identify the biological bases of the important dimensions of personality. The field had to start someplace, and Eysenck had the nerve to suggest a possible place to begin. He proposed, quite reasonably, that two basic properties of the brain are arousal and stability, hypothesized a specific mechanism behind each, and developed a system for classifying personality based on the interactions of these mechanisms. The challenge that Eysenck presents for the rest of personality psychology is to prove him wrong and—a more difficult challenge—to come up with a better theory.

APPROACH AND INHIBITION: GRAY

One researcher who has tried to improve on Eysenck's theory is a neuropsychologist named Jeffrey Gray (e.g., 1981). Gray extrapolated the findings of his early research on animals to human personality. As a result, Gray's hypotheses about the anatomical structures that underlie certain aspects of personality are more specific and may be better supported than Eysenck's (Zuckerman, 1991).

Like Eysenck, Gray proposes that personality is based on the interaction of two basic systems. Gray's two systems revolve around approach and inhibition, however. The "approach" system, said to be based in the **septal area** of the brain (a thin sheet of tissue deep within the brain that connects the hippocampus and the hypothalamus) and the **lateral hypothalamus,** causes one to be both sensitive to potential rewards and motivated to seek those rewards. An attraction to a chocolate cake or to a particular member of the opposite sex, as well as the concomitant motivation to approach that cake or that person, comes from this system. When the approach system functions in high gear, it can lead a person to be impulsive. When it is in low gear, a person feels little motivation to seek out anything.

The other, independent system is the inhibition or "stop" system. This system, said to be controlled by the **septo-hippocampus,** causes one to be both sensitive to potential punishments and motivated to avoid those punishments. A fear of a snake or of rejection by a member of the opposite sex, and the corresponding motivation to avoid these things, comes from this system. When the inhibition system functions in high gear, it can lead a person to be inhibited and anxious. When it is in low gear, the individual puts little effort into anticipating or avoiding negative outcomes. These two systems, when combined, yield the two-dimensional scheme outlined in Figure 8.6.

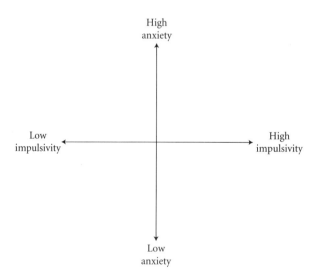

FIGURE 8.6 GRAY'S TWO-DIMENSIONAL DESCRIPTION OF PERSONALITY
The psychologist Jeffrey Gray theorizes that the two main, biologically based dimensions of personality are anxiety and impulsivity.

Notice how Gray assumes these two systems are independent or "orthogonal." Their location at 90° to each other means that being high or low on one does not necessarily imply anything about one's position on the other. The kind of person you are depends upon your position on both dimensions taken together.

Gray also postulates a third system, based on the "fight vs. flight" system found in animals, which controls the tendency to become aroused and aggressive. This system, which Gray contends is located in the amygdala, controls one's overall level of arousal, and corresponds roughly to Eysenck's psychoticism dimension.

The first two systems in Gray's theory can be mapped onto the first two dimensions of Eysenck's scheme as shown in Figure 8.7. It has been pointed out that Gray's scheme can be viewed as a 45° rotation of Eysenck's, whereby high anxiety in Gray's system, for example, can be seen as a blend of Eysenck's dimensions of neuroticism and introversion, whereas extraversion in Eysenck's system can be seen as a blend of Gray's dimensions of high impulsivity and low anxiety.

The schemes of Eysenck and Gray, which fit together so elegantly, provide a useful starting place for those who would base a theory of personality on

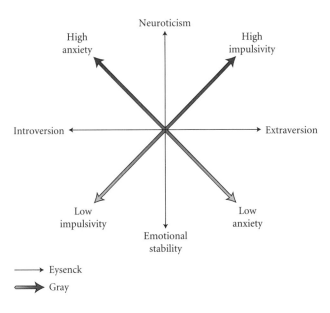

FIGURE 8.7 INTEGRATION OF EYSENCK'S AND GRAY'S FRAMEWORKS The first two dimensions of Eysenck's description and both dimensions of Gray's description of personality can be mapped onto each other as shown. For example, to be highly neurotic in Eysenck's scheme is to be high on anxiety and impulsivity in Gray's scheme.

mechanisms of the brain. And, indeed, both have stimulated a good deal of research. Yet, these two approaches need to be kept in perspective. The evidence in support of each is uneven and difficult to gather. A particularly difficult, yet necessary, task is to devise behavioral and physiological methods to evaluate these theories. For example, researchers have yet to specify the behaviors and the brain processes associated with such constructs as neuroticism, anxiety, inhibition, or even arousal. As psychophysiological research becomes more sophisticated and more active, we will learn more about how structures and processes of the brain underlie some of the major dimensions of personality.

A SYNTHESIS: ZUCKERMAN

The most recent major player in the research of brain mechanisms is Marvin Zuckerman (e.g., 1991). Zuckerman has tried to update the insights of Eysenck and Gray with a synthesis of current knowledge about brain function. For example, Zuckerman believes that both Eysenck's concept of instability and Gray's concept of the "stop" system are both part of a more general mechanism that regulates emotionality. The evidence from human and animal studies indicates that this mechanism is located in the amygdala and that it regulates positive emotions such as sociability as well as negative emotions such as anxiety and fear. Zuckerman has also reinterpreted the dimension called "psychoticism" by Eysenck and "fight-flight" by Gray as a basic failure to inhibit impulses, a function that Zuckerman locates to some degree in the hippocampus. According to Zuckerman, when the hippocampus is inactive in its duty to inhibit impulse, the result is a personality trait called "impulsive unsocialized sensation-seeking." Some rock musicians seem to have a lot of this trait.

To his credit, Zuckerman, unlike some of his colleagues, is modest about the limits of current knowledge about the biological basis of personality. He points out that animals and humans are adapted for such different environments that it is hazardous to draw too many parallels between what a structure does in an animal's brain and its function in the human brain. Furthermore, research on the human limbic system is quite rare; most research that has been performed on the human brain concentrates on the cortex.

Even in studies with animals, it is difficult to draw strong conclusions about the function of brain structures. For example, removing or damaging an animal's amygdala does seem to affect the animal's emotional functioning. Does this mean the amygdala is the seat of the emotions? Not necessarily. Removing a person's legs would lower his or her level of activity, but this does not mean the legs are the basis of one's activity level (Zuckerman, 1991). Similarly, removing a major brain structure such as the amygdala can have all kinds of adverse consequences, and it is difficult to be sure that emotions are particularly affected.

Still, Zuckerman has done an admirable job of building on the prior theories of Eysenck and Gray and of integrating them with the very latest that has been learned about the functioning of the brain.

The Brain and Personality

It is remarkable how much has been learned about the relationship between the brain and personality in spite of the difficulties in doing the relevant research. An important degree of continuity between human and animal brains has been identified. The general locations of the major functions of the brain—planning, foresight, emotion, motivation, motor control—have been mapped. And some speculative but also stimulating hypotheses have been offered about the relationship between brain structures and some of the important traits of personality. Whereas a few years ago it would have been reasonable to study personality while ignoring brain function altogether, such a practice is no longer reasonable. Personality psychologists must pay attention to the brain.

THE BIOCHEMISTRY OF PERSONALITY

The physical basis of personality comprises not only anatomy, but also biochemistry. The biological chemicals that are distributed in the brain and throughout the body have important effects. These chemicals fall into two groups: neurotransmitters and hormones. Their effects are quite complex, but knowledge about them is accumulating at a rapid rate.

Galen's Ancient Theory

Chemical approaches to the study of personality have a long history. The ancient Greek physician Galen (who lived between 130 and 200 A.D., practicing mostly in Rome), building on an earlier proposal by Hippocrates, theorized that personality was dependent on the balance between four "humors," or fluids in the body. These humors were blood, black bile, yellow bile (also called choler), and phlegm. A person who had a lot of blood relative to the other three humors, Galen conjectured, tended to be "sanguine" (cheerful), ruddy, and robust. An excess of black bile caused a person to be depressed and melancholy; an excess of yellow bile caused a person to be "choleric," angry, and bitter; and an excess of phlegm made one "phlegmatic," cold, and apathetic.

The terms "sanguine," "melancholic," "choleric," and "phlegmatic" survive in the English language to this day, carrying roughly the same psychological meaning that Galen ascribed. Even more remarkably, this four-fold typology is undergoing something of a revival among health psychologists, who are finding it useful in connecting personality with disease (Friedman, 1991, 1992). The choleric or chronically hostile person, for example, seems to be at extra risk for heart attack. But modern research suggests the basis of this risk is not the person's yellow bile, but rather the stress produced by a life filled with arguments and fights.

Modern Research Complications

Modern-day research on the chemical basis of personality has not paid much attention to phelgm or bile; it has focused instead on neurotransmitters and hormones.

In principle, it might seem fairly simple to do research on the chemistry of personality. The scientist measures some biochemical in a sample of people, then measures some aspect of their personalities, and then checks to see how one measurement is related to the other. For example, if people with higher levels of a certain chemical—the hormone testosterone, perhaps—tend to be more aggressive, then it would seem reasonable to conclude that a chemical basis for aggressiveness has been discovered. One might even announce, "testosterone causes aggressiveness."

In practice, however, this kind of research is much more difficult than it appears. For one thing, the measurement of personality is no simple matter, as we saw in Chapters 4 through 7. It is seldom easy to find a dependable measure of aggressiveness or of any other important trait.

For another thing, many chemicals that are behaviorally important are also difficult to measure. Testosterone can be measured from a small amount of saliva, but measuring the level of other chemicals requires blood to be drawn or cerebrospinal fluid to be tapped. These procedures are more difficult, expensive, and subjects are (understandably) often reluctant to participate. Furthermore, techniques have not been developed to measure all the important biochemicals in the body, and indeed many chemicals important to behavior may not even have been identified yet. Yet another complication is the hazard of assuming that chemicals in the body cause behavior; sometimes the reverse is true. As will be discussed below, for example, the experience of victory can raise a person's testosterone level.

This last complication—how to know which came first, the behavior or the chemical—is not present in a second method for studying the relationship between chemistry and personality: the use of drugs. A wide variety of psychoactive drugs exists, and many of them are known to affect other chemicals that are important to behavior. For example, L-Dopa (a drug used to treat Parkinson's disease) increases levels of the neurotransmitter dopamine, and Prozac (a drug used to treat depression) increases levels of the neurotransmitter serotonin.

Drugs have their complications, too, however. For one thing, they typically have more effects than just raising the level of one or another substance. Some of these side effects may be harmful; others just make it difficult to determine for sure how the drug affects behavior. Moreover, it is also not certain that *all* the effects a given drug has on the body and nervous system are completely known.

All these complications lead to a couple of conclusions. First, this is an extremely new and difficult research area, and one can only admire the persistence and ingenuity with which psychologists are making progress anyway. Second, it is important to appreciate how relatively little is known about the biochemistry of the nervous system, compared with what remains to be learned. Those chemical influences on behavior that we do know are not the only and are probably not even the most important ones. They are just the ones psychology happened to find first.

Neurotransmitters

The physical basis of behavior is the nervous system. The nervous system is made up of billions of cells, called nerve cells or **neurons**, which are connected with one another through complex pathways. The brain is a thick bundle of neurons; other neurons form the medulla oblongata and the spinal cord, which connect the brain to muscles and sensory receptors all over the body. The essence of neuronal activity is communication: Neurons communicate with one another, allowing sensations to travel from the far reaches of the body into the brain; allowing these sensations to be connected with feelings, memories, and plans in the brain; and allowing behavioral impulses to be sent back out to the muscles, causing the body to move.

Communication between neurons is based upon substances called **neurotransmitters**. As illustrated in Figure 8.8, an impulse generated by a neuron causes neurotransmitter chemicals to be released at the end of the neuron. These neurotransmitters travel across the synapse to the next neuron in line, where they cause a chemical reaction that results in that second neuron firing an impulse that causes the neurotransmitter chemicals at *its* other end to be released, and so on down the neural network, all the way to the brain or to the tip of the big toe.

Many neurotransmitter chemicals have been discovered, and more are still being identified. Different neurotransmitters are associated with different neural subsystems, and so have different effects on behavior. For example, the neurotransmitters norepinephrine and dopamine work almost exclusively in the **central nervous system**—the brain and spinal cord. By contrast, very little of the neurotransmitter epinephrine is found in the brain. Epinephrine is mostly found in the **peripheral nervous system**, the neuronal networks that extend all over the body. As another complication, some neurotransmitters cause adjacent neurons to fire, while others inhibit the neuronal impulse. For example, the body's own natural painkilling system is based on endogenous opiates, or **endorphins**. These special neurotransmitters work by inhibiting rather than facilitating the neuronal transmission of pain.

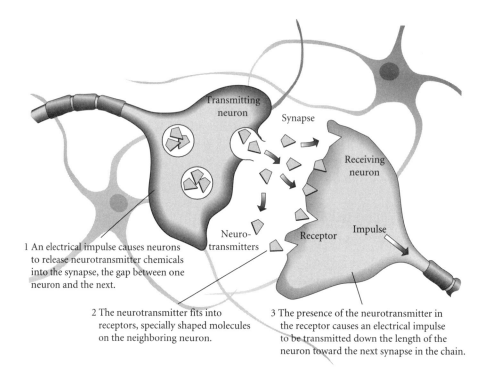

1 An electrical impulse causes neurons to release neurotransmitter chemicals into the synapse, the gap between one neuron and the next.

2 The neurotransmitter fits into receptors, specially shaped molecules on the neighboring neuron.

3 The presence of the neurotransmitter in the receptor causes an electrical impulse to be transmitted down the length of the neuron toward the next synapse in the chain.

FIGURE 8.8 COMMUNICATION BETWEEN NEURONS   The transmission of impulses throughout the nervous system is mediated by electrical and chemical processes.

Many aspects of biochemistry are important in neural communication. As we have just seen, the neurotransmitter chemicals themselves play a large role in transmitting impulses. But the chemicals out of which neurotransmitters are made are also important, as are other chemicals that cause neurotransmitters to be broken down into their constituent chemical parts after they have traveled across the synaptic gap. Drugs that affect behavior may do so by affecting any or all of these different chemicals. For example, the anti-anxiety drug Prozac is said to increase the amount of serotonin in the body by inhibiting the activity of the chemical that ordinarily causes serotonin to break down (Kramer, 1993).

The functioning of the various parts of the nervous system is affected in important ways by the amounts of various neurotransmitters available at the moment. This availability can vary as a function of what the individual is doing, and indeed can fluctuate quite widely over short periods of time. But people also seem to differ from each other in their *average* levels of various transmitters, and these differences seem to be associated with various personality traits.

CATECHOLAMINES

One important class of neurotransmitters is the catecholamines. This class includes, most notably, norepinephrine and dopamine. Norepinephrine can raise heart rate, blood pressure, and energy level, and seems to be involved in the experience of both anxiety and anger. People with chronically high levels of norepinephrine seem to be anxiety-prone, dependent, and sociable (e.g., Gray, 1987). Low levels of norepinephrine seem to be associated to some degree with disinhibition and impulsivity, and people with chronically low levels seem to be nonconformist and socially detached (Zuckerman, 1991).

Dopamine is important for the mechanisms that allow the brain to control body movements, and is also involved in systems that cause one to approach attractive objects and people. (Dopamine is also an important part of the chemical process that produces norepinephrine.) This neurotransmitter is theorized to be part of the basis of sociability and of general activity level. A severe lack of dopamine is the basis of Parkinson's disease.

In a famous case (described, with artistic license, in the movie *Awakenings*), a group of patients who developed Parkinson's as a result of an epidemic of encephalitis during World War I were given the new drug L-dopa forty years later, during the 1960s. L-dopa increases the brain's production of dopamine, and for some patients, who had been nearly catatonic for years, the results were dramatic. Suddenly they not only could move around much better than before, but they also were able once again to experience positive emotions, motivation, sociability, and interest in and awareness of their environments.

Sadly, over time, most of these patients' conditions worsened again. They went from normal enthusiasm and energy levels into hypomanic excitement, restlessness, and grandiosity. Then, like manic-depressive patients, they would "crash" into deep depressions (Sacks, 1983; Zuckerman, 1991). These effects suggest that dopamine systems might also have something to do with manic-depressive disorder. Perhaps even more important, they suggest that dopamine might be relevant to the personality traits of extraversion, impulsivity, and perhaps some others.

SEROTONIN

Serotonin is another important neurotransmitter that has a chemical base different from that of the catecholamines. Serotonin seems to play a role in the inhibition of behavioral impulses (e.g., in stopping you from doing something attractive yet dangerous). Serotonin is particularly relevant to the inhibition of emotional impulses. A person who has abnormally low levels of serotonin available will, according to one author, suffer from "serotonin depletion" (Metzner,

1994). The symptoms of serotonin depletion include irrational anger, hypersensitivity to rejection, chronic pessimism, obsessive worry, and fear of risk-taking.

The effects of serotonin and the reality of serrotonin depletion have become a topic of public discussion in recent years. The pharmaceutical company Eli Lilly in 1993 sold $1.2 billion worth of Prozac, which is a "selective serotonin re-uptake inhibitor" (SSRI). The physical effect of Prozac seems fairly clear—it raises the serotonin levels in the nervous system of the person who takes it. The psychological effects, however, are more controversial.

In his best-selling book, *Listening to Prozac,* psychiatrist Peter Kramer claims that Prozac can give many people entirely new personalities. It can stop one from needlessly worrying and from being oversensitive to minor stresses, and can provide a newly cheerful outlook on life. Some individuals who take Prozac claim that it makes them more like "themselves"; they don't feel like different people, they feel like *better* people. They get more work done and they become more attractive to members of the opposite sex.

Kramer raises the possibility that Prozac and other drugs might show that personality is primarily a matter of chemicals. Just as remarkably, Kramer also suggests that "cosmetic psychopharmacology" might become the psychiatric equivalent of plastic surgery. Just as people with perfectly good noses sometimes go to a surgeon to obtain even-better noses (they think), so too might people with perfectly adequate personalities begin to take Prozac and other drugs to obtain even-better personalities.

This possibility gives rise to several issues. First, some authorities claim that the term "cosmetic psychopharmacology" is misleading because Prozac does not work on people with adequate personalities (Metzner, 1994). They claim that unless you suffer from a disease—serotonin depletion—Prozac will have no effect. Since the diagnosis of this syndrome is far from clear-cut, this claim is difficult to evaluate.

A second issue is that although chemicals clearly influence personality, the idea that personality is so specifically based on chemicals that it can be precisely adjusted is surely an exaggeration. For one thing, Kramer's own book clearly states that the effects that Prozac will have on a given individual are difficult to predict and can change over time. Moreover, the effects of Prozac and other drugs can vary according to other factors in the patient's life, including the administration of psychotherapy. Kramer's and other psychiatrists' prescription strategies seem to be to give troubled patients some Prozac, see what happens, and then adjust the dosage of the drug accordingly, while also providing some psychotherapy on the side. This technique is a far cry from giving someone a "designer personality" by having him or her take a pill.

For now, we can conclude only that serotonin has important effects on personality, and that its levels may have something to do with certain kinds of psychological problems. Prozac and other drugs that affect serotonin have widely varying effects on different individuals, and these drugs do not create a predictable, new personality in the way a plastic surgeon can promise to make your nose a certain shape. That said, these drugs do have effects that are sometimes remarkably beneficial for certain individuals. It is simply difficult to predict who these individuals will be.

Hormones

A **hormone** is a biological chemical that, by definition, affects parts of the body far from where it was produced (Cutler, 1976). Many hormones have important effects on behavior, stimulating the activity of neurons in many locations in the brain and in the body at the same time. Hormones that are important for behavior are released by the hypothalamus (part of the limbic system of the brain), the gonads (testes and ovaries), and the adrenal cortex (part of the adrenal gland that sits atop the kidneys). Hormones in a sense make up a second nervous system, because they allow behaviorally relevant messages to be sent from one location in the body to another—they just travel through the bloodstream rather than along neuronal pathways.

Testosterone

The most studied and probably best-known hormones are the gonadal or sex hormones: testosterone in males and estrogen in females (although all humans in fact have both kinds of hormone in their bodies). It has long been observed that males seem generally to be more aggressive than females (e.g., Kagan, 1978; Maccoby & Jacklin, 1974), and males certainly have more testosterone in their bodies. To be exact, normal human females have about 40 nanograms of testosterone in each deciliter, of their blood; normal males have between 300 and 1000 nanograms per deciliter, or a ten times greater concentration of testosterone.

This set of observations has led some psychologists to hypothesize that testosterone is the cause of aggressive behavior, and many studies have pursued this idea. Some of these studies found that human males who have higher levels of testosterone are indeed more likely to have aggressive and other behavioral control problems than are those with lower testosterone levels. In one study, for example, male American military veterans were asked about their past behaviors. Those with higher testosterone levels reported more often having had trouble with their parents, teachers, and classmates; having assaulted others; having used hard drugs, marijuana, or alcohol; having had numerous sexual partners; and having a "general tendency toward excessive behavior" (Dabbs & Morris, 1990, p. 209).

It should be noted that findings like these, though provocative, are not always consistent from one study to the next (Zuckerman, 1991). They are also complex. For example, we should bear in mind that nearly all studies in this area—including the one just quoted above—measure aggressive or even criminal behavior solely through self-reporting (S data); they do not account for those people who engage in such activities but will not admit it. A more basic consideration is that while males of many species are more aggressive than females of the same species, this is not always the case. Males are *not* more aggressive than females among gibbons, wolves, rabbits, hamsters, or even laboratory rats (Floody, 1983).

Beyond the difficulty in getting good data in this area, there is yet another important complexity. Although some extreme criminal types (e.g., rapists who also commit other kinds of bodily harm) may be likely to have high levels of testosterone (Rada, Laws, & Kellner, 1976), the reverse does not seem to be true: men with high levels of testosterone are *not* necessarily aggressive, and they are certainly not all aggravated rapists. Furthermore, it has sometimes been reported that the relationship between testosterone level and physical aggression holds only (or holds more strongly) for relatively uneducated men from low economic classes (Dabbs & Morris, 1990). The presumed reason is that more educated men in the higher classes have been taught to express their aggressive impulses in less physical ways (maybe by saying something elegantly sarcastic or initiating a hostile takeover of your company). Yet another body of evidence indicates that higher testosterone levels can be a *result* of aggression, especially of successful aggression (i.e., when you win; Zuckerman, 1991).

Other studies indicate that males high in testosterone are higher in "stable extraversion," that is, sociability, self-acceptance, and dominance. Such males also report having more sexual experience and more sexual partners. But again, higher testosterone levels may be a result rather than a cause of sexual activity (Zuckerman, 1991).

And we should not forget that women have testosterone as well. In women, testosterone is produced by the adrenal cortex, and has important behavioral effects. For example, one study showed that female prisoners who had committed "unprovoked" violent crimes had higher levels of testosterone than did women who had been violent after provocation or who had committed nonviolent crimes (Dabbs, Ruback, Frady, Hopper, & Sgoritas, 1988). Other research has shown that women with impaired adrenocortical functioning, who therefore produce less testosterone, seem to become less interested in sex. Moreover, the administration of testosterone injections to women can sometimes produce dramatic increases in sexual desire (Zuckerman, 1991). These results suggest that testosterone is a chemical basis of sexual arousal in women as well as in men.

Higher levels of testosterone in women also have been found to be associated with higher levels of self-reported sociability and with impulsivity, lack of inhibition, and lack of conformity. In support of this conclusion, one study found that women who held professional and managerial jobs had higher testosterone levels than homemakers or those with clerical jobs (Purifoy & Koopermans,

1979). However, even if one accepts the reasoning behind this conclusion, it is once again difficult to separate cause and effect. Perhaps it was the "power rush" of holding a managerial job that raised women's testosterone levels, not the testosterone levels making certain women more likely to enter such a job.

Further evidence concerning the effects of testosterone comes from body-builders and athletes who take anabolic steroids to promote muscular development (Carver & Scheier, 1992). Anabolic steroids are synthetic testosterone; their effects include not only speedier muscle development but also a whole host of troublesome side effects. Steroid users frequently experience erratic and uncontrolled aggressiveness and sexuality. For example, male steroid users may experience erections without stimulation, but also seem to have a lower overall sex drive and to be prone to impotence and sterility. Ben Johnson, the Canadian sprinter whose Olympic gold medal was taken away when he was found (through blood tests) to have used steroids, seemed to experience difficulty controlling aggression: he got into a lot of fights with reporters (then again, maybe that behavior was not abnormal).

What can we conclude from all this? It would be an oversimplification to conclude that testosterone causes either male aggression *or* sexuality in any simple or direct way. Instead, it seems more accurate to surmise that testosterone plays a role in the control and inhibition of aggressiveness and sexuality, including normal assertiveness and perhaps even generalized activity level, as well as the normal range of sexual function and responsiveness in both sexes. Recall the comment quoted above that males with high testosterone levels were prone to "excessive" behavior. In general, the evidence suggests that when this hormone is present in abnormally high proportions, such as occurs naturally in certain individuals and artificially in steroid users, aggression and sexuality are not so much enhanced as they are messed up. Both may occur at inappropriate times, and fail to occur at appropriate times. But the simple belief that testosterone makes you either more aggressive or more sexy is probably not true.

CORTISOL

Cortisol is another hormone that has important effects on the body and on behavior. Sometimes called the "fight-flight" hormone, it is released into the bloodstream by the adrenal cortex as a response to physical or psychological stress. (It is also an important part of several normal metabolic processes.) It can speed the heart rate, raise blood pressure, stimulate muscle strength, and metabolize fat, and has many other effects. Cortisol is thought to be part of the alarm system that alerts and prepares the mind and body to face a potential threat (Selye, 1956).

Individuals with chronically high levels of cortisol in their blood sometimes suffer from severe depression or other painful results of psychological stress. Of course, their cortisol levels could well be the result, rather than the cause, of their distress. Individuals with abnormally low levels of cortisol may be impulsive sensation-seekers who are disinclined to follow the rules of society (Zuckerman, 1991). This latter pattern may arise because the lack of cortisol causes such individuals to fail to respond normally to the signs of danger associated with such activities as bungee jumping and shoplifting.

A Synthesis

The evidence concerning the effects of brain mechanisms and biochemicals on behavior is still tentative and spotty, and it may be premature to attempt a summary or synthesis. The personality psychologist Marvin Zuckerman (1991) has recently made an attempt to do so, however. The structure of his theory appears in Figure 8.9. It is an attempt to integrate ideas such as those of Eysenck and Gray with some of the neurobiological evidence we have just surveyed.

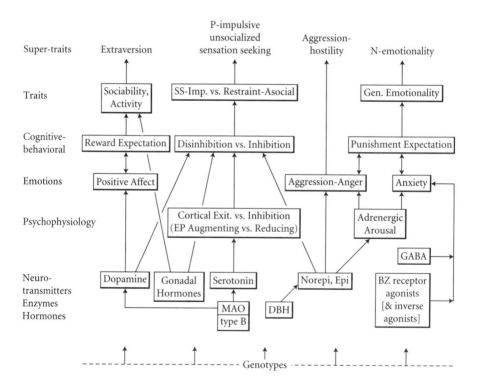

FIGURE 8.9 ZUCKERMAN'S HIERARCHICAL MODEL OF THE BIOLOGICAL BASIS OF PERSONALITY Zuckerman's model of how different biological processes contribute to personality is highly complex, but it provides a useful map of what psychologists have learned so far and can be helpful in organizing future research.

Zuckerman's theory is hierarchical, in the sense that it tries to move from extremely broad patterns of behavior down to very small, precise influences on specific neural activities. The theory organizes the biology of personality into five levels of analysis. At the first, highest, broadest level are what Zuckerman calls "supertraits." These are the most general attributes of personality, and are the ultimate, long-term result of the interaction between a person's experience and his or her biological makeup. These supertraits include the dimensions of extraversion, neuroticism, impulsiveness, and anxiety proposed by Eysenck and Gray. These traits are produced by general mechanisms of the sort that Eysenck and Gray described, but also can be seen as concatenations of more specific traits. The second level of analysis, then, consists of the narrower traits such as sociability, activity, or assertiveness out of which the supertraits are built. These more specific traits are themselves derived from patterns of behavior and emotional experience, which are at the third level of analysis. For example, positive affect (a pattern of emotional experience) seems to help produce sociability (a personality trait). The fourth level of analysis takes us to the psychophysiological processes that produce patterns of behavior and emotional experience. These psychophysiological processes, in turn, are based on the functioning of neurotransmitters and hormones, such as dopamine and testosterone, which lie at the fifth and lowest level of analysis.

This framework illustrates why the most useful research strategy is to relate a given process or attribute at one level to the *next* level, up or down, but not to skip too many levels at once. For example, it is feasible and worthwhile to show how the supertrait of extraversion is related to the more specific trait of sociability, but to research how extraversion is a function of testosterone level may require too great a jump. The most important contribution of Zuckerman's theory, therefore, is to organize the vast and unwieldy array of research on the biology of behavior into a manageable hierarchy of interconnected levels. It provides a useful starting place and a map for the further research on the biology of personality that is likely to thrive in the coming decades.

SUMMARY

Brain anatomy and neurophysiology are both relevant to personality. Observations of animals suggest that the human brain is really three brains in one: a reptilian, a paleomammalian, and a neomammalian brain. This structure suggests that humans and animals have many basic brain functions in common. What we know about brain functioning in humans comes from the observation of people who have suffered accidental brain damage or undergone brain surgery. Damage to the frontal lobes, for example, seems to affect planning, foresight, and emotional regulation. The amygdala is important for emotions, and the two cerebral hemispheres seem to have different functions: the right hemisphere is more intuitive and the left hemisphere is more analytic. For a time, surgery was used on the frontal lobes and other areas of the brain in an attempt to affect behavior, but this did not turn out to be a worthwhile approach. Theories by Hans Eysenck and Jeffrey Gray describe postulated brain mechanisms, such as arousal or inhibitory systems, that affect major dimensions of personality, such as extraversion and anxiety. These theories remain unproven, but provide a useful starting point for theorizing about the relationship between personality and brain function.

Research on the physiology of personality has explored the effects of neurotransmitters such as norepiniphrine, dopamine and serotonin. Other research has examined the effects of hormones—primarily the male sex hormone testosterone and the "stress" hormone cortisol—on personality. The relationship between anatomy, physiology, and personality is complex, but an integrative model by Zuckerman provides a start toward organizing and understanding them by describing the interactions between five levels of psychological and biological functioning.

CHAPTER

THE INHERITANCE
OF PERSONALITY:
BEHAVIORAL GENETICS AND
EVOLUTIONARY THEORY

Two other approaches to explaining personality are very different from those considered in the preceding chapter, but still are essentially biological. Both address how personality might be biologically inherited, that is, how characteristic patterns of behavior might be encoded on genes and passed from parents to children across generations. The first of these approaches, behavioral genetics, attempts to explain how individual differences in behavior—personality traits—are passed from parent to child and thus are shared by biological relatives. The second of these approaches, evolutionary biology, attempts to explain how patterns of behavior that are characteristic of the entire human species had their origins in the survival value these characteristics had for our ancestors.

BEHAVIORAL GENETICS

Behavioral genetics studies the way inherited biological material, i.e., genes, can influence broad patterns of behavior. A pattern of behavior that is relevant to more than one situation—the only kind of pattern worth considering—is, by definition, a personality trait (Plomin, Chipuer, & Loehlin, 1990).[1] Thus "be-

---

[1]Moreover, research in behavioral genetics relies almost exclusively on self-report personality tests (S data) to measure behavior.

havioral" genetics might more accurately be called "trait" genetics, but I will stick with the traditional term in this presentation.

Calculating Heritabilities

The basic methodology of behavioral genetics is to compare similarities in personality between individuals who are and are not genetically related, or who are related to each other to different degrees. The classic technique is to look at twins. As you probably know, human twins come in two kinds: identical (also called monozygotic or MZ) twins, and fraternal (also called dizygotic or DZ) twins. Monozygotic ("one-egg") twins come from a splitting of a single fertilized egg, and therefore are genetically identical. Dizygotic ("two-egg") twins come from two eggs fertilized by two different sperm, and so, although born at the same time, they are related genetically no more than any other two siblings.

Humans are highly similar to each other genetically. Many human genes— about 90 percent of them—are identical from one individual to another. Behavioral genetics concentrates on the approximately 10 percent of the human genome that does vary. MZ twins are identical in all of these varying genes; DZ twins share about one-half of them, on average. Thus when it is said, for example, that a mother shares 50 percent of her genetic material with her child, this statement really means that she shares 50 percent of the material that varies across individuals. This rather technical point highlights an important fact: behavioral genetics, like trait psychology (see Chapters 4–7), with which it is so closely aligned, focuses exclusively on aspects of personality that *differ* from one individual to another. The inheritance of "species-specific" traits that all humans share is addressed by evolutionary biology, which is discussed in the latter section of this chapter (Tooby & Cosmides, 1990).

Research on behavioral genetics has made great efforts to find twins of both types (MZ and DZ), and also to seek out the rare cases of twins who were separated at birth and reared apart from each other. Once such twins are found, their personalities are measured, usually with self-report instruments such as were discussed in Chapters 5 and 6 (the Eysenck Personality Questionnaire and the California Psychological Inventory are particular favorites). The next step is to compute the correlation coefficients (see Chapter 3) across each pair of twins.[2] The basic assumption of behavioral genetics is that if a trait is influenced by genes, then it ought to be more highly correlated across pairs of identical (MZ) twins than across pairs of fraternal (DZ) twins, and more highly correlated across closer genetic relatives than across more distant genetic relatives.

---

[2]For technical reasons, a certain kind of coefficient, called the intraclass correlation, is used.

	TABLE 9.1		

CALCULATING HERITABILITIES

	Identical Twins		Fraternal Twins	
	Score of First Twin	Score of Second Twin	Score of First Twin	Score of Second Twin
Pair #1	54	53	52	49
Pair #2	41	40	41	53
Pair #3	49	51	49	52
...	x_4	y_4	x_4	y_4
...	x_5	y_5	x_5	y_5
	$r = .50$		$r = .30$	

Calculation: $.50 - .30 = .20$
$\quad\quad\quad .20 \times 2 \;\; = .40$

Conclusion: Heritability $= 40\%$

A statistic called the **heritability coefficient** is computed to reflect this influence (see the hypothetical example in Table 9.1). In the case of twins, one simple formula is (MZr − DZr) × 2. Across many, many traits, the average correlation across MZ twins is about .50, and across DZ twins is about .30. The difference between these figures is .20; multiply that by 2 and you arrive at a heritability coefficient of .40. This means that, according to twin studies, the average heritability of a good many traits of personality is about .40, which is interpreted to mean that the proportion of phenotypic (behavioral) variance that can be explained by genetic variance is 40 percent (e.g., Plomin, Chipuer, & Loehlin, 1990).

Twin studies are not the only way to calculate heritabilities. Such studies are simple and elegant, because MZ twins share exactly twice as many genes as do DZ twins, but other kinds of relatives also vary in their degree of shared genes. For example, children share, on average, 50 percent of their genes with their biological parents, whereas adopted children (presumably) share none of their personality-relevant genes with their adoptive parents. Full siblings also share 50 percent of the genes that vary, on average, whereas half siblings (who have one parent in common) share only 25 percent. Calculating similarities in personality across these relatives provides an alternative way to derive heritability estimates. Interestingly, the estimates of heritability for most traits garnered from non-twin studies is about 20 percent, or half that estimated from twin studies (Plomin, Chipuer, & Loehlin, 1990).

Why this difference? One possible explanation is that the effects of genes are multiplicative rather than additive. That is, the twin-study calculation assumes that because DZ twins share half the genes that MZ twins do, they are half as similar in genetic expression. But if genes act not just by independently adding up, but also by interacting with one another, then DZ twins' similarity in genetic expression will be less than 50 percent. While they share 50 percent of the genes, they share only 25 percent of the interactions among those genes. As a result, in terms of genetic expression identical twins will be four times as similar to each other as are fraternal twins, instead of just twice as similar. If this line of reasoning is correct, then the 20 percent figure for the heritability of many traits is probably a better estimate than the 40 percent figure often quoted.

WHAT HERITABILITIES CAN TELL YOU

Admittedly these heritability calculations are rather technical, and there is a more basic question we should be asking: Regardless of how you compute it, what does a heritability tell you? Three things.

First, heritabilities tell you that genes matter. For years, psychologists commonly presumed that all of personality was determined environmentally—that is, by early experiences and parental practices. Heritabilities challenge that presumption whenever they turn out to be greater than zero—and they nearly always do. So not all of the determination of personality is environmental; some of it comes from the individual's genes. This important realization is rather new to psychology, and is still not accepted by everyone.

Second, heritabilities can sometimes tell you whether specific behavioral or mental disorders are part of the normal range or are pathologically distinctive. One of the more interesting findings to emerge so far from the behavioral genetics literature is that severe mental retardation (defined as an IQ below 50, when 100 is the average) apparently is *not* heritable. The average IQ of the sibling of a severely retarded child is a perfectly normal 103. However, moderate mental retardation (IQs ranging from 50 to 69) does seem to be heritable; the average IQ of the sibling of a moderately retarded child is 85. These findings show that severe mental retardation involves more than just extremely low IQ. The fact that its pattern of heritability is different from that of mere low IQ suggests that severe retardation is caused by a different mechanism and can be expected to have a fundamentally different etiology (e.g., it may be due to prenatal trauma or infection, or other nongenetic influences; Plomin, Chipuer, & Loehlin, 1990).

A third thing that heritability studies can do is provide a window into how the early environment does—or does not—operate in determining later personality. According to some researchers in this area, the major finding of behavioral genetics so far is this: The personality traits of adoptive siblings who are all raised in the same family resemble each other with a correlation of only .05, which means that a mere 5 percent of the variation in their personalities is due to their common family environment. More important, it seems, is the nonshared portion of their early environments. This includes effects of their birth order (e.g., the degree to which firstborns are treated differently from later-borns), friendships outside the home, and other outside interests and activities (Loehlin, Willerman, & Horn, 1985, 1989).

Of course, these are just speculations. Research on behavioral genetics does not tell us *which* aspects of a child's early environment are important. But it does suggest that whatever they are, they are not aspects that are shared across members of a family.

If correct, this is a stunning conclusion. It implies that aspects of the family environment that siblings share, such as their neighborhood, their home environment, their income level, their nutritional level, their parents' styles of child-rearing, and so forth, are *not* important in the determination of each child's adult personality.

A number of questions could be raised about this conclusion, however. First, it does seem to directly contradict many decades of research in developmental psychology that document effects of child-rearing, family environment, and even social class on personality (Baumrind, 1993; Bergeman et al., 1993; Funder, Parke, Tomlinson-Keasey, & Widaman, 1993; Hetherington, 1983). On the other hand, it must be admitted that research on how parental styles affect children has been confounded, to use a methodological term, by the fact that parents and their children are genetically related. So some of the effects that psychologists have believed were due to the way parents raise their children may instead be due to the genes that parents share with their children. Still, it is difficult to believe that having an alcoholic parent, or living in substandard housing, or having parents who encourage all their children to do well are factors that have no importance for how a child turns out.

Another complication with this conclusion is that the personality measures used in these studies—mostly self-report scales like the CPI—may fail to capture the essence of personality as it emerges from family experience (Shweder & Sullivan, 1990). Perhaps the result of family experience is a view of the world or a set of values not measured by standard personality questionnaires.

A third complication is that because they are often screened, chosen, and even arranged by social service agencies, the environments fostered by adoptive families may be more similar to each other than are the environments encountered in families at large. To the extent the families in these studies in fact resemble each other, estimates of the effects of family environment upon personality will tend to be underestimates. (The technical reason is that the range has been restricted on the family environment variable, lowering its chance of demonstrating an effect on any other variable.)

Despite these complications, behavioral genetics research should get credit for having raised this provocative issue, and much further research remains to be done to ascertain the true role of the family environment in personality development.

WHAT HERITABILITIES CANNOT TELL YOU

Now let's consider what heritability studies *cannot* tell you.

First, the heritability coefficient is not the "nature-nurture ratio"; it cannot tell you how much a trait is determined by genes as opposed to the environment. Even professional researchers in the area seem to forget this from time to time. Ever since scientists realized the effects that heredity might have on behavior, they have longed for a simple number that would resolve the nature-nurture debate by telling you what percentage of any given trait was due to nature (or heredity), and what percentage was due to nurture (or upbringing and environment). To some, the heritability coefficient has seemed like that number, since it indeed yields a percentage figure that is supposed to reflect the percentage of the variation in a trait that is due to genes.

But consider, as an example, the number of arms you have. Was this number determined by your genes or by your childhood environment? Well, let's calculate the heritability of this trait. Looking again at Table 9.1, plug in for the first member of the first pair of twins the number of arms he or she has, which we will presume is 2. Then do the same thing for the other twin of that pair. Then do this for all the other individuals in both parts of the table (we'll assume all of these numbers are 2). Then calculate the correlations. Actually you cannot do that in either case, because the formula to calculate the correlation (not shown in Table 9.1) will, in this case, require a division by zero (the result of which is undefined in mathematics). So, the difference between these correlations is 0; multiply that by 2 and you still get 0—the heritability of having two arms is 0. Does that mean this trait is determined entirely by the environment? Well . . . .

What went wrong in this calculation? The problem is that on the trait of arm quantity there is practically no variation across individuals; nearly everyone has two. Because heritability is the proportion of *variation* due to genetic influences, if there is no variation then the heritability will approach zero. Generally, the less variation there is on a trait across individuals, then the lower the heritability is likely to be. This means that if a given trait has a high heritability, one of two things is possible: that trait might vary more across individuals, or it might be a trait for which genes are important, in an absolute sense. Likewise, if a given trait has a low heritability, that trait might vary *less* across individuals, or it may be a trait that is less dependent on one's genes.

Some recent theorizing maintains—somewhat surprisingly, at first glance— that traits with high heritabilities are likely to be those that have *not* been important for survival or reproductive fitness. The reason is that harmful traits should have been selected out of the gene pool through the process of evolution, and helpful traits should have been magnified. The result would be that important traits should vary less across individuals in the present generation. Everyone should have those traits that are extremely helpful to survival; nobody should have those traits that are extremely harmful. So, those traits that still have large variances after all these years, and which thereby manifest high heritabilities, must not have been very important, evolutionarily speaking (Tooby & Cosmides, 1990).

A second, related limitation of the heritability coefficient is that it can vary as a function of many different extraneous influences. For example, the more diverse the genes in a given population are, the higher the heritabilities that will be calculated based on members of that population. Also, the more diverse the environments experienced by a group of individuals, the lower the heritabilities will be. This means, for example, that if a study includes only individuals who live in Minnesota, the heritabilities that will be calculated will tend to be higher than if the same study included Minnesotans along with natives of Moscow, Pago Pago, and Mongolia. Indeed, the fact that the human gene pool is dispersed fairly uniformly around the globe, whereas important cultural differences still exist, implies that heritability studies done within single, homogeneous cultures (as nearly all such studies are) may tend to overestimate genetic influence.

A third limitation of heritability coefficients is that, no matter who they are derived from and how they are calculated, these statistics do not yield conceptual understanding of *how* personality develops. At best, they can tell you that genes are involved, somehow.

Consider the recent finding that television-watching is heritable to a statistically significant degree (Plomin, Corley, DeFries, & Fulker, 1990). Does this mean there is a biologically active gene in your DNA that causes you to watch television? Presumably not. Rather, there must be some more basic propensity— perhaps sensation-seeking, perhaps lethargy, perhaps a craving for blue light— that has some genetic component. And this component, interacting somehow with early experience, creates in some people a propensity to watch a lot of television. The research on this has not yet examined any of these interactions, however, and does not offer even a hint as to what exactly is inherited or how it influences television-watching. Indeed, as the researchers who presented this finding admitted, "it is likely to be difficult to find specific mechanisms of genetic influence on television viewing because genetic mechanisms have not as yet been uncovered for *any* complex behavioral trait, including cognitive abilities and personality" (Plomin, Corley, DeFries, & Fuller, 1990, p. 376; emphasis added).

Part of the problem is that while this study did measure television-watching and did measure genetic similarity (via degree of relatedness), it reported no measures of the environments in which its subjects grew up, and very few behavioral measures other than that of television-watching. Thus, from this study, too, all we learn is that genes are involved somehow.

Even very recent molecular studies suffer from a related shortcoming. Consider the recent study by Hamer and Copeland (1994), which apparently has come close to identifying a gene (on the X chromosome) associated with homosexuality in males. This study did two things. First, it found a group of homosexuals who were related to various degrees. Then, using microbiological techniques, it identified a pattern of genetic similarity that most (but not all) of the homosexuals shared, but that was not found in heterosexual members of the same family. They concluded that this genetic similarity was the basis of the homosexuality.

The authors admitted that this is still not a full explanation of homosexuality, in part because *not all* of the homosexuals in their study shared the same DNA pattern. But even if this pattern were found in all of them, it would not explain their homosexuality because it would not show us *how* this behavior pattern is inherited. That is, which brain structures or hormones or neurotransmitters differ as a result of this genetic code, what kind of nervous system is the result, and how does this nervous system interact with the social environment to produce a lifelong pattern of homosexual interest and behavior? The study offers not a clue in answer to these questions. All we have is DNA, on the one hand, and behavior, on the other. And so all we really learn, once again, is that genes are involved, somehow. (A theory presented at the end of this chapter attempts to provide a more complete picture of how genes might influence sexual orientation.)

So far, we have only a few hints about just how genes affect behavior. Genes themselves cannot cause anybody to do anything. They can only affect behavior by influencing biological structure and physiology. The challenge is to find the aspects of the nervous system that are affected by genes, then to understand how those aspects interact with environmental experience to affect behavior. Researchers have found that some behaviorally relevant physiology is heritable. For example, the heritability of an individual's level of the neurotransmitter noradrenaline (see Chapter 8) is extremely high, perhaps .80 or even greater (Oxenstierna et al., 1986; Zuckerman, 1991). Patterns of electrical activity of the brain, as measured through electroencephalographs (EEGs), also are highly heritable (e.g., Claridge, Canter, & Hume, 1973; Zuckerman, 1991). Findings such as these provide a hint about the kinds of biological mechanisms through which personality can be inherited, but much more remains to be learned.

Gene-Environment Interactions

Although the *zeitgeist* is tending to give more emphasis to the effects that genetic inheritance can have on personality, it is worth remembering that genes can influence the development of behavior only in people who live in some kind of environment. Without an environment there would be no behavior at all, regardless of what genes were present. And the reverse is true about the environment: without a person (built by genes) to affect, no behavior can occur, no matter what the environment. The point has been made many times but seems always to need re-emphasis: In the determination of personality, genes and the environment *interact*.

Genes and the environment can interact in several ways (Scarr & McCartney,

1983). For example, a child who as a result of his genes is shorter than his peers may be teased in school; this teasing could have long-term effects on his personality. These effects are in part due to his genes, but they came about only through an interaction between the genetic expression and the social environment that resulted. Without both, there would have been no effect.

Another way genes and environment can interact is through the way people choose their environments. A person who inherits a tendency towards sensation-seeking, for example, may as a result take dangerous drugs. This practice might harm that person's health, or involve the person in the drug culture, either of which could have long-lasting effects on his or her experience and the development of his or her personality. Let's say the person develops a criminal personality. This result is not really a fault of the inherited trait of sensation-seeking; it comes about through the interaction of the inherited trait with the environment that the person seeks out because of that trait.

The most important way in which genes and environments interact is that the same environment can affect different individuals in different ways. A stressful environment may lead a genetically predisposed individual to develop mental illness, for example, while leaving individuals without that predisposition psychologically unscathed. More generally, the same environmental circumstances might be perceived as stressful, or enjoyable, or boring, depending on the genetic predispositions of the individuals involved; these variations in perception can lead to very different behavioral results and, over time, to the development of different personality traits.

The most significant news from the study of behavioral genetics over the past few years is that genes are important in the determination of personality. This is quite a change from the conventional view held only a few years ago. The future of behavioral genetics, however, does not lie in further documenting this fact. The job for behavioral genetics is, first, to explain how genes create brain structures and aspects of physiology that are important to personality, and second, to explain how a person's genetically determined tendencies interact with his or her environment to determine how he or she behaves.

EVOLUTIONARY THEORY

An important part of the foundation of all of modern biology is evolutionary theory. Modern extensions of the theorizing that began with Charles Darwin's *Origin of the Species* (1859/1967) are used to organize the entire field, providing a way to compare one species of animal or plant to another, to explain the functional significance of various aspects of anatomy and behavior, and to understand how animals function within their particular environments.

In recent years, an increasing number of attempts have been made to apply the same kind of theorizing and reasoning to the understanding of human behavior and even social structure. One landmark book, E. O. Wilson's *Sociobiology: The New Synthesis* (1975), applied evolutionary theory to psychology and sociology. Other, earlier efforts, such as Konrad Lorenz's *On Aggression* (1966), also have tried to explain human behavior by analogies to animals and their evolution.

In general, the evolutionary approach to human behavior assumes that behaviors seen in people are present because, in the evolutionary history of the human species, these behaviors were helpful or necessary for survival. The more a behavior helps an individual to survive and reproduce, according to evolutionary theory, the more likely the behavior is to occur in subsequent generations. The evolutionary approach to explaining behavior, therefore, is to identify a common behavior pattern and then ask how that pattern could have been adaptive (i.e., beneficial to survival and reproduction) during the development of the human species. The focus is not on individual differences, but on patterns of behavior that are held to be common to all people and thus part of "human nature" (Tooby & Cosmides, 1990).

A wide range of human behavior has been examined through this evolutionary lens. For example, the possibly necessary—and sometimes harmful—role of the instinct toward aggression throughout human history was discussed by Lorenz (1966). The biologist Richard Dawkins (1976) closely considered the evolutionary roots of the opposite behavior, altruism, and described how a general tendency to aid and protect other people, especially close relatives, might help assure the survival of one's own genes into succeeding generations (an outcome called inclusive fitness). It pays to be nice to your relatives, according to this analysis, because if the people who share your genes survive, then some of your genes may make it into the next generation through these relatives' children, even if you produce no offspring.

Sex Differences in Mating Behavior

A behavioral pattern that has received particular attention from evolutionary psychologists has been the differences in sexual behavior between human males and females. Particular differences can be identified in the behaviors of **mate selection**—what one looks for in the opposite sex—and **mating strategies**—how one handles heterosexual relationships.

MATE SELECTION

First consider mate selection. When looking for someone of the opposite sex with whom to form a relationship, are you more interested in that person's (a) physical attractiveness or (b) financial security? Across a wide variety of cultures, including most emphatically late-twentieth-century North America, men are more likely than women to place a higher value on physical attractiveness (Buss, 1989). In these same cultures, by contrast, women are more likely to value economic security in their potential mates. Moreover, men are likely to desire (and typically do find) mates who are several years younger than themselves (the average age difference is about three years, and gets larger as men get older), whereas women tend to seek mates who are older than themselves (of course).

One can document this difference through marriage statistics and even through "personal" ads. For example when an age is specified in a personal ad, men advertising for women usually specify an age younger than their own, whereas women will specify an age that is greater than their own. The other effect can also be found in personals: Men are more likely to describe themselves as financially secure than as physically attractive, whereas women are more likely to describe their physical charms than their financial ones (Kenrick & Keefe, 1992). Presumably, each sex is acting this way because it knows what the other sex is looking for, and is trying to maximize its own attractiveness.

The evolutionary explanation of these and other differences is that, essentially, men and women are seeking the same thing: the greatest possible likelihood of mating with someone with whom they will have healthy offspring who themselves will survive to reproduce. But each sex contributes to and seeks this goal differently, and thus the optimal mate for each is different. Women bear and nurse children, and so their youth and physical health is essential. Attractiveness, according to the evolutionary explanation, is simply a cue that informs men that a woman is indeed young, healthy, and fit to bear children (Buss & Barnes, 1986; Symons, 1979).

A man's biological contribution to reproduction is relatively minimal, in contrast. Viable sperm can be produced by male bodies of a wide range of ages, physical conditions, and appearances. For women, what *is* essential in a mate is his capacity to provide an environment and resources conducive to her children's survival and thriving until their own reproductive years. Thus, since a woman seeks a mate to optimize her children's chances, she will seek someone with resources (and perhaps attitudes) that will support a family, whereas a man seeks a mate who will provide his children with the optimal degree of physical health.

We can see already that these explanations gloss over some obvious complications. For example, a woman who lacks a certain percentage of body fat will stop menstruating and will therefore be unable to conceive children, yet many women considered by men to be highly physically attractive are thin nearly to the point of anorexia. In previous eras, much heavier women were considered the ideal of physical attractiveness. Thus culture does seem to influence concepts of physical attractiveness, and although it is far from clear where those ideas come from, reproductive fitness is not always the sole determinant.

Likewise, male physical attractiveness is more important to many women than the standard evolutionary explanation seems to allow. However, it must be admitted that physical attractiveness does not seem to be as important to women as it is to men. The general trends in what men and women favor in each other are difficult to deny, despite occasional exceptions and complications.

MATING STRATEGIES

Once they have completed their mutual selection process and have mated, men and women still differ in their subsequent behavior. According to the evolutionary account, men tend to want to have more sexual partners and are neither particularly faithful nor particularly picky about those women with whom they will mate. Women, in contrast, are much more selective about their mating partners and, having mated, seem to have a greater desire for monogamy and a stable relationship.

These differences can also be explained in terms of reproductive success. A male may seek to have the greatest number of children who reproduce to subsequent generations—which evolutionarily speaking is the only important outcome—by having as many children by as many different women as possible. In a reproductive sense, it is a waste of his time to stay with one woman and one set of children; if he leaves them they will probably survive somehow and he can spend his valuable reproductive time trying to impregnate somebody else. A woman, however, is more likely to have viable offspring if she can convince the man to stay and provide support for her and the family they create. In that case her children will survive, thrive, and eventually themselves reproduce her genes.

Another, related behavioral difference is found in the ways in which men and women approach sexual jealousy. In one study, for example, men and women were asked to respond to the following vignette (Buss, Larsen, Westen & Semmelroth, 1992):

Please think of a serious committed relationship that you have had in the past, that you currently have, or that you would like to have. Imagine that the person with whom you've become seriously involved became interested in someone else. What would distress or upset you more: (Circle only one)
(a) Imagining your partner forming a deep emotional attachment to that person, or
(b) Imagining your partner enjoying passionate sexual intercourse with that person?"

In this study, 60 percent of males chose option (b), whereas 82 percent of females chose option (a). In a follow-up study, the final question was changed slightly:

What would upset you more:
(a) Imagining your partner trying different sexual positions with that other person, or
(b) Imagining your partner falling in love with that other person?"

Here, 45 percent of males chose (a), whereas only 12 percent of females chose (a). In other words, option (b) was chosen by 55 percent of males, and by 88 percent of females. Notice that this question does not produce a complete reversal between the sexes; most members of each sex find their partner falling in love with someone else more threatening than their partner having intercourse with another person. But this difference is much stronger among women than it is among men.

Why is this? Evolutionarily speaking, a man's greatest worry—especially for a man who has decided to stay with one woman and support her family—is that he might not really be the biological father of the children he is supporting. This makes sexual infidelity in his mate his greatest worry and her greatest sin, from a biological point of view. For a woman, however, the greatest worry is that the development of an emotional bond between her mate and some other woman will cause the support of her and her children to be withdrawn or, almost as bad, that her mate will share resources that would otherwise belong only to her and her children with some other woman and *her* children. This makes emotional infidelity a greater threat than mere sexual infidelity, from the woman's biological point of view.

A related evolutionary logic can even be used to explain some seeming paradoxes or exceptions to these general tendencies. For example, why do some women seem to seek out men who are obviously unstable? Consider the situation described by the typical country-western song. Some women prefer to mate with men who may be highly attractive physically (and/or own motorcycles) even when such men have no intention of forming a serious relationship, and are just "roaming around." I have no idea how common this situation is, but from an evolutionary standpoint it should *never* happen, right?

Wrong. The theory is rescued here by what has been called the "sexy son" hypothesis" (Gangestad, 1989). This hypothesis proposes that some women follow a different reproductive strategy from most of their sisters (Gangestad & Simpson, 1990). Instead of seeking to maximize the reproductive viability of their offspring by mating with a stable (but perhaps unexciting) male, they instead choose to take their chances with an unstable but attractive one. The theory is that if they produce a boy, even if the father then leaves, the son will be just like dad. When he grows up, this "sexy son" will himself spread numerous children (who of course will also be the woman's grandchildren) across the landscape, in the same ruthless and irresponsible manner as his father.

Objections and Responses

I can just imagine some readers seething as they read the preceding section. Indeed, many objections have been raised to sociobiology and the evolutionary approach to the explanation of human behavior in general, and of sex differences in mating behavior in particular. These theories seem particularly interesting to some, but are particularly objectionable to others. At least five objections to this approach can be identified.

METHODOLOGY

The first objection concerns scientific methodology. It may be interesting to speculate "backward" in the way that evolutionary theorists do, by wondering about what in the past might have produced a behavioral pattern we see today. But how can such speculations be put to empirical test? What sort of experiment could one do, for example, to see whether men seek multiple sexual partners in order to maximize their genetic propogation?

Evolutionary theorists usually acknowledge that this is a fair criticism, up to a point, but they do have a response: Whole, complex theories in science are seldom subjected to one crucial, "up or down" study; instead, bits and pieces of these theories are tested as methods to do so become available. Similarly, complex evolutionary theories of behavior may be difficult to prove or disprove in their entirety, but empirical research *can* be designed to address various parts of them. For example, the evolutionary theory of sex differences implies that males in general should be older than their sexual partners across all cultures, because the evolutionary hypothesis is that this difference is a biological and not a cultural product (Kenrick & Keefe, 1992). In the cultures examined by researchers so far (which have included India, the United States, and many others) the hypothesis seems to have been supported. This finding constitutes some encouraging empirical data, even if it does not prove that the reproductive motives described by evolutionary theory are the cause of the age differences.

REPRODUCTIVE INSTINCT

A second objection is that there is something strange about assuming that everybody wants as many children as possible in an age where many people practice birth control and abortion to limit their own reproduction. The response to this objection is that for evolutionary theorizing about behavior to be correct, it is not necessary for people to be *consciously* trying to do what the theory says they are *really* trying to do (Wakefield, 1989). All that is required is for people in the past who followed a behavioral pattern to have left more children in the present generation than did people who did not follow the pattern (Dawkins, 1976).

Thus, although you might or might not want children, and you might even practice birth control, it cannot be denied that you would not be here unless *somebody* (your ancestors) had children. (Sterility does not run in anyone's family.) The same tendencies (e.g., sexual urges) that caused them to reproduce offspring are also present in you. Thus your sexual urges are based on a reproductive instinct, even though you might not consciously wish to reproduce. After all, your sexual urges *do* increase your chances of reproducing (birth control methods can sometimes fail). In general, according to evolutionary theory, people have a tendency to do what they do because of the effect similar behavior in past generations has had on reproductive outcomes, not because they necessarily intend to reproduce in any conscious sense.

HUMAN FLEXIBILITY

A third, related objection is that evolutionary accounts seem to describe a lot of complex behavior as genetically programmed into the brain, whereas a general lesson of psychology is that humans are extraordinary flexible creatures with a minimum of instinctive behavior patterns, compared with other species. Indeed, we saw in Chapter 8 that the neomammalian brain, the outer cortex that is unique to humans, has the function of planning and thinking in ways that go beyond fixed action patterns and other simple responses. Yet evolutionary accounts such as that of sex differences seem to come close to postulating built-in patterns of behavior that cannot be overcome by conscious, rational thought.

Evolutionary theorists seem fairly untroubled by this criticism, and point to the evidence we have already reviewed that genetics seems to be relevant to, although not responsible for, all sorts of complex behavioral patterns. Nevertheless, I must confess I personally find this particular criticism rather telling. The human behavioral repertoire is amazingly complex, and all of it is learned in interactions with the physical and social environment beginning at birth (Funder, 1991). The postulation of strong effects of brain biology on behavior, effects that arise independently of the environment in which a child is raised, seems unlikely to be valid given what we know about the causation of behavior otherwise.

For their part, evolutionary theorists would probably respond that this is not how it works. The history of the species, and the differences between those of our ancestors who survived and the potential ancestors who did not, create the human organisms you see today. And among their attributes are two hands, ten fingers, and a whole variety of behaviors that those humans are more and less likely to perform.

CONSERVATISM

A fourth criticism of the evolutionary approach to behavior is that it seems to embody a certain conservative bias (Alper, Beckwith, & Miller, 1978; Kircher, 1985). It tends to assume that whatever exists in human behavior today must be here because of the past environments experienced by the species, and that whatever exists is rooted in our biology. These assumptions imply that the current behavioral order was not only inevitable, but it is probably also unchangeable. This conservative implication annoys some people who think the male mating behavior described above is rather reprehensible (they are correct, of course), and others who think that human tendencies toward aggression, for example, must and can be changed.

This criticism disturbs many academics, who tend to be politically liberal. Evolutionary theorists do not seem particularly troubled by this criticism, however; they maintain that political objections are irrelevant from a scientific standpoint (see the discussion of research ethics in Chapter 3). As the evolutionary theorist Daniel Dennett has said, "evolutionary psychologists are absolutely not concerned with the moral justification or condemnation of particular features of the human psyche. They're just concerned with their existence" (Flint, 1995).

TELEOLOGICAL FALLACY

A final criticism of the evolutionary approach is more complex. The criticism asserts that evolutionary theorizing commits the **teleological fallacy**, which is the assumption that everything that exists today exists *because of its effects* (Maryanski & Turner, 1992). This assumption, which is sometimes referred to less pejoratively as "functionalism," was popular in nineteenth-century social science. It led theorists of that day to note that, for example, the existence of wealthy people means that large amounts of capital are under particular individuals' control, which makes large-scale investment possible. The functionalist conclusion: wealthy people exist because of their necessary role in investment (which implies, in turn, that wealthy people are necessary and even inevitable). Or, because the growth of cities allows large numbers of people to communicate rapidly with one another because of their close proximity, the functionalists would conclude that cities arose in order to facilitate rapid communication.

By the early twentieth century functionalism had been thoroughly discredited as a tool of social science (Maryanski & Turner, 1992). The short explanation for this is that social scientists became aware of the law of unintended consequences: events tend to have consequences that could not possibly have been foreseen, therefore such consequences could not have been the reason why these events occurred. When certain people become wealthy it is because they have the skills (and often the ruthlessness) required to accumulate wealth; they do not become wealthy in order to promote investment. Cities arise because of geographical features, trade routes, and so on; nobody decided to build Chicago because of the possibility of rapid intracity communication. Investment and communication are simply byproducts.

Maryanski and Turner argue that the same fallacy is commonly committed today in evolutionary theorizing. The example they focus on is the evolution of language. Theorists have put a great deal of effort into explaining how the development of language gave early humans reproductive advantages that explain why language exists in our species today. Maryanski and Turner challenge this theory and propose instead that the early humanoid brain was forced to solve complex problems of spatial and social relations and developed to such a degree that its propensity to language was just an accidental byproduct. Any brain of a certain complexity is likely to develop language, they argue, but that does not mean that the brain developed its complexity *in order* to develop language. Of course, Maryanski and Turner's conjecture is not proven either, but just by making their argument they point out that it is not safe to assume that any phenomenon exists *because of* the effects it produces.

The same reasoning could be applied to the sex differences in mating behavior. The usual evolutionary explanation of the behavioral differences between men and women is that they were phylogenetically crucial for the reproductive fitness of each sex. Another possibility is that the sex differences in behavior—to the extent they exist and are biologically based—might be accidental byproducts of other, more evolutionarily important facts. For example, perhaps they arise because men are generally larger and stronger than women, or because anatomical differences make it easier for a man to rape a woman than vice versa.[3] Again, there is no way to test this kind of conjecture, but it is probably sufficient—and is also extremely useful—to realize that just because a plausible theory can be constructed about how a behavioral pattern may have been evolutionarily adaptive, it does *not* necessarily follow that evolutionary needs forced the behavioral pattern (see Kircher, 1985). If research is ever able to prove that a behavioral pattern—such as sex differences—was *not* evolutionarily significant in its own right, that it was not inevitable after all, then we might be encouraged to turn our research toward ways to change such behaviors.

WILL BIOLOGY REPLACE PSYCHOLOGY?

In the past two chapters we have reviewed the implications for personality of four different areas of biology: anatomy, physiology, genetics, and evolution. Each of these areas had a lot to say about personality. Indeed, each can be taken to imply that personality is biologically based. This implication was anticipated by Gordon Allport's classic definition of personality, which predated by many years nearly all the research just surveyed. Allport wrote that personality is "the dynamic organization within the individual of those *psychophysical systems* that determine his [or her] characteristic behavior or thought" (originally offered in 1937; also in 1961, p. 18; emphasis added).

---

[3]When Freud explained sex differences by saying "anatomy is destiny," it is this kind of influence, not evolutionary history, he seems to have had in mind.

The rapid progress made by biological approaches to psychology in recent years has led some observers to speculate that, as an independent field of study, psychology is doomed. Because personality is a "psychophysical" system, once everything is known about brain structure and physiology, there will be nothing left for psychology to do! This point of view is called "biological reductionism"—in the final analysis, everything about the mind is reduced to biology.

Obviously your author has a vested interest in this issue, but nevertheless I will state that I do not think biology is going to replace psychology. It certainly will not do so soon. As we have seen, there are too many huge gaps in our knowledge about the functioning of the nervous system to use it to replace the other approaches to human personality—yet.

But what about the future? I don't think so, and the reason is fundamental. Biological approaches to psychology, by themselves, generally tell us much more about biology than about psychology. This biology is extremely interesting, but it does not provide a description of how people act in their daily social environments, or of the important consistencies that can be found in their behavior (topics that were considered in Part 2 of this book). A purely biological approach to psychology will never describe what psychological conflict feels like, or how such conflict might be revealed through accidental behavior, or what it means to face one's existential anxiety (topics to be considered in Parts 4 and 5 of this book). Nor does a purely biological approach address how an individual's environment can determine what he or she does, nor does it explain how an individual interprets his or her environment or plans a strategy for success (topics to be considered in Part 6 of this book). It cannot even say much about what is on your mind at this moment.

For example, the evolutionary process as it has affected males has given them a biological mechanism that makes them tend to be unfaithful to their mates (according to one theory). But what happens inside the male's head at the moment he is being unfaithful? What does he perceive, think, feel, and, above all, want? Evolutionary psychology not only fails to answer this question, it fails to ask it. Similarly, the other biological approaches describe how brain structures, neurochemicals, or genes affect behavior, without considering the psychological processes that lie between the brain, neurochemicals, or genes on the one hand, and behavior on the other.

One theme of this book is that the different approaches to personality are not different answers to the same question, but different questions. Thus there is little danger of any one of them completely taking over—not even the biological approach. The biological approach to personality is important and is becoming more so all the time. But it will never supersede all the other approaches by showing how behavior is "really" caused by biological mechanisms. The greatest promise of the biological approach lies elsewhere, in the way it can sometimes explain how biology interacts with social processes to determine what people do.

PUTTING IT ALL TOGETHER: SEXUAL ORIENTATION

Consider sexual orientation, for example. What causes a person to become heterosexual, homosexual, or bisexual? A novel theory by the psychologist Daryl Bem has recently shown how anatomical, neurochemical, evolutionary, and genetic perspectives can be combined with social psychology and even sociology to explain the processes that determine this interesting and important psychological outcome (Bem, 1996).

At the outset, Bem observes that the right question to ask is not, what is the cause of homosexuality? but rather, what directs sexual orientation in general? Bem shares this point of view with Freud, who said that homosexuality and heterosexuality were equally difficult to understand, and who also speculated that the same basic processes might underlie both (Freud, 1962/1905). So Bem's theory tries to account for the development of *all* varieties of sexual orientation. The theory is outlined in Figure 9.1.

First, biological influences such as genes and prenatal hormones produce children with particular childhood personalities (Bem calls them "temperaments"); some children are aggressive and active, while others are more quietly sociable. These temperaments interact with the structure of childhood society, which strongly segregates boy and girl playgroups beginning at about age five. A boy who enjoys rough-and-tumble play will fit in well with groups of other boys. A boy who for reasons of his temperament does not enjoy these activities, however, may seek out the company of girls. So the first boy will grow up around other boys; the second boy will grow up around girls. As a result, the first boy will come to see girls—with whom he has little experience in childhood—as relatively unfamiliar and "exotic" (to use Bem's term). The second boy will come to see other *boys*—with whom he may have as little experience—as exotic.

At this point psychological mechanisms that are common to all members of the human species come into play. People are physically aroused by novel stimuli; when one sees something unusual or strange, one's heartbeat increases and one's blood pressure rises. But people interpret what their arousal *means* based upon the environmental context and who and what is present in it. For example, one classic study showed that men who were aroused by standing on a high, swaying bridge apparently came to believe they were sexually attracted to a woman standing on the bridge with them (Dutton & Aron, 1974)!

These processes lead the boy who grew up around other boys to be aroused, later in life, by the novelty of the presence of girls and, as he enters puberty, to label this arousal as sexual attraction. But the boy who grew up around girls is aroused by the novelty of the presence of boys, and through a parallel path comes to label this arousal as sexual attraction. Now you can see why Bem calls this theory "Exotic becomes erotic." People who belong to the group (male or fe-

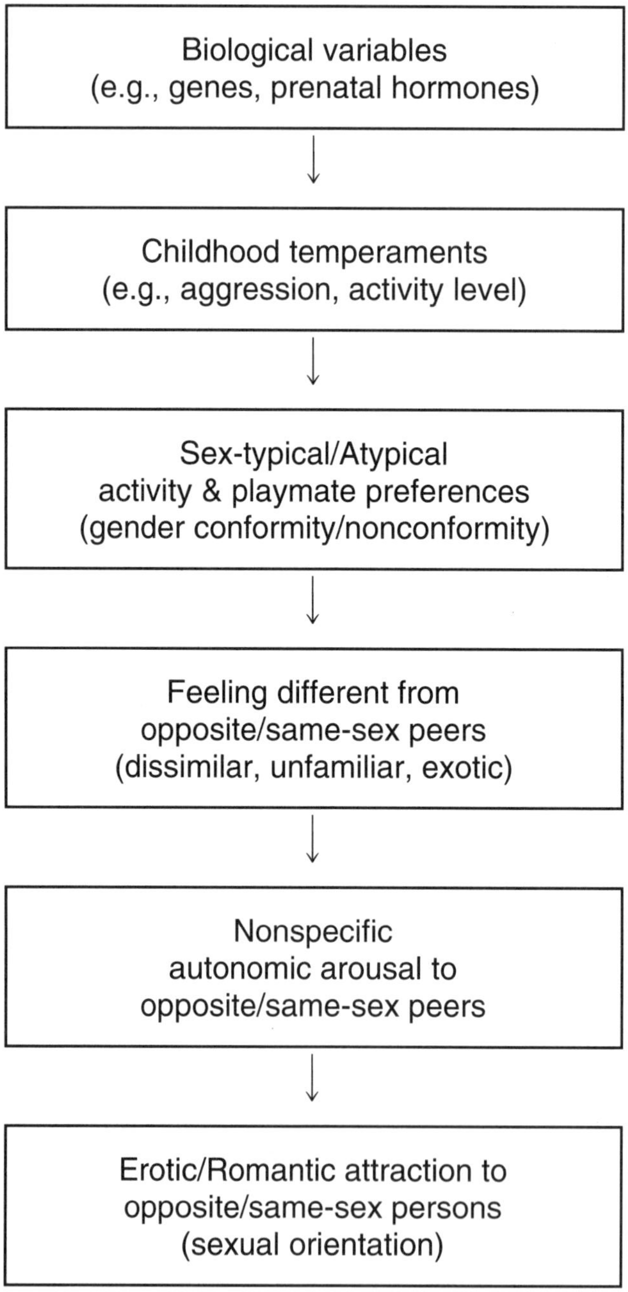

Biological variables
(e.g., genes, prenatal hormones)

↓

Childhood temperaments
(e.g., aggression, activity level)

↓

Sex-typical/Atypical
activity & playmate preferences
(gender conformity/nonconformity)

↓

Feeling different from
opposite/same-sex peers
(dissimilar, unfamiliar, exotic)

↓

Nonspecific
autonomic arousal to
opposite/same-sex peers

↓

Erotic/Romantic attraction to
opposite/same-sex persons
(sexual orientation)

FIGURE 9.1 BEM'S "EXOTIC BECOMES EROTIC" THEORY OF SEXUAL ORIENTATION This figure describes the sequence of events over the course of development that produce the sexual orientation of most men and women in a culture that accentuates sex differences and segregates the sexes during much of childhood.

male) seen as exotic become seen as erotically stimulating, too. For most people, the exotic sex is the opposite one; for a substantial minority, the reverse is the case.

Notice that Bem's theory has several components, some of which are biological and others of which are social and even sociological. All four of the biological approaches we have considered in this chapter and in the preceding chapter are included at least briefly. Bem assumes that hormones and the anatomical structure of the brain produce basic patterns of behavior concerning energy level, activity preferences, and so on. At another level of analysis, he assumes that these basic patterns of behavior are heritable. And he also assumes that there are some psychological mechanisms that everybody shares, that are "built in" as the result of evolution—specifically, the mechanisms that cause arousal in response to novel stimuli and that cause arousal to be interpreted according to the situation. The truly novel aspect of Bem's theory is the way he puts all these components together and integrates them with the experiences of a child who is growing up in the usual cultural context.

The evidence for Bem's theory is reasonably good. For example, 63 percent of homosexual men report not having enjoyed typical "boy" activities in childhood, while only 10 percent of heterosexual men make the same report. The trend for women is almost as strong. Among lesbian women, 63 percent report not having enjoyed typical "girl" activities in childhood, while this is true of only 15 percent of heterosexual women. Parallel trends are found among many other variables that, according to Bem's theory, ought to be precursors of sexual orientation.

These figures are consistent with the theory, but they do not *prove* it, and the same is true about the rest of the evidence Bem cites. A complete test of his model would require a longitudinal study that followed a sample of boy and girl children with varying temperaments, activity preferences, and playmate groups from childhood to adulthood, and tracked their sexual orientation as it developed. Such a study would be difficult to carry out and is not likely to be available any time soon. Moreover, a complete proof of a theory this complex is probably not possible.

But for present purposes, the proof or disproof of Bem's theory of sexual orientation is not really the issue. The most important aspect of Bem's theory may be the way it shows what a biologically informed theory of personality should look like—but almost never does. Notice how many different kinds of elements interact: The child begins with genes and hormones, which produce personality styles, which interact with the structure of society and the formation of childhood groups, which leads to certain feelings about members of the same and opposite sexes, which become eroticized through a universal emotional mechanism, which produces the sexual orientation of the adult. Wow!

Biological approaches to personality have come a long way. Their further progress will come from showing how biological influences interact with behavioral styles, social interaction, and the structure of society to produce the people we become. This could and should be done with many important personality outcomes, not just sexual orientation. Bem has shown us a way to do it.

SUMMARY

Behavioral genetics and evolutionary biology both concern how personality might be inherited from one's parents and ancestors. Behavioral genetics addresses individual differences in behavioral traits and examines how parents transmit traits to their children and how biological relatives tend to be psychologically similar. Many personality traits are heritable in this sense, but this finding does not mean that personality is genetically determined. The environment remains critically important. Evolutionary biology explains patterns of behavior that are characteristic of the entire species, such as aggression, altruism, and mating, as being those that have been useful for reproductive success as the human species evolved. Some of these explanations are controversial. But research on evolutionary biology and behavioral genetics does imply that biology and genetic inheritance are involved in the determination of human personality. Biology will never take over the functions of other areas of personality research and theory. As exemplified by Bem's theory of the development of sexual orientation, the promise of the biological approaches comes from their potential to illuminate the interactions between biological, personality, social, and sociological influences on behavior.

SUGGESTED READINGS:
BIOLOGICAL APPROACHES

Zuckerman, M. (1991). *Psychobiology of personality*. Cambridge, England: Cambridge University Press.

> *An impressively thorough and up-to-date summary of nearly everything biological research can contribute to the study of personality. The book is not easy reading, but it is worth the effort. The book includes the author's own synthesis.*

Valenstein, E. S. (1973). *Brain control*. New York: Wiley.

Valenstein, E. S. (1986). *Great and desperate cures: The rise and decline of psychosurgery and other radical treatments for mental illness*. New York: Basic Books.

> *These two books are lively histories of psychosurgery, electroshock therapy, and other drastic, biologically based "psychotherapeutic" interventions that have been tried over the years. Along the way, much is taught about both biology and about the sociology of psychology and medicine.*

Plomin, R., Chipuer, H. M., & Loehlin, J. C. (1990). Behavioral genetics and personality. In L. Pervin (Ed.), *Handbook of personality: Theory and research* (pp. 225–243). New York: Guilford.

> *A good summary of how behavioral genetics research is performed and what its principal findings are.*

Wilson, E. O. (1975). *Sociobiology: The new synthesis*. Cambridge, MA: Harvard University Press.

> *The book that sparked the revival of interest in using evolutionary theory to explain human behavior.*

Buss, D. M. (1994). *The evolution of desire: Strategies of human mating*. New York: Basic Books.

> *A clearly written and engaging tour of that ever-popular topic, sex, from the viewpoint of evolutionary psychology. Includes a good summary of the author's controversial ideas about the different approaches of men and women to mating.*

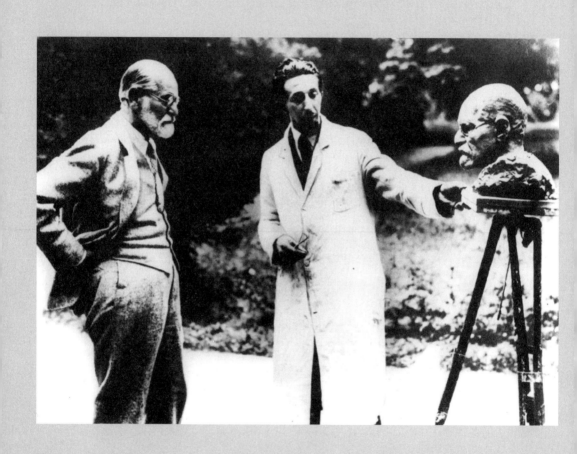

PART IV

The Hidden World of the Mind: The Psychoanalytic Approach

The following dispatch was transmitted by the Associated Press on March 12, 1992. I have changed only the name of the protagonist of this story—I am sure he has suffered enough.

ST. LOUIS—The city's prosecutor, who has crusaded against prostitution and pornography, was charged Thursday with soliciting a prostitute.

Circuit Attorney John Smith was charged with soliciting an undercover police officer at the St. Louis Airport Marriott Hotel on Tuesday night, said St. Louis County Prosecutor Robert McCulloch. . . .

Smith, 49, at first denied the charge, but on Thursday apologized and said he was "ready for any consequences." . . . But he added he wouldn't step down from the office he's held since 1979.

Smith has been a crusader against pornography, and a strong supporter of sting operations to crack down on prostitution in the city. He led a recent crackdown on the rental of pornographic movies at video stores.

Last June, the Board of Aldermen adopted mandatory jail terms for prostitutes, pimps and customers on a second conviction. Smith said then that the measure would make the customers of prostitutes "scared to death."

The seeming paradox of a case like this makes one ask, how could this happen? How could someone who is a loud and public opponent of pornography and prostitution, and a professional prosecutor of both, turn out to be a customer of prostitutes himself? This is not just an isolated case, either. You can probably recall reading in the news about various evangelical preachers and sanctimonious politicians who turned out to be regular practitioners of exactly the same vices they made careers of denouncing. There seem to be new and similar instances all the time. They beg to be explained, and providing such explanations would seem to be a natural job for a psychologist.

It might surprise you, therefore, to learn that most approaches to personality psychology have little or nothing to say when confronted by strange and paradoxical cases like these. For example, more than fifty years ago, the psychologist Henry Murray issued a complaint about the trait approach, which we reviewed in Chapters 4 through 7:

... trait psychology is over-concerned with recurrences, with consistency, with what is clearly manifested (the surface of personality), with what is conscious, ordered, and rational.... It stops short at the point precisely where a psychology is needed, the point at which it begins to be difficult to understand what is going on (Murray, 1938, p. 715).

This same complaint applies just as much, if not more so, to the rest of psychology.

There is one one approach, however, that *has* taken up the challenge of explaining what is going on when what is going on is difficult to understand. The approach is psychoanalysis, and it is based on the writings of Sigmund Freud. Psychoanalysis is more than just "Freudian" psychology, however; Freud changed his mind about many points over the course of his career, and his ideas have been translated, interpreted, and extended by many other psychologists for nearly a century. The key concern of the psychoanalytic approach is the part of the mind that is hidden from view and, in some cases, seemingly irrational, contradictory, or absurd.

The next four chapters describe the psychoanalytic approach to the study of personality. Chapter 10 provides a general introduction to Freud and to psychoanalytic thought, Chapter 11 describes the structure and development of the mind, and Chapter 12 describes defense mechanisms, parapraxes (slips), and humor. Finally, Chapter 13 brings psychoanalysis into the present day by surveying the work of some of the latter-day "neoFreudians," as well as some relatively recent empirical research that is relevant to a psychodynamic account of personality.

CHAPTER  10

INTRODUCTION TO THE PSYCHOANALYTIC APPROACH

The psychoanalytic approach offers an extraordinarily complex view of personality, but one of its primary attractions is that all of its complexity is built upon a relatively small number of key ideas. The four ideas that make up the foundation of psychoanalysis are psychic determinism, internal structure, mental energy, and psychic conflict.

PSYCHIC DETERMINISM

First and probably most fundamental to the psychoanalytic approach is the assumption of **psychic determinism** (Brenner, 1974). Determinism, a basic tenet of science, is the idea that everything that happens has a cause that can be identified by someone diligent and clever enough. The *psychic* determinism at the root of the psychoanalytic approach is the assumption that everything that happens in a person's mind, and therefore everything that a person does, also has a specific cause that can, in principle, be identified.

This means that psychoanalysis has no room for accidents, miracles, or free will. If it did, the entire approach would be stalled at the starting line. The key faith (and that is really what it is—faith) of a psychoanalyst is that even something as bizarre as the behavior of a prostitute-patronizing city prosecutor can be explained, if one uses enough diligence and insight.

The nondeterministic alternative would be to say something like, "he just decided to get a prostitute of his own free will, despite what he said," or "he's just inconsistent." Those statements might be true, but you would never hear either one from a psychoanalyst. Only slightly better, from a psychoanalytic point of view, would be the observation that "this prosecutor is just a typical hypocritical politician doing what is popular in order to get elected, but doing whatever he wants to on the side." This explanation also might be true, but would still beg the question of why, given the number of law enforcement issues that a prosecutor might exploit, did this particular prosecutor select prostitution instead of, say, home burglary. There *must* be a reason, and psychoanalysts would argue that the reason is rooted somewhere in the structure and dynamics of the prosecutor's personality. The only trick is to find it.

From a psychoanalytic perspective, all seeming contradictions of mind and behavior can be resolved; nothing is ever really accidental. There is a reason why you preached one way and acted another; there is also a reason you forgot that name, dropped that dish, or said a word you did not intend to say. The purpose of psychoanalysis is to do the deep digging usually required to figure out what those reasons are. Usually, the reason lies in the unconscious and hidden processes of the mind. The assumption of psychic determinism, therefore, leads directly to the conclusion that many of the important things that go on in the mind are **unconscious**.[1]

INTERNAL STRUCTURE

A second key assumption of psychoanalysis is that the mind has an internal structure. It is important to remember the distinction between the mind and the brain: the brain is a physical organ, whereas the mind is the psychological *result* of what the brain (and the rest of the body) does. The mind is divided into three parts that will probably sound familiar to you. They are usually given the Latinized labels **id**, **ego**, and **superego**. These terms pertain to the irrational and emotional part of the mind, the rational part of the mind, and the moral part of the mind, respectively.[2]

MENTAL ENERGY

A third key assumption of the psychoanalytic approach is that the psychological apparatus of the mind needs some kind of energy to make it go. This special

---

[1]Freud believed that the assumption of determinism led so directly and necessarily to the postulation of unconscious mental processes that to assume the first (determinism) was to assume the second (the unconscious). That is why, following Freud, I do not treat the postulation of the unconscious as a fifth and separate foundation of psychoanalytic thought.

[2]Bruno Bettelheim (1982) argues that these terms mistranslate the labels Freud used in his original German, but because of the wide use of these terms today, it is probably too late to correct that mistake here. For what it's worth, Bettelheim's preferred translations for id, ego, and superego are the It, the I, and the Over-I.

kind of energy is sometimes called **psychic energy**, or **libido**. The import of this metaphor is that at any moment the mind has a finite amount of psychic energy available to it. Therefore, energy powering one part of the apparatus is not available to make the other parts go; energy that your mind spends doing one thing (such as pushing uncomfortable ideas out of memory) is unavailable for other purposes (such as having new and creative ideas). The principle of the conservation of energy applies to the mind as it does to the physical world. One purpose of psychoanalysis, from the client's perspective, is to free up more psychic energy for the challenges of daily living, by removing the neurotic energy drains one by one.

PSYCHIC CONFLICT

The fourth assumption of the psychoanalytic approach is that because the mind is divided into distinct structural parts, it can be in conflict with itself. This is a truly distinctive insight of this approach; **psychic conflict** is nowhere to be found in any of the others. Psychoanalysts believe that your ego can want one thing, your superego another thing, and your id a third thing. Maybe your id wants ice cream. Your superego thinks you do not deserve it because you have not studied all week. It might fall to your ego to make a compromise: you get to have an ice cream, *after* you have finished this chapter. The idea of psychic conflict might also explain why a prosecutor might choose to patronize a prostitute. In this case his id seems to have won out, at least temporarily, over his superego.

UNIQUE ASPECTS OF PSYCHOANALYTIC THEORY

Psychoanalytic theory offers a view of human nature that is unusual, challenging, surprising, and to some people even offensive. Several aspects of the psychoanalytic approach are unique.

Controversy

From its inception the psychoanalytic approach, more than any of the other approaches to personality psychology, has stirred controversy and has been seen by some as dangerous. The insults flung at psychoanalysis by its critics have changed with the times. The Victorians, looking at Freud's emphasis on sex and sexual energy as an important underpinning of all behavior, complained that his theory was "dirty." More enlightened folk in the 1990s have looked at Freud's emphasis on that which cannot be seen and cannot be conclusively proven, and complained that his theory is "unscientific." The bases of the criticisms seem to change but in every age, it seems, a lot of people just don't like Freud's theory.

Freud anticipated this and sometimes even seemed to revel in it. He pointed out that Copernicus became unpopular for pointing out that the earth is not the center of the universe and that Darwin was derided for showing that humans are just another species in the animal kingdom. His own insights that human nature is largely hidden from view and that the motivations that drive many of our behaviors are base and irrational were not ideas he expected would win him any popularity contests, and he was right. Psychoanalytic theory bothers a great number of people.

Let's bring this down to a personal level. Before launching into an exposition of the psychoanalytic approach, consider two cautionary tales. They both exemplify the discomfort that psychoanalytic insights can cause, and the dangers of providing them unsolicited.

The first takes us way, way back to the time when I decided to major in psychology. I broke the news to my family in the traditional fashion. Returning home from college for Thanksgiving break, I waited for the inevitable question: "Have you decided on a major yet?" "Psychology," I replied. As many others making this choice have discovered, my family was not exactly thrilled by the news. After a stunned silence, my sister spoke first. "OK," she said, "but so help me, if you ever psych me out, I will *never* speak to you again!"

Her comment is more pertinent than you might think. Learning about personality psychology, and particularly the psychoanalytic approach, can make irresistible the urge to analyze the behavior and thoughts of those around us. It's all part of the fun. The advice you should take from my sister's warning, however, is to keep the fun private. People are typically *not* grateful to be analyzed. Sharing your insights into why your friends "really" did something can be the start of real trouble. This is true even if your insights are completely accurate—Freud thought this was true *especially* when one's insights are accurate.

My second tale is a specific example concerning psychoanalysis. When I get to the part of my courses in which I teach about Freud, I try to do so as an advocate. I make the best, most convincing case for psychoanalytic theory that I can. Who knows what effect this sales job has on my students, but one person I never fail to convince is myself. Thus for a few weeks each academic year, I turn into a raving Freudian. One side effect of this is that I become temporarily unable to avoid analyzing every slip, mistake, and accident I see.

I did this once, several years ago, while on a date. In the course of a casual conversation, my dinner companion related something she had forgotten to do that day. Being deep in the Freudian phase of my syllabus, I immediately offered a complex—and I thought convincing—interpretation of the unconscious anxieties and conflicts that probably caused her memory lapse. My perception was not well received, however. My date vehemently replied that my interpretation was ridiculous and that in the future I could keep my absurd Freudianisms to myself. Gesturing for emphasis, she knocked a glass of ice water into my lap. Picking up the ice cubes, but still in a Freudian frame of mind, all I could do was acknowledge the vivid, symbolic nature of the warning I had received.[3]

The moral of these two stories is the same: Keep your clever analyses of other people to yourself! If you are wrong, and especially if you are right, it will make them mad. It is a little like what they say at stunt demonstrations: "We are trained professionals. Do not try this at home."

Distinct from Other Approaches

The psychoanalytic approach assumes that everything you think and do has an identifiable cause. It further assumes that this cause usually is located in your mind, not in the external world, and that it often is hidden from you, as well. Psychoanalysts tend to believe that overt behavior and even conscious thinking are unimportant in themselves; behavior and thought serve only as clues to what is actually going on in the hidden recesses of the mind. You will find many psychoanalysts surprisingly uninterested in what you do, and even in what you think you think. Their job, they believe, is to get beyond all that.

This belief is just one way in which the psychoanalytic approach is fundamentally different from all the other approaches to personality. Instead of locating the psychological "action" in the interplay between behavior, the environment, and conscious thought—like most of the other approaches try to do— the psychoanalytic approach sees the real action as being *all in the mind*. While other approaches tend to neglect mental life and the unconscious, the psychoanalytic approach focuses on it almost to the exclusion of everything else.

Another big difference is that several of the other approaches are based upon rigorous, controlled, and rather narrow experiments, sometimes performed on animals. The psychoanalytic approach, by contrast, is based originally on the verbal meanderings of upper-middle-class European neurotics around the turn of the century, as filtered through the mind of (and informed by the introspections of) one the few bona fide geniuses of the twentieth century. Even to the present day, the "database" of psychoanalysis consists largely of therapists' experiences with their clients and their own introspections. Controlled research is rare in this approach. Moreover, when somebody does try to do rigorous research on psychoanalytic theory, other psychoanalysts often treat it as having missed the point. (More will be said about this in Chapter 13.)

Another, related attribute of the psychoanalytic approach is its heavy emphasis on practical application (although Freud himself became less interested in that aspect over the years). Most psychoanalysts are practicing psychothera-

---

[3]We eventually married each other, anyway.

pists who see clients every day and thereby earn their living (no small point). This experience gives them a pragmatic approach. Like most medical practitioners, they tend to rely on their own experience more than on what they read, and find case studies more convincing than controlled science. This orientation may arise because to a practitioner in the "trenches," dealing with real patients with urgent problems, the results of controlled science often seem artificial and rather divorced from reality.

It is not a coincidence, I suspect, that most psychoanalysts are so indifferent to the usual canons of science *and* that so many of them are MDs. (The American tradition, unlike that in Europe, is for psychoanalysts to be medical doctors, even though Freud himself objected that medical training is irrelevant to psychoanalytic practice.) As was discussed in Chapter 3, medical training is more technical than scientific; it emphasizes the application rather than the discovery of knowledge. Some psychoanalysts, trained in this tradition, seem more comfortable applying what they have been taught than questioning or extending it.

Finally, the most distinctive attribute of the psychoanalytic approach to personality is that it focuses on behaviors and thoughts that are *irrational*—i.e., that do not follow the normal dictates of logic. Murray's complaint, quoted in the introduction to Part 4 of this book, was apt. Every other approach, it seems, makes a basic if usually unstated assumption that human thought follows paths that are basically logical, and that the task of psychology is to understand and to make explicit that logic. The psychoanalytic approach, in contrast, explicitly acknowledges that the mind works by a fundamentally different "psycho-logic," much of which operates outside of conscious awareness. The fundamental task of psychoanalysis is to decode this psycho-logic—to make sense of the strange and irrational activities of our minds.

A Beautiful Theory

It is important to know something about psychoanalysis for two reasons. The first has to do with the theory itself. Psychoanalytic theory deals with real cases and complex situations and therefore can be vastly more dramatic and colorful than any other approach to psychology. Reading psychoanalytic case studies can be an experience akin to reading a novel. One of the appealing aspects of these case studies is that unlike all the other approaches, the psychoanalytic formulation seems to do the case justice; it never tries to boil the situation down to just a few abstract variables. Psychoanalytic case studies delve deep into details and texture. Other approaches to psychology do not have this knack—they seem to have lost something along the way.

Moreover, Freud's psychoanalytic theory is one of the most amazing theories of anything that anybody has ever developed. Unlike any other psychological theory, psychoanalysis tries to explain infancy, parenting, the causes of war, the workings of memory, the roots of sexuality, the meaning of dreams, the thought processes of psychotics, the practice of psychotherapy, and many other topics. Other theories, if they are very good, might provide a persuasive account of one or at most two of these topics and be justifiably proud. Freud's theory tackles *all* of them.

Moreover, Freud handles all these diverse topics not just by listing his opinion of what is going on with each, but by fitting all of these pieces together. The theory of dreams is connected to the theory of psychotic thought, which is connected to the theory of memory, which is connected to the practice of psychotherapy, and so on. Everything fits with everything else. A theory that is so richly interconnected is sometimes said to be "elegant" or even "beautiful." No matter what else can be said about Freud, his theory is beautiful. No other can touch it.

Psychoanalysis and Western Culture

The second reason why psychoanalysis is important is its influence on Western culture. One index of the widespread popularity of psychoanalysis is its representation in the media. If you find an article about psychology in one of America's tonier magazines, such as the *New Yorker* or the *Atlantic*, it will almost certainly not have anything to do with what most modern research psychologists are doing; it will instead be about Freud or psychoanalysis.

Another reason for the wide influence of psychoanalysis is that a number— uncounted but certainly large—of the most powerful, influential people in this country are currently undergoing psychoanalytic treatment. Psychoanalysis is a widespread therapy in places like Manhattan and Beverly Hills; it is less common in places like Houston and Indianapolis. It is an elite therapy because it is so expensive—it takes a large amount of the therapist's (and the patient's) time, it takes years, and sometimes never ends. It also requires a cooperative and intelligent client. Most of clinical psychology is dominated by behavioristic, drug-based therapies; these alternatives are cheaper to administer and get much better results in the short term. (Psychoanalysts continue to insist that their results are better in the long term, although satisfactory evidence to settle the argument has proved impossible to obtain.)

The influence of psychoanalysis on clinical psychology extends beyond the orthodox Freudian analysts. Psychoanalytic ideas affect the practice of many psychoanalytically inclined therapsts who do not consider themselves true Freudians. And, as will be described later in this chapter, several of Freud's ideas of how psychotherapy should be practiced influence nearly every therapist, including many who think they are *anti*-Freudian. One survey indicated that about 75 percent of today's practicing psychotherapists report relying to some degree on psychoanalytic ideas (Pope, Tabachnick, & Keith-Spiegel, 1987).

An even more important source of the influence of psychoanalysis is the way Freud has made it into the mainstream of our everyday psychological thought in ways we might not always recognize. You might find yourself asking, "what's the *real* reason you did that?" For instance, suppose you give somebody an expensive present. The next time you visit the person, the present is nowhere in sight. "What ever happened to . . . ?" you ask. "Oh," your friend replies nonchalantly, "I broke it and threw it away. An accident." How does this make you feel? If it makes you feel bad (and of course it does), one reason might be that you have made a Freudian interpretation of your friend's behavior—and attitude—without even knowing that you have done so.

Sometimes our everyday thought is even more explicitly Freudian. Have you ever heard somebody hypothesize that "she only goes out with that older guy because he's a father figure," or "he's all messed up because of the way that his parents treated him when he was little," or "he never sees anybody because all his energy goes into programming his computer," or "she's got too much invested in him [psychologically] to walk out now?" These are all basically Freudian analyses.

So, it is probably the case that you already know more psychoanalytic theory than you realize, and you may even use it every day. One result can be that Freud's ideas sometimes might not sound as original as they should. There is an old joke about the person who went to see one of Shakespeare's plays for the first time, but walked out halfway through. "It was boring," he complained, "too full of clichés." Of course, much of Shakespeare *is* full of clichés because so many of his lines ("to be or not to be," for example) have made it into everyday speech. Some of Freud's most original ideas might sound rather mundane after all these years, for the same unfair reason.

FREUD HIMSELF

In this book, I have specifically tried to avoid the trap of writing about theorists instead of about theories—I have never liked the suggestion that psychology consists simply of "what psychologists do." An exception must be made for Freud, though. No other psychological approach is at once so important and influential, and so closely identified with one particular individual. Freud is one of the most interesting and important people to have lived in the past couple of centuries. So let's take a moment and consider Freud and how he developed his ideas.

Sigmund Freud was a medical doctor who practiced in Vienna, Austria, from the 1890s until almost 1940. (He lived from 1856 to 1939.) He was Jewish and had to flee his native country after Hitler came to power in the 1930s; he spent the last years of his life in London. Freud died in a pessimistic frame of mind, convinced that the impending world war, following so closely on the heels of the unbelievably destructive and tragic First World War, proved that humans had an aggressive, destructive urge that in the end would destroy them.

One of Freud's less important yet enduring cultural legacies is our collective, stereotypical image of what a psychotherapist should be like. He had a beard and small eyeglasses. He favored three-piece suits, with a watch chain hanging from the vest. When he spoke English it was, of course, with a Viennese accent. He had a couch in his office. And it was Freud who originated the practice of charging patients for their missed appointments!

Freud began his career as a research neurologist. He went to France for a time to study the newly developing field of hypnosis with Jean-Martin Charcot. He gradually moved into the practice of psychiatry, in part so he could make a living and get married. Then, as now, medical practice paid much better than theoretical research.

In his clinical practice, Freud made a simple but fundamental discovery: When his patients talked about their psychological problems, sometimes that was enough to make them better or even cure them. At first, Freud used hypnosis to get his patients to talk about difficult topics. Later, he turned to the use of free association (instructing the patient to say whatever comes to mind) for the same purpose. One of Freud's grateful patients dubbed the results of such therapy the "talking cure." The talking cure must be seen as Freud's greatest contribution to psychotherapy. By now, it is ubiquitous. A fundamental assumption of nearly every school of psychotherapy—including many whose followers claim they have nothing in common with Freud—is that "talking about it helps."

Freud thought he knew why talking helps. In part, it is because making one's thoughts and fears explicit by saying them out loud brings them out into the light of day where one's conscious, rational mind can better deal with them. (Your crazy thoughts won't make you so crazy once you have had a chance to think them through rationally.) The other reason is that the psychotherapist can provide emotional support during the patient's difficult task of trying to figure out what is going on. In a letter to Carl Jung, Freud wrote that "psychoanalysis is in essence a cure through love" (cited in Bettelheim, 1982). Again, many schools of psychotherapy—including non-Freudian ones—share these two ideas.

Freud attracted numerous disciples whom he encouraged to help him spread the ideas of psychoanalysis. Many of his disciples had strong minds of their own, however, which led to some famous quarrels and splits over the years. Carl Jung and Alfred Adler were the most famous of Freud's followers who eventually split with their mentor (see Chapter 13).

Freud's ideas came from the cases he treated and, even more importantly, from his observations of the workings of his own mind. This is something the psychoanalytic approach has in common with the humanistic approach, which will be considered later in this book. Psychoanalysts and humanists both begin the psychological endeavor with the attempt to know themselves first. (An important part of traditional psychoanalytic training is being psychoanalyzed oneself.) Other psychologists do not attempt to do this; in fact, they seem actively to avoid it. Trait psychologists and behaviorists, for example, stay safely outside of their own minds.

Freud's ideas were certainly influenced by the time and place in which he lived and by the patients he saw. Most were well-to-do women, a surprising number of whom reported having been sexually abused by their fathers when they were young. Freud at first believed them and saw this early abuse as a common source of early-life trauma. Later he changed his mind, however, and decided that these memories of early abuse were fantasies that, for psychological reasons, had come to seem real.[4]

FREUD AND THE ENGLISH DEPARTMENT

Psychoanalysis is still employed by a large number of practicing psychotherapists. As will be discussed in Chapter 13, these range all the way from diehard psychoanalysts who are more orthodox in following Freud's theories than was Freud himself, to those who use psychoanalytic ideas when they seem useful, to those numerous therapists who often use psychoanalytically derived ideas without realizing their ultimate source (Pope et al, 1987).

However, academic research psychologists by and large have shunned Freud for many years. I have been a faculty member in three different psychology departments, and there is only one professor out of all these departments who I even *suspect* of being a Freudian. I am not a Freudian, either, although I am much more sympathetic toward Freudian analysis than many of my colleagues are. Psychoanalysis does not come close to attaining the empirical rigor that most research psychologists value. But, as I mentioned earlier, there may be more to it than that. Freud seems to make many research psychologists anxious, and as any good Freudian would expect, that produces in them a typical defense mechanism, contempt.

Nevertheless, at almost any big university you *will* find several committed Freudians on the faculty—they just won't be in the psychology department. They'll most likely be found in the *English* department![5]

---

[4]Jeffrey Masson (1984) has argued that this latter conclusion was a fundamental mistake, because it led Freud to look increasingly inside the mind, instead of outside at the world, for the causes of his patients' psychological problems.

[5]I am deliberately sidestepping the fact that medical schools, some of which are affiliated with universities, occasionally have Freudian psychoanalysts practicing within their departments of psychiatry. In my experience, university medical schools seldom have much to do with the academic activities elsewhere on campus (often the medical school isn't even on campus), and in particular almost never have any impact on undergraduate education.

This location for the headquarters of academic interest in Freud has always struck me as slightly anomalous. For one thing, although he was fluent Freud rarely wrote in English; almost all of his important writings are in German. For another, it seems strange that so often in any university students of people— i.e., psychologists—turn their backs on Freud, while students of literature focus on him.

But in the end, the interest makes sense. Serious students of literature use psychoanalysis to understand complex texts in the same way that Freud used it to understand complex persons. Psychoanalytic theory provides a way to understand what symbols mean and to decode the underlying themes and meanings. English professors use psychoanalysis to unpack the meaning of texts just as Freud used it to unpack the meaning of lives. In the next chapter we will begin to consider how psychoanalysis works.

SUMMARY

Unlike many other approaches to personality, the psychoanalytic approach concentrates on the cases where the cause of behavior is mysterious and hidden. Psychoanalytic theory is complex, but it is based on a relatively small number of key ideas, including psychic determinism, internal structure, mental energy, and psychic conflict. Of these, probably the most important is the idea of psychic determinism, that everything you think and do has a cause that, in principle, is knowable. Throughout its history psychoanalysis has been controversial, although the nature of the controversy has changed with the times. The theory is truly distinct from the other approaches to personality; it can be regarded as elegant and aesthetically pleasing, and it has had a variety of influences on Western culture. Freud himself was one of the geniuses of the twentieth century. Although psychoanalytically influenced clinical practice is still widespread, academic and scientific psychology has shunned psychoanalysis in recent years. Freud's theory, however, is still an important part of intellectual life on university campuses, most often in the English department.

CHAPTER

STRUCTURE AND DEVELOPMENT

As we saw in Chapter 10, a fundamental tenet of the psychoanalytic approach is the idea of **psychic energy**. The mind is a large and complex apparatus, but without psychic energy, according to this approach, it would be much like a powerful automobile with an empty gas tank—it wouldn't go.

LIFE AND DEATH

The psychic energy that makes our minds "go" comes from two drives, one that impels toward life and the other that impels toward death. Both forces are always present and forever competing. In the end, the death drive always wins.

The life drive is sometimes called **libido**, and is also referred to as the "sexual drive" (which is what "libido" means in ordinary conversation). In psychoanalytic writings by Freud and by those who came later, libido receives a great deal of attention. But I think it is also widely misunderstood, perhaps because so many people are so easily distracted by any reference to sex. In the final analysis, sex is simply life. Sex is necessary for the creation of children (biological interventions aside), and its enjoyment can be an important part of being alive. It is in this sense that libido is a sexual drive—Freud meant that it had to do with the creation, protection, and enjoyment of life, and with creativity, productivity, and growth. This fundamental force exists within every living person, Freud believed, and he called this force libido.[1]

---

[1] Here, as elsewhere, I am interpreting Freud, who said many different things about libido and many other topics. I think this rendition is true to the spirit of what Freud thought was important about libido. I must admit, however, that Freud frequently talked about libido in its literally sexual sense, and several later psychoanalytic thinkers, notably Jung, thought Freud overemphasized sexuality at the expense of a broader interpretation of libido as a life force.

Relatively late in his career, Freud posited a second fundamental drive, that toward death. He called it **Thanatos**. Although he probably did not mean to claim the existence of a "death wish," he held a fundamental belief in the duality of nature, or the idea that everything contains its own opposite. Freud observed not only that people seem to engage in a good deal of destructive activity that does not seem to have a rational basis (wars are a good example), but also that, in the end, everybody does die. It was to account for these facts that he introduced the death drive.

This drive, too, is sometimes misunderstood. Freud probably was not as morbid as his idea of a drive toward death makes him sound. I suspect that Freud really had in mind something like the concept of entropy, the basic force in the universe toward randomness and disorder. Ordered systems tend toward disorder and, according to physics, this trend is inevitable; local, short-term increases in order only result in widespread, long-term increases in disorder. Freud viewed the human mind and life itself in similar terms. We try desperately throughout our lives to make our thoughts and our worlds orderly and to maintain creativity and growth. But the fundamental force of entropy dooms these efforts to failure in the end, although we may have a pretty good ride in the meantime. So, I think Freud's ultimate view of life was far from morbid; it may be better described as tragic.

The opposition of libido and Thanatos derives from another basic idea that arises repeatedly in psychoanalytic thinking; the **doctrine of opposites**. This doctrine states that everything contains its opposite—life must contain death, happiness contains sadness, and so forth. Although this idea may sound a little strange to you at first, the longer you think about it the more reasonable it becomes. Indeed, the doctrine seems to hold true in a surprisingly wide range of contexts.

One application of the doctrine of opposites is the idea that extremes on any dimension tend to be more like each other than either is with the middle. For example, compare the leaders of antipornography censorship campaigns with pornographers. The doctrine of opposites would claim that they have more in common with each other than either does with those in the middle. Pornographers and censorship crusaders share not only extremism, but a certain fascination with pornographic material. Those in the middle, by contrast, may have a distaste for pornography but are not so excited by its existence to make its prohibition one of the burning issues of the age. Or consider an antiprostitution crusader and a regular patron of prostitutes. They could not be more different, right? Now re-read the AP dispatch on page 203 of this book. Or consider what happens when one person stops loving another. Does his or her new attitude move to the middle of the continuum, to something like "mild liking"? No—surprisingly often, it changes to the extreme of something closer to hate.

The juxtaposition of the life drive with the death drive is also consistent with the doctrine of opposites. But the death drive came as a sort of afterthought to Freud, and he never worked it fully into the fabric of his theory—most modern analysts do not really believe in it. (Personally, I find the idea useful.) When I talk about psychic energy in this chapter and the next, therefore, I will be referring to life energy, or libido.

Freud thought that the energy metaphor was apt in several ways. Psychic energy, like physical energy, follows the conservation principle: energy can be neither created nor destroyed. In the psychological realm, this means that (1) psychic energy used for one purpose is not available for any other purpose, and (2) all psychic energy must be expressed somehow—it cannot be bottled up forever.

The energy metaphor should not be taken too literally, however. My first teaching job was at a college of engineering and science. (I recommend to my psychologist colleagues such a bracing experience.) My class of engineers was dozing politely through one of my lectures on Freud when I mentioned psychic energy. They immediately perked up, and one student, grabbing his notebook, quickly asked, "Psychic energy—in what units is that measured?"

Psychic energy is not something that Freud ever proposed to measure in "units" of any kind. It was just a metaphor that applied in some respects but, as my engineering students quickly discovered, not in others. And none too precisely in any case. At that answer, the students all sighed, slouched back into their chairs, and no doubt privately redoubled their determination to become engineers and not psychologists.

PSYCHOLOGICAL DEVELOPMENT: "FOLLOW THE MONEY"

In the movie (and book) *All the President's Men*, the reporter Bob Woodward asked his secret source, Deep Throat, how to get to the bottom of the Watergate affair. Deep Throat replied, "Follow the money." By this he meant that Woodward should find out who controlled a large sum of secret cash at the Committee to Re-elect the President and find out how that money was spent. Woodward later said that this tip allowed him and Carl Bernstein to crack the case.

When trying to understand the workings and the development of the human mind, Freud gives us similar advice. His version is "follow the energy." For like money, psychic energy is always both absolutely limited and absolutely necessary, so the story of where it goes tends to be the story of what is really happening.

This principle comes into play particularly in Freud's account of how the mind of an infant gradually develops into the mind of an adult. The story of psychological development is the story of how life energy, libido, becomes invested and then redirected over an individual's early years. A new baby fairly bubbles with life energy, but that energy is without focus or direction. As the baby develops into a child and an adult, the energy begins to focus, first on one outlet (called an "object") and then another. As the focus shifts and shifts again, the style and type of gratification that the child seeks continually changes. But no matter where it is focused at any moment, it is still libido, the same old psychic energy.

The focal points for psychic energy serve to define the *stages* of psychological development. You have probably heard of them: the oral, anal, phallic, and genital stages. Each stage has three aspects: (1) a physical focus, where energy is concentrated and gratification obtained; (2) a psychological theme, related both to the physical focus and to the demands being made on the child by the outside world as he or she develops; and (3) an adult character type that is associated with being "fixated," or to some degree stalled, in that particular stage, rather than fully developing toward the next one. If an individual fails to resolve the psychological issues that arise at a particular stage, that person will always have some psychological scar tissue in that location, and those issues will continue to be troublesome to him or her throughout life.

Oral Stage

A newborn baby is essentially helpless. It flails its arms and legs around. It cannot see clearly and cannot reach out and grab something it wants. It cannot crawl or even turn over. A baby's lack of motor control and physical coordination is almost total.

Almost. There is one thing a newborn baby can do as well at birth as any grown person will ever be able to do: suck. This action is quite complex; it requires a baby to develop suction with the muscles of the mouth and to bring the resulting food into the stomach without cutting off his or her supply of air. In a full-term baby, the neuronal networks and muscles necessary for sucking are present and in working order at the moment of birth. (One of the many problems premature babies can have is that this complex mechanism may not yet be functional.)

So now ask yourself, how does a new baby have any fun? It is not from anything done with the arms or legs because they do not work fully yet. The primary source of pleasure for a newborn, and the one place on his or her body where the newborn has any control, is right there in the mouth. It stands to reason, therefore, that the mouth will be the first place psychic energy is focused.

The **oral stage** of psychological development lasts from birth to about eighteen months. Like every stage, it has a physical focus, a psychological theme, and an associated adult character type.

The physical focus of the oral stage, as we just discussed, is on the mouth, lips, and tongue. Freud sometimes said at this stage these are sexual organs, another remark that seems almost deliberately designed to be misunderstood.

What Freud meant was that during this stage the organs of the mouth are where the life force and primary feelings of pleasure are concentrated. Eating is an important source of pleasure, but so too are sucking on things and exploring the world with one's mouth.

When a baby begins to get control over his hands and arms, and sees some small, interesting object, what is the first thing he does? He puts the object in his mouth—often to the distress of his parents. Many parents assume the baby is trying to eat the ball, or the pencil, or the dead cockroach. But that is not the baby's real intention. His hands are simply not developed enough to be helpful for exploration. When *you* pick up something interesting, you fondle it, turn it around, feel its texture and its heft. None of this works for a baby, because too many fine motor skills are required. For a baby, putting the object in his mouth can be much more informative and interesting, because his mouth is far more developed than his hands.

The psychological theme of the oral stage is dependency. A small baby is utterly, even pathetically, dependent on others for everything she needs to live. The baby is passive in the sense that there is very little she can do for herself (though she may be far from passive in her demands about what others should do). The main psychological experience of this stage, therefore, is lying back and having others either provide everything she needs, or not. Either way, there is not much she can do about it, besides make noise.

If a baby's needs at this stage of life are fulfilled to a reasonable degree then her attention and psychic energy will move along in due course to the next stage. Two things might go wrong, however. One is that her needs might *not* be fulfilled. Her caretakers might be so uncaring, incompetent, or irresponsible that she is not fed when she is hungry, covered when she is cold, or comforted when she is upset. If this happens, she may develop a basic mistrust of the world and never be able to deal adequately with dependency relationships. The idea of depending on other people—or of being betrayed or abandoned by them—will forever make her upset, although she might not realize why.

A second thing that might happen is that a baby's needs are fulfilled so instantly and automatically that it never occurs to her that the world could respond differently. The increasing demands—and poor service—the world later provides, therefore, come as quite a shock. She may wish she was back at the oral stage, where all she had to do was want something, and it immediately appeared. Again, any issue that comes up in her life involving dependency, passivity, and activity might make her very anxious, though again she may be unaware as to just why.

Here we see the principle of opposites again. (It will resurface many, many times.) Either one extreme style of child-rearing or its exact opposite will, according to Freud, yield the same results. The extremes are therefore alike. The ideal, Freud believed, was in the middle; he was suspicious of extremes of any sort. For a child-rearing strategy, then, Freud would advocate that one make reasonable efforts to fulfill a child's wants and needs at the oral stage, but not go overboard by making sure every wish is instantly gratified, *nor* neglect the child so much that it starts to doubt that it will get what it really needs.

I find it surprising that Freud gets so little credit for having been such a consistent and profound moderate. He disliked like extremes of any kind—of behavior, of child-rearing styles, of personality types, of attitudes—in part because he saw both ends of most scales as equivalently pathological. Freud's ideal was always the golden mean; his adherence to this ideal is one of the most consistent and praiseworthy aspects of his theory. In his theory of child-rearing we see one example of Freud as the quintessential moderate.

The adult personality type Freud thought was the result of either extreme style of child-rearing at this stage is the oral character. If you are starting to get used to how Freud thought about things, you will not be surprised to learn that the oral character comes in one of two extreme types. Both extremes share an obsession, discomfort, and fundamental irrationality about any issue related to dependency and passivity. As one extreme are the supposedly independent souls who refuse to accept help from anyone, who are determined to go it alone no matter what the cost. To these people, no accomplishment means anything unless it is done without assistance. At the other extreme are the passive individuals who wait around, seemingly forever, for their ships to come in. They do nothing to better their situation, yet are continually bewildered—and sometimes angry—about their failure to get what they want. To them, wanting something should be enough to make it appear. That is how it works for babies, after all; they feel hunger or some other need, cry, and somebody takes care of them. It is almost as if, as adults, oral characters expect the same strategy to work.

Both types are oral types, and at the roots they are equivalent, Freud believed. One interesting sign of their equivalence is how such people flip from one type to another. When they change, they go not to the middle but to the other end of the scale, which psychologically is closer to their original position. Someone who is aggressively independent, for example, may suddenly become completely passive and dependent when things do not go right. Someone who is completely passive may one day conclude that things are not going as they should and may move, not to the middle but to the other extreme, disdaining help and trying to be independent to a degree that is not sensible.

I have a relative who while in his thirties was thought of by many as the world's oldest sixteen-year-old (which is actually an insult to many sixteen-year-olds). He is a very intelligent and likable person, but seems utterly unable to connect what he wants with what he must do. A few years ago he announced at a family gathering that he had finally formulated a career goal. We waited to hear what it was with some anticipation. He announced that he had thought about it carefully, worked out all the figures, and decided that he wanted a job that paid $100,000 a year—*after taxes.* That would be enough to give him everything he wanted. And what would the job be? we asked. He seemed surprised by the question; he had not worked that part through, he said, but he did know what the job had to give him.

This is a classic attitude of an oral character. I think he believed, perhaps at some unconscious level, that all he had to do to get something was to make it clear that he wanted it. The idea that more might be required was somehow foreign. In general, oral characters seem to spend much more time thinking about *what* they want than about *how* to get it.

Some students show a related attitude. They plead for a higher grade in a course on the grounds that they need it. Often, they make an eloquent case for why they *really* need it. That should be enough, they seem to feel. The idea that attending class and doing the necessary work was the way to get what they wanted, rather than simply demanding it after the semester was over, seems not to have occurred to them.

The reverse kind of oral character, the person who is chronically and patho-logically independent, seems for some reason to be more rare. Yet I have seen the same relative that I described above disdain even the most minor help in preparing a cookout or fixing a car. Perhaps we all know people who insist "I can do it myself" when in the midst of utter failure.

Again, the ideal is the middle. A person who has resolved the oral stage accepts help gracefully but is not utterly dependent on it and understands that people are ultimately responsible for their own outcomes.

Anal Stage

The glory of life at the oral stage is that you do not have to do anything. Because you can do nothing for yourself, you are not expected to. You do and express whatever you feel like (and whatever you can), whenever you want. This bliss does not last, however. The world starts to cramp your style surprisingly early.

Many breast-feeding mothers have had the experience of their baby, sucking away, suddenly trying out his or her new teeth with a good, strong bite. You can imagine how mom reacts: she yells "yow!" (or something stronger), and instantly pulls the baby off. And you know how the baby reacts: it cries with outrage, anger, frustration, and maybe even fear (if mom yelled loudly enough). The reaction and consequences of its action come to the baby as a rude shock. What do you mean, I can't bite when I feel like it? Moreover, the baby will quickly discover that until he or she can muster enough self-control to stop biting, the groceries will fail to be forthcoming. This is a very early and rather ominous forewarning to the baby of what later life holds in store.

As the baby grows a little older, the demands that the world makes on him or her rapidly escalate. The baby becomes expected to do a few things for him or herself—to control his or her emotions to some degree, for example. As the baby begins to understand language, he or she will begin to be expected to do as he or she is told. The baby will be taught the word "no"—a new and alarming concept. And—something that famously got Freud's attention—the baby begins to be expected to control his or her bowels and processes of elimination. Toilet training begins.

The physical focus of the **anal stage** is, of course, the anus and associated eliminative organs. Learning the sensations of "having to go" and dealing with them appropriately is an important task of this stage. Freud and others have pointed out that a good deal of everyday language seems to reveal an emotional resonance with the processes and products of elimination. This includes not only many standard insults and expletives with which I am sure you are familiar, but also descriptions of some people (anal characters as it turns out) as "uptight," or the common advice to "let it all out" (which of course is advice to relax self-control and act "naturally").

But here I am going to bend Freud a bit (in the direction of Eriksonian theory; see Chapter 13). I think in the classical theory there is a misleading degree of emphasis on literal defecation and the supposed physical pleasures thereof. Toilet training is an important part of life during the anal stage, and seems to be the source of some powerful symbolic language. But it is just one example, among many, of the increasing demands for obedience and self-control that are made of a child beginning around the age of eighteen months. As the baby develops the capacity to control his or her bowels, the parents, tired of diapers, are eager to have the baby use that control. But this applies to many other things as well, from "get your own drink of water" to "don't touch that!" All of these experiences, happening at once and for the very first time, are part of a dramatic turning point in life that is tied to a powerful set of psychological themes.

The primary psychological theme of the anal stage is self-control and its corollary, obedience. You begin, at about eighteen months of age, to locomote efficiently and to be able to do other things for yourself; you also begin to have the ability to control your own urges, including the urge to defecate, but including other urges as well, such as the urge to cry, or to grab a forbidden object, or to hit your baby sister. Authority figures—usually your parents—begin to insist that you use your new self-control capacities.

There is a lot to work out at the anal stage and things do not always go smoothly. Typically, a child will try to figure out just how much power the authority figures in his life really have, as opposed to how much he gets to decide for himself. The child does this by testing his parents, by repeatedly experimenting to find the boundaries of what he can get away with. What happens if I pull the cat's tail after being told not to? If my parents say no more cookies, what happens if I take one?

In the folklore of parenthood, this stage of testing is known as the "terrible twos." At this point a child often begins to seem like a little monster. But really, the child's behavior is perfectly rational. How will the child figure out how the world really works without doing some experimenting? It can be trying, but it is normal, and probably even necessary.

Two things can go wrong at the anal stage. As always in psychoanalytic thinking, the two mistakes are polar opposites, and the ideal is in the middle. Too much control of a child can be traumatic. If demands are insistently made that the child is simply not capable of meeting—for example, demanding that the child *never* cry, or *always* obey, or hold her bowels longer than she is physically capable of—the result can be a psychological trauma with long-lasting consequences. And the opposite—never demanding that the child control her urges, neglecting toilet training altogether—can be equally problematic.

As at every stage, the developmental task of the child is to figure out what is going on in the world and how to deal with it. At the anal stage, the child must figure out how and how much to control herself, and how and how much to allow herself to be controlled by those in authority. This is a thorny issue to resolve, even for an adult. A child will never work it through sufficiently if her environment is too harsh *or* too lenient.

Relatively recent research that followed a sample of children from childhood into late adolescence has basically confirmed this Freudian view. The parents of these children were classified as authoritarian (extremely rigid and obedience-oriented), permissive (weak and lacking control), or authoritative (having found a compromise between firm control and allowing their children freedom). As Freud would have anticipated, it was the authoritative parents—the ones in the middle—whose children fared the best later in life (Baumrind, 1971, 1991).

Psychological mishaps at the anal stage produce the adult anal character. The anal character has a personality overly organized around issues concerning control. As always, this might go either of two ways. An anal character might be obsessive, compulsive, stingy, orderly, rigid, and subservient to authority. This person insists on being able to control every aspect of his or her life, and often seems equally happy to be controlled, in turn, by an authority figure. This type of person cannot tolerate disorganization or ambiguity. Long ago, one of my old abnormal psychology professors said he had a one-item test for detecting an anal character: go to that person's room, and you will see on the desk a row of pencils or other items aligned in a perfectly straight line. Reach over casually and turn one of the pencils at a ninety-degree angle. If within two minutes the person has quietly reached over and moved the pencil back, he or she is an anal character. (This is too facile, of course, but you get the idea.)

The other type of anal character is exactly the opposite. This person may have little or no self-control, be unable to do anything on time or because it is necessary, be chaotic and disorganized, and have a compulsive need to defy authority. Freud saw this type of person as psychologically equivalent to the other type of anal character and further believed that it was more likely that such individuals would flip from one anal extreme to the other than that either would attain the ideal position, which is in the middle.

There is a lame joke dating from the 1970s that expresses the equivalence of the two anal types beautifully. The two-part joke goes like this:

Q: Why did the short-hair cross the road?
A: Because somebody told him to.
Q: Why did the long-hair cross the road?
A: Because somebody told him not to.[2]

The point of this joke is that crossing the road *either* because somebody told you to *or* because somebody told you not to is equally and equivalently foolish. In both cases, your behavior is under the control of somebody else. The ideal is to cross the road because *you* want to, because it is the best and most reasonable thing to do.

Freud's point is similar. If you are rigidly organized and obedient because you must be, you have a problem. If you are completely disorganized and disobedient because you cannot help it, you also have a problem—in fact, you have the *same* problem. Self-control and relations to authority should be means to ends, not ends in themselves. The ideal is to determine how, whether, and to what degree to organize your life and how you relate to authority, in order to move toward the goals that are important in your life.

Phallic Stage

The next stage of development begins with a realization: Boys and girls are different. According to psychoanalytic theory, this realization begins to sink in at around three-and-a-half to four years of age, and dominates psychological development until about the age of seven, when the child enters a "latency" phase. The latency phase is sort of a psychological respite to allow the child to do much of the learning he or she will need in adult life. This rest stop comes to a screeching halt at puberty, when the next phase begins.

The specific realization that occurs at the **phallic stage**, according to Freud, is that boys have penises and girls do not—hence the name of the stage. (Maybe this is not as universal as Freud thought. I once asked one of my daughters, then not quite four years old, what the difference was between boys and girls. "Boys do not have crotches," she instantly replied.) Coming to terms with sex differences and all that they imply is the basic developmental task of the phallic stage.

According to Freud, the physical focus of the phallic stage, for either sex, is the penis. Boys, having noticed that girls do not have one, wonder what happened and if the same thing could happen to them. Girls just wonder what happened.

---

[2]The meaning of this joke rests on a stereotypical image held almost universally by college students during the latter days of the Vietnam War: people with short hair were conservative and subservient to authority; people with long hair were radical and disobedient.

Hard-core adherents of orthodox psychoanalysis launch into a pretty complicated story at this point. It involves boys' fear of castration by their fathers in a rivalry for the affection of the mother, and girls' grief over a castration that has supposedly already occurred. To resolve this anxiety, or grief, each child identifies with the same-sex parent, taking on many of his or her values and ideals while lessening feelings of rivalry and jealousy that might otherwise reach a critical level. The full story of the Oedipal crisis (referring to the Greek myth of the man who unknowingly killed his father and married his mother) is rich and fascinating, and the summary just presented does not really do it justice. Nevertheless, I will not say much more about the Oedipus story here, in part because it is so well told elsewhere. The best rendition in English is probably that provided by Bettelheim (1982). A more important reason for not getting too deeply into the traditional story of the phallic stage is that it has not held up well in the light of empirical research (Sears, 1947). So, I will discuss what happens at this point in development in simpler and more modern terms.[3]

It seems obvious that the realization that the sexes differ must be an important milestone in psychological development. It also seems only natural that with this realization comes the realization that one parent is male and the other female. I do not think it is far-fetched to think that children wonder about the essence of the attraction between their two parents, and that they fantasize to some degree about what a relationship with their opposite-sex parent would be like. And, although this may push the envelope a bit, I even think it plausible that children feel guilty to some degree, at some level, about having such fantasies. They probably seem rather outlandish even to the child, and they probably suspect their same-sex parent would not exactly be thrilled if he or she knew what the child was thinking.

The psychological theme of the phallic stage is the need to figure out what it means to be a boy or girl. For most children, the best, or at least most obvious, examples in their immediate vicinity are their mother and father.[4] One easy way to be a girl is to act like mom. To be a boy, act like dad. This can mean taking

---

[3]Here is yet another place where I am straying from what Freud literally said, and substituting a contemporary rendition that strikes me as consistent with the spirit of what he said.

[4]Here is a point where the personal lives of students often intersect with the content of a course. It is common to be asked, "what happens at this stage if a child is from a single-parent family?" In this day and age, when students raise such questions, they are hardly being hypothetical or theoretical. I wish I had a good answer; the best I can manage—is that these children look elsewhere for examples of maleness and female-ness, perhaps to relatives, friends, teachers, or (shudder) the mass media.

on many of their attitudes, values, and ways of relating to the opposite sex. This is the process Freud called **identification**.

Related psychological themes of the phallic stage include love, sexuality, fear, and jealousy. The adult consequences of what happens at the phallic stage include the development of morality, which Freud saw as a byproduct of the process of identification; you take on the values of your same-sex parent as the beginning of your own moral outlook. Another adult consequence is the eventual development of sexuality—what kind of person you find attractive, how you handle sexual competition, and the overall role and importance of sexuality in your life all have their roots at this stage. The most important result of the phallic stage is an image of oneself as masculine or feminine, along with whatever that comes to mean.

The adult character type labeled "phallic" is a person who has gone to one extreme or the other on these issues. Someone who is extremely active and promiscuous in his or her sexual behavior might be a phallic type. So too might someone who becomes completely asexual. Male homosexuality might have its roots here, although psychoanalysis does not, in my opinion, offer a very convincing detailed account of just how. (The story basically involves a boy who falls so deeply in love with his mother that all other women become intolerable rivals. To avoid disloyalty to mom, he then turns to members of his own gender for sexual gratification.) An extremely "loose" pattern of sexual behavior might be one manifestation of a phallic character; so too might an overly rigid and puritanical one. As always, Freud was suspicious of the extremes; he viewed the middle as the healthy place to be.

Genital Stage

After the phallic stage, a child gets a chance to take a developmental breath and concentrate on the important learning tasks of childhood, such as learning to read, the names of the state capitals, arithmetic, and all that other important stuff you get in elementary school. As this few years' respite begins to come to an end, puberty kicks in. It is not accidental, I suspect, that the American school system traditionally moves students to a different school beginning around the seventh grade. At that time, things are becoming importantly different, and these kids do not really belong in the same school as the little ones. Just a couple of years later, some important changes have been completed and it seems necessary to move these kids again, to high school. The American school system doesn't usually advertise this way but it works like this: elementary school = pre-puberty; intermediate school = process of puberty; high school = physically adult (psychological adulthood is another matter, of course).

The **genital stage** of development is fundamentally different from all of the others because Freud saw it not as something individuals necessarily pass through, but something they must *attain*. Sometime after physical puberty, if all goes well, a person develops a mature attitude about sexuality and other aspects of adulthood. Freud is not explicit about when this happens; in some people, apparently, it never happens.

The physical focus of the genital stage is, of course, the genitals, but notice how this label differs from that for the phallic stage. "Genital" describes not just a physical organ; the word also refers to the process of reproduction or giving life. The genitals, at this stage, become not just organs of physical pleasure, but the source of new life and the basis of a new psychological theme.

The psychological theme of the genital stage is the creation and enhancement of life. True maturity, Freud believed, entailed the ability to bring new life into the world and to nurture its growth. This of course includes children, but it can also include other kinds of creativity, such as intellectual, artistic, or scientific contributions. The developmental task of the genital stage is to learn how to add something constructive to life and to society, and to take on the adult responsibility to do just that. In that sense, the psychological theme of the genital stage is maturity. And, as I mentioned, not everybody attains it.

The genital character is unlike all the others, because it does not represent a fixation at an earlier stage but a successful development into the final stage. The genital character is psychologically well adjusted and—here comes the key term—balanced. The well-adjusted genital character is, as always, somebody who has found the golden mean.

Freud made one trip to America, early in this century, where much to his dismay he found himself trailed by newspaper reporters who apparently found some of his sexual theories titillating, especially after they had finished distorting them. Freud's lifelong aversion to America and anything American seems only to have been boosted by this experience. But his trip was not a total loss. At one point, a reporter asked him the following question: "Dr. Freud, what is your definition of mental health?" Freud's off-the-cuff reply remains, to this day, the single best answer that anybody has ever come up with for this question. He said the essence of **mental health** is the ability "to love and to work."

The most important word in this definition is *and*. Freud thought it was important to love, to have a family that you care for and nurture. He also thought it was important to work, to do something useful and constructive for society. The good life, Freud thought, would always contain *both*. To do just one was to be an incomplete person. The truly mature person—the one who has attained the genital stage—has learned to balance both kinds of generativity, love *and* work.

Today we hear accounts of the difficulties many women have in balancing families and careers. In our society, one seems to conflict with the other, it seems, and to have it all is a nearly insurmountable challenge. Freud would have approved of the way women make this struggle, I think. After all, the balance of those two things is what life is all about.[5]

Consider today's men, by contrast. The word "workaholic" has been coined to describe what many have become. These men experience little conflict between work and home because they have simply given up on, or delegated, the home part. Are they better off? Freud would not think so. To leave out one of the two things you must balance in life is not psychological health—it's arrested development. The balance many women are trying to achieve, therefore, implies that they are psychologically more fully developed than the men who gave up on the struggle before it even started.

I had just finished making this point in class one day when a (female) student startled me by asking, "Does this imply that women are psychologically healthier than men?" I had not thought about it quite that way, but pushed for an answer I said "yes." On reflection, I still think that answer is correct. When you consider what the ideal genital character is supposed to be like, more women get there than men.

Moving through Stages

Freud once used the analogy that a mind progressing through the stages of psychological development is a little like an army conquering a hostile territory. Periodically it encounters opposition and difficulty and at that point a battle ensues. To secure the ground after the battle is over, some troops are left behind as the army advances. If the battle was particularly bitter and if the local resistance remains strong, a larger part of the army must be left behind—leaving less, of course, with which to advance. Moreover, if the main army encounters severe problems later, it is likely to retreat to one of its strongholds, which will be the site of a former battle.

The store of libido is the army in this analogy. It encounters "battles" at each of the developmental stages. If the battle of the oral or anal or phallic stage is not completely won, libidinal energy must be left behind at that point. The result will be an adult personality that is dominated by issues from that stage, and a person who tends to retreat to that stage even more strongly when under stress. An oral character under stress becomes passive, dependent, and may even suck his or her thumb. An anal character under stress becomes even more rigid (or even more disorganized) than usual. A phallic character under stress may engage in promiscuous behavior (or become completely asexual).

---

[5]Actually, perhaps Freud would *not* have approved; in his personal life he seems to have been a typical conservative, Victorian sexist. But I think the spirit of Freudian thought, its essence, is exactly compatible with what many modern women are trying to accomplish.

FIXATION

Leaving a disproportionate share of one's libido behind at a childhood stage of development is called **fixation**; a person might be said to be fixated at the oral stage, for example. You will recall that fixation can happen for either of two, opposite reasons. A person's needs may have been overly indulged at a stage, in which case the libido is unwilling to leave completely. Another (and I would guess more common) possibility is that the issues raised at this stage (dependency, control, or sexuality) were never completely resolved and so the battle is not over. As a result, not all of the libido is free to move on to more adult concerns. Ideally, at each stage you are not overly protected from the issues that arise, you face them directly, and you deal with them successfully. That allows you to move on or, more precisely, allows most of your libido to move on.

Yet Freud believed that a little libido *always* gets left behind. The events at each stage are so important and leave such deep marks that some of you—ideally, a small amount of you—remains forever camped in the oral, anal, and phallic stages. One result is that every normal adult can still enjoy gratifications related to the earlier stages. There is something to be said for sucking on a popsicle, having a really good bowel movement, and having one's genitals directly stimulated. A lot of human life revolves around our needs for dependency and independence, our needs to control our lives and those of other people and to resist being overly controlled, and our sexual and social identities as women and men.

REGRESSION

People under stress will often retreat, sometimes almost literally, to the childhood stage at which their libido was fixated. As mentioned above, this can cause problems (e.g., an oral character might become completely passive), and may even result in severe psychopathology. This retreat to an earlier stage of development is called **regression**.

Freud thought some regression could be good; he believed that moving backward to an earlier stage, occasionally and temporarily, was "regression in service of the ego." Such regression can allow a person to be, for a while, psychologically like a child again. Indeed, this can be a boon to creativity: Freud thought that artists often used this kind of regression to free their thinking from adult and societal constraints.

Such good regression can also lead to play. Adults who can act like kids again can enjoy life in a way that is impossible otherwise. Regressing together and playing together can be a way to develop emotional intimacy. For example, I frequently take my two young daughters to the parks in the city where I live. When I look around the playground, the adults I see fall into one of two groups. The larger group comprises the watchful parents, like me, of the kids who are playing on the swings and other equipment. But occasionally, a young couple wanders in from the nearby university campus. Although they may be in their twenties, they laugh and giggle, splash each other with water from the drinking fountain and push each other on the swings. This is not adult behavior! But regressing to childhood together in this way is an important way for this couple to grow closer to each other emotionally. Thus it is a good thing to do. (And besides, it's awfully cute.)

Within limits. Remember, Freud was the quintessential moderate. He thought some fixation was good, but not too much. In his view, too much fixation resulted from either an overemphasis or underemphasis on the issues of a particular stage. And he thought regression was good, but only if done occasionally, temporarily, and for sufficient reason. Play is good, but on Monday morning one should get back to work.

THE STRUCTURE OF THE MIND

The result of psychological development is a mind that has a structure. At birth, the mind is a disorganized and chaotic thing; it is mainly a pool of unfocused libidinal (life) energy. But with the very first conflicts and difficulties of life, a structure begins to establish itself. The result is a mind divided into three parts that will sound familiar: the **id**, the **ego**, and the **superego**. These three parts correspond, roughly, to the physical, the cognitive, and the ethical sectors of one's being.

Freud was originally trained as a neurologist, so it is not surprising that his tripartite division of the mind is consistent with what was known then—and still is believed today—about the basic structure of the brain. As was reviewed in Chapter 8, the human brain is sometimes viewed by neuropsychologists as three brains in one. The innermost, reptilian brain seems to handle basic emotions and motivation; at the next layer a paleomammalian brain offers more flexible control of behavior; and the outermost cortex or neomammalian brain is uniquely human and may be the seat of the "higher" thought processes. These very basic structures were known even in Freud's time and can be considered approximately analogous to the id, ego, and superego, respectively. This is a rough analogy, to be sure. What Freud considered ego functions are almost certainly located in the cortex, for example—not in the middle brain. But the rough similarity been Freud's three parts of the mind and the three basic parts of the human brain is surely more than just coincidence.

The Id

Draw a big circle and label it "id." At birth a baby's mind is all id. In that sense the id is the primitive mind. It contains all the basic, unverbalized needs and feelings that are at the core of being alive. It is also the source for libido. The new baby is a seething mass of needs and feelings—all id.

The id follows one simple rule, the "pleasure principle," which can also be expressed by the title of a song by a (now-forgotten) rock band called the Tubes: "I Want It All Now." Every word of this slogan is important. I want it *all*; I am not interested in foregoing one thing to get another. I want it *now*; I am not interested in waiting, not even for a moment. The id cannot even conceive of wanting less than everything immediately. This is the essence of childish (or more accurately infantile) thought, and the id will always think this way throughout life. The id's thought processes follow what is called "primary process thinking," about which more will be said later in this chapter.

The Ego

The infant soon learns that life is not nearly as simple as the id would have it. Needs are not instantly fulfilled, and the baby also finds out that it cannot always do whatever it wants—such as bite Mommy during breast-feeding, as mentioned earlier. These disillusioning experiences begin very early, and really begin to cascade at the onset of the anal stage.

The result of these experiences is the development of a new structure, the ego, out of the id. (Now draw a slice out of the id and label it "ego.") The ego develops as a result of an increasing awareness that you do not always instantly get what you want and that you sometimes have to forego doing something you like so that you can get something you like even more. (Some people never quite learn these lessons, of course. In psychological jargon, they are said to have "insufficient ego development.") Ego development begins in the oral stage, as the baby first experiences frustration, but it develops much faster in the anal stage, especially when outside authority starts trying to control what the baby wants to do. Thus the ego and the anal stage are closely linked.

The function of the ego is to deal with the real world. It operates by the "reality principle," as opposed to the pleasure principle by which the id operates. The reality principle recognizes that the way to get the most gratification in the long run is to make certain compromises. One might have to delay gratification or substitute a more attainable and less dangerous gratification for one that cannot be attained or is too risky.

Indeed, modern "ego psychologists" believe that compromise formation is one of the most important functions of the ego (Brenner, 1982). When different parts of the mind want different things, the ego may seek a compromise that allows all of them to get a little of what they want. For example, imagine a person whose superego strongly condemns pornography while his id loves the stuff. His ego might formulate a compromise in which he becomes an active antipornography crusader. He then can satisfy his superego by loudly and frequently condemning the evils of pornography, while at the same time collecting and viewing large amounts of pornography, all in reluctant service of the battle against it.

The ego takes some libidinal energy away from the id and uses this energy to plan, to think, to perceive, and to control the id itself. The ego is in a sense an agent or executant for the id; its job is to get the pleasures the id wants, but to be more reasonable—and less self-defeating—than the id is capable of being. So although in some ways the ego opposes the id (by denying it instant gratification, for instance), in the long run it helps the id (by planning how to obtain gratification eventually).

Modern ego psychologists, notably Jane Loevinger, give the ego an even more central role. According to Loevinger, the ego's function is to make sense of everything that a person experiences (Loevinger, 1987). Moreover, to Loevinger the story of development is essentially the story of the development of the ego itself. Early in life the ego struggles to understand how the individual is separate from the world and from his or her mother; later the ego grapples with such issues as how to relate to society, how to achieve personal autonomy, and how to appreciate the autonomy of others. According to a personality test designed by Loevinger to measure individuals' levels of "ego development," most people never get much farther than learning society's basic rules and appreciating that some of those rules have exceptions (Holt, 1980). Very few get to the point of being truly independent people who can appreciate and support the independence of those around them.

In a way, the ego is the most familiar part of our mind, because among its functions are conscious and rational thought. All that we ordinarily call "thinking" happens in the ego. The ego is also responsible for arranging compromises to conflicts among different parts of the mind—such as handling opposing directives from the pleasure principle (I want to run outside right now) and the reality principle (I must finish this chapter first).

The Superego

Recall that, according to Freud, at the phallic stage of development the child develops a love for the opposite-sex parent and a corresponding jealous fear of the same-sex parent, a fear that is resolved through taking on the values and worldview of the same-sex parent (the process of **identification**). As was already described, a watered-down but perhaps more plausible version of what happens at the phallic stage is that the child begins to be aware of sex differences and, as a guide to appropriate behavior, begins to take on as many attributes of the same-sex parent as possible. Either way, the result is identification.

Other identifications are possible and even likely as well. A child might take on the values and behaviors of an admired teacher, relative, or religious leader, or of a rock or sports star. A child usually identifies with someone because he or she loves and admires the person. In some bizarre circumstances an individual might even identify with someone he or she loathes and fears. World War II concentration camp inmates apparently sometimes identified with their guards, making Nazi armbands and uniforms from scraps and giving each other the "Heil Hitler" salute. This seemingly strange behavior was an adaptation to deal with their profound (and realistic) fear of the guards; to become more like the guards was to fear them less. I suspect milder forms of this same behavior—trying to become more like the people you most fear—are actually rather common, and are probably one basis for the development of the superego. People sometimes identify with a teacher they hate, a coach they fear, an older student who hazes them, or a drill sergeant (or an entire branch of the military) who gives them nothing but abuse. In the process, these characters become less fearful while the person becomes a little more like them.

The agglomeration of a person's identifications, whatever their source, is a psychological structure called the superego. It is sometimes viewed as the moral voice of the mind, but morality is not exactly what the superego embodies. Its function is to store and enforce rules; these rules might be part of a moral code drawn from a parent or religious leader, or they may be various injunctions and prohibitions that have only the vaguest connection with morality but that are strictly enforced nonetheless. My grandmother saw card-playing and dancing as immoral; her explanations of what was wrong with these behaviors were never very clear, but explanations were not the point; her parents and the culture in which she was raised (northern Illinois around 1900) prohibited these activities, and that was reason enough.

The superego's power to enforce its rules comes from its ability to create anxiety. Sometimes this anxiety is consciously felt as guilt; other times all one feels is psychological discomfort without knowing why. We will speak more about anxiety of unknown origin in the next chapter.

PRIMARY AND SECONDARY PROCESS THINKING

According to psychoanalytic theory the mind has two distinct modes of thinking: secondary process thinking and primary process thinking. **Secondary process thinking** is what we ordinarily mean by the word "think." The conscious part of the ego thinks this way; it is thought that is rational, practical, prudent, and that can delay or redirect gratification. It is "secondary" in two senses. First, it develops only as the ego begins to develop; a newborn has no secondary process thinking. The other sense in which it is secondary is that Freud believed primary process thinking was more interesting, important, and powerful throughout life, not just in infancy.

Primary process thinking is the way in which the unconscious mind operates, and how the infant's (and later adult's) id operates. It is a strange sort of thinking. The fundamental aspect of primary process thinking is that it does not contain the word (or even the idea) of "No." It is thought that contains no negatives, no qualifications, no sense of time, or of any of practicalities, necessities, or dangers of life. It has one goal: immediate gratification of every desire.

Primary process thinking operates by a strange shorthand. It can tie disparate feelings closely together. Your feeling about your family can affect how you feel about your house, for example. Primary processing thinking can use **displacement** to replace one idea or image with another: your anger toward your father might be replaced by anger with all authority figures, or your anger toward an authority might be transformed into anger at your father. **Condensation** can cause several ideas to be compressed into one; an image of a house or of a woman might contain within it a complex set of memories, thoughts, and emotions. And **symbolization** might have one thing stand for another in primary process thought.

At one point in his career, Freud thought there might be a universal symbolic grammar of the unconscious mind, in which certain symbols meant the same thing to everybody the world over. Some of these are included in the little paperback books on dream analysis you can get at the supermarket, and include lists like this:

house = human body
smooth-fronted house = male body
house with ledges and balconies = female body
king and queen = parents
little animals = children
children = genitals
playing with children = you fill in this one
going on a journey = dying
clothes = nakedness
going up stairs = having sex
bath = birth

As it happens, Freud later dropped the idea of universal symbols. He decided that their meaning varies for every individual. The idea of unconscious universal ideas was picked up with a vengeance, however, by Carl Jung (see Chapter 13).

Primary process thinking is a very interesting kind of thinking, but one might reasonably ask where, if it is a property of the unconscious mind, it is ever seen. Freud thought that primary process thinking could emerge into consciousness under several limited circumstances. He thought the conscious thought of very small children operates according to primary process, but because they have developed secondary process thinking by the time they can talk this idea is difficult to verify (actually it is impossible). He also thought primary process thinking can become conscious during fever deliriums and during dreams. This is consistent with the experience of many people that in dreams (or deliriums) one has no sense of time, one person can change into another, images serve as symbols of other things, and so on. Freud also thought that psychotics sometimes experience primary process thinking; if you ever listen to the speech of a schizophrenic for any length of time you will see where Freud got this idea.

But instances in which primary process thinking emerges directly into consciousness are relatively rare. More important, Freud believed, are the more ordinary and indirect ways that primary process thinking can be seen to influence people's conscious thought and overt behavior. The results of primary process thinking often "leak" into slips of the tongue, accidents, lapses of memory, and the like (see Chapter 12). Freud also believed that when a person "free associates," or says without self-censorship everything that comes to mind, that eventually the way in which the person jumps from one topic to another will reveal the unconscious workings of primary process thought.

I know of one psychoanalyst who, following these precepts, explains to his patients that they should tell him whatever comes to mind, because their thoughts, feelings, and motives are all connected with one another along complex networks of associations. We often lack conscious access to these networks, but they can be uncovered. One goal of psychoanalysis is to map these networks in order to see the context in which a symptom is embedded and to get a better idea of how the patient's mind works (Drew Westen, personal communication, April 28, 1994).

CONSCIOUSNESS

Freud believed that except under unusual circumstances, such as dreams or delirium, conscious thought is a secondary process. He saw consciousness as a relatively unimportant byproduct of a small part of the ego. The really important psychological action, Freud believed, happens outside of awareness, in the unconscious.

Freud posited three levels to consciousness in what is sometimes called his "topographic" model. (Topography refers to elevation; a topographic map is one that shows the elevations of the hills and valleys over an expanse of territory.) The smallest and topmost layer is the conscious mind, that part of our mental functioning we can observe when we simply turn our attention inward. A second layer, the preconscious, consists of those things we are not thinking about at the moment, but that we could bring into consciousness easily if we wished. For example, how is the weather outside right now? What did you have for breakfast?

Where is your car parked? Who is the president of the United States? None of these things was in your conscious mind until I asked (presumably), but you probably had little trouble bringing them into your conscious awareness.

The third, the biggest, and, Freud thought, the most important layer of the mind is the unconscious. The unconscious includes all the id and superego and most of the ego. The unconscious is buried deep; the only way to bring it to the surface is by digging. One method of digging that Freud used early in his career is hypnosis. Another method is the technique of free association, in which a person is encouraged to say whatever comes to mind in relation to some concern or issue. Freud thought the wanderings of free association were never random (he never thought *anything* was random), and that the way a person jumps from one thought to another can provide important clues about his or her unconscious. Other clues can come from slips of the tongue, accidents, and lapses of memory. All have their causes in mental processes that occur outside of consciousness.

PSYCHOANALYTIC THERAPY

The use of clues to uncover the unconscious is the core purpose of psychoanalytic therapy. The problems that make most people anxious and unhappy, Freud believed, have their roots in conflicts within the unconscious mind. The way to resolve these conflicts is to bring them into the open, through dream analysis, free association, and analysis of slips and lapses. Once an unconscious conflict is brought into consciousness, Freud believed, the rational part of the ego is able to deal with it and the conflict will no longer pose a problem. In the long run of therapy, Freud believed that to achieve insight into oneself was to attain rational control of oneself. (Freud was nothing if not a rationalist.)

Of course, the process is more complicated than that. The conflict must be dealt with not just rationally, but *emotionally*, which takes time and can be painful. As people bring their conflicts to the surface, they often begin to feel *worse* anxiety in the short run; the prospect of losing one's neuroses can be surprisingly disconcerting. Many people avoid dealing with their unconscious anxieties for this reason; Freud called the phenomenon of running away from the solution to one's psychological problems the "flight from health."

To comfort, guide, and support the client through this healing process, Freud believed, there must be an emotional bond between therapist and client. The development of this bond is called the "therapeutic alliance." This alliance gets its power through a phenomenon called **transference**, which is the tendency to bring ways of thinking, feeling, and behaving that developed with one important person into a later relationship with a different person. One might relate to a teacher in the same way one learned to relate, years earlier, to one's father, for example. Transference is particulary important in psychotherapy, because the emotional relationship the patient develops with the therapist is built on the model of that patient's past relationships with other important people.

The development of transference in therapy is important, but it can also be dangerous. Freud was perhaps the first psychotherapist to note that sexual attractions between psychotherapists and clients are quite common. He was absolutely adamant that it was the duty of the therapist to resist acting on this attraction. The patient *must* get emotionally involved for the therapy to work, Freud believed, but the therapist must *avoid* such involvement at all costs.

Psychoanalysis is often criticized for its allegedly low (or even zero) demonstrable cure rate, and for the fact that it can last for many years and perhaps never end. Many psychoanalysts have become heavily involved in a debate over the therapeutic efficacy of their techniques, but late in his career Freud himself began to see it all as beside the point:

After forty-one years of medical activities, my self-knowledge tells me that I have not been a physician in the proper sense. . . . [my real interests are] the events of the history of man, the mutual influences between man's nature, the development of culture, and those residues of prehistoric events of which religion is the foremost representation . . . studies which originate with psychoanalysis but go way beyond it. (from *The Question of Lay Analysis*, as translated by Bettelheim, 1982, p. 48).

In the end, Freud was surprisingly uninterested in psychoanalysis as a medical or therapeutic technique.[6] He saw its real importance as a tool for better understanding human nature and culture.

SUMMARY

Freud's psychoanalytic theory posits two drives, a life drive, or libido, and a drive towards death and destruction. Libido is a much more important part of the theory; many modern analysts see it as the only important drive. Libido produces psychic energy, and the story of psychological development is the story of how this energy is focused in different areas at four different stages of life. The main issue for the oral stage is dependency; for the anal stage it is obedience and self-control; for the phallic stage it is gender identity and sexuality; and for the genital stage it is maturity, in which ideally one learns to balance "love and work" and to be productive in both domains. Fixation occurs when an individual gets "stuck" in one of these stages into adulthood; regression is a movement backward from a later psychological stage to an earlier one.

---

[6]Some modern practicing psychoanalysts are also surprisingly uninterested in whether their technique makes their patients any better (Bader, 1994).

Freud's theory divides the mind into three parts: the id, ego, and superego. These parts correspond roughly to emotions, cognition, and conscience, respectively. Primary process thinking is a primitive style of unconscious thought, characterized by association, displacement, symbolization, and an irrational, uncompromising drive toward immediate gratification. Secondary process thinking is ordinary, rational, conscious thought. There are three layers to consciousness: the conscious mind, the preconscious, and the unconscious. The essence of psychoanalytic therapy, performed through techniques such as dream analysis and free association in the context of a therapeutic alliance between patient and therapist, is to bring the unconcious thoughts that are the source of an individual's problems into the open, where the conscious, rational mind can deal with them.

CHAPTER

DEFENSES AND SLIPS

Anxiety is unpleasant, and one important function of the ego is to prevent an individual from feeling it too strongly. The real world presents many threats to our well-being that provide a realistic source of anxiety. Freud never seemed particularly interested in the anxiety produced by the stresses and strains of the real world, however. He concentrated instead on the anxiety that comes from within.

ANXIETY AND DEFENSE

We saw in the previous chapter that, according to psychoanalytic theory, the mind is divided into three parts, each with its own purposes, its own way of thinking, and, most important, its own store of psychic energy. Just as having your own money can make you independent, having its own psychic energy makes each part of the mind independent. The independence of the id, ego, and superego leads them often—and perhaps typically—to be in conflict with each other. "Psychic conflict" is what goes on in a mind battling with itself. The result is anxiety.

Sources of Anxiety

A typical conflict arises when the id formulates a desire that the ego or the superego or perhaps both are inclined to forbid. Recall that in its primary process thinking, the id wants everything it sees, now. The ego will object if the desire seems impractical. The superego will object if the desire seems immoral (if it violates whatever system of rules and prohibitions the superego has internalized).

Suppose you see a small boy, standing with his mother and holding a delicious-looking piece of candy. You may not be aware of the feeling, but your id will immediately want that candy and will create an impulse to reach out and grab it. But both the ego and superego will swing quickly into action. The ego will realize that grabbing candy from a child in full view of his mother is likely to lead to serious difficulties, such as being yelled at or possibly even arrested. The superego will be horrified at the idea that the id would even think of doing such a despicable thing. Both object, but for different reasons; the ego cares about practical consequences rather than right and wrong, and the superego cares about right and wrong rather than practical consequences.

In this example both the ego and superego will probably use their energy to push the id's impulse back down not only below the threshold of action, but below the threshold of awareness. You will probably never know you wanted to grab the candy. But consider what might happen if the problematic impulse and its prohibitions were particular strong. Imagine a married person, deeply committed to his or her family, who experiences strong, lustful impulses toward an attractive individual of the opposite sex. This impulse creates problems, because although the temptation is real, the ego will probably calculate that acting on the impulse will cause terrible damage to the person's family and other areas of his or her life. On top of that, the superego might weigh in with a realization that acting on this impulse would violate every value the person holds dear. As a result of these strong oppositions, the impulse might be pushed almost completely out of awareness, and the person might be conscious only of a vague feeling of uneasiness, anxiety, or guilt. Later on, the person might be unable to remember ever having met this attractive individual. (If he or she were to remember, that might cause renewed anxiety.) The person may never know where the anxiety came from nor understand why what seemed like a routine encounter was so quickly forgotten.

Freud believed one particular conflict to be quite common. He believed that most people at times feel sexual attraction toward members of their own sex and that these latent homosexual feelings are pushed out of action and awareness by both the ego, on practical grounds, and the superego, on moral grounds (most people in Freud's era—and perhaps today as well—were raised with the idea that homosexuality is abhorrent and immoral). This constant but prohibited impulse is a persistent source of anxiety in many individuals, Freud believed, although they may never become consciously aware of the source of their discomfort.

Indeed, vague anxiety of unknown origin is a quintessential Freudian symptom. Psychologists from other approaches tend to throw up their hands when a client presents the complaint "I feel bad and don't know why." A psychoanalyst, however, settles into the problem with relish. The whole purpose of psychoanalysis is to uncover—and eventually to relieve—hidden sources of anxiety.

Defense Mechanisms

Anxiety is unpleasant, whether it comes from realistic sources in the external world or from conflict within one's own mind. An important function of the ego is to operate **defense mechanisms** designed to protect against anxiety and other related negative emotions such as guilt and shame. Freud emphasized how these mechanisms defend against the anxiety produced by psychic conflict, but I think they also function to keep us from worrying too much about the real world.

The ego's defense strategies are varied and ingenious. The discussion that follows will consider eight of them: denial, repression, reaction formation, projection, rationalization, intellectualization, displacement, and sublimation.

DENIAL

Denial is the simplest defense mechanism: One simply denies that the source of anxiety exists. This tactic is common and effective in the short run, but if used for very long can lead to a serious lack of contact with reality.

My office was at one time located directly across the hall from the location where grades for introductory psychology exams are posted. So I occasionally observed when someone discovered he or she had failed an exam. How could I tell? By the audible defense mechanism of denial: these students would jump back from the grade roster and shout (at themselves more than at anybody else), "No!"

For most of these students, denial is just a temporary tactic. By refusing to believe what they have just seen, they give themselves a psychological breather to collect themselves and make a second run at the problem. As time passes they will probably acknowledge that, yes, they really failed the exam. They may even come back to the grade roster, in a somewhat calmer frame of mind, to double-check their score. At that point they will either deal realistically with the problem—study harder next time, for example—or invoke one or more of the more permanent defense mechanisms to deal with the anxiety of academic failure.

Denial can also be used to defend against anxiety that comes from within. Suppose you unintentionally blurt out something that causes you anxiety. Your next statement might be, "I didn't say that!" Or suppose you do something of which you are ashamed. You might try to deny, even to yourself, that you did it.

In extreme cases, denial persists. Occasionally somebody's permanent solution to an anxiety-producing situation is simply to deny it even exists. This may be a sign of serious psychopathology. It is a classic symptom of alcoholism, for example. (Have you ever tried to tell an alcoholic that he or she has a drinking problem?) But the primary purpose of denial is to keep us from being overwhelmed by the initial shock—at something that has happened or at something we have done—as we muster our psychological resources to do something more permanent about it.

REPRESSION

The defense mechanism of repression is more complex, farther reaching, and longer lasting than denial. Denial generally refers to pushing out of awareness things that *currently* exist, such as anxiety-producing events or feelings. **Repression**, in contrast, refers to banishing the past from present awareness, and therefore tends to involves less outright negation of reality. With repression, you do not deny outright that something exists, you just do not think about it.

Like denial, the ultimate purpose of repression is to keep out of action and out of consciousness a problematical impulse of the id, an unpleasant thought, feeling, or memory, or something in the real world that is a potential source of stress.

Freud believed that many forbidden impulses are quite common. For example, it is not unusual for college students in their early twenties to resent their continued financial dependence upon their parents. The ego finds this feeling of resentment to be problematical, however, because its direct expression (calling your parents and telling them you hate them) is likely to endanger one's financial support. Moreover, the superego also finds the resentment problematical, because it seems shamefully ungrateful after all that your parents have sacrificed for you. If the resentment were somehow to become conscious—and even more if it were to be overtly expressed—its disapproval by both the ego and superego would cause anxiety. The defense mechanism of repression may kick in to prevent this from happening.

The most direct action of repression will be to bar from consciousness any negative thoughts about your parents, which should also prevent any overt negative behaviors. But repression takes no chances; it may also bar from consciousness anything that might *remind* you of how you resent your parents. (In fact, it will build a wider and deeper repressive wall the stronger and more dangerous the resentment is.) You might find yourself forgetting to call them as you have promised, because remembering to call them reminds you they exist, which raises the possibility of becoming aware that you resent them. Or you might even forget their names! It can go further: You might forget your roommate's parents' names, because remembering her parents will remind you of your parents, which might remind you of how you resent them. Or you might forget to watch a favorite television show because it is also your father's favorite show . . . —you get the idea. Such elaborate secondary protection from anxiety-arousing stimuli can cause a wide range of slips and memory lapses, and the connection between what is forgotten and what is being defended against can be so indirect that a good deal of psychoanalytic digging can be required to find the cause. For instance, to figure out the real reason you forgot your roommate's mother's phone message might take a long time and a lot of work.

Thus repression is much more complicated than simple denial. The same complex process can work with memories as well. Suppose you did something a month ago, the memory of which would cause you anxiety, perhaps because it was dangerous (an ego judgment), immoral (a super-ego judgment), or both. Repression might cause you not only to forget what you did, but to forget other things that might possibly remind you of what you did. If you did something stupid with your car that would be stressful to remember, for example, you might find that you have forgotten where you parked it.

If the feeling, memory, or impulse is successfully kept deep in the unconscious then you are successfully defended against the anxiety it would otherwise cause. But here is the rub: Such defense does not come free. The ego has a limited store of psychic energy that it has taken from the id. Every forbidden feeling, memory, or impulse has a certain amount of id energy associated with it that impels it toward the surface, toward consciousness and behavioral expression. In repression, the ego must oppose that impulse with an equal amount of its own energy. If the ego runs low on energy, or tries to defend against too many impulses at once, it can start to lose the struggle and these forbidden things will work their way toward consciousness again. As these forbidden impulses begin to move up, you will feel anxiety, typically without knowing why.

You can imagine the danger of this situation. If ego energy fails for some reason—e.g., illness, stress, or some trauma—a whole array of forbidden impulses might suddenly come to consciousness and even action all at once. Or they might burst forth simply because they are too numerous and too strong, as a dam can suddenly break after years of slowly increasing water pressure behind it. The result can be violent lashing-out, emotional binges, and a wide variety of irrational behaviors.

For example, an ordinarily meek and mild person might absorb insults and humiliations for many years. Each insult and humiliation may have been successfully repressed so that he does not have to feel the associated anxiety, until one day it has gone on too long. The defenses fail, the dam breaks, and he goes on a murderous rampage. "He was always so quiet," comment the (surviving) neighbors in the newspaper the next day (see Megargee, 1966).

The danger of repression can be more subtle, as well. The ego's energy store is limited; the more it has tied up in repression the less it has available for other purposes. A severe shortage of free psychic energy can lead to depression, Freud believed. Clinical depression is much more than just being sad all the time. It produces a near-total lack of motivation and energy. One purpose of psychoanalysis is to locate the loci of repression, remove their causes, and free up more psychic energy for more constructive and creative purposes.

Repression is a sort of brute force defense mechanism; it tries to build a psychological wall between you and potential sources of anxiety. But any wall can hold back only so much for so long. Repression is not a defense mechanism that can be used too often, therefore. Fortunately, the ego has several other tactics in its playbook.

REACTION FORMATION

Reaction formation is even more complex than repression. It keeps forbidden thoughts, feelings, and impulses out of awareness and action by instigating their *opposites*. The ego is particularly likely to use this tactic if the forbidden impulse is very dangerous or very strong, and an extra measure of defense seems necessary. Doing (or thinking) the opposite of the forbidden impulse builds a sort of safety margin, ensuring that the impulse never reaches consciousness or action.

Again, unconscious homosexual impulses provide a good example. These very common (according to Freud) impulses are considered problematical by both the ego and the superego, but ordinarily are suppressed by repression. If the homosexual impulse is particularly strong, however, or if the superego has developed particularly strong prohibitions against it (as might a superego that developed in a rigidly puritanical environment), then reaction formation may become necessary to be sure the impulse is never felt or acted upon.

The most obvious manifestation of reaction formation in such a case would be what is called "gay-bashing." The person might loudly denounce homosexuals and describe them with epithets; might write "death to queers" on bathroom walls; might tell "fag" jokes frequently and loudly; or in an extreme case might physically attack gays.

The indication that these behaviors might be signs of reaction formation is the disproportion and gratuitousness of the anti-gay behavior. Reaction formation is *not* revealed by saying something like "some aspects of one common gay lifestyle can lead to serious problems in an age of AIDS." Such a statement might well express a sincere and reasonable attitude. But the demonstrated need to insult, to belittle, to characterize with obscenities, and perhaps even to physically assault is not. *No* reasonable attitude about gays leads to such behaviors. Thus we are led to suspect a deeper, psychological source.

Consider another example. I lived for several years in a small, peaceful, almost bucolic college town in the Midwest. The local television news one night showed a preacher who was crusading in front of the town's (apparently) one-and-only pornographic bookstore, which was located in such an obscure location—even in such a small town—that until I saw it on television I didn't know it existed. The preacher was screaming the dangers of smut. His face was red, his voice was hoarse, the veins stood out on his neck: The store was Sin and it was a Danger!

Again, notice that we are not talking about somebody who is calmly saying, "the images of women and of sexuality in most pornography are not the sorts of things to which we would wish to expose our children." Such a statement, although you might agree or disagree, is certainly reasonable. It is the almost absurd exaggeration of the response to the bookstore that makes us suspicious of the preacher's psychological motives. How big a danger is this store, really? What is it actually doing to the town, if many townspeople do not even know it exists? The vehemence of this crusader's reaction suggests that the source of his emotion is not any danger the store realistically poses, but rather his own temptation to rush in and buy the place out. He effectively prevents himself from doing this, of course, by standing out front with a megaphone and a picket sign. Such is the purpose and mechanism of reaction formation.

The giveaway is always a lack of proportion between the provocation and the response. Both homosexuality and pornography are legitimate targets of discussion and perhaps even complaint. But when so much emotion is involved we must become suspicious. It can be informative, but also brave to the point of being foolhardy (thus I do not recommend it) to ask such a crusader this question: Why do you care about this so much? The response is unlikely to be reasonable; it will be angry, anxious, and defensive.

A more mundane but even more common manifestation of reaction for-mation, Freud believed, occurs in nearly every family. When a new baby comes home from the hospital, the natural reaction of the older sibling is hate—this is called sibling rivalry, and it may be biologically based. But the older sibling soon discovers that his or her parents are protective of the baby and any attempts to harm it are met with punishment and loss of parental love, which is quite threat-ening. The sibling learns to repress his or her hate for little brother or sister and, if sufficiently threatened (or if the impulse to harm is sufficiently strong), may engage in some elaborate demonstrations of affection. "I love my little brother!" she might say, giving him a big kiss. In this way she can keep herself from strangling him. The parents may approve of this affectionate behavior, but if they are sensitive they may also realize that it rings a little false. Behavior driven by reaction formation often appears odd; somehow, it does not look right.

Hamlet's mother said, "methinks the lady doth protest too much." She was talking about reaction formation.

PROJECTION

Like reaction formation, **projection** is a defense mechanism that protects against unwanted impulses by causing a behavior that, at first glance, appears to be opposite. It is the tactic of attributing a thought or impulse to somebody else that is feared in oneself. You announce, to yourself as much as to others, "It's not me who feels that ways (or is like that), it's *him*."

Homosexuality again provides a prototypical example. Freud believed that one way some people deal with threatening, latent homosexual impulses of their own is to project homosexual intent onto everybody else. "Gay-bashers" like those described above are quick to claim to have spotted "another one," and may even tell you that they can infallibly identify any homosexual at a glance. They are wrong, of course, but it is revealing that they believe this.

Other kinds of self-doubt can lead to projection. People who doubt their own intelligence often deal with the anxiety of realizing their own inadequacy by claiming to be surrounded by morons. It seems to make them feel better, and for the short term the tactic of pointing out other people as stupid seems to make them seem smarter than they would appear otherwise (Amabile & Glazebrook, 1982.).

Not all negative opinions you have of other people are due to projection, of course. Ask yourself this: Do you *often* characterize other people in this particular way? Are you constantly detecting "fags," "morons," "lazy freeloaders," or whatever? And does making this judgment about somebody else make *you* feel better in some way? If so, it is fair to suspect the workings of projection. The negative attribute with which you are tagging other people may be something that you actually (albeit unconsciously) fear characterizes yourself.

RATIONALIZATION

Rationalization may be the most frequently used defense mechanism of all. **Rationalization** defends against the anxiety aroused by having done something of which you would otherwise feel ashamed by concocting a seemingly rational case for why it was something you just had to do. An (annoying) hit song a decade or two ago proclaimed that "You've got to be cruel to be kind." That's a rationalization.

Rationalization can be seen everywhere. Parents who harshly punish their children claim it is for their own good. Wealthy people give themselves tax breaks while raising the burden on the poor, then claim they are trying to promote economic growth for the benefit of everybody. People cheat and tell lies, then claim it was harmless, or even necessary for a greater good.

The remarkable facts about such rationalizations are that (1) they are obviously rationalizations, and (2) the people who use them seem to believe them anyway. If the reasoning were not so obviously flawed we might be tempted to think that these people actually believe what they say. It is the ability and even eagerness of otherwise intelligent people to believe the implausible that identifies rationalization. Deep inside, these people are all ashamed of themselves. Rationalization protects them from the anxiety they would feel if they realized their shame.

INTELLECTUALIZATION

Yet another way to deal with a threatening emotion is to turn the feeling into a thought. This is the defense mechanism of **intellectualization**. Intellectualization turns heated and anxiety-provoking issues into something cold, intellectual, and analytical. An aid to intellectualization is the development of a technical vocabulary that allows one to talk about horrifying things without using everyday, emotionally arousing language.

You see a lot of intellectualization in war. During the Persian Gulf war, for example, television screens were filled with retired generals and colonels expounding on military strategy. It was remarkable how seldom they used words like "kill" or "die," even though those are the defining attributes of war. They used words like "suffer" and "bleed" even more rarely. Instead, their analyses used maps and charts and pointers to tell an interesting story that had much of the same appeal as a good game of chess. But to truly enjoy the show—and maybe even just to plot strategy—you had to forget about what was really going on.

The medical profession must do this, too. Surgeons talk about "this gall bladder" rather than "this person," and their vocabulary is so technical as to be virtually inaccessible to the layperson. That is on purpose. Physicians are reluctant to talk about pain (they prefer the term "discomfort") and death (you really just "expire").

I don't mean to belittle the military or medical professions here. When you strip away pretense and technical blather, they both deal on a daily basis with situations that are truly horrifying. It is unlikely they could function at all without the defense of intellectualization. If the surgeon thought too directly about the life of the child on whom she is operating, it is doubtful she could get through the operation successfully. A general who dwells too much on the deaths his work will cause might be unable to formulate a winning strategy. Unadorned reality can be too painful to deal with effectively. The purpose of intellectualization and the other defense mechanisms is to build a useful barrier between you and reality, so that you can go on with what you need to do.

All the defense mechanisms have costs, however, and intellectualization is no exception. A general who forgets he is killing might be an effective strategist, but also might sacrifice life needlessly or even come to enjoy war so much as an intellectual exercise that he unnecessarily prolongs it. A physician who finds surgery enjoyable and comes to forget she is cutting real people might also forget that patients have not only physical needs, but also emotional needs that are important components of the healing process.

Intellectualization is a particular occupational hazard of psychologists. I suspect that part of the field's appeal lies in the way it takes potent issues of emotion and experience and puts them into an abstract theoretical framework. This is useful and even necessary; Freud himself seems to have built his theory as a gigantic exercise in intellectualization. But to the extent that it begins to shield one from the realities of everyday psychological life, psychology itself can become a defense mechanism that distorts reality.

DISPLACEMENT

Displacement is a less-intellectual defense mechanism that is based on a property of primary process thinking. Among the attributes of the primary process by which the infantile id operates is a capacity for **displacement**, or replacing one object of emotion with another. A feeling about your family might be displaced upon your house, for example, or a feeling about a parent might be displaced onto a boss, or vice versa. The defense mechanism of displacement relocates the object of an emotional response or desire from an unsafe target to a safe one. A simple example might be the desire, based in a mild fixation in the oral stage, that an adult might have to suck his thumb. Of course, this is not acceptable behavior at a business meeting, so displacement might lead our executive to chew thoughtfully, and with impeccable dignity, on his pen or pipe instead.

The direction of displacement depends upon two things. Generally an id impulse will be displaced upon the available target that is most similar to the actually desired object but that is also socially acceptable. Acceptably similar substitutes for sucking one's thumb (itself a displacement from sucking mother's breast) might include both a toe and a pipe stem. However, only the pipe is acceptable in public (it also requires less flexibility), so that is where the impulse is relocated.

Aggression is frequently displaced in this manner. You might become angry at your boss but fear losing your job if you confront him. So you go home and kick your dog (especially if your dog looks like your boss). Many student dormitory rooms contain professor dart boards. It is safe and legal to throw darts at a piece of cork decorated with a disliked professor's picture, and dart-throwing can partially gratify an aggressive impulse. But it is not the same thing as throwing pointed darts at the professor herself; that is why the behavior is said to manifest displacement.

Like all defense mechanisms, displacement has its uses and its dangers. It is useful in redirecting forbidden and even dangerous impulses onto safe targets. It can be a problem if it becomes a substitute for necessary direct action. Displacement can also be a problem if it causes aggression to be directed onto innocent targets. It is not the dog's fault that your boss is a jerk, and cruelty to animals at home is no solution to difficulties at work.

In addition, displacement is not always effective, if it ever is. Experimental research since the time of Freud suggests that a person who expresses aggression at a displaced target may become *more*, not less, inclined to be aggressive in general (Berkowitz, 1962). This suggests that rather than being one of the ego's defense mechanisms, in some cases displacement might be a more primitive function of the id's primary process thinking. People who kick the wall when they are angry at someone may do so not for any rational reason, but because they cannot help it. At a basic and primitive level, they are just built that way.

SUBLIMATION

To be sublime is to be elevated and noble. **Sublimation** is the defense mechanism by which base and possibly forbidden impulses are transformed into constructive behaviors. Sublimation is a type of displacement in which the object of an impulse is relocated such that the result is the accomplishment of some kind of high cultural attainment. For example, Freud believed that the production of great works of art by people such as Leonardo da Vinci and Michelangelo was strongly influenced by psychological traumas they had experienced in early childhood. Freud also believed that Leonardo's prolific scientific investigations, in particular, constituted a sublimation of his sexual passions.[1]

Occupational choice is a more mundane place to look for sublimation. It can be psychologically useful to channel one's otherwise unacceptable impulses into a lifelong work that will accomplish constructive ends. For example, if what you really want is to cut people, poke them with needles, or see them with their clothes off, you might consider a career in medicine, particularly surgery. If your deep urges are to express hostility and to argue, then perhaps you should become a lawyer. If you want to spend your life trying to get everybody to love you, then consider a career in politics. If you have anally based urges to smear feces (and, via displacement, paint), then you might become an artist. And, if what you really want to do is pry into other people's minds, then you perhaps should consider a career in clinical psychology.

Perhaps this all sounds rather silly to you, but there is a kernel of truth here. Every person has a unique pattern of fixations left over from childhood, and as result has a unique pattern of desires and interests. People who are both wise and lucky may find constructive careers that allow the expression of these desires and interests.

It is important to realize that Freud saw sublimation as a *positive* thing. It is a part of normal functioning and a useful way to translate into constructive outcomes urges that otherwise could cause problems. Unlike the other defense mechanisms, sublimation does not have a down side. It is what allows human psychic energy to be channeled into useful pursuits and allows the development of society, culture, civilization, and achievement of all sorts. We need to sublimate more often. To do this, we probably need to know ourselves better.

THE EXPRESSION OF IMPULSE

Defense mechanisms work to prevent forbidden impulses from being acted upon or even thought about. But sometimes feelings and thoughts that the ego and

---

[1]Freud's interpretation was presented in a short book entitled *Leonardo da Vinci and a Memory of his Childhood*. This work is discussed in detail by Gay (1988, pp. 268–77).

superego are trying to suppress make it into the open anyway. This leakage might be uncontrolled and haphazard, or it might be carefully channeled. Uncontrolled, it creates a slip of some kind, or a parapraxis. Controlled, it can be the basis of wit and humor.

Parapraxes

A **parapraxis** is another name for what is commonly called a Freudian slip: a leakage from the unconscious mind into an overt manifestation such as a mistake, accident, omission, or memory lapse. Both common sense and psychoanalytic theory view such slips as revealing. You give someone you care about an expensive present. The person almost immediately has an accident, dropping and breaking the gift. How do you feel? If you feel that a hidden animosity toward you might just have been revealed, then you are following exactly the kind of logic used in the analysis of parapraxes in general.

Remember that Freud was a determinist—he thought everything had a cause. This belief comes directly into play when considering the causes of accidents and other slips. Freud was never willing to believe that they just happened.

Forgetting

Forgetting something is a manifestation of an unconscious conflict revealing itself in your overt behavior. The slip or parapraxis is the failure to recall something you needed to remember or do something you needed to do, either of which can have consequences ranging from embarrassment to much worse. These consequences make the lapse a parapraxis; in service of the suppression of something in your unconscious mind, your slip manages to mess up something in your real life.

Usually this is a result of repression. To avoid thinking about something painful or anxiety-producing, you fail to remember it. You make a date and then have second thoughts, so you forget you made it. Although you might have saved yourself some immediate anxiety, when you run into your erstwhile date the next week in the cafeteria you will have a serious social problem to deal with. Many college students manage to forget the dates that exams are held and term papers are due. Failing to remember such things may make the students less anxious in the short run, but can produce serious problems in the long run. Occasionally a student will make an appointment with me to discuss a difficulty he or she is having in class. In each case, I know the odds are no better than 50 percent that the student will actually show up at the appointed time. When I see the student later the explanation is always the same: "I forgot."

These examples are all fairly obvious. But Freud insisted that *all* lapses of this kind reveal unconscious conflicts. Now the theoretical going gets a little tougher: what about when you just forget something for no reason? No such thing, acording to Freud. The psychoanalytic faith declares that through long psychotherapy using free association, a therapist can eventually (and perhaps at great expense) figure out the cause of *any* memory lapse. The root system may be quite complex: You may have forgotten to do something because it reminds you of something else that through primary process thinking has come to symbolize yet something else, which makes you anxious.

In one case, a psychoanalyst reported that a patient forgot the name of an acquaintance who had the same name as an enemy of his. Moreover, the acquaintance was physically handicapped, which reminded the patient of the harm he wished to do the enemy of the same name. To defend against the superego-induced guilt produced by this wish, he forgot the name of his perfectly innocent acquaintance (Brenner, 1974).

SLIPS

Slips are unintended actions that are caused by the leakage of suppressed impulses. Many of them appear in speech, and can be as simple as a failure to suppress what one really means to say. In one of the first courses on psychoanalysis I took in college, the professor one day was mentioning the students who come see him during his office hours. "When infants come to see me . . . , " he said, then (very revealingly) his face turned bright red. His students could not have failed to understand this revelation of what he really thought of them.

A more common slip is to say one name when you mean to say another. Saying the name of one's *former* boyfriend or girlfriend at important and delicate moments with one's *current* boyfriend or girlfriend is a common and extremely embarrassing slip. Explanations are often demanded: "Why did you say her name?" "I just slipped! It didn't mean anything!" This reply is no more likely to be accepted by one's current "significant other" than it would have been by Sigmund Freud himself.

An interesting slip occurred during the 1992 presidential election campaign. One of the candidates was making a speech in which he meant to attack his opponent's proposal to increase taxes on those making more than $200,000 per year. Most people making that kind of money are not actually millionaires, he intended to say, but mom-and-pop operators—small-business owners. Alliteration can be dangerous though; it can open the door to what you *really* believe. "These people making $200,000 are not mom-and-po . . . , " he began—then corrected himself. Watch for slips like that; they can be very revealing.

Slips can occur in action as well as in speech. Accidentally breaking something can be a leakage of hostility against the person who owns the object, who gave you the object, or whom the object (for some reason) symbolizes. A more pleasant slip to think about is the standard interpretation when somebody accidentally leaves something behind at your house after a visit: It means the person did not want to leave, and hopes to come back.

As already noted, the person who commits these slips of speech or action will often deny that the slip had any meaning. Not only does psychoanalysis not take such a denial seriously, but the louder and more vehement the person's denial, the more likely it will be that a Freudian will suspect a powerfully dangerous and important impulse behind it.

But what about accidents that happen just because you are tired, not paying attention, in a hurry, or excited? Not accidents, according to Freud. These factors make slips more likely, but they do not cause them. Freud compared the operation of such factors to the way darkness helps a robber. A dark street might make a burglary more likely, but dark streets do not *cause* burglaries; you still need a burglar. Similarly, fatigue, inattention, and other factors might make it easier for a suppressed impulse to leak into behavior, but they are not the basis of the impulse itself.

Does this mean, then, that there really are no accidents? Freud believed so. Any failure to do something you ordinarily can do—such as drive a car safely— is due to the leakage of a suppressed impulse, according to Freud. Some examples have been quite prominent. In the Winter Olympics a few years ago, a skier on the way to an important downhill race managed to crash into a member of the ski patrol and break her leg. This was an accident, of course, but it is also reasonable to ask, How often does an Olympic-level skier crash into somebody else? How often does any skier crash into a member of the ski patrol? And, of all mornings of this skier's life, why did the accident happen on this morning? One is led to wonder if this skier did not want to show up for her race, and why.

An even more dramatic incident at the 1988 Olympics involved the speed skater Dan Jansen, whose sister had died of leukemia just five hours before he was scheduled to compete in the 500-meter event. Jansen was favored for the gold medal, and his sister had insisted he go to the Olympics even though all knew she had not long to live. He fell just ten seconds into the race. Four days later, in his second event, the 1,000-meter, he fell again. A psychoanalytic perspective on these accidents makes one wonder whether Jansen really wanted to come home bedecked in gold medals at such a time. Had he wanted to succeed, it seems unlikely that he would have fallen down in both of the two most important athletic events of his life to that point. (The sports world breathed a sigh of relief when, in the 1994 Olympics, Jansen finally resolved matters, both taking the gold medal in the 1000-meter event and setting a world record.)

In Chapter 10 I mentioned that there often are a lot of Freudians in the English Department. Freudians also can be found in another place on campus— the P.E. Department. They may not think about themselves that way, but coaches are often orthodox Freudians. Coaches worry about instilling in their athletes the right mental attitude, a will to win. When an athlete at the free-throw line "blows it" or "chokes" by missing a shot he or she can make twenty times in a row in practice, any good coach knows the solution is not more free-throw practice; there is something about the athlete's attitude or desire that needs work. If the player had wanted to make the basket, the ball would have gone in. The player missed, so in some way he or she must not have really wanted to win. Ask any coach which team will win any given game. The coach will reply, "The team that wants it more." And Freud would say, "Exactly right."

The next time you fail to perform to your ability, in sports, in academics, at work, or wherever, take a moment and ask yourself this: Did you *really* want to succeed? Why not?

Wit

Parapraxes are more or less random leaks; they appear wherever defenses are weak. In wit, however, a forbidden impulse comes out in a controlled manner. Freud saw wit as essentially a form of sublimation: An impulse that otherwise would be anxiety-provoking or even harmful is vented in such a way that it can be safely enjoyed. Wit, therefore, is the safe expression of evil, according to Freud. It is no accident that the most common themes of humor are sex, violence, and bodily elimination.

THE PURPOSE OF HUMOR

Humor allows otherwise problematical impulses to be enjoyed by using the tactic of surprise. In a successful joke, the impulse is disguised until the last possible moment. Then—Bang!—the impulse is expressed, and enjoyed, before you have a chance to be worried about it. A few seconds later, you might even feel a bit sheepish or even guilty about what made you laugh, but the deed is done. The impulse was expressed, and enjoyed.

In one of the Pink Panther movies, Peter Sellers sees a dog standing next to a desk and asks the clerk, "Does your dog bite?" The clerk answers, "No, never." Sellers reaches down to pet the dog, and his hand is savagely bitten. "I thought you said your dog doesn't bite!" he cries, jumping up and down. "That," replies the clerk, "is not my dog."

Someone who laughs at this scene is enjoying the spectacle of a person being fooled into being physically harmed by an unexpectedly vicious animal. What's funny about that? Everything, apparently. The reason this scene works is that what is going on is carefully concealed until the last moment, when it is suddenly revealed. The situation is enjoyed with a burst of laughter before the superego's censors can point out how reprehensible the whole situation really is.

A comedian named Emo tells the following story: "When I was a child, my parents always said to me, 'Emo, whatever you do, don't open the cellar door. *Never* open the cellar door.' But I was curious, and after a few years I finally snuck over and opened the cellar door. What I saw was amazing—things I had never seen before. Trees. Birds. The sky."

This is a child abuse joke! What could be funny about locking a child in the basement for the first years of his life? Some evil impulse to enjoy such a situation seems to exist, however, and it leaks out and causes surprised laughter before we have a chance to realize that this situation is tragic, not funny. Moreover, this is a better joke than the Peter Sellers scene for two reasons. First, child abuse is ordinarily more reprehensible than dog bites, so the release of the impulse causes a stronger emotional response. Second (and this is really the key), Emo's disguise around the impulse is deeper than Sellers's. It is less as apparent at the beginning where Emo's joke is going, and when I tell it to classes there are always several students who don't get it until someone explains it.

The purpose of a joke is to allow a forbidden impulse to be released in such a way that anxiety can be avoided. For this reason, most (maybe all) jokes, when examined closely, are what you might call "sick" jokes, based on sexual or hostile impulses. Many involve people being made to look stupid; others express some kind of obscenity in an indirect, disguised, sudden fashion.

BAD JOKES

So, the enjoyment of a joke depends upon the safely disguised or surprise expression of a forbidden impulse. This theory allows us to predict when a joke *won't* work.

A joke can fail to be funny for any of several reasons. If you do not have the impulse in the first place, the joke will not be funny to you. Some people enjoy hostile jokes more than others do, for example. Presumably, this is partly because some people have stronger hostile impulses that are seeking expression. The same probably goes for sexual jokes. A particularly noticeable individual difference appears in the enjoyment of racist and sexist jokes. Their enjoyment depends upon the existence of underlying hostility toward the targeted minority group or gender. Someone who does not have such underlying hostility may find such jokes mystifying rather than funny. I know someone who is uptight and generally rule-bound—a real "anal" character. Her favorite form of humor? Toilet jokes. Children who are still not far beyond the anal stage themselves also greatly enjoy bathroom humor. But as their libidos move into later stages, most adults find that the appeal of potty humor fades a bit.

Political humor is another problematical area. We are more likely to laugh at jokes about politicians we oppose than those we support. A political humorist, therefore, must choose whether to be a blatant partisan, and thereby limit his audience, or to try to joke about politicians of all persuasions. (Johnny Carson became an American comedy icon to a large degree because he had the rare ability to do just that.)

A joke can also fail by being too direct. If a joke fails to disguise sufficiently the impulse or fails to surprise the hearer, when the impulse is expressed it will cause discomfort rather than enjoyment. This is why the more times you have heard a joke, the less funny it becomes. As the element of surprise is taken away, the impulse can no longer be enjoyed. Some jokes are not even surprising at *first* hearing. If you can see the punch line coming, it won't be very funny.

Some "jokes" do not even try to disguise the impulses they express. Some jokes rely simply on saying obscene words or describing sexual acts in graphic terms. Some people find them funny; most do not. Other jokes amount to the almost completely undisguised expression of hostility. Jokes like these are the ones that make most people squirm instead of laugh. That response, of course, defeats the whole purpose of humor.

One category of joke is both common and unfunny: sexist jokes that are told in the workplace by male bosses to and about female employees. By commenting lasciviously and loudly on his secretary's physical attributes or personal life, the boss gets to express at least two impulses at once. One is sexual, and the other is a sadistic expression of power. The boss—and those who happen to share his unenlightened attitudes—may laugh loudly; the employee may be miserable. There are two reasons why such jokes are not funny. The first is that they are usually too obvious. An obscene comment about a subordinate's body lacks the necessary disguise for the release of impulse. The second reason is that the impulse may not be widely shared. Surely the subordinate herself is unlikely to enjoy the boss's expression of his sexual and power impulses. Co-workers, including male co-workers, who also do not share these impulses toward the employee will similarly find the boss's "humor" unfunny.

Practical jokes can be problematical in a similar manner. A harmless prank can express mild hostility in an enjoyable way, but there is a fine line between playing a prank, which can be funny, and seriously harming somebody, which is not. When I was in college, a group of men in my dorm developed a degree of hostility toward a certain female resident. For her birthday, they decided to stage an elaborate surprise party. At its climax they ceremoniously presented her with a gift, which turned out to be an oversized, battery-powered dildo. This was meant to be funny; it was not. It was one of the most depressing and humiliating moments I have ever witnessed. The hostility and contempt that was felt—unfairly—toward this woman was expressed too directly, too publicly, and too cruelly.

A well-known example of the same kind of problem is presented by the long-running television program *America's Funniest Home Videos*. Most of the home videos shown on this program portray people, including children, as they fall down, break things, and make huge messes. Some people—myself included—feel uncomfortable rather than entertained by this program. The events portrayed come a little too close to the line that separates a humorous incident from an event that is humiliating, disturbing, or painful.

After these examples, I should re-iterate that from the psychoanalytic perspective, humor is *good*. It allows forbidden impulses that otherwise would have to be repressed or defended against to be vented harmlessly. But humor is also a delicate business. The impulse must be shared, and it must be suitably disguised. To succeed on both of these bases is the art of humor.

Parapraxes vs. Wit

Both parapraxes and wit express an otherwise unconscious impulse in speech and perhaps in behavior. In both cases, the impulse might be transformed or symbolized via primary process thinking. But there is an important difference between the two. In a parapraxis, the impulse simply leaks out in an uncontrolled manner. In humor, the expression of the impulse is carefully crafted to allow it to come out full force, but also in complete safety. A parapraxis, therefore, is a failure of the ego. Humor, by contrast, is one of its most important successes.

PSYCHOANALYTIC THEORY: AN EVALUATION

Throughout Part Four of this book, I have tried to sell you Freud. Psychoanalytic theory has much to offer in understanding important aspects of daily life. The theory is dramatic and insightful, it is comprehensive, it is aesthetic.

Perhaps the most remarkable aspect of Freud's theory is that, to the present day, it is the only *complete* theory of personality ever proposed. Freud knew what he wanted to explain: aggression, sexuality, development, energy, conflict, neurosis, dreams, humor, accidents—the list goes on. His theory accounts for all of them. Whether he is right or wrong about every aspect of the theory, it does provide a roadmap of all the right questions, the questions that personality psychologists have been asking ever since. It is a truism that in science the important thing is not really answering questions, but figuring out the right ones to ask. In this regard, Freud's theory of personality is a triumph that may stand for all time.

Having said all that, let me warn you against taking Freud too seriously. When a student comes up to me after class and says, "What happens to sexual development if a boy is raised solely by his mother in a single-parent family?" what I really want to reply is, "Hey! Don't take this stuff to heart! Freud has a neat theory here, and it's fun to play around with, but don't start using it to evaluate your life." Psychoanalytic theory is far from being received truth. So, having praised Freud, let me now bury him for a bit. There are at least five important shortcomings to psychoanalytic theory.

Lack of Parsimony

First of all, Freud's theory is nonparsimonious (to put it mildly). A basic principle of science, sometimes called Occam's Razor, is that less is more: all other things being equal, the simplest explanation for something is the best. Suppose we want to explain why small boys take on many of the values and attitudes of their fathers. One possibility is that they look for guides in the world around them and choose the most obvious and prominent. Freud's theory, however, says that boys sexually desire their mothers, they worry that their fathers will be jealous and castrate them in punishment, so they identify with their fathers to vicariously enjoy the mother and lessen the threat from the father. This is intriguing, and just maybe it is even correct, but is it the simplest possible explanation of the known facts? No way.

Case Study Method

A second fundamental tenet of science is that all data must be public. The basis of one's conclusions must be laid out so that scientists can evaluate the evidence together. Psychoanalytic theory almost never does this. It is based on analysts' (including Freud's) introspections, and on insights drawn from working with single therapeutic cases, which are themselves (by law) confidential. Freud himself repeatedly complained that the *real* proof of his theory lay in the details of case studies that he could never reveal because of the need to protect his patients' privacy. The fact that this case study method is uncheckable means that it may be biased. This bias may arise out of what psychoanalysts and their patients (such as Freud's turn-of-the-century, Viennese hysterics) are like. Or perhaps the reasoning the theorist employs distorts what really happens in his or her cases. Because the data are forever private, no one can ever be sure. Psychoanalytic theory's attitude toward empirical proof could be summarized by this slogan: "Take it or leave it."

Poor Definitions

Another conventional scientific canon is the operational definition. In other words, a scientific concept should be defined largely in terms of the operations or procedures by which it can be identified and measured. Psychoanalytic theory almost never does this; its concepts are often poorly defined. Take the idea of psychic energy. I mentioned that a student once asked me what units it was measured in. There are no units, of course, and looked at closely it is not entirely clear what Freud meant by psychic energy at all: Was he being literal, or is energy just a loose metaphor? Exactly how much psychic energy—what percent, say— needs to be left behind at the oral stage to develop an oral character? As repressions accumulate, at what point will one run out of energy for daily living? Psychoanalytic theory does not come even close to offering concrete answers to questions like these.

Untestability

Freud's theory is also untestable. In science, a theory should be "disconfirmable"; that is, a theory should imply a set of observations or results that, if found, would prove it to be false. (This is the difference between religion and science. There is no conceivable set of observations or results that would prove that God does not exist. He always might just be hiding. Therefore, the existence of God is not a scientific issue.) But psychoanalytic theory is so complicated that there is no set of observations that it cannot explain after the fact. Because there is no imaginable experiment that would prove the theory wrong, the theory is in that sense unscientific.[2]

Still, no single experiment is sufficient to prove or disprove *any* complex theory. So one could conclude that the real question is not whether psycholoanalysis is testable in a strict sense, but rather whether the theory leads to hypotheses that can be tested individually. In the case of psychoanalysis, the best answer to this question is sometimes yes, and sometimes no.

Sexism

Psychoanalytic theory is sexist. This cannot be denied; even those modern writers who are highly sympathetic to Freud admit it (e.g., Gay, 1988). In psychoanalytic writing it is abundantly clear that Freud considers males to be normal and bases his theorizing on their psychology. He then considers females, if he considers them at all, as aberrations or deviations from the male model. For example, his Oedipal theory of sex-typing (which I have not emphasized in this book) is much more coherent for males than for females, who seem to have been added almost as an afterthought.

Freud's view of females is that they are essentially castrated males, rather than being whole in their own right. They spend much of their lives grieving for not having a penis. The side effects of being female, in psychoanalytic theory, include having less self-esteem, less creativity, and less moral fiber. Much of a female's life, according to Freud, is based on her struggle to come to terms with the tragedy that she is not male.

---

[2]Early in his career Freud frequently expressed the desire that psychoanalytic theory be considered scientific. As he grew older this criterion became less important to him (Bettelheim, 1982).

The Theory Is Valuable Anyway

Do all these limitations imply that Freud's psychoanalytic theory is worthless? I hope it is clear by now that I do not think so. The theory offers a template for what an ultimate theory of personality might someday look like, and it does ask all the right questions. Moreover, scattered throughout Freud's theory are important kernels of truth concerning such matters as the doctrine of opposites, the descriptions of defense mechanisms, and explanations of slips and humor. The theory might be unscientific according to certain canons, but perhaps there is room in our understanding of ourselves for theories that are not conventionally scientific.

The criterion by which the psychoanalytic approach to psychology and every other approach should be evaluated is not whether it is right or wrong (because all theories are wrong in the end), nor even whether it is scientific. Instead we should evaluate it by asking, Does the approach give you insight into something you did not understand as well before, and is it in that sense useful? On that question, psychoanalytic theory gets more than a passing grade.

SUMMARY

Anxiety can have its origins in the real world or in inner, psychic conflict, such as that produced by an impulse of the id that the ego and superego try to combat. The ego has several defense mechanisms to protect against the conscious experience of excessive anxiety and its associated negative emotions, such as shame and guilt. These defense mechanisms include denial, repression, reaction formation, projection, rationalization, intellectualization, displacement, and sublimation.

Forbidden impulses of the id can occasionally be expressed in thought and behavior in two ways. Parapraxes are accidental ventings of forbidden impulses in the kind of accidents of speech or action commonly called "Freudian slips." In wit, a forbidden impulse is deeply disguised in such a way as to permit its enjoyment without anxiety. A joke is not funny when this disguise is insufficient.

Psychoanalytic theory violates several of the conventional canons of science, but remains valuable because of the questions that it raises and the unique view of human nature that it provides.

CHAPTER

PSYCHOANALYSIS AFTER FREUD

Sigmund Freud died in 1939. His theory of the human mind did not die with him, however, nor did his style of theorizing or his general approach to psychodynamics. Although Freudian theory and psychoanalysis are not and really never have been the dominant theme in academic research psychology, more than a few modern psychologists continue to keep Freud's legacy alive, sometimes just by continuing to argue about it.

MODERN REACTIONS TO FREUD

The debate surrounding psychoanalysis today is a little like that over the U.S. Constitution, a two-century-old document that remains the legal basis of the U.S. government. Some people think this document must be read, word for word, as closely to its original meaning as possible. They take its prescriptions literally, and try to change nothing. Others try to read the Constitution in the context of modern times, ignoring provisions that made sense years ago but that no longer seem apt, and reinterpreting two-century-old legal language in light of modern needs. Still others would prefer to scrap the Constitution and start over with a whole new basis for government that, to them, would make more sense.[1]

This issue is hardly abstract. The argument over the constitutional "right to bear arms" is fought on just this ground. Some take this provision literally, as meaning that every American has an irrevocable right to keep any weapon at all—even assault rifles, machine guns, and hand grenades, for example—in his

---

[1]A similar analogy could be drawn about reactions to the Bible. Some people want it read (and obeyed) to the letter, others try to modify its interpretation for the modern age, and others would rather ignore it altogether.

or her home, for any purpose. Others believe that this phrase, written in a vastly different political context in a time of much-simpler and less-dangerous weapons, needs to be interpreted in light of the modern reality. Small arms kept around for hunting and target shooting may be protected by the Constitution, these people suggest, but assault rifles and private militias are not. Still others believe the whole phrase about bearing arms is outdated to the point of being senseless.

Similarly, post-Freudians can be sorted into three types: those who want to maintain the theory inviolate, those who want to reinterpret and revise it for the modern context, and those who would replace it altogether.

Maintaining the Theory Inviolate

The first group of post-Freudians comprises those orthodox psychoanalysts who continue to read Freud's original works closely and try to apply the truths of the master as faithfully to his original thinking as they possibly can. For example, consider the story of the Oedipal crisis, described briefly in Chapter 11. Orthodox psychoanalysts take the whole thing quite literally; they believe that small boys fall sexually in love with their mothers, fear retaliatory castration from their fathers, and as a defense identify with their fathers and try to become like them. After all, this is what Freud said.

The orthodox analysts are, in a sense, "more Freudian than Freud," because although Freud himself often changed his theory, these followers never do. There are several thousand strict Freudians in clinical practice, and they publish a number of psychoanalytic journals. But to a large extent this group has become irrelevant to the wider psychological community, because these orthodox analysts seem only to want to talk to, and are listened to by, one another.

Interpreting Freud

A second group of post-Freudians actively interprets and revises Freud's theory. For example, they might try to reinterpret the Oedipal story in light of modern evidence. Like I did in Chapter 11, they might describe how children unsure of their gender roles look to obvious role models, such as their same-sex parents, for guidance. The result is still that small boys identify with their fathers, but the dynamic process is different from the one Freud originally envisioned.

As in constitutional law, the activities of interpreting and revising a theory are separated only by a fuzzy boundary. Freud wrote hundreds of articles and dozens of books over many years (his career spanned more than six decades), and he changed his mind more than once about important issues. So it is no small or insignificant activity to interpret what he said or meant to say, or to determine the overall meaning of his work, or how it can best be summarized.

A particular challenge is to interpret Freud's theory in a way that makes sense in the modern context. The original theory is, after all, nearly a century old.

Many psychologists and historians have taken on this task, with widely varying results. Peter Gay's (1988) monumental biography of Freud includes a thorough and insightful survey of the development of Freud's theory. Charles Brenner's (1974) outline of psychoanalysis is a complex merging of Freud's own ideas with Brenner's own insights and updates. The preceding three chapters of this book likewise constitute more of an interpretation than a literal rendition of Freud. I have merged what Freud said with what I think he *meant* to say or *should* have said in some cases, and have even mixed in some ideas that are probably better traced to later thinkers in the same tradition.

For example, as mentioned above, I altered the traditional rendition of the Oedipal crisis because I think the original makes little sense in light of years of research about socialization. Thus my version changes (some would say distorts) what Freud actually said. I also interpreted libido by describing it as the life drive, rather than limiting it to something exclusively sexual in nature. Again, this changes, and in fact, directly contradicts, what Freud said in some of his own writings, but I prefer to interpret what he said in terms of what makes sense to me today.

The more you become tempted to "fix" Freud in your rendition, to mix in other thinkers and ideas from other sources, and the more you find yourself having ideas of your own about Freudian theory, the more you become an active developer of psychoanalytic theory yourself. Anna Freud wrote a masterful survey of the defense mechanisms about a decade after her father's death (these mechanisms were summarized in Chapter 12). It is probably safe to say he would have approved (he apparently approved of everything his favorite daughter did), as she did not deviate from the spirit of his theorizing. But such an explicit rendering of defenses is not to be found in Freud's own writings. Many other, more minor figures have also continued to write about psychoanalysis in a manner that tries to stay true to Freud's theory, while still extending it in some way.

Replacing Freud

A third group of post-Freudians would discard Freudian theory altogether if they could. For example, they treat the Oedipal story as an excellent illustration of just how wrong Freud was about everything and find many other reasons to reject his entire theory.

Some of these rejecting post-Freudians, small in number today, have developed psychoanalytic theories of their own, in explicit opposition to Freud. The aim of these theories is not just to improve Freud's psychoanalysis, but to replace it. Carl Jung and Alfred Adler, who will be discussed later in this chapter, are the two most famous examples. For his part, Freud was not shy in pointing out how both of his former disciples—and others he thought had wandered from the true path—had gone fundamentally astray.

Modern individuals in this category differ from Jung and Adler in that they seldom have replacement theories of their own. Rather, they indulge in the seemingly never-ending task of debunking Freud, proving he was wrong about nearly everything from the beginning. A few years ago a book by the flamboyant psychoanalyst Jeffrey Masson made a stir in the popular media by using dredged-up material about some of Freud's questionable friends to call Freud's whole theory into question (Masson, 1984).[2] Works with similar intent continue to appear on a regular basis.[3]

I shall start the rest of this chapter by describing some of the more prominent of the psychoanalytic alternatives to and important refinements on Freud, namely those of the major psychoanalysts Alfred Adler, Carl Jung, Karen Horney, and Erik Erikson. Only the first two of these came to think of themselves as "anti-Freudians," but all of them provided important revisions and extensions of psychoanalytic theory, some of which influenced the general summary of psychoanalysis you have read in the preceding chapters.

Then I will briefly summarize some research that is trying to bring Freud and psychoanalysis *back* into the scientific mainstream of academic psychology. Some researchers in this tradition, such as Drew Westen and Dan Weinberger, base their hypotheses on a general psychoanalytic viewpoint that is an amalgam of Freud, Jung, Adler, Horney, Erikson, and others, and try to test their hypotheses according to the rigorous standards of modern psychological research. Other researchers are promoting psychoanalytic ideas by studying such topics as how some perceptions and memories can exist in what is called the "cognitive unconscious," or how the child-rearing style of one's parents can affect one's adult personality.

NEO-FREUDIAN ISSUES AND THEORISTS

The theorists who continued the development of psychoanalytic theory after Freud are an impressive crew. They include Anna Freud, Bruno Bettelheim, Erik Erikson, Carl Jung, Alfred Adler, Karen Horney, Harry Stack Sullivan, and Henry Murray. You have probably heard of several of them; Erikson, Jung, and Adler all number among the major intellectual figures of the twentieth century. But it

---

[2]Masson also received extensive publicity for his lawsuit against the *New Yorker* magazine, which he claimed libeled him in a personality profile. He lost the case.

[3]See, for example, Sulloway (1979). Robinson (1993) offers a summary of the arguments of these critics and a defense of Freud against them.

is also important to note that every single one of the individuals just named is deceased. Although neo-Freudians still exist and are practicing to this day, the "golden age" of neo-Freudianism seems to have passed.

Most neo-Freudians—including all the ones just mentioned—used the same research "method" as Freud himself. They saw patients, looked into themselves, read widely in history and literature, and drew conclusions. This is just as true of some of Freud's most vehement critics, such as Jung, an early dissenter, and Jeffrey Masson, a recent dissenter, as it is of those more sympathetic to him, such as Bruno Bettelheim and Anna Freud.

This method gives psychoanalysts the ability to cover a lot of theoretical ground and to develop opinions about almost everything. It also invokes a style of argument that more traditionally scientific psychologists tend to find frustrating. When Jung argued with Freud, for example, he basically said that his cases and introspection showed *A*, and Freud would reply no, his own cases and introspection lead clearly to conclusion *B*, to which Jung would reply that anybody can see it's really *A* . . . and so forth. Anyone looking for a crucial experiment to settle the matter will search in vain; even if somebody were clever enough to come up with one, neither Freud nor Jung—nor any other neo-Freudian—would admit that a mere experiment could settle anything about such profound matters. You can only read these other thinkers, think about it yourself, and be intrigued, provoked, and maybe even convinced. But no brand of psychoanalysis seems to be science in the usual sense.

In general, the neo-Freudians differ from Freud in three major respects. First, in one way or another, nearly all of them place less emphasis on the explicitly sexual nature of libido as the wellspring of all thought and behavior and reinterpret libido as a more general kind of motivation toward life and creativity. You have seen such a reinterpretation in the preceding chapters of this text. I view this change of emphasis as a permissible modern reinterpretation of an old theory; other theorists view this issue as an example of one place where Freud was simply wrong.

Freud's explicit emphasis on sexuality—even in children—was always one of the most unsettling and controversial aspects of his theory. Thus it should not be surprising that so many later theorists have tried to "clean up" psychoanalysis in this area. Freud himself believed that those who wished to deemphasize the importance of sex were doing so because of their own anxiety about the topic. Their defenses made them unable to face the importance of sex directly, and caused them to see the important bases of behavior elsewhere. This kind of argument is not easily settled. If I say you disagree with me because of your own anxiety, psychopathology, and defense mechanisms, how can you reply except, perhaps, by saying the same thing about me?

A second common deviation of the neo-Freudians is to put more emphasis on interpersonal relations as the source of psychological difficulties, and less emphasis on childhood history and the internal workings of the mind. By modern psychological standards, Freud showed little interest in the social lives of his patients. Whereas a modern therapist would want to know the details of a client's day-to-day interactions with his or her spouse, for example, Freud would be more interested in the history of that client's relations with his or her opposite-sex parent during childhood. Adler and Erikson, to name two, both emphasized the way psychological problems can arise from the difficulties people have relating with other people and with society.

A third deviation by some neo-Freudians is to put less emphasis on the unconscious processes of the mind, and more emphasis on the conscious processes of thought. Modern "ego psychologists," for example, are interested in explaining the ego processes behind the perception and conscious comprehension of reality (e.g., Hartmann, 1964; Loevinger, 1976; Rapaport, 1960; Klein, 1970; the ego psychology of Loevinger was briefly described in Chapter 11). Ego psychology looks a little less like classical psychoanalysis and a little more like the rest of psychology, because instead of focusing on sexuality, psychic conflict and the unconscious, it focuses on perception, memory, learning, and (rational) thinking.

Inferiority and Compensation: Adler

Alfred Adler (1870–1937) was the first major disciple of Freud to end up at odds with the master. Like many others at the time and since, Adler thought that Freud was much too focused on sex as the ultimate motivator and organizer of thought and behavior. Of equal or greater importance than sex, Adler thought, was what he called "social interest," or the desire to relate positively and productively with other people (Adler, 1939).

Adler said that individuals are motivated to attain equality with or superiority over other people, and that they try to accomplish this in order to compensate for whatever they felt, in childhood, was their weakest aspect. This idea, called **organ inferiority**, leads one to expect that someone who felt physically weak as a child will grow into an adult who strives for physical strength, that a child who feels stupid will grow into an adult obsessed with proving himself or herself to be smarter than everyone else, and so on. It matters little whether the child *was* physically weak or relatively unintelligent; more important is how the child was made to *feel.*

A particular kind of such compensation for the past is seen in the desire of an adult to act and become powerful, as the result of feeling inadequate or inferior. Adler called this kind of overcompensating behavior the **masculine protest** (he applied this term to both men and women). Your various compensations for your perceived inferiorities coalesce into a particular mode of behavior, which Adler called your "style of life." Two terms with roots in Adlerian thought that have made it into everyday speech are "inferiority complex" and "lifestyle."

The Collective Unconscious, Persona, and Personality: Jung

The next major rebel from psychoanalysis was Carl Jung (1875–1961; see Jung, 1971a, for a reader). His feud with Freud was even more dramatic and bitter than Adler's, because Freud had high hopes for Jung, who was one of Freud's earliest disciples. Indeed, Jung and Freud had close contacts for many years; they wrote each other numerous letters and even traveled to America together. Freud declared Jung to be his "crown prince" and made him the very first president of the International Psychoanalytic Association.

But over the years Jung's theorizing deviated more and more from Freud's, to the point that neither of them could reconcile their views. Perhaps Jung's most irritating deviation, from Freud's point of view, was his increasing interest in mystical and spiritual matters. Freud, a devout atheist, found Jung's ideas concerning an inner rythm to the universe ("synchronicity"), transcendental experiences, and a collective unconscious rather hard to take. These ideas became extremely important to Jung, however, and they are probably the reason he is so famous today.

Jung's most famous idea is that of the **collective unconscious**. Jung believed that as a result of the history of the human race as a species, we all share certain inborn "racial" (by which he meant "species-specific") memories and ideas, most of which reside in our unconscious. Some of these are fundamental images, called **archetypes**, that Jung believed went to the core of how people think about the world at both conscious and unconscious levels. They include the earth mother, the hero, the devil, and the supreme being. Images of these archetypes, sometimes disguised behind symbols, show up repeatedly in our dreams, in our thoughts, in mythology all over the world, and even in modern literature. (Indeed, a school of literary criticism active to this day entails finding Jungian archetypes in novels, plays, and cinema.)

Another lasting idea of Jung's is the **persona**, which was his term for the social mask one wears in public dealings. He pointed out that to some degree one's persona is always a false self, because everyone tries to keep some aspects of their real selves private, or at least fails to advertise all aspects of their selves equally. This idea survives today in modern social psychology and sociology (e.g., see Goffman, 1959). The danger, according to Jung, is that you might come to identify more with your persona than with your real self. You may become obsessed with your "image" instead of who you really are and what you really feel, and thus become a shallow person with no aims or purposes in life deeper than becoming socially successful. You become a creature of society instead of an individual true to yourself.

Another influential Jungian concept is that of the anima and animus. The **anima** is the idea, or protypical conceptualization, of the female, as held in the mind of a male. The **animus** is the idealized image of the male as held in the mind of a female. These two images cause members of each sex to have some aspects of the opposite sex in their own psychological makeup: a male's anima is the root of his "feminine side"; a female's animus is the basis of her "masculine side." These concepts also determine how each responds to the other sex: a man understands (or misunderstands) women through the psychological lens of his anima; a woman likewise understands or misunderstands men according to her view through her animus. This can lead to real problems if the idealized woman or man in one's mind turns out to match poorly or not at all with the *real* women and men in one's life. This is a common problem, Jung believed, and daily experience would seem to support him on this.

Another key idea of Jung that survives is his distinction between people who are turned in on themselves (introverts) and those who are oriented outward toward the world and other people (extraverts). As we saw in the trait section of this book, the dimension of extraversion-introversion is one of the Big Five dimensions of personality, and has been found again and again in a wide range of psychometric research programs.

Yet another Jungian idea that many people still find useful is his classification of four basic ways of thinking: rational thinking, feeling, sensing, and intuiting. As Jung wrote,

Sensation establishes what is actually present, [rational] thinking enables us to recognize its meaning, feeling tells us its value, and intuition points to possibilities as to whence it came and whither it is going in a given situation (Jung, 1971b/1931, p. 540).

Jung believed that everybody uses all four kinds of thinking, but that people vary in which kind predominates. An engineer might emphasize rational thinking, for example, while an artist emphasizes feeling, a detective emphasizes sensation, and a religious person emphasizes intuition. A modern personality test, the Myers-Briggs Type Indicator (of course also known as the MBTI; Myers, 1962), is sometimes used to determine which kind of thinking is dominant in a particular individual. This test is used frequently by vocational guidance counselors.

Jung believed that ideally one would achieve a balance between all four types of thinking, although he acknowledged that such an achievement is difficult and rare. (The distinction between Jung and Freud, by the way, could be summed up by saying that Freud emphasized rational thinking, whereas Jung was more intuitive.)

Feminine Psychology and Basic Anxiety: Horney

Karen Horney (1885–1952) did not begin writing publicly about psychoanalysis until late in Freud's career, and unlike Adler and Jung she never feuded with the master. She is one of the two influential women in the history of psycho-analysis—the other is Freud's brilliant and devoted daughter Anna. Horney wrote widely about psychoanalytical topics, and some of her books are among the best works one can read for an introduction to psychoanalytic thought (see Horney, 1937, 1950). She also wrote about self-analysis, which she thought people could use to help them through their own psychological difficulties at times when the services of a professional psychoanalyst are impractical or impossible to obtain (Horney, 1942).

Horney's principle deviation from Freud is over an aspect of his theory that many other people have also found objectionable. She disagreed with Freud's portrayal of women as being obsessed by their "penis envy" and their desire to be male. As was mentioned in Chapter 12, in many of his writings Freud seemed to view women as damaged creatures, as men-without-penises, instead of as whole persons in their own right. Like many others since, Horney found this view implausible and objectionable. If some women wish to be men, she theorized, it is probably because they see men as more free and more able to pursue their own interests and ambitions than women are. Although women might lack confidence and seek self-fulfillment to an excessive degree through their love relationships with men, these are the results of the structure of society rather than of the structure of bodies.

Horney's other contributions fit better into the conventional Freudian mode. She emphasized how much adult behavior is based on efforts to overcome the basic anxiety acquired in childhood: the fear of being alone and helpless in a hostile world. Attempts to avoid such anxiety can lead to a number of what Horney called "neurotic needs," needs that people feel but that are neither realistic nor truly desirable. These include the needs to find a life partner who will solve all of one's love-related problems and take over and fix one's life, to be loved by everybody, to dominate everybody, and to be independent of everybody. Not only are these needs unrealistic, they are mutually contradictory. But our mind often unconsciously tries to pursue all of them anyway, which can lead to problems in relating to other people.

Psychosocial Development: Erikson

Erik Erikson (1902–1994) always claimed to be a faithful, orthodox Freudian, but his innovations in psychoanalytic theory make him perhaps the most interesting of the neo-Freudians (his most important book was Erikson, 1968). For example, he pointed out persuasively that not all conflicts take place in the unconscious regions of the mind—many conflicts are conscious ones. For example, you might have to choose between two (or more) activities, two careers, even two lovers. These conflicts can be real, painful, and consequential, as well as completely conscious.

Erikson believed that certain basic kinds of conflict arose at various stages of one's life. This insight led Erikson to develop his own version of Freud's theory of psychological development, in which Erikson emphasized not the physical location of libido at each stage, but rather the conflicts that are experienced at each stage and their possible outcomes. For that reason, his theory of development is referred to as "psychosocial" as opposed to Freud's "psychosexual" approach. (Erikson's psychosocial approach heavily influenced the psychoanalytic view of development that was presented in Chapter 11.) Erikson's developmental theory covers not just childhood, but development throughout one's life.

The first stage, according to Erikson, is "basic trust versus mistrust." This corresponds to Freud's oral stage of very early childhood, where the utterly dependent child learns whether his or her needs and wants will be met, ignored, or overindulged. If the appropriate ratio of satisfaction and temporary frustration is experienced, the child develops "hope" (which in Erikson's terminology refers to a positive but not arrogant attitude toward life) and a confidence—but not overconfidence—that his or her basic needs will be met.

The next stage, corresponding to Freud's anal stage, is that of "autonomy versus shame and doubt." As the child becomes able to control his or her bowels and other physical activities, learns language, and begins to receive orders from adult authorities, an inevitable conflict arises: Who's in charge here? On the one hand, adults put strong pressure on a child to obey, but on the other hand, that child has a desire to take control of his or her own life. The outcome can go either way, leading in some cases to the anal character described in Chapter 11.

Erikson's third stage, corresponding to Freud's phallic stage, is that of "initiative versus guilt." The child begins to anticipate and fantasize about what life as an adult might eventually be like. These fantasies will inevitably include sexual ones, as well as various tactics and plans to get ahead in life. Such fantasies are good for a child, Erikson believed, but can if not responded to well by adults lead the child to feel guilty and to back off from taking initiative in his or her development toward adulthood. Ideally, the child will begin to develop a sense of right and wrong, derived from adult teachings but also true to the child's developing sense of self. This will lead, in adulthood, to a true and principled morality rather than a merely conformist pseudo-morality. You may have noticed that this stage is a reinterpretation of Freud's phallic stage without the full Oedipal crisis (see Chapter 11).

The fourth stage is "industry vs. inferiority," during which one begins to develop the skills and attitudes to succeed in the world of work or otherwise make a positive contribution to society, or not. At this time the child must begin to control his or her exuberant imagination and unfocused energy and get on with tasks of developing competence, workmanship, and a way of organizing the various tasks of life. This stage corresponds roughly to Freud's latency period.

At Erikson's fifth stage, development begins to deviate more widely from the path laid out by Freud. The Freudian account of psychological development, recounted in Chapter 11, basically stops with the genital stage, which is reached, if at all, at some unspecified time after puberty. But in Erikson's view, development continues throughout life. The next crisis to be encountered involves "identity versus identity confusion," as the adolescent strives to figure out who he or she is and what is and is not important. The task at this stage is to begin to choose values and goals that are consistent, personally meaningful, and useful.

Close on the heels of the identity conflict comes the conflict of "intimacy versus isolation." The task here, for young adulthood, is to find an intimate life partner with whom you can share important experiences and your further development, as opposed to becoming isolated and lonely.

As one enters middle age, Erikson said, the next crisis to be faced is the conflict of "generativity versus stagnation." As your own position in life becomes set with increasing firmness, do you settle in and become comfortable and passive, or do you begin to turn your concerns to the next generation? The challenge here is to avoid the temptation to stagnate, and instead to raise and nurture children and more generally to do what you can to assure the progress of the next generation. One is reminded here of the modern phenomenon of American retirees, living in trailer parks and retirement communities, voting overwhelmingly against taxes to support schools. At a younger age, we see "Yuppies" (young urban professionals) who either don't have children because they tend to slow down one's career, or do have children but hire other people to raise them because they "don't have time" to do it themselves. Which choice do you think these people have made between generativity and stagnation?

The final crisis in life occurs in late old age, as one begins to face the prospect of death. The choice here is between "integrity" and "despair." Do you despair about the mistakes you made in your life and feel that, basically, you blew it? Or from your long experience have you developed wisdom? The test of that is: After seventy, eighty, or ninety years of life, have you anything of interest and value to say to the next generation? Or not?

As we have seen, one progresses from one crisis to another in Erikson's scheme *not* according to processes of physical or genital maturation, but according to the different developmental tasks that are necessary at different times of life because of the structure of human society. This insight about the societal basis of development is the first of the two major contributions of Erikson's theory of development. The second major contribution is that this scheme is Erikson's pioneering venture into what modern psychology calls "life span development." This idea proposes that development is not something that only little children do; it is an never-ending task and opportunity across life from childhood through middle and old age. Modern developmental psychology is heavily influenced by this idea.

Where Have All the Neo-Freudian Theorists Gone?

As I mentioned earlier, they all seem to be dead. In fact, the chapters in personality textbooks that survey Freud and the neo-Freudians are sometimes sardonically called, in the business, the "tour of the graveyard." Certainly no one of the stature of Jung, Adler, Horney, or Erikson seems to be actively developing psychoanalytic theory today, and it seems doubtful that any great psychoanalytic theorists will emerge in the future. This kind of theorizing, based ultimately on informal observation, clinical experience, and insight, seems to be the wave of the past. The future of psychoanalysis seems to lie not in the direction of further theoretical development of the kind just surveyed, but rather in increased attempts to do experimental and correlational research of the more conventional sort in an attempt to scientifically confirm, disprove, or alter psychoanalytic theory on the basis of the same kind of evidence employed by psychology more generally.

MODERN PSYCHOANALYTIC RESEARCH

Almost all conventional psychological research—that is, experimental and correlational studies with data that can be publicly reported—is conducted by academic psychologists with positions at universities or research institutes. Over the years, the relationship between these psychologists and their colleagues who practice psychoanalysis in clinical settings has ranged from uneasy to downright hostile. Most university psychology departments, where researchers are trained, have no Freudians in them at all, so there is a remarkable amount of ignorance about psychoanalysis on the part of many research psychologists. Where would they learn about it? And even when academic psychologists do encounter psychoanalytic research that meets their usual standards of empirical validity, they often seem unprepared to believe any evidence that shows any aspect of psychoanalytic thought as having value.

For their part, the psychoanalysts are at least equally guilty (Bachrach, Galatzer-Levy, Skolnikoff, & Waldron, 1991). They typically have very little interest in conventional scientific research, preferring to exchange anecdotal evidence: "I had a patient once who. . . ." Freud himself thought that psychodynamic processes could only be seen through clinical case study; most modern psychoanalysts likewise seem to regard experimental and correlational research as irrelevant. For example, one psychoanalyst recently wrote the following about experimental research:

I have been singularly uninterested in, if not contemptuous of, anything that the "number crunchers" had to say. . . . The phrase "meaningful statistical data" was, to me, an oxymoron of hilarious proportions (Tansey, 1992, p. 539).

The result of this mutual myopia is that psychoanalytic psychologists and non-psychoanalytic psychologists ignore each other most of the time, and when they do interact, they attack or at best lecture each other without listening to the other side.

This sorry situation may be starting to change, however. A few brave psychologists are pursuing research that is relevant to psychoanalysis, and many more are doing so without knowing that is what they are doing. One of the first of these new researchers, Drew Westen, has pointed out that while few psychologists research Freud or even psychoanalysis directly, the work of many of them can nevertheless be considered relevant to these topics (1990). He proposes that any research is psychoanalytic to the extent that it includes

1. an examination of independent mental processes that occur simultaneously in the same mind and can conflict with one another;
2. mental processes that are unconscious;
3. compromises among mental processes that are negotiated out of consciousness;
4. self-defensive thought processes and self-deception;
5. the influence of the past on current functioning, especially patterns laid down in childhood that endure into adulthood; or
6. sexual or aggressive wishes as they consciously or unconsciously influence thought, feeling, and behavior.

While very little experimental or correlational research includes *all* of these concerns, a great deal is relevant to at least one or some of them. Westen contends that if a given piece of research addresses any one of these issues, it is at least a little bit psychoanalytic. The more of these issues a piece of research includes, the more psychoanalytic that research becomes—knowingly or not. Westen's observation is extremely important because it implies that conventional, experimental, and correlational research may not be as irrelevant to psychoanalysis as psychologists on both sides of the fence have long assumed.

Testing Psychoanalytic Hypotheses

In light of Westen's conclusion, it is possible to find a large amount of research in the psychological literature that addresses psychoanalytic hypotheses. Most of this research did not explicitly set out to test psychoanalysis, and sometimes when the research is reported psychoanalysis *per se* is not even mentioned. But if one wants to find research documenting some ideas that can be traced back to Freud and the variants on the psychoanalysis he invented, a fair amount of support can be found.

For example, a large amount of research over the years has shown that the unconscious part of a person's mind can perceive some things without the conscious mind being aware of it (Erdelyi, 1974). It appears that the unconscious mind can keep a perception out of consciousness in order to protect the individual from experiencing anxiety—a classic defense mechanism. In one study an obscene word, which might upset the values of the superego, was flashed on a screen in front of a subject. The person reported being unable to perceive what the word was. Then another word, the same length as the first but innocuous rather than obscene, was flashed. The person could read it immediately. This finding implies that some part of the mind recognized that the first word was obscene *before* it was consciously perceived, and apparently decided to keep this recognition out of conscious awareness. Furthermore, people who avoid reporting unpleasant perceptions are not just trying to look good, but appear to be actively pushing their experience of negative emotions out of conscious awareness (Weinberger & Davidson, 1994). This is the process Freud called repression.

Many modern cognitive psychologists have concluded that most of what the mind does is unconscious (they usually report their findings without acknowledging Freud, however). One currently dominant model of cognitive processing, called parallel distributed processing, or PDP, posits that the mind does many things at once, all outside of consciousness. Only the result and the compromise between these simultaneous mental processes becomes represented in conscious awareness (Rumelhart, McClelland, & the PDP Research Group, 1986). This finding recalls Freud's idea that consciousness is just the tip of the mental iceberg, with most of its determinants hidden from view.

Other psychoanalytic ideas have also been supported by modern research. The character traits of the anal personality—stinginess, orderliness, rigidity, and so on—have been demonstrated to be correlated with each other just as Freud said they were, and the traits of the oral character also seem to be intercorrelated as Freud predicted, though perhaps to a weaker degree (Westen, 1990). The process Freud called catharsis, which involves getting one's psychological disturbances out into the open, has been proved to be helpful both for psychological and even physical health (Erdelyi, 1994; Hughes, Uhlmann, & Pennebaker, 1994). Modern laboratory studies also have demonstrated transference, Freud's term for taking patterns of behavior and emotion developed with somebody in the past and applying them to one's relations with somebody new (Andersen & Baum, 1994).

Not all Freudian ideas have fared so well, however. Notably, as I mentioned earlier, research has failed to support Freud's story of the Oedipal crisis at the phallic stage (Kihlstrom, 1994; Sears, 1947). Apparently this part of Freud's theory is wrong, which is why Chapter 11 offered a different account of what happens at the phallic stage. Some psychologists claim that those psychoanalytic ideas that have been supported by research, such as the existence of the unconscious, would have been thought of even had Freud never lived, and that most of those ideas that seem unique to Freud, such as the Oedipal crisis, have been shown to be wrong. These psychologists conclude that Freud has contributed nothing to our modern understanding of human psychology (Kihlstrom, 1994).

This view seems unduly harsh to me. The edifice of Freudian theory has influenced modern thinking and modern psychology many, many ways. Indeed, it is difficult to imagine what modern psychology would look like had Freud never lived. Moreover, the completeness and persuasiveness of the original Freudian accounts of human nature, along with some of the revisions offered by the neo-Freudians and a bit of modern interpretation, convince me that Freudian theory has a great deal to offer toward trying to understand the complex nature of others and ourselves.

Attachment and Romantic Love

One particularly interesting area of modern research that acknowledges a heavy debt to psychoanalytic thought is the study of attachment and romantic love. The English psychoanalyst John Bowlby was heavily influenced by Freud's theory, but became frustrated by the sheerly speculative way some of his analytic colleagues wrote about the nature of love. He was even more frustrated by what he saw as their failure to understand how a person's early experiences in love—those in infancy, usually with his or her mother—could shape one's entire future outlook on emotional attachments.

Bowlby's description of the origins of love is similar to some of the theorizing by evolutionary biologists that was described in Chapter 9. Bowlby hypothesizes that in the risky environment in which the human species developed over thousands of years, humans (and actually all primates) evolved a strong and basic fear of being alone, especially when in unusual, dark, or dangerous places, and especially when tired, injured, or sick. This fear motivates us to desire someone to protect us, preferably someone who has a particular interest in our survival and well-being. In other words, we want someone who loves us. This desire is especially strong in infancy and early childhood, but it never truly goes away; it is the basis of many of our most important interpersonal relationships (Bowlby, 1969/1982).

This desire for protection leads us to develop what Bowlby called "attachments." The first attachment relationship is formed with one's primary caregiver, usually one's mother. The term "primary" implies that a child generally has other caregivers as well, even if one is preferred—all of those relationships are important. If everything goes well, the attachments he or she develops provide a child with both a safe haven from danger and a secure base from which to explore in happier times.

Unfortunately, everything does not always go well. As a result of his or her interactions with the primary and other caregivers, and the degree to which they meet his or her basic needs, the child develops expectations about what attachment relationships are like and what can be expected from them. Bowlby pointed out that a child draws two lessons from these early experiences. First, the child develops a belief about whether the people to whom he or she becomes attached will generally be reliable. Second, and perhaps more important, the child develops a belief about whether his or her own self is the kind of person to whom attachment figures are likely to respond in a helpful way. In other words, if a child learns that she does not usually receive the necessary amount of love and care, she might conclude this is because she is not lovable or worth caring about. This inference is not logical, of course: just because a child fails to be loved by a negligent caregiver, this does not mean the child would not be lovable to others. But Bowlby believed children draw this kind of inference nonetheless.

The American psychologist Mary Ainsworth tried to make the consequences of these expectations and conclusions concrete and visible. She invented an experimental procedure called the "strange situation," in which a child is briefly separated from and then reunited with his or her mother. Ainsworth believed that a good deal could be gleaned from observing how the child reacted both to the separation and the reunion. In particular, one could determine the type of attachment relationship the child had developed (Ainsworth, Blehar, Waters, & Wall, 1978). From her research, Ainsworth classified children into three types, depending on the kinds of expectations they had developed about their primary caregivers and how they acted in the strange situation.

Anxious-ambivalent children come from home situations where their caregivers' behavior is "inconsistent, hit-or-miss, or chaotic" (Sroufe, Carlson & Shulman, 1993, p. 320). These children are vigilant about their mother's presence and grow very upset when she disappears even for a few minutes. In their school situation, they are often victimized by other children and attempt to cling onto teachers and peers in a way that backfires—it only drives them away—and leads to further hurt feelings, anger, and insecurity.

Avoidant children come from homes where they have repeatedly been rebuffed in their attempts to enjoy contact or reassurance. According to one study, their mothers tend to dislike hugs and other bodily contact (Main, 1990). In the strange situation, they do not appear distressed, but if their heart rate is measured one sees definite signs of tension and anxiety (Sroufe & Waters, 1977). When their mother returns from the brief separation, they simply ignore her. In their school situations these children are often hostile and defiant, and manage to alienate both their teachers and their peers. As they grow older they develop an angry self-reliance and cold and distant attitudes toward other people.

The more lucky ones, secure children, have managed to develop a confident faith in themselves and their caregivers. When their mother returns in the strange situation, they greet her happily, with open arms. When upset, they are easily soothed, and they are active in exploring their environment, returning frequently to the primary caregiver for comfort and encouragement. They are sure of the caregiver's support and do not worry about it. This positive attitude carries over into the other relationships in their lives.

One remarkable aspect of these attachment styles is their self-fulfilling nature (Shaver & Clark, 1994). The anxious, clingy child drives people away; the avoidant child makes people angry; the secure child is easy to be with and attracts both caregivers and friends. Thus a child's developing attachment style will affect his or her outcomes throughout life.

In fact, research is beginning to examine in detail what happens to these children as they grow into adults and try to develop satisfying romantic relationships. There are at least twenty-one different methods to assess one's "adult attachment style," the grown-up version of the childhood pattern described above. One of the simplest goes like this:

Which of these descriptions fits you best?

1. I am somewhat uncomfortable being close to others; I find it difficult to trust them completely, difficult to allow myself to depend on them. I am nervous when anyone gets too close, and often, love partners want me to be more intimate than I feel comfortable being.

2. I find that others are reluctant to get as close as I would like. I often worry that my partner doesn't really love me or won't want to stay with me. I want to get very close to my partner, and this sometimes scares people away.

3. I find it relatively easy to get close to others and am comfortable depending on them. I don't often worry about being abandoned or about someone getting too close to me. (Shaver & Clark, 1994, p. 120)

According to this measure, if you checked item 1 you are avoidant, if item 2 you are anxious-ambivalent, and if item 3 you are secure. When this survey was published in a Denver newspaper, 55 percent of the respondents described themselves as secure, 25 percent as avoidant, and 20 percent as anxious—the same percentages found in American infants studied by Ainsworth in the strange situation (Campos, Barrett, Lamb, Goldsmith, & Stenberg, 1983).

More detailed studies have found that avoidant individuals are relatively uninterested in romantic relationships, are more likely (than secure individuals) to have the relationships they enter break up, and grieve less after a relationship ends, even though they admit to being lonely (Shaver & Clark, 1994). They like to work alone, and sometimes use their work as an excuse to detach themselves from their emotional relationships. They describe their parents as having been rejecting and cold, or else describe them in vaguely positive ways (e.g., as "nice") without being able to provide specific examples. (For example, when asked "What did your mother do that was *particularly* nice?" they are typically unable to give a convincing answer.) Avoidant individuals withdraw from their romantic partners when under stress, and instead tend to cope with their stress by ignoring it or denying it exists. They do not often share personal information with other people, and they tend to dislike other people who do share such information.

According to attachment theory, this pattern arises from a life and especially a childhood history of being rejected and ignored by important attachment figures. As a defense, the child (and then the adult) has learned to deny being vulnerable to this kind of rejection, and tries to believe that emotional relationships are not necessary and do not matter. (That way, they cannot be hurt.)

Anxious-ambivalent adults are obsessed with their romantic partners—they think about them all the time, and have trouble allowing them to have their own lives. They suffer from extreme jealousy, report a high rate of relationship failures (not surprisingly), and sometimes exhibit the repeating cycle of breaking up and getting back together with the same romantic partner. Anxious-ambivalents tend to have low and unstable self-esteem, like to work with other people, but typically feel unappreciated by their co-workers. They are highly emotional under stress, and have to work hard to keep their emotions under control. They describe their parents as having been intrusive, unfair, and inconsistent.

Attachment theory traces this pattern to a history of attachment figures who were unlikely to respond to the child unless he or she displayed anger or anxiety loudly and dramatically. Anything less was ignored. The expectations the child developed from this experience carried over into his or her adult life.

You will be relieved to learn that secure adults tend to enjoy long, stable romantic relationships characterized by deep trust and friendship. They have high self-esteem as well as high regard for others. When under stress, they seek out others and in particular their romantic partners for emotional support. They are also loyal in supporting their romantic partners when they are under stress. They describe their parents in positive but realistic terms, which they are able to back up with specific examples. In sum, they are people who are easy to be with (Shaver & Clark, 1994).

Secure individuals can deal with reality in a direct manner because their attachment experience has been positive and reliable. They have always had a safe refuge from danger and a secure base from which to explore the world. This idyllic pattern does not mean that secure people never cry, become angry, or worry about abandonment. But they do not need to distort reality to deal with their sadness, anger, or insecurity.

According to attachment theory, all of these patterns are learned in early childhood and reinforced in an increasingly self-fulfilling manner across young adulthood. This pattern of transference can persist across one's entire life span. If one is unlucky enough to learn an avoidant or anxious-ambivalent style, change is difficult but perhaps not impossible. Psychotherapists informed by attachment theory try to teach these people the origins of their relationship styles, the way these styles lead to self-defeating outcomes, and constructive, positive ways to relate to others (Shaver & Clark, 1994).

Attachment theory, originated by a psychoanalyst (Bowlby) who considered himself a neo-Freudian, has diverged a long way from its psychoanalytic roots. Indeed, it is possible to say that it is no longer really Freudian (Kihlstrom, 1994).

But one can also see it is as an example of how far a group of creatively thinking psychologists can develop a basic Freudian precept. In this case, the Freudian precept is that early relationships with one's parents form a template for how one conducts other emotionally important relationships thoughout life.

THE FUTURE OF PSYCHOANALYSIS

It has been said that the function of genius is to raise questions that time and mediocre minds eventually will answer. If Freud is the genius, you can see where this saying leaves the rest of us. But it is true that even today Freud's theorizing raises questions that psychology would be better off trying to answer than continuing to ignore.

For example, Drew Westen points out that "one can read a thousand pages of social-cognitive theory [arguably the dominant paradigm in social psychology today] and never know that people have genitals—or even, for that matter, that they have bodies—let alone fantasies" (1990, p. 54). Freud's function in the Victorian age, as well as today, was to raise questions that others found too uncomfortable to think about. Freud was convinced that much of the resistance he experienced early in this century was a result of the sexual hang-ups of his critics, who were uncomfortable hearing what he had to say. Would Freud's opinion of his critics today be much different?

My crystal ball for the future of psychoanalytic theory is cloudy. But I will offer two predictions. First, I think the classic neo-Freudians—the Jungs, Adlers, and Eriksons—are gone and their kind will not be seen again. Their thinking will continue to influence psychoanalytic theory for years to come, but it seems highly unlikely that some future genius is going to come out of the clinic with a new set of insights to turn the psychoanalytic world on its ear.

Second, research on cognitive and perceptual processes and on personality functioning in daily life will gradually and slowly become integrated with one or more tenets of psychoanalytic theory. As Westen has pointed out, a surprising amount of such research is doing so already, although the investigators in question do not always acknowledge it. Cognitive psychology, in particular, has developed some extraordinarily clever methods for studying mental functioning that may eventually elucidate some of the unconscious processes of thought that so interested Freud.

Thus the future of research relevant to psychoanalysis is in principle highly promising and intriguing. But before this promise can be fulfilled, some formidable scientific and institutional obstacles must be overcome. Psychoanalysts will have to become more open to empirical evidence, and empirical researchers will have to learn more about psychoanalysis.

SUMMARY

Freud died more than half a century ago, but his theory lives on in a variety of ways. Some psychoanalysts try to preserve his theory in its pure form, while other post-Freudians continue to interpret, update, revise, and argue about Freud's basic theory. Others have attempted to develop their own, distinct kinds of psychoanalytic theory. Still others content themselves with debunking Freud without offering a real alternative. Neo-Freudians who have offered theories of their own include such famous individuals as Alfred Adler, Carl Jung, Karen Horney, and Erik Erikson. The kind of theoretical development these individuals worked on seems to have been relegated to the past, however. Modern psychologists interested in psychoanalysis are trying to bring rigorous research methodology to bear on some of the hundreds of hypotheses that could be derived from psychoanalytic theory. Some of these hypotheses seem to have been confirmed, such as the existence of unconscious mental processes and phenomena such as repression and transference. A particularly fruitful area of research has studied the connection between childhood patterns of attachment and adult patterns of romantic love. If more researchers conduct this kind of research, and manage to overcome some significant obstacles, then the future of psychoanalysis could become bright indeed.

Suggested Readings: Psychoanalysis

Brenner, C. (1974). *An elementary textbook of psychoanalysis.* Garden City, NY: Doubleday/Anchor.
  An excellent secondary source for a thorough summary of psychoanalysis.

Bettelheim, B. (1988). *A good enough parent.* New York: Vintage.
  Bettelheim is one of the more important psychoanalysts of the latter part of this century. This is a fascinating look at child-rearing from a psychoanalytic point of view. It is never blindly orthodox, however, and is filled with nuggets of wisdom that would be of interest to any parent.

Horney, K. (1942). *Self-analysis.* New York: Norton.

Horney, K. (1950). *Neurosis and human growth.* New York: Norton.
  These two books, by an important neo-Freudian in her own right, make fascinating reading for their insights into human nature, especially the unrealistic ways people think about themselves and their goals. These are "self-help" books, but intellectually they are much richer than more recent writing in this category.

Gay, P. (1988). *Freud: A life for our time.* New York: Norton.
  A masterful, thorough, well-written biography of Freud that includes a tour not just of his life, but of the development of psychoanalytic thought. The author is clearly sympathetic to Freud and psychoanalysis.

Gay, P. (Ed.). (1989). *The Freud reader.* New York: Norton.
  An excellent collection of Freud's original writings, including some unusual selections translated for the first time for this volume.

Sulloway, F. J. (1979). *Freud, biologist of the mind: Beyond the psychoanalytic legend.* New York: Basic Books.
  A summary and discussion of Freud's biological ideas, from a somewhat unsympathetic modern viewpoint.

Robinson, P. (1993). *Freud and his critics.* Berkeley: University of California Press.
  An interesting attempt to defend Freud from some of his prominent modern attackers, including Frank Sulloway and Jeffrey Masson.

PART V

Experience and Awareness: Humanistic and Cross-Cultural Psychology

Every individual has a unique point of view. The way you see the world is different, at least slightly and sometimes deeply, from the way other people see it. Fans of opposing teams may watch the same game yet come away with drastically different impressions of who fouled whom and which side the referees unfairly favored (Hastorf & Cantril, 1954). Or, more consequential, where one person sees a woman exercising a free choice, another person, observing exactly the same behavior, may see the murder of an unborn child.

Your individual experience of the world—what you see, hear, feel, and think from moment to moment—is called your phenomenology. The phenomenological approach to personality psychology, which is the subject of Chapter 14, is based on the premise that to understand a person you must understand his or her unique view of reality. This approach, more than any other, also emphasizes that the object of the psychologist's scrutiny and analysis is a person who can scrutinize right back and form his or her own opinions. Whereas the other basic approaches to personality tend to regard people, implicitly if not explicitly, as things to be dispassionately examined, the phenomenological approach emphasizes that people are beings who feel, think, and experience, and indeed these attributes are what make humans unique. For this reason, the phenomenological approach is also known as humanistic psychology.

One interesting question raised by a phenomenological approach is this: If everybody's view of the world is different, which one is right? Or, in the midst of all these shifting perceptions, where is reality? Either way you ask it, the question turns out to be unanswerable, but it is critically important nonetheless. For to ask this question is to acknowledge that none of us has an exclusive ownership of truth, and that other points of view—even those that seem drastically different, foreign, or strange—may also be valid.

This latter insight is the basis of the cross-cultural study of personality, the topic of Chapter 15. Not only do different individuals have different views of reality, but so do different cultures. A behavior seen as polite by a Japanese may seem horribly inefficient to a North American, and the same action seen as ordinary by an American may seem deeply immoral to an Indian. Psychologists are just beginning to examine the degree to which theories of personality forged in Western culture apply to people in very different cultures around the world. They are also compelled to address the same issue raised by the phenomenological approach to personality: If different cultures have very different views of the world, where is reality?

The following two chapters, therefore, address the same basic phenomenological premise—that the way you view and experience the world is the most important psychological fact about you. The first, Chapter 14, examines this premise at the individual level, and the second, Chapter 15, examines this premise at the cultural level. In both cases, the difficult challenge is to try to see the world the way someone else does, be that someone a close friend or the native of a different culture. From a phenomenological perspective, this is the only way to begin truly to understand that person.

CHAPTER 14

EXISTENCE, EXPERIENCE, AND FREE WILL: THE PHENOMENOLOGICAL APPROACH

The story is told of how Watergate burglar G. Gordon Liddy liked to impress people by holding his hand steadily above a lit candle as his flesh burned.

"How can you do that? Doesn't it hurt?" he was asked.

"Of course it hurts. The trick," he replied, "is not to care."[1]

A HUMANISTIC PSYCHOLOGY

Psychology is sometimes accused of having "physics envy." Many psychologists seem to covet the prestige of being considered "real" scientists, and many more believe that the best way to understand the human mind is through an enterprise modeled on the physical sciences, one that follows the same canons of public data, objective analysis, repeatability, and so on. This belief underlies the trait, behavioral, and cognitive approaches, and sometimes psychoanalysis as well.

The phenomenological approach is a glaring exception—in fact, *the* glaring exception—to this belief. Most adherents of the phenomenological approach vehemently disagree with the idea that the study of the mind is just another science or that it in any way does, could, or should resemble physics or chemistry. They believe that the subject matter of psychology is fundamentally different from that of any of the conventional sciences. As an object of study, they argue,

---

[1] I heard this existential fable from Lily Tomlin, who told it during a performance of *Search for Signs of Intelligent Life in the Universe*. Ms. Tomlin seems reliable on other matters, so perhaps this story is true.

the mind is not only different from things such as molecules or atoms, it is *fundamentally* different.

It is fundamentally different because, unlike anything else, the human mind is *aware*. It knows it is being studied, for instance, and has opinions about itself that affect the way it is studied. The field of psychology amounts to the human mind attempting to understand the human mind. This complication does not arise in the study of molecules or atoms; they just lie there, unaware and without purpose—and they don't seem to have opinions about their own nature.[2] The term "phenomenological" refers to the emphasis of this approach on the phenomenology, or conscious experience, of the aware mind. And since the aware mind is usually assumed to be a uniquely human possession, the term "humanistic" is also sometimes used for this general point of view. A third term associated with this approach is "existential," because it has roots in the branch of philosophy, called existentialism, that puts the experience of one's existence at the core of things. In this chapter I shall use all three terms—phenomenological, humanistic, or existential—depending upon which aspect of the approach is being emphasized at the moment.

A Diverse Approach

The use of three different terms to refer to one approach highlights another important fact: phenomenological/humanistic/existential psychologists share less of a common core of beliefs than adherents of the other approaches considered in this book. Whereas trait psychology had Gordon Allport, psychoanalysis had Sigmund Freud, and behaviorism had B. F. Skinner to lay down a foundation from which to start, there is no single person or theory that unites this three-headed perspective. The debates within phenomenological psychology sometimes seem unusually bitter, involving strong disagreement about fundamental points. Part of the reason is that adherents have included not just empirically trained psychologists, but artists, poets, novelists, philosophers, and even members of the clergy—some of whom like to argue (Hall & Lindzey, 1978).

Nonetheless, I think it is worth considering these diverse perspectives together because there are certain important themes that run across them and make them fundamentally different from the rest of psychology. These include an emphasis on conscious experience as the fundamental phenomenon that psychology must address, an emphasis on free will and the responsibilities that free will entails, and, perhaps above all, an insistence that we not forget that the

---

[2]Presumably. Although before this chapter is over, even this presumption will be questioned!

objects of our study are human beings. As this chapter shall discuss, humans have unique existential and phenomenological concerns that do not seem to apply to rocks, trees, or other animals, and these concerns are important to humans' psychological functioning.

Awareness Is Everything

To say that the phenomenological approach emphasizes conscious experience is perhaps an understatement. Proponents of the approach often seem to believe that one's immediate, conscious experience is *all* that matters. They believe that your conscious thoughts and feelings are the cause of everything you do. Everything that has happened to you in the past, everything that is true about you at this moment, and anything that might happen in the future can influence you only in the way that it affects your thoughts and feelings at this moment. Indeed, from the phenomenological viewpoint, the only place and time in which you really *exist* is in your consciousness, at this moment. The past, the future, other people, and other places are no more than ideas and, in a sense, illusions. The sense is this: a broader reality might exist, but only the part of it that you perceive—or invent—will ever matter to you.

This may all sound rather New Age, but phenomenological analysis is not a new idea. The Talmud says, "We do not see things as they are. We see them as *we* are." Epictetus, a Greek Stoic philosopher who lived two thousand years ago, said, "It is not things in themselves that trouble us, but our opinions of things." More recently, but still nearly half a century ago, Carl Rogers wrote, "I do not react to some absolute reality, but to my perception of this reality. It is this perception which for me *is* reality" (Rogers, 1951, p. 484). All of these quotes express basic tenets of the phenomenological approach (McAdams, 1990).

It is hard to overemphasize how different these ideas are from those espoused by any other approach to psychology. As was already mentioned, every other approach regards people basically as objects to be scientifically studied, much as anything else (a plant, a star, a seismic fault) might be studied. The phenomenological approach, in contrast, says that the only thing interesting about people is something that is not even located in the objective world: the subjective, conscious, experiencing mind.

The psychoanalytic approach places the causes of thought and behavior largely in the unconscious mind. The trait approach concentrates on stable differences between people and how they affect the way those people think and act differently. Behavioristic approaches locate the important causes of action in the rewards and punishments afforded by the social and physical environment. (The behavioristic approaches will be considered in Chapters 16–18.) From the phenomenological perspective, however, all of these influences are secondary. They matter only if you think about them *now*, and if you decide to *let* them influence you. Otherwise, they might as well not (or maybe in some sense they really do not) exist.

Free Will

All the other basic approaches to personality can agree on at least one thing: People do not have free will. People's behavior is a function of how their traits interact with situations, or of their neurotransmitters and hormones, or the workings of their unconscious minds, or the structure of the rewards and punishments in their environment.

Phenomenologists disagree. Their belief that your conscious experience is the crux of personality means that you *do* have free will. What your unconscious mind contains cannot begin to matter until it becomes conscious in some way. And nothing in the world nor anything that has ever happened to you can affect your mind, if you choose not to let it. As Gordon Liddy said, the trick is not to care.

Your own particular experience of the world is called your **construal**. Because construals are interpretations rather than reflections of reality, they are freely chosen. These freely chosen construals are the basis for your choice about which goals in life you will pursue. So it is through choosing how you wish to construe the world that you achieve free will (Boss, 1963). And it is by abdicating this choice, to other people or to society, that you can lose free will (I'll say more about this later).

Understanding Others

A corollary of the phenomenological view is that to understand another person, you must understand his or her construals (Kelly, 1955). You can only comprehend the mind of someone else to the extent that you can imagine how the world appears from his or her perspective. The adage "Do not judge me until you have walked a mile in my shoes" expresses the general idea.

This principle tends to discourage being judgmental about others. It implies that if only you could see the world through others' eyes, you would realize that their actions and attitudes, which may seem incomprehensible and even evil from your perspective, are the natural consequences of their own view of reality. Furthermore, there is no way to prove that your view of reality is right and other views are wrong. Thus it is a fundamental mistake to assume that others view the world the same way you do, or that there is only one correct way to view the world. The views of others, no matter how strange they may seem, must be considered just as valid as your own. (Extremists such as Thomas Szasz (1960, 1974) have sometimes argued that this is even true about the people usually considered to be mentally ill; they merely have an alternative and equally valid construal of reality. But, this is an extreme position.)

One direct consequence of the phenomenological view is a far-reaching cultural and even moral relativism. We cannot judge the practices of other cultures from the perspective of our own (more will be said about this claim in Chapter 15). Nor can we judge the moral codes of other people through our own moral code. For when all is said and done, there is no objective reality—or, if there is, there is no way for us to know it. There are only varying construals of reality, all equally valid and equally invalid.

EXISTENTIALISM

The philosophical root of the phenomenological approach to personality is existentialism. Existentialism is not only a ten-dollar word, it is a broad philosophical movement that can be traced to Europe in the mid-1800s. Søren Kierkegaard, the Danish theologian, was one of its early proponents, as were Freidrich Nietzsche, Martin Heidegger, and, more recently, Ludwig Binswanger, Medard Boss, and Jean-Paul Sartre.

Existentialism arose as a reaction against European rationalism, science, and even the industrial revolution. The existentialists thought that by the late nineteenth century rationality had gone too far in its attempt to account for everything. In particular, they thought that science, technology, and rational philosophy had lost touch with human experience. This point of view began to attract a dramatically larger following in Europe after World War II. The purpose of existential philosophy was to regain contact with the experience of being alive and aware.

Existential analysis begins with the concrete and specific experience of a single human being *existing* at a particular moment in time and space. An excellent example is you, right now. I mean, then, back when you read the words "right now," although that is already past, so maybe we should concentrate on right now, instead. Too late. The point is, your experience of existence exists only one infinitesimally small moment at a time, which is then gone, to be followed by another.

The key existential questions are the following: What is the nature of existence? How does it feel? And what does it mean?

Three Parts of Experience

The attempt to understand how existence feels is called **phenomenology**. According to the existential psychologist Ludwig Binswanger, if you look deeply into your own mind, you will find that the conscious experience of being alive has three components (Binswanger, 1958).

The first component is biological experience, or **Umwelt**, which consists of the sensations that you feel by virtue of being a biological organism that is a part of nature. *Umwelt* includes pleasure, pain, heat, cold, and all the other sensations your body experiences. It also includes the sensations of your eyes, ears, tongue, nose, and skin. Poke your finger with a pin: what you experience is *Umwelt*.

The second component is social experience, or **Mitwelt**, which consists of what you think and feel as a social being who relates to other people. Your emotions and thoughts about other people, and the emotions and thoughts that you receive from them, make up *Mitwelt*. Think about someone you love, fear, or admire. What you experience is *Mitwelt*.

The third component is inner, psychological experience, or **Eigenwelt**. In a sense, this is the experience of experience itself. It consists of how you feel and think when you try to understand yourself, your own mind, and your own existence. *Eigenwelt* is the experience of introspection (and is something we can presume Binswanger felt strongly when trying to figure out the components of experience). Try to watch yourself having the experience of a pin prick, or the experience of feeling love, or even the experience of reading this paragraph. When you observe your own mind and feelings in this way the (often confusing) experience you have is *Eigenwelt*.

''Thrown-ness'' and Angst

An important basis of your experience is your **thrown-ness**—Heidegger used the German word *Geworfenheit*. This term refers to the time, place, and circumstances into which you happened to have been thrown at birth (Heidegger, 1927/1962). One's experience clearly depends in large part upon whether one was born into a medieval slave society, or a seventeenth-century Native American society, or late-twentieth-century North American society.

From an existential perspective, this last way of being thrown—yours—is particularly difficult. Existence in modern society is difficult because we have been thrown into a world that seems to have no overarching meaning or purpose. Organized religion plays a relatively small role in providing a meaning to existence, compared to the role it played in the past. Its modern substitutes—science, art, and philosophy—have all failed to provide an alternative worldview that can tell us the two things we most need to know:

1. Why are we here?
2. What should we be doing?

Indeed, modern existential philosophy only tells us that there are no answers to these two concerns beyond those we invent for ourselves!

When you do not have answers to these two questions, you experience anxiety about what your life means, if anything, and whether you are spending yours the right way. After all, life is finite, even short, and you only get one—waste it, and you waste everything. The unpleasant feelings one can get from the contemplation of these concerns is called existential anxiety, or **Angst**. According to Sartre (1965), this *Angst* can be analyzed into three other sensations: anguish, forelornness, and despair.

Every conscious human must feel anguish because the choices we inevitably must make are never perfect. A choice to do good in one way will always lead to bad outcomes in other ways. For example, deciding to aid one person can result in harm to others who are not aided. Such tradeoffs are inevitable, according to Sartre, and so the resulting anguish is inevitable, too.

Furthermore, nothing and no one—no god, no unquestionable set of rules or values—can guide our choices or let us off the hook for what we have decided. Our choices are ours, and ours alone. (Sartre also says that even if there is a God who will tell you what to do, you still need to decide whether or not to do what God says—and so you are still alone in your choice.) Furthermore, there is no escape from this existential solitude: there you are, *forelorn*, alone with your existential choices.

Finally, any aware person realizes that there are many things and many important outcomes that he or she cannot hope to change or even to affect. These outcomes include some of the most important elements of our lives, such as the fate of ourselves and our loved ones. If we are honest in acknowledging this momentous and regrettable fact, then we will also feel despair at our inability to change all aspects of the world. This inability, according to Sartre, only redoubles our responsibility to affect those aspects of the world that we can influence.

Bad Faith

What should you do about *Angst* and all these other unpleasant-sounding experiences? According to existentialists such as Sartre, you must face them directly. It is a moral imperative, they believe, to face the facts of your own mortality and the apparent meaninglessness of life, and to seek meaning for your existence nonetheless. This is your existential responsibility, which requires existential courage, or what Sartre called "optimistic toughness" (1965, p. 49).

Of course, there is a way out, at least temporariliy, that requires neither courage nor toughness: simply avoid the topic and the problem altogether. Quit worrying about what life means, get a good job, buy a big car, and advance your social status. Do not try to think about fundamental issues for yourself. Instead, simply do as you are told by society, convention, your peer group, political propaganda, religious dogma, and advertising. Lead the unexamined life.

Existentialists call this head-in-the-sand approach "living in bad faith." Although the strategy of ignoring existential issues is of course very common, the existentialists say there are three problems with it.

The first problem, they say, is that to ignore the troubling facts of existence is to live a cowardly lie; it is immoral and amounts to selling your soul for comfort. Each of us is given just one short life to experience, and in a sense we are giving it away by refusing to examine the substance and meaning of that experience. If one surrenders one's experience of self, the existentialists believe, one might as well not be alive. Existentially speaking, you might as well be a rock.

In his novel *Cat's Cradle*, Kurt Vonnegut Jr. proposes that a person really is just a pile of so much lucky mud (Vonnegut, 1963). After all, the human body is not all that chemically different from the dirt on which it walks, plus a lot of water (the body is about 70 percent water). The only difference is that this mass of mud is up and walking around. And, more important, it has awareness, so it gets to look around and experience the world. The other mud, that stuff under one's feet, does not get to do that. It just lies there, ignorant of all the interesting things happening above.

And that is Vonnegut's good news. The bad news, of course, is that this luck does not last long. Sooner or later, the chemicals that make up the body will break back down (generally at death) and turn right back into earth. The Bible says we come from the earth and return to it; that is Vonnegut's point as well.

What is imperative, therefore, is to not blow this brief period of lucky awareness. As long as you are alive and aware mud, and not just regular mud, your obligation is to experience as much of the world as possible as vividly as possible. In particular, you need to be aware of your luck and know that it won't last— this is the only chance you will get. The tragedy, from an existential perspective, is that many people never do this. They lead the unexamined life, they never realize how lucky they are to be alive and aware, and they eventually lose their awareness never having realized what a special gift it was.

A second, more pragmatic problem with living in bad faith is that even if you manage not to be aware of troubling existential issues, you still will not be happy. Even the most smug and unthinking person wakes up occasionally late at night, the existentialists believe, and realizes that he or she will soon be dead without having done anything meaningful in life beyond acquiring material possessions. Such a person might have a brief, tantalizing, frustrating glimpse of what could have been if he or she had made different choices in life. These dark moments of the soul may pass quickly, but until one has taken one's existential responsibility in hand, they will continue to sneak up when least expected.

The third problem with the ostrich approach to existential issues is that it is impossible, because choosing *not* to worry about existential issues and to surrender one's choices to external authorities is itself a *choice*. As Sartre put it, "What is not possible is not to choose. . . . If I do not choose, I am still choosing" (1965, p. 54). Thus there is no exit from the existential dilemma, even if you can fool yourself into thinking that there is.

Authentic Existence

The preferred alternative is to courageously come to terms with your existence in the world. Rather than dodging your existential responsibility, face the facts that you are mortal, your life will be short, and you are master of your own destiny (within those limits). This approach is called **authentic existence** (Binswanger, 1963); it entails being honest, insightful, and morally correct.

Authentic existence will not relieve you from loneliness and unhappiness, however; such a courageous examination of conscious experience reveals the awful truth that each of us is forever alone and doomed to die. Life has no meaning beyond what we give it, which means that any apparent meaning life might have is only an illusion. The essence of the human experience is this discovery: The human being is the only animal that knows it must die.

This is pretty stern stuff. Existentialism is not for wimps (McAdams, 1990). It takes moral courage to peer into the void of mortality and meaningless. When the existentialist philosopher Friedrich Nietszche did this, he decided the only logical response was to rise above it all and become a "superman." This was easier said than done, however: instead of becoming a superman, Nietszche went insane and died in an asylum.

Jean-Paul Sartre tried to be both more realistic and a little more optimistic. He sometimes expressed annoyance with people who viewed existentialism as a gloomy philosophy, although one wonders what else he could expect, given his claim that the three essential experiences of life are anguish, despair, and forelornness. Sartre lightened this load a little with his claim that only through existential analysis can people regain their awareness of their freedom. He wrote that existential theory "is the only one which gives man dignity, the only one which does not reduce him to an object" (1965, p. 51). The existential challenge, he preached, was not to give up, but to do all you can to better the human condition, even in the face of all its uncertainties. This is how you can regain your dignity and your freedom and still find meaning in life, and is the ultimate benefit of Sartre's optimistic toughness.

THE MODERN AND MORE CHEERFUL HUMANISTS

Sartre did his best to find a positive message in the midst of an essentially disconcerting existential analysis. But his maneuvers did not come close to accomplishing what happened when existentialism crossed the Atlantic in the early 1950s. It has often been noted that the basic outlook of American culture tends to be optimistic, so it may be no coincidence that the new American adherents applied existentialism and phenomenology to psychology with a decidedly more cheerful tone.

Existential Optimism: Rogers and Maslow

The two pioneers who introduced phenomenological analysis into North American psychology were Carl Rogers and Abraham Maslow. These psychologists developed somewhat different phenomenological theories, but they shared a common optimism about human nature and the possibilities of existence.

SELF-ACTUALIZATION: ROGERS

Although Carl Rogers was a phenomenologist, by adding one optimistic assumption to the phenomenological approach, he changed its entire tone and much of its message. His added assumption was this: People are basically good. Or, to quote him directly, "The organism has one basic tendency and striving—to actualize, maintain and enhance the experiencing organism" (1951, p. 487).

According to Rogers's theory, a person can be understood only from the perspective of his or her "phenomenal field," which is the entire panorama of the person's conscious experience. Conscious experience is where everything comes together—unconscious conflicts, environmental influences, memories of the past, hopes for the future, and so on. These experiences continually combine in different ways at every moment of a person's life, and the result of their combination is what you experience at *this* moment. So far, this is standard phenomenological fare of the sort we considered earlier.

Rogers added a new aspect, however, when he posited that all people have a basic need to actualize, that is, to maintain and enhance life. (This need has much in common with Freud's notion of libido as it was interpreted in Chapter 10.) The goal of existence is to satisfy this need. This assumption led Rogers to differ sharply with the existentialists who believed that existence has no intrinsic goal.

THE HIERARCHY OF NEEDS: MASLOW

Abraham Maslow was a contemporary of Rogers and almost equally influential (e.g., Maslow, 1987). His theory begins with the same basic assumption as Rogers: that your ultimate need or motive is to self-actualize. However, Maslow claimed that this motive becomes active if and only if your other, more basic needs are met. According to Maslow, human motivation is characterized by a hierarchy of needs. First, one requires food, water, safety and the other basic elements of survival. When those are in hand, one then seeks sex, meaningful relationships, prestige, and money. Only when enough of those things are in hand does one turn to the quest for self-actualization. In other words, someone starving to death is not particularly concerned with the higher aspects of existence. In this belief, Maslow too is at odds with the existentialists who would believe that, even if starving, you have free choice in what to concern yourself with.

THE FULLY FUNCTIONING PERSON

Maslow and Rogers both believed that the best way to live is to become more clearly aware of reality and of yourself. If you can perceive everything in the world accurately and without neurotic distortion, and if you then take responsibility for the choices you make in life, then you become what Rogers called a fully functioning person. A fully functioning person lives what the existentialists called an authentic existence, except that the fully functioning person is happy.

The only way you can become a fully functioning person is to face the world without fear, self-doubt, or neurotic defenses. This becomes possible, Rogers believed, only if you have experienced "unconditional positive regard" from the important people in your life, especially during your childhood. Maslow disagreed slightly with this premise; he believed that anybody from any background could become a fully functioning person. But Rogers thought that if you come to feel that other people value you only if you are smart, successful, attractive, or good, then you will develop "conditions of worth."

Conditions of worth are bad because they limit your freedom to act and to think. If you believe you are valuable only if certain things about you are true, then you will distort your perception of reality to believe that those things are true, even if they are not. If you think you are valuable only if your behavior conforms to certain rules, then you will lose your ability to choose what to do. Both of these limitations violate the existential imperatives to see the world as it is, to choose freely, and to take total responsibility for all of your actions.

A person who has experienced unconditional positive regard from parents and other important people in his or her life does not develop such conditions of worth. This leads to an existence that is free from anxiety, because that person is confident of his or her value. The experience of a fully functioning person is also rich in emotion and self-discovery, and such a person is reflective, spontaneous, flexible, adaptable, confident, trusting, creative, self-reliant, ethical, open-minded. . . .—you get the idea.

The fundamental belief of humanism is that people are basically good. If left alone and not burdened with conditions of worth, humans will develop into healthy, happy, and wise people. Moreover, they will become nicer to one another: when you can perceive and accept all the experience that life has to offer, without filtering some experiences to protect your self-image, you will become "more understanding of *others* and more accepting of others as separate individuals" (Rogers, 1951, p. 520, emphasis added).

PSYCHOTHERAPY

The goal of Rogerian psychotherapy, and humanistic psychotherapy in general, is to help a person to become a fully functioning person. This goal is achieved through the therapist's providing unconditional positive regard for the client. This somewhat infamous technique is sometimes caricatured: the patient says something like "I would really like to kill you with a knife," and the therapist—reluctant to impose conditions of worth—replies "You feel you want to kill me with a knife. Uh huh."

This portrayal is probably unfair—Rogers did once state he would stop a murderer—but it captures the basic idea that the therapist's job is (a) to help the client perceive his or her own thoughts and feelings without trying to change them in any way, and (b) to make the client feel positively regarded no matter what he or she thinks, says, or does. This process allows insight and the removal of conditions of worth, the theory goes, and the eventual result will be a fully functioning person.

Rogerian psychotherapy requires enormous amounts of time and, on the part of the therapist, the patience (and sometimes also the courage) of a saint. What is the result of this kind of therapy? Although research on the effects of any kind of psychotherapy is extraordinarily difficult, Rogers and his followers have tried to document the effects of Rogerian treatment.

In a typical study, a group of people about to begin psychotherapy and a group of people who were not interested in undergoing therapy were asked to describe themselves and then to describe their ideal person. The results showed that these two descriptions diverged more among those who felt they needed therapy. When the therapy group repeated this procedure after completing a program of Rogerian treatment, their real and ideal selves were more closely in alignment—although still not as closely as those of the people who did not seek therapy (Butler & Haigh, 1954).

Results like these—and they have been obtained frequently over the years—seem to imply that one result of Rogerian psychotherapy is that people become more like the people they wish they were. But two problems with this conclusion have been noted. First, the results seem to be due about equally to the clients' changing their own self-views and to their changing their ideal views. That is, they not only change what they think they are like, they also change what they wish they were (Rudikoff, 1954). Second, it is not certain that reporting oneself to resemble one's ideal person is good measure of psychological adjustment. One study found that the self-views of paranoid schizophrenics were reasonably close to their ideal persons, and concluded that "to employ a high correlation between the self and ideal-self conceptions as a sole criterion of adjustment . . . would lead to the categorization of many people, particularly paranoid schizophrenics, as adjusted" (I. Friedman, 1955, p. 73).

It seems there is more to mental health than being the person you want to be (Wylie, 1974). Since that is the criterion employed by Rogerian psychotherapy, whether its clients truly become psychologically healthier is a subject of debate. Despite this ambiguity about outcome, one important and lasting contribution can be traced directly to Rogerian psychotherapy: the promulgation of the idea that the first job of any psychotherapist is to listen to the client. Although not all therapists will respond "Uh huh" to statements such as those of our hypothetical client above, many have been influenced by the Rogerian example to be more patient in listening and more hesitant to impose their own values than they might have been otherwise.

Personal Constructs: Kelly

Another important phenomenological psychologist, George Kelly, also thought that a person's personal experience of the world was the most important part of his or her psychology. Kelly's unique spin was to emphasize how one's "cognitive" or thinking system builds one's experience of reality out of a unique set of ideas about the world called one's "personal constructs." Accordingly, his theory of personality is called Personal Construct Theory.

Kelly viewed constructs as bipolar dimensions along which people or objects can be arranged. These constructs can be nearly anything: the idea of good vs. bad, or large vs. small, or weak vs. strong, or conservative vs. liberal, for example. If weak vs. strong is one of your constructs, you might tend to see everything and everybody in your world in terms of whether they are weak or strong. Each individual has a unique set of constructs that make up his or her personal construct system.

There are many ways one could assess someone's personal construct system, but Kelly favored a method called the Role Construct Repertory Test, or Rep test. The Rep test asks you to identify three people who are or have been important in your life. Then it asks you to describe how any two of them seem to you to be similar to each other and different from the third. Then you do the same with three ideas important to you, three things you admire, and so on. In each case the second question is the same: How are two of these similar to each other and different from the third?

Kelly believed that the ways you discriminate among these objects, people, or ideas reveal the constructs through which you view the world. For example, if you frequently state that two of the objects are strong whereas the third is weak (or vice versa), then strong vs. weak is probably one of your important personal constructs. Therefore, because you use it to relate different aspects of the world, this dimension is an important part of how you frame and experience reality.

Recent research has shown that certain constructs are more readily brought to mind by certain individuals. These have been called "chronically accessible constructs" (Bargh, Lombardi, & Higgins, 1988). For example, for one person the idea of devastating failure might be chronically accessible, and in everything he undertakes or even considers undertaking, the idea that it will all turn into a catastrophe is never far from his mind. For another person, the idea of interpersonal power might be chronically accessible, and in every relationship she observes or enters, the idea "who is in charge here?" frequently comes to mind and frames her view of these relationships.

Where do these constructs come from? Kelly believed that they come from past experience, although they are not determined by past experience. What does that mean? Kelly leaned heavily on the metaphor that every person is, in a sense, a scientist. A scientist obtains data and tries to come up with a theory that can explain the data. But the data never determine the theory the scientist formulates; any pattern of data is always consistent with at least two and perhaps even an infinite number of alternative theories. (This observation comes from elementary philosophy of science.) Which theory to use to explain the data, therefore, is always the scientist's *choice*. To be sure, science has developed canons, such as the principle of parsimony (the idea that all other things being equal, the simplest theory is the best). But these canons do not ensure the right choice (sometimes the most complex theory is actually the best). Which theory the scientist chooses is a judgment call.

Kelly believed that everything that has ever happened to us and everything that we have ever seen or heard provide the data from which we must develop an interpretation, or theory, of what the world is like. This theory is your personal construct system, which becomes the framework for your perception of and thinking about the world. This system is determined not by your past experience, therefore, but by your interpretation of past experience, and this interpretation is freely chosen. No matter what has happened to you in the past, you *could* have chosen to draw different conclusions from it than you did. In fact, you still can.

For example, suppose you had a miserable childhood; perhaps you were even abused. You could draw from this history a personal construct system that tells you the world is evil and abusive and there is nothing you can do about it. That would be a conclusion entirely consistent with the data of your life experience. But, just as well, you could draw the conclusion that no matter what life throws at you, you will survive it. That conclusion—since you did survive—is also entirely consistent with your data. Therefore, which conclusion you draw and the world view you develop is up to you.

A corollary of personal construct theory, which Kelly called the "sociality corollary," holds that if you wish to understand another person, you must understand his or her personal construct system or view of the world; you must be able to look at the world through that person's eyes. Actions that appear incomprehensible or even evil can make sense, Kelly believed, if you can see them from the point of view of the person who did them. In addition, Kelly believed that helping the client to achieve self-understanding was the primary duty of a psychotherapist, and his Rep test was designed to be a tool psycho-therapists could use for doing that.

Construals and Reality

The basic lesson of Kelly's theory is that any pattern of experience can lead to numerous construals—perhaps an infinite number. That means the construal you have is one you chose, not one that was forced upon you, because others were equally possible. Kelly called this view **constructive alternativism**, which means that your personal reality does not simply exist; it is *constructed* in your mind. Furthermore, there are always alternative ways you could choose to construct reality, besides the way you happen to be using at this moment.

This lesson has far-reaching implications. Kelly's theory draws on a part of the philosophy of science that scientists themselves sometimes forget. Scientific paradigms are different frameworks for construing the meaning of data. The basic approaches to personality considered in this book—trait, psychoanalytic, phenomenological, and so on—are paradigms in that sense. Each is perfectly sensible, I believe, and each is consistent with the data it regards as important, but each also represents a choice: to focus on some aspects of human psychology and to ignore others. This implies two things about scientific paradigms: (1) The choice between them is not between which is right and which is wrong, but rather of which one addresses the topic you are interested in understanding; and (2) You need all of them, because any one of them always leaves out something important.[3]

There are many other systems of constructs, or paradigms, to which the same two lessons also apply. Most of us have developed systems of belief that affect how we interpret and understand politics, and morality, and economics, and many other important matters. These belief systems are useful and even necessary, but a myopic devotion to just one paradigm can make us forget (or worse, deny) that other construals of reality—other belief systems—are equally plausible.

My personal favorite example concerns the economic concept of "opportunity costs," which in my opinion (according to my personal belief system) is one of the most dangerous ideas ever invented. The concept deals with this question of what something costs. The lay person's answer to this question is that the cost of something is the amount of resources required to get it. A second and different answer, however, is taught in business schools: the cost of some-

---

[3]This does not mean they can or need all be applied simultaneously; that exercise would lead only to incoherence. Rather, one needs to apply the appropriate paradigm for the question at hand while keeping the rest in reserve, lest the question of interest change.

thing is the difference between what it brings you and what you could have gotten had you spent your resources on something else. The difference between these two figures is not your ordinary cost, but your opportunity cost.

These two definitions of cost derive from two different construals of the goal of economic life. The first construes the goal as doing what you want as long as you can pay for it. This is sometimes called a "satisficing" goal. The second maintains that you must maximize your gain, and that unless you make as much money as possible you have failed. This is an "optimizing" goal. Both goals are reasonable, but different, and neither is intrinsically right or wrong. Yet business schools often teach the second goal as being sophisticated and correct, and the first as hopelessly naive.

The consequences of one's construal can be real and concrete. A few years ago, I read an article in the *Boston Globe* about a mom-and-pop grocery store located on the ground floor of a building in Beacon Hill, which has developed into a fashionable neighborhood in recent years. The store, which had been there for decades, was being evicted. The longtime owner of the building had discovered that he could get more rent from a clothing boutique. When neighbors protested, the owner said, apparently with a straight face, "I couldn't afford to keep that grocery store there any longer with property values going up so high."

He may have actually believed what he said, but from another point of view this man's statement is absurd: as long as he could afford to keep the building he could afford to keep the store. He never claimed the grocery paid him less than he needed to pay for the building or to live well himself. Rather, he focused upon the fact that by evicting the grocer he could make more money, and thought of the difference between what he was making and what he could make as a "cost" that he could not "afford."

This viewpoint is the reverse of a remarkably silly television commercial that an automobile maker ran a few years ago. The theme of the commercial was "What will you do with all the money you save by buying our car?" In one ad, a happy woman says that with the money she saved, she is going to Hawaii!

I have news for this person: Nobody ever went to Hawaii with the money saved by buying a car. The news for the Boston landlord is, nobody ever went broke from opportunity costs. You can *choose* to think about these situations that way, but you are kidding yourself if you think you are getting rich by spending money, or getting poor by not collecting as much money as possible.

The Boston landlord and the car buyer in the commercial had each absorbed a particular construct about money and come to think of that construct as real. The result was a behavior on the part of the landlord that was immoral from the perspective of another construct system, and an action on the part of the car buyer that was silly according to a different construct system. Beware of the construals of reality taught in business school, in science classes, or anywhere else (including in this book); other construals are also possible and you have the ability, the right, and perhaps even the duty to choose your own.

Flow: Csikszentmihalyi

The heart of the phenomenological approach is the conscious experience of being alive, moment to moment. The research of Mihalyi Csikszentmihalyi provides a renewed focus on this fundamental concern (Csikszentmihalyi & Csikszentmihalyi, 1988). As a good phenomenologist, Csikszentmihalyi believes that your moment-to-moment experience is what really matters in life; his concern is how to make the most of it. His work focuses on "optimal experience"—what it is and how to achieve it.

Csikszentmihalyi investigated the experiences of artists, athletes, writers, and so forth as they did what they enjoy most. He concluded that the best way to spend your time is in autotelic activities, or activities that are enjoyable for their own sake. The subjective experience a person has during an autotelic activity—the enjoyment itself—is what Csikszentmihalyi calls "flow."

Flow is not the same thing as joy, happiness, or other more familiar terms for subjective well-being. Rather, the experience of flow is characterized by tremendous concentration, utterly no distractibility, and no thoughts of anything but the activity itself. One's mood is elevated slightly (although not to the point of ecstasy or anything like it), and time seems to pass very quickly. This flow is what is experienced—when all goes well—by a writer writing, a painter painting, a gardener gardening, or a baseball player waiting for the next pitch. Flow has been reported by surgeons, by dancers, and by chess players in the midst of an intense match. Computers induce flow in many people. Perhaps you have seen an individual playing Sim City on the computer far into the night, seemingly oblivious to any distraction or to the passage of time itself. What he or she is experiencing, I would presume, is flow. I often experience flow when lecturing to a class, and sometimes while writing. To me, a fifty-minute class feels like it ends about a minute and a half after it begins. (I know it does not feel this way to my students.) This sense of losing track of time is one sign that you have been experiencing flow.

According to Csikszentmihalyi, the defining attribute of flow is that it is a focused and ordered state of consciousness that arises when your activity entails a balanced ratio of skills to challenges. If an activity is too difficult or too confusing, you will experience anxiety, worry, and frustration. If the activity is too easy, you will experience boredom and (again) anxiety. But when skills and challenges are balanced, you experience flow.

Csikszentmihalyi thinks that the secret for enhancing the quality of one's life is to spend as much time in flow as possible. Achieving flow entails finding something you find worthwhile and enjoyable, and becoming good at it. This is not a bad prescription for happiness, come to think of it, whether you are a phenomenologist or not. (Achieving flow also entails staying away from television. Csikszentmihalyi found that watching television disrupts and prevents flow for long periods of time.)

On the other hand, Csikszentmihalyi seems to be describing a rather solitary kind of happiness. In that respect Csikszentmihalyi is a true existentialist, perhaps not dwelling on our forelornness like Sartre did, but still regarding experience as something that happens alone. (Csikszentmihalyi does describe flow as it can occur during sexual relations, but the emphasis even here is on the experience of one individual during such an encounter.) The drawback with flow is that somebody experiencing it can be difficult to interact with; he or she may not hear you, may seem distracted, and in general may be poor company. Interrupt somebody engrossed in a novel, or a computer game, and you will see what I mean.

HUMANISTIC PSYCHOLOGY TODAY

The research of modern humanistic psychologists is distinctive in that it tries to focus on the conscious experiences of individuals, rather than on hidden mental processes, group trends, or anything that might look like a psychological law. For example, one humanistic psychologist did a research project that turned out to be an introspective account of what a hard time he had thinking up a suitable research project!

Surely, I am just stuck momentarily; stay with the task, I exhort myself. But I cannot stave off the negativity. The phenomenon I sought to describe has slipped through my fingers (Shapiro, 1985; quoted by Rychlak, 1988, p. 464).

Another humanistic psychologist once presented an account of the experience of a father who gave a cherished chess set to his son. The son turned out to be delighted with the gift, but only because he could slice the pieces open and remove the weights inside, not because he cared about chess. The father was at first upset, then came to appreciate the gift from the son's point of view, and decided to take the view of St. Thomas Aquinas that the quality of a gift lies in what the receiver appreciates about it, not in the intentions of the giver (this indeed strikes me as a saintly point of view; Giorgi, 1985). Both of the projects just described are existential, phenomenological, and humanistic analyses of experience and how particular people construe it. Such analyses are the meat and potatoes of the humanistic approach.

It is safe to say, however, that this kind of research is not taking the broader field of psychology by storm. The insights it yields can be interesting, but seem so particular to individual cases that to many psychologists—including me, frankly—they leave much to be desired. Even Joseph Rychlak, a prominent humanistic psychologist, surveys the field this way:

An Association for Humanistic Psychology now exists, with an accompanying *Journal of Humanistic Psychology*. . . . The papers which appear in this journal do not necessarily follow the format of an experiment . . . but are usually discursive surveys, case-history reports, or personal observations. [They believe] the intuition of the investigator [is] above the validation of an experiment in any rank ordering of steps in the scientific enterprise (Rychlak, 1988, p. 190).

The tone of this description is clear, but later on Rychlak removes all doubt as to how he feels about this work:

A humanistic outlook which is internally hostile to research design seems more harmful than helpful. . . . To expect a scientist to run after each person's phenomenal reality in hopes of capturing each possibility that might be subjectively concocted is surely unnecessary and a waste of time (pp. 192–93, 201).

Rychlak's most telling complaint about his fellow humanists is that

[they] tend to attract students who are in fact not interested in developing the necessary self-discipline and exerting the effort that a scientific career demands (p. 194).

Rychlak is not trying to destroy humanistic psychology with these criticisms, of course. He is trying to reform it into something he calls "rigorous humanism," a humanistic psychology that sees the essential cause of human behavior as being its purpose, rather than its antecedent causes. (This kind of analysis of behavior in terms of its purposes is called teleological analysis.) The purpose of a behavior, in turn, is a function of the individual's freely chosen construal of reality. Rychlak has tried hard, even writing a very long book, to develop a rigorous, internally consistent theory of humanism.

In an attempt to defend his belief that purpose and free will have an important place in psychology, Rychlak turns to physics, of all places. He cites an idea of the physicist Neils Bohr, who, according to the historian Lewis Feuer, suggested that

every change in the state of an atom should be regarded as an individual process, incapable of more detailed description. . . . An atom in a stationary state may in general even be said to possess a free choice between various possible transitions to other stable states (Feuer, 1974, p. 137, as quoted by Rychlak, 1988, p. 241).

Rychlak is enthusiastic about this passage and this line of reasoning. He recommends it highly to "all modern psychologists who find telic [free will] commentary improper in the scientific context." Yet I find it slightly disappointing that Rychlak used this quote. Too many psychologists have physics envy already; they seem to employ analogies between psychology and the "harder" sciences in attempts to justify the former by trading off of the prestige of the latter. Psychology can and should be justified on its own terms. A humanist would be the last person I would expect to succumb to physics envy.

Moreover, when it comes to research, it is not clear that Rychlak is much better off than the less rigorous humanists he criticizes. To his credit, he does not publish rambling accounts of his own existential anxieties. But most of the studies he does are experiments of the standard variety, showing that whether people value stimuli as good or bad affects how they perceive and respond to those stimuli. For example, words one likes are sometimes remembered better than words one does not like (Rychlak & Marceil, 1986). Since deciding to like a word is an existential choice, Rychlak claims, this kind of study shows how one's construal of the world is a cause of how one perceives and remembers it. This is an interesting finding, to be sure, but the gap between this experiment and humanistic theory seems rather large. Experiments like these *begin* with humanistic presumptions, rather than demonstrate the validity of those assumptions.

Of course, an existentialist would argue that is all that any kind of study can do. One's theoretical presuppositions are built into the questions one decides to study and the way in which one decides to study them, and so are built into the results well before any actual data are gathered. Such a point of view may be reasonable, but it does not exactly encourage research efforts. Although its general point of view continues to be influential, the specific research currently called "humanistic psychology" seems to be headed toward a dead end. Its prospects of becoming dominant in psychology at large are certainly dim.

CONCLUSION

All of the phenomenologists, the philosophers as well as the psychologists, agree that the key to human existence is the experience of being alive as it happens one moment at a time. They agree that you have free will precisely because each moment of experience exists separately—the past is always the past and the future is always the future. The past and future only affect you if you let them; at the present moment you can always choose.

On Happiness

But they also differ among themselves on a fundamental point. The original, philosophical existentialists, such as Kierkegaard and Nietzsche, found that the fact of existence moment-to-moment, together with the fact of mortality, implied that life was finally meaningless. Sartre, not as pessimistic, still claimed that the inescapable human fate consisted of anguish, forelornness, and despair, none of which sounds like much fun. Carl Rogers, by contrast, adding just one assumption, drew an opposite conclusion. He assumed that people have an instinctive drive to grow and to create, and if people are allowed to develop naturally and learn to face experience directly, they will experience not existential despair, but contentment and happiness—and, adds Csikszentmihalyi, maybe even flow.

This fundamental divergence in point of view seems to prove that another phenomenologist, George Kelly, was correct all along. Kelly said that the same reality can lead, equally well, to fundamentally different construals. The philosophical existentialists view life as something that can consist, at best, of a sort of gloomy courage. The humanistic psychologist Rogers, however, holds out the hope that you can happily relate to a warm and wonderful world. How can these thinkers, each one a phenomenologist, come to such opposite conclusions? Kelly's theory of constructive alternativism explains it all—they simply have different personal construct systems.

The Mystery of Experience

It is difficult to emphasize sufficiently how different the phenomenological approach to psychology is from any other part of psychology or of science. Its fundamental difference comes from its focus on moment-to-moment, alive, aware, conscious experience. The essential fact that phenomenologists grasp, which all other basic paradigms fail to address, is that this experience is the basic mystery of life. It cannot be explained or even very well described by science or even by words. And when words are tried, poetry works better than prose. You cannot describe what it is to be aware and alive, but you know what it is.

Science and psychology usually choose not to address the fact that something so commonplace should also be so mysterious; they just ignore the mystery. That is fine, to a point. The point is reached when science and psychology seem to assume that conscious awareness is not important or seem even to pretend it does not exist. It is nearly as bad when psychology treats conscious experience simply as an interesting form of information processing, no different in kind than that done by a computer (Rychlak, 1988). Some theories proposed by cognitive psychologists, for example, claim that consciousness is a higher-order cognitive process that organizes thoughts and allows flexible decision-making. Other theories suggest that consciousness is simply a memory tag for "I've been here before." Beyond these functions, say these theories, consciousness is just a feeling (Dennett, 1994; Dennett & Weiner, 1991; Ornstein, 1977).

Of course, to say consciousness is "just a feeling" begs the main question: what does it mean to be able to consciously experience feeling? In fact, conscious awareness is not at all similar to the kind of information processing that a computer performs, even if it does fulfill some of the same functions. Awareness is a human experience, and science can neither credibly deny that it exists, nor explain just where it comes from.

It is only natural, therefore, that phenomenological analysis sometimes drifts into speculations that are not only philosophical, but also religious and spiritual. Because *science cannot account for consciousness.*

The Influence of the Phenomenological Approach

Despite the self-imposed isolation of modern humanistic psychology, the more general phenomenological approach continues to have an impact. Its key precept—that the most important thing to understand about a person is his or her construal of reality—is an idea that will not go away. Furthermore, this idea has a strong influence on cognitive approaches to personality, which will be considered in Chapter 18. It also leads directly into the comparison of the different construals of reality held by different cultures, which will be considered in the next chapter.

SUMMARY

The phenomenological approach to personality concentrates on the experience, or phenomenology, of being alive and aware from moment to moment. This emphasis makes the approach humanistic, because it concentrates on that which makes the study of humans different from the study of objects or animals. The phenomenological approach asserts that each moment of experience is all that matters, an assertion that implies that individuals have free will, and that the only way to understand another person is to understand his or her experience of the world. The approach has philosophical roots in existentialism, which breaks experience into three parts (of the world, of others, and of one's own experience), claims that a close analysis of existence implies that it has no meaning beyond what we give it, and concludes that a failure to face this fact constitutes living in bad faith. As an alternative, existentialism prescribes living an authentic existence, which entails coming to terms with existential dilemmas and taking responsibility for one's choices in life.

Modern humanist psychologists, such as Rogers, Maslow, and Kelly, are more optimistic than their existentialist forebears. Rogers and Maslow assert that a person who faces his or her experience directly can become a fully functioning person; Rogers believed this outcome could only occur for individuals who had received unconditional positive regard from the important people in their lives. Kelly's theory says that each person's experience of the world is organized by a unique set of personal constructs, or general themes. Scientific paradigms have much in common with these personal constructs. Csikszentmihalyi's recent theory says that the best state of existence is to be in a state of flow, in which challenges and capabilities are well balanced. Although modern humanistic psychology continues to maintain that the rest of psychology makes a fundamental mistake by ignoring that which makes humans unique among objects of study, the field has so far offered only non-rigorous, introspective accounts, which psychologists with a scientific approach find unconvincing. Humanistic psychologists and philosophers still have not settled the issue of whether directly confronting the facts of one's existence should make you happy or miserable. Nevertheless, they must be given credit for providing the only approach that even attempts to address the mystery of human experience and awareness. The phenomenological approach has had an important impact on the practice of psychotherapy, on modern cognitive views of personality, and on the study of psychology across cultures.

CULTURAL VARIATION IN EXPERIENCE, BEHAVIOR, AND PERSONALITY

What the world actually contains may matter less than how an individual sees or construes it, and the only real way to understand a person is to understand his or her construals. We saw the phenomenologists make a pretty good case to this effect in Chapter 14. In recent years, psychologists have paid increasing attention to the ways interpretations or construals of reality vary, not just across individuals, but across cultures. The same behavior that is the epitome of politeness in one culture can be seen as rude by another. The seemingly same idea may take on drastically different meanings in different cultural contexts. And, perhaps most important, cultures seem to vary in some of their most basic values. For example, members of some cultures seem to believe that the individual is more important than the society of which he or she is a part, whereas members of other cultures seem to believe just the opposite—that the importance of the group overwhelms the interests of the individual.

THE IMPORTANCE OF CROSS-CULTURAL DIFFERENCES

Psychologists have three very good reasons for being interested in cross-cultural differences like these.

Possible Limits on Generalizability

The psychological theorizing of Sigmund Freud was largely based on his experiences treating upper-middle-class, hysteric women who lived in turn-of-the-century Vienna, plus his own introspections. It is not particularly original to observe that his view of humanity may have been skewed by the limited nature of this database.[1] This problem is not limited to Freud, of course. As was discussed in Chapter 3, a basic worry about generalizability concerns the degree to which the results of modern empirical research, obtained in large part from college students residing in North America, can be applied to humanity at large. The only real way to alleviate this worry is to include not only nonstudents in psychological research, but people around the world.

Cross-Cultural Conflict

A second reason to be concerned with cross-cultural differences is that the different attitudes, values, and behavioral styles of members of different cultures frequently cause misunderstandings. The consequences can range from the trivial to the extremely serious.

Near the trivial end of the spectrum, the cultural psychologist Harry Triandis has described a misunderstanding with an Indian hotel clerk that resulted from a contrast between the American practice of putting an "X" next to the part of a form that *does* apply, and the Indian practice of putting an "X" at the part that does *not* apply. He received a postcard with an "X" next to "we have no rooms available," and thought he did not have a hotel reservation when he did (Triandis, 1994). This episode was surely inconvenient, but it was no major tragedy.

Somewhat more serious results arise from the Thai tendency to try to save the face of everybody involved in a negotiation, or the Japanese insistence on knowing a potential business partner well on a personal level before beginning to draw up a contract. When these styles encounter the relatively brash, direct, and even insensitive American style of business, the result is more conflict and probably less profit than would have occurred with a little more mutual understanding and accomodation.

In 1994, an American teenager living with his parents in Singapore learned another hard lesson about cross-cultural differences. After being convicted of spray-painting some parked cars, an act that in the United States would be treated as petty vandalism and for which he might not even have been punished if it were his first offense, he was sentenced by the Singapore courts to pay

---

[1]A very early tradition in cross-cultural psychology involved trying to construct psychoanalytic interpretations of other cultures. Gorer (1943), for example, claimed that the Japanese people are anal-compulsive because Japanese children are subjected to early and severe toilet training. Today, this interpretation seems ethnocentric; theorizing by modern cultural psychologists is quite different. In particular, it is seldom Freudian.

restitution, spend several months in jail, and—most surprising from an American perspective—to be hit several times with a bamboo cane, which can split open the skin and cause permanent scarring. This sentence caused an international uproar.

Even more serious cases of cross-cultural misunderstanding occur in international diplomacy. On January 9, 1991, James Baker, the American secretary of state, met in Geneva with a number of Iraqi officials, including the half-brother of Saddam Hussein, the president of Iraq. Baker told the Iraqis in no uncertain terms that unless they left Kuwait (which they had recently invaded) immediately, the United States would attack. But he said it calmly, using his best Western diplomatic manners. As a result, Hussein's half-brother telephoned home saying, "The Americans will not attack. They are weak. They are calm. They are not angry. They are only talking" (Triandis, 1994, p. 29). The Iraqis did not withdraw and within a few days Operation Desert Storm was unleashed. It left 175,000 Iraqi citizens dead and $200 billion in property destroyed.

Judging American behavior from the perspective of their own culture, the Iraqis made the mistake of thinking that calm words cannot go with aggressive intent. If Baker had wanted to impress his point effectively, according to Triandis, he would have done better to throw the Geneva telephone book at Tariq Aziz, the Iraqi foreign minister. But he did not, and the resulting cross-cultural misunderstanding had dire consequences.

Cross-cultural misunderstandings can occur within as well as across international borders. In the inner cities of North America, a subculture of violence, fear, and degradation has led to an extreme valuation being put on receiving proper "respect." Anything that threatens such respect can literally threaten one's life, and so outward tokens such as stylish clothing, a fear-producing appearance, and even an advertised willingness to kill become much more valued than they are in other settings (Anderson, 1994). Nonverbal expressions take on an added meaning, too. For example, to gaze for more than a second or so at a person from this subculture is to express disrespect, and invites a violent response. The teenage daughter of an acquaintance of mine, newly enrolled in a high school in which many students held such values, found herself in several fairly serious fights until she finally learned this lesson.

Varieties of Human Experience

A third and more deeply theoretical issue also helps drive interest in cross-cultural psychology. This issue is existential, and stems from a curiosity about the possible varieties of human experience and the degree to which being alive, aware, and human is the same or different across cultures. A moment's reflection is sufficient to tell us that the way we see and construe the world around us is, to a considerable degree, a product of our experience and cultural background.

An intriguing possibility to consider is that, were we from some other cultural background, the world might look entirely different. Things that are invisible to us now might become visible, and things we see and take for granted might become invisible.

For example, a visitor from a South American rain forest community might look at a tree and immediately "see" the uses to which it, its bark, and its sap might be put. But that same visitor might look at an automobile or a computer and have no idea about how it could be used. A native of Western culture, however, while he or she might immediately "see" the transportation and informational possibilities in the car and the computer, might see little potential on beholding a teak. A ride around the block might be sufficient to acquaint the visitor from the rain forest with the possibilities of cars; getting him or her to understand what computers are for might be a bit more difficult. By the same token, if you were to visit *their* community in the rain forest, there might be artifacts or objects they would find difficult to explain to you.

So, a cross-cultural perspective raises a profound existential question: Does the human experience of life vary fundamentally across cultures? Do people raised and living in very different cultural environments see the same colors, feel the same emotions, desire the same goals, or organize their thoughts in comparable ways? The cultural anthropologist and psychologist Richard Shweder calls these aspects of psychology experience near constructs and proposes they are the most fitting subject matter for a cross-cultural psychology (Shweder & Sullivan, 1993). In a somewhat more accessible phrase, Harry Triandis claims that "culture imposes a set of lenses for seeing the world" (1994, p. 13). If that description of culture is valid, and it probably is, then the natural next question is, how different are these lenses? Do they lead to views of the world that are fundamentally different, or more or less comparable?

In its ultimate form, this question is probably unanswerable. We can never know for certain what the experience of another individual in our own culture comprises, much less enter fully into the experience of members of a different culture. Still, if you recall Funder's Third Law (Chapter 2) you will know that your author prefers something over nothing, usually. In this case, the fact that the basic question of cross-cultural comparability is unanswerable does not mean that it is not worthwhile to study how cultures are psychologically different and similar. And indeed, cross-cultural research is a small, but lively and apparently rapidly growing area of psychology.

DIFFICULTIES OF CROSS-CULTURAL RESEARCH

Several factors conspire to make research in the psychology of different cultures exceptionally difficult to do well.

Ethnocentrism

One source of difficulty is that any observation made of another culture almost certainly will be colored by the observer's own cultural background, no matter how hard he or she tries to avoid it. A truly objective point of view, free from any cultural bias, is difficult to attain, and some anthropologists argue that such a point of view is impossible in principle. As Harry Triandis points out, we are most in danger of committing ethnocentrism (judging another culture from the point of view of our own) when the "real" nature of the situation seems most obvious (Triandis, 1994). As an example, he asks us to consider two interviews concerning behavior described as "a widow in your community eats fish two or three times a week." First, a Hindu Indian was interviewed:

Q: Is the widow's behavior wrong?
A: Yes. Widows should not eat fish, meat, onions or garlic, or any "hot" foods. . . .
Q: How serious is the violation?
A: A very serious violation. . . .
Q: Is it a sin?
A: Yes. It's a "great" sin.
Q: What if no one knew this had been done? It was done in private or secretly. Would it be wrong then?
A: What difference does it make if it is done while alone? It is wrong. A widow should spend her time seeking salvation—seeking to be reunited with the soul of her husband. Hot foods will distract her. They will stimulate her sexual appetite. . . . She will want sex and behave like a whore.

Then an American interview is reported:

Q: Is the widow's behavior wrong?
A: No. She can eat fish if she wants to.
Q: How serious is the violation?
A: It is not a violation.
Q: Is it a sin?
A: No.
Q: What if no one knew this had been done? It was done in private or secretly. Would it be wrong then?
A: It is not wrong, in private or public.
(Shweder, Mahapatra, & Miller, 1990, pp. 168–70).

Triandis points out that the responses of the Indian informant may seem absurd and somewhat amusing, whereas those of the American informant seem perfectly obvious and even boring. It takes a real intellectual struggle to consider seriously the possibility that the Indian's responses are just as reasonable as the American's, and differ only by starting with an unfamiliar set of cultural assumptions. The principal Indian assumption underlying the conversation above is that relationships such as that between a husband and a wife exist for all eternity, whereas the American assumption is that after a husband's death a widow is a free and independent individual. (The Indian interview also contains some assumptions about the aphrodisiac properties of fish and certain other foods.) The American assumption is the one we are more used to, of course, but the Indian assumption is not necessarily false.

The point of this example is not that we should begin worrying about widows who eat garlic, but that it is difficult, and perhaps impossible, to cast off the lenses on reality provided by our own cultural background.

Outgroup Bias

A second potential pitfall of cross-cultural research into which many researchers have fallen over the years, is to assume that all members of a given culture are alike. It is sometimes reported that everybody in India, or Japan, or China has a certain view of the world (sometimes it is even claimed that Indians, Japanese, and Chinese all have the *same*, "Eastern" view of the world) as if it were true that everybody in these cultures thinks in the same way. Given the size and diversity of these populations, any such blanket statement seems extremely unlikely to be correct.

The phenomenon to beware of here is one that social psychologists call the **outgroup homogeneity bias** (e.g., Linville & Jones, 1980; Lorenzi-Cioldi, 1993; Park & Rothbart, 1982). A group to which one belongs naturally seems to contain individuals who differ widely from each other. But members of those groups to which one does *not* belong seem to be "all the same." Even cross-cultural psychologists and anthropologists, who of all people should know better, sometimes seem to fall into this bias trap. We should remember that in our *own* culture, individuals can be very different from each other. This fact is surely no less true within other cultures.

Going Native, and Other Hazards

Many other factors make cross-cultural research especially difficult. For example, to study another culture well, one needs to spend a considerable amount of time living in it, and of course also needs to learn the local language. Yet researchers do not always do this, choosing instead to fly into a vastly different cultural world, grab some data, and fly out. One critic has called this style "research by 747."

Another difficulty is that, although it is difficult to do research on a representative sample of North Americans, as was discussed in Chapter 3, it is probably even more difficult to do research on a representative sample of Chinese.

One survey reported that 50 percent of "cross-cultural" studies conducted in China used college students as subjects. Yet Chinese college students are even more elite, select, and unrepresentative of the Chinese people at large than are American college students of the American people. College students in China are relatively modern, wealthy, and (ironically, considering their status as subjects in studies of Chinese culture) Westernized, as compared to other Chinese (Gabrenya & Hwang, 1995).

A final danger of cross-cultural research is the propensity of some researchers to "go native," or fall in love with the other culture they study. This can lead the culture to be portrayed in a romanticized manner. For example, some researchers write as if the "collective" worldview of Asian cultures is a perfect approach to life, and certainly superior to the "individualist" worldview of Western culture. One pair of investigators wrote that collectivist cultures, unlike individualistic ones, appreciate "the fundamental connectedness of human beings to each other" (Markus & Kitayama, 1991, p. 227), which certainly sounds romantic. But, as we will see later in this chapter, each worldview has its pros *and* cons, and collectivism definitely has its drawbacks.

None of these difficulties imply that cross-cultural psychology is not worthwhile; they simply underline how difficult it is to do it well. This might be a good place to invoke yet again Funder's Third Law, about something usually beating nothing. As difficult as this work is, the only alternative to accepting its many difficulties is to ignore cross-cultural differences altogether. That would be unfortunate. There is a good deal to be said for investigating the degree to which our research results generalize to other cultural contexts, for trying to alleviate sources of cross-cultural misunderstanding, and for trying to understand how members of other cultures experience the world, even if an ultimate understanding will probably elude us.

THREE APPROACHES TO CROSS-CULTURAL PSYCHOLOGY
Ignoring Cross-Cultural Issues

Psychologists have taken three different approaches to cross-cultural issues. The first—and still the most common—is to ignore them. Most of this neglect is fairly benign, of the sort you see in the other chapters of this book. Rather than worry about cross-cultural variation at every step, especially in the absence of much real, relevant data, most psychologists usually limit themselves to doing their best to describe and explain the phenomenon at hand in the context of their own culture. Freud did not worry too much about cross-cultural concerns; he found hysteric Viennese women complicated enough. Likewise, the measurement of individual differences and the exploration of the laws of behavior change have proceeded primarily within the Western cultural context. The research has proven to be both interesting enough and difficult enough to prevent the international application of these topics from rising to the top of most researchers' agendas.

In fact, research such as that just described does not intend to claim that its findings are universal. Most approaches to personality psychology have simply not yet gotten around to addressing cross-cultural issues; most psychologists are content to leave such issues to the anthropologists, at least for the time being.

But a few investigators are more aggressive in making absolutist claims of universal relevance. The psychologist Hans Eysenck and his associates, for example, have measured personality within various cultures around the world using the explicit assumption that the same traits can be used to describe anybody anywhere (e.g., H. Eysenck & S. Eysenck, 1983; S. Eysenck, 1983; H. Eysenck, 1986; Hanin, S. Eysenck, H. Eysenck, & Barrett, 1991). They have been roundly criticized for this practice by psychologists who believe you cannot simply import a trait idea, unchanged, from one culture to another. At least some adjustment for the specific cultural context is generally required (Bijnen & Poortinga, 1988; Bijnen, Van der Net, & Poortinga, 1986).

Deconstructionism

A second approach claims that cultures are so fundamentally different that they cannot be compared with each other, because no common frame of reference exists. This view derives from a general intellectual approach, sometimes called deconstructionism, that claims that nothing in the world has any meaning or essence apart from the interpretations imposed upon it by each observer. The meaning of a thing is never preordained; it is always invented or "constructed." The task of *de*constructionism is to see beyond these inventions by showing how meaning is essentially arbitrary. In literary theory, for example, deconstructionism leads to the attitude that the meaning of a "text," such as a novel, lies not in its content nor even in the author's intention, but in each reader's interpretation. In cross-cultural psychology, the deconstructionists argue that there is no lens-free way to look at any culture, and that each culture's view of reality is entire in itself and is not judgeable from any other point of view. In the words of prominent advocates of this idea,

Cultural psychology [their name for their preferred approach] has grown up in an intellectual climate [deconstructionism] suspicious of a one-sided emphasis on fixed essences, intrinsic features, and universally necessary truths—an intellectual climate disposed to revalue processes and constraints that are local, variable, context-dependent, contingent, and in some sense made up (Shweder & Sullivan, 1993, p. 500).

THE SEMIOTIC SUBJECT

The deconstructionist brand of cultural psychology described in the preceding quote conceptualizes people as being "semiotic subjects" who do *not* have traits, mental states, or psychological processes that are independent from culture. "Semiotic" in this context refers to the human capacity to invent and use symbol systems such as language. To invent a symbol is to invent also the *meaning* for that symbol, and the fundamental, "semiotic" human capacity, according to Richard Shweder, one of the most prominent of the deconstructionist cross-cultural psychologists, is to decide what the world consists of, what it means, and how to talk and think about it. As language and other symbols change across cultures, so too does human experience.

What, then, can cross-cultural researchers do under this set of assumptions? Two things. The first is travel among foreign cultures and come back with what they call "thick," detailed reports of how other peoples interpret and symbolize reality. These reports include investigations of how members of different cultures have (or do not have) a sense of self, or how they experience emotions, or whether they believe that individual personalities exist separately from society (e.g., Shweder, 1992; Shweder & Bourne, 1982).

The other activity common to this brand of cross-cultural psychology is to spend some energy berating the rest of psychology for any attempt to understand the whole world through a common set of categories. Each culture must be examined in its own terms, says this argument; to compare one culture to another profoundly misses the point, because any system of categorization that allowed such comparison to occur would itself be ethnocentric. Even comparing one individual with another is profoundly misguided, according to this view, because each individual is not a mere "vessel" for psychological states, but a meaning-producing system in his or her own right. Such a semiotic subject, to use that term again, can be understood only in his or her own terms, in regard to his or her unique experience of the world (Shweder & Sullivan, 1990).

THE INDIAN SENSE OF SELF

A particular mistake of ordinary, non-cross-cultural psychology, from this point of view, is to impose the Western notion of the "self" on members of other cultures. This notion sees the individual personality, or self, as distinct from other individuals and as separate from the world in which it lives, and as having properties (e.g., emotions and personality traits) of its own. As obvious as this idea might seem to our Western minds, according to Shweder and Bourne (1982) it is far from universal. In particular, they claim, people do not think this way in India.

From their study of the Hindu Indian culture, Shweder and Bourne conclude that its holistic outlook leads Indians to think of themselves in a fundamentally different way than we do in our Western culture. Westerners, and perhaps especially Americans, see the individual as the fundamental human unit. Indians, by contrast, think in terms of the group to which they belong, typically the family. For them, an individual cannot be set apart from this wider group. One manifestation of this, according to Shweder and Bourne, is that Indians do not speak of each others' psychological properties, that is, they do not have conceptions, as we do, of each others' personality traits.

To demonstrate this point, Shweder and Bourne (1982) performed a very simple experiment: they asked Hindu Indian and American informants to describe people they knew. The answers they got differed significantly. While an American might say, "She is friendly," an Indian would say, "She brings cakes to my family on festival days." An American might say, "He is cheap," while an Indian said, "He has trouble giving things to his family." And where an American might say, "He is kind," an Indian is more likely to say, "Whoever becomes his friend he remembers him forever and will always help him out of his troubles." Overall, whereas descriptions of acquaintances offered by Americans consisted of about 50 percent personality trait terms (such as friendly, cheap and kind), descriptions by Indians were only about 20 percent comprised of such traits. The conclusion reached by Shweder and Bourne is that Americans' frequent use of trait terms to describe properties of persons, and even the very idea of self, is not shared by Hindus in India.

IS THE SELF A CULTURAL ARTIFACT?

The concept of self is extremely important. Every other chapter in this book describes a personality psychology that throughout its diverse approaches uniformly assumes—if it uniformly assumes nothing else—that individuals are separate from one another and from the society of which they are a part. Furthermore, all of personality psychology also assumes that these individuals have properties, whether conceived as traits, learning patterns, or mental structures, that belong to or characterize each of them. Yet Shweder and Bourne claim that this fundamental idea is an arbitrary artifact of Western culture, and have even found a culture, India, where they claim this idea is not held. They need only one such culture to make their point and to cast the rest of psychology down the river. If anybody anywhere fails to see individual persons as separate entities in their own right, then all of Western personality psychology (and much of Western thought, in general) is little more than an arbitrary social construction.

This kind of sweeping philosophical claim makes it important to take cultural psychology seriously. If this claim is really true, then many ideas that have been taken for granted for many years should be discarded or revised. Among these are the ideas of personality development, self-interest, morality, and personal responsibility, to name a few. It would also be necessary to thoroughly revise all of personality psychology. I gather that such a project is exactly what

Shweder has in mind (e.g., Shweder & Sullivan, 1990). But before we get started on the re-invention of Western psychology, a few points are worth considering.

First, despite all the rather dramatic claims made about and by this research, the evidence presented in favor of Shweder and Bourne's basic claim is not very compelling. Consider the key experiment that they report, in which Indian and American subjects were asked to describe people they knew, and in which Americans usually answered with traits while Indians more often used complex and contextualized phrases. As the social psychologist John Sabini points out, "it would be rash to impute a very different concept of the self on the basis of this kind of evidence" (Sabini, 1995, p. 264). First of all, the finding that 20 percent of the Indians' descriptions of people *were* personality trait terms shows that the idea of individual traits is not exactly foreign to them—if I may be forgiven the pun. Moreover, it is not clear that even the colorful phrases used by the Indian informants are fundamentally different from the Americans' descriptions. They may be just longer and more vivid ways to make the same point.

Sabini recalls the description offered by the former governor of Texas, Ann Richards, of then-President George Bush: "Poor George, he can't help it—he was born with a silver foot in his mouth." Ann Richards is nothing if not Western, and her description is certainly a description—and a vivid one—of an aspect she perceived of Bush's personality.[2] There is nothing Eastern, or fundamentally denying of the separateness of Bush's self, about this description.

Now consider the Indian's description of his kind acquaintance as being someone who "remembers [his friend] forever and will always help him out of his troubles." This description is less caustic than Richards's, but similarly provides a vivid description of the habitual behavioral style—the trait of kindness, in this case—of a person he knows well.

Even more fundamentally, Shweder's Indian informants apparently had no trouble identifying the individuals they were to describe. They were not describing any random person in their collective culture; with ease they were describing a particular individual. Within the description of the kind person, they did not find it strange or difficult to distinguish the person who was always willing to help a friend from the friend he was willing to help. These descriptions by Indians of Indians, on closer examination, do not seem very different from those we are used to, after all (Sabini, 1995).

However, the difference between the 20 percent Indian vs. 50 percent American usage of trait terms remains large enough to deserve attention. It does seem to be the case that in India and some other Eastern cultures trait terms are used less often than they are in North America and Europe (Bond & Cheung, 1983;

---

[2]In case a trait translation is necessary, Richards was calling Bush an inarticulate, over-privileged bumbler.

Cousins, 1989). Even if this difference does not reflect a fundamentally different concept of self, it is a real cross-cultural variation. Members of different cultures do seem to vary in their ways of describing each other. But do Indians have no sense of self, or even of personality? The evidence on this point is dubious.

ON CATEGORIZATION

In its essence, Shweder and Bourne's argument is the same one that was made by the American personality psychologist Gordon Allport (1937) when he argued in favor of what is sometimes called **idiographic assessment**. No two people ever have the same experiences (or genetic makeup), Allport argued, so it is always to some degree a distortion to see them in common terms, or even to categorize them as varying along common dimensions. As we saw in the preceding chapter, George Kelly (1955) also claimed that no two people have the same personal constructs through which they view the world and so also believed that it makes little sense to try to classify people or to compare them along common dimensions. Shweder and Bourne seem not only to endorse this point of view, but to raise it to the cultural level by bringing in an even broader, deconstructionist viewpoint: One individual cannot be compared with another; one culture cannot be compared with another; nothing really can be compared with anything. Everything must be understood in its *own* terms.

This is an interesting and even challenging point of view, but it is not without problems of its own. For one thing, it contains something of an internal contradiction. On the one hand, Shweder and Bourne are claiming that no two cultures or individuals are even comparable, much less identical. Yet they also seem to be categorizing individual members of cultures quite broadly. They write, for example, as if *nobody* in India has a separate sense of self, whereas *everybody* in the United States does. But their basic argument would seem to prohibit categorizing the semiotic inhabitants of India and of the United States into groups whose members all see the world in the same way.

An even more devastating difficulty with a deconstructionist approach is that it comes dangerously close to making cross-cultural psychology impossible. An exclusive focus on the uniqueness of every individual and every culture seems to foreclose any possibility of coming to general understandings about people or cultures. I once heard the psychologist Henry Gleitman claim, "If we understood a rose in its own terms, botany would be impossible." He meant that certain things about roses—and even each individual rose—are unique, to be sure. But we can only achieve a general understanding of plants, including roses, by being willing to classify and compare on the basis of important differences, while ignoring small differences.

The deconstructionist approach to cross-cultural psychology tends to leave one in a swirl of details about particular, individual cultures—details that can be very interesting. But because it eschews comparisons between cultures, the approach leads to few broad conclusions beyond the broad conclusion that broad conclusions are impossible. The approach also seems to lend itself more to philosophical debate than to empirical research, as is perhaps already apparent.

The Comparative Cultural Approach

An increasing number of psychologists are following a third approach that does attempt to tackle directly the task of comparing and classifying cultures. The major proponent of this approach, Harry Triandis, calls it "cross-cultural psychology." This term is unfortunately similar to the label Richard Shweder applies to his own, very different, deconstructionist approach, which is "cultural psychology." So I have chosen to use a different term to describe research comparing different cultures along common dimensions: the "comparative cultural approach."

EMICS AND ETICS

According to Triandis, any idea or concept has both aspects that are the same across cultures and aspects that are particular to a specific culture. (This claim makes him a moderate in the never-ending debate between the absolutists and the deconstructionists.) The universal components of an idea are called **etics** and the particular aspects are called **emics**.[3]

For example, all cultures have some conception of self-reliance, the idea that a person should be responsible for doing what he or she is supposed to do. But beyond this basic, etic idea, collectivist cultures (such as China) have the emic notion that the essence of self-reliance is to be a dependable and contributing member of one's *group*, whereas Westerners have the equally emic notion that self-reliance entails rising *above* the crowd and establishing ourselves as individuals.

A particular topic in which the distinction between emics and etics has received close attention concerns the cross-cultural generality of personality traits. As was discussed in Chapter 7, many personality psychologists have concluded that five basic traits account for much of the variation from one individual to another (McCrae & Costa, 1987): These so-called Big Five are extraversion, neuroticism, conscientiousness, agreeableness, and openness to experience (the exact terms vary somewhat from one investigator to another). This is by no means an uncontroversial conclusion (see Block, 1995, and Chapter 7), but let us accept it for a moment. An obvious next question is, Are these basic traits

---

[3]These terms are also sometimes used to refer to the insider (emic) versus the outsider (etic) perspective on a person or group, or to an objective (etic) versus a subjective (emic) view of the world (see Headland, Pike, & Harris, 1990).

applicable across different cultures, or are they limited to the North American and European cultures in which they were originally demonstrated?

In one attempt to answer this question, investigators assembled a group of Chinese words that are used to describe personality, and then asked Chinese subjects to rate several other people using these words. These ratings were factor analyzed (see Chapter 3), and five factors were extracted. As was mentioned in Chapter 7, the Chinese Big Five turned out to be social orientation, competence, expressiveness, self-control, and optimism (Yang and Bond, 1990). It is possible to view social orientation as similar to what American psychology often calls agreeableness; competence seems related (negatively) to neuroticism; expressiveness seems related to extraversion; self-control is related to agreeableness as well as conscientiousness (the Chinese version of self-control seems to involve the inhibition of negative emotions such as anger); and optimism seems related to both extraversion and (negatively) to neuroticism (cf. McCrae & Costa, 1987).

Do these findings mean that the Western Big Five are in fact universal, or etic, dimensions of personality, as some have suggested (e.g., Goldberg, 1981)? Sort of. Here is Triandis's conclusion:

If one takes into account the unreliability of measurements, which are inevitable in any measurement, the correlations are "not bad," but they are certainly "not good." You have to decide for yourself if the Big Five are etic. (Triandis, in press, p. 20 of ms.)

DIFFERENCES AMONG CULTURES

Research of the sort just described, which attempts to distinguish emics from etics, explores how constructs such as personality traits vary across cultures. A second kind of research explores how cultures vary along constructs. Such studies begin by conceptualizing a way in which one culture might be different from another, perform research to see how cultures vary in this way, and then examine the consequences.

One pioneering effort nearly half a century ago produced the conclusion that some cultures are "tough" whereas others are "easy" (Arsenian & Arsenian, 1948). Notice the common dimension of tough/easy is here applied to *all* cultures, and the focus is on how different cultures vary along this common dimension. Tough cultures are strict and demanding, especially on children; easy cultures are more tolerant, and their children seem to have an easier time growing up.

Another pioneer in this field was David McClelland (1961), one of the first personality psychologists to make serious efforts to apply his ideas in different cultures. McClelland assessed cultural attitudes toward achievement by examining the stories that are traditionally told to children. Some cultures, such as the American one, tell their children many stories along the lines of "The little engine that could," and so reflect a high cultural need for achievement. Other cultures tell more stories in which needs for love or, to use McClelland's term, affiliation, are more prominent. Cultures whose stories manifest a high need for achievement, according to McClelland, can be expected to have more rapid industrial growth than those that manifest less of this kind of achievement orientation.

More recently, Triandis (1994, in press) has proposed that cultures vary along three basic dimensions: complexity, tightness vs. looseness, and collectivism vs. individualism. One can compare one culture to another by assessing the position of each on these "cultural trait" scales.

Complexity The first trait describes some cultures as more complicated than others. In particular, Triandis writes of the difference between "modern, industrial, affluent cultures [and] the simpler cultures, such as the hunters and gatherers, or the residents of a monastery" (in press, p. 6 of ms.). This difference seems plausible, but we must be careful here. Recall the phenomenon of out-group bias, in which the group to which one actually belongs seems to be more diverse and complicated than other groups (Linville & Jones, 1980). Members of the National Rifle Association, classical violinists, and residents of California all see themselves as diverse and complex groups. Nonmembers of these and other groups, however, show a distinct tendency to see group members as all the same and to believe—incorrectly—that members of such groups are simple to characterize. We must not fall into the same trap by assuming that other cultures are easier to characterize and thus are less complex than our own.

Moreover, it might be reasonable to ask whether modern industrial society is in fact more complex than hunter-gatherer cultures. Although they may not be very visible to an outsider, it is reasonable to suspect that such cultures have their own patterns of interpersonal relationships and political struggles—when it comes time to choose a new chief, for example—that are themselves fairly complex. One has grounds to wonder, too, whether monastery life looks as simple from the inside as it does from the outside.

Tightness The tightness/looseness dimension contrasts cultures in which very little deviation from proper behavior is tolerated (tight cultures) with those in which fairly large deviations from cultural norms are allowed (loose cultures). Triandis claims that ethnically homogenous and densely populated societies tend to be tighter than societies that are more diverse or where the people are more spread out. This is because, Triandis assumes, to enforce norms strictly people must be similar enough to one another to agree on what those norms should be, and because strict norms of behavior are more necessary when people must live close together.

The United States, historically a diverse and geographically spread-out society, is a classic example of a loose culture. But even here it varies. Having lived in both places, I can testify that east-central Illinois is a much tighter culture than Berkeley, California, even though both are in the United States. Berkeley is more densely populated than is downstate Illinois, but it is also more diverse. This observation suggests that diversity might be more important than density as a determinant of tightness and looseness.

Boston, where I have also lived, is an even more interesting case. Tightness and looseness can vary by block. In Boston, homogenous, ethnic Italian and Irish neighborhoods (the North End and South Boston, respectively), where mores are quite tight, abut more diverse neighborhoods (such as Back Bay), where standards are much looser. Again, diversity seems to be key. All of these neighborhoods are about equally crowded. But whereas South Boston and the North End are populated largely by people who were born and raised there, nearly everybody I met in Back Bay seemed to be from another state—usually California!

An interesting way to index the tightness of a culture is to examine left- and right-handedness. Biologically, about 12 percent of the world's population should be left-handed. But almost all cultures (including our own) prefer for people to be right-handed, and use various tactics to coerce use of the right hand. One cross-cultural survey found that Eskimos and Australian Aborigines were about 10 to 12 percent left-handed, showing a minor coercion toward right-handedness in those two relatively loose cultures. In Western European samples the rate was about 6 percent, and in Hong Kong the rate was near 1 percent, suggesting that those cultures are much tighter. Interestingly, the percentage of "lefties" among women enrolled at the University of Hong Kong was zero, suggesting that they are subjected to particularly strong cultural coercion (Dawson, 1974).

A failure to appreciate cultural tightness vs. looseness can be quite hazardous, as the American teenager who was caned for spray-painting cars in Singapore found out. This episode seems rather exceptional, however. Often, tight cultures impose strict codes of conduct on their natives, but are tolerant of foreigners (who are not expected to know better). This is the case in Japan, for example (Triandis, 1994). Anglo-Americans travelling or living in Japan have relatively few difficulties living up to Japanese expectations. However, I have known Japanese who came to the United States to work for several years in research laboratories, and who found their return to Japan quite traumatic. They had gotten out of the rhythm of the complex, ritualistic nature of Japanese life, and found themselves prone to make faux pas that were not quickly or easily forgiven. *They* were expected to know better. Some of these Japanese eventually migrated back to the United States permanently, not so much because they preferred it here, but because they had lost the knack of living in Japan.

Collectivism and Individualism   The dimension of cultural variation that has received the most attention in recent years is the distinction between collectivism and individualism (Markus & Kitayama, 1991). In collectivist cultures, such as

Japan, the needs of the "collective" or group seem to be more important than the needs of the individuals in the group. In fact, some investigators have claimed that the boundary between the individual self and the others in one's group is relatively fuzzy in such a culture. (As has already been discussed, Shweder and Bourne [1982] go even further, claiming that natives of India literally do not have a sense of the self as being separate from others.) For example, the Japanese word for self, *jibun*, refers to "one's share of the shared life space." Japanese also exhibit a general desire to sink inconspicuously into the group; a Japanese proverb says, "the nail that stands out gets pounded down" (Markus & Kitayama, 1991, pp. 224, 228).

In individualistic cultures, such as the United States, the individual is more important. People are viewed as separate from those around them, and independence and individual prominence are important virtues. Individual rights take precedence over group interests, and one has a right—indeed, an obligation—to make moral choices that are independent, not merely guided by cultural tradition. The willingness to stand up for one's rights as an individual is all-important, and an American proverb teaches that "the squeaky wheel gets the grease" (Markus & Kitayama, 1991).

Japan is the most frequently discussed example of a collectivist culture and the United States seems like the most obvious—or glaring—example of an individualist culture. A survey of employees of IBM (which has native employees all over the world), found that natives of Taiwan, Peru, Pakistan, Columbia, and Venezuela were more collectivist and less individualistic in outlook than were natives of Australia, Britain, Canada, the Netherlands, and, of course, the United States (Hofstede, 1984). Within the United States, Hispanics, Asians, and African Americans are all more collectivist than Anglos (Triandis, 1994). Also within the United States, women seem to be more collectivist than men (Lykes, 1985).

Differences in Behavior   Many differences between individualistic and collectivist cultures have been pointed out by various commentators. More autobiographies are written in individualistic countries, and more histories of the group are written in collectivist countries (Triandis, in press). People in individualistic countries report experiencing more self-focused emotions (such as anger), compared with people in collectivist countries, who are more likely to report experiencing other-focused emotions (such as sympathy; Markus & Kitayama, 1991).

People from a collectivist culture strictly observe social hierarchies. In India, a person who is even one day older than another is supposed to receive more respect from the younger friend than the other way around (Triandis, in press). People in an individualistic culture, by contrast, are less attentive to differences in status. In the United States, many students call their professors by their first names; this would not happen in China, Japan, or India. (It also would not have happened in the United States fifty years ago, although it is not clear whether this means that our society used to be more collectivist than it is now.)

People in collectivist cultures are more likely to engage in social bathing and skiing in groups; in individualistic cultures people are more likely to prefer these activities alone (Brandt, 1974). Arranged marriages are relatively common in collectivist cultures; members of individualist cultures usually marry "for love." In general, members of individualistic cultures spend less time with more people; members of collectivist cultures spend more time with fewer people (Wheeler, Reise, & Bond, 1989). The cocktail party, where one is supposed to circulate and meet as many people as possible, is a Western invention. While Easterners may be relatively standoffish and shy at such a gathering, they also tend to have a few relationships, *not* casually entered into, that are more intimate than usual Western friendships.

Differences in Values   Styles of moral reasoning also differ from collectivist to individualistic cultures (Miller, Bersoff, & Harwood, 1990). The individualistic cultural ethos emphasizes "my rights" and "my needs," whereas the collectivist cultural ethos emphasizes obligations, reciprocity, and one's duties to the group (Miller & Bersoff, 1992). The collectivist style of moral reasoning imposes a group norm; the individualistic style emphasizes independent and individual choice. We can see this distinction even within our own culture. For example, even though individualism is often viewed as a Western cultural attribute, the Roman Catholic Church—a Western institution if ever there was one—is profoundly collectivist in outlook. Individualism is really a Protestant, northwestern European idea, whereas collectivism is more Catholic, southeastern European (Sabini, 1995). Martin Luther broke with the Catholic Church over the right of an individual to come to his own interpretation of the Scriptures. The Catholic view was—and still is—that any interpretation must come from the Church itself.

We can hear echoes of this ancient argument, as well as of the distinction between individualism and collectivism, in the modern debate over abortion. The individualistic point of view, endorsed by many (though not all) Protestant and Jewish denominations, is that abortion is a matter of individual moral responsibility and choice. One might deplore abortion and regard it as a tragic occurrence, but still endorse the idea that it is the pregnant woman who is most centrally involved, and in the end it all comes down to her own free, moral choice. Those who endorse the right to safe, legal abortions do not like to be called "pro-abortion"; they prefer the term "pro-choice."

The very different, collectivist point of view, strongly espoused by the Catholic Church and some of the more conservative Protestant denominations, is that abortion is morally wrong, period. The unborn fetus is already a person— a member in good standing of the collective, if you will. To kill that fetus with an abortion is to kill a member of the collective, something no individual member—not even the fetus's mother—has a right to do. Indeed, it is the duty of the collective, institutionalized in the church or the state, to prohibit any such act. The matter does not come down to personal choice at all. It comes down to a collectively determined issue of right and wrong.

No wonder this debate shows no signs of subsiding, and no wonder, too, that grounds for reasonable compromise seem nonexistent. In the abortion debate we are seeing a head-on collision between two fundamentally different ways of addressing moral issues. Elements of both co-exist, uneasily, in our own culture, but you cannot map one of them onto the other. From either a collectivist or individualistic point of view on the abortion debate, the other point of view is simply wrong.

The Pros and Cons of Collectivism and Individualism This observation leads us to a broader point, which is that it is important not to romanticize individualism or collectivism. Individualist cultures value freedom and equal opportunity, but also promote selfishness and greed. The currently high rates of divorce, child neglect, and crime in the United States, together with our failure to take responsibility for the accumulated national debt and for the decay of the (collectively owned) infrastructure of schools, roads, and parks might all be traced to our dominant, individualistic culture (Triandis, 1994). Collectivist cultures, in contrast, are more likely to be responsible about the husbanding of their shared resources, but such cultures also put little value on personal freedom and make strong distinctions between members of in-groups and out-groups. For example, consider the ancient system that rigidly divides Indians into castes, including a group of "untouchables" that everybody else is supposed to avoid.

Ironically, an individualistic culture may be less likely than a collectivist one to create barriers between groups, because it views the individual as the unit of analysis, rather than the group to which the individual happens to belong. Collectivist cultures promote caring for members of one's group, typically the extended family, but such charity does not extend to non-members. Walled communities, within which neighbors are kind to each other but which aggressively keep all outsiders at bay, are collectivist minicultures. Genocide—the systematic killing of persons who belong to a particular group—is a more extreme, but related practice that is not rare among collectivist, tribal cultures. We have seen it recently in Bosnia and in Rwanda. It is always going on somewhere.

Cultural Assessment and Personality Assessment A fairly close analogy can be drawn between assessing a culture along the three dimensions just described and assessing the personality of an individual. Indeed, the three basic dimensions of cultural variation are also dimensions along which individuals differ from one another. The complexity dimension is analogous to the personality trait of cognitive complexity; cultural tightness resembles the traits of conscientiousness and intolerance for ambiguity; the collectivist/individualist distinction is analogous to idiocentrism vs. allocentrism, a dimension of personal values that focuses on whether one believes that the individual is more important than the group, or vice versa. It seems that complexity, tightness, and collectivity are all traits of individuals as well as of cultures.

THE QUESTION OF ORIGIN

I am sure it is obvious by now that cross-cultural differences in personality, behavior, and experience are real and profound. Where do these differences come from?

The Deconstructionist Dodge

This obvious and fundamental question seems to have received less attention than it deserves. The deconstructionist cultural psychologists seem particularly prone to avoid this question, probably because their basic approach tends to foreclose any answer to it. Recall that the deconstructionist critique claims that reality cannot be known apart from culturally determined perceptions or constructions of it (e.g., Shweder & Sullivan, 1990). Therefore, one's view of reality must always *follow* culture; it is not determined before there is any culture.

This viewpoint strikes me as akin to answering the old chicken-or-egg question with "chicken," *without* then explaining where that first chicken came from. The existentialists who were discussed in Chapter 14 would say that even a cultural view of reality is never actually imposed on the individual; it is freely chosen. But the deconstructionist cultural psychologists do not seem to be claiming that cultures or individuals have free will, just that their constructions are arbitrary. According to them, the way a culture views reality cannot depend on anything that preceded the culture itself. Frankly, this is not much of an answer to the origin question.

The Ecological Approach

Comparative cultural psychologists have tried to provide serious answers to the origin question, although so far their answers must be classified as speculative rather than proven. Triandis (1994) proposes a straightforward model that can be diagrammed as

ecology $\rightarrow$ culture $\rightarrow$ socialization $\rightarrow$ personality $\rightarrow$ behavior.

In this model, behavior comes from personality, which is a result of what one has been explicitly and implicity taught during one's upbringing (socialization), which is a product of the culture. These steps we have already discussed. The first term in Triandis's model is ecology, by which he means the physical layout and resources of the land where the culture originated, together with the distinctive tasks this culture has needed to accomplish. Part of the collectivist nature of the Chinese culture, for example, might be traceable to their need, thousands of years ago, to develop complex agricultural projects and water systems that required the coordination of many people. In the same historical period, people who lived in hunting or gathering societies did not develop the same collectivist outlook or complex social system. In a similar vein, mentioned earlier in this chapter was Triandis's hypothesis that people who live in ethnically homogenous and densely populated environments tend to develop tight cultures, whereas people who live in more diverse or less densely populated environments tend to develop loose cultures.

Even small differences in ecology can lead to large differences in personality. For example, Truk and Tahiti, both small islands in the South Pacific with cultures heavily dependent on fishing, have evolved different patterns of gender roles and aggressive behavior (Gilmore, 1990). In Truk, fish can only be caught by those who are willing to venture out to sea, which is quite hazardous. The result is a culture in which the men who must do this learn to be brave, violent, and physical, and also dominating of women. In Tahiti, fish can be caught easily in the home lagoon, which is not dangerous at all. The men in this culture tend to be gentle, to ignore insults, and to be very slow to fight, and also to be respectful of women. Apparently, all this is merely a result of where the fish are!

Of course, there is no way to prove that this interpretation of the source of the differences between the culture on Truk and Tahiti is correct. If it sounds reasonable to you, fine; if it does not, also fine. Nearly all interpretations of the origins of cross-cultural differences must be taken with a similar grain of salt; there are no experiments one can do to prove them right or wrong. But it is still worthwhile to try to formulate such explanations, especially given the fact that the only alternative is to ignore the origins question altogether.

It is also possible to see the development of subcultures within larger cultures, as a function of particular conditions experienced by members of that subculture. As was mentioned earlier, extreme poverty and decades of racial discrimination have led some ethnic subcultures within the United States to develop styles of self-presentation (it being essential for young males to appear tough and threatening) and self-definition (through identification with gangs and other sources of social support and physical protection) that stand in strong contrast with that of the mainstream culture (Anderson, 1994). Other aspects of minority subcultures in the United States stem from distinct ethnic heritages rooted in Asia, Africa, or Latin America, which have been more or less imported onto the North American continent.

IMPLICATIONS OF CULTURAL PSYCHOLOGY
The Culture and the Individual

As was mentioned at the beginning of this chapter, the members of any given culture are not identical. Our own culture contains both individualists and collectivists, for example, and the same is surely true about China or India or anyplace else. Somebody who says that "nobody in India has a sense of the self as separate" is falling into exactly the same trap as somebody who says "everybody in the world senses the self as separate." Variations between individuals within a culture are as important as variations between cultures; in fact, they may be more important.

Interestingly, to think that variations between individuals within a culture are important is an individualistic view. To think that variations between cultures, taken as a whole, are more important, is a collectivist view.[4] Which view is yours?

Cultures and Values

Unless one is careful, cultural psychology sometimes has a way of leading to cultural relativism. Relativism is the phenomenologically based idea that all cultural views of reality are equally valid, and that it is impossible and presumptuous to judge any of them as good or bad, because any such judgment would inevitably be ethnocentric.

This point of view seems fine until you begin to consider some examples. In some areas of Africa and Asia, female genitals are mutilated as part of a cultural tradition intended to preserve purity and thereby improve chances for marriage. Typically, elderly village women use a razor blade or piece of glass, under unhygienic conditions and without anesthesia, to remove the clitoris or the clitoris and labia minora of a young girl. Each year, this procedure is performed on about two million girls between the ages of four and fifteen. Opposition expressed by the World Health Organization and some international human rights groups has sometimes been denounced as ethnocentric (Associated Press, 1994). But does our necessarily different cultural perspective truly mean that we have no valid grounds on which to condemn this cultural tradition?

Steven Spielberg's movie *Schindler's List* describes the career of Oskar Schin-

---

[4]This definition implies that cross-cultural psychology—especially the subset that regards one's cultural membership as more important than one's properties as an individual (e.g., Shweder & Sullivan, 1990)—is itself collectivist in orientation. The rest of psychology, by contrast, can be seen as individualist.

dler, who was by the standards of the dominant culture of his day (the Nazi culture) a misfit and an outlaw. One of the fascinating things about this movie is that it suggests that Schindler might not have been completely well-adjusted, psychologically. He is shown as disorganized, deceitful, impulsive, and not very good at calculating risks. Yet it is precisely these traits that allowed him to engage in behavior—a complex and dangerous scheme to save thousands of Jewish lives over a period of several years—that today is regarded as heroic. Being a misfit in one's culture is not always a bad thing.

The dangers of cultural relativism have been compellingly described by the psychologists Jack and Jeanne Block, who have written,

> If the absolute definition [of psychological adjustment and of right and wrong] risks the danger of a parochial arrogance, the relative definition may be advocating the value of valuelessness. . . . To the extent that relativism implies one culture is as good as another . . . relativism provides a rationale for tolerance that is also a rationale for perpetuation of what is, rather than what might be (Block, Block, Siegelman, & von der Lippe, 1971, p. 328).

Process and Content

As we have seen, the basic issue that arises from applying psychology to different cultures is this: To what degree and in what ways are people the same around the world? And to what degree and in what ways are they different?

One way to answer this question might be in terms of the difference between psychological **process** and **content**. Psychological processes include basic mechanisms such as perception, memory, and motivation. These are all aspects of the way the mind works. Psychological content, on the other hand, consists of the ideas on which these processes work. They might include one's system of political beliefs or moral values, or even the exact categories one uses to organize one's perceptions of the world.

Notice how the last example, perceptual categories, seems to hover on the blurry edge between process and content. The distinction gets more difficult the more closely you examine it, but it may be crucial because psychological *processes* are assumed to be universal across social class, gender, ethnic group, and culture, whereas content varies. Everybody sees and remembers according to the same basic design, for example, and everybody needs to eat and wants to avoid pain. Content, on the other hand, varies importantly across all of these divisions. Rich and poor, women and men, blacks and whites, Americans and Indians—all sometimes have ideas and values that differ in fundamental ways.

The distinction is worth bearing in mind, but its application is not always clear. One reason, as we have already seen, is that the distinction between process and content is not always obvious. Another reason is that cultural psychologists themselves are not always clear about whether they wish to claim that two cultures have somewhat different ideas laid atop a basic similarity of perception and cognition, or that the worldviews of the two cultures are fundamentally different. Nevertheless, this is the fundamental question we should be asking.

The Universal Human Condition

According to the existential philosopher Sartre, who was discussed in Chapter 14, one universal fact applies across all individuals and all cultures. That fact comprises the "*a priori* limits which outline man's fundamental situation in the universe." Sartre writes,

Historical situations vary; a man may be born a slave in a pagan society or a feudal lord or a proletarian. What does not vary is the necessity for him to exist in the world, to be at work there, to be there in the midst of other people, and to be a mortal there. . . . In this sense we may say that there is a universality of man (Sartre, 1965, pp. 52–53).

I once heard the psychologist Brian Little relate an unpublished result from a cross-cultural research project. He was interested in the goals or "personal projects" people pursue, and the degree to which they might vary cross-culturally. Little teaches at a university in Canada, and it was easy for him to ask his students to describe their current personal projects. At considerable expense and difficulty, he managed to have a group of Chinese students, in China, surveyed on a similar question. Great pains were taken to translate the question into Chinese, then to "back-translate" it into English to make sure it correctly crossed the cultural divide,[5] and the same efforts were expended on translating the students' answers. Almost uniformly, the results were disappointing for anyone who expected large differences. The goals—get good grades, shop for tonight's dinner, find a new girlfriend—seemed more universal than culturally specific. Then, to his great excitement, Little read one particular Chinese student's response: one of her current projects, she reported, was to "work on my guilt."

Little reports his initial reaction as: Wow, what a profoundly different, non-Western type of goal. What interesting insight a goal like working on one's guilt provides into the fundamentally contrasting, collectivist Chinese worldview. And, not least of all, what a publication this will make!

Then, good scientist that he is, Little did some checking. The statement turned out to be a typographical error. The Chinese student was making a blanket for herself, and she was trying to find time to work on her *quilt*. Sometimes,

---

[5]In back translation, the researcher takes a phrase in one language and translates it into a second language, then has a separate person translate it back into the first language. Then a native speaker of the first language judges whether the statements are identical (as they should be, if the translations were done correctly).

cross-cultural differences in personality are more difficult to find than one might expect.

SUMMARY

If, as the phenomenologists claim, a person's construal of the world is all-important, a logical next question concerns the ways in which such construals of reality vary across different cultures. This topic is addressed by cross-cultural psychology. It is important to know whether psychological research and theorizing that originates in one culture can be applied to another, because misunderstandings across cultures can lead to conflict and even war, and because to understand how other peoples view reality can expand our own understanding of the world. Hazards of cross-cultural research include ethnocentrism, outgroup bias, and the unfortunate fact that ultimately one person can never fully comprehend the experience of another.

   Some psychologists ignore cross-cultural issues. A second group, the deconstructionists, argues that comparing cultures is impossible; we must seek to understand each culture in its own terms. Some deconstructionists have even claimed that the Western sense of self is a cultural artifact. A third group of psychologists follows a comparative approach, contrasting etics, or elements that all cultures have in common, with emics, or elements that make them different. Cultures have been compared on emic dimensions including complexity, tightness, and collectivism. Deconstructionists avoid the question of where these differences originate, but one comparative approach sees the ultimate origin of cultural differences in the differing ecologies to which groups around the world must adapt. Despite the importance of cross-cultural psychology, it is important to bear in mind that individuals vary within as well as across cultures, that cultural relativism can be taken too far, and that beneath all cultural differences there may be a universal human condition in an existential sense: the need to exist, to work, to relate to other people, and ultimately to die.

SUGGESTED READINGS:
EXPERIENCE AND AWARENESS

Lonner, W. J., & Lapass, R. S. (1994). *Psychology and culture.* Needham Heights, MA: Allyn & Bacon.
> *A good general introduction to cross-cultural psychology.*

Maslow, A. H. (1987). *Motivation and personality* (3rd ed.). New York: Harper & Row.
> *This is one of the most accessible—and briefest—thorough presentations of American humanistic psychology by one of its two historically most important figures (the other being Carl Rogers). Maslow's writing is passionate and persuasive.*

Rogers, C. R. (1961). *On becoming a person.* Boston: Houghton Mifflin.
> *The classic statement of the ultimate optimistic phenomenologist.*

Rychlak, J. F. (1988). *The psychology of rigorous humanism* (2nd ed.). New York: New York University Press.
> *This is a difficult (and very long) book, but it provides a thorough presentation of the modern approach to humanistic psychology, written by the foremost person in the field.*

Sartre, J. P. (1965). The humanism of existentialism. In W. Baskin (Ed.), *Essays in existentialism* (pp. 31–62). Secaucus, NJ: Citadel Press.
> *A surprisingly readable and interesting exposition of existentialism, from one of the important historical figures of the approach.*

Shweder, R. A., & Sullivan, M. A. (1993). Cultural psychology: Who needs it? *Annual Review of Psychology, 44,* 497–523.
> *An opinionated presentation of the view of cultural psychology that, in this text, I have called "deconstructionist."*

Triandis, H. C. (1994). *Culture and social behavior.* New York: McGraw-Hill.
> *A thorough and readable introduction to comparative cross-cultural psychology.*

PART VI

Behavior and Thought: Behaviorist, Social Learning, and Cognitive Approaches

Many research psychologists are scientifically inclined people who entered psychology to fulfull a particular goal: to help develop an actual science of the human mind. They believe that psychology is not and should not be art, or literature, or poetry. It is and should be science. And what makes psychology scientific can only be its unique *objectivity*, its basis in concrete facts rather than personal points of view. The worldview of these scientifically inclined individuals—and certainly their approach to psychology—is exactly the opposite of that of the humanists described in Chapter 14.

The desire for objectivity has led some of these psychologists, namely the behaviorists, to concentrate their science upon aspects of the mind and behavior that can be directly observed. They are more reluctant than the practitioners of the other approaches described in this book to see personality as residing in the unconscious mind, the ephemeral moment of experience, or even the biological system and personality traits. For none of these underpinnings of personality can be seen, even if they do exist.

Instead, these psychologists concentrate on the only two things relevant to personality that *can* be observed: behavior and the environment. Behavioral psychologists try to show how people's behavior is a direct result of their environment, particularly the rewards and punishments that environment contains. Chapter 16 will review the philosophical underpinnings and classic findings of behaviorism and basic learning theory, along with some of its notable applications.

Behaviorism was and remains a successful approach for many purposes. But eventually, some researchers grew dissatisfied with its rigidity and lack of completeness, and so extended behaviorism into what became called social learning theories. Chapter 17 will describe three different social learning theories, those of John Dollard and Neal Miller, Julian Rotter, and Albert Bandura.

More recently, social learning theorists have become increasingly attentive to the cognitive or memory system, and how information is processed by the human mind. They have developed the cognitive approaches to personality. The final chapter in this section (Chapter 18) will outline the evolution of the later social learning theories into the cognitively oriented approaches to personality that are driving the research of many psychologists today.

Across these three chapters, there will be places where elements of the trait approach, the psychoanalytic approach, and even the phenomenological approach can be seen to have an important degree of influence. Still, the lineage is fairly direct: Behaviorism begat social learning theory, which begat the modern cognitive approaches. The ironic aspect of this progression is that the end is very different from the beginning. Whereas the hallmark of behaviorism was its insistence that everything studied be concrete and observable, its intellectual grandchild, the cognitive approach, is organized around mentalistic concepts of schemas, strategies, and representations, none of which can be directly observed. It turns out that even for the most scientifically inclined psychologist, the temptation to get inside the human mind is difficult to resist.

CHAPTER 16

How the World Creates Who You Are: Behaviorism and the View from Outside

The behaviorist credo, as exemplified in the beliefs of prototypic, historical figures such as John Watson and B. F. Skinner, can be distilled into a belief that the best angle from which to view a person is from the outside. Although the behaviorists do not have an official slogan that expresses this belief, I will happily make one up for them: "We can only know that which we can see, and we can see everything we need to know."

Consider the two parts of this epigram separately. First, the behaviorist believes that knowledge that does not come from direct, public observation is illusory. Introspection is invalid as a source of knowledge because nobody else can verify what you claim to introspect. Attempting to tap other peoples' thoughts is similarly suspect. The only valid way to know something about somebody is to watch what he or she can be seen to *do*—the person's behavior. That, of course, is why the approach is called behaviorism.

When applied to the study of personality, this idea implies that your personality is simply the sum total of everything you do. Nothing else. Personality does not include traits, unconscious conflicts, psychodynamic processes, conscious experiences, nor anything else that cannot be directly observed. If such unobservables even exist (which behaviorists tend to doubt), they are not important.

Close on the heels of this belief comes a further belief that the causes of behavior can be observed as directly as behavior itself can be. That is because these causes are not hidden away in the mind; they are to be found in the individual's environment. In this context, "environment" refers not to the trees and rivers of nature, but to the rewards and punishments that are contained in the physical and social world.

Thus, the behaviorists tell us, personality and all its causes can be directly observed by looking at two very visible things: A person's behavior, and a person's environment.

FUNCTIONAL ANALYSIS

The purpose of behavioristic psychology, as a science, is to connect the first of these fundamental observables to the second: In what way, the behaviorists ask, is behavior a function of the environment? The answer to this question is called a **functional analysis**, and the behaviorists' work to explain in this way what people do has yielded a vast edifice of theory and data.

Behaviorism can be diagrammed like this:

$$\text{environment} \longrightarrow \text{behavior}$$
$$\text{(learning)}$$

As the diagram shows, the connector between the stimuli of the environment and what the person[1] does is called **learning**. Learning consists of any change in behavior as a function of one's experience with the environment. It is *the* key theoretical idea—some might say the only theoretical idea—in behaviorism. But notice how behaviorists use this term in a special, technical, and narrow way. In classical behaviorism, learning refers to the acquisition *not* of knowledge and understanding (the usual, wider meaning of the word) but of the effect of the observable environment upon observable behavior.

I have long been amused by a small wooden building, with green, peeling paint, that sits just north of the bell tower near the center of the enormous university campus at Berkeley. On the wall of this small building is a small sign: "Institute of Human Learning." The sign amuses me because, by most people's definition, the entire campus, and not this pathetic structure, is an "institute of human learning." But the sign refers to the technical meaning of the term—it houses a behaviorist laboratory. When you see or hear the term "learning" in a behavioristic analysis, it might be helpful to remember that little green building. It represents the narrow meaning of the term in this context, not its broader meaning as represented by the rest of the university.

From the behaviorist perspective, your personality is your behavior. Moreover, your behavior is a function of the rewards and punishments that are and have been present in your environment. Therefore, *you* are a direct result of

---

[1]Or animal; traditionally either type of subject is called the "organism" in behavioral theory.

your present and past environments. For this reason, behaviorism could just as well have been called environmentalism (although that term is now being put to different and perhaps better use by the Sierra Club). Behavior is just the result, after all; the environment is the ultimate and only cause.

THE PHILOSOPHICAL ROOTS OF BEHAVIORISM

Behaviorism can be regarded as the American, twentieth-century, scientific manifestation of some very old philosophical ideas. Three ideas in particular are fundmental to the approach: empiricism, associationism, and hedonism.

Empiricism

Empiricism is the idea that everything we know comes from our experience. Experience, in this analysis, is not something that exists separately from or that can produce reality, as the phenomenologists described in Chapter 14 would argue. Rather, experience is the direct product of reality itself. The contents of our minds—and, by extension, our behavior—are caused by the contents of the world and how it has impinged upon us, producing what we have seen, heard, and felt in life. In this way, the structure of reality determines the structure of the mind.

The opposing view, rationalism, holds that exactly the reverse is true: The structure of the mind determines our experience of reality. We saw this latter belief in the views of the phenomenologists discussed in Chapter 14, as well as the deconstructionists and some of the cultural psychologists considered in Chapter 15. Empiricism—and behaviorism—is emphatically neither phenomenological nor deconstructionist.

Taken to its logical conclusion, empiricism implies that the mind, at birth, is essentially empty. The nineteenth-century philosopher John Locke called the newborn mind a *tabula rasa*, or blank slate, ready to be written on by experience. Only as one encounters reality does one begin to accumulate experiences and thereby build a way of reacting to the world, i.e., a personality.

Associationism

A second key philosophical idea explains how this process happens. **Associationism** is the claim that two things, or two ideas, or a thing and an idea, become mentally associated into one thing if they are repeatedly experienced close together in time. Often, but not always, this closeness in time occurs as the result of a cause-and-effect relationship. The lightning flashes, and then the thunder booms. Thunder and lightning become associated in the mind of all who experience this combination. Other combinations are more psychological: a smile of a certain kind is followed by a kiss. Still other combinations are completely arbitrary, or even artifically imposed. A bell rings, and then you are fed (try to imagine yourself as a dog for this example). In each of these cases, the two things tend to become one in the mind. The thought of one will conjure up the other, and the way a person reacts to one will tend to become the way he or she reacts to the other.

Philosophers such as Thomas Hobbes, John Locke, and David Hume believed that these two ideas, empiricism and associationism, were sufficient to explain the basis of all knowledge (Bower & Hilgard, 1981). Even the most complex ideas in one's mind are no more than the combination of simple ideas, and these ideas have become attached to each other because they have been experienced close together in time. Simple ideas, such as thunder and lightning, and more complex ideas, such as justice or the meaning of life, are all associations of a few or many simple elements.

This is not an uncontroversial notion, even after all these years. A particular school of objectors were the *Gestalt* (German for "whole pattern") psychologists, whose point of view is partially captured by the well-known phrase, "the whole is different from the sum of its parts" (Koffka, 1935; Kohler, 1925).[2] They accumulated numerous cases where the result of a combination of elements was not predictable from the elements taken one at a time. A classic example is water. No matter how much you know about hydrogen and oxygen, you would never predict that their combination would be wet. Thus, the whole (water) is fundamentally different from just the sum of its parts (2 hydrogen atoms + 1 oxygen atom). The broader and more psychological claim of the Gestaltists is that our perceptions of the world are not built merely from the pieces we perceive; the mind imposes on complicated stimuli a general form that has a meaning different from its parts.

Nonetheless, the associationist perspective remains that the whole is *exactly* the sum of its parts. In general, this perspective on knowledge has not fared well over the years, and the Gestaltist view has tended to prevail (Bower & Hilgard, 1981). Psychologists who study perception have shown repeatedly and convincingly that our impressions of the world are different from and in fact go far beyond what you would get from adding up the simple sensory inputs to the perceptual system (e.g., Gregory, 1968). For example, as you move about a room your perception of its shape and contents remains about the same, even though the bits of information coming through your eyes constantly change. But despite this general and widely accepted conclusion, many basic ideas derived from associationism remain highly influential.

For example, the conceptualization of knowledge as comprising simple as-

---

[2]This principle is often misquoted as "the whole is *greater* than the sum of its parts."

sociations between small facts leads to the research strategy called reductionism. In this strategy, every large phenomenon is to be understood by breaking it down into its smaller, constituent components. Thus, one would conceptualize personality as consisting of a person's inventory of learned associations, or (reducing further) even his or her basic physiological mechanisms, perhaps considered one nerve cell at a time.

Reductionism is an active force in psychology today, not only in behaviorism but in some biological approaches as well. As we saw in Chapter 8, some researchers try to explain mental illness, or even personality itself, as the result of the combination of basic biological processes. (We also saw in Chapter 8 some problems inherent in this reductionist approach.) The behaviorists' strategy for explaining personality is similar; they break a human's entire complex psychology into the many, many small elements—such as associations between stimuli and responses—of which behaviorism assumes it consists.

Hedonism and Utilitarianism

Taken together, empiricism and associationism form the core of the behaviorist explanation of where personality comes from and of what it is made: it comes from experience and consists of the resulting associations between simple ideas. A third philosophical belief, called **hedonism**, provides the remaining piece of the puzzle: motivation. Hedonism provides an answer for *why* people behave at all.

In this context, hedonism claims that people (and "organisms" in general) learn in order to do just two things: seek pleasure and avoid pain. These fundamental motivations explain why rewards and punishments are able to shape people's behavior. They also form the basis of a value system that guides the technology of behavioral change that is behaviorism's proudest achievement.

Hedonism is not a new idea. Epicurus, a Greek philosopher who lived from 341–270 B.C., claimed that the purpose of life is to be free of pain and to pursue what he called "gentle" pleasure, or aesthetic enjoyment and peace of mind. This simple idea led to a surprisingly powerful principle for morality and ethics: Whatever produces the most pleasure for the most people in the long run is good. Whatever does the reverse is bad. Actions are judged to be ethically wrong solely on the basis of the pain they ultimately and inevitably cause.

The power to build a moral code from this principle stems from the distinction between outcomes for the few and those for the many, and between short-term outcomes and long-term outcomes. Immoral actions become those that benefit one person or just a few while harming many more, or that might produce short-term pleasure but long-term harm.

A large variety of actions commonly regarded as unethical or immoral fall under this umbrella. Theft, for example, benefits the thief and harms the victim, which could be said to cancel out, but it also harms the social order that allows commerce and other good things to happen. So theft is, on balance, harmful. In a very different example, marital infidelity might produce short-term pleasure, but it damages a more important marital relationship (thus causing long-term harm to the individual) and may possibly damage an entire family (thus harming the many for the advantage of the few). Lying, cheating, and even more complicated actions such as polluting the environment for short-term profit, or concentrating power and money in the hands of a few at the expense of the many, can all be judged immoral by the same pragmatic standard. In general, the Epicurean ideal leads to a social philosophy called **utilitarianism**, which claims that the best society is the social arrangement that creates the most happiness for the largest number of people.

This idea might sound uncontroversial and innocuous, and in the examples just listed it seems pretty compelling. But it is not without problems of its own. One complication is that utilitarianism puts the goal of the most happiness for the most people above *all others*, including truth, freedom, and dignity. These latter values are viewed as worthwhile only to the extent they promote happiness. The behaviorist and latter-day utilitarian B. F. Skinner wrote a book, called *Walden II*, about a fictional utopia (Skinner, 1948). In this utopia everybody was happy, but nobody was free and considerations such as dignity and truth were treated as irrelevant.

Would you give up your freedom to be happy? A utilitarian would (and would believe freedom to be an illusion, anyway). An existentialist, by contrast, would surely not. As you will recalled from Chapter 14, the ultimate purpose of life for an existentialist is to understand and to face truth at all costs, not to be happy.

Another implication of utilitarianism is less controversial in modern American culture than it once was (or still is, in many places on Earth). When combined with the empiricist idea that a person is born psychologically empty, as a *tabula rasa*, and that therefore a properly designed society should be able to erase differences between individuals, utilitarianism leads to the conclusion that the most happiness for the most people will be best served by treating every person equally. Since equal treatment will ensure equal outcomes, the best way to make everybody happy is to distribute the rewards of society (material goods and power) as uniformly as possible. For this reason, the early utilitarians were pioneers in opposing racial and sexual discrimination.

The behaviorists, who came later, became notorious for pushing the belief in equality to its limit. The founder of modern American behaviorism, John Watson, published the following statement in 1925:

Give me a dozen healthy infants, well-formed, and my own specified world to bring them up in and I'll guarantee to take any one at random and train him to become any type of specialist I might select—doctor, lawyer, artist, merchant, chief and yes, even beggarman and thief, regardless of his talents, penchants, tendencies, vocations, and race of his ancestors. There is no such thing as an inheritance of capacity, talent, temperament, mental constitution, and behavioral characteristics (Watson, 1925).

If this statement sounds radical now, it was even more so seventy years ago.

THREE KINDS OF LEARNING

Recall that in behaviorist terminology, learning refers to any change in behavior as a function of experience. Construed in this way, three types of learning are traditionally identified. They are habituation, classical (or respondent) conditioning, and operant conditioning.

Habituation

Sneak up behind someone and ring a bell. The person will probably jump, perhaps high in the air. Then ring it again. The second jump will not be as high. Then ring it again. The third jump (assuming the person has not snatched the bell out of your hand by now) will be still lower. Eventually, the bell will produce almost no response at all.

This kind of learning is called **habituation**. It is the simplest way in which behavior changes as a result of experience. A crayfish, which has only a few neurons, can do it. Habituation can even be seen in amoebas and single neurons. If you repeatedly poke a crayfish, or electrically stimulate a neuron, the response diminishes with each repetition, until it disappears almost entirely.

Despite its simplicity, habituation can be a powerful mechanism of behavioral change. When my wife and I moved to Boston some years ago, we had been in our new Back Bay apartment just a few minutes when we heard an earsplitting whooping and clanging sound outside. I ran to the window and saw a new Mercedes parked across the street, its alarm in full uproar. Nobody was near it. Eventually, the alarm stopped. A few minutes later, it went off again. Again I went to the window, but a little more slowly this time. Then again, a few minutes after that. And again. After a few weeks, only by noticing the looks on our guests' faces did I become aware that another car alarm was going off. The same kind of thing happens with people who live near railroad tracks or airport glide paths.

Experimental research on habituation has shown that a response nearly as strong as the original *can* be maintained, but only if the stimulus is changed or increased with every repetition. Obviously there is a limit to how much a given stimulus can be increased. But the limit is sometimes tested. At some point in the last few years, some genius apparently discovered that if graphic details of a murder were shown on the television news, people would react emotionally, become interested, and stop changing the channel. And ratings would go up.

But soon every station was doing it, and the reactions of the audience began to habituate. The only thing left to do, of course, was to make the murder footage even more graphic, and to display it even more prominently. As one news director was quoted, "if it bleeds, it leads." If one watches television news today, it seems that the theoretical maximum for this sort of thing has just about been reached (I hope I am not simply displaying a lack of imagination here). If so, then there is hope: people will (eventually) stop responding to even the most graphic images of violence and that will stop being a sure-fire way to enhance ratings. At that point, television news will have to reinstate the response by varying the stimuli—it will have to find some other way to garner viewer interest. (One possibility is to cover truly important events, although that outcome seems unlikely.)

Violence on television is just one example; others include media portrayal of sexuality and the extremity of fashion design. Constant portrayals of war, or even of genocide, eventually begin to elicit less and less reaction. The horrifying images of ethnic "cleansing" in Rwanda and Bosnia shown on television in the mid-1990s may make viewers less sensitive the next time such atrocities take place.

People who are chronically habituated are commonly called "jaded" (this is *not* a technical term). Jaded people have seen it all, and done it all. It is hard to get them excited about anything; extreme or novel stimuli are required to get any reaction whatsoever. Among other things, habituation may be a price of gluttony.

Classical Conditioning

You moved away ten years ago and have not been back since, but one day you find yourself near the old neighborhood, so you drop by. As you walk down the street you used to walk every day, a host of long-forgotten images and feelings floods your mind. It can be a strange sensation, a little like traveling back in time. You might feel emotions you cannot label but know you have not felt in years; you might surprise yourself with the strength of your reaction to seeing a familiar mailbox or your own old front door; you might even in some hard-to-describe way feel ten years younger! What is going on here? You are experiencing the results of **classical conditioning**.

Classical conditioning is usually described in very different contexts, often involving animals—traditionally dogs. The well-known and nearly legendary story of classical conditioning involves the Russian scientist Ivan Pavlov, who was originally interested in studying the physiology of digestion. (He won a Nobel Prize for his work on that subject in 1904.) His subjects were dogs, which he hooked up to an apparatus that measured their salivation as they were fed.

He discovered such research to be complicated, but in a different way than he had expected. He wanted to study how dogs salivated *as* they were fed, but inconveniently often they started salivating *before* they were fed! They might salivate at the sight of the assistant who usually brought their food, or at the sound of the streetcar that passed outside at feeding time. This complicated Pavlov's research, because it forced his investigations out of the realm of pure physiology and into the realm of psychology. Against the advice of some of his physiological colleagues, Pavlov decided that the psychological issues were more interesting than the physiological ones, and turned his attention to the circumstances under which salivation and other physical responses could be elicited with psychological rather than physical stimuli.

Pavlov's investigations developed into the study of what is now called classical conditioning. Classical conditioning begins with a built-in response to a stimulus that an animal emits *before* being taught in any way. For example, meat put into a dog's mouth causes the dog to salivate. In this example the meat is the **unconditioned stimulus**, or UCS, and the salivation in response to biting the meat is the **unconditioned response**, or UCR. But if the same person always feeds the dog, then the very sight of the person might begin to cause the dog to salivate. The person has become a **conditioned stimulus**, or CS, and the response of the dog is now called the **conditioned response**, or CR.

Pavlov was not the first to discover this kind of conditioning. The basic existence of the "conditioned reflex" was known at least one hundred years earlier (Bower & Hilgard, 1981). And classical conditioning is closely related to the philosophical ideas of associationism, discussed above, which had been around even longer. Associationism had always held that two things that happen together will become related in the mind and responded to as if they were the same thing; that is more or less what Pavlov demonstrated.

Pavlov's contribution to what was already known was an elaborate research program that yielded very specific principles about how responses can be conditioned. One of his first findings forced an important change in the principle of associationism. It turns out that a bell begins to elicit salivation most quickly and reliably not if it is rung simultaneously with feeding, but if it is rung just slightly before. (If it is rung too early, it also loses its effectiveness.) Associationism had held that two things become combined in the mind by being experienced *together*; Pavlov's finding, however, showed that matters are more complicated than that.

The implication of Pavlov's finding is that conditioning is not in fact a simple pairing of one stimulus with another, but involves teaching the animal that one stimulus (the bell) is a warning or signal of the other (the food). The difference in interpretation—which, by the way, Pavlov did not make much of—is subtle but fundamental. Pavlov's result forced a reinterpretation of the combining of concepts from a simple, mechanical matter of attaching one concept to another, to a mechanism by which the meaning of one concept changes the meaning of the other. The bell used to mean nothing. Now it means, "food is coming."

Pavlov worked out many details of how conditioning proceeds, and developed a number of subsidiary ideas. For example, if after initial training such as just described, a stimulus such as a bell fails to be followed by food enough times, the animal will stop responding to the bell. This phenomenon is called **extinction**. If you wait a while, without giving food with the bell, the response will probably come back by itself, temporarily; you have witnessed **spontaneous recovery**. The speed with which a response is acquired and the length of time it will persist under extinction are functions of the rate and manner in which it was originally paired with the unconditioned stimulus. The detailed rules of how this process works describe **schedules of reinforcement**.

Two other principles are particularly relevant to the use of classical conditioning for understanding human behavior. One of these principles is **second-order conditioning**, which refers to the fact that something else that is paired with the bell can itself begin to elicit the bell's response. If, after training with the bell, the bell is then preceded by a tone, then the tone will begin to produce salivation. The other principle is **stimulus generalization**, which refers to the fact that stimuli that are *not* the bell, but are in some way *like* the bell, will tend to elicit the same response as the bell. Drop a wrench on the floor with a clang, and the dog will probably salivate—not as much as with the bell, to be sure, but enough to be detectable.

These two principles help explain a wide range of human reactions. People respond powerfully to a broad array of stimuli that are associated with primary, unconditioned stimuli *only via* very long, indirect chains mediated by second-order conditioning and generalization. Consider one's reaction to a smile, for example. "There are smiles that make us happy, there are smiles that make us blue . . ."—so goes an old song. We react in an emotional way, usually pleasantly, to the smile of another person, including a person we have never seen before. This means our reaction must be generalized from the smiles we have seen before. And the smile itself takes on a pleasant meaning because of its assocation with previous pleasant experiences, which themselves may be generalizations and second-order responses to still earlier (and more basic) unconditioned stimuli.

This phenomenon can work in a negative direction as well. Many people have stereotypes of members of other ethnic groups that have not only a cognitive component (e.g., an opinion about what "such people" are like), but also a powerful emotional component (e.g., hate or fear). This kind of reaction, too, depends critically on the mechanisms of generalization and second-order conditioning from what may have been negative experiences with actual members of that group, or (perhaps more often) from media or cultural portrayals.

Classical conditioning affects emotional responses and low-level behavioral responses such as salivating, as we have seen. Some research has also suggested that many organs of the body not usually considered to be under psychological control can be classically conditioned. Some "behaviors" that researchers report having been able to classically condition include insulin release by the pancreas, glycogen uptake by the liver, the speed of the heartbeat, and the flow of secretions in the stomach, gall bladder, and endocrine glands (Bykov, 1957; Bower & Hilgard, 1981). These findings raise some interesting possibilities concerning the way one's experiences in life, and perhaps psychological training, might affect physical health (Dworkin, 1993; King & Husband, 1991).

On an even broader level, classical conditioning can help to explain where certain personality traits—those that involve emotional reactions—originate. For example, if throughout early life, a child has only unpleasant experiences with other people, he or she can be expected to develop a trait of social anxiety, of responding with nervousness and fear to the presence of other people. Likewise, a person who always succeeds at sports is likely to find that playing, watching, or even thinking about sports is a pleasant experience.

So far we have considered what happens when a person learns that one stimulus is associated with another. What about the cases where one stimulus is *not* associated with another—where both seem to happen randomly? This might seem like a nonsensical question; it seems there is nothing to learn in this case. But in fact there is an important lesson here: The world is unpredictable. If one experiences occasional, unpleasant shocks, for example, *without* any stimulus to provide advance warning, one learns this: You are never safe (Gleitman, 1995).

Such a sense of unpredictability is not only unpleasant, it can have important consequences. If one group of rats is given periodic electric shocks, with each shock preceded by a warning light, and another group of rats is given the exact same shocks at the exact same times, but without any warning, the second (unwarned) group becomes much more likely to develop stomach ulcers (Seligman, 1968; Weiss, 1970, 1977). On a psychological level, this may be an example of the difference between fear and anxiety. One feels fear when one knows what the danger is, and has a reason to think that danger is impending. One feels anxiety when it is not clear exactly what the danger is, or when one has no idea when the danger might actually arrive. A chronically anxious person—and there are many such people in this world—may be somebody who has experienced no more than the usual ration of "hard knocks," but who has never been able to learn when they are coming.

Much of what can be said about such conditioning seems—and is—little more than common sense. A person learns that a bell, or a lightning flash, or a smile, is soon followed by something else, and so learns to anticipate it. That seems like a fairly obvious and rational conclusion for the person to draw.

But not all of classical conditioning is sensible in this way; something about it seems more primitive. The psychologist Henry Gleitman gives the example of a concentration camp survivor revisiting the scene of his torment. The survivor knows that World War II is long over; Germany lost, Hitler is dead. And yet he feels a chill, and perhaps real fear. The mechanism that produces the survivor's emotional reaction is more basic, and in some sense more primitive, than his or her rational analysis of any danger that might still exist (Gleitman, 1995).

A less powerful but more common example of the same principle is an old aphorism that says, "It is worth scheming to be the bearer of good tidings." Why? If you tell someone a piece of good news, even a piece of news you had nothing to do with ("you've won the lottery!"), you as a stimulus become paired with the good news and the person may come to feel better about you for that reason alone. Conversely, to be the bearer of bad tidings has long been known to be dangerous. (In some ancient cultures, according to legend, the messenger who told of defeat in battle was put to death.) You become paired with bad news and may become shunned or disliked for that reason. In either case, whether you deserve any credit or blame is beside the point; it matters no more than it mattered to Pavlov's dogs whether the bell deserved credit for the dog being fed.

Classical conditioning also provides an explanation for phobias, as well as a technique for removing them. Presumably an irrational fear is based upon a past, unfortunate, arbitrary pairing of the feared object with an unpleasant experience. (Behaviorists believe phobias must result from such associations, even though such traumatic events cannot always be found for every phobia.) The way to remove the phobia is to expose the individual to the stimulus repeatedly, until the fear response becomes extinct.

One way to do this is to surround the phobic with the feared stimulus. Put the acrophobic atop a mountain; place the snake phobic in a snake pit; strap the person who is afraid of flying into the cockpit of an F-15 doing barrel rolls. This is a real—although rarely used—technique called exhaustion, or flooding (Guthrie, 1935; Bower & Hilgard, 1981; Stampfl & Levis, 1967). It may actually help remove the phobia—if the phobic survives the treatment.

More gently, and more commonly, one can use systematic desensitization to accustom the patient to the fear stimulus a little at a time. The psychology department at Stanford, where I went to graduate school, used to have a program to cure people of snake phobia.[3] The snake is introduced across the room from the phobic. Each time, the snake is brought a little closer, and gradually, over a long period of time, the client learns to hold the snake. To give an extra boost to the treatment, one can add "counterconditioning," in which a person is trained to *relax* in response to the (formerly) feared stimulus. One thinks of

---

[3]Most of the patients were Palo Alto–area housewives who had such a deep fear of snakes they could no longer do gardening or take out the garbage. In the four years I lived in Palo Alto myself, I never saw a snake (outside of the departmental lab). Yet apparently it was easier to train these clients to like snakes than it was to convince them that there actually *were* no snakes around. Interestingly, a behavioristic analysis has a difficult time accounting for so much snake phobia in a relatively snake-free part of the world. For that, one might have to turn to other approaches, such as evolutionary biology or even psychoanalysis.

snakes at the same time one thinks of a favorite vacation place, for example. This technique has been used to treat other common phobias as well, including fear of heights, flying, and the outdoors. It works reasonably well.

Although the examples just cited are usually described as an example of the application of classical conditioning, notice how they resemble the even simpler form of learning—habituation—that was considered earlier. The repeated exposure to a stimulus lessens the organism's response to that stimulus. This is a simple principle, but it remains powerful and, as we have just seen, useful.

Operant Conditioning

A good cook likes to experiment. He or she rarely does exactly the same thing twice, varying ingredients, cooking times, and methods. Nonetheless, every good cook also has a fairly consistent style that evolves from this process of continual experimentation. Things that worked are done more often. Things that do not work are dropped from the cook's repertoire. As a result, and through experience, the cook's creations constantly change and constantly improve.

The Law of Effect: Thorndike

This kind of learning-from-experience is not limited to cooks or even to humans. A classic, early example involved cats. Even before Pavlov began his studies of hungry dogs, the American psychologist Edward Thorndike was putting hungry cats in a device he called the puzzle box. The cats could escape from this box only by doing some specific, simple act, such as pulling on a wire or pressing a bar. Doing so would cause the box suddenly to spring open, and the cat would jump out to find a bit of food nearby. Then Thorndike would put the cat back in the box, to try again (Thorndike, 1911).

Thorndike found that gradually, the cat began to escape from the box more and more quickly. What originally took three minutes, after twenty-five trials or so, occurred in less than fifteen seconds. It is important to note that this change in escape time developed *gradually*, because Thorndike's explanation was not that the cat came to "understand" how to get out of the box, but rather that the specific response, such as pressing a bar, that was associated with escape became mechanically "strengthened" through its pairing with a pleasant outcome—escape and food.

When the German psychologist Heinz Kohler later argued that the chimpanzees he studied actually came to *understand* their situation—to have insight—his evidence was that once they learned what would work to get them a banana, they learned it *immediately*, not gradually (Kohler, 1925; Gleitman, 1995). Such immediate acquisition of knowledge can be considered insight or an "aha" effect. Thorndike's cats did not gain insight—maybe because due to the design of the box there was no way for them to figure out what was happening. They learned gradually, and the visible manifestation of the gradual strengthening of the correct response is that the cats began to press the bar earlier and more frequently.

Thorndike did not view this kind of learning by cats as fundamentally different from the classical conditioning that Pavlov did in his lab. He thought his cats pressed the bar (which was followed by food) for basically the same reason that Pavlov's dogs salivated at the bell (which was followed by food). Thorndike's "Law of Effect" shows the similarity:

Of several responses made to the same situation, those which are accompanied or closely followed by satisfaction to the animal will, other things being equal, be more firmly connected with the situation; . . . those which are accompanied by discomfort to the animal will, other things being equal, have their connections with that situation weakened" (Thorndike, 1911; cited by Bower & Hilgard, 1981, p. 24).

Notice how this "law" makes no reference to the state of the animal. This is an important omission; Thorndike did not use just any cat at any time; he preferred hungry cats. The motivational state of the organism has an important influence on the possibilities for conditioning.

NEEDS AND CRAVINGS: HULL

Working a couple of decades after Thorndike, Clark Hull remedied this omission. He pointed out that behavior is a function not just of events in the environment, but also of properties of the organism itself. These might include the organism's history of prior training, its biological need states (such as hunger), its health status and level of fatigue, and so forth. These are potentially intervening variables that lie between the environment and the organisms' behavior, and can determine whether and how much the environment affects that behavior.

Hull's specific motivational theory was that all animals, including humans, have certain needs, such as the need for food. Each need creates a drive, and reducing that drive (by eating, perhaps) reinforces the behavior (eating). Later on, Hull acknowledged that people do not just have needs, we have what he called "cravings," which are desires for reinforcement even when they do not satisfy a need (Hull, 1943). An obese person may eat even when full, for example, and many people will consume products with saccharine (artificial sugar) even though such products have no calories and no nutritional value and fulfill no real need at all.

Thorndike and Hull and their contemporary learning theorists all conceived of learning in terms of stimuli and responses. In a process not really different from classical conditioning, responses to stimuli that were followed by reinforcement became strengthened, meaning they became more likely. A bell rings, the dog salivates, the food arrives. A cat sees the inside of a puzzle box, she pulls a wire, the box opens, revealing food. The mechanisms by which salivation and wire-pulling are reinforced and learned seem similar, and were lumped together in the Law of Effect as formulated by Thorndike.

OPERANT BEHAVIOR: SKINNER

It was left to B. F. Skinner (e.g., 1938) to insist that the two situations are very different. In the case of Pavlov's dogs, their salivating actually has no effect on their environment. It is a response that, after training, happens to be followed by meat. Even if a dog were not to salivate, the meat would still arrive. But when Thorndike's cats pushed the lever that opened their cage, they changed the state of their world. A door once closed became open, allowing their escape.

Skinner called the first kind of learning **respondent conditioning**, meaning that what is conditioned is an essentially passive response that has no impact of its own. The second kind of learning, in which he was much more interested, he called **operant conditioning**, meaning that the animal learns to operate on its world in such a way as to change it to that animal's advantage. It is the consequence of this operant behavior that produces the reinforcement.

To work out the laws of operant conditioning, Skinner invented a device that became known as the Skinner box. In principle, this invention is much like Thorndike's puzzle box, but it is simpler in design and is usually used with simpler animals, such as rats and pigeons. The Skinner box contains little but a bar and a chute for delivering food pellets. Put a pigeon in there and it immediately begins to bump around. It does a little dance, it preens its feathers, and, eventually, it pushes the bar. A food pellet immediately rolls down the chute. The pigeon eats it and then—pigeons not being terribly bright—goes back to its pigeon activities. It dances around some more, preens some more, and again eventually hits the bar. Another food pellet. The pigeon dimly begins to catch on. At a steadily increasing rate, the pigeon will begin to hit the bar more often, sometimes (depending upon the frequency of reinforcement) to the point where it does little else.

The cook with which we began this section and the pigeon just mentioned are not all that different, believe the behaviorists. Both learn from experience through the mechanism of operant conditioning. If an animal or a person emits a behavior, and the behavior is followed by a reinforcement, the behavior becomes more likely than it was before. If the behavior is followed by a punishment, it becomes less likely.

Despite Skinner's claims about how reinforcement derives from the organism's effect on its environment, the results of operant conditioning are not necessarily logical. It will work on any behavior, regardless of what the real connection is between it and the consequences that follow. For example, if a student happens to wear red socks the day of an important exam, and then gets an A+, he or she might *always* wear red socks on future exam days. If the student fails the exam, however, the red socks might go straight into the trash. Superstitious behaviors like this are quite common, and are explained as well by the earlier and simpler theories of Pavlov and Thorndike as by Skinner's theory of operant conditioning.

Shaping Behavior   One has to admire the way Skinner developed his notions of operant conditioning into a practical technology of behavioral change. The techniques he invented work on both animals and humans, and the results can be complex and impressive. Skinner's basic approach takes advantage of the fact that organisms are constantly doing things and varying what they do; Skinner said, "It is in the nature of organisms to emit behaviors" (1938). These actions all have consequences, positive or negative, so their relative frequencies are constantly changing. The results might be gradual but can be powerful.

Consider shaping. A sculptor shapes a piece of clay into a statue by gradually shaving off clay here and there until a square block comes to represent a person or an animal. The process is gradual and moves in small steps, but the ultimate result is very different from where the sculptor started.

Behavior can be shaped in a similar manner. One can reward a pigeon for hitting a bar, but then raise the criterion. Now, to get rewarded, the pigeon must step forward and back, and *then* hit the bar. (Because a pigeon is constantly emitting different behaviors, it will do this eventually.) The behavior is then rewarded, and gradually becomes more frequent. Then the criterion can be raised again. Before too long, you can produce a pigeon who is doing a fairly complicated dance there inside the Skinner box.

According to legend, the same technique was once shown to be effective on Skinner himself. The story, advertised as true when told to me but probably apocryphal, is that Skinner was teaching a course on behaviorism at Harvard when his students decided to try out Skinner's principles on their esteemed instructor. They decided that they wanted him to stop giving lectures from the podium, and instead deliver them from a spot near the door, with one foot in the outside hallway. As Skinner began his lecture, they all looked bored and shuffled their feet. The first time he happened to step away from the podium, they all perked up noticeably. When he stepped back, they all returned to an apathetic slouch. After Skinner had learned to lecture from a step away, the students raised the criterion. Now they did not look alert until he was *two* steps away from the podium. By the end of the semester, B. F. Skinner was indeed delivering his lectures from the doorway, with one foot in the hall, only running occasionally to the podium to glance at his notes, then running back to the doorway to continue lecturing.

And now, the punch line. A departmental colleague happened to pass the class one day while it was meeting. Seeing Skinner later in a faculty lounge, he asked why he had been lecturing from the doorway, instead of from the podium. Skinner replied, "the light is *much* better in the doorway."

Another example, which I know is true because I was there, concerns my old college roommate, Rick. A psychology major long before I was (and now a successful fireman in Idaho—who says you can't have a valuable career with a BA in psychology?), Rick was given the assignment of using shaping in a real-life context. He chose the dorm lounge where, every night at 6 P.M., most of the residents gathered to watch Star Trek. Rick was a stereo buff as well as a psychology major. He attached a wire to the innards of the television, ran the wire under the carpet to the back of the room, and there connected the wire to a box with a button. When he pressed the button, the television picture scrambled as if the antenna was misaligned.

Now he was ready to strike. That evening, as the crowd gathered to watch Star Trek, he silently selected his victim: that person, he decided, was going to stand by the television with one hand on top, one hand raised straight up in the air, and one foot lifted off the floor. It was easy enough to do. As the program began to get interesting, Rick pushed the button and scrambled the picture. Various people leapt up to fix things, but the picture cleared only when his victim stood. It scrambled again when she sat down. After she was standing, he raised the criterion. Now she had to stand closer, and then even closer to the television to clear the picture. Well before 7 P.M., Rick's victim was standing like Skinner himself, by the television with one hand on top, one up in the air, and one foot off the floor.

After Star Trek ended, Rick approached his victim and asked, innocently, why she had been standing like that. "Oh, don't you know," she replied, "the body acts like a natural antenna."

The Causes of Behavior A number of morals can be derived from these stories including, perhaps, the moral that neither psychologists nor their students are to be trusted (see Chapter 3). A deeper moral is that people may do things for very simple reasons without knowing those reasons. They can make up elaborate rationales for their actions that have little or nothing to do with the real causes (Nisbett & Wilson, 1977).

Try this bit of introspection, if you dare. Ask yourself why you are dating someone (if you are), why you are going to college (if you are), or even why you are reading this book (I *know* you are). You may come up with some plausible reasons, but then ask yourself, is that *really* why you are doing it? (Don't do this with anybody but yourself; people frequently become angry when their reasons for doing something are questioned.) Consider the possibility that you do these things simply because of a long (and perhaps now obscure) history of reward and punishment in your life. Consider, too, the possibility that the reasons you first gave are no more the basis of your actions than was Skinner's "better light" or the dorm resident's "natural antenna." Maybe you are reading this book not to learn about psychology but because, as a child, you were sent to bed without your supper unless you finished your homework!

But let's not get too carried away here. The human mind has many processes that *occasionally* lead to errors, but usually lead to correct outcomes (Funder, 1987). The fact that sometimes we don't know the real reasons for our actions could be an example. One can fool somebody—like Skinner or the dorm resident—into doing something without knowing the reasons why. But under most circumstances, it is a good bet that we *do* know why we do certain things. In part, this is because rewards are not usually so hidden. The paycheck that causes many people to go to work is an effective and obvious reinforcement.

Classical and Operant Conditioning Compared

Classical conditioning and operant conditioning are both forms of learning by the behaviorist definition. And in most matters they seem more similar than different. A number of general principles work exactly the same in both kinds of learning, such as reinforcement schedules, extinction, and generalization.

But Skinner's belief that they are fundamentally different seems to be correct in at least one very important sense. Classical conditioning is better for explaining *reactions*. Operant conditioning is better for explaining *actions*.

In classical conditioning, nothing in the world changes as a result of your behavior. Rather, your own responses to things change as a function of what has happened to you. The sound of a bell makes the dog salivate. The sight of your old street makes you feel twelve years old again. The sight of someone who has given you bad news in the past makes your stomach hurt. Or, people have always been mean to you so the sight of nearly anybody makes your stomach hurt.

In operant conditioning the organism's role—i.e., your role—is more active. The world is (perhaps in a very small way) different because of what you have done. A bar, previously unpressed, becomes pressed. A soup that otherwise would not have garlic in it is now full of garlic because you put it there. These are changes to the world that will now have consequences. A food pellet will or will not appear. The soup will or will not be palatable. The consequences will affect the chances that the action will ever be repeated. If a food pellet appears, the pigeon will probably press the bar again. If the soup is delicious, the cook may put in even more garlic next time. Or perhaps you have won nearly every argument you have ever entered, and really enjoyed winning. So now you seek out opportunities to argue, and as a result have the personality trait of being "argumentative."

Psychologists have engaged in a long and complex debate about how classical and operant conditioning are different, if they are. For what it is worth, my own resolution is this: Classical and operant conditioning are similar in structure, but deal with fundamentally different kinds of psychological phenomena. Classical conditioning explains changes in the way you *react to* the world. Operant conditioning explains changes in the way you *act upon* the world. Classical conditioning is better for explaining emotion. Operant conditioning is better for explaining behavior. At the level of personality, classical conditioning better explains emotionally relevant personality traits, like anxiousness. Operant conditioning offers a better account of behaviorally relevant personality traits, like argumentativeness.

PUNISHMENT

He that spareth the rod hateth his own son.

—Proverbs 13:24

I will end this survey of behavioristic approaches by considering a technique that millions of people use every day to try to control behavior: punishment. Despite its wide (and probably eternal) popularity, a close psychological analysis of punishment reveals that it has some definite dangers. Or, to be more precise, punishment works well if it is done right. The only problem is, it is almost never done right.

A **punishment** is an aversive consequence that follows an act in order to stop it and prevent its repetition. Punishment is frequently used by three kinds of people: parents, teachers, and bosses. In fact, there is much that these three roles have in common. It turns out, for example, that many principles for good parenting also apply to being a good teacher or a good boss. Moreover, principles for being a good manager also apply to being a good teacher and a good parent. This may be because people in all three roles are trying to do three things:

1. start some behaviors
2. maintain some behaviors
3. prevent some behaviors.

The usual tactic for achieving goal 1 and goal 2, of course, is to use reward. Teachers use gold stars and grades, parents use allowances and treats, and bosses use raises and bonuses. All of them (if they are good at what they do) use praise. (Praise is an excellent behavior modification technique because it is effective, and it is free.) But what about goal 3? Many people believe the only way to stop or prevent somebody from doing something is to punish them for doing it.

Wrong. One can use reward for this purpose, too. All you have to do is find a response that is incompatible with the one you are trying to get rid of, and reward that incompatible response, instead. Reward a child for reading, instead of punishing the child for watching television. Or, if you want to stop and prevent drug abuse, provide opportunities for rewarding activities that are not drug-related. Provide would-be drug users with recreation, and entertainment, and education, and with useful work. Make these other activities as rewarding as possible (spend some money on it!) and you will find that drug use becomes less attractive than it used to be.

Consider the famous anti-drug campaign called "Just Say No." Saying no is a pretty limited life. It is difficult to just say no to drugs without being able to say yes to something else. Yet (if I may editorialize) our society seems much more interested in punishing drug use than in providing rewarding alternatives. The reason is not a matter of saving money—it costs taxpayers 1.5 times as much to house a prisoner for a year than it does to house *and* educate a student at the University of California. Budget savings from closing schools, parks, basketball courts, and community-service programs are more than eaten up in jail construction. I think it has to do with a generally punitive attitude, coupled with a profound lack of imagination—and a lack of psychological education. Although I can do nothing about punitive attitudes or lack of imagination, I do what I can about psychological education—writing this book, for example.

Reward in the workplace is also not used as much as it should be. A friend of mine from graduate school now is a psychological consultant for businesses. One of his first clients was a lumber mill. The mill operated along classic, old-style management principles. The supervisor sat in a glass booth high in the rafters, from which he could see the entire production line. He scanned the line with binoculars until he saw something go wrong. Then he came down, yelled at the worker who was responsible, and sometimes demoted or even fired the worker on the spot. Not surprisingly, the workers dreaded the supervisor's approach. Moreover, they did what they could to conceal their activities from the supervisor's view. Morale was low. Absenteeism and turnover were high. Occasionally even sabotage took place.

My friend's first action was to gather the supervisors together and instruct them to do something different. (He charged a high fee, to make sure that the company would order them to follow his advice.) He told them they were forbidden to punish workers, effective immediately. Instead, they were to sit in their little glass booth until they saw a worker doing something *perfectly*. They were then to come down and praise the worker. Occasionally, if the perfection was truly exemplary, they were to award a bonus or a day off on the spot.

The supervisors were perplexed and resistant to this seemingly crazy plan. But they followed corporate orders, and you can guess the results. At first the workers were terrified; they thought they knew what the supervisor's approach meant. But gradually they came to look forward to instead of dread his visits. Then they went one step further: they started to try to show the supervisor what they were doing, in case it might be good enough to merit a reward or just some praise. They started to like the supervisor better, and they started to like their jobs better. Absenteeism and turnover declined. Productivity skyrocketed. My friend earned every cent of his fee.

Okay, maybe this story is not entirely accurate. It sounds a little too good to be true. Accept it as an instructive fable, at least. Punishment has all sorts of unintended consequences, some of which you may not see until you stop using it, if you ever do.

How to Punish

One way to see how punishment works, or fails to work, is to examine the rules that must be followed in order to apply it correctly. The classic behavioristic analysis says that five principles are most important (Azrin & Holz, 1966).

1. Availability of alternatives   An alternative response to the behavior that is being punished must be available. This alternative response must not be punished, and should be rewarded. If you want to threaten kids with punishment for Halloween pranks, be certain some other activity is available that will not be punished, or will even be rewarding, such as a Halloween party. The best tactic, of course, is to not use punishment at all. Instead, reward a behavior that cannot be done at the same time as the behavior you want to prevent. If the party is attractive enough, threats about the consequences of pranks will not be necessary. The kids will be too busy having fun at the party.

2. Behavioral and situational specificity   Be clear about exactly what behavior you are punishing and the circumstances under which it will and will not be punished. This rule is the basis of the advice, commonly given to parents, never to punish a child for being a "bad boy" or "bad girl." You must be much more specific. Instead, punish "staying out after curfew" or "cursing at Grandma." A child who is unsure exactly why he or she is being punished may, just to be safe, become generally inhibited and fearful, daring to do little because he or she is not quite sure what is right and what is wrong. You may have seen the same phenomenon in a classroom or a workplace where the teacher or boss likes to punish, but never quite conveys clearly what does and does not get punished. People will be afraid, and will do as little as possible.

3. Timing and consistency   To be most effective—or to be effective at all— a punishment needs to be applied *immediately* after the behavior you wish to prevent, *every* time that behavior occurs. Otherwise, the person (or animal) being punished may not clearly understand exactly what behavior is forbidden. And again, if a person (or animal) is punished but does not understand why, the result will be general inhibition instead of specific behavior change.

Have you ever made this mistake? You come home from a hard day at work and discover your dog has dug out the kitchen trash and spread it across the living room. The dog bounds to greet you, and you swat it. This is, one supposes, punishment for scattering trash, but consider the situation from the dog's point of view. The trash-scattering occurred hours ago. What the dog did just before being punished was greet you. What behavior change will result? This kind of error is very common, and shows the danger of applying punishment when you are angry. The punishment might vent *your* emotions, but is likely to be counterproductive in the way it affects behavior.

4. Condition secondary punishing stimuli   One can lessen the actual use of punishment by conditioning secondary stimuli to it. I once had a cat who liked to scratch the furniture. I went out and bought myself a plastic squirt bottle and filled it with water, and then kept it nearby. Whenever the cat started to claw the sofa, I made a hissing noise and then immediately squirted the cat. Soon I did not need the squirt bottle; my "hissss" was sufficient to make the cat immediately drop what she was doing. With people, verbal warnings can serve the same purpose. Many a parent has discovered this technique: "If you don't stop, when I get to three, you'll be sorry. 1, 2, . . ." It works reasonably well.

5. Avoid displays of sympathy and affection   This is a particular warning to parents. Sometimes after punishing a child the parent can feel so guilty that he or she picks the child up for a cuddle. This is a mistake. Under the worst circumstances, the child might start to misbehave just to get the cuddle that follows the punishment. If you must punish, then do it. Do not mix your message.

A variant on this problem occurs when one parent plays off against the other. The father punishes the child, for example, and the child then goes to the mother for sympathy, or vice versa. This can produce the same counterproductive result. Parents should act together, and avoid mixing the message.

Dangers of Punishment

The reason that punishment is such a dangerous technique for behavioral modification is that *all* of the rules just listed must be followed. Usually, most of them are not. A punisher has to be extremely disciplined to follow all these rules, for several reasons.

1. Punishment arouses emotion   The first and perhaps most important danger is that punishment creates emotion. In the punisher, it can arouse excitement, satisfaction, and even further aggressive impulses. The result is that the punisher may get carried away. Anybody who has seen the much-broadcast videotape of the Los Angeles police officers beating Rodney King has seen a good example of punishment getting out of hand. The emotions that beating King aroused in the officers seemed to cause them to lose all semblance of self-control.

Several emotions are aroused in the punishee, too. By definition, a punishment is aversive, which means that the punishee feels pain, discomfort, or humiliation. Punishment also usually arouses fear, hate for the punisher, a desire to escape (which may indeed become possible later), and possibly self-contempt. These are all powerful emotions, and are not conducive to clear thinking.

As a result, the punishee is unlikely to "learn a lesson," which is supposedly the purpose of punishment. How do you learn a lesson when you are fearful, in pain, confused, and humiliated? Often punishers think the person they are punishing is learning what behavior not to do again. But the punishee is much too unhappy and confused to think anything beyond "let me out of here!"

2. It is hard to be consistent   Another reason why punishment is so difficult to apply correctly is that it is difficult to be clear and consistent. Punishments tend to vary according to the mood of the punisher. Imagine that, in one day at work, you lost a big account, got yelled at by your boss, spilled ketchup on your pants, and found a new dent in your car. When you arrive home, you find that your child has thrown a baseball through your living-room window. What do you do?

Now imagine another day, when you landed a big account, got promoted by your boss, and took delivery on a beautiful new car that cost $5,000 less than you had expected. You arrive home and find a baseball through the window. Now, what do you do?

Very few people would react to the child's behavior the same way under both circumstances. (Those who can are saints.) Yet the child's behavior was exactly the same in both cases. Punishment tends to vary with the punisher's mood, which is one big reason why it is rarely applied with consistency.

3. It is hard to gauge severity A third danger of punishment is that it is difficult for the punisher to gauge accurately the severity of the punishment. This holds true whether the punishment is physical or psychological. Many cases of child abuse have occurred when what a parent thought was a mild but painful slap caused a broken bone or worse. Parents are bigger than children: this is not always easy to take into account, especially if the parent is angry.

Words can hurt, too. A rebuke from a parent, teacher, or boss can be a severe humiliation. It can cause more psychological distress than the punisher may imagine, and can provoke desires for revenge or escape that will only make the situation worse.

4. Punishment teaches about power A fourth problem with punishment is that, whether or not it teaches the lesson intended, it *always* teaches one lesson quite well: Big, powerful people get to hurt smaller, less-powerful people. As a result, the punishee may think, I can't wait to be big and powerful so that I can punish too!

Thus parents who were abused as children sometimes become child abusers themselves (Hemenway, Solnick, & Carter, 1994; Widom, 1989). And any worker can tell you that a boss who brags about his or her own experiences in the "school of hard knocks" is going to be trouble. Even college fraternity initiations carry a powerful, implicit message: It is better to be an upperclassman than a pledge, because the former gets to abuse the latter.

Why does abuse get transmitted "generationally" in this manner? One reason is that the punishee's experience creates hostility and resentment that eventually gets vented on an available target, perhaps years later. A more important reason may be simply that the experience of being punished gives one knowledge about punishment, and a model of someone who thinks punishment is justified. A punishing act can create victims far beyond the person immediately punished, therefore. It may also lead to harm to the punishee's own, eventual victims.

5. Punishment motivates concealment A fifth problem with punishment is that it motivates concealment, especially if it has been applied inconsistently. The prospective punishee has good reasons to try to conceal from the punisher anything that conceivably might be punished. Have you ever been in an office where the boss rules through the use of punishment? Nobody talks to anybody, least of all the boss, if they can avoid it, and the boss soon becomes very detached from what is really going on in his or her own office. (This was the case in the lumber mill described earlier.)

The use of reward has just the reverse effect. When workers anticipate being rewarded for good work instead of being punished for bad work, they are naturally motivated to bring to the boss's attention everything they are doing, in case it might merit reward. They will have no reason to conceal anything that is going on, and the boss will be in much better contact with the operation he or she is supposed to be running.

This works in the home, as well. A child who expects punishment from his or her parent soon cuts off as much contact and communication as possible. A child who expects the reverse, naturally does the reverse. Thus, at home or at work, one important side effect of punishment is that it tends to cut off communication.

The Bottom Line

Punishment, if used correctly, is an effective technique for behavioral control. But to use it correctly is nearly impossible. Correct application of punishment requires that the punisher understand and consistently apply *all* of the rules just listed. It also requires that the punisher's own emotions and other personal needs not affect his or her actions, which is even more difficult.

So the bottom line is this: *Punishment works great if you apply it correctly. But in order to apply it correctly, you need to be a genius and you need to be a saint.* If you have any shortcomings in either department, you might be best advised to stay away from it.

CONTRIBUTIONS AND SHORTCOMINGS OF BEHAVIORISM

Behaviorism has much of value to contribute to personality psychology. It offers a useful technology of behavior change and important insights into the application of reward and punishment. Behaviorism's most important intellectual contribution may be its insistence that we discard from psychological analysis everything that is not truly necessary for changing or predicting behavior; if it isn't visible, you don't need it. All you need for a complete psychology is reward, punishment, and behavior. This claim has forced the field of psychology as a whole to rethink and defend notions such as perception, thought, emotion, and even the mind.

Yet, as we would predict from Funder's First Law (the one about advantages being disadvantages), it is this distinctive contribution that makes behaviorism so dissatisfying and vulnerable to criticism. It is easy to come up with a list of potentially important topics that behaviorist approaches leave out. To name just a few, behaviorism has nothing to say about mental life and thought, conscious experience, emotions, free will, or the unconscious. In the next two chapters, we will review several efforts by "social learning theorists" and the later "cognitive social learning theorists" to broaden behaviorism to account for some of these neglected topics.

Summary

Behaviorism's key tenet is that we can only know about what we can see, and we can see everything we need to know. This translates into a basic belief that all of behavior is a function of the rewards and punishments in one's past and present environment, and how behavior is a function of the environment can be seen through a functional analysis. The philosophical roots of behaviorism include empiricism, a belief that all knowledge comes from experience; associationism, a belief that two stimuli paired together will come to be seen as one; hedonism, the belief that the goal of life is "gentle pleasure"; and utilitarianism, the belief that the best society is the social arrangement that creates the most happiness for the most people. In behaviorist terminology, learning is any change in behavior that results from experience. Basic principles of learning include habituation, classical conditioning, and operant conditioning. Classical conditioning affects emotions and feelings; operant conditioning affects behavior. Key figures in the development of operant conditioning include Edward Thorndike, Clark Hull, and B. F. Skinner. Punishment is a useful technique of operant conditioning if it is applied correctly, which it almost never is. Behaviorism has contributed a useful technology of behavioral change, and has forced the rest of the field to clarify and defend its use of mentalistic concepts (such as thought and mind). But behaviorism neglects important topics such as motivation, emotion, and cognition.

CHAPTER

MOTIVATION, THOUGHT, AND BEHAVIOR: THE SOCIAL LEARNING THEORIES

It is neat, tidy, and easy to describe behavior as a simple result of accumulated rewards and punishments. However, we saw at the end of Chapter 16 that as a model of personality, the behavioristic account leaves a lot unexplained. A natural response to these omissions is to try to come up with a theory that retains behaviorism's empirical rigor and some of its basic principles, but extends its reach to account for what is missing. Three different theories have been developed by psychologists who began with a basic affinity for behaviorism but who nonetheless recognized important shortcomings in the classic version. The purpose of each of these "social learning theories" is to remedy these shortcomings.

WHAT BEHAVIORISM LEAVES OUT

The most obvious shortcoming of classic behaviorism is the way it ignores motivation, thought, and cognition. In fact, sometimes behaviorism tries to make a virtue of such ignorance. The writings of B. F. Skinner and his followers, for example, often deny that thinking is important and sometimes have even denied that it exists. They certainly never conduct research on it. Social learning theorists, by contrast, claim that the way people think, plan, perceive, and believe is an important part of learning, and that research must address these processes.

Second, classic behaviorism is to a surprisingly large extent based upon animals. Much of Skinner's own work was done with rats and pigeons; Thorndike favored cats; Pavlov used dogs. The reason behaviorists so often study animals is that they hope to formulate general laws of learning that are relevant to all species. This is a laudable goal, but according to the social learning theorists it has led behaviorists to concentrate too much on elements of learning that are important for animals, such as reinforcement, and not enough on elements of learning that may be uniquely important to humans, such as solving a problem by thinking about it.

A third shortcoming of classic behaviorism is that it ignores the social dimension of learning. The typical rat or pigeon in the Skinner box is in there *alone*. It cannot interact with, learn from, or influence any other animal. Ordinary learning by humans, however, tends to be social. We learn by watching others, for example—something an isolated pigeon is in no position to do even if it were capable. The social learning theorists, as their label implies, are highly sensitive to this issue.

A fourth shortcoming of classic behaviorism is that it treats the organism as essentially passive. How does a rat or pigeon get into a Skinner box in the first place? Easy—it is put there. Once there, the contingencies of the box are iron-clad and may even be automated. The pigeon did not ask to be put in the box, but there it is, and unless it pushes the bar there will be no food pellets. It is that simple. For humans, however, real life is not like that. To an important (if not unlimited) degree, we *choose* what environments to enter, and these environments then change as a result of what we do in them.

Imagine if rats were allowed to choose which of several Skinner boxes to jump into, and then had a way of changing the reinforcement contingencies once they got inside. A party might bring out certain behavior you do not emit otherwise, but you can choose whether to go to the party. Moreover, once you are there the party changes as a result of your presence. These facts complicate any analysis of how the environment can affect behavior. This complication is welcomed and focused upon by modern social learning theorists.

Three major theories of personality have been invented in order to expand behaviorism to remedy one or more of these shortcomings. It seems somewhat ironic—and more than a little confusing—that although the three theories are importantly different from each other, all three were named "social learning theory" by their inventors. The three different theories of social learning were developed by John Dollard and Neal Miller, by Julian Rotter, and by Albert Bandura.

DOLLARD AND MILLER'S SOCIAL LEARNING THEORY

Even while behaviorism racked up its most impressive accomplishments in both the analysis and the modification and control of behavior, it developed—until about the late 1940s—in some isolation from the rest of psychology. Behaviorism was a free-standing enterprise, with much to say about its chosen topic of interest, which is learning. But it said little or nothing about many of the major phenomena of psychopathology, such as repression, conflict, and anxiety, and it also largely ignored the fact that people do not just respond to stimuli in a passive manner; they also think and understand.

John Dollard and Neal Miller were psychologists at Yale during the 1940s and 1950s who embarked on an extraordinarily ambitious project to extend behaviorism to these heretofore neglected and even forbidden topics. The breadth of their ambition can be seen in the dedication to their principal work, a book they published together in 1950. The remarkable dedication reads, "To Freud and Pavlov and Their Students" (Dollard & Miller, 1950, p. vii).

Dollard and Miller sought to deal with issues of cognition and motivation that behaviorists had ignored, and even hoped to provide a behaviorist account for some phenomena that only Freud had tackled before. Their "social" theory of learning was a pioneering effort to bend and stretch behaviorism as far as they could take it.

Dollard and Miller's key idea is that of the **habit hierarchy**. An individual's habit hierarchy is made up of all of the behaviors that that individual might ever do, ranked from most to least probable. The behavior you are most likely to perform at this moment resides at the top of your habit hierarchy. Your least likely behavior is at the bottom. As a result of learning, some behaviors become more likely and others become less likely. The effect of rewards, punishments, and learning, therefore, is to rearrange your habit hierarchy.

Notice how Dollard and Miller have already deviated from classic behaviorism in a major way. Skinner would claim that the effect of learning is to change *behavior*. Dollard and Miller claim that the effect of learning is a change in an unobservable, psychological entity, the habit hierarchy. In some cases behavior will not change at all. This is just the beginning of a fundamentally different way of looking at the basic principles of behavior.

In order to learn, that is, in order for its habit hierarchy to change, according to Miller and Dollard (1941, p. 2), an organism "must want something, notice something, do something, and get something." Consider the simple example of a pigeon in a Skinner box. To learn, the pigeon must *want* food. If it is not hungry, the food reward will not produce behavior change. The pigeon must *notice* the bar. If the pigeon never sees it, the pigeon will never emit the necessary behavior. The pigeon must *do* a bar press. For a response to be reinforced, it must first occur. Finally, the pigeon must *get* a food pellet. That is the reinforcement that makes subsequent bar-pressing more likely.

Dollard and Miller's simple-sounding formula brings four components into behavioral analysis: motivation (wanting something), attention and perception (noticing something), behavior (doing something), and reinforcement (getting something). Only the latter two are included in classic behaviorism. Dollard and Miller have added motivation and cognition.

Motivation and Drives

What do you want, and why do you want it? These are questions of motivation. According to Dollard and Miller, the answer to this question is to be found in needs, which produce psychological **drives**. Borrowing this idea from Clark Hull (see Chapter 16), they described a drive as a state of psychological tension that feels good when it is reduced. The pleasure comes from the satisfaction of the need that produced the drive.

Two kinds of drive are important. **Primary drives** include those to get food, to get water, to obtain physical comfort, to avoid physical pain, to obtain sexual gratification, and so on. They are the various *biologically* built-in drives to survive or to perpetuate the species. **Secondary drives** include those for love, prestige, money, and power, as well as negative drives such as fear and humiliation. They are *psychologically* based and derive from the organism having learned through experience that the fulfillment of these drives can lead indirectly to the satisfaction of one or more of the primary drives.

Both primary and secondary drives have the power to guide and shape behavior, and Dollard and Miller believed that for humans secondary drives are ordinarily more important. We are more likely to spend our days seeking money or power or love, for example, than more directly seeking food or sex, even though the former goals can lead indirectly (and sometimes more directly) to the latter goals.

According to Dollard and Miller, there can be no reinforcement (and hence no behavior change) without some kind of drive reduction occurring, whether it be primary or secondary. In other words, for a reward to be rewarding, and thereby have the power to make the behavior it rewards more likely, the reward must satisfy a need.

This principle is not as straightforward or obvious as it may sound, because it raises an important question: Is the goal of all behavior (and hence of life) really just to satisfy every desire and get to a state of "zero need"? So far, the analysis seems to imply that the ideal state of existence is one in which all needs have been satisfied, so you have no motivation to do anything, and can just sit in an inert, satisfied lump. This is a questionable implication because people often seem to go out of their way to *raise* their level of need.

For example, if you are going out this evening for a dinner at a four-star restaurant that will cost you $120, you are unlikely to eat a bag of potato chips at 6 P.M., even if you are hungry. Why not? Because it would "spoil your appetite," as your mother always said. The meal will be less fun and will hardly seem worth the expense if you are not hungry for it. But why would that matter, if the goal is simply to attain a state of zero hunger?

Sexual arousal and gratification is another obvious example. People go out of their way to seek sexual arousal, not just gratification. The greater the arousal and degree of sexual need, it seems, the more gratifying the ultimate satisfaction of that need will be.

Secondary drives may also work this way, but in a more complex fashion. Many people do not only try to finish the work they have been assigned, for example, but actively seek new work to do. It seems they are constantly creating new needs—starting projects that will need to be finished—as they continue to complete projects they started earlier.

Observations such as these require a modification of drive-reduction theory. Perhaps what is reinforcing is not a state of zero need, but rather the *movement* from a state of higher need to a state of lower need. It is the *distance* between the initial and final state that matters, according to this proposition, not simply the attainment of a state of zero need. This principle explains why people might actually try to create new needs in themselves as well as try to satisfy existing needs.

Thus, the person who skips the potato chips so as to better enjoy dinner puts himself in a higher state of need, so the distance travelled to a state of lesser need during the meal is greater, and therefore the satisfaction is greater. The more sexually aroused a person is, the more distance she travels toward a state of lesser arousal as a function of gratification, and the more satisfying the end result. And, in order to continue to experience the satisfaction of completing work projects, not only do you need to finish the projects you start, but you must continually start new ones.

Frustration and Aggression

If your roommate has had a frustrating experience—failing an exam, say, or being turned down for a date—watch out. He or she will be in a bad mood, which means he or she is likely to be angry. It hardly matters at what. It could be at you, if you are not careful. If your socks are on the sofa, you will get yelled at. If you present no such opportunity to be the object of anger, then your roommate might just pound the wall instead, or steam loudly about the professor or person who supposedly caused the problem.

Not everybody reacts this way all the time, of course, but such a reaction is not uncommon. When it does happen, the interesting psychological question is, why the anger? Specifically, why does the person vent anger on targets that had nothing to do with the source of the problem, such as an innocent roommate or a wall? Dollard and Miller's answer to this question is called the **frustration-aggression hypothesis**. According to this hypothesis, the natural reaction of any person (or animal, for that matter) to being blocked from a goal, or frustrated, will be an urge to lash out and injure. The more important the blocked goal, the greater will be the frustration, and the greater will be the aggressive impulse.

The preferred target of the impulse will be the source of the frustration—the person or thing that stopped you from getting what you wanted. But Dollard and Miller borrow Freud's idea of displacement to describe how the aggressive impulse can be redirected elsewhere as well. If your boss unfairly denies you a raise, this might lead to frustration and anger but you are unlikely to vent it at the boss, if you want to keep your job. So you might come home and kick the dog or criticize your spouse, all in anger that is displaced from its original target, your boss.

Dollard and Miller believed that the link between frustration and aggression is built in at a biological level. The natural response to frustration is to want to lash out, even if no reasonable target is at hand. Many instances of aggressive behavior do not seem to make any sense, and this idea helps explain why they happen, even at the mass level. When members of a community get word of an injustice that seems directed at them, such as the acquittal of police officers who beat up a neighbor, they may riot, producing the self-defeating outcome of destroying much of their own community and sometimes their own property. This makes no sense, but Dollard and Miller would explain that it is only natural.

How can irrational, misdirected aggression be prevented? Dollard and Miller's theory offers only a couple of hints. One is that if frustration can be minimized aggression will be too. The amount of aggressive behavior in a community will be lessened to the extent that frustrations involving economics and police behavior can be lessened. A second possibility is to displace aggressive impulses onto a constructive target—what Freud called sublimation. Perhaps anger can be vented in political action, or nonviolent protest, or even sports activities. The impulse must be vented somehow, so a high priority should be to find a safe target.

Give your roommate a dart board. When he or she comes home in a bad mood, hand over the darts and leave. This cannot hurt, but also recall the research mentioned in Chapter 12, which suggests that this kind of dart-board catharsis might make someone feel good *without* making later aggression less likely (Berkowitz, 1962). When you get back, your roommate might feel better, but may also still be dangerous.

Psychological Conflict

Things that are fun can also be frightening. Take bungee jumping, for example. A while back, a student of mine signed up for a Sunday bungee jump. It cost him money and he signed up of his own free will, so he must have thought it would be fun. As the day approached, however, he became noticeably more nervous (the funeral plans being made by his fellow students may not have been helpful). In the end it seemed a near thing whether he would go or not. In this case he did (and survived, I should add).

This kind of conflict between desire and fear, and how it can change over time, was addressed by Dollard and Miller's theorizing on **approach-avoidance**

conflict. (This theorizing can get technical, mind you.) Consider the five key assumptions of this theory:

1. An increase in drive strength will increase the tendency to approach or avoid a goal.
2. Whenever there are two competing responses, the stronger one (the one with greater drive strength behind it) will win out.
3. The tendency to approach a positive goal increases the closer one is to the goal.
4. The tendency to avoid a negative goal also increases the closer one is to the goal.
5. (most important) Tendency 4 is stronger than 3. That is, the tendency to avoid a negative goal becomes *stronger*, with nearness, than does the corresponding tendency to approach a positive goal. To put this technically (I warned you it would get technical), the avoidance gradient is steeper than the approach gradient (see Figure 17.1).

This set of principles yields some interesting predictions, particularly involving conflicted goals that have both positive and negative elements. Such a goal might be a bungee jump, an airplane trip you are both looking forward to

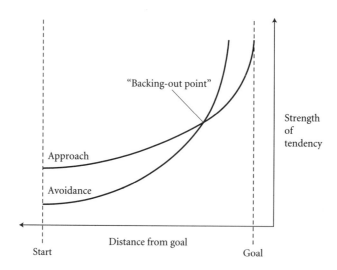

FIGURE 17.1 DOLLARD AND MILLER'S CONCEPT OF APPROACH AND AVOIDANCE An illustration of how tendencies to approach and avoid a conflicted goal (e.g., a bungee jump) might change over time. According to Dollard and Miller, while tendencies to approach and avoid both increase as the goal gets closer, the avoidance gradient is steeper than the approach gradient. In this example, the person will try to withdraw, or back out, of the act after the approach and avoidance gradients cross.

(for the vacation) and fearing (because you are afraid of flying), or a talk you have volunteered to give because you need the practice, but that you also dread. Dollard and Miller's five-part theory first predicts that in each case you will be relatively willing to commit yourself to these behaviors if they are far off in time. But as the moment of truth approaches, you will start to regret having agreed to do it. Even though the bungee jump, plane trip, or talk seemed like a good idea last week, as the activity approaches the negative aspects will become more prominent than to the positive aspects. In the end, you may not be able to go through with it.

This can be a useful principle. If you are responsible for arranging a series of speakers before a group, for example, you are wise to schedule your speakers and get iron-clad commitments from them as far in advance as possible. Something somebody will commit to six months in advance might be flatly refused if you ask the day before. Bungee jump companies often require nonrefundable deposits, and Dollard and Miller may have discovered the real reason that dentists schedule their appointments and airlines encourage ticket purchases so far in advance.

Defense Mechanisms

One particular goal that Dollard and Miller set for themselves was to use learning theory to explain psychological phenomena that previously only psychoanalysis had addressed. For example, they developed explanations of how the law of effect—the simple idea that rewards make a behavior more likely and punishments make it less likely—could account for the Freudian defense mechanisms.

Dollard and Miller interpreted defense mechanisms primarily in terms of negative reinforcement. Let me emphasize the definition of this term, because most people and even many textbooks get it wrong. "Negative reinforcement" is *not* a technical term for punishment. The technical term for punishment, in behavioral theory, is "punishment." Negative reinforcement, by contrast, is a *reward* that consists of the withdrawal of an aversive stimulus. The pleasure you experience when you stop hitting yourself on the head with a hammer is a negative reinforcement. More seriously, any cessation of pain, discomfort, or anxiety is negatively reinforcing, which means that the behavior that came just before such cessation will become more likely.

Defense mechanisms, according to Dollard and Miller, are cognitive behaviors that are negatively reinforced because they remove anxiety. For example, repression is the pushing of a disturbing idea out of consciousness. You stop thinking about it, you are no longer disturbed, and you enjoy negative reinforcement. Thus repression becomes even more likely next time, because of the law of effect. The other defense mechanisms—rationalization, projection, reaction formation, and the others listed in Chapter 12—can also lessen your anxiety and so be (negatively) reinforced.

The point Dollard and Miller are making is that Freud may have been on the right track, but he created a theory that was more complex than really necessary. One does not need to set up an elaborate mesh of conflicts and patterns of energy channelling between invisible entities such as the id, ego, and superego to explain the defense mechanisms, they argued. Defense mechanisms make you feel better. All you need to explain why we use them, is Thorndike's basic law of effect, modified a little by Dollard and Miller.

ROTTER'S SOCIAL LEARNING THEORY

Julian Rotter's version of social learning theory, developed a little later than Dollard and Miller's, has a less psychodynamic flavor (Rotter, 1954, 1982). Whereas Dollard and Miller were concerned with motivation, anxiety and defense, Rotter concerned himself primarily with the process of decision making.

The Expectancy Value Theory of Decision Making

Consider the following example. A woman about to graduate from college scans the placement center's list of companies that are interviewing on campus. The center's policy is that she is allowed to interview for one job, and she narrows her choice down to two. One pays $35,000 a year to start, and the other pays $20,000. Which one will she sign up for? Classic, straightforward, unadorned behaviorism predicts that of course she will choose the $35,000 job. But, according to Rotter's social learning theory, there is another factor to consider that behaviorism leaves out: What if she does not think she would *get* the $35,000 job if she interviewed for it, but thinks the chances are excellent that she would get the $20,000 job?

Rotter claims you can work out her choice mathematically. Suppose she thinks her chances of getting the $35,000 job are 50/50, whereas she thinks she is certain to get the $20,000 job. The "expected value" of the $35,000 job then becomes .50 × $35,000, or $17,500. The expected value of the other job is 1 × $20,000, or $20,000. The second job has a higher expected value and, under these circumstances, is the interview she would be predicted to choose.

The core of Rotter's approach is **expectancy value theory**, which was just illustrated above. The basic assumption of this theory is that your behavioral decisions are determined not just by the presence or size of reinforcements, but by your beliefs about what the results of your behavior are likely to be. Even if a reinforcement is very attractive, according to this theory, you are not likely to pursue it if your chances of success seem slim. Conversely, even something that is not particularly desirable might motivate behavior, if the chances of getting it are good enough. Rotter translated this theory into a quasi-mathematical formula that includes several key concepts.

BEHAVIOR POTENTIAL

Behavior potential (BP) is the probability that in the situation under analysis you will perform the behavior in question. The higher an action's BP, the more likely you are to do it. BPs vary with situations. In class, a student's BP for note-taking is higher than his or her BP for beer-drinking, but the reverse is probably true at a party. In theory, *every* possible behavior has a BP in *every* situation, however improbable some of these behaviors are. In that sense, BP is much like Dollard and Miller's concept of the habit hierarchy. Notice that BP is a probabilistic term; the other variables in the equation influence the probability of an action, but they do not absolutely determine it. Sometimes people do unlikely things. Nevertheless, the behavior with the highest BP is the one that *probably* will be performed.

In any college class, each student has a unique BP for attendance. Some show up for class nearly every day. Some show up only on the first day, the last day, and on exam day. Others are in between. The ratio of the number of classes one attends to the number that are held is one's BP for class attendance. Again, the BP is probabilistic; even a student with a high attendance BP (better than 90 percent, say) may miss class occasionally. And even students with low BPs can surprise you, occasionally, by showing up when you least expect them.

Or suppose you are considering asking someone out on a date. Will you actually make the move? The answer depends on your BP for this behavior, which is a function of the other terms in the equation. Read on.

EXPECTANCY

An individual's **expectancy** for a behavior is his or her belief, or subjective probability, about how likely he or she thinks the behavior is to attain its goal. If you ask that person out, what is the probability the person will say yes? If I apply for that job (and forego others), will I get it? If I go to class, will that really make a difference in how well I do on the final exam? What are the chances? The expectancy is your belief as to the odds that an action will pay off.

Because an expectancy is a *belief*, it may be right or wrong. Rotter's theory says that the actual, objective odds of success actually matter less to your behavior than what you think the odds are. It does not matter whether something is actually likely to succeed or not; if you think it will, you will try. The same goes for something that actually would succeed, if you only gave the effort; if you think it will not work, you will not even try.

Here lies the key difference with classic behaviorism: The classical view focuses on the *actual* rewards and punishments in the environment and how they affect behavior. Rotter's social learning variant focuses on what people *believe* the rewards and punishments in the environment are likely to be. It is these beliefs that shape behavior, Rotter claims, even when they do not map accurately onto reality. At this point in Rotter's social learning theory, a little wisp of phenomenology drifts in (recall Chapter 14): He is saying that a person's impressions of reality are more important than reality itself!

Rotter claims that people actually have two kinds of expectancies: specific and general. A specific expectancy is the belief that a certain behavior, at a certain time and place, will lead to a specific outcome. For example, if just after lunch on Tuesday I ask Mary for a date on Friday night, will she say yes? The expected answer may depend on all of these factors—when the question is asked, who is asked, and when the date is scheduled. In another example, if I attend class this Monday, what are the chances I will pick up something helpful for the exam? From reading the syllabus, you might have reason to think that Monday's material is going to be essential for the exam, but that Wednesday's class can safely be skipped. Specific expectancies like these are denoted, in Rotter's system, as E' (E-prime).

At the other extreme, people also have generalized expectancies, denoted GE. These are general beliefs about whether *anything* you do is likely to make a difference. Some people, according to Rotter, essentially believe that they have very little control over what happens to them; they have low GEs. Others believe that the reinforcements they enjoy (and the punishments they avoid) are directly a function of what they do; these people have high GEs. Not surprisingly, people with high GEs tend to be energetic and highly motivated; those with low GEs are more likely to be lethargic and depressed. GE is a general personality variable, and in fact can be considered a trait exactly like those discussed in Chapters 4 through 7.

Specific expectancies (E's) and general expectancies (GEs) can feed into each other in complex ways. For example, as you start college, your approach toward studying is likely to be shaped by your GE, because you do not yet have relevant experience in the college domain. But as experience accumulates, you will start to develop more specific expectancies about what you can do (e.g., you discover that you are better at chemistry than at psychology), and these will start to take over the direction of your behavior.

The result of this interaction is that people who have generally high or low GEs might still have lower or higher E's in different specific situations, depending upon their experiences. Rotter sometimes referred to GE as "locus of control." People with internal locus of control are those with high GEs who think that what they do can affect what happens to them. Those with external locus of control have low GEs and tend to think that what they do will not make much difference. Later investigators have emphasized how locus of control (and GE) can vary across the domains of one's life. For example, some people have internal academic locus of control (they believe they have control over their academic outcomes), but external locus of control otherwise. Other psychologists have studied health locus of control, which involves the difference between people who believe that their daily actions importantly affect their own health, as opposed to those who think they have very little control over whether they are sick or well (e.g., Rosolack & Hampson, 1991; Lau, 1988). Even dating locus of control can be variable. Maybe you are right to think that not *everybody* is willing to go out with you, but *somebody*, somewhere is eager to do so.

REINFORCEMENT VALUE

What's it worth to you? The subjective benefit of a reward is its **reinforcement value** (RV), which is Rotter's conception of motivation. The question here is how much an individual really cares whether he or she gets a job, or gets good grades, or graduates, or has good health, or goes out on dates. In the abstract, of course, probably almost everybody wants all of these things. But the real issue is, how badly do you want it, and compared to what?

One of my psychological mentors, Jack Block, once pointed out to me that if you ask someone the following three important questions you will get predictable and boring answers:

1. Do you want to be healthy?
2. Do you want to be wealthy?
3. Do you want to be wise?

The answers will be boring and uninformative because in each case anybody will say yes. More interesting, said Block, is to ask the person to rank the three choices. Which of these three matters the most, and which the least? The answer to that requires some difficult decisions, and is therefore much more revealing.

Thus the *relative* reinforcement value of different outcomes is what is important. All students want to get good grades. They also all want to sleep late, and have fun with their friends. Which they want *more*, however, is the important variable that seems to drive both academic and other life outcomes.

PSYCHOLOGICAL SITUATION

The last variable in Rotter's formula is the psychological situation (S). The inclusion of this term is Rotter's way of acknowledging that the values of every other term in the prediction equation can change as a function of situation. Obviously, everything changes as one moves from a party to a classroom, but more subtle changes in the situation can affect expectancies and reinforcement values as well. Something that seems likely to be achieved (high E') in one situation might suddenly seem unlikely if the situation changes. Likewise, something that seems highly desirable (high RV) in one situation might seem positively aversive in another.

ROTTER'S PREDICTION FORMULA

Rotter combined all of the terms just considered into the following behavioral prediction formula:

$$BP_{x,S1,Ra} = f(E_{x,Ra,S1} \ \& \ RV_{a,S1})$$

In other words, "The potential for behavior x to occur in situation 1 in relation to reinforcement a is a function of the expectancy of the occurrence of reinforcement a following behavior x in situation 1 and the value of reinforcement a in situation 1." (f is a standard mathematical term for "function"; the ampersand [&] is a non-mathematical symbol meant to convey that the two terms in parentheses interact, but not in any strictly numerical fashion.)

When used by psychologists, equations like this can be both helpful and misleading, and I confess that my feelings about them are mixed at best. The usefulness of this equation is that it serves as a short-hand way of conveying the essence of Rotter's theory. It also may make it a little easier to think about his theory in a precise way.

The disadvantage of a formula like this is that it is not obvious what the formula offers that a simple verbal statement of the same ideas does not. An English translation of the formula above might be "what you are likely to do depends upon whether you think you can get something and how badly you want it, under the circumstances." The translation might miss some of the nuances, but it is not far off.

Formulas are all well and good, but their usefulness may be rather limited in psychology. Sometimes they can be a smoke screen for simple ideas; they can also make psychological analysis seem more precise and better quantified than it really is. Almost never is it possible to plug any actual numbers into these formulas. There is no way to do so in the example above. So, I would advise you to use Rotter's formula—and any other "formula" you see presented by a psychologist—only to the extent it aids your thinking about these matters. Otherwise, try not to take them too seriously.

Adjustment and Maladjustment

Rotter's theory yields several insights concerning psychological adjustment and maladjustment. For example, it draws attention to cases in which an individual has a low expectancy but a high reinforcement value for the same outcome. This is a recipe for depression and worse. It describes the case of wanting something desperately, but thinking that nothing you can do will help you get it. This can lead to serious behavioral and emotional problems.

Consider a person who desperately wants a normal heterosexual relationship but considers himself to be so unattractive that he doubts it will ever happen. This can lead not only to depression but to avoidance of or hostility toward the opposite sex, a failure to perform even minimal behaviors that might improve the situation (e.g., he might not show up for a blind date, or may not bathe before going on one), excessive time spent in fantasy, a failure to develop appropriate social skills, and so on. All of these reactions are direct results of high motivation paired with low expectancy, and they will all postpone or even prevent progress toward solving the problem.

The same destructive pattern can be seen in other areas of life. Many students are academic "underachievers" because as much as they might desire success, they have simply decided that they "cannot do math" or that otherwise their efforts will be fruitless. In the health domain, as well, when people give up on the idea that they have the ability and responsibility to influence their own health outcomes, their situation will only become worse (Lau, 1988).

Rotter's theory also addresses Freud's idea of psychological conflict from a different perspective. To Rotter, conflict arises when two (or more) behaviors both have high RVs. For example, a person might have a high RV both for getting good grades *and* for going to the beach every day. He or she not only will experience conflict, but his or her behavior is likely to become erratic and unpredictable. Conflict can arise on broader issues, as well. As was discussed in Chapter 7, for some people the most important outcome in life is to get along— to be popular and to have positive social experiences. For others, it matters more to get ahead—to become the best or most dominant person in their group. If both desires are strong, conflict results, because the two desires are incompatible. To maximize your popularity you will not be able to maximize the degree to which you compete successfully with others, and vice versa. Another common form of conflict involves the old Freudian pairing of love and work. As was discussed in the psychoanalytic section of this book, many people today find themselves torn between strong desires to have a positive family life and to succeed in the occupational arena. In Rotter's terms, this kind of double–high RV again leads to the experience of conflict and, unless resolved, might in some cases lead to erratic behavior, in which the person veers wildly between ignoring work or ignoring family, depending upon his or her mood of the moment.

Rotter was particularly concerned with one particular byproduct of low E's, that of "lack of competency." If people do not think that efforts to get what they want will be successful, they will avoid any activity in that area, and then will fail to perform the practice necessary to get better at that activity. Somebody with a low E' for dating, for example, might avoid the opposite sex and therefore never develop necessary social skills. A student with a low E' for academic success might (and in my experience often does) stop going to class, which only ensures the outcome the student fears. Low E's are dangerous, Rotter believes, because they can produce behavior patterns that become self-fulfilling prophecies.

Rotter also pointed out the importance of the "minimal goal level," or the lowest RV that is still sufficient to motivate an individual's behavior. There are problems if this is set either too high or too low. Some people refuse to get interested in dating somebody who is not the most attractive person for miles around. Others will settle for *anybody*, including people who might be abusive. Both patterns are self-defeating. In general, if one's minimal goal level is set too high, the result will be frustration; if it is set too low, one may fail to attain what one easily could.

Psychotherapy

Rotterian psychotherapy follows directly from the principles considered above. It is directed at the conscious, rational mind. The client is encouraged to understand better the nature of his or her goals and expectancies, and the degree to which they might be unrealistic or conflicted. The objective is to help the client to plan more realistically the life he or she wants to lead. Social skills training might be included, because Rotter believes that an important byproduct of low E's can be a failure to engage in the world sufficiently to develop such skills. Overall, Rotterian therapy involves helping the client answer these questions: What can you do? What do you want? How do you get from your capacities to your desires? These are excellent questions for anybody to consider.

BANDURA'S SOCIAL LEARNING THEORY

The most recent development that goes by the name "social learning theory" comes from the Stanford psychologist Albert Bandura. Bandura's version of social learning builds directly upon Rotter's (Bandura, 1971, 1977). Many of the same ideas appear in both theories. Indeed, the two theories are more similar than different and it is probably worth noting, historically, that Rotter's came first.

But there are also some important differences. Rotter's concept of generalized expectancies and locus of control leads to theorizing about and measurement of individual differences. Bandura's theory does not give the same amount of emphasis to stable differences between people—in fact, it generally ignores them. Where Bandura has gone beyond Rotter lies in his emphasis upon the social nature of learning, and upon the way people interact with the situations in their lives.

Efficacy Expectations

What Rotter called "expectancies," Bandura reinterpreted slightly as **efficacy expectations**. Both terms refer to the belief that one can accomplish something successfully, and have the mildly phenomenological (in fact, Kellyan) flavor that how one reinterprets reality matters more than what reality actually contains. The two concepts are not exactly the same, however. Rotter's "expectancy" is the perceived conditional probability that if you do something, you will attain your goal. Bandura's "efficacy" is the perceived nonconditional probability that you can do something in the first place.

Recall the example of the woman deciding which job to seek. Rotter's analysis assumes that she *can* apply for any job; that is not the issue. To Rotter, the issue is whether she thinks she will get the job if she applies. It is her perception of the probable result of her behavior that determines what she will do.

A more typical case for Bandura's analysis is that of a snake phobic. He wishes not to be so afraid of snakes, yet does not believe he could ever get near one. If this belief changes, he will be able to approach snakes and be over his phobia. The issue for Bandura is not what happens after he handles a snake, but rather whether he can get close to a snake in the first place.

What can be seen by comparing Bandura's theorizing to Rotter's is a further step away from the classic behaviorism with which both theories began. Rotter's expectancy is a belief about reinforcement, which was classically seen as the key agent of behavioral change. Bandura's efficacy expectation is a belief about the *self*, about what the person himself or herself is capable of doing.

Bandura emphasizes that such efficacy expectations should be the key target for therapeutic interventions. If you can achieve a better match between what you *think* you can accomplish and what you really *can* accomplish, Bandura believes, your life will be lived in a more rational and productive manner. Moreover, your efficacies can themselves create capacities. A snake phobic who is persuaded, by whatever means, that he *can* handle a snake, subsequently *will* be able to handle a snake. The target of therapy for a snake phobic, therefore, should be not the *behavior* of handling a snake, but the client's *beliefs* about his ability to handle a snake.

A psychotherapist in Bandura's mold uses whatever tactic can be found to change a client's efficacy expectations, including verbal persuasion ("you can do it!") and modeling, which means allowing the client to watch somebody else (the model) do it. Part of the therapy for snake phobics is for them to watch somebody else cheerfully handle a snake. The most powerful technique, of course, is to actually have the person perform the behavior. The goal of therapy for fear of snakes, therefore, is to build up to the point where the client can actually have the experience of handling a snake. There is no more powerful way of convincing the client that such a thing is possible.

Bandura's prescription for self-change follows the same pattern. If you are afraid to do something, force yourself to do it. You will then become less afraid, and it will be less difficult next time. A small example: suppose you know you should exercise more, but do not think you are really the type to exercise. Take control of your life and go exercise anyway. This experience, if you can keep it up, will change your view of yourself in such a way that exercise will come to seem a natural part of your life rather than something strange that you must force yourself to do. In its brilliant way, Madison Avenue recently created a commercial for an athletic shoe that boils this principle down to three words: Just Do It. According to Bandura, that is good advice; the rest will follow, usually.

Observational Learning

A key innovation of Bandura's theory is the emphasis on vicarious or observational learning, that is, learning a behavior by seeing someone else do it. It is very different from what happens in a Skinner box, and may be something that is uniquely human (this point is controversial). Learning by songbirds is a frequently cited counterexample. Some species of bird seem to learn their songs simply by listening to adult birds, without any rewards or punishments being involved. We also have all seen *National Geographic* television specials that show lion cubs learning to hunt by watching Momma Lion. Apparently, some animals *do* learn by observation. The difference, if there is one, is that for humans nearly *everything* we learn is by observation.

An efficient way of learning an attitude or skill is to imitate somebody who already has it. We take on many of our parents' values by watching them closely throughout our early years. And who knows what children learn by watching the mayhem portrayed daily on television.

Bandura provided a classic demonstration of how this process can work with his "Bobo doll" studies. A Bobo doll is a large clown doll, on a round, weighted base, that bounces back when it is hit. In a series of studies, Bandura showed that a child who watches an adult hit the doll is likely to later hit the doll him or herself, especially if the adult is rewarded for the aggressive behavior (Bandura, Ross, & Ross, 1963). The extrapolation to the probable effects of television seems rather direct. A person—particularly a child—who day after day watches violence glamorized and rewarded may indeed become more likely to engage in such behavior.

The mechanism of observational learning can also be used for positive purposes. A positive role model can provide a whole array of useful and desirable behaviors for a young person to emulate. More specifically in the psychotherapeutic context, Bandura has shown that one way to persuade a snake phobic to handle the feared reptile is to let him watch a research assistant handling a snake first. This kind of vicarious experience—which, as we have seen, Bandura calls modeling—can make the next step, actually handling the snake, easier to take.

Reciprocal Determinism and the Self

A third and more recent innovation in Bandura's version of social learning theory is the idea of **reciprocal determinism**, which is an analysis of how people can shape their own environments (Bandura, 1978, 1989). Classic versions of behaviorism, and even Rotter's refinement, tend to view reinforcements and the environments that contain them as influences that are inflicted upon people; the people themselves remain basically passive. Bandura's analysis points out that this view is an oversimplification. You are not just placed in the environments in your life, in the way that a rat is placed into a Skinner box. In many circumstances you choose the environments that influence you. If you go to college, all sorts of reinforcement contingencies will be invoked that are designed to cause you to study, attend class, read books, and do other things you might not otherwise have done. But none of these contingencies come into effect until you voluntarily step upon the campus. Similarly, if you join a gang, or the army, or a law firm, various environmental rules and contingencies will immediately start to reshape your life. Do not underestimate their power; understand the implications of choosing to enter different social environments.

A second aspect of reciprocal determinism is that the social situations in your life are changed, at least a little and perhaps importantly, *because* you are there. The party livens up (or calms down) when you arrive. The class discussion switches to a new topic because of something you contribute. Your home environment is to a large extent a function of what you do there. It is in this sense that we control many of the environmental contingencies that in turn influence our behavior. The influence runs both directions.

The third aspect of reciprocal determinism is perhaps the most important. Bandura's deepest departure from behaviorism is his claim that a *self system* develops that has its own effects on behavior, independent of the environment. Here Bandura is forging a middle course between the phenomenologists considered in Chapter 14 and the behaviorists considered in Chapter 16:

Unidirectional environmental determinism is carried to its extreme in the more radical forms of behaviorism . . . [but] humanists and existentialists, who stress the human capacity for conscious judgment and intentional action, contend that individuals determine what they become by their own free choices. Most psychologists find conceptions of human behavior in terms of unidirectional personal determinism as unsatisfying as those espousing unidirectional environmental determinism. To contend that mind creates reality fails to acknowledge that environmental influences partly determine what people attend to, perceive, and think (Bandura, 1978, pp. 344–345).[1]

---

[1]In a further slap at the humanists, Bandura adds, "To contend further that the methods of natural science are incapable of dealing with personal determinants of behavior does not enlist many supporters from the ranks of those who are moved more by empirical evidence than by philosophic discourse" (Bandura, 1978, p. 345).

Bandura's middle course posits that the self system arises from experience, but then takes on an autonomous existence of its own. The self system is what shapes your perceptions, determines your efficacies, and chooses which environments you enter, and thereby determines what you do. This behavior has its consequences, of course, and these consequences—good or bad—further shape the self system, which then determines future behavior. It is this two-way influence—environmental consequences shape the self, then the self acts on the environment, then the environment reacts with consequences that alter the self, and so on—that Bandura calls "reciprocal determinism."

If you trace Bandura's analysis back to its origin, it is clear that underneath all this talk of the self system he remains a behaviorist at heart. Think of the self system in reciprocal determinism as a chicken-egg problem. You have the environment affecting the self, which affects the environment, which affects the self.... But which came first? Bandura's answer is quite clear, and essentially behaviorist: the environment.

Still, social learning theory, and especially Bandura's version, has brought behaviorism a long way. Watson and Skinner emphasized how our environment shapes our behavior. Bandura describes how our behavior shapes our environment. Very little influences you that you do not yourself influence. The causes of what you do cannot be located solely in the world (as the behaviorists would have it) *or* in your mind (as the humanists would have it); they originate somewhere in the interaction between the two.

SUMMARY

Three different social learning theories have been constructed by psychologists trying to extend behaviorism's basic tenets and empirical approach to cover topics that classical behaviorism leaves out. Dollard and Miller's social learning theory explains motivation as the result of primary and secondary drives, aggression as the result of frustration, and psychological conflict as the result of the interplay of motivations to approach and avoid a goal. Dollard and Miller also offer a reinforcement-based explanation of some psychoanalytic defense mechanisms.

Rotter's social learning theory offers an explanation of how people make decisions. His expectancy value theory describes an individual's behavioral potential (tendency to do something) as a function of his or her expectancies, the reinforcement value of the goal, and the particular situation. This theory is presented in the form of a quasi-mathematical formula. Rotter also offers an account of psychological maladjustment and prescriptions for psychotherapy.

Bandura's social learning theory includes a notion of efficacy expectations that closely resembles Rotter's expectancies. Bandura's theory goes beyond Rotter's, however, in two important ways. Bandura describes the process of observational learning, in which one learns by watching the behaviors and outcomes of others, and he also describes the process of reciprocal determinism, in which one's actions are determined by a self system that originates in the environment, then changes the environment, which in turn affects the self system.

CHAPTER  18

COGNITION AND PERSONALITY

Cognitive psychology is a branch of the field, distinct from personality psychology, that deals with basic mental processes such as perception and memory. It has produced some impressive and complex findings about the ways people recognize physical objects and remember events and facts. Much of this research has used computers and other sophisticated hardware, as well as mathematics and other advanced analytic techniques. An important direction in modern personality psychology involves an attempt to integrate some of the methods, findings, and theories of cognitive psychology into our understanding of human personality.

THE ROOTS OF THE COGNITIVE APPROACH

The cognitive approach to personality is an outgrowth of the social learning theories considered in Chapter 17, especially Rotter's and Bandura's versions. Rotter's theory emphasized that that your beliefs about the *environment* determine your expectations about the probable results of different behaviors; these expectations are in turn the basis for what you decide to do. Bandura's theory, slightly different, emphasized that your beliefs about *yourself* determine your expectations of what you are capable of doing in the first place, which also help determine what you will attempt to do. These key components of social learning theory—beliefs and expectations—are essentially cognitive concepts. The next logical step, then, is to try to be more specific about how the cognitive system affects personality and behavior.

Because social learning theory developed from behaviorism, some behaviorist influence is also always lurking in the background of the cognitive approach. The law of effect is still present, for example, though it is not always prominently mentioned. Cognitive representations of reinforcements often play a central role. Moreover, while cognitive theorists are rather free in their use of mentalistic concepts like "schemas" and "scripts," as we shall see, they still manifest the behaviorist's reluctance to see people as possessing consistent personality traits.

Another, rather surprising connection can sometimes be drawn between modern cognitive research and psychoanalysis (see Chapters 10–13). Some of Freud's notions of consciousness, particularly the preconscious and the unconscious, find their counterparts in modern theories of the functioning of the cognitive system.

Yet another important influence on modern cognitive approaches is the phenomenological approach considered in Chapter 14, particularly the ideas of George Kelly (1955). Kelly emphasized the way one's concepts for thinking about the world shape one's personality and behavior. This idea was an important influence on the social learning theories of Rotter and Bandura, as we saw in Chapter 17, and it provides another natural point for cognitive research to enter the study of personality.

A GENERAL COGNITIVE MODEL

Attempts to integrate cognitive theory and personality psychology are all based, more or less, on the same basic idea about what the cognitive system looks like and how it functions. The cognitive system is a mechanism for processing, retaining, and accessing information. In other words, it is a system for creating and using memory. This information-processing function intersects in many places with the patterns of perception, thought, and action that make up human personality.[1]

A useful way to begin consideration of cognitive approaches to personality, therefore, may be to describe in general terms how the cognitive system is believed to work. Figure 18.1 shows a rather standard, "generic" model of cognitive function. From this model I will try to foreshadow how each stage of thinking and memory can be relevant to personality.

This model is not really original; it is a distillation of what I think is the consensus of numerous cognitive psychologists about the basic outline of the cognitive system. The essence of mental functioning, from the cognitive perspective, is how information enters into and is retained in or discarded by the mind. In the figure, each arrow represents both information transfer and information loss. In fact, *most* information is probably lost at each transfer, because

---

[1]Some "cognitive approaches to personality" are really about the way people use and understand trait words or other topics that are not centrally relevant to personality functioning. These are not considered in this chapter.

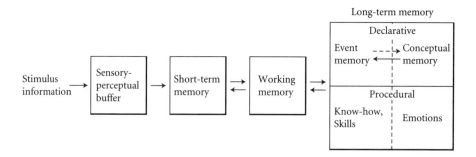

FIGURE 18.1 A GENERIC MODEL OF THE COGNITIVE SYSTEM This model diagrams a typical view of the human cognitive system in terms of the stages and functions of memory. Each arrow represents information transfer (and loss). That is, information is almost always lost in the process of being transferred from one stage of memory to another.

memory is highly selective. Each box in the figure represents a stage in the memory or cognitive system.

It is important to remember this is a model of the *mind*, not the brain. These boxes are not physical places in the brain or nervous system. They represent stages of mental processing; the physical location of the organs that perform the functions of each stage might be—and probably are—spread throughout the nervous system.

The Sensory/Perceptual Buffer

Information comes from the environment in "raw" form via our sense organs, the eyes, ears, tongue, nose, and skin. Each of these organs is constantly transmitting vast amounts of information at a high rate. Every sight, sound, taste, smell, and feeling that impinges upon you triggers a sensory response that transmits an impulse to the brain. This vast stream of information enters the first stage of processing: the **sensory buffer**.

The sensory buffer holds all information from the senses for a very short period of time—a couple of seconds at most, usually less. The information it holds is unanalyzed, a little like information stored on a cassette tape. It is there, but very little processing has taken place to find out what it means.

One way to demonstrate how this buffer works is to put you in a completely dark room and place an object in front of you. If we flash a strobe light, perhaps for a couple of milliseconds, you will not know what you see while you are seeing it; there simply is not enough time to figure it out. But if you are allowed to sit and think about it for a couple of seconds, you may then be able to describe what you saw. This easily demonstrated effect shows that you still have the visual information in your mind, even if you do not yet know what it means. It also shows that you can continue to work on and analyze the information even after the stimulus itself is gone.

Clever experiments have been performed to figure out just how long it takes for the mind to figure out what it has seen, after the object is gone. In "backward masking" studies, *another* object is flashed *after* the one you are to identify. If the second object (or sometimes a random pattern) is flashed (using a device called a tachistoscope) immediately after the first, you will not be able to say what the first one was. But if the experimenter waits a half-second or so after the first object is gone before flashing the second object, you will then be able to identify the first object. This kind of study shows that it takes a little time to interpret what an object is, and specific variants can provide precise measurements of how long it takes to identify different kinds of objects.

The same kind of experiment can be done with sounds, too. Follow a sound immediately with a second, very different sound, and the first will be nearly impossible to identify. Give the person a little time between sounds, however, and he or she will be able to identify both.

Of course, most information that enters the sensory buffer is never identified at all. As one of my former professors once said, "I urge you to consider your backside." If you are sitting as you read this, then sensations of the chair against your bottom are steadily being transmitted as you read. But as long as you are paying attention to what you are reading, those sensations flow out again at the same rate they flow in, without causing any reaction. But if you suddenly shift your attention—consider your backside; now come back to reading, please— you can become aware that you have been ignoring quite a bit of complex information.

The information we do notice is determined by the focus of our attention. Attention can be directed at a book, at your backside, or at a noise outside, and can make you acutely aware of those stimuli. But, just as everything outside the beam of a spotlight remains in the dark, everything that you do not attend to might as well not exist. Information that comes into the sensory buffer will go right out again unless some attention is paid to it.

At one time it was thought that this information "in the dark" was not processed at all before it was lost forever (Broadbent, 1958). Some fascinating studies of the "cocktail party effect," however, show that this belief is an oversimplification. This effect is one you have probably experienced in a crowded room, such as a cafeteria, or at a cocktail party. You are engrossed in talking with someone right next to you, and are fairly oblivious to the hum of conversation all around. Suddenly, somebody at the other end of the room speaks your name. What happens? Your attention to your companion lapses for at least a moment as your attention shifts across the room. The interesting thing is that not only do you become immediately aware that your name was included in a conversation to which you *thought* you were not listening, but you probably can now retrieve the two or three or four words that person spoke *before* saying your name. This information—the words that were spoken before your attention even shifted—presumably has been drawn out of your sensory buffer.

This effect, which can be demonstrated experimentally (e.g., Moray, 1959; Triesman, 1964), shows two things. First, you are constantly monitoring the non-attended information in your sensory buffer, at some level. The information is being processed to the extent that your mind is checking to see if your name was there, for example. Other things are being screened as well. If somebody across the room speaks a foul obscenity, your attention is likely to shift. Or you might be driving down the highway, not really paying attention to what you are seeing, when suddenly a truck comes at you from an unexpected direction. Your attention is likely to switch to it immediately—a good thing!

The purpose of this low-level processing of information in the sensory buffer seems to be to scan for things to which you need to switch your attention, such as somebody talking about you, or a careening truck. Some evidence suggests that another function might be to screen and prevent you from perceiving stimuli that might make you anxious or uncomfortable.

Indeed, the functions of the sensory-perceptual buffer have sometimes been viewed as relevant to the psychoanalytic notion of perceptual defense. This is the idea that the ego will prevent stimuli that the superego finds threatening from entering awareness (recall the discussion of defense mechanisms in Chapter 12). The hypothesis is that although all stimuli enter the buffer, defense mechanisms will screen out those that might cause anxiety. Attempts have been made to test this hypothesis experimentally.

In one early experiment, words were presented extremely briefly to subjects on a tachistoscope, as described above. Some of these words were neutral, such as "apple," "child," and "dance." Others were sexually charged words, such as "penis," "rape," and "whore." Over successive trials, words of both types were presented for longer and longer durations, beginning with flashes so brief nobody could perceive them, until the exposures were so long everybody could perceive them. Subjects' detection of the words was measured two ways. One was simply to ask them, "can you read that?" after each presentation. The minimal amount of exposure time required to perceive each word was recorded. The second way was by measuring the subjects' sweat-gland activity; when they began to sweat in response to a word like "rape," subjects were assumed to have detected it.

The interesting finding was that these two ways of measuring perception did not exactly coincide. In particular, subjects' sweat glands would react to emotionally charged words sooner than would their verbal reports. In other words, they were physically reacting to words that they were claiming they could not read (McGinnies, 1949).

Results like this suggest that something much like an ego defense mechanism may prevent certain stimuli from entering consciousness even while other aspects of the mind are well aware of and responding to them. These results also suggest that we might be able to avoid becoming consciously aware of aspects of the world that might feel threatening, even when they are right in front of us.

Although many investigators have obtained results more or less like the ones just described, their interpretation has been controversial. One obvious possibility is that subjects in fact can read the word "penis" just fine, they are just embarrassed to tell the investigator. It is difficult and perhaps impossible to be 100 percent sure, but taken as a whole the evidence seems persuasive that the mind has mechanisms, located somewhere in the sensory-perceptual buffer, that not only selectively attend to certain stimuli, but actively screen out other stimuli that might cause anxiety if they were to enter consciousness (Erdelyi, 1974, 1985).

Short-Term Memory

Information that, for whatever reason, is extracted from the sensory buffer then moves to the next stage, which is **short-term memory**, or STM. STM is roughly equivalent to consciousness; it comprises whatever you have in mind at the moment. Thus, STM is where thinking takes place, and is where the fundamental contact between mind and world, so important to the phenomenologists discussed in Chapter 14, is located.

The capacity of STM is specifically limited. To demonstrate this limit in class, I sometimes start to read a list of numbers to my students, asking them to hold *all* of them in memory as I go. I ask them to raise their hands when their "brains are full." (Try it with a friend; read slowly the numbers 4, 6, 2, 3, 7, 6, 2, 8, 7 . . . .) The results are highly consistent. The hands begin to go up after about five numbers, most are up by seven, and by nine I have everybody.

This experiment shows the capacity of STM, which is said to be "7, plus or minus 2" (Miller, 1956). The next question, of course, is seven *what*? The answer is that the capacity of STM is about seven "chunks" of information. A chunk is any piece of information that can be thought of as a unit. It can vary with learning and experience. Seven random numbers, for example, comprise seven chunks. But your own phone number, which also consists of seven numbers, is just one chunk; it is known to you as one piece of information, not seven pieces. It seems to be about as easy to hold in STM seven phone numbers you have previously memorized (or forty-nine digits in all) as seven random digits you have never seen in that sequence before.

Chunking can work with ideas, too. If you know what "liberalism" is, or "existential philosophy," or "overdrive," or "water pressure," these complex ideas can be contained within single chunks. This is important because the limit to STM implies that you can only think about seven things at a time and that all new ideas you have must come from the interaction of these seven things. The more rich and complex each of the ideas in STM is, the more rich and complex your thinking can be.

This is the best argument I know of for education. What education provides, at best, is more and better chunks to use for thinking. You learn complicated ideas and concepts one small piece at a time, often slowly and painfully. But when you've finally learned them, complicated patterns of information and thinking become contained within single chunks, which you can now manipulate and contrast in your mind simultaneously with other such chunks. Once you learn all of the many ideas that make up "conservatism" and "liberalism," you will then be in a position to compare the two basic philosophies. By now, you should be able to say something about the basic differences between psychoanalysis and phenomenology, whereas before you understood these ideas you might have been able to compare only one aspect of each at a time. And until you really understand what water pressure is and can use it as a single idea, you will never be able to design a plumbing system.

This is the logic behind **Funder's Fifth Law**: *The purpose of education is not to teach facts, or even ideas. It is to create new chunks.* That is the only way to expand your ability to think.

Because your thinking consists of the comparison and contrast of the chunks of information and philosophy you have collected from your experience and your education, your thinking will be different from anyone else's. No other person's chunks of information are likely to be exactly like yours, so your thoughts will always have a unique cast. This must be an important aspect of personality. Some psychologists have examined the "schemas" that organize our knowledge (schemas are somewhat like chunks; Markus, 1977). People who see themselves as dominant, for example, seem to organize their perceptions not just of themselves but of other people in terms of how dominant they are perceived to be. This example should remind you of Kelly's personal construct theory (Chapter 14), which claimed that the critical aspect of cognition is the "constructs" out of which we build our unique views of the world.

The idea of STM as consciousness has interesting parallels in other basic approaches to personality. Freud believed that consciousness was by far the smallest part of the mind. In the usual cognitive model, too, STM is the smallest part of the mind—for one thing, it is the only part with a specifically limited capacity. The phenomenologists believe that what matters in psychology is what you are conscious of *now*. Research on STM suggests that right now you are conscious of about seven things—a suprisingly exact upper limit to the capacity of human awareness.

Working Memory

STM is closely attached to **working memory**, which contains a vast store of information that is just barely out of consciousness. Examples of information in your working memory at this moment (although we will now extract it and move it into STM) are where did you last park your car?, is rain expected tomorrow?, and what did you have for breakfast? None of these pieces of information (presumably) was difficult to retrieve into consciousness, even though it is unlikely you were thinking of any of them before I asked. You might recognize working memory as similar to what Freud called the preconscious.

The principal purpose of working memory is to maintain close at hand a constantly updated representation of your current environment. It keeps track of information you might need to know at a moment's notice but that does not need to be kept actively in your consciousness. That is why it holds the information of where your car is parked, for example. You do not want or need to think about it all day, but when you go out to the parking lot at 5:30, it would be nice to be able to remember.

Because it is constantly updated, working memory is a representation of the *current* environment and the various things you need, temporarily, to keep at your mental fingertips. It probably remembers where your car is today, but not where you parked it last Tuesday. Working memory also contains a list of the things you are currently trying to accomplish or are worried about.

Research on individuals' current concerns shows that at any given moment people will list around half a dozen matters that are frequently coming to mind, as thoughts move from working memory to STM and back again (Klinger, 1977). They might include a job you hope to get, a term paper you need to be working on, a phone call you expect will be returned soon, and so forth. Some of these current concerns can make you emotionally aroused when you think about them consciously, and you will find many of them drifting into your daydreams (Gold & Reilly, 1985; Nikula, Klinger, & Larson-Gutman, 1993). But what were you trying to accomplish or what were you worried about three weeks ago? It is not the job of working memory to know or to care. Once the concern is resolved—when that person finally calls you back—working memory can and will erase all record of it.

The essential difference between working memory and STM is not really one of kind, but of size. Material constantly moves back and forth between them, and the same sort of chunks likely fill both. So like STM, working memory can be expected to contain personally relevant ideas such as schemas, goals, and personal constructs; these ideas are both a function and a cause of the kind of person you are.

One theory describes the process of thinking using the analogy of a workbench. On your workbench is what you are currently building, and hanging on the wall nearby is a wide assortment of tools. You take down a tool when you need it, but because the work bench is small, every time you get a tool down you must hang another one up. (The workbench has room for, say, seven tools, plus or minus two).

In this analogy, of course, the workbench is STM and the wall where the many other tools are stored is working memory. Information remains in STM only while it is being used, then it goes back to working memory so that another piece of necessary information can be considered for a while. Personal computers of a sort now rapidly becoming obsolete work the same way. They have a limited CPU (central processing unit), where all the computer's "thinking" takes place, but its capacity is expanded through the use of floppy disks that can store information nearby. Such a computer constantly swaps information back and forth from the CPU onto the floppy and back again as it needs different data for its analysis. If you watch these old machines at work, you will hear the floppy drive go whirr, whirr, then pause, then whirr again, and again, until the answer is ready. The computer is swapping from CPU to floppy and back with each whirr, just as a person (less audibly) swaps information back and forth between STM and working memory.

The Movement from Short-Term to Long-Term Memory

How does information make it into the final information storage compartment, **long-term memory** (LTM)? An old theory was that if you repeated something over and over in your mind, such "rehearsal" was sufficient to move it into LTM. Later research showed that this idea is not quite correct. The only way to get information into LTM, it turns out, is not to repeat it to yourself, but to really *think* about it. The longer and more elaborate the processing that a piece of information receives, the more likely it is to transfer into LTM (Craik & Watkins, 1973; Craik & Tulving, 1975).

This principle of cognitive psychology yields some useful advice about how to study. A common strategy, and one that usually fails dismally, is the rote repetition technique. We have all seen college students with their yellow highlighter pens, marking passages in the textbook they think will be on the exam. To study, they go back through the book and reread everything highlighted; if they have time, they do it again and even again.

A much better strategy would be to take each of these highlighted strategies, pause, and ask yourself several questions. Do I agree with this statement? Why? Does this statement remind me of anything in my life? Is it useful for anything? Does it contradict anything else I know from experience or have learned in this course? If you can generate an answer to each of these questions, you are more likely to remember the statement you are asking them about. Moreover, you might learn something.

Long-Term Memory

According to most theories of long-term memory, this part of the mind is both permanent and of unlimited capacity. David Starr Jordan, a turn-of-the-century ichthyologist[2] and president of Stanford University, in his later years refused to learn anybody's name. Every time he learned a new name, he complained, he forgot a fish.

Apparently, Jordan was a better ichthyologist than he was a cognitive psychologist. The consensus of modern cognitive theories is that any information that makes it into LTM is there forever (although it might be hard to retrieve), and that LTM never runs out of room. In this view, LTM is much like an infinite attic. You can keep storing stuff in there, and you will never fill it. But there is no guarantee that, when you go up there, you will be able to find that snorkel you put away at the end of last summer. Whether you can find anything or not will depend upon how well the attic is organized. The same is true about LTM. The better organized its contents, the easier information is to retrieve.

Recall that George Kelly thought that your mind is organized by its personal constructs (Kelly, 1955; see Chapter 14). These constructs may get their power to affect experience, thought, and behavior by their ability to determine what you are and are not able to find in the attic of your mind. To push this attic analogy a little further, it is as if your mental attic is divided into storage bins, each of which is labelled with a personal construct. Perhaps at the back of the attic is a large bin labeled "miscellaneous." Clearly, something that goes in one of the construct-labeled bins will be easier to find than something tossed into the miscellaneous bin. Moreover, the information you are more easily able to find, of course, will have more influence on how you think about the world.

The representation of LTM in Figure 18.1 shows it divided into two parts, each of which is further divided in two. The two main parts are the areas of LTM that contain declarative and procedural knowledge. The distinction comes from the philosopher Gilbert Ryle (1949), who said there were two forms of knowledge, which he called "knowing that" and "knowing how." You might know *that* Little Rock is the capital of Arkansas, but you know *how* to ride a bicycle. These two forms of knowledge are, according to Ryle and modern cognitive theory, fundamentally different.

DECLARATIVE KNOWLEDGE

Declarative knowledge is "knowing that." It includes your knowledge about everything you can talk about, or declare. In Figure 18.1, this kind of knowledge is represented in two kinds of memory, event and conceptual.

---

[2]An ichthyologist is a person who studies fish.

Event Memory   **Event memory** contains almost everything you might refer to by saying, "I remember. . . ." It includes events, such as what happened on your first date, as well as specific facts, such as the state capitals, your mother's first name, the number of inches in a foot, and (I hope) the essential tenets of psychoanalysis. These are all specific items of information that you can talk about.

Declarative knowledge is the place where your "verbalizable" knowledge about yourself resides. These also are things you can talk about. The important, formative experiences of your life—those you remember—sit here more or less permanently, and have an influence on your personality that can last throughout your life. This is how a particularly traumatic or delightful episode can continue to affect your outlook on life, your emotions, and your behavior, even years after it happens.

Conceptual Memory   **Conceptual memory** contains your more general knowledge of the world. It refers not to specific events or facts about specific things, but rather to the knowledge you have abstracted from experience about how the world works (e.g., Schank & Abelson, 1977).

For example, you probably have never been told explicitly what happens at McDonald's. Yet you know the rules. You know that if you go into a McDonald's, sit down, and expect a waiter to take your order, you might eventually starve to death. From your experience of having gone there many times, you know what to expect, and how to follow what some cognitive psychologists call the implicit "McDonald's script." Furthermore, not only have you developed a knowledge base about all the specific things you have done in life, but you have also abstracted from those behaviors a general view of the kind of person you are (the "self-schema"). The shy person remembers not only various past social disasters, but has a general—and powerfully influential—view of the self as shy (Cantor, 1990).

Your conceptual knowledge might be used to fill gaps in your event memory (which is why there is an arrow on Figure 18.1 that leads from conceptual to event knowledge). For example, consider the following scenario: A person walks into McDonald's, orders a hamburger, fries, and a Coke, gets the food, sits down and eats it, then leaves. Now here is a question: Did the person pay for the food? Not only will almost anybody respond "yes," after just a few minutes many people will think that they *remember* being told that the person paid. Of course, they were not told that—they inferred it, from their general knowledge that the McDonald's Corporation regards payment as an essential part of every transaction.

This is a reasonable piece of information to infer, and in general the practice of using conceptual knowledge to fill in gaps in event knowledge is probably quite useful. But it can also lead to errors. For example, someone who has in his or her conceptual knowledge an image of what members of a certain ethnic group are like might "remember" facts about members of that group that never really happened. Trial lawyers know that eyewitnesses to a crime are likely to confuse what they *actually* saw with what they *assumed* they saw, based on how they think a bank robbery or mugging usually proceeds, or even based upon what they expect a person who looks like the suspect to do (e.g., Loftus, 1992; Loftus, Greene, & Doyle, 1989). In a similar manner, a shy person might fill in gaps in his memory of an unpleasant social encounter with details that did not really happen, but that serve to increase his humiliation.

Our store of conceptual knowledge contains many general scripts and stereotypes. For example, we have strong ideas about waitresses and librarians. Consider these questions: Which one, the waitress or the librarian, drinks wine and which one drinks beer? Which one drives an old Volvo, and which one drives a pick-up truck? Which one likes classical music, and which one prefers country-western? We may have abstracted these stereotypes from experience (this is the basis of the arrow leading from event to conceptual knowledge in Figure 18.1) and many of them probably have a kernel of truth (Lee, Jussim, & McCauley, 1995).

Indeed, if all stereotypes were abstractions from firsthand experience, they might not be a problem. Generalizations are useful, after all. But we also form stereotypes and general views of the world from sources that are *not* valid. One significant source is the mass media. Movies and television programs portray the world as a place where large numbers of people are armed and dangerous and where violence is a frequent event. They also show images of what dangerous people look like, and thereby communicate stereotypes about how dangerous people act, how they dress, and to which ethnic groups they belong. An unfortunate recent trend is for politicians to scapegoat stereotyped groups— "illegal immigrants" or "welfare mothers"—as the source of all of society's ills. These images are conveyed repeatedly through the media, and the result is that many citizens think they know all about immigrants and welfare recipients, even if they have never knowingly met an individual of either type. Most worrisome of all, many children watch hours of television every day. Think a moment about the image of reality they must be assembling on the basis of their contact with this fantasy land.

In principle, false conceptual knowledge can be undone. The method would be the same by which the knowledge was acquired in the first place—experience. If television shows were to change their portrayal of the world, children's general images might eventually change, too. More powerfully, there is no better way to remove a negative stereotype about an ethnic group than having experience with real, living, breathing members of that group (Pettigrew, 1986). A shy person, given enough successful—or even just non-aversive—social interactions, might become less shy. However, the process by which daily experience and event knowledge affect conceptual knowledge is very slow. That is why a *dotted* arrow connects event to conceptual knowledge in Figure 18.1.

PROCEDURAL KNOWLEDGE

Procedural knowledge is what you know but cannot really talk about. Rather than words or statements, it consists of knowledge about ways of doing things, or procedures, which is why it is called "knowing how." As with declarative knowledge, procedural knowledge can also be divided into two parts.

Know-How   The first is simply all those skills we ordinarily call "know-how." Examples include knowing how to read, to ride a bicycle, to close a business deal, to analyze a set of data, or to ask someone out on a date. For the most part—by which I mean about 98 percent of the time—these skills are learned by *doing* them. You can talk about each of them, and people of course do. But if somebody merely tells you how to do any of these things, without giving you a chance to actually do it, you will not learn the skill. Furthermore, if you try to describe how you do any of these things, you may find something to say, but your words will fail to capture the essence of the activity.

A classic example is bike riding. I can tell you how to ride a bike: Get on the saddle, grab the handlebars, pump the pedals up and down, and maintain balance so you will not fall off. There might be a little more I could say, but no matter how much I talk, it will never be enough to teach you how to ride a bicycle, or even to let you know what riding one is really like. You can only learn how to ride a bicycle by doing it, and by getting practice and feedback.

The usual analysis of procedural knowledge stops here, but it can be applied in many different contexts. Consider how one learns to think (assuming one ever does). A number of colleges now have courses on "How to think." In these courses, instructors explain the rules of logic, describe tactics for organizing one's thinking, teach brainstorming methods, and so on. I am not a big fan of these courses, because I believe that in a college *every* course ought to be about how to think. They do it (or should do it) by giving you something to think about. You then formulate ideas and get feedback on them (such as the instructor or a fellow student saying, "good!" or "very interesting!"). Practice and feedback are how you learn to think.

It is sometimes claimed that less than a year after taking the final exam, few college students remember any of the facts they supposedly learned in a course. Does this make college education a waste of time? I have heard this claim made. Such a conclusion not only puts my livelihood in jeopardy, it profoundly misunderstands the purpose of college education. The role of a course is to provoke practice and feedback at thinking, not to impart facts for their own sake. You can get smarter by thinking about literature, or chemistry, or even psychology. You will not get smarter if all you do in your courses is memorize poems, the periodic table, or a list of experiments. And if you cannot remember these specific details a year later, that does not mean you learned nothing.

Every semester, when term papers are assigned, students ask me, "How do I come up with a topic, and what should I write about it?" They are often frustrated by my answer, which is always the same: "Come up with something you think is worthwhile and interesting, and write what you think about it." Students believe I am holding out on them, that there is some secret formula for how to come up with a topic and analyze it that I am refusing to tell them.

There is no formula. The *only* way to learn how to find a worthwhile topic is to try to find one. You will find out later—through feedback—whether it was worthwhile. Then, later (or in another course), you will try again, much like when you learned to ride a bicycle: you fell off again and again, until one day you did not fall off.

Good teachers of procedural knowledge are often not particularly good themselves at what they are teaching. Sports coaches are an excellent example. The legendary coaches of football and basketball typically were *not* great athletes during their own playing years. But top skills are not necessary for coaches. The role of a coach is to provide two things, motivation and feedback. The coach must get his or her players to practice, and then tell them when they are getting better and when they are getting worse. (Although of course it is not as easy as this description might make it sound.)

To get back to personality, the general styles and strategies we use to approach life make up part of our base of procedural knowledge (Cantor, 1990). We all have well-practiced routines for dealing with various aspects of life, and sometimes these routines kick in without our conscious intention (Langer, 1992, 1994). For example, as was mentioned in Chapter 2, you probably developed over the years some very specific patterns in the way you interact with your parents. You may even forget these patterns exist, until you visit home after a long absence. Before you know it, you are falling into the same old well-rehearsed childhood routine (Cantor, 1990).

Teachers of singing, dancing, violin-playing and other forms of procedural knowledge play exactly the same role as coaches. In some cases, their activities are no different from those of a psychotherapist trying to help you change your characteristic behavioral patterns. First, they must motivate their students (or clients) to practice that which they want to learn to do. Second, they must provide feedback on how their students (or clients) are doing.

Now you can see the *big* difference between declarative and procedural knowledge. The first can be taught by lecturing; the second only through practice and feedback. The first requires a teacher good at what is being taught; you cannot learn Russian history from somebody who does not know Russian history. But you can learn to sing from somebody whose own voice is hoarse, or learn to bat from a middle-aged coach with slow reflexes and a beer gut. You might even get some help in developing your personality from someone who has not yet worked out all of his or her *own* personal problems.

Emotions   Emotions are a separate category of procedural knowledge. You cannot learn about emotions by reading about them, nor can you describe an emotion in words. But everybody knows what they are.

Our knowledge of emotion and feeling is not verbal, nor is it verbalizable, although both psychologists and poets have tried. Verbal descriptions of emotions certainly exist, but always seem to miss the point a little (Frijda, 1986). Even poetry, when it works, communicates by evoking an emotion in the reader or listener, rather than by actually describing the emotion itself. Emotions cannot be fully described in words because our most important knowledge about them is procedural, not declarative.

For example, consider the emotion of anger. In the course of experiencing this emotion, a person does a wide variety of things. His heart rate accelerates and his blood pressure rises; he may get red in the face and his fist and jaw may clench. His thoughts are taken over by the way the object of his anger mistreated or threatened him, and he makes plans to get even or lashes out without thinking. He may or may not recognize that *everything* he is doing is part of the emotion of anger. That is, he will not necessarily say to himself, "Boy am I angry." But that is what all the other activities of his body and mind amount to.

Thus, an emotion is a set of procedures of the body and mind. It is something you *do*, not merely a set of verbal concepts or a passive experience (Ekman & Davidson, 1994). And you learn about emotion by experiencing it, not by talking about it. It may be the most important learning we do.

COGNITIVE SOCIAL LEARNING THEORY: MISCHEL

The tour of the general cognitive model we just completed revealed many places where cognitive processes intersect with aspects of personality. A few theorists—an increasing number in recent years—have tried to develop theories of personality that are based explicitly upon what psychology has learned about the cognitive system.

The first of these theorists was George Kelly, whose work on "personal constructs" was described in Chapter 14 (Kelly, 1955). These constructs are the ideas about the world that guide an individual's perceptions and thoughts. Kelly's theory was essentially cognitive in nature. For example, as was mentioned above, personal constructs presumably reside in long-term memory, affect the formation of chunks in short-term memory, and determine which pieces of information that enter the sensory-perceptual buffer will make it further into consciousness. Kelly's career came before the explosion of research in cognitive psychology in the late 1960s, however, and he never tied his ideas about constructs very closely to the cognitive psychology of his own day.

One of Kelly's students eventually did connect constructs and cognitive theory. The name of this student might surprise you, if you recall the material presented in Chapter 4: Walter Mischel—yes, the very same Walter Mischel who triggered the person-situation controversy by claiming that personality traits are not important and that situations are much more powerful determinants of behavior. He can also be considered the first modern cognitive theorist of personality.

Mischel introduced his theory in 1973, calling it a "cognitive social learning reconceptualization of personality" (Mischel, 1973). This cumbersome title is revealing in several ways. First, notice he called his theory a *re*-conceptualization. Why the prefix? It is a residue from his involvement in the person-situation debate, I believe. When Mischel claimed that personality traits account for little of the variance in human behavior, his greater goal was to replace trait units such as "sociability" or "dominance" with new units of his own invention. Instead of conceptualizing personality in terms of traits, he is saying, we need to conceptualize it in some other way.

The other way he espouses is based closely on the social learning theories of Rotter and Bandura, as Mischel's title further reveals. His intention was to combine social learning theory with the knowledge about mental processes that cognitive psychology was so rapidly accumulating. And always, in the background, we can sense the continuing influence of the personal construct theory developed by his mentor, George Kelly.

Cognitive Person Variables

Mischel claimed that individual differences in personality could best be described in terms of four "person variables":

1. Cognitive and behavioral construction competencies. These competencies comprise an individual's mental abilities and behavioral skills, so might include such properties as one's IQ, creativity, social skills, and occupational abilities. In general, these would comprise procedural knowledge in the cognitive model described earlier.

2. Encoding strategies and personal constructs The tie to Kelly's personal construct theory could not be more clear than this variable indicates. These aspects of personality include a person's ideas about how the world can be categorized (one's Kellyan personal construct system) and one's efficacy expectations, or beliefs about one's own capabilities. They also might include other beliefs about oneself, such as "I am a shy person." These beliefs are usually of the sort that can be verbally described, so would reside in the declarative knowledge section of LTM in the model described earlier.

3. Subjective stimulus values This idea to some degree resembles the notion of expectancies in Rotter's social learning theory—an individual's beliefs about the probabilities of attaining a goal if it were to be pursued. It also includes the values people put on different rewarding outcomes; for one person money is more important than prestige, for example, whereas another person's priorities might be just the reverse.

4. *Self-regulatory systems and plans*   These are another kind of procedural knowledge in LTM, and are closely related to what Bandura called the "self system," as described in Chapter 17. Recall that Bandura's self system is a set of procedures for the control of behavior, including self-reinforcement, the selection of situations, and the purposeful alteration of situational circumstances. This is more or less what Mischel had in mind, but Mischel was also interested in how one might directly control one's own thoughts.

An example Mischel addressed many times in his research concerned a child who is trying to delay gratification. As was described in Chapter 7, most experiments of this sort present a child with two rewards, such as marshmallows and pretzels. The child is told his less-preferred reward can be had immediately, but he can have the better reward if he is able to wait for a few minutes. Mischel was interested in the strategies the child might use to help him or herself through the waiting period.

One strategy he proposed to the waiting children was to mentally transform the object that presumably was being so eagerly awaited. For example, if a child's preferred treat was the marshmallow, he might hardly be able to wait if he thought about its "chewy, sweet, soft taste." But if he instead thought about the marshmallow as a cloud, the waiting period could go much longer without difficulty. If a child's preferred treat was the pretzel, her tolerance for waiting would end quickly if she concentrated on its "crunchy, salty taste." But if she thought about the pretzel as a brown log, the waiting was much easier.

Mischel drew from this research not only some pointers on how to help children delay gratification, but a deeper moral that fits right into the point of view of the phenomenologists considered in Chapter 14:

The results [of the research just described] clearly show that what is in the children's heads—not what is physically in front of them—determines their ability to delay (Mischel, 1973, p. 260).

The Personality System

Twenty-two years after his pioneering effort, and after a good deal of progress in cognitive psychology and a great deal of research by many investigators tying cognition to personality, Mischel (and his own student Yuichi Shoda) issued an updated version of his original theory. Perhaps the most remarkable aspect of the updated theory was how little it had changed over more than two decades. Instead of four person variables, the new version had five; the new variable was "affects," or feelings and emotions. This new variable was added because, by 1995, research had made it "clear that affects and emotions profoundly influence social information processing and coping behavior" (Mischel & Shoda, 1995, p. 252).

Another wrinkle introduced in the new version of the theory was a description of personality as a "cognitive-affective system." With a nod toward modern cognitive models of "parallel distributed processing," which assume that the mind does many different things at the same time (Rumelhart, McClelland, & PDP Research Group, 1986), Mischel's revised theory claims that the most important aspect of the (now) five cognitive social learning person variables is the way in which they simultaneously interact. Personality, then, is "a stable system that mediates how the individual selects, construes, and processes social information and generates social behaviors" (Mischel & Shoda, 1995, p. 246). Mischel offers the following example:

Suppose that while waiting for the results of medical tests, an individual scans for and focuses on a specific configuration of features in the situation, which activate the encoding that this is a health threat to the self, and concurrently trigger anxiety, which activates further scanning of and for those features, and simultaneously feeds back to reactivate the encoded health threat. The perceived threat activates the belief that this situation is uncontrollable, which triggers further anxiety and also negative outcome expectations. Both the negative expectancies and the anxiety concurrently activate defensive plans and scripts that generate a pattern of multiple behaviors at varying levels of strength. These events occur concurrently, in parallel activation within the system. The behaviors ultimately generated depend both on the situational features and on the organization of the network of cognitions and affects that become involved (Mischel & Shoda, 1995, p. 255).

There is no substitute for the experience of reading the paragraph just quoted, for appreciating what happens when cognitive psychology—one of the drier subfields of our discipline, frankly—is combined with personality theory. The jargon in this paragraph, some of which you encountered in the description of the general cognitive model, is largely borrowed from cognitive psychology. And notice how the focus of this example is on the abstract mental processes that all happen at once, not on the behavior that ultimately results. From reading this paragraph, you have *no* idea what the individual in the example, or for that matter any individual, will do in the face of the anxiety generated while waiting for his or her prognosis.

Cognitive vs. Trait Approaches

Not surprisingly, Mischel places his cognitive theory in explicit opposition to the "traditional trait theory" (as he usually calls it) that he has battled for almost three decades. First, he argues that the cognitive person variables in his theory are superior to the ordinary trait terms in the English language because they express scientific rather than lay understanding. Mischel and his followers have always tended to be skeptical of the validity of human psychological judgments; one Mischelian has even dubbed the tendency of people to see personality traits in each other "the fundamental attribution error" (Ross, 1977). In this light, it seems to them an important advance to move theorizing about personality out of lay conceptualizations like "irritability" and into more scientific-sounding conceptualizations like "encoding competency."

A second way in which Mischel sees his theory as an advance over the trait approach is that his person variables are aimed at the psychological processes underlying behavior, rather than at the behaviors themselves. That is, a trait like "irritability" describes a pattern of action in the world, specifically, in this example, responding with hostility to minor inconveniences. By contrast, an "encoding competency" or a "self-regulatory plan" describes a mental process by which a person comes to understand the world or generate behavior. As was seen in the medical-test example quoted above, this description does not always generate an obvious behavioral prediction, but it does attempt to describe what is going on in the mind.

A third advantage Mischel sees in his approach is that individual differences in behavior become conceptualized not as average levels, but as patterns. For example, rather than measuring a child's overall level of hostility, one might focus on the fact that two children with equal overall levels are hostile under different circumstances. Whereas one child is most hostile when approached by peers, the other is most hostile when warned by an adult. A measurement of overall level of hostility could obscure the potentially important difference between these two patterns (Mischel & Shoda, 1995).

A skeptic, however, or an unreconstructed trait theorist, like your author, could find grounds to doubt the superiority of Mischel's cognitive approach over the trait approach, and could argue that in some respects the two approaches are not all that different. First, the detachment of cognitive social learning theory's person variables from the ordinary language of personality is not an unmitigated advantage. Lay language may contain folk wisdom that is deliberately bypassed by cognitive jargon. Perhaps even more important, a personality psychology based on concepts such as "encoding competency" rather than "irritability" forgoes any possibility of addressing the accuracy of lay personality judgments (see Chapter 6). If scientific personality theory is ever to have something to say about lay personality theory (or vice versa), they will have to speak the same language to some extent (Funder, 1991).

A second ground for skepticism is that cognitive social learning theory is not completely consistent in its avoidance of ordinary trait concepts. Specifically, the latest version of Mischel's theory allows for the influence of "temperaments"—basic aspects of personality that are visible early in life. These include variables such as "activity, irritability, tension, distress, and emotional lability" (Mischel & Shoda, 1995, p. 260). Of course, these are personality traits, and in fact Mischel's own list, just quoted, encompasses three of the Big Five basic traits that were discussed in Chapter 7 (specifically, extraversion, neuroticism, and agreeableness).

Finally, consider the two aspects of cognitive person variables that Mischel regards as their most important advantages over traits. First, he emphasizes that his variables describe psychological processes rather than just behavioral content. But take a quick look back at Chapter 7, and see how trait theorists describe the psychological processes behind self-control, self-monitoring, and authoritarianism, for example. Second, Mischel emphasizes that his theory treats individual differences in behavior as manifested through complex patterns rather than average levels. But let me refer again to two particular trait theories described in Chapter 7. Self-monitoring describes how a high self-monitor can have the same overall level of behavior as a low self-monitor, but adjust it differently in response to different situations. And authoritarians are "inconsistent" in that they treat superiors with deference and subordinates with contempt—a pattern that is a definitive manifestation of the authoritarian trait. Thus, many trait theories already embody the same complexity that Mischel touts as an exclusive virtue of his cognitive theory.

In my own view, Mischel would have been better off if he had not gone out of his way to place his theory in opposition to trait psychology, for his ideas do have much to offer. Mischel's theory triggered a large amount of research and theorizing to integrate the study of personality with cognitive psychology. Furthermore, although trait theories often include descriptions of psychological processes, Mischel's theory puts such processes at the center of the picture. His approach thereby changes somewhat the basic question for personality psychology, from asking "what do you do in general," to Mischel's "what processes are determining what you are doing right now?" In that way, in the trenchant phrase of Mischel's student Nancy Cantor, personality moves from being something you *have*, to being something you *do* (Cantor, 1990).

SOCIAL INTELLIGENCE: CANTOR AND KIHLSTROM

Mischel's influence goes beyond his own cognitive social learning theory. One of the most promising of the recent cognitive approaches to personality is the work by Nancy Cantor and her colleague John Kihlstrom on "social intelligence" (Cantor & Kihlstrom, 1987). Their basic idea, highly similar to Mischel's, is that the personality trait terms so often used to describe people may not be well suited for describing the mental processes that are important in determining how people differ from one another. Cantor and Kihlstrom suggest that descriptive terms such as "dominant," "cheerful," or "shy" instead should be replaced by more process-oriented terms—terms that describe how people develop beliefs about the environment, expectations about their behaviors, and the strategies they pursue. Cantor and Kihlstrom's theory of social intelligence is based on three key terms of this sort: schemas, goals, and strategies.

Schemas

The first important term in the theory of social intelligence is the **schema**, which is a mental structure of knowledge. For example, everything you know about parties, or about introverts, or about sociology, forms a schema in your mind. Schemas function much like Kelly's personal constructs; they filter and color and to some extent direct the way we perceive reality (Cantor, 1990).

Cantor and Kihlstrom propose that your mind contains two importantly different kinds of schema. One kind is general schemas such as those just mentioned; these contain your overall knowledge of the world. In the general cognitive model presented earlier in this chapter, this kind of knowledge was described as conceptual memory in the declarative section of LTM.

A more specific kind of knowledge is the self schema, which is the mental structure of everything you know about yourself. The self schema is particularly important, Cantor and Kihlstrom claim, because it contains our ideas about what we are like and what we are capable of doing (Markus & Nurius, 1986). These ideas, in turn, affect our behavior. If we think we are sociable we are more likely to seek out other people. If we think we are academically capable, we are more likely to go to college.

In another example, Cantor points out that the person with a "self-as-shy" schema has an elaborate structure of knowledge about how he or she has behaved in awkward ways in social situations in the past, and is always ready to interpret his or her new social experiences in the light of this special self-knowledge. In a sense, the shy person is an "expert" about shyness. Work elsewhere in cognitive psychology has shown that experts in any domain—chess or mechanical engineering, for example—can quickly remember relevant information in their domain of expertise, tend to see the world in terms dictated by their expertise, and have a ready and almost automatic plan of action that can be invoked in relevant situations (Chase & Simon, 1973; Larkin, McDermott, Simon, & Simon, 1980). This kind of expertise can have some obvious advantages—it can help one to be a better chess player or engineer—but can also cause one to limit one's view of the world, to view things too rigidly, and to fail to test possibilities beyond the limits of one's expertise. A person who is an "expert" about his or her shyness is probably over-ready to see his or her social experiences as organized around his or her social deficiencies.

How then does a person ever change? One possibility, by using one's imagination, is to conjure up other "possible selves," to visualize the other, perhaps better persons one could be (Markus & Nurius, 1986). This possible other self can then serve as a goal that directs your behavior. A less-pleasant way to change is to experience a serious and upsetting trauma, such as a serious illness or rape

(Janoff-Bulman, 1989). This kind of experience can cause a person to doubt things about the world that were previously taken for granted, and can lead to drastic changes in one's self-view. These changes are not necessarily positive.

Goals

The second cognitive term Cantor and Kihlstrom use is **goal**. A goal, in their technical usage of this everyday word, is your mental representation (thought) about something you want. It might be a specific project: I want to finish this paper by Thursday; I want to mow the lawn. Or, it can be more general: I want to save the environment; I want to contribute to world peace; I want to be a better person; I want to change Western civilization (Little, 1989).

Goals often can be arranged hierarchically. You might have the goal of impressing your neighbors. Toward that goal, you want to have a beautiful yard. Toward *that* goal, you mow your lawn today. Or, perhaps you want to be financially secure. Toward that goal, you must graduate from college. Toward that goal, you must pass this course. Toward that goal, you must finish reading this book.

Keeping your eye on a long-term goal can help you choose wisely and organize short-term goals. You have probably heard the old story about the two medieval workers who were asked what they were doing. One said, "I'm laying down these here bricks." Another said, "I am building a cathedral." (Of course, they were actually doing exactly the same thing.) When one's goal structures are well organized, life can be lived fairly smoothly and with clear purpose. If you know what your general goals are, then everything you do on a daily basis can be organized to help reach these goals.

Many people are not so fortunate, however. When a person has few or no general goals, or spends time in activities that do *not* serve the general goals one has, then life is chaotic and disorganized, and nothing that really matters seems to get done. Moreover, if you lack general goals or any clear connection between your daily activities and your general goals, your general motivation may suffer. Indeed, you may become depressed.

But the relationship between general and specific goals must not be too one-sided. The potential disadvantage of a general, cathedral-type goal is that if you focus *too* much on the cathedral (which after all may not be finished for another hundred years), you may forget or lose your motivation to lay the few bricks you can today. And you might become too inflexible to accomplish important short-term goals that do not serve the long-term goal. If your attention is rigidly focused on building the cathedral, you might not be able to find the time or energy to fix the leaky roof on your hut. If your general goal is to promote world peace, you might forget to be kind to your friends. So, an ability to shift flexibly between long-term and short-term goals is a useful skill (Vallacher & Wegner, 1987).

While discussing psychoanalysis, we saw that psychological conflict and problems of performance can arise when one's goals are not mutually compatible (see Chapters 10–13). This idea also appeared prominently in Dollard and Miller's social learning theory (Chapter 17). The same lesson can be derived from Cantor and Kihlstrom's cognitive theory. First, be clear about what you want. Then your behaviors are likely to be effective. But if you are not clear about what you want, your behaviors are likely to become inefficient, unproductive, and perhaps mutually defeating.

Strategies

The third part of Cantor and Kihlstrom's cognitive triad is the **strategy**. A strategy is a plan for connecting actions to goals. In Cantor's words, "strategies form a core of highly practiced procedural knowledge about *how* to react when certain life conditions are met." (Recall that procedural knowledge was located in LTM in the cognitive model presented earlier in this chapter.)

Different people use different strategies, sometimes for the same ends. This is an important point, because it stands in contrast to trait approaches, which seem to assume, for example, that everybody who acts in an extraverted fashion is basically the same. The more explicitly process-oriented cognitive approaches emphasize that different people may reach the same behavioral ends through drastically different cognitive routes.

For example, Cantor's student Julie Norem has found that some college students deal with anxiety about exams by optimistically expecting to do their best (Norem, 1989). Others deal with anxiety by expecting the worst, so they can be pleasantly surprised when the worst does not happen (Norem calls these latter students "defensive pessimists"). Norem's interesting finding is that both groups of students seem to succeed about equally well in coping with anxiety and with exam performance (although, admittedly, the optimists seem to enjoy life more). The two kinds of strategists have simply chosen different routes to that common goal.

Several years ago, a friend of mine was waiting anxiously for his wife to have a baby. The pregnancy had been difficult and the delivery was expected to be complicated. Many people would deal with the potential anxiety from this situation by hoping for the best, convincing oneself that the mother was a strong person who would do fine, that the doctors can take care of everything, and so on. My friend did just the reverse. An extremely defensive pessimist, he expected nothing but the worst from the very beginning. The night before the baby was born, he cornered the pediatrician and asked, "What is the worst outcome that can possibly happen tomorrow?" Understandably, the pediatrician was taken aback, but under continued prodding finally acknowledged that, well, the worst thing that could happen would be for the mother to die and for the baby to be born dead. My friend seemed strangely satisfied with this answer.

The next day, all did not go smoothly, but nor did the worst happen. My friend seemed to maintain his own equilibrium through his constant awareness that things could be worse. And when, in the end, mother and baby came through fine, he seemed to have gotten through the trauma not much worse for the wear.

Apparently, his insistence on imagining the worst was just an exaggerated version of the strategy pursued by Norem's defensive pessimists. He reduced the anxiety that might be produced by bad news by imagining, in advance, the very worst possible news. Then, even as unpleasant news arrived, he could always compare it against this worst-case scenario and feel relieved.

A Cognitive Approach to Motivation: Dweck

Motivation concerns what you want and why you want it. In the terminology we have been using in this chapter, this motivational issue naturally ties into the notion of goals. To understand the goals a person is pursuing is to understand much of what drives and organizes his or her behavior.

Performance and Learning Goals

The most prominent cognitive theory of motivation, at present, is that of Carol Dweck (Dweck & Leggett, 1988). Dweck theorizes that all the goals that a person might pursue fall into two basic types: performance goals and learning goals. A **performance goal** is one in which the individual is concerned with gaining favorable judgments of his or her competence. For example, a student might want to do well on a term paper in order to get a high grade and prove to herself and to others that she is a smart, capable person. A **learning goal** is one in which the individual is more concerned with increasing his or her competence. Rather than being focused on the grade, the student might care more about the specific feedback and suggestions she gets on her term paper, in order to be able to do better next time.

These two goals are importantly different because they produce different reactions to failure (and everybody fails sometimes). A person with a learning goal will respond to failure with what Dweck calls a "mastery-oriented" pattern of behavior, in which he or she tries even harder the next time. The student might get a poor grade on her paper, but be eager to take what she has learned from the experience to do a better job on her next paper. In contrast, a person with a performance goal is vulnerable to respond to failure with what Dweck calls the "helpless pattern": Rather than try harder in response to failure, this individual simply concludes "I can't do it," and gives up. Of course, this kind of response only guarantees future failure.

As a college professor, I see both patterns all the time, but the latter is especially poignant. In casual conversation, I have sometimes referred to the latter pattern as "the famous disappearing student trick." A student performs poorly on an exam early in the course. The logical thing to do is to try harder next time. But all too many students do the reverse, and simply disappear. It is remarkable how many students who do poorly on the midterm exam stop coming to class, and apparently also stop doing the course readings, and are not seen again until the day of the final exam. Unsurprisingly, they do even worse on the final.

Entity and Incremental Theories

Where do these dramatic differences in behavior come from? Dweck believes they originate in fundamentally different implicit theories—personal constructs, if you will—about the nature of the world. Some people hold what Dweck calls **entity theories**, and believe that personal qualities such as intelligence and ability are fixed and unchangeable. This belief makes such people anxious to prove that they are intelligent and able, and thus drives them to have performance goals. But failure makes these individuals conclude they just do not have what it takes, so they give up.

Other people hold what Dweck calls **incremental theories**, and believe that intelligence and ability can change over time and with experience. Their goal, therefore, is not to prove their competence, but to increase it. They accept failure as a learning experience, and are motivated to try even harder next time, taking advantage of their new knowledge. One young boy in Dweck's research, following a failure to solve an experimental puzzle, "pulled up his chair, rubbed his hands together, smacked his lips, and exclaimed, 'I love a challenge!' " (Dweck & Leggett, 1988, p. 258).

Research and Measurement

Nearly all of the research on Dweck's theory has occurred in academic contexts, or simulations of such contexts. For example, the responses of children to their failure to solve word puzzles have been repeatedly examined. Dweck and her students have consistently found that children who are incremental theorists, as described above, do better in the face of failure than do entity theorists (e.g., Diener & Dweck, 1978; Goetz & Dweck, 1980).

How are these young "theorists" identified? In the time-honored method of trait psychology, identification is accomplished using a self-report questionnaire (S data, in the terminology introduced in Chapter 2). For example, subjects have been asked to choose between options such as:

1. Smartness is something you can increase as much as you want to, or
2. You can learn new things, but how smart you are stays pretty much the same.

If you choose the first option you are an incremental theorist; if you choose the second you are an entity theorist (Dweck & Leggett, 1988, p. 263).

Another method is to give subjects a questionnaire that describes a series of hypothetical social situations, all of which involve rejection. For example, a subject might be asked, "Suppose you move to a new neighborhood. A person you meet does not like you very much. Why would this happen to you?" If the subject responds that the likely reason is that he or she is socially incompetent, then the subject is assumed to be an entity theorist (Goetz & Dweck, 1980).

Entity and Incremental Theories Reconsidered

The core of Dweck's theory is expressed in the following statement:

For any personal attribute that the individual values, viewing it as a fixed trait will lead to a desire to document the adequacy of that trait, whereas viewing it as a malleable quality will foster a desire to develop that quality (Dweck & Leggett, 1988, p. 266).

This entity or incremental orientation, in turn, will lead to bad or good responses to failure, respectively. But let us conclude by probing some apparent weak spots in this theory.

First, is being an incremental theorist always better than being an entity theorist? This is certainly what Dweck implies, but her empirical research has focused nearly exclusively on responses to failure. What about responses to success? Dweck's formulation would seem to predict that for an incremental theorist the result of success—from which one learns nothing except that one is good at the task—should be *decreased* motivation, whereas entity theorists should be newly infused with energy and enthusiasm to document their ability even further. Here, then, being an entity theorist would seem to produce a more positive result.

Even in the case of failure, being an entity theorist may not always cause problems. I think I am an entity theorist myself (maybe that is why I am defensive on this point) and so can report some self-observation. An important part of my job involves applying for federal research grants. These are extremely difficult to get, and many failures are interspersed with a few successes. Yet I think it is my entity-oriented belief in my own ability that causes me to press on, and to believe that eventually I will be successful. My introspection tells me that what I expect to change is not me (as I am an entity theorist), but my product. I am as smart (or as dumb) as I will ever be. But I do believe that if I pay attention to the feedback I receive, my next grant proposal will be better.

This is an incremental theory, to be sure, but of a different sort than described by Dweck.

A final observation about Dweck's theory is that it contains a significant irony, maybe even a self-contradiction. Her theory about entity vs. incremental theorists is itself an entity theory; that is, a person is either an entity or an incremental theorist, period. Which one you are can be measured by a questionnaire of the standard trait-assessment variety, and very little is said about how you got to be one of these theorists in the first place, or how you could ever change.

THE COGNITIVE APPROACH AND ITS INTERSECTIONS

The cognitive approach to personality was considered here, near the end of this book, for several reasons.

The first reason is that the cognitive approach to personality is the newest one. It generates much if not most of the empirical research currently being done on personality. Together, the trait and cognitive approaches account for nearly all modern personality studies. Much, much less research is currently being performed within the psychoanalytic, humanistic, or behaviorist approaches, for example (this fact does not make these latter approaches wrong or irrelevant, of course).

A more important reason to present the cognitive approach last is that, perhaps because it is the most recently developed one, it makes the most reference to all of the other approaches. As we have seen, the cognitive approach to personality intersects at various points with the trait, behaviorist, social learning, and even psychodynamic and phenomenological approaches. (It probably has the least contact with biological approaches but that, too, will eventually come.) As a result, it would be difficult to understand the cognitive approach without having studied these others first.

Moreover, this consideration of the cognitive approach has brought us nearly full circle. Recall that the first basic approach to personality presented in this book was the trait approach. Here in the last section of the book, we have seen Mischel's persistent devaluation of personality traits, Cantor's formulation that personality is something we do rather than have, and Dweck's unflattering portrayal of a lay entity approach that looks very much like trait theory.

Despite all this, I really believe that the cognitive approach and the modern trait approach to personality are not only valuable, but more similar than they are different. Both are continuing to generate a large amount of empirical research that documents the complex nature of individual differences in behavior. Both try to outline the psychological processes that produce those differences.

And both are trying to come to terms with the origin of these differences, in genetics and in experience. So in that way, this book ends in a place not so different from where it began.

SUMMARY

The cognitive approach consists of various attempts to combine recent developments in cognitive psychology with the concerns of personality psychology. Modern cognitive psychology describes the mind as a system for organizing and storing information—memory, in short. A general model of this system was described, in which information passes through the sensory/perceptual buffer into short-term memory, working memory, and long-term memory. Long-term memory includes both declarative and procedural knowledge. Several important modern theorists are extending the terminology and ideas in this model into the domain of personality. Mischel's cognitive social learning theory, and its recent amendment, describes five cognitive person variables and describes the individual differences produced by these variables as patterns of behaviors that vary across situations. Cantor and Kihlstrom describe personality as social intelligence, which comprises everything you know about the world and your skills for using that knowledge. In the terms of social intelligence theory, schemas are mental structures that hold factual knowledge, goals are desired ends that organize and motivate behavior, and strategies are characteristic means of attaining goals. The same goal can be approached through different strategies. Dweck's cognitive approach to motivation distinguishes between two kinds of individual. Entity theorists believe personality attributes and abilities are fixed, desire to prove their competence, and respond to failure with helplessness. Incremental theorists believe attributes and abilities can be changed, desire to improve, and respond to failure with even greater effort. In the final analysis, the cognitive approach is more similar to than different from the trait approach. Even though they use somewhat different terminology, both approaches try to describe patterns of individual differences in behavior and the psychological processes behind them.

SUGGESTED READINGS:
BEHAVIOR AND THOUGHT

Skinner, B. F. (1966). *The behavior of organisms: An experimental analysis.* New York: Appleton-Century-Crofts (originally published 1938).

> *Nearly every college or university library has a copy of this book (either the original or reprinted edition), and it is worth seeking. It is the original and still the best comprehensive survey of the thinking of this pre-eminent behaviorist and major intellectual figure of the century.*

Skinner, B. F. (1948). *Walden Two.* New York: Macmillan.

> *Not many research psychologists write novels. But Skinner did. It describes how the "perfect" society looks from a behaviorist point of view. Some find Walden Two a scary place. You decide.*

Bandura, A. (1978). The self system in reciprocal determinism. *American Psychologist, 33,* 344–358.

> *This article is a relatively user-friendly presentation of Bandura's notion of self-control. It tries to explain how the notion of self-control can be integrated with a basically behavioristic point of view.*

Mischel, W., & Shoda, Y. (1995). A cognitive-affective system theory of personality: Reconceptualizing situations, dispositions, dynamics, and invariance in personality structure. *Psychological Review, 102,* 246–268.

> *This is a fairly difficult article. Still, it is the latest statement by the originator of the cognitive approach to personality, and along with presenting the latest version of Mischel's theory it manages to provide a good survey of most of the other modern cognitive approaches.*

Cantor, N., & Kihlstrom, J. F. (1987). *Personality and social intelligence.* Englewood Cliffs, NJ: Prentice-Hall.

> *This book is fairly difficult to read, but if you want to thoroughly understand what Cantor means when she says personality is something you "do," not something you "have," you need to read it.*

CHAPTER

LOOKING BACK AND LOOKING AHEAD

This book began with the observation that personality is the study of the whole person. Personality is where all the other strands of psychology come—or should come—together in a view of how real individuals function in their social and physical worlds. A problem with this goal was identified immediately, however: It is overwhelming. In fact, it is impossible. You cannot really look at everything all at once; you must limit yourself to a certain perspective and to certain questions and variables that seem most important. The only alternative to such self-limitation, probably, is hopeless confusion.

The rest of the book has tried to translate this advice into action. It laid out five basic approaches, which are also sometimes called "paradigms," through which personality psychologists have tried to view the whole person.

THE DIFFERENT APPROACHES

Each basic approach, we saw, conceptualizes individuals and their psychological life by focusing on a limited number of key concerns *and*, just as importantly, by ignoring pretty much everything else. The trait approach focused upon individual differences, the personality traits that make people psychologically different from one another and that make every individual unique. The biological approach concentrated on the architecture and function of the nervous system and on the inheritance and evolutionary history of behavioral patterns. The psychoanalytic approach focused upon the unconscious mind and the complicated ways in which motivations and conflicts of which we are not even aware might affect what we think, feel, and do. The humanistic approach focused upon the moment-to-moment conscious experience of being alive, and how the fact that we experience life one moment at a time might give us free will and the ability to choose how we see reality. The behavioristic approach focused on how rewards and punishments in the environment shape behavior, and its social learning variant added an emphasis on how we learn from observing others and how our actions are shaped by the way we evaluate ourselves. The cognitive variant focused upon processes of thinking, memory, and construal and how they mediate the way environment shapes behavior.

Which One Is Right?

Anybody with the experience of teaching a course in personality psychology, after a semester of presenting these approaches in sequence, has had a bright but confused student approach and ask, "yes, but which one is *right*?" By now, you probably can predict that professors flounder around when they try to answer this question, because the question is not really answerable. To be able to say which one is "right," the different approaches of personality psychology would have to be different answers to the same question. But they are not. Rather, *they are different questions.* Each lives or dies not by being right or wrong, because in the end, all theories are wrong, but rather by being useful in accounting for a delimited area of known facts, for having application in the real world, and for clarifying important facets of human nature.

Thus we cannot choose between the different approaches to personality on the grounds of which one is right. A better criterion for evaluating a psychological approach is this: Does it offer us a way to seek an answer to a question we feel is worth asking? The trait approach asks about individual differences; the psychoanalytic approach asks about the unconscious; the biological approach asks about physical mechanisms; the humanistic approach asks about consciousness, free will, and individual construals of reality; and the behavioristic approaches ask about behavioral acquisition and change. Which do you need or want to know about?

The Order of Approaches

One interesting decision that any author of a book like this gets to make—amid much conflicting advice—is the order in which to present the chapters. This might seem like a trivial decision, but it can reveal much about the author's view of the field of personality.

One surprisingly common method is to begin with the author's least favorite approach, and end by describing the author's most favorite approach. But such books leave the impression that the whole world was just marking time until the right approach came along. At the end, the author can triumphantly announce, At last, the truth was discovered!

I have already explained why I am not a fan of such invidious comparisons.

Portraying one approach as right and the others as wrong misses the whole point of why different approaches continue to exist. So it should not be surprising that I did not choose this strategy of chapter arrangement.

A second common strategy is more even-handed. The author arranges the chapters in more or less chronological order. I say "more or less" because it is not an easy matter to settle which are the older and newer approaches. The philosophical tradition behind behaviorism is extremely old, but the research is comparatively new; the reverse could be said about psychoanalysis. One problem with this strategy is that a strict chronological ordering (assuming one can be settled upon) is not necessarily intellectually coherent. Another problem is that such a book tends also to acquire a "psychology marches on" flavor that I think is somewhat misleading.

The final strategy I will mention—and not coincidentally the one I chose—is to arrange the approaches in the order in which they are most teachable. It is sometimes claimed that, unlike other sciences, psychology is not cumulative; its findings do not build in an orderly manner, one upon the other, as they do in physics, for example.[1] But psychology is cumulative in another way. The approaches branch off from, react to, and interact with each other in such a way that does suggest an order in which to present them.

So this book began with a review of the data and research methods of personality psychology. This laid a base for everything that followed. Then, the trait approach was presented first, because it raises a basic issue (does personality exist?) that seems to come before all others, and because its focus on how people differ can be presented without much reference to the other approaches. The biological approaches considered next are direct outgrowths of the trait approach; they examine how neurostructure, biochemicals, genes, or evolutionary histories produce the broad patterns of behavior called personality traits.

By then, a close reader could begin to suspect that these trait and biological approaches neglect some of the more mysterious aspects of the mind, such as the workings of the unconscious (recall that this was Henry Murray's complaint about the trait approach). So the psychoanalytic approach was presented next. The psychoanalytic view of behavior as driven by irrational and even mysterious impulses is countered in an interesting way by the humanistic approach, which was considered in the following section. The humanists believe we can (even must) choose our construals of reality. We also saw that some cross-cultural psychologists believe that members of different cultures construe reality so differently that they cannot really be compared with each other (we also saw some reasons to doubt this belief).

---

[1] I believe this claim simultaneously underestimates the cumulativeness of psychology and overestimates the cumulativeness of physics, but that is another story.

The final set of chapters presented approaches that are all basically behaviorist. First we considered classical behaviorism, then looked at the social learning theories that grew directly out of behaviorism. Finally we considered the modern cognitive approaches, which are an outgrowth of behaviorism themselves (via social learning theory), but which also are influenced in an interesting way by trait, psychoanalytic, and even humanistic perspectives. I presented the cognitive approach last because, as I mentioned in Chapter 18, to appreciate it fully I think you need some familiarity with all these other approaches. I also think that considering the cognitive approach last brings us full circle, because it has so much in common with the trait approach.

Conclusions

Having now completed our survey of the five basic approaches to personality, it is time to draw some conclusions.

No Single Perspective Accounts for Everything

I have been saying this all along, and by now I hope you know what I mean. Einstein's theory of relativity has managed to unify physics. Darwin's theory of evolution has managed to unify biology. But psychology has no Darwin or Einstein. The nearest contender is probably Freud, but you have already seen the problems there. As broad as Freud's theory is, it still does not address the key concerns of the other approaches, such as conscious experience, free will, individual differences, or learning from experience.

This lack of a single unifying perspective for psychology is often lamented, and is an important source of the "physics envy" so often suffered by psychologists. So let me rock the boat a little: I think it's a good thing. I say this for two reasons.

The first reason is that any approach that tried to account for *all* the key concerns of what are now five basic approaches would almost inevitably be unwieldy, confusing, and incoherent. The limitations that each basic approach imposes on observation and theorizing is not a *fault*; it is their very *purpose*. The purpose of the self-limitation of each basic approach is to avoid being overwhelmed and confused. The prospect of some new approach that combined all these disparate concerns is, to me, not particularly attractive. As I have reiterated several times, the five basic approaches are in an important sense five different topics.

The second reason is that the existence of alternative basic viewpoints can keep us open-minded toward phenomena that any one of them may fail to account for. Intellectual competition is good. It can prevent dogmatism and closed minds. No matter how emphatically a Freudian or a behaviorist believes that his or her approach accounts for everything, he or she also knows that a substantial number of psychologists believe him or her to be dead wrong. I think that kind of knowledge is good for any person.

I even fantasize, sometimes, that biology and physics might be better off if they had not settled so firmly on a single, unifying approach. What phenomena are being missed because they do not happen to fit relativity or evolutionary theory? Biologists and physicists might never find out what their theories and methods neglect because, as we have seen in this book, adherence to one basic approach tends to blind you to many things that are perfectly obvious from other perspectives. I enjoy personality psychology's lack of a single, basic, unifying approach. This lack leaves a lot of room for free thought and theorizing. Other sciences have always seemed a bit too closed for my taste. If you feel the same way, you might enjoy being a personality psychologist, too.

You Probably Must Choose

There is a natural temptation, faced with all these of approaches, each with strengths and weaknesses, to want to blend them. Maybe we could take the good parts of each, remove the bad parts of each, and create some sort of powerful hybrid theory. Dollard and Miller tried that, you will recall, when they thought that some key aspects of the psychodynamic approach could be combined with learning theory.

I have already described several reasons why I do not hope for a single, unifying theory in personality psychology. There is another factor that I have not yet mentioned: Theoretical blends have an unfortunate tendency to remove exactly what is most fascinating and compelling about each of the theories being combined, yielding a stew that is often tasteless and bland. Dollard and Miller were brilliant psychologists, but their blend of psychoanalysis and behaviorism lacks both the deep insight of psychoanalytic case study *and* the crisp, clean logic of classical behaviorism. The result, in my opinion, is an unsatisfying muddle. I would rather read about psychoanalysis *or* behaviorism, depending upon my interests and purposes that day, than about a semi-successful attempt to blend the two.

So in the end, you probably must choose (McAdams, 1990). If you are to become a personality psychologist or even to devote some serious thought to the topic, you must choose which lens you want to look through—the trait, biological, psychoanalytic, humanistic, or behaviorist approach.

I will repeat that this choice *cannot* be based upon which one is right or wrong, because all of them are both right and wrong. Rather, the choice should be made on the basis of two (perhaps three) criteria. The first is, What do you want to understand—free will, individual differences, the unconscious mind, or the shaping of behavior? The second is even more personal: Which approach is the most interesting to you? If one of them really turns you on, maybe you *should* become a personality psychologist. And if you do become a personality psychologist, then a third criterion comes into play: Which basic approach seems to offer the best potential to do interesting work that can add to knowledge?

My own choice has been the trait approach, mostly on the basis of this third criterion. Much though I admire psychoanalysis, for example, and even find it useful in my own daily life, I find it hard to imagine what kind of research can tell us more about it, and the case study method is, to me, unsatisfying. The trait approach, by contrast, has managed to keep me busy in a research career for the past dozen years and will continue, I hope, for many years to come.

Nevertheless, I try to take a vacation from my favored approach now and then. One occasion for such a trip is when I teach a personality course, or when I was writing this book. I get the opportunity, for a time, to look once more at the psychological world through several different sets of unaccustomed lenses. I think about questions I usually ignore—like what is free will?—and entertain alternative visions of reality. I think this variation is good for me, and it is also fun.

No matter which basic approach one chooses, there are four reasons why one should always maintain an awareness and knowledge of the alternatives. The first is simply to avoid arrogance and to prevent starting to think that you know it all. The second is to understand the proper basis for evaluating alternative approaches. Remember that each of the basic approaches to personality, brilliant though it is, tends to look irrelevant and even foolish from the point of view of the other approaches. The third reason is to have a way of dealing with those psychological phenomena you will run across, from time to time, that do not fit into your favorite approach. I once heard the psychologist E. R. Hilgard say that we must not be in the position of the entomologist who found a bug he could not classify, so he stepped on it. The fourth reason is to give yourself the chance to change your mind later. If your interests change, if your goals change, or if the phenomena you encounter keep refusing to fit your favorite approach, you will have some place to go.

THE FUTURE OF PERSONALITY PSYCHOLOGY

No book on personality psychology is complete without some predictions of the future. So here are several of mine.

Further Development
of the Cognitive Approach

Cognitive psychology is one of the more successful branches of psychology, and despite the work surveyed in Chapter 18, a great deal more remains to be done to integrate it in a convincing way into the realm of personality. Chapter 18 described some ways in which a general model of the cognitive system can be used to illuminate aspects of personality functioning. It also surveyed modern research that uses higher-order cognitive concepts such as schemas, strategies, and goals to explain why people act the way they do. I think the future of the cognitive approach to personality lies in further demonstration and explanation of how the basic mechanisms of perception and memory interact with these more general mechanisms to affect how we behave with one another.

A further promising lead in the cognitive domain concerns the computer simulation of personality. In cognitive psychology it is now becoming routine to test theories of how people perceive or process information by translating the theory into a computer program, and then seeing if the program works. The same thing has been tried, but only in a very crude fashion, with personality processes, and not enough progress has yet been made to merit a mention in Chapter 18. I think the more distant future of personality psychology will yield computer simulations of how, for example, an extravert perceives the world, that will lead to explicit predictions of how an extravert will behave under various circumstances. This work will help enormously toward our understanding of when and how personality dispositions affect behavior.

Renewed Attention to Emotion
and Experience

Cognitive research can be expected eventually to make a great deal of progress in explaining the ways in which the human mind operates like a computer. That work will be useful, but in the end we will have to face the fact that people are not computers. They are something else altogether. Indeed, as cognitive models and even computer simulations of personality become more sophisticated, their shortcomings will become increasingly obvious.

People are different from computers in two fundamental ways. People are aware, computers are not. And people experience emotions, computers do not.

As in the future this pair of realizations begins to sink in, the long-neglected humanistic/phenomenological approaches to personality may enjoy a surprising resurgence. We will need to address anew questions such as what is awareness and what does it mean, exactly, to experience an emotion? We may also see a return to animal research. Before there were computers, psychologists in search of simple systems they could use to establish general laws studied rats and pigeons. But computers are easier to use, they do not bite or have to be fed, and nobody from the "computer rights league" will ever picket psychology laboratories. Still, as we return to the realization that people are in the end animals, not computers, animal research may become popular again.

Biology

Another beneficiary of the eventual realization that people are animals and not computers will be the biological approaches to personality. Computers are electrical devices, and computer programs are not even specific to particular devices. People, however, are biological organisms. This must be an important fact for understanding personality, but so far its potential has just begun to be explored (as we saw in Chapters 8 and 9).

One aspect of biology that has received much increased attention from personality psychologists in recent years is behavioral genetics. This rapidly developing field shows that personality traits are to some extent affected by heredity. However, it seems to me that the vague insight that "genes are somewhat important" is, at present, all that the study of quantitative behavioral genetics can contribute. Similarly, evolutionary biology offers plausible stories of the origin of some human behavioral patterns, but almost nothing is known about how such patterns could be genetically transmitted or influenced by the anatomy and physiology of the nervous system. What is needed from a biological approach to personality is a better understanding of how genetics and evolutionary development work through basic biological *processes,* such as physiological arousal, metabolism, and development, and interact with experience to determine personality. At present very little is known about such matters, except that they must be relevant. Someday—perhaps not soon—personality psychology will make important progress in this area.

Cross-Cultural Psychology

The past few years have seen an increasing interest in the question of which psychological phenomena are found in all cultures, in some cultures, or just in Western culture. For example, as we saw in Chapter 15, some writers have even proposed that the very idea of personality itself is a Western, "individualistic" idea not held in any remotely comparable way among members of Eastern, "collectivist" cultures. (A book like the one you are holding in your hands presumably could not exist—or at least would not mean anything—in those cultures, according to this point of view.)

Cross-cultural concerns are and will remain important, because people do vary importantly around the world; a "one-size-fits-all" psychology is probably no better for cultures than it is for individuals. Still, I think the more radical versions of cross-cultural psychology, the ones that doubt the very meaning or existence of personality, for instance, contain within them the seeds of their own eventual downfall.

One of those seeds is a tendency they sometimes show to romanticize non-Western cultural views. In Chapter 15 we saw how "collectivist" and "individualistic" orientations are often compared. The Western, individualistic view of personality is presented as something that artificially isolates humans from each other and prevents them from working together for the common good. But Eastern collectivism has its drawbacks, too. Collectivist views of the world regard group norms as more important than individual choices. The freedom to choose one's own destiny—or even one's own spouse—is not generally well appreciated. And I could go on. The moment one starts romanticizing the alternative views of other cultures, one will find that every such comparison is a two-edged sword.

A second seed of the downfall of the more extreme forms of cross-cultural psychology is that they seem to deny the possibility of real comparison or analysis of different cultures. If any view of any other culture is always to be hopelessly colored by our own background in our own culture, then what is the point of trying to do cross-cultural psychology at all? I have not seen a good answer to this question.

The future of cross-cultural psychology, my wager is, is in work like that of Harry Triandis, discussed in Chapter 15. The ultimate challenge for a cross-cultural psychology is *not*, as some would have it, to see each solely "in its own terms"—that is not a useful mission, and may not even be possible. The challenge is to come up with a set of constructs that are general enough and penetrating enough for us to compare one culture's psychology in a meaningful way with the psychology of another.

Integration of Personality, Social, and Cognitive Psychology

An area in which progress can be expected more immediately is in our understanding of how accurately people judge each others' personalities. It is obvious that we all make exceedingly complex inferences about each other every day, all the time. We infer the presence of complicated traits on the basis of complex patterns of behavior viewed bits at a time across time and diverse situations. How do we do it? The answer is still surprisingly poorly understood.

Yet the answer is highly relevant to social psychology and its concern with social relationships, to cognitive psychology and its concern with how people process information, and to personality psychology and its concern with the connection between personality dispositions and social behavior. I believe that examining how accurate perceptions of personality can be arrived at by everyday observers leads directly to the two, interrelated questions that lie near the heart of personality psychology:

1. What does behavior reveal about personality?
2. How does personality affect behavior?

THE QUEST FOR UNDERSTANDING

Remember L, I, S and T data (Chapter 2)? To learn about a person you have no alternative but to watch what he or she does and listen to what he or she says. These are behaviors, and in the end must be the basis of what you conclude about personality, whether your approach be trait, biological, psychoanalytic, behaviorist, cognitive, or even humanistic. By the same token, if you think you understand an individual's personality, the only way to find out whether you are right or wrong is to try to use your understanding to explain (and sometimes to predict) what the person does or says. Again, this is true no matter which basic approach you follow.

Ultimately, our minds are forever sealed off from each other. We can only know each other from watching what we each do. From that observation, we can try to infer the nature of each others' personalities. And that inference, in turn, is the basis of how we try to understand each other. So personality psychology is, in the final analysis, a quest for mutual understanding.

SUMMARY

Each of the different approaches to personality psychology has aspects of the person it explains rather well, and other aspects it does not explain or ignores entirely. Thus, the choice between them depends not upon which one is right, but what one wishes to know. To make progress as a personality psychologist it is probably necessary to choose one of these approaches, but one should try to stay open to alternative approaches when necessary. The future of personality psychology may include further development of the cognitive approach, renewed attention to emotion and experience, progress in biology and better understanding of its limits, a reconceptualization of cross-cultural approaches, and an increased integration of personality, social, and cognitive psychology. In the end, personality psychology is an attempt to turn our observations of each other into mutual understanding.

REFERENCES

Adler, A. (1939). *Social interest.* New York: Putnam.

Adorno, T. W. (1950). Politics and economics in the interview material. In T. W. Adorno, E. Frenkel-Brunswik, D. Levinson, & N. Sanford (Eds.), *The authoritarian personality* (pp. 654–726). New York: Harper.

Adorno, T. W., Frenkel-Brunswik, E., Levinson, D., & Sanford, N. (1950). *The authoritarian personality.* New York: Harper.

Ahadi, S., & Diener, E. (1989). Multiple determinants and effect size. *Journal of Personality and Social Psychology, 56,* 398–406.

Ainsworth, M. D. S., Blehar, M. C., Waters, E., & Wall, S. (1978). *Patterns of attachment: Assessed in the strange situation and at home.* Hillsdale, NJ: Erlbaum.

Allport, G. W. (1937). *Personality: A psychological interpretation.* New York: Holt, Rinehart, & Winston.

Allport, G. W. (1958). What units shall we employ? In G. Lindzey (Ed.), *Assessment of human motives* (pp. 239–260). New York: Rinehart.

Allport, G. W. (1961). *Pattern and growth in personality.* New York: Holt, Rinehart, & Winston.

Allport, G. W., & Odbert, H. S. (1936). Trait-names: A psycho-lexical study. *Psychological Monographs: General and Applied, 47,* 171–220. (1, Whole No. 211).

Allport, G. W., & Vernon, P. E. (1933). *Studies in expressive movement.* New York: Macmillan.

Alper, J., Beckwith, J., & Miller, L. G. (1978). Sociobiology is a political issue. In A. L. Caplan (Ed.), *The sociobiology debate: Readings on ethical and scientific issues* (pp. 476–488). New York: Harper & Row.

Amabile, T. M., & Glazebrook, A. H. (1982). A negativity bias in interpersonal evaluation. *Journal of Experimental Social Psychology, 18,* 1–22.

Andersen, S. M. (1984). Self-knowledge and social inference: II. The diagnosticity of cognitive/affective and behavioral data. *Journal of Personality and Social Psychology, 46,* 294–307.

Andersen, S. M., & Baum, A. (1994). Transference in interpersonal relations: Inferences and affect based on significant-other representations. *Journal of Personality, 62,* 459–499.

Andersen, S. M., & Bem, S. L. (1981). Sex typing and androgyny in dyadic interaction:

Individual differences in responsiveness to physical attractiveness. *Journal of Personality and Social Psychology, 41,* 74–86.

Anderson, E. (1994). The code of the streets. *Atlantic Monthly, 273,* 80–94.

Aronson, E. (1972). *The social animal.* San Francisco: Freeman.

Arsenian, J., & Arsenian, J. M. (1948). Tough and easy cultures: A conceptual analysis. *Psychiatry, 11,* 377–385.

Associated Press (1994, May 5). African emigrants spread practice. Online: Prodigy service.

Azrin, N. H., & Holz, W. C. (1966). Punishment. In W. K. Honig (Ed.), *Operant behavior: Areas of research and application* (pp. 380–447). New York: Appleton-Century-Crofts.

Bachrach, H. M., Galatzer-Levy, R., Skolnikoff, A., & Waldron, S. (1991). On the efficacy of psychoanalysis. *Journal of the American Psychoanalytic Association, 39,* 871–916.

Bader, M. J. (1994). The tendency to neglect therapeutic aims in psychoanalysis. *Psychoanalytic Quarterly, 63,* 246–269.

Bailey, K. G. (1987). *Human paleopsychology applications to aggression.* Hillsdale, NJ: Erlbaum.

Bandura, A. (1971). *Social learning theory.* New York: General Learning Press.

Bandura, A. (1977). *Social learning theory.* Englewood Cliffs, NJ: Prentice-Hall.

Bandura, A. (1978). The self system in reciprocal determinism. *American Psychologist, 33,* 344–358.

Bandura, A. (1989). Human agency in social cognitive theory. *American Psychologist, 44,* 1175–1184.

Bandura, A., Ross, D., & Ross, S. A. (1963). Imitation of film-mediated aggressive models. *Journal of Abnornal and Social Psychology, 66,* 3–11.

Bargh, J. A., Lombardi, W. J., & Higgins, E. T. (1988). Automaticity of chronically accessible constructs in person x situation effects on person perception: It's just a matter of time. *Journal of Personality and Social Psychology, 55,* 599–605.

Barron, J. W., Eagle, M. N., & Wolitzky, D. L. (Eds.). *Interface of psychoanalysis and psychology.* Washington, DC: American Psychological Association.

Baumeister, R. F., & Tice, D. M. (1988). Metatraits. *Journal of Personality, 56,* 571–598.

Baumrind, D. (1971). Current patterns of parental authority. *Developmental Psychology, 4,* 1–103.

Baumrind, D. (1985). Research using intentional deception: Ethical issues revisited. *American Psychologist, 40,* 165–174.

Baumrind, D. (1989). Rearing competent children. In W. Damon (Ed.), *Child development today and tomorrow* (pp. 349–378). San Francisco: Jossey-Bass.

Baumrind, D. (1991). The influence of parenting style on adolescent competence and substance use. *Journal of Early Adolescence, 11,* 56–95.

Baumrind, D. (1993). The average expectable environment is not good enough: A response to Scarr. *Child Development, 64,* 1299–1317.

Bem, D. J. (1996). Exotic becomes erotic: A developmental theory of sexual orientation. *Psychological Review, 103* (forthcoming).

Bem, D. J., & Allen, A. (1974). On predicting some of the people some of the time: The search for cross-situational consistencies in behavior. *Psychological Review, 81,* 506–520.

Bem, D. J., & Funder, D. C. (1978). Predicting more of the people more of the time: Assessing the personality of situations. *Psychological Review, 85,* 485–501.

Bergeman, C. S., Chipuer, H. M., Plomin, R., Pedersen, N. L., McClearn, G. E., Nesselroade, J. R., Costa, P. T., Jr., & McCrae, R. R. (1993). Genetic and environmental effects on openness to experience, agreeableness, and conscientiousness: An adoption/twin study. *Journal of Personality, 61,* 159–179.

Berkowitz, L. (1962). *Aggression: A social psychological analysis.* New York: McGraw-Hill.

Berry, D. S., & Finch Wero, J. W. (1993). Accuracy in face perception: A view from ecological psychology. *Journal of Personality, 61,* 497–520.

Berry, D. S., & Pennebaker, J. W. (1993). Nonverbal and verbal emotional expression and health. *Psychotherapy and psychosomatics, 59,* 11–19.

Bettelheim, B. (1982). *Freud and man's soul.* New York: Vintage.

Bijnen, E. J., & Poortinga, Y. H. (1988). The questionable value of cross-cultural comparisons with the Eysenck Personality Questionnaire. *Journal of Cross-cultural Psychology, 19,* 193–202.

Bijnen, E. J., Van der Net, Z. J., & Poortinga, Y. H. (1986). On cross-cultural comparative studies with the Eysenck Personality Questionnaire. *Journal of Cross-cultural Psychology, 17,* 3–16.

Binswanger, L. (1958). The case of Ellen West. In R. May, E. Angel, & H. F. Ellenberger (Eds.), *Existence* (pp. 237–364). New York: Basic Books.

Binswanger, L. (1963). *Being-in-the-world: Selected papers of Ludwig Binswanger.* New York: Basic Books.

Block, J. (1977). Advancing the science of psychology: Paradigmatic shift or improving the quality of research? In D. Magnusson & N. S. Endler (Eds.), *Personality at the crossroads: Current issues in interactional psychology* (pp. 37–64). Hillsdale, NJ: Erlbaum.

Block, J. (1978). *The Q-sort method in personality assessment and psychiatric research.* Palo Alto, CA: Consulting Psychologists Press (originally published 1961).

Block, J. (1989). Critique of the act frequency approach to personality. *Journal of Personality and Social Psychology, 56,* 234–245.

Block, J. (1993). Studying personality the long way. In D. C. Funder, R. D. Parke, C. Tomlinson-Keasey, & K. Widaman (Eds.), *Studying lives through time: Personality and development* (pp. 9–41). Washington, DC: American Psychological Association.

Block, J. (1995). A contrarian view of the five-factor approach to personality description. *Psychological Bulletin, 117,* 187–215.

Block, J., Block, J. H., & Keyes, S. (1988). Longitudinally foretelling drug usage in adolescence: Early childhood personality and environmental precursors. *Child Development, 59,* 336–355.

Block, J., Block, J. H., Siegelman, E., & von der Lippe, A. (1971). Optimal psychological adjustment: Response to Miller's and Bronfenbrenner's discussions. *Journal of Consulting and Clinical Psychology, 36,* 325–328.

Block, J., Gjerde, P. F., & Block, J. H. (1991). Personality antecedents of depressive tendencies in 18-year-olds: A prospective study. *Journal of Personality and Social Psychology, 60,* 726–738.

Block, J. H. (1973). Conceptions of sex role: Some cross-cultural and longitudinal perspectives. *American Psychologist, 28,* 512–526.

Block, J. H., & Block, J. (1980). The role of ego-control and ego-resiliency in the organization of behavior. In W.A. Collins (Ed.), *Development of cognition, affect, and social relations: The Minnesota symposia on child psychology* (Vol. 13, pp. 40–101). Hillsdale, NJ: Erlbaum.

Bond, M. H. (1979). Dimensions of personality used in perceiving peers: Cross-cultural comparisons of Hong Kong, Japanese, American, and Filipino university students. *International Journal of Psychology, 14,* 47–56.

Bond, M. II., & Cheung, T. (1983). College students' spontaneous self-concept: The effect of culture among respondents in Hong Kong, Japan, and the United States. *Journal of Cross-cultural Psychology, 14,* 153–171.

Bond, M. H., Nakazato, H., & Shiraishi, D. (1975). Universality and distinctiveness in dimensions of Japanese person perception. *Journal of Cross-cultural Psychology, 6,* 346–357.

Borkenau, P., & Liebler, A. (1993). Consensus and self-other agreement for trait inferences from minimal information. *Journal of Personality, 61,* 477–496.

Boss, M. (1963). *Psychoanalysis and daseinsanalysis.* New York: Basic Books.

Bower, G. H., & Hilgard, E. R. (1981). *Theories of learning* (5th ed.). Englewood Cliffs, NJ: Prentice-Hall.

Bowers, K. S. (1973). Situationism in psychology: An analysis and critique. *Psychological Review, 80,* 307–336.

Bowlby, J. (1982). *Attachment and loss: Vol. I. Attachment* (2nd ed.). New York: Basic. (Original work published 1969).

Brandt, V. S. (1974). Skiing cross-culturally. *Current Anthropology, 15,* 64–66.

Brenner, C. (1974). *An elementary textbook of psychoanalysis.* Garden City, NY: Doubleday/Anchor.

Brenner, C. (1982). *The mind in conflict.* New York: International Universities Press.

Briggs, S. R. (1989). The optimal level of measurement for personality constructs. In D. Buss & N. Cantor (Eds.), *Personality psychology: Recent trends and emerging directions* (pp. 246–260). New York: Springer-Verlag.

Briggs, S. R., & Cheek, J. M. (1986). The role of factor analysis in the development and evaluation of personality scales. *Journal of Personality, 54,* 106–148.

Briggs, S. R., Cheek, J. M., & Buss, A. H. (1980). An analysis of the Self-Monitoring Scale. *Journal of Personality and Social Psychology, 38,* 679–686.

Broadbent, D. E. (1958). *Perception and communication.* London: Pergamon.

Brunswik, E. (1956). *Perception and the representative design of psychological experiments.* Berkeley: University of California Press.

Bullock, W. A., & Gilliland, K. (1993). Eysenck's arousal theory of introversion-extraversion: A converging measures investigation. *Journal of Personality and Social Psychology, 64,* 113–123.

Burnett, J. D. (1974). Parallel measurements and the Spearman-Brown formula. *Educational and Psychological Measurement, 34,* 785–788.

Burwen, L. S., & Campbell, D. T. (1957). The generality of attitudes toward authority and nonauthority figures. *Journal of Abnormal and Social Psychology, 54,* 24–31.

Buss, D. M. (1989). Sex differences in human mate preferences: Evolutionary hypotheses tested in 37 cultures. *Behavioral and Brain Sciences, 12,* 1–49.

Buss, D. M., & Barnes, M. F. (1986). Preferences in human mate selection. *Journal of Personality and Social Psychology, 50,* 559–570.

Buss, D. M., Larsen, R. J., Westen, D., & Semmelroth, J. (1992). Sex differences in jealousy: Evolution, physiology and psychology. *Psychological Science, 3,* 251–255.

Butler, J. M., & Haigh, G. V. (1954). Changes in the relation between self-concepts and ideal concepts consequent upon client-centered counseling. In C. R. Rogers & R. F. Dymond (Eds.), *Psychotherapy and personality change: Co-ordinated studies in the client-centered approach* (pp. 55–76). Chicago: University of Chicago Press.

Bykov, K. M. (1957). *The cerebral cortex and the internal organs* (W. H. Gantt, Trans.). New York: Chemical Publishing.

Campbell, A., Converse, P. E., Miller, W. E., & Stokes, D. E. (1960). *The American voter.* New York: Wiley.

Campos, J. J., Barrett, K., Lamb, M. E., Goldsmith, H. H., & Stenberg, C. (1983). Socioemotional development. In M. M. Haith & J. J. Campos (Eds.), *Handbook of child psychology: Vol. 2. Infancy and psychobiology* (pp. 783–916). New York: Wiley.

Cantor, N. (1990). From thought to behavior: "Having" and "doing" in the study of personality and cognition. *American Psychologist, 45,* 735–750.

Cantor, N., & Kihlstrom, J. F. (1987). *Personality and social intelligence.* Englewood Cliffs, NJ: Prentice-Hall.

Carver, C. S., & Scheier, M. F. (1992). *Perspectives on personality* (2nd ed.). Boston: Allyn & Bacon.

Cattell, R. B. (1952). *Factor analysis.* New York: Harper.

Cattell, R. B. (1957). *Personality and motivation structure and measurement.* New York: World Book.

Cattell, R. B. (1965). *The scientific analysis of personality.* Baltimore: Penguin.

Cattell, R. B., & Eber, H. W. (1961). *The Sixteen Personality Factor Questionnaire* (3rd ed.). Champaign, IL: Institute for Personality and Ability Testing.

Chaplin, W. F. (1991). The next generation of moderator research in personality psychology. *Journal of Personality, 59,* 143–178.

Chaplin, W. F., & Goldberg, L. R. (1985). A failure to replicate the Bem and Allen study of individual differences in cross-situational consistency. *Journal of Personality and Social Psychology, 47,* 1074–1090.

Chase, W. G., & Simon, H. A. (1973). The mind's eye in chess. In W. G. Chase (Ed.), *Visual information processing* (pp. 215–281). New York: Academic Press.

Cheek, J. M. (1990b). Shyness, self-esteem, and self-consciousness. In H. Leitenberg (Ed.), *Handbook of social and evaluation anxiety* (pp. 47–82). New York: Plenum.

Claridge, G. S., Canter, S., & Hume, W. I. (1973). *Personality differences and biological variations: A study of twins.* Oxford, England: Pergamon.

Clark, H. H., & Clark, E. V. (1977). *Psychology and language: An introduction to psycholinguistics.* New York: Harcourt Brace Jovanovich.

Clark, J. M., & Paivio, A. (1989). Observational and theoretical terms in psychology: A cognitive perspective on scientific language. *American Psychologist, 44,* 500–512.

Cohen, J. (1994). The earth is round ($p < .05$). *American Psychologist, 49,* 997–1003.

Colvin, C. R. (1993a). Childhood antecedents of young-adult judgability. *Journal of Personality, 61,* 611–635.

Colvin, C. R. (1993b). "Judgable" people: Personality, behavior, and competing explanations. *Journal of Personality and Social Psychology, 64,* 861–873.

Colvin, C. R., & Funder, D. C. (1991). Predicting personality and behavior: A boundary on the acquaintanceship effect. *Journal of Personality and Social Psychology, 60,* 884–894.

Cook, T. D., & Campbell, D. T. (Eds.). (1979). *The design and analysis of quasi-experiments for field settings.* Chicago: Rand-McNally.

Costa, P. T., Jr., & McCrae, R. R. (1985). *The NEO Personality Inventory Manual.* Odessa, FL: Psychological Assessment Resources.

Cousins, S. D. (1989). Culture and self-perception in Japan and the United States. *Journal of Personality and Social Psychology, 56,* 124–131.

Craik, F. I. M., & Tulving, E. (1975). Depth of processing and the retention of words in episodic memory. *Journal of Experimental Psychology: General, 104,* 268–294.

Craik, F. I. M., & Watkins, M. J. (1973). The role of rehearsal in short-term memory. *Journal of Verbal Learning and Verbal Behavior, 12,* 599–607.

Cronbach, L. J. (1955). Processes affecting scores on "understanding of others" and "assumed similarity." *Psychological Bulletin, 52,* 177–193.

Cronbach, L. J., Gleser, G. C., Nanda, H., & Rajaratnam, N. (1972). *The dependability of behavioral measurements: Theory of generalizability for scores and profiles.* New York: Wiley.

Cronbach, L. J., & Meehl, P. E. (1955). Construct validity in psychological tests. *Psychological Bulletin, 52,* 281–302.

Csikszentmihalyi, M., & Csikszentmihalyi, I. S. (Eds.). (1988). *Optimal experience: Psychological studies of flow in consciousness.* New York: Cambridge University Press.

Csikszentmihalyi, M., & Larson, R. (1992). Validity and reliabilty of the Experience Sampling Method. In M. V. deVries (Ed.), *The experience of psychopathology: Investigating mental disorders in their natural settings,* (pp. 43–57). Cambridge, England: Cambridge University Press.

Cutler, A. G. (Ed.). (1976). *Stedman's medical dictionary.* Baltimore: Williams & Wilkins.

Dabbs, J. M., Jr., & Morris, R. (1990). Testosterone, social class, and antisocial behavior in a sample of 4462 men. *Psychological Science, 1,* 209–211.

Dabbs, J. M., Jr., Ruback, R. B., Frady, R. L., Hopper, C. H., & Sgoritas, D. S. (1988). Saliva testosterone and criminal violence among women. *Personality and Individual Differences, 9,* 269–275.

Dahlstrom, W. G., & Welsh, G. S. (1960). *An MMPI handbook: A guide to use in clinical practice and research.* Minneapolis: University of Minnesota Press.

Darley, J. M., & Batson, C. D. (1967). "From Jerusalem to Jericho": A study of situational and dispositional variables in helping behavior. *Journal of Personality and Social Psychology, 27,* 100–108.

Darley, J. M., & Latane, B. (1968). Bystander intervention in emergencies: Diffusion of responsibility. *Journal of Personality and Social Psychology, 28,* 377–383.

Darwin, C. (1967). *On the origin of the species by means of natural selection, or the preservation of favoured races in the struggle for life.* New York: Modern Library. (Original work published 1859.)

Dawkins, R. (1976). *The selfish gene.* New York: Oxford University Press.

Dawson, J. L. M. (1974). Ecology, social pressures toward conformity, and left-handedness: A bio-social psychological approach. In J. L. M. Dawson & K. W. J. Lonner (Eds.), *Readings in cross-cultural psychology* (pp. 124–149). Hong Kong: University of Hong Kong Press.

Dennett, D. C. (1994). Real consciousness. In A. Revonsuo & M. Kamppinen (Eds.), *Consciousness in philosophy and cognitive neuroscience.* Hillsdale, NJ: Erlbaum.

Dennett, D. C., & Weiner, P. (1991). *Consciousness explained.* Boston: Little, Brown.

Diener, C. I., & Dweck, C. S. (1978). An analysis of learned helplessness: Continuous changes in performance, strategy and achievement cognitions following failure. *Journal of Personality and Social Psychology, 36,* 451–462.

Dillehay, R. C. (1978). Authoritarianism. In H. London & J. E. Exner (Eds.), *Dimensions of personality* (pp. 85–127). New York: Wiley.

Dollard, J., & Miller, N. E. (1950). *Personality and psychotherapy: An analysis in terms of learning, thinking, and culture.* New York: McGraw-Hill.

Dutton, D., & Aron, A. (1974). Some evidence for heightened sexual attraction under conditions of high anxiety. *Journal of Personality and Social Psychology, 30,* 510–517.

Dweck, C. S., & Leggett, E. L. (1988). A social-cognitive approach to personality and motivation. *Psychological Review, 95,* 256–273.

Dworkin, B. R. (1993). *Learning and physiological regulation.* Chicago: University of Chicago Press.

Ekman, P., & Davidson, R. J. (Eds.). (1994). *The nature of emotion: Fundamental questions.* New York: Oxford University Press.

Elder, G. (1974). *Children of the Great Depression*. Chicago: University of Chicago Press.

Elms, A. C., & Milgram, S. (1966). Personality characteristics associated with obedience and defiance toward authoritative command. *Journal of Experimental Research in Personality, 1,* 282–289.

Emmons, R. A., & King, L. A. (1988). Conflict among personal strivings: Immediate and long-term implications for psychological and physical well-being. *Journal of Personality and Social Psychology, 54,* 1040–1048.

Emmons, R. A., & McAdams, D. P. (1991). Personal strivings and motive dispositions: Exploring the links. *Personality and Social Psychology Bulletin, 6,* 648–654.

Epstein, S. (1979). The stability of behavior: I. On predicting most of the people much of the time. *Journal of Personality and Social Psychology, 37,* 1097–1126.

Epstein, S. (1980). The stability of behavior: II. Implications for psychological research. *American Psychologist, 35,* 790–806.

Erdelyi, M. H. (1974). A "new look" at the New Look in perception. *Psychological Review, 81,* 1–25.

Erdelyi, M. H. (1985). *Psychoanalysis: Freud's cognitive psychology*. San Francisco: Freeman.

Erdelyi, M. H. (1994). Commentary: Integrating a dissociation-prone psychology. *Journal of Personality, 62,* 669–680.

Erikson, E. (1968). *Identity: Youth and crisis*. New York: Norton.

Exner, J. E., Jr. (1993). *The Rorschach: A comprehensive system: Vol. 1. Basic foundations* (3rd ed.). New York: Wiley.

Eysenck, H. J. (1947). *Dimensions of personality*. London: Routledge & Kegan Paul.

Eysenck, H. J. (1967). *The biological basis of personality*. Springfield, IL: Charles C. Thomas.

Eysenck, H. J. (1976). *Sex and personality*. Austin: University of Texas Press.

Eysenck, H. J. (1986). Cross-cultural comparisions: The validity of assessment by indices of factor comparison. *Journal of Cross-cultural Psychology, 17,* 506–517.

Eysenck, H. J. (1987). Arousal and personality: The origins of a theory. In J. Strelau & H. J. Eysenck (Eds.), *Personality dimensions and arousal* (pp. 1–13). New York: Plenum.

Eysenck, H. J., & Eysenck, S. B. G. (1976). *Psychoticism as a dimension of personality*. London: Hodder & Stoughton.

Eysenck, H. J., & Eysenck, S. B. G. (1983). Recent advances in the cross-cultural study of personality. In J. N. Butcher & C. D. Speilberger (Eds.), *Advances in personality assessment* (Vol. 2, pp. 41–69). Hillsdale, NJ: Erlbaum.

Eysenck, S. B. (1983). One approach to cross-cultural studies of personality. *Australian Journal of Psychology, 35,* 381–391.

Eysenck, S. B. G., & Eysenck, H. J. (1967). Salivary response to lemon juice as a measure of introversion. *Perceptual and Motor Skills, 24,* 1047–1053.

Eysenck, S. B. G., Eysenck, H. J., & Barrett, P. (1985). A revised version of the psychoticism scale. *Personality and Individual Differences, 6,* 21–29.

Eysenck, S. B. G., & Long, F. Y. (1986). A cross-cultural comparison of personality in adults and children: Singapore and England. *Journal of Personality and Social Psychology, 58,* 281–291.

Fenz, W. D., & Epstein, S. (1967). Gradients of physiological arousal of experienced and novice parachutists as a function of an approaching jump. *Psychosomatic Medicine, 29,* 33–51.

Festinger, L., & Carlsmith, J. M. (1959). Cognitive consequences of forced compliance. *Journal of Abnormal and Social Psychology, 58,* 203–210.

Feuer, L. S. (1974). *Einstein and the generations of science.* New York: Basic Books.

Fishbein, M., & Ajzen, I. (1974). Attitudes toward objects as predictors of single and multiple behavioral criteria. *Psychological Review, 81,* 59–74.

Flint, A. (1995, October 25). Stone age weighs us down today. *Press-Enterprise* (Riverside, CA), p. D1.

Floody, O. R. (1983). Hormones and aggression in female mammals. In B. B. Svare (Ed.), *Hormones and aggressive behavior* (pp. 39–89). New York: Plenum.

Flor-Henry, P. (1969). Schizophrenia-like reactions and affective psychoses associated with temporal lobe epilepsy: Etiological factors. *American Journal of Psychiatry, 126,* 148–152.

Freeman, W., & Watts, J. W. (1950). *Psychosurgery: In the treatment of mental disorders and intractable pain* (2nd. ed.). Springfield, IL: Charles C. Thomas.

Freud, S. (1962). *Three essays on the theory of sexuality.* New York: Basic Books. (Originally published 1905.)

Friedman, H. S. (1992). Disease-prone and self-healing personalities. *Hospital and Community Psychiatry, 43,* 1177–1179.

Friedman, H. S. (Ed.). (1991). *Hostility, coping, and health.* Washington, DC: American Psychological Association.

Friedman, H. S., Hall, J. A., & Harris, M. J. (1985). Type A behavior, non-verbal expressive style, and health. *Journal of Personality and Social Psychology, 48,* 1299–1315.

Friedman, H. S., Tucker, J. S., Tomlinson-Keasey, C., Schwartz, J. E., Wingard, D. L., & Criqui, M. H. (1993). Does childhood personality predict longevity? *Journal of Personality and Social Psychology, 65,* 176–185.

Friedman, I. (1955). Phenomenal, ideal, and projected conception of self. *Journal of Abnormal and Social Psychology, 51,* 109–120.

Frijda, N. H. (1986). *The emotions.* Cambridge, England: Cambridge University Press.

Fromm, E. (1941). *Escape from freedom.* New York: Holt, Rinehart, & Winston.

Funder, D. C. (1982). On the accuracy of dispositional versus situational attributions. *Social Cognition, 3,* 205–222.

Funder, D. C. (1983). Three issues in predicting more of the people: A reply to Mischel and Peake. *Psychological Review, 90,* 283–289.

Funder, D. C. (1987). Errors and mistakes: Evaluating the accuracy of social judgment. *Psychological Bulletin, 101,* 75–90.

Funder, D. C. (1991). Global traits: A neo-Allportian approach to personality. *Psychological Science, 2,* 31–39.

Funder, D. C. (1993). Judgments as data for personality and developmental psychology: Error vs. accuracy. In D. C. Funder, R. D. Parke, C. Tomlinson-Keasey, & K. Widaman (Eds.), *Studying lives through time: Personality and development* (pp. 121–146). Washington, DC: American Psychological Association.

Funder, D. C. (1995). On the accuracy of personality judgment: A realistic approach. *Psychological Review, 102,* 652–670.

Funder, D. C., & Block, J. (1989). The role of ego-control, ego-resiliency, and IQ in delay of gratification in adolescence. *Journal of Personality and Social Psychology, 57,* 1041–1050.

Funder, D. C., Block, J. H., & Block, J. (1983). Delay of gratification: Some longitudinal personality correlates. *Journal of Personality and Social Psychology, 44,* 1198–1213.

Funder, D. C., & Colvin, C. R. (1988). Friends and strangers: Acquaintanceship, agreement, and the accuracy of personality judgment. *Journal of Personality and Social Psychology, 55,* 149–158.

Funder, D. C., & Colvin, C. R. (1991). Explorations in behavioral consistency: Properties of persons, situations, and behaviors. *Journal of Personality and Social Psychology, 60*, 773–794.

Funder, D. C., & Dobroth, K. M. (1987). Differences between traits: Properties associated with inter-judge agreement. *Journal of Personality and Social Psychology, 52*, 409–418.

Funder, D. C., & Harris, M. J. (1986). On the several facets of personality assessment: The case of social acuity. *Journal of Personality, 54*, 528–550.

Funder, D. C., & Ozer, D. J. (1983). Behavior as a function of the situation. *Journal of Personality and Social Psychology, 44*, 107–112.

Funder, D. C., Parke, R. D., Tomlinson-Keasey, C., & Widaman, K. (Eds.). (1993) *Studying lives through time: Personality and development.* Washington, DC: American Psychological Association.

Funder, D. C., & Sneed, C. D. (1993). Behavioral manifestations of personality: An ecological approach to judgmental accuracy. *Journal of Personality and Social Psychology, 64*, 479–490.

Funder, D. C., & West, S. G. (1993). Consensus, self-other agreement, and accuracy in personality judgment: An introduction. *Journal of Personality, 61*, 457–807.

Gangestad, S. W. (1989). The evolutionary history of genetic variation: An emerging issue in the behavioral genetic study of personality. In D. Buss & N. Cantor (Eds.), *Personality psychology: Recent trends and emerging directions* (pp. 320–332). New York: Springer-Verlag.

Gangestad, S. W., & Simpson, J. A. (1990). Toward an evolutionary history of female sociosexual variation. *Journal of Personality, 58*, 69–96.

Gangestad, S. W., Simpson, J. A., DiGeronimo, K., & Biek, M. (1992). Differential accuracy in person perception across traits: Examination of a functional hypothesis. *Journal of Personality and Social Psychology, 62*, 688–698.

Gangestad, S. W., & Snyder, M. (1985). "To carve nature at its joints": On the existence of discrete classes in personality. *Psychological Review, 92*, 317–349.

Gabrenya, W. K., Jr., & Hwang, K. K. (1995). Chinese social interaction: Harmony and hierarchy on the good earth. In M. Bond (Ed.), *Handbook of Chinese psychology.* Hong Kong: Oxford University Press.

Gay, P. (1988). *Freud: A life for our time.* New York: Norton.

Gergen, K. (1973). Social psychology as history. *Journal of Personality and Social Psychology, 26*, 309–320.

Gigerenzer, G., Hoffrage, U., & Kleinbolting, H. (1991). Probabilistic mental models: A Brunswikian theory of confidence. *Psychological Review, 98*, 506–528.

Gilmore, D. D. (1990). *Manhood in the making.* New Haven, CT: Yale University Press.

Giorgi, A. (1985). Sketch of a psychological phenomenological method. In A. Giorgi (Ed.), *Phenomenology and psychological research* (pp. 8–22). Pittsburgh: Duquesne University Press.

Gleitman, H. (1995). *Psychology* (4th ed.). New York: Norton.

Goetz, T. E., & Dweck, C. S. (1980). Learned helplessness in social situation. *Journal of Personality and Social Psychology, 39*, 246–255.

Goffman, E. (1959). *The presentation of self in everyday life.* Garden City, NY: Doubleday (Anchor).

Gold, S. R., & Reilly, J. P. (1985). Daydreaming, current concerns and personality. *Imagination, Cognition and Personality, 5*, 117–125.

Goldberg, L. R. (1981). Language and individual differences: The search for universals in personality lexicons. In L. Wheeler (Ed.), *Review of Personality and Social Psychology* (Vol. 2, pp. 141–166). Beverly Hills, CA: Sage.

Goldberg, L. R. (1992). The social psychology of personality. *Psychological Inquiry, 3,* 89–94.

Goldman, W., & Lewis, P. (1977). Beautiful is good: Evidence that the physically attractive are more socially skillful. *Journal of Experimental Social Psychology, 13,* 125–130.

Gorer, G. (1943). Themes in Japanese culture. *New York Academy of Sciences, 5,* 106–124.

Gough, H. G. (1968). An interpreter's syllabus for the California Psychological Inventory. In P. McReynolds (Ed.), *Advances in psychological assessment* (Vol. 1, pp. 55–79). Palo Alto, CA: Science and Behavior Books.

Gough, H. G. (1995). Career assessment and the California Psychological Inventory. *Journal of Career Assessment, 3,* 101–122.

Gray, J. A. (1981). A critique of Eysenck's theory of personality, In H. J. Eysenck (Ed.), *A model for personality* (pp. 246–276). New York: Springer-Verlag.

Gray, J. A. (1987). *The psychology of fear and stress* (2nd ed.). Cambridge, England: Cambridge University Press.

Greenberg, J., & Folger, R. (1988). *Controversial issues in social research methods.* New York: Springer-Verlag.

Gregory, R. L. (1968). Visual illusions. *Scientific American, 219,* 66–76.

Guilford, J. P. & Zimmerman, W. S. (1956). Fourteen dimensions of temperament. *Psychological Monographs, 70,* no. 417.

Guthrie, E. R. (1935). *The psychology of learning.* New York: Harper & Row.

Guthrie, G. M., & Bennett, A. B. (1971). Cultural differences in implicit personality theory. *International Journal of Psychology, 6,* 305–312.

Hall, C. S., & Lindzey, G. (1978). *Theories of personality* (3rd ed.). New York: Wiley.

Hamer, D. H., & Copeland, P. (1994). *The science of desire: The search for the gay gene and the biology of behavior.* New York: Simon & Schuster.

Hammond, K. R., Harvey, L. O., Jr., & Hastie, R. (1992). Making better use of scientific knowledge: Separating truth from justice. *Psychological Science, 62,* 80–87.

Hammond, K. R., Householder, J. E., & Castellan, N. J. (1970). *Introduction to the statistical method: Foundations and use in the behavioral sciences* (2nd ed.). New York: Knopf.

Hanin, Y., Eysenck, S. B., Eysenck, H. J., & Barrett, P. (1991). A cross-cultural study of personality: Russia and England. *Personality and Individual Differences, 12,* 265–271.

Hanson, F. A. (1993). *Testing testing: Social consequences of the examined life.* Berkeley: University of California Press.

Hartmann, H. (1964). *Essays on ego psychology: Selected problems in psychoanalytic theory.* New York: International Universities Press.

Hastie, R., & Rasinski, K. A. (1988). The concept of accuracy in social judgment. In D. Bar-Tal & A. W. Kruglanski (Eds.), *The social psychology of knowledge* (pp. 193–208). Cambridge, England: Cambridge University Press.

Hastorf, A. H., & Cantril, H. (1954). They saw a game: A case study. *Journal of Abnormal and Social Psychology, 47,* 574–576.

Hathaway, S. R., & Meehl, P. E. (1951). *An atlas for the clinical use of the MMPI.* Minneapolis: University of Minnesota Press.

Headland, T. N., Pike, K. L., & Harris, M. (Eds.). (1990). *Emics and etics: The insider/ outsider debate.* Newbury Park, CA: Sage.

Heidegger, M. (1962). *Being and time.* New York: Harper & Row (originally published 1927).

Hemenway, D., Solnick, S., & Carter, J. (1994). Child-rearing violence. *Child Abuse & Neglect, 18,* 1011–1020.

Hetherington, E.M. (Ed.). (1983) *Socialization, personality, and social development.* New York: Wiley.

Hilton, T. L., & Berglund, G. W. (1974). Sex differences in mathematics achievement: A longitudinal study. *Journal of Educational Research, 67,* 231–237.

Hofstede, G. (1984). The cultural relativity of the quality of life concept. *Academy of Management Review, 9,* 389–398.

Hogan, R. (1969). Development of an empathy scale. *Journal of Consulting and Clinical Psychology, 33,* 307–316.

Hogan, R. (1992, August). *A socioanalytic interpretation of Factor V.* Paper presented at the Annual Meetings of the American Psychological Association, Washington, DC.

Holt, R. R. (1980). Loevinger's measure of ego development: Reliability and national norms for male and female short forms. *Journal of Personality and Social Psychology, 39,* 909–920.

Horney, K. (1937). *The neurotic personality of our time.* New York: Norton.

Horney, K. (1942). *Self-analysis.* New York: Norton.

Horney, K. (1950). *Neurosis and human growth.* New York: Norton.

Hughes, C. F., Uhlmann, C., & Pennebaker, J. W. (1994). The body's response to emotional trauma: Linking verbal text with autonomic activity. *Journal of Personality, 62,* 565–586.

Hull, C. L. (1943). *Principles of behavior: An introduction to behavior theory.* New York: Appleton-Century-Crofts.

Jackson, D. N. (1967). *Personality Research Form manual.* Goshen, NY: Research Psychologists Press.

Jackson, D. N. (1971). The dynamics of structured personality tests: 1971. *Psychological Review, 78,* 229–248.

Jackson, D. N., Neill, J. A., & Bevan, A. R. (1973). An evaluation of forced-choice and true-false formats in personality assessment. *Journal of Research in Personality, 7,* 21–30.

Janoff-Bulman, R. (1989). Assumptive worlds and the stress of traumatic events: Applications of the schema construct. *Social Cognition, 7,* 113–136.

John, O. P. (1990). The "Big Five" factor taxonomy: Dimensions of personality in the natural language and in questionnaires. In L. Pervin (Ed.), *Handbook of personality: Theory and research* (pp. 66–100). New York: Guilford.

John, O. P., & Robins, R. W. (1994). Accuracy and bias in self-perception: Individual differences in self-enhancement and narcissism. *Journal of Personality and Social Psychology, 66,* 206–219.

Jones, E. E., & Nisbett, R. E. (1971). *The actor and the observer: Divergent perceptions of the causes of behavior.* Morristown, NJ: General Learning Press.

Jourard, S. M. (1971). *Self-disclosure: An experimental analysis of the transparent self.* New York: Wiley.

Jung, C. G. (1933). *Psychological Types.* New York: Harcourt, Brace, and World.

Jung, C. G. (1971a). *The portable Jung* (J. Campbell, Ed.). New York: Viking.

Jung, C. G. (1971b). A psychological theory of types. In H. Read, M. Fordham, & G. Adler (Eds.), *Collected Works of C. G. Jung* (Vol. 20, pp. 524–541). Princeton, N.J.: Princeton University Press. (German original published 1931.)

Jussim, L. (1991). Social perception and social reality: A reflection-construction model. *Psychological Review, 98,* 54–73.

Jussim, L., & Eccles, J. (1992). Teacher expectations II: Construction and reflection of student achievement. *Journal of Personality and Social Psychology, 63,* 947–961.

Kagan, J. (1978). Sex differences in the human infant. In T. E. McGill, D. A. Dewsburg, & B. D. Sachs (Eds.), *Sex and behavior* (pp. 305–316). New York: Plenum.

Kelly, G. A. (1955). *The psychology of personal constructs* (Vols. 1 and 2). New York: Norton.

Kenny, D. A. (1991). A general model of consensus and accuracy in interpersonal perception. *Psychological Review, 98,* 155–163.

Kenrick, D. T., & Funder, D. C. (1988). Profiting from controversy: Lessons from the person-situation debate. *American Psychologist, 43,* 23–34.

Kenrick, D. T., & Keefe, R. C. (1992). Age preferences in mates reflect sex differences in human reproductive strategies. *Behavioral and Brain Sciences, 15,* 75–91).

Kihlstrom, J. F. (1994). Commentary: Psychodynamics and social cognition: Notes on the fusion of psychoanalysis and psychology. *Journal of Personality, 62,* 681–696.

King, M. G., & Husband, A. J. (1991). Altered immunity through behavioral conditioning. In J. G. Carlson & A. R. Seifert (Eds.), *International perspectives in behavioral psychophysiology and medicine* (pp. 197–204). New York: Plenum.

Kircher, P. (1985). *Vaulting ambition: Sociobiology and the quest for human nature.* Cambridge, MA: MIT Press.

Klein, G. S. (1970). *Perception, motives, and personality.* New York: Knopf.

Klinger, E. (1977). *Meaning and void: Inner experience and the incentives in people's lives.* Minneapolis: University of Minnesota Press.

Kluckhohn, C., & Murray, H. A. (1961). Personality formation: The determinants. In C. Kluckhohn, H. A. Murray, & D. M. Schneider (Eds.), *Personality in nature, society, and culture* (2nd ed., pp. 53–67). New York: Knopf.

Koffka, K. (1935). *Principles of Gestalt psychology.* New York: Harcourt, Brace, & World.

Kohler, W. (1925). *The mentality of apes* (E. Winter, Trans.). New York: Harcourt, Brace, & World.

Kolar, D. W., Funder, D. C., & Colvin, C. R. (in press). Comparing the accuracy of personality judgments by the self and knowledgable others. *Journal of Personality.*

Kramer, P. D. (1993). *Listening to Prozac.* New York: Viking.

Kruglanski, A. W. (1989). The psychology of being "right": The problem of accuracy in social perception and cognition. *Psychological Bulletin, 106,* 395–409.

Langer, E. J. (1992). Matters of mind: Mindfulness/mindlessness in perspective. *Consciousness and Cognition, 1,* 289–305.

Langer, E. J. (1994). The illusion of calculated decisions. In R. C. Schank & E. Langer (Eds.), *Beliefs, reasoning, and decision making: Psycho-logic in honor of Bob Abelson* (pp. 33–53). Hillsdale, NJ: Erlbaum.

Larkin, J. H., McDermott, J., Simon, D. P., & Simon, H. A. (1980). Models of competence in solving physics problems. *Science, 200,* 1335–1342.

Lau, R. R. (1988). Beliefs about control and health behavior. In D. S. Gochman (Ed.), *Health behavior: Emerging research perspectives* (pp. 43–63). New York: Plenum.

Lee, Y.-T., Jussim, L. J., & McCauley, C. R. (1995). *Stereotype accuracy: Toward appreciating group differences.* Washington, DC: American Psychological Association.

Linville, P., & Jones, E. E. (1980). Polarized appraisals of out-group members. *Journal of Personality and Social Psychology, 38,* 689–703.

Little, B. R. (1989). Personal projects analysis: Trivial pursuits, magnificent obsessions, and the search for coherence. In D. M. Buss & N. Cantor (Eds.), *Personality psychology: Recent trends and emerging directions* (pp. 15–31). New York: Springer-Verlag.

Loehlin, J. C., Willerman, L., & Horn, J. M. (1985). Personality resemblances in adoptive families when the children are late-adolescent or adult. *Journal of Personality and Social Psychology, 48,* 376–392.

Loehlin, J. C., Willerman, L., & Horn, J. M. (1989). Personality resemblance in adoptive families: A 10-year follow-up. *Journal of Personality and Social Psychology, 53,* 961–969.

Loevinger, J. (1976). *Ego development: Conceptions and theories.* San Francisco: Jossey-Bass.

Loevinger, J. (1987). *Paradigms of personality.* New York: Freeman.

Loftus, E. F. (1992). When a lie becomes memory's truth: Memory distortion after exposure to misinformation. *Current Directions in Psychological Science, 1,* 121–123.

Loftus, E. F., Greene, E. L., & Doyle, J. M. (1989). The psychology of eyewitness testimony. In D. C. Raskin (Ed.), *Psychological methods in criminal investigation and evidence* (pp. 3–45). New York: Springer.

Lorenz, K. (1966). *On aggression.* New York: Harcourt, Brace, & World.

Lorenzi-Cioldi, F. (1993). They all look alike, but so do we . . . sometimes: Perceptions of in-group and out-group homogeneity as a function of sex and context. *British Journal of Social Psychology, 32,* 111–124.

Lykes, M. B. (1985). Gender and individualistic vs. collectivist bases for notions about the self. *Journal of Personality, 53,* 356–383.

Maccoby, E. (1966). Sex differences in intellectual functioning. In E. Maccoby (Ed.), *The development of sex differences.* Stanford, CA: Stanford University Press.

Maccoby, E. E., & Jacklin, C. N. (1974). *The psychology of sex differences.* Stanford, CA: Stanford University Press.

Machover, K. (1949). *Personality projection in the drawing of the human figure.* Springfield, IL: Charles C. Thomas.

MacLean, P. D. (1982). On the origin and progressive evolution of the triune brain. In R. G. Grenell & S. Gabay (Eds.), *Biological foundations of psychiatry* (pp. 177–198). New York: Raven.

Main, M. (1990). Parental aversion to infant-initiated contact is correlated with the parent's own rejection during childhood: The effects of experience on signals of security with respect to attachment. In K. E. Barnard & T. B. Brazelton (Eds.), *Touch: The foundation of experience* (pp. 461–495). Madison, CT: International Universities Press.

Markus, H. R. (1977). Self-schemata and processing information about the self. *Journal of Personality and Social Psychology, 35,* 63–78.

Markus, H. R., & Kitayama, S. (1991). Culture and the self: Implications for cognition, emotion, and motivation. *Psychological Review, 98,* 224–253.

Markus, H. R., & Nurius, P. (1986). Possible selves. *American Psychologist, 41,* 954–969.

Maryanski, A., & Turner, J. H. (1992). *The social cage: Human nature and the evolution of society.* Stanford, CA: Stanford University Press.

Maslow, A. H. (1987). *Motivation and personality* (3rd ed.). New York: Harper & Row.

Masson, J. M. (1984). *The assault on truth: Freud's suppression of the seduction theory.* New York: Farrar, Straus, Giroux.

McAdams, D. P. (1990). *The person.* San Diego, CA: Harcourt Brace Jovanovich.

McAdams, D. P. (1992). The five-factor model of personality: A critical appraisal. *Journal of Personality, 60,* 329–361.

McClelland, D. C. (1961). *The achieving society.* Princeton, NJ: Van Nostrand.

McClelland, D. C. (1972). Opinions reflect opinions: So what else is new? *Journal of Consulting and Clinical Psychology, 38,* 325–326.

McClelland, D. C. (1975). Love and power: The psychological signals of war. *Psychology Today, 8,* 44–48.

McClelland, D. C. (1984). *Motives, personality, and society.* New York: Praeger.

McCrae, R. R. (1994). The counterpoint of personality assessment: Self-reports and observer ratings. *Assessment, 1,* 159–172.

McCrae, R. R., & Costa, P. T., Jr. (1987). Validation of the five-factor model of personality across instruments and observers. *Journal of Personality and Social Psychology, 52,* 81–90.

McCrae, R. R., & Costa, P. T., Jr. (1991). Adding Liebe und Arbeit: The full five-factor model and well-being. *Personality and Social Psychology Bulletin, 17,* 227–232.

McCrae, R. R., & John, O. P. (1992). An introduction to the five-factor model and its applications. *Journal of Personality, 60,* 175–215.

McGinnies, E. (1949). Emotionality and perceptual defense. *Psychological Review, 56,* 244–251.

McKay, J. R., O'Farrell, T. J., Maisto, S. A., Connors, G. J., & Funder, D. C. (1989). Biases in relapse attributions made by alcoholics and their wives. *Addictive Behaviors, 14,* 513–522.

Meehl, P. E. (1992). Factors and taxa, traits and types, differences of degree and differences in kind. *Journal of Personality, 60,* 117–174.

Megargee, E. I. (1966). Undercontrolled and overcontrolled personality types in extreme antisocial aggression. In E. I. Megargee & J. I. Moranson (Eds.), *Psychological Monographs.* New York: Harper & Row.

Metzner, R. J. (1994, March 14). Prozac is medicine, not a miracle. *Los Angeles Times,* p. B7.

Michigan Department of Education (1989). *The Michigan employability survey.*

Milgram, S. (1975). *Obedience to authority.* New York: Harper & Row.

Miller, G. A. (1956). The magical number seven plus or minus two: Some limits on our capacity for processing information. *Psychological Review, 63,* 81–97.

Miller, J. G., & Bersoff, D. M. (1992). Culture and moral judgment: How are conflicts between justice and interpersonal responsibilities resolved? *Journal of Personality and Social Psychology, 62,* 541–554.

Miller, J. G., Bersoff, D. M., & Harwood, R. L. (1990). Perceptions of social responsibilities in India and in the United States: Moral imperatives or personal decisions? *Journal of Personality and Social Psychology, 58,* 33–47.

Miller, N. E., & Dollard, J. (1941). *Social learning and imitation.* New Haven, CT: Yale University Press.

Mischel, W. (1968). *Personality and assessment.* New York: Wiley.

Mischel, W. (1973). Toward a cognitive social learning reconceptualization of personality. *Psychological Review, 80,* 252–283.

Mischel, W., & Ebbesen, E. (1970). Attention in delay of gratification. *Journal of Personality and Social Psychology, 16,* 329–337.

Mischel, W., & Shoda, Y. (1995). A cognitive-affective system theory of personality: Reconceptualizing situations, dispositions, dynamics, and invariance in personality structure. *Psychological Review, 102,* 246–268.

Mischel, W., Shoda, Y., & Peake, P. K. (1988). The nature of adolescent competencies predicted by preschool delay of gratification. *Journal of Personality and Social Psychology, 54,* 687–696.

Moray, N. (1959). Attention in dichotic listening: Affective cues and the influence of instructions. *Quarterly Journal of Experimental Psychology, 11,* 56–60.

Morgan, C. D., & Murray, H. A. (1935). A method for investigating fantasies: The Thematic Apperception Test. *Archives of Neurology and Psychiatry, 34,* 289–306.

Murray, H. A. (1938). *Explorations in personality.* New York: Oxford University Press.

Murray, H. A. (1943). *Thematic Apperception Test manual.* Cambridge, MA: Harvard University Press.

Myers, I. B. (1962). *The Myers-Briggs Type Indicator.* Princeton, NJ: Educational Testing Service.

Nikula, R., Klinger, E., & Larson-Gutman, M. K. (1993). Current concerns and electrodermal reactivity: Responses to words and thoughts. *Journal of Personality, 61,* 63–84.

Nisbett, R. E. (1980). The trait construct in lay and professional psychology. In L. Festinger (Ed.), *Retrospections on social psychology* (pp. 109–130). New York: Oxford University Press.

Nisbett, R. E., & Wilson, T. D. (1977). Telling more than we can know: Verbal reports on mental processes. *Psychological Review, 84,* 231–259.

Norem, J. K. (1989). Cognitive strategies as personality: Effectiveness, specificity, flexibility, and change. In D. M. Buss & N. Cantor (Eds.), *Personality psychology: Recent trends and emerging directions* (pp. 45–60). New York: Springer-Verlag.

Norem, J. K., & Cantor, N. (1986). Defensive pessimism: "Harnessing" anxiety as motivation. *Journal of Personality and Social Psychology, 51,* 1208–1217.

Norman, W. T. (1963). Toward an adequate taxonomy of personality attributes: Replicated factor structure in peer nomination personality ratings. *Journal of Abnormal and Social Psychology, 66,* 574–583.

O'Bannon, R. M., Goldinger, L. A., & Appleby, G. S. (1989). *Honesty and integrity testing.* Atlanta, GA: Applied Information Resources.

Ones, D. S., Viswesvaran, C., & Schmidt, F. L. (1993). Comprehensive meta-analysis of integrity test validities: Findings and implications for personnel selection and theories of job performance. *Journal of Applied Psychology, 78,* 679–703.

Ornstein, R. E. (1977). *The psychology of consciousness* (2nd ed.). New York: Harcourt Brace Jovanovich.

Oxenstierna, G., Edman, G., Iselius, L., Oreland, L., Ross, S. B., & Sedvall, G. (1986). Concentrations of monamine metabolites in the cerebrospinal fluid of twins and unrelated individuals: A genetic study. *Journal of Psychiatric Research, 20,* 19–20.

Ozer, D. J. (1985). Correlation and the coefficient of determination. *Psychological Bulletin, 97,* 307–315.

Park, B., & Rothbart, M. (1982). Perceptions of out-group homogeneity and levels of social categorization: Memory for the subordinate attributes of in-group and outgroup members. *Journal of Personality and Social Psychology, 42,* 1051–1068.

Peabody, D. (1966). Authoritarianism scales and response bias. *Psychological Bulletin, 65,* 11–23.

Pennebaker, J. W. (1992). Inhibition as the linchpin of health. In H. S. Friedman (Ed.), *Hostility, coping, and health* (pp. 127–139). Washington, DC: American Psychological Association.

Pettigrew, T. F. (1986). The intergroup contact hypothesis reconsidered. In M. Hewstone & R. Brown (Eds.), *Contact and conflict in interpersonal encounters* (pp. 169–195). Oxford, England: Basic Blackwell.

Plomin, R., Chipuer, H. M., & Loehlin, J. C. (1990). Behavioral genetics and personality. In L. Pervin (Ed.), *Handbook of personality: Theory and research* (pp. 225–243). New York: Guilford.

Plomin, R., Corley, R., DeFries, J. C., & Fulker, D. W. (1990). Individual differences in television viewing in early childhood: Nature as well as nurture. *Psychological Science, 1*, 371–377.

Pope, K. S., Tabachnick, B., & Keith-Spiegel, P. (1987). Ethics of practice: The beliefs and behaviors of psychologists as therapists. *American Psychologist, 42*, 993–1006.

Price, R. H., & Bouffard, D. L. (1974). Behavioral appropriateness and situational constraint as dimensions of social behavior. *Journal of Personality and Social Psychology, 30*, 579–586.

Public Health Service (1991). *Application for Public Health Service Grant* (PHS 398; OMB No. 0925–0001). Washington, DC: U.S. Government Printing Office.

Purifoy, P. E., & Koopermans, L. H. (1979). Androstenedione, testosterone, and free testosterone concentration in women of various occupations. *Social Biology, 26*, 179–188.

Rada, R. T., Laws, D. R., & Kellner, R. (1976). Plasma testosterone levels in the rapist. *Psychosomatic Medicine, 38*, 257–258.

Rapaport, D. (1960). *The structure of psychoanalytic theory: A systematizing attempt.* New York: International Universities Press.

Robinson, P. (1993). *Freud and his critics.* Berkeley: University of California Press.

Rogers, C. R. (1951). *Client-centered therapy: Its current practice, implications, and theory.* Boston: Houghton Mifflin.

Rokeach, M. (1960). *The open and closed mind.* New York: Basic.

Rorer, L. G. (1965). The great response-style myth. *Psychological Bulletin, 63*, 129–156.

Rorer, L. G. (1990). Personality assessment: A conceptual survey. In L. Pervin (Ed.), *Handbook of personality: Theory and research.* New York: Guilford.

Rorschach, H. (1921). *Psychodiagnostik.* Bern, Switzerland: Huber.

Rosenthal, R. (1973). Estimating effective reliabilities in studies that employ judges' ratings. *Journal of Clinical Psychology, 29*, 342–345.

Rosenthal, R. (Ed.). (1980). *Quantitative analysis of research domains.* New directions for methodology of social and behavioral science, no. 5. San Francisco: Jossey-Bass.

Rosenthal, R., & Jacobson, L. (1968). *Pygmalion in the classroom: Teacher expectation and pupils' intellectual development.* New York: Holt, Rinehart, & Winston.

Rosenthal, R., & Rosnow, R. L. (1991). *Essentials of behavioral research: Methods and data analysis* (2nd ed.). New York: McGraw-Hill.

Rosenthal, R., & Rubin, D. B. (1982). A simple, general purpose display of magnitude of experimental effect. *Journal of Educational Psychology, 74*, 166–169.

Rosolack, T. K., & Hampson, S. E. (1991). A new typology of health behaviors for personality-health predictions: The case of locus of control. *European Journal of Personality, 5*, 151–168.

Ross, L. (1977). The intuitive psychologist and his shortcomings. In L. Berkowitz (Ed.), *Advances in experimental social psychology* (Vol. 10, pp. 174–214). New York: Academic Press.

Ross, L., Greene, D., & House, P. (1977). The false consensus phenomenon: An attributional bias in self-perception and social perception processes. *Journal of Experimental Social Psychology, 13*, 279–301.

Ross, L., Lepper, M. R., & Hubbard, M. (1975). Perseverance in self perception and social perception: Biased attribution processes in the debriefing paradigm. *Journal of Personality and Social Psychology, 32*, 880–892.

Ross, L., & Nisbett, R. E. (1991). *The person and the situation: Perspectives of social psychology.* New York: McGraw-Hill.

Rotter, J. B. (1954). *Social learning and clinical psychology.* Englewood Cliffs, NJ: Prentice-Hall.

Rotter, J. B. (1982). *The development and applications of social learning theory: Selected papers.* New York: Praeger.

Rudikoff, E. C. (1954). A comparative study of the changes in the concepts of the self, the ordinary person, and the ideal in eight cases. In C. R. Rogers & R. F. Dymond (Eds.), *Psychotherapy and personality change: Co-ordinated studies in the client-centered approach* (pp. 85–98). Chicago: University of Chicago Press.

Rumelhart, D. E., McClelland, J. L., & the PDP Research Group (1986). *Parallel distributed processing: Explorations in the microstructure of cognition: Vol. 1. Foundations.* Cambridge, MA: MIT Press.

Rychlak, J. F. (1988). *The psychology of rigorous humanism* (2nd ed.). New York: New York University Press.

Rychlak, J. F., & Marceil, J. C. (1986). Task predication and affective learning style. *Journal of Social Behavior and Personality, 1,* 557–564.

Ryle, G. (1949). *The concept of mind.* New York: Harper & Row.

Sabini, J. (1995). *Social psychology* (2nd ed.). New York: Norton.

Sackett, P. R., Burris, L. R., & Callahan, C. (1989). Integrity testing for personnel selection: An update. *Personnel Psychology, 42,* 491–529.

Sacks, O. W. (1983). *Awakenings.* New York: Dutton.

Sartre, J. P. (1965). The humanism of existentialism. In W. Baskin (Ed.), *Essays in existentialism* (pp. 31–62). Secaucus, NJ: Citadel Press.

Scarr, S. (1981). *Race, social class, and individual differences in IQ.* Hillsdale, NJ: Erlbaum.

Scarr, S., & McCartney, K. (1983). How people make their own environments: A theory of genotype-environment interactions. *Child Development, 54,* 424–435.

Schank, R. C., & Abelson, R. P. (1977). *Scripts, plans, goals, and understanding.* Hillsdale, NJ: Erlbaum.

Scherer, K. R. (1978). Personality inference from voice quality: The loud voice of extraversion. *European Journal of Social Psychology, 8,* 467–487.

Schmidt, F. L., & Hunter, J. E. (1992). Development of causal models of processes determining job performance. *Current Directions in Psychological Science, 1,* 89–92.

Sears, D. O. (1986). College students in the laboratory: Influences of a narrow data base on social psychology's view of human nature. *Journal of Personality and Social Psychology, 51,* 515–530.

Sears, R. R. (1947). *Survey of objective studies of psychoanalytic concepts.* New York: Social Science Research Council.

Seligman, M. E. P. (1968). Chronic fear produced by unpredictable electric shock. *Journal of Comparative and Physiological Psychology, 66,* 402–411.

Selye, H. (1956). *The stress of life.* New York: McGraw-Hill.

Shanahan, J. (1995). Television viewing and adolescent authoritarianism. *Journal of Adolescence, 18,* 271–288.

Shapiro, K. J. (1985). *Bodily reflective modes: A phenomenological method for psychology.* Durham, NC: Duke University Press.

Sharpe, D., Adair, J. G., & Roese, N. J. (1992). Twenty years of deception research: A decline in subjects' trust? *Personality and Social Psychology Bulletin, 18,* 585–590.

Shaver, P. R., & Clark, C. L. (1994). The psychodynamics of adult romantic attachment. In J. M. Masling & R. F. Bornstein (Eds.), *Empirical perspectives on object relations theory* (pp. 105–156). Washington, DC: American Psychological Association.

Shedler, J., & Block, J. (1990). Adolescent drug use and psychological health: A longitudinal inquiry. *American Psychologist, 45,* 612–630.

Shils, E. A. (1954). Authoritarianism: Right and left. In R. Christie & M. Jahoda (Eds.),

Studies in the scope and method of "The authoritarian personality." Glencoe, IL: Free Press.

Shweder, R. A. (1975). How relevant is an individual-difference theory of personality? *Journal of Personality, 43,* 455–485.

Shweder, R. A. (1992). The cultural psychology of the emotions. In M. Lewis & J. Haviland (Eds.), *Handbook of the emotions.* New York: Guilford.

Shweder, R. A., & Bourne, E. J. (1982). Does the concept of person vary cross-culturally? In A. J. Marsella & G. M. White (Eds.), *Cultural conceptions of mental health and therapy* (pp. 97–137). London: Reidel.

Shweder, R. A., Mahapatra, M., & Miller, J. G. (1990). Culture and moral development. In J. W. Stigler, R. A. Shweder, & G. Herdt (Eds.), *Cultural psychology* (pp. 130–204). New York: Cambridge University Press.

Shweder, R. A., & Sullivan, M. A. (1990). The semiotic subject of cultural psychology. In L. A. Pervin (Ed.), *Handbook of personality: Theory and research* (pp. 399–416). New York: Guilford.

Shweder, R. A., & Sullivan, M. A. (1993). Cultural psychology: Who needs it? *Annual Review of Psychology, 44,* 497–523.

Silverstein, S. (1993, July 10). Target to pay $2 million in testing case. *Los Angeles Times,* pp. D1–D2.

Skinner, B. F. (1938). *The behavior of organisms: An experimental analysis.* New York: Macmillan.

Skinner, B. F. (1948). *Walden Two.* New York: Macmillan.

Skinner, B. F. (1971). *Beyond freedom and dignity.* New York: Knopf.

Snyder, M. (1974). The self-monitoring of expressive behavior. *Journal of Personality and Social Psychology, 30,* 526–537.

Snyder, M. (1987). *Public appearances, private realities: The psychology of self-monitoring.* New York: Freeman.

Snyder, M., & Ickes, W. (1985). Personality and social behavior. In G. Lindzey & E. Aronson (Eds.), *Handbook of social psychology* (3rd ed., Vol. 2, pp. 883–948). Reading, MA: Addison-Wesley.

Snyder, M., & Monson, T. C. (1975). Persons, situations, and the control of social behavior. *Journal of Personality and Social Psychology, 32,* 637–644.

Snyder, M., Tanke, E. D., & Berscheid, E. (1977). Social perception and interpersonal behavior: On the self-fulfilling nature of social stereotypes. *Journal of Personality and Social Psychology, 44,* 510–517.

Spain, J. (1994). *Personality and daily life experience: Evaluating the accuracy of personality judgments.* Unpublished Ph.D. dissertation, University of California, Riverside.

Sroufe, L. A., Carlson, E., & Shulman, S. (1993). Individuals in relationships: Development from infancy through adolescence. In D. C. Funder, R. D. Parke, C. Tomlinson-Keasey, & K. Widaman (Ed.), *Studying lives through time* (pp. 315–342). Washington, DC: American Psychological Association.

Sroufe, L. A., & Waters, E. (1977). Heart rate as a convergent measure in clinical and developmental research. *Merrill-Palmer Quarterly, 23,* 3–27.

Stampfl, T. G., & Levis, D. J. (1967). Essentials of implosive therapy: A learning-theory-based psychodynamic behavior therapy. *Journal of Abnormal Psychology, 72,* 496–503.

Stanovich, K. E. (1991). Cognitive science meets beginning reading. *Psychological Science, 2,* 70–81.

Sternberg, R. J. (1995). For whom the bell curve tolls. [Review of *The Bell Curve.*] *Psychological Science, 6,* 257–261.

Stipek, D. J., & Gralinski, J. H. (1991). Gender differences in children's achievement-related beliefs and emotional response to success and failure in mathematics. *Journal of Educational Psychology, 83,* 361–371.

Strong, E. K., Jr. (1959). *Strong Vocational Interest Blank.* Palo Alto, CA: Consulting Psychologists Press.

Sulloway, F. J. (1979). *Freud: Biologist of the mind.* New York: Basic Books.

Sundberg, N. D. (1977). *The assessment of persons.* Englewood Cliffs, NJ: Prentice-Hall.

Symons, D. (1979). *The evolution of human sexuality.* New York: Oxford University Press.

Szasz, T. S. (1960). The myth of mental illness. *American Psychologist, 15,* 113–118.

Szasz, T. S. (1974). *The myth of mental illness: Foundations of a theory of personal conduct* (rev. ed.). New York: Harper & Row.

Taft, R. (1955). The ability to judge people. *Psychological Bulletin, 52,* 1–23.

Tansey, M. J. (1992). Countertransference theory, quantitative research, and the problem of therapist-patient sexual abuse. In J. W. Barron, M. N. Eagle, & D. L. Wolitzky (Eds.), *Interface of psychoanalysis and psychology* (pp. 539–557). Washington, DC: American Psychological Association.

Thompson, C. (1995, July 19). Kennedy secretary writes of Rosemary. *Press-Enterprise,* p. A2.

Thorndike, E. L. (1911). *Animal intelligence.* New York: Macmillan.

Tooby, J., & Cosmides, L. (1990). On the universality of human nature and the uniqueness of the individual: The role of genetics and adaptation. *Journal of Personality, 58,* 17–67.

Triandis, H. C. (1994). *Culture and social behavior.* New York: McGraw-Hill.

Triandis, H. C. (in press). Cross-cultural perspectives on personality. In R. Hogan, J. Johnson, & S. Briggs (Eds.), *Handbook of personality psychology.* San Diego, CA: Academic Press.

Triesman, A. M. (1964). Selective attention in man. *British Medical Bulletin, 20,* 12–16.

Tversky, A., & Kahneman, D. (1973). Availability: A heuristic for judging frequency and probability. *Cognitive Psychology, 5,* 207–232.

Valenstein, E. S. (1973). *Brain control.* New York: Wiley.

Valenstein, E. S. (1986). *Great and desperate cure: The rise and decline of psychosurgery and other radical treatments for mental illness.* New York: Basic Books.

Vallacher, R., & Wegner, D. (1987). What do people think they're doing? Action identification and human behavior. *Psychological Review, 94,* 3–15.

Vonnegut, K., Jr. (1963). *Cat's cradle.* New York: Holt, Rinehart & Winston.

Vonnegut, K., Jr. (1966). *Mother night.* New York: Delacorte.

Wakefield, J. C. (1989). Levels of explanation in personality theory. In D. Buss & N. Cantor (Eds.), *Personality psychology: Recent trends and emerging directions* (pp. 333–346). New York: Springer-Verlag.

Waller, D. (1993, April 12). A tour through "hell week." *Newsweek,* 33.

Watson, D. (1989). Strangers' ratings of five robust personality factors: Evidence of a surprising convergence with self-report. *Journal of Personality and Social Psychology, 57,* 120–128.

Watson, D., & Clark, L. A. (1984). Negative affectivity: The disposition to experience aversive emotional states. *Psychological Bulletin, 96,* 465–490.

Watson, J. B. (1925). *Behaviorism.* New York: Norton.

Weinberger, D. A., & Davidson, M. N. (1994). Styles of inhibiting emotional expression: Distinguishing repressive coping from impression management. *Journal of Personality, 62,* 587–614.

Weiss, J. M. (1970). Somatic effects of predictable and unpredictable shock. *Psychosomatic Medicine, 32,* 397–408.

Weiss, J. M. (1977). Psychological and behavioral influences on gastrointestinal lesions in animal models. In J. D. Maser & M. E. P. Seligman (Eds.), *Psychopathology: Experimental Models* (pp. 232–269). San Francisco: Freeman.

Westen, D. (1990). Psychoanalytic approaches to personality. In L. Pervin (Ed.), *Handbook of personality: Theory and research* (pp. 21–65). New York: Guilford.

Wheeler, L., Reise, H. T., & Bond, M. H. (1989). Collectivism-individualism in everyday social life: The Middle Kingdom and the melting pot. *Journal of Personality and Social Psychology, 57,* 79–86.

Whorf, B. L. (1956). Science and linguistics. In J. B. Carroll (Ed.), *Language, thought, and reality* (pp. 207–219). Cambridge, MA: MIT Press.

Widom, C. S. (1989). The cycle of violence. *Science, 244,* 160–166.

Wiggins, J. S. (1973). *Personality and prediction: Principles of personality assessment.* Reading, MA: Addison-Wesley.

Wilson, E. O. (1975). *Sociobiology: The new synthesis.* Cambridge, MA: Harvard University Press.

Wilson, G. D. (1978). Introversion/extraversion. In H. London and J. E. Exner (Eds.), *Dimensions of personality.* New York: Wiley.

Woodworth, R. S. (1917). *Personal Data Sheet.* Chicago: Stoelting.

Wylie, R. C. (1974). *The self concept* (Vols. 1 and 2). Lincoln: University of Nebraska Press.

Yang, K. S., & Bond, M. H. (1990). Exploring implicit personality theories with indigenous or imported constructs: The Chinese case. *Journal of Personality and Social Psychology, 58,* 1087–1095.

Zimbardo, P. G. (1977). *Shyness.* New York: Jove/Harcourt Brace Jovanovich.

Zuckerman, M. (1984). Sensation seeking: A comparative approach to a human trait. *Behavioral and Brain Sciences, 7,* 413–471.

Zuckerman, M. (1991). *Psychobiology of personality.* Cambridge, England: Cambridge University Press.

Zuckerman, M., Koestner, R., DeBoy, T., Garcia, K. T., Maresca, B. C., & Sartoris, J. M. (1988). To predict some of the people some of the time: A reexamination of the moderator variable approach in personality theory. *Journal of Personality and Social Psychology, 54,* 1006–1019.

GLOSSARY

acquiscence response set The tendency to respond "true" to any personality test item, no matter how ludicrous.

aggregation The combining of different measurements, such as by averaging them.

amygdala A part of the *limbic system*, located near the base of the brain, that is believed to play a role in emotion, especially negative emotions such as anger and fear.

anal stage In psychoanalytic theory, the stage of psychosexual development, from about eighteen months to three-and-a-half or four years of age, in which the physical focus of the *libido* is located in the anus and associated eliminative organs.

Angst In existential philosophy, the anxiety that stems from doubts about the meaning and purpose of life.

anima In Jung's version of psychoanalysis, the idea of the typical female as held in the mind of a male.

animus In Jung's version of psychoanalysis, the idea of the typical male as held in the mind of a female.

approach-avoidance conflict In Dollard and Miller's social learning theory, the conflict induced by a stimulus that is at once attractive and aversive.

archetypes In Jung's version of psychoanalysis, the fundamental images of people that are contained in the *collective unconscious*, including the earth mother, the hero, the devil, and so forth.

association cortex The areas of the *cerebral cortex* believed to combine inputs from the various senses and parts of the brain in order to make sense of and act upon them.

associationism The idea that all complex ideas are combinations of two or more simple ideas.

authentic existence In existential philosophy, living with an awareness of the dilemmas concerning the meaning of life, mortality, and free will.

basic approach (to personality) A theoretical view of personality that focuses on some phenomena and ignores others. In personality, the basic approaches are trait, biological, psychoanalytic, phenomenological, and behavioral.

behavior potential In Rotter's social learning theory, the probability of a behavior under a particular set of circumstances.

behavioral prediction The degree to which a judgment or measurement can predict the behavior of the person in question.

behavioristic approach The theoretical view of personality that focuses on overt behavior and the ways in which it can be affected by rewards and punishments in the environment. Modern variants include the social learning approach, which adds a concern with how behavior is affected by observation, self-evaluation, and social interaction; and the cognitive approach, which adds a concern with the mental processes that establish goals and mediate between the environment and behavior.

Binomial Effect Size Display (BESD) One method for displaying and understanding more clearly the magnitude of an effect reported as a correlation.

biological approach The view of personality that focuses on the way behavior and personality are influenced by neuroanatomy, biochemistry, genetics, or evolution.

California Q-set A set of 100 descriptive items (e.g., "Is critical, skeptical, not easily impressed") that comprehensively cover the personality domain.

central nervous system The brain and spinal cord.

cerebral cortex The outer layers of the *cerebral hemispheres;* thought to be the location of higher mental processes.

cerebral hemispheres The two large, roughly half-spherical, upper structures of the brain.

classical conditioning The kind of learning through which a response elicited by an *unconditioned stimulus* becomes elicited also through a new, *conditioned stimulus.*

cognitive dissonance The unpleasant feeling that one is holding two conflicting attitudes at the same time. This feeling is held by some theorists to be an important mechanism underlying attitude change.

cohort effect The tendency for a research finding to be limited to one group or "cohort" of people, such as people all living during a particular era or in a particular location.

collective unconscious In Jung's version of psychoanalysis, the proposition that all people share certain unconscious ideas because of the history of the human species.

conceptual memory The section of declarative memory that stores what we know about general aspects of the environment (e.g., what happens at McDonald's, or what an extravert is).

condensation In psychoanalytic theory, the process of *primary process thinking* in which several ideas are compressed into one.

conditioned response (CR) A learned response to a *conditioned stimulus* (CS).

conditioned stimulus (CS) A stimulus that, after learning, elicits a *conditioned response* (CR).

construal An individual's particular experience of the world or way of interpreting reality.

constructivism The philosophical view that reality, as a concrete entity, does not exist, and that only ideas or "constructions" of reality exist.

construct validation The strategy of establishing the validity of a measure by comparing it to a wide range of other measures.

content (psychological) The ideas on which mental processes work, such as beliefs, perceptions, and categories.

convergent validation The process of assembling diverse pieces of information that converge on a common conclusion.

correlation coefficient A number between -1 and $+1$ that reflects the degree to which one variable, traditionally called Y, is a linear function of another, traditionally called X. A negative correlation means that as X goes up Y goes down; a positive correlation means that as X goes up, so does Y; a zero correlation means that X and Y are unrelated.

cortex The outside portion of an organ; in the context of this book the reference is to the outer layers of the brain.

critical realism The philosophical view that the absence of perfect, infallible criteria for truth does not imply that all interpretations of reality are equally valid; instead, one can use empirical evidence to determine which views of reality are more or less likely to be valid.

declarative knowledge The part of *long-term memory* that includes verbalizable information; sometimes called "knowing that."

defense mechanisms In psychoanalytic theory, the mechanisms of the *ego* that serve to protect an individual from experiencing anxiety produced by conflicts with the *id, superego*, or reality.

denial In psychoanalytic theory, the *defense mechanism* that denies a current source of anxiety exists.

displacement In psychoanalytic theory, the *defense mechanism* that redirects an impulse from a dangerous target to a safe one.

doctrine of opposites In psychoanalytic theory, the idea that everything implies or contains its opposite.

drive In learning theories, a state of psychological tension, the reduction of which feels good.

effect size A number that reflects the degree to which one variable affects or is related to another.

efficacy expectation In Bandura's social learning theory, one's belief that one can perform a given goal-directed behavior.

ego In psychoanalytic theory, the relatively rational part of the mind that takes on the job of balancing competing claims of the *id*, the *superego*, and reality.

Eigenwelt In Binswanger's phenomenological analysis, the experience of experience itself; the result of introspection.

emics The locally relevant components of an idea. In cross-cultural psychology, the reference is to aspects of a phenomenon that are specific to a particular culture.

empiricism The idea that everything we know comes from experience.

endorphins The body's own pain-killing chemicals, which operate by blocking the transmission of pain messages.

entity theory In Dweck's theory of motivation, an individual's belief that abilities are fixed and unchangeable.

etics The universal components of an idea. In cross-cultural psychology, the reference is to phenomena that all cultures have in common.

event memory The section of *declarative memory* that stores what we remember about specific events and facts.

expectancy In Rotter's social learning theory, an individual's subjective probability for how likely a behavior is to attain its goal.

expectancy effect The tendency for a person to become the kind of person others expect him or her to be. Also known as a "self-fulfilling prophecy."

expectancy value theory Rotter's theory of how the value and perceived attainability of a goal combine to affect the probability of a goal-seeking behavior.

existential approach The approach to personality that emphasizes the nature and meaning of human existence. Closely related to the *humanistic* and *phenomenological approaches.*

extinction The dying out of a *conditioned response* following enough trials without reinforcement or (in classical conditioning) without the pairing of the *conditioned stimulus* with the *unconditioned stimulus.*

face validity The degree to which an assessment instrument, such as a questionnaire, on its face appears to measure what it is intended to measure. For example, a face valid measure of sociability might ask about attendance at parties.

factor analysis A statistical technique for finding clusters of related traits, tests, or items.

fixation In psychoanalytic theory, leaving a disproportionate share of one's *libido* behind at an earlier stage of development.

frustration-aggression hypothesis In Dollard and Miller's social learning theory, the hypothesis that frustration automatically creates an impulse toward aggression.

functional analysis In behaviorism, a description of how a behavior is a function of the environment of the person or animal that performs it.

Funder's First Law Great strengths are usually great weaknesses, and surprisingly often the opposite is true as well.

Funder's Second Law There are no perfect indicators of personality; there are only clues, and clues are always ambiguous.

Funder's Third Law Something beats nothing, two times out of three.

Funder's Fourth Law There are only two kinds of data, Terrible Data and No Data.

Funder's Fifth Law The purpose of education is not to teach facts, or even ideas. It is to create new "chunks."

generalizability The degree to which a measurement can be found under diverse circumstances, such as time, context, subject population, and so on. In modern psychometrics, this term subsumes both *reliability* and *validity*.

genital stage In psychoanalytic theory, the final stage of psychosexual development, in which the physical focus of the *libido* is the genitals, with an emphasis on heterosexual relationships. The stage begins at about puberty, but is only fully attained when and if the individual achieves psychological maturity.

goal A mental representation (thought) about something one wants.

habit hierarchy In Dollard and Miller's social learning theory, all of the behaviors an individual might do ranked in order from most to least probable.

habituation The decrease in response to a *stimulus* on repeated applications; this is the simplest kind of learning.

hedonism The idea that people are motivated to seek pleasure and avoid pain.

heritability coefficient A statistic that reflects the percent of the variance of a trait that is controlled by genetic factors.

hippocampus A complex structure deep within the brain that forms an important part of the *limbic system.*

hormone A biological chemical that affects parts of the body some distance from where it is produced.

humanistic approach The approach to personality that emphasizes aspects of psychology that are distinctly human. Closely related to the *phenomenological* and *existential approaches.*

hypothalamus A complex structure deep within the brain, part of the *limbic system,* that has direct connections to many other parts of the brain and also is involved in the production of psychologically important hormones; thought to be important for mood and motivation.

id In psychoanalytic theory, the repository of the drives, the emotions, and the primitive, unconscious part of the mind that wants everything now.

I data "Informants' data"; judgments, by knowledgeable human informants, of general attributes of an individual's personality.

identification In psychoanalytic theory, taking on the values and worldview of another person (such as a parent).

idiographic assessment Personality assessment centered upon individuals taken one at a time, rather than upon differences between two or more individuals. Contrasts with nomothetic assessment.

incremental theory In Dweck's theory of motivation, an individual's belief that abilities can increase with experience and practice.

intellectualization In psychoanalytic theory, the defense mechanism by which thoughts that otherwise would cause anxiety are translated into cold, analytic, nonarousing terms.

inter-judge agreement The degree to which two (or more) judges of the same person provide the same description of his or her personality.

judgeability The extent to which an individual's personality can be judged accurately by others.

judgments Data that derive, in the final analysis, from someone using his or her common sense and observations to rate personality or behavior.

lateral hypothalamus The side portions of the hypothalamus, an organ in the *limbic system*; thought by Gray to be the location of part of the "approach system."

L data "Life data"; more or less easily verifiable, concrete, real-life outcomes of possible psychological significance.

learning In behaviorism, a change in behavior as a result of experience.

learning goal In Dweck's theory, a goal to learn from one's failures as well as successes in order to increase one's competence.

libido In psychoanalytic theory, the drive towards the creation, nurturing, and enhancement of life (including but not limited to sex); or the energy stemming from this drive.

limbic system An evolutionary ancient collection of structures deep within the brain thought to underlie motivation and emotion; these structures include the *hippocampus* and *amygdala* and their connections with the *hypothalamus* and *septal area*.

long-term memory (LTM) The final stage of information processing, in which a nearly unlimited amount of information can be permanently stored in an organized manner; this information may not always be accessible, however, depending on how it was stored and how it is looked for.

masculine protest In Adler's version of psychoanalysis, the idea that one particular urge in adulthood is to compensate for the powerlessness one felt in childhood.

mate selection What a person looks for in the opposite sex.

mating strategies How individuals handle heterosexual relationships.

measurement error The variation of a set of measurements around their true mean.

mental health According to Freud's definition, the ability to love and to work.

Minnesota Multiphasic Personality Inventory (MMPI) A widely used test derived through the empirical method. Originally designed for the diagnosis of psychopathology, it is today used to measure a wide range of personality attributes.

Mitwelt In Binswanger's phenomenological analysis, social experience; feelings and thoughts about others and yourself in relation to them.

moderator variable A variable that affects the relationship between two other variables.

neuron A cell of the nervous system.

neurotransmitters The chemicals that allow one *neuron* to affect, or communicate with, another.

objective test A personality test that consists of a list of questions to be answered by the subject as "true or false" or on a numeric scale.

operant conditioning Skinner's term for the process by which an organism's behavior is shaped by the consequences for the organism of that behavior's effect on the environment.

oral stage In psychoanalytic theory, the stage of psychosexual development, from birth to about eighteen months of age, in which the physical focus of the *libido* is located in the mouth, lips, and tongue.

organ inferiority In Adler's version of psychoanalysis, the idea that one is motivated to succeed in adulthood in order to compensate for whatever one felt, in childhood, was his or her weakest aspect.

outgroup homogeneity bias The social psychological phenomenon by which members of a group to which one does not belong seem more alike than members of a group to which one does belong.

parapraxis An unintentional utterance or action caused by a leakage from the unconscious parts of the mind; a "Freudian slip."

performance goal In Dweck's theory, a goal to perform well in order to attain the favorable judgment of others and of oneself.

peripheral nervous system The system of nerves running throughout the body, not including the brain and spinal cord.

perseveration A behavioral pattern in which an individual is unable to stop doing one thing in order to begin doing another.

persona In Jung's version of psychoanalysis, the social mask one wears in public dealings.

personality An individual's characteristic patterns of thought, emotion, and behavior, together with the psychological motivations behind those patterns.

phallic stage In psychoanalytic theory, the stage of psychosexual development, from about four to seven years of age, in which the physical focus of the *libido* is the penis (or for girls, in their lack thereof).

phenomenological approach The theoretical view of personality that emphasizes experience, free will, and the meaning of life. Closely related to the humanistic approach and the existential approach.

phenomenology The study of conscious experience. Often, conscious experience itself is referred to as an individual's "phenomenology."

predictive validity The degree to which one measure can be used to predict another.

primary drive A drive that is innate to an organism, such as the hunger drive.

primary process thinking In psychoanalytic theory, the term for the strange and primitive style of unconscious thinking manifested by the *id*.

procedural knowledge What you know but cannot really talk about; sometimes called "knowing how."

process (psychological) The way the mental system works; the mechanisms of perception, memory, and motivation.

projection In psychoanalytic theory, the defense mechanism of attributing a thought or impulse that is feared in oneself to somebody else.

projective test A test that presents a subject with an ambiguous *stimulus*, such as a picture or inkblot, and asks him or her to describe what is seen. The answer is held by some psychologists to reveal inner psychological states or attributes of which the subject himself or herself may be unaware.

psychic conflict The phenomenon of one part of the mind being at cross-purposes with another part of the mind.

psychic determinism The assumption that everything psychological has a cause that is, in principle, identifiable.

psychic energy In psychoanalytic theory, the energy that allows the psychological system to function. Also called *libido*.

psychoanalytic approach The theoretical view of personality, based on the writings of Sigmund Freud, that emphasizes the unconscious processes of the mind.

psychometrics The technology of psychological measurement.

punishment An aversive consequence that follows an act in order to stop the act and prevent its repetition.

rationalization In psychoanalytic theory, the *defense mechanism* that produces a seemingly logical rationale for an impulse or thought that otherwise would cause anxiety.

reaction formation In psychoanalytic theory, the *defense mechanism* that keeps an anxiety-producing impulse or thought in check by producing its opposite.

reciprocal determinism Bandura's term for the way people affect their environments even while their environments affect them.

regression In psychoanalytic theory, a movement back to an earlier stage of psychosexual development.

reinforcement In operant conditioning, a reward that, when applied following a behavior, increases the frequency of that behavior. In classical conditioning, this term refers to the pairing of a *conditioned stimulus* with the *unconditioned stimulus*.

reinforcement value In Rotter's social learning theory, how much a given reinforcement is worth.

reliability In measurement, the tendency of an instrument to provide the same comparative information on repeated occasions.

repression In psychoanalytic theory, the *defense mechanism* that banishes the past from current awareness.

respondent conditioning Skinner's term for *classical conditioning*.

response Anything a person or animal does as a result of a *stimulus*.

Rorschach Test A projective test that asks subjects to interpret blots of ink.

schedule of reinforcement The rate and frequency with which a *reinforcement* is applied.

schema A mental structure of knowledge.

S data "Self judgments"; ratings that people provide of their own personality attributes or behavior.

secondary drive A drive that is learned through its association with *primary drives*—for example, the drive for prestige.

secondary process thinking In psychoanalytic theory, the term for rational and conscious processes of ordinary thought.

second-order conditioning The training of a new *conditioned response* to a previously acquired *conditioned stimulus*.

self-concept A person's knowledge and opinions about himself or herself.

self-efficacy A person's beliefs about the degree to which he or she will be able to accomplish what he or she sets out to do, if he or she tries.

sensory buffer The first stage of information processing in which nearly all stimulus information is held, in unprocessed form, for a very short period of time (also called perceptual buffer).

septal area (of the brain) A thin sheet of brain tissue underneath the *cerebral hemispheres* that connects the *hippocampus* and the *hypothalamus;* said by Gray to be the location of part of the approach system.

septo-hippocampus The connective area between the *hippocampus* and the *septal area;* this brain tissue is part of the *limbic system.*

short-term memory (STM) The second stage of information processing, in which the person is consciously aware of a small amount of information (about seven "chunks") as long as that information continues to be actively processed.

spontaneous recovery The reappearance of an extinguished response without further *reinforcement.*

state A temporary psychological event, such as an emotion, thought, or perception.

stimulus Anything in the environment that impinges upon the nervous system. The plural form is stimuli.

stimulus generalization The phenomenon of responding to a *stimulus* that resembles a *conditioned stimulus* (CS) nearly as if it were the CS itself.

strategy In Cantor and Kihlstrom's theory, procedural knowledge about how to react under certain circumstances to attain a particular goal.

sublimation In psychoanalytic theory, the *defense mechanism* that turns otherwise dangerous or anxiety-producing impulses to constructive ends.

superego In psychoanalytic theory, the location of conscience and the individual's system of internalized rules of conduct, or morality.

symbolization In psychoanalytic theory, the process of *primary process thinking* in which one thing stands for another.

synapse The space between two *neurons* across which impulses are carried by *neurotransmitters.*

T data "Test data"; direct observations of another's behavior that are translated directly or nearly directly into numerical form. T data can be gathered in natural or contrived (experimental) settings, and include some (but not most) standard personality tests.

teleological fallacy The assumption that everything that exists today exists because of its effects. Also known as "functionalism."

Thanatos In psychoanalytic theory, another term for the drive toward death, destruction, and decay.

Thematic Apperception Test (TAT) A *projective test* that asks subjects to make up stories about pictures.

thrown-ness In Heidegger's existential analysis, the era, location, and situation into which you happened to be born.

trait A relatively stable and long-lasting attribute of personality.

trait approach The theoretical view of personality that focuses on individual differences in personality and behavior, and the psychological processes behind them.

transference In psychoanalytic theory, the tendency to bring ways of thinking, feeling, and behavior that developed with one important person into later relationships with different persons.

Umwelt In Binswanger's phenomenological analysis, biological experience; the sensations you feel of being a live animal.

unconditioned response (UCR) A response to an *unconditioned stimulus* (UCS) that is elicited even prior to learning.

unconditioned stimulus (UCS) A stimulus that elicits a built-in response (UCR) even prior to learning.

unconscious (mind) Those areas and processes of the mind of which a person is not aware.

utilitarianism The idea that the best society is that which creates the most happiness for the largest number of people.

validity In measurement, the degree to which a measurement actually reflects what it is intended to measure.

working memory The third stage of information processing, which contains a large amount of information, including a representation of the current environment, in easily accessible form just out of consciousness.

NAME INDEX

Abelson, R. P., 392
Adair, J. G., 53
Adler, A., 266
Adorno, T. W., 130, 135
Ahadi, S., 70
Ainsworth, M. D. S., 276
Ajzen, I., 67
Allen, A., 62, 67
Allport, G. W., 41, 57, 60, 67, 76, 88–89, 109, 119, 143, 195, 319
Alper, J., 193
Amabile, T. M., 247
Andersen, S. M., 101n, 113, 274
Anderson, E., 310, 328
Appleby, G. S., 137
Aron, A., 197
Aronson, E., 70
Arsenian, J., 321
Arsenian, J. M., 321
Associated Press, 329
Azrin, N. H., 357

Bachrach, H. M., 272
Bader, M. J., 238n
Bailey, K. G., 154
Bandura, A., 104, 376, 378, 379, 379n
Bargh, J. A., 297
Barnes, M. F., 189
Barrett, K., 277
Barrett, P., 162, 315
Batson, C. D. 72
Baum, A., 274
Baumeister, R. F., 62
Baumrind, D., 53, 183, 224
Beckwith, J., 193
Bem, D. J., 31, 62, 67, 119, 121, 197
Bem, S. L., 101n
Bennett, A. B., 145
Bergeman, C. S., 88, 183
Berkowitz, L., 249, 367
Berlund, G. W., 104
Berry, D. S., 110, 113
Berscheid, E., 100
Bersoff, D. M., 325
Bettelheim, B., 213, 226, 259n
Bevan, A. R., 113
Biek, M., 111
Bijnen, E. J., 315
Binswanger, L., 289, 293
Blehar, M. C., 276
Block, J., 13n, 66, 88, 89, 106, 119, 120, 122, 124, 125, 128, 144, 320, 330
Block, J. H., 13n, 121, 122, 124, 128, 330

Bond, M. H., 145, 145–46, 318, 321, 325
Borkenau, P., 113
Boss, M., 288
Bouffard, D. L., 61
Bourne, E. J., 316, 317, 324
Bower, G. H., 340, 345, 347, 348, 350
Bowers, K. S., 64
Bowlby, J., 275
Brandt, V. S., 325
Brenner, C., 205, 232, 252, 263
Briggs, S. R., 89, 93, 142, 143, 145
Broadbent, D. E., 385
Brunswik, E., 43–44, 114
Bullock, W. A., 162–63
Burnett, J. D., 38
Burris, L. R., 138
Burwen, L. S., 66, 67
Buss, A. H., 142
Buss, D. M., 189, 190
Butler, J. M., 296
Bykov, K. M., 347

Callahan, C., 138
Campbell, A., 135
Campbell, D. T., 66, 67, 106
Campos, J. J., 277
Canter, S., 186
Cantor, N., 85, 86, 401, 402
Cantril, H., 283
Carlsmith, J. M., 71
Carlson, E., 276
Carter, J., 359
Carver, C. S., 175
Castellan, N. J., 36
Cattell, R. B., 13n, 74, 86, 87, 143
Chaplin, W. F., 67n, 68
Chase, W. G., 402
Cheek, J. M., 89, 93, 99, 142, 143
Cheung, T., 318
Chipuer, H. M., 179, 181, 182
Claridge, G. S., 186
Clark, C. L., 103, 277, 278
Clark, E. V., 73
Clark, H. H., 73
Clark, J. M., 111
Clark, L. A., 144
Cohen, J., 47
Colvin, C. R., 25, 28, 67, 73, 107, 108, 109, 109n, 110, 112, 113, 139
Converse, P. E., 135
Cook, T. D., 106
Copeland, P., 185
Corley, R., 185

Cosmides, L., 180, 185, 188
Costa, P. T., Jr., 87, 144, 145, 320, 321
Cousins, S. D., 319
Craik, F. I. M., 390
Cronbach, L. J., 39, 40, 106, 107
Csikszentmihalyi, I. S., 301
Csikszentmihalyi, M., 27, 301
Cutler, A. G., 173

Dabbs, J. M., Jr., 173, 174
Dahlstrom, W. G., 28
Darley, J. M., 72
Davidson, M. N., 274
Davidson, R. J., 396
Dawkins, R., 188, 192
Dawson, J. L. M., 323
DeFries, J. C., 185
Dennett, D. C., 305
Diener, C. I., 406
Diener, E., 70
DiGeronimo, K., 111
Dillehay, R. C., 130, 134, 134–35
Dobroth, K. M., 110
Dollard, J., 364
Doyle, J. M., 393
Dutton, D., 197
Dweck, C. S., 405, 406, 407
Dworkin, B. R., 347

Ebbesen, E., 31
Eber, H. W., 143
Eccles, J., 102
Ekman, P., 396
Elder, G., 42
Elms, A. C., 135
Emmons, R. A., 22, 86
Epstein, S., 38, 39, 67
Erdelyi, M. H., 274, 387
Erikson, E., 269
Exner, J. E., Jr., 80, 81, 82
Eysenck, H. J., 87, 143, 160, 162, 315
Eysenck, S. B. G., 143, 162, 315

Fenz, W. D., 67
Festinger, L., 71
Feuer, L. S., 303
Finch Wero, J. W., 113
Fishbein, M., 67
Flint, A., 194
Floody, O. R., 174
Flor-Henry, P., 160
Folger, R., 53
Frady, R. L., 174
Freeman, W., 158
Frenkel-Brunswik, E., 130
Freud, S., 197, 238
Friedman, H. S., 13, 138, 167
Friedman, I., 296
Frijda, N. H., 396
Fromm, E., 129
Fulker, D. W., 185
Funder, D. C., 15, 16, 25, 28, 31, 48, 49, 59, 62,
    63, 67, 71, 73, 74, 77, 105, 106, 107, 108,
    109n, 110, 112, 113, 114n, 115, 116, 119,
    121, 122, 124, 125, 139, 183, 193, 354, 400

Gabrenya, W. K., Jr., 314
Galatzer-Levy, R., 272
Gangestad, S. W., 111, 143, 191
Gay, P., 250n, 259, 263

Gergen, K., 42
Gigerenzer, G., 47
Gilliland, K., 162–63
Gilmore, D. D., 328
Giorgi, A., 302
Gjerde, P. F., 128
Glazebrook, A. H., 247
Gleitman, H., 347, 349
Goetz, T. E., 406, 407
Goffman, E., 267
Gold, S. R., 389
Goldberg, L. R., 67n, 70, 145, 321
Goldinger, L. A., 137
Goldman, W., 102
Goldsmith, H. H., 277
Gorer, G., 309n
Gough, H. G., 59, 82, 83
Gralinski, J. H., 104
Gray, J. A., 163, 171
Greenberg, J., 53
Greene, D., 108, 109n
Greene, E. L., 393
Gregory, R. L., 340
Guilford, J. P., 88
Guthrie, E. R., 348
Guthrie, G. M., 145

Haigh, G. V., 296
Hall, C. S., 286
Hall, J. A., 13
Hamer, D. H., 185
Hammond, K. R., 36, 44
Hampson, S. E., 373
Hanin, Y., 315
Hanson, F. A., 93, 95
Harlow, H., 156
Harris, M., 320n
Harris, M. J., 13, 139
Hartmann, H., 266
Harwood, R. L., 325
Hastie, R., 105
Hastorf, A. H., 283
Hathaway, S. R., 90
Headland, T. N., 320n
Heidegger, M., 290
Hemenway, D., 359
Hetherington, E. M., 183
Higgins, E. T., 297
Hilgard, E. R., 63, 340, 345, 347, 348, 350
Hilton, T. L., 104
Hofstede, G., 324
Hogan, R., 17
Holt, R. R., 233
Holz, W. C., 357
Hopper, C. H., 174
Horn, J. M., 183
Horney, K., 268, 269
House, P., 108, 109n
Householder, J. E., 36
Hubbard, M., 53
Hughes, C. F., 274
Hull, C. L., 350
Hume, W. I., 186
Hunter, J. E., 138
Husband, A. J., 347
Hwang, K. K., 314

Ickes, W., 61

Jacklin, C. N., 173

Jackson, D. N., 84, 93, 113
Jacobson, L., 100
Janoff-Bulman, R., 403
John, O. P., 25, 107, 144, 145
Jones, E. E., 109n, 313, 322
Jourard, S. M., 110
Jung, C. G., 267, 268
Jussim, L., 100, 102, 393

Kagan, J., 173
Kahneman, D., 21
Keefe, R. C., 189, 192
Keith-Spiegel, P., 211
Kellner, R., 174
Kelly, G. A., 288, 319, 383, 391, 396
Kenny, D. A., 111
Kenrick, D. T., 62, 74, 189, 192
Keyes, S., 128
Kihlstrom, J. F., 274, 275, 278, 401
King, L. A., 22, 86
King, M. G., 347
Kircher, P., 193, 195
Kitayama, S., 314, 323, 324
Klein, G. S., 266
Klinger, E., 389
Kluckhohn, C., 60
Koffka, K., 340
Kohler, W., 340, 349
Kolar, D. W., 25, 107, 108, 109n
Koopermans, L. H., 174–75
Kramer, P. D., 170, 172
Kruglanski, A. W., 105

Lamb, M. E., 277
Langer, E. J., 395
Larkin, J. H., 402
Larsen, R. J., 190
Larson, R., 27
Larson-Gutman, M. K., 389
Latane, B., 72
Lau, R. R., 373, 375
Laws, D. R., 174
Lee, Y.-T., 393
Leggett, E. L., 405, 406, 407
Lepper, M. R., 53
Levinson, D., 130
Levis, D. J., 348
Lewis, P., 102
Liebler, A., 113
Lindzey, G., 286
Linville, P., 313, 322
Little, B. R., 403
Loehlin, J. C., 179, 181, 182, 183
Loevinger, J., 233, 266
Loftus, E. F., 393
Lombardi, W. J., 297
Long, F. Y., 143
Lorenz, K., 188
Lorenzi-Cioldi, F., 313
Lykes, M. B., 324

McAdams, D. P., 22, 86, 145, 287, 293, 415
McCartney, K., 186
McCauley, C. R., 393
McClelland, D. C., 81, 111, 321
McClelland, J. L., 274, 399
Maccoby, E., 121, 173
McCrae, R. R., 20, 87, 144, 145, 320, 321
McDermott, J., 402
McGinnies, E., 386

Machover, K., 81
McKay, J. R., 108
MacLean, P. D., 151
Mahapatra, M., 312
Main, M., 276
Marceil, J. C., 304
Markus, H. R., 314, 323, 324, 388, 402
Maryanski, A., 194
Maslow, A. H., 294
Masson, J. M., 214n, 264
Meehl, P. E., 39, 90, 106, 134
Megargee, E. I., 244
Metzner, R. J., 171–72, 172
Michigan Department of Education, 137
Milgram, S., 52, 72, 135
Miller, G. A., 387
Miller, J. G., 312, 325
Miller, L. G., 193
Miller, N. E., 364
Miller, W. E., 135
Mischel, W., 31, 62, 63, 65, 70, 124, 397, 398,
    399, 400
Monson, T. C., 62, 142
Moray, N., 386
Morgan, C. D., 81
Morris, R., 173, 174
Murray, H. A., 29, 41, 60, 80, 81, 143, 204
Myers, I. B., 268

Nakazato, H., 145
Neill, J. A., 113
Nikula, R., 389
Nisbett, R. E., 62, 65, 109n, 353
Norem, J. K., 85, 86, 404
Norman, W. T., 144
Nurius, P., 402

O'Bannon, R. M., 137
Odbert, H. S., 57, 119, 143
Ones, D. S., 94, 96, 137, 138
Ornstein, R. E., 160, 305
Oxenstierna, G., 186
Ozer, D. J., 48, 49, 71

Paivio, A., 111
Park, B., 313
Parke, R. D., 183
Peabody, D., 136
Peake, P. K., 124
Pennebaker, J. W., 110, 274
Pettigrew, T. F., 393
Pike, K. L., 320n
Plomin, R., 179, 181, 182, 185
Poortinga, Y. H., 315
Pope, K. S., 211, 214
Price, R. H., 61
Public Health Service, 43
Purifoy, P. E., 174–75

Rada, R. T., 174
Rapaport, D., 266
Rasinski, K. A., 105
Reilly, J. P., 389
Reise, H. T., 325
Robins, R. W., 25, 107
Robinson, P., 264n
Roese, N. J., 53
Rogers, C. R., 287, 294, 295
Rokeach, M., 136
Rorer, L. G., 105, 136

Rorschach, H., 29, 80
Rosenthal, R., 36, 38, 48n, 49, 66, 69, 100, 102
Rosnow, R. L., 36, 48n
Rosolack, T. K., 373
Ross, L., 53, 62, 108, 109n, 400
Ross, S. A., 378
Rothbart, M., 313
Rotter, J. B., 104, 370
Ross, D., 378
Ruback, R. B., 174
Rubin, D. B., 49, 69
Rudikoff, E. C., 296
Rumelhart, D. E., 274, 399
Rychlak, J. F., 302, 303, 304, 305
Ryle, G., 391

Sabini, J., 135, 136–37, 318, 325
Sackett, P. R., 138
Sacks, O. W., 171
Sanford, N., 130
Sartre, J. P., 291, 292, 293, 331
Scarr, S., 136, 186
Schank, R. C., 392
Scheier, M. F., 175
Scherer, K. R., 113
Schmidt, F. L., 94, 138
Sears, D. O., 41
Sears, R. R., 226, 274
Seligman, M. E. P., 347
Selye, H., 175
Semmelroth, J., 190
Sgoritas, D. S., 174
Shanahan, J., 135
Shapiro, K. J., 302
Sharpe, D., 53
Shaver, P. R., 103, 277, 278
Shedler, J., 128
Shils, E. A., 136
Shiraishi, D., 145
Shoda, Y., 63, 124, 399, 400
Shulman, S., 276
Shweder, R. A., 30, 183, 311, 312, 315, 316, 317, 318, 324, 327, 329n
Siegelman, E., 330
Silverstein, S., 92
Simon, D. P., 402
Simon, H. A., 402
Simpson, J. A., 111, 191
Skinner, B. F., 51, 342, 351, 352
Skolnikoff, A., 272
Sneed, C. D., 113, 114n, 115, 116
Snyder, M., 61, 62, 67, 100, 139, 142, 143
Solnick, S., 359
Spain, J., 27
Sroufe, L. A., 276
Stampfl, T. G., 348
Stanovich, K. E., 105
Stenberg, C., 277
Sternberg, R. J., 138
Stipek, D. J., 104
Stokes, D. E., 135
Strong, E. K., Jr., 91
Sullivan, M. A., 183, 311, 315, 316, 318, 327, 329n
Sulloway, F. J., 264n

Sundberg, N. D., 81
Symons, D., 189
Szasz, T. S., 288

Tabachnick, B., 211
Taft, R., 107
Tanke, E. D., 100
Tansey, M. J., 272
Thompson, C., 157
Thorndike, E. L., 349, 350
Tice, D. M., 62
Tomlinson-Keasey, C., 183
Tooby, J., 180, 185, 188
Triandis, H. C., 43, 309, 310, 311, 312, 321, 322, 323, 324, 326, 327
Triesman, A. M., 386
Tulving, E., 390
Turner, J. H., 194
Tversky, A., 21

Uhlmann, C., 274

Valenstein, E. S., 156, 157, 158, 159
Vallacher, R., 403
Van der Net, Z. J., 315
Vernon, P. E., 67
Viswesvaran, C., 94
von der Lippe, A., 330
Vonnegut, K., Jr., 3, 292

Wakefield, J. C., 192
Waldron, S., 272
Wall, S., 276
Waller, D., 94
Waters, E., 276
Watkins, M. J., 390
Watson, D., 110, 144
Watson, J. B., 343
Watts, J. W., 158
Wegner, D., 403
Weinberger, D. A., 274
Weiner, P., 305
Weiss, J. M., 347
Welsh, G. S., 28
West, S. G., 105, 107
Westen, D., 190, 236, 237, 274, 279
Wheeler, L., 325
Whorf, B. L., 73
Widaman, K., 183
Widom, C. S., 359
Wiggins, J. S., 59, 81, 82, 84, 91
Willerman, L., 183
Wilson, E. O., 188
Wilson, G. D., 162
Wilson, T. D., 353
Woodworth, R. S., 84
Wylie, R. C., 297

Yang, K. S., 145–46, 321

Zimbardo, P. G., 99
Zimmerman, W. S., 88
Zuckerman, M., 67n, 154, 155, 157, 158, 159, 161, 162, 163, 164, 166, 171, 173, 174, 176, 186

SUBJECT INDEX

abortion, and individualism vs. collectivism, 325–26
accidents, psychoanalysis denial of, 206, 253
accuracy, 116
  of lay judgments of personality, 105–16
  see also validity
achievement, cultural attitudes toward, 321–22
acquaintanceship effect, 112
actor-observer effect, 109n
adjustment, psychological, Rotter on, 374–76
Adler, Alfred, 213, 263, 264, 266
  and interpersonal relations, 266
adoption studies, 182–83
adult attachment style, 277–78
affiliation, cultural attitudes toward, 322
African Americans, 138
aggregation (averaging), 37–39
aggressiveness (aggression), 176
  displacement of, 249
  and Freud, 212
  frustration-aggression hypothesis, 366–67
  and testosterone, 168, 173–74, 175
agreeableness, 119
"aha" effect, 349
Ainsworth, Mary, 276–77
alcoholism
  and denial, 242
  and self-judgment, 108
allocentrism, 326–27
Allport, Gordon, 41, 57, 195, 286
American Psychological Association (APA), convention of, 78
America's Funniest Home Videos, 256
amygdala, 159, 162, 166
anal stage, 222–25
anatomical approach, 150, 151
  see also biological approach
Angst, 290–91
anima and animus (Jung), 267–68
animal research, 417–18
anti-Semitism, 130, 134, 135
anxiety, 347
  and amygdala, 159
  and brain function, 166
  in Dollard and Miller's theory, 369, 370
  existential, 290–91
  Horney on, 269
  and perceptual defense, 274, 386
  and psychoanalytic theory
    in defense mechanisms, 242–50
    sources of, 240–41
    and superego, 234
  and supertraits, 177

  and test performance (research design), 45–46
  and unconditional positive regard (Rogers), 295
anxious-ambivalent children, 276
approach-avoidance conflict, 367–68
approach system, in brain, 164
ARAS (Ascending Reticulocortical Activating System), 160–61, 162, 163
archetypes, 267
Aristotle, 149
Army, U.S., personality test of, 84–85
arousal
  interpretation of, 197
  neurological, 163
  sexual arousal sought (Dollard and Miller), 365–66
Ascending Reticulocortical Activating System (ARAS), 160–61, 162, 163
associationism, 339–41
  and classical conditioning, 345
attachment, modern psychoanalytic research on, 275–79
authentic existence, 293, 295
authoritarianism, 129–37, 144, 401
  as parenting style, 224
authoritative parenting style, 224
authority
  and anal stage, 223–25
  Milgram study on, 52–53, 72
autonomy
  in ego psychology (Loevinger), 233
  in Erikson's theory, 270
autotelic activities, 301
avoidant children, 276
awareness
  in phenomenological approach, 286, 287, 305
  see also consciousness
Aziz, Tariq, 310

"backward masking" studies, 385
bad faith, 291–92
Baker, James, 310
Bandura, Albert, 376–80, 382, 383, 398
Barry, Dave, xxiv
bathroom humor, 255
beeper method of data collection, 26–27
behavior
  causes of, 353–54
  personality judgments based on, 420
  shaping of, 352–53
behavioral genetics, 5, 150, 179–87
  future of, 418
  in sexual-orientation explanation, 197–200

behaviorism and behavioristic approach, xxv, 2, 6, 7n, 335, 337–38, 412
    and actual vs. expected reward or punishment, 371–72
    and Bandura on determinism, 379
    and chronological order of approaches, 413
    and cognitive approach, 3n, 382
    contributions of, 360–61
    Dollard and Miller's extension of, 364
    ethical questions in, 51
    as functional analysis, 338–39
    as isolated program, 363–64
    and passivity, 379
    vs. phenomenological approach, 287
    philosophical roots of, 339–43
    and punishment, 355–60
    self-knowledge avoided in, 214
    shortcomings of, 361, 362–63
    and social learning theory, 3n, 336, 363
    see also biological approach
behavior potential, 371
Bem, Daryl, 134, 197, 199
Berkeley group, 130, 131, 136
Bernstein, Carl, 218
BESD (binomial effect size display), 49–51, 69
Bettelheim, Bruno, 206n, 264, 265
bias
    gender, 41–42
    in informant (I) data, 20–21
    outgroup, 313
Bible
    Freudian doctrine analogous to, 261n
    Proverbs quoted, 355
Big Five (group of traits), 119, 144–46, 320, 321
Big Five, Chinese, 145–46, 321
binomial effect size display (BESD), 49–51, 69
Binswanger, Ludwig, 289
biochemistry of personality, 150, 167–77
    in sexual-orientation explanation, 197–200
biological approach(es), xxv, 2, 149–50, 151, 411, 413
    behavioral genetics, 5, 150, 179–87, 197–200, 418
    and biochemistry of personality, 150, 167–77
    and brain, 151–67 (see also brain)
    and chronological order of approaches, 413
    evolutionary theory, 5, 111, 150, 180, 184–85, 187–95, 197–200, 275
    future of, 418
    as replacement for psychology, 195–96
    and sexual-orientation explanation, 197–200
biological reductionism, 149, 196
Block, Jack, 373
Bohr, Neils, 303
Boss, Medard, 289
Bowlby, John, 275, 278
brain
    anatomy and function of, 151
        human brain, 155–60
        neomammalian brain, 153–55, 193, 231
        paleomammalian brain, 152–53, 231
        reptilian brain, 151–52, 231
    and behavior patterns, 158, 159
    difficulties in study of, 149
    and Freudian theory, 231
    functions of, 160
        approach and inhibition (Gray), 163–66
        inhibition and excitation (Eysenck), 160–63
        synthetic view on, 166–67
    and language, 159, 195
    left and right halves of, 159–60
    and mind, 149, 206
    and personality, 167
    and sexual-orientation explanation, 199
Brunswik, Egon, 43–44, 114
"Brunswikians," 44
burden of proof, on generalizability, 43
Bush, George, 318, 318n
bystander intervention research, 72

California F scale, 130–31, 132–33
California Psychological Inventory (CPI), 79, 82–83, 180
California Q-set. See Q-sort
Cantor, Nancy, 401–5
Carson, Johnny, 255
case study method, 416
    in psychoanalytic theory, 210, 258
cassette player, as brain-mind analogy, 149
catecholamines, 171
categorizing or classifying, 6–7
    and cognitive person variables, 397
    and cross-cultural psychology, 319–20
    Hilgard on, v
    as test purpose, 93–96
catharsis, 274, 367
causality, and experimental method, 45–46
Central Intelligence Agency (CIA), 94
cerebral cortex, 153–54
cerebral hemispheres, 159–60
character type, and Freudian stages, 219
    anal, 224, 274
    genital, 228
    oral, 221–22, 274
    phallic, 227
Charcot, Jean-Martin, 213
child abuse
    joke about, 255
    sexual abuse, 96, 214, 214n
child-rearing
    Freud's theory of, 221
        and anal stage, 223–24
        and oral stage, 220–21
    styles of, 224
        and authoritarianism, 135, 224
Chinese culture
    as collectivist, 320, 328
    difficulties in research on, 313–14
    personality traits in, 145–46, 321
    personal projects of students in, 331
choice
    and existentialists, 291
    and human environment, 363
chunks of information, 387–88
classical conditioning, 344–49
    vs. operant conditioning, 354–55
clinical psychology
    psychoanalysis and alternatives in, 209–10, 211
    as sublimation, 250
coaches
    as Freudians, 253–54
    and procedural knowledge, 395
cocktail party, as Western invention, 325
"cocktail party effect," 385
cognitive approach(es), 3, 3n, 6, 335–36, 382–84, 412
    cognitive social learning theory, 396–401
    future development of, 417
    intersections of, 408–9
    and long-term memory, 391–96

to motivation, 405–8
and perception of personality, 419
and sensory/perceptual buffer, 384–87
and short-term memory, 387–88
and short-term to long-term memory
movement, 390
and social intelligence, 401–5
and working memory, 389–90
cognitive complexity, 326
cognitive dissonance, and forced- compliance
study, 71–72
cognitive person variables, 397–98, 399–400
cognitive processing, 274
cognitive psychology, 279, 382
as combined with personality theory, 399
cognitive social learning theory, 396–401
cognitive unconscious, 264
cohort effects, 42
collective unconscious (Jung), 267
collectivist cultures, 323–26, 419
and idea of personality, 418
romanticization of, 314, 419
and self-reliance, 320
college students
dependency of, 243
"helpless patterns" of, 406
personal projects of (China), 331–32
as research subjects, 15, 40–41, 42, 87
as research subjects (China), 314
commonality scale, 83
comparative cultural approach, 320–27
comparisons, of individual differences, 60
compartmentalization
and I data, 18–20
and self-judgments, 23
compensation, in Adler's theory, 266
complexity, as cultural trait, 322, 326–27
computers, and flow, 301
computer simulation of personality, 417
conceptual memory, 392–93
conditioned reflex, 345
conditioned response (CR), 345
conditioned stimulus (CS), 345
conditioning
classical, 344–49, 354–55
operant, 349–355
conditions of worth, 295, 296
conflict, psychic
Dollard and Miller on, 367–69
in psychoanalytic view, 207
and anxiety, 240–41
and Erikson, 269–71
conscientiousness, 137–38, 144
on Big Five list, 119, 144
and cultural tightness, 326
and integrity tests, 94, 95, 144
significance of, 13
conscious experience, and phenomenological
approach, 286, 287, 294, 305
consciousness, 305
Freudian view of, 236–37, 388
short-term memory as, 388
conservatism
of evolutionary biology, 193–94
and pseudoconservatism, 131, 131n, 135, 136
consistency controversy, 38, 62–74
Constitution of U.S., Freudian doctrine
analogous to, 261–62
construals, variation in, 308
constructive alternativism, 299–300

constructivism, 105
and deconstructionism, 315–20, 327, 339
construct validation, 39–40
content vs. process in psychology, 330–31
control, personality tests for, 94–95
convergent validation, 106
Copernicus, and Freud, 208
correlational methods, 44–46
correlation coefficient, 47–49, 65, 71
cortisol, 175–76
cosmetic psychopharmacology, 172
counterconditioning, 348–49
CPI (California Psychological Inventory), 79,
82–83, 180
cravings, Hull on, 350
critical realism, 105
cross-cultural differences, 308–11
approaches to
comparative-cultural, 320–27
deconstructionism, 315–20, 327, 339
neglect, 314–15
origins of, 327–29
and process vs. content, 330–31
and universal human condition, 331–32
and variations within culture, 329–30
cross-cultural psychology, xxv, 320
in future, 418–19
cross-cultural research, difficulties of, 311–14
cross-cultural study of personality, 283–84
Csikszentmihalyi, Mihalyi, 301–2, 304
cultural psychology, implications of, 329–32
cultural relativism, see relativism
culture, vs. values, 329–30

Darwin, Charles, 187, 208, 414
data quality, 36
generalizability, 40–44
reliability, 36–39
validity, 39–40
data types, 11–13
informant (I data), 15–21
life outcomes (L data), 13–14
self-judgments (S data), 21–25, 103–4 (see also
self-judgments)
test (T data), 25–32, 64, 80, 81
death drive (Freud), 217–18
deception, in research, 52–54
decision making, expectancy value theory of,
370–74, 377
declarative knowledge, 391–93
deconstructionism
and cross-cultural psychology, 315–20, 327
as rationalist, 339
Deep Throat, 218
defense mechanisms, 242
cognitive understanding of, 386–87
denial, 242–43, 253
displacement, 249, 367
Dollard and Miller on, 369–70
intellectualization, 247–48
and leakages, 250–51
projection, 246–47
psychology departments' resort to, 214
rationalization, 247
reaction formation, 245–46
repression, 24, 243–45, 274, 369
research on, 274
sublimation, 250, 254, 367
defensive pessimists, 404
definitions, and Freudian theory, 258–59

delay of gratification, 31–32, 118, 121–25, 398
denial, 242–43
  of slips, 242, 253
Dennett, Daniel, 194
dependency
  of college students, 243
  and oral stage, 220
depression, 128
  and psychic energy, 244
  and Rotter's theory, 374
desensitization, systematic, 348
designer personality, 172
determinism, 205, 206n
  reciprocal, 379–80
  and slips, 251
developmental psychology
  for ego psychology, 233
  Eriksonian, 270–71
  Freudian-psychoanalytic, 218–19, 229–31
    anal stage, 222–25
    genital stage, 227–29
    oral stage, 219–22
    phallic stage, 225–27, 270, 274
diaries, as data source, 26–27
"disappearing student trick," 406
discrimination, racial and sexual, utilitarians as
    opposing, 342
displacement, 249
  and frustration-aggression hypothesis, 367
doctrine or principle of opposites, 217–18,
    220–21
dogmatism, 136
Dollard, John, 364–70, 415
dopamine, 168, 171, 176, 177
double-blind drug trial, 52n
dream analysis, 237
drives, in Dollard and Miller theory, 365–66
drug abuse, 125, 128
  and punishment vs. reward, 356
drugs, psychoactive, 168–69
Dweck, Carol, 405–8

easy cultures, 321
ecological approach, to cross-cultural differences,
    327–29
Edelman, Gerald, on questioning, v
education
  expectancy in, 100
  purposes of, 394
    and chunks of information, 388
    as study of facts vs. method, 34–35
    scientific, 35–36
  see also lecturing
effect sizes, 47
  and correlation coefficient, 47–49, 71
  and significance vs. importance, 46–47
efficacy expectations, 104, 377–78, 397
ego, 232–33
  and brain, 231
  and psychic conflict, 240–41
ego control, 124
ego psychologists, 232, 233, 266
ego resiliency, 124
Eigenwelt, 290
emics, 320–21
emotions
  behaviorist rethinking of, 360–61
  future attention to, 417–18
  as procedural knowledge, 396
empirical method, of test construction, 89–93

empiricism, 339, 340
endorphins, 169
entity theories, 406, 407–8
entropy, 217
environment
  in behaviorist viewpoint, 337–39
  and expectations, 382
  genes in interaction with, 186–87 (see also
    behavioral genetics)
  humans' ability to choose, 363
  and psychoanalytic approach, 209
    and Masson critique, 214n
  and reciprocal determinism, 379–80
  roles as function of, 19–20
  see also situation, influence of
Epictetus, 287
Epicurus, 341
Erikson, Erik, 264, 269–71
  and anal stage, 223, 270
  and interpersonal relations, 266
error variance, 37
essential-trait approach to understanding of
    behavior, 143–46
ethics, of psychological research, 51–54
ethnic diversity, and generalizability of data,
    42
ethnic groups
  generalization from experience with, 346
  and stereotypes, 393
ethnic subcultures in inner city, 310, 328
ethnocentrism, 312–13
  and genital mutilation denunciation, 329
etics, 320–21
event memory, 392
evolutionary theory, 5, 150, 187–95
  and Bowlby on love, 275
  and heritabilities, 184–85
  in sexual-orientation explanation, 197–200
  and sociosexuality, 111
  and species-specific traits, 180
existential anxiety, 290–91
existentialism, 286, 289–93
expectancy effects, 18, 100–103
expectancy value theory of decision making,
    370–74, 377
expectations
  as cognitive, 382
  and compartmentalization, 18–19
  efficacy, 104, 377–78, 397
experience
  future attention to, 417–18
  mystery of, 305
  see also conscious experience
experimental methods, 44–46
experiments, 27–28
  and humanistic theory, 304
  and psychoanalytic approach, 209, 265
external locus of control, 104, 372
extraversion
  and ARAS, 161, 162–63
  on Big Five list, 119, 144
  as essential trait, 143
  and Gray's scheme, 165
  Jung on, 268
  and self-monitoring, 142
  as supertrait, 177
  and testosterone, 174
Eysenck, Hans, 143, 160–63, 166, 167, 176–77,
    315
Eysenck Personality Questionnaire, 163, 180

face validity, 90
factor analytic method, of test construction, 86–89, 93
false consensus effect, 109n
Fascism, and authoritarianism, 129
   see also authoritarianism
fear
   and amygdala, 159
   vs. anxiety, 347
   and brain function, 166
   and phallic stage, 227
female genital mutilation, 329
fight vs. flight system, 165, 166
   and cortisol, 175
fish-and-water effect, 25
fixation, 219, 230, 250
fixed action patterns, in reptiles, 152, 154–55
flow, 301–2
forced compliance effect, 71
forgetting, in Freudian view, 251–52
free association, 213, 236, 237
freedom, and authoritarianism, 129–30
free will, 288
   and phenomenological approach, 4, 288, 304
      and atoms (Rychlak), 303
   as question, 416
Freud, Anna, 263, 264, 265, 269
Freud, Sigmund, 212–14, 261, 286
   on anatomy as destiny, 195n
   and anxiety, 240
   on artistic production, 250, 250n
   on consciousness, 236–37, 388
   and controversy, 207–8
   and cross-cultural concerns, 314
   as determinist, 206n, 251
   and Erikson, 270
   intellectualization of, 248
   and Jung, 267, 268
   and libido, 216n
   limitations in database of, 308–9
   on love and work, 228
   on medical training, 210
   as moderate, 221, 231
   modern reactions to, 261–64
   presentation of, xxiv
   as rationalist, 213, 237, 268
   and sexual orientation, 197, 241
   on significance of therapy, 238
   and single perspective, 414
   and therapeutic value, 238
   and tragic view of life, 217
   and transference, 238
   and women, 228–29, 229n, 259, 269
   see also psychoanalytic approach and theory
Fromm, Erich, 129–30
frontal lobes, 155–59
frustration-aggression hypothesis, 366–67
fully functioning person, 295, 296
functional analysis, 338–39
functionalism, 194
fundamental attribution error, 400
Funder's First Law, 4, 7, 12, 25, 60
Funder's Second Law, 11, 163
Funder's Third Law, 12, 25, 33, 311, 314
Funder's Fourth Law, 32–33
Funder's Fifth Law, 388

Gage, Phineas, 155–56, 157
Galen, 167
gender bias, 41–42

generalizability
   of data, 40–44
   of research results, 308–9
generalization, 393
   stimulus, 346
generativity, as Eriksonian stage, 271
genetic basis, for authoritarianism, 136
genetics, behavioral, see behavioral genetics
genital stage, 227–29
genocide, 326
Gestalt, 340
Geworfenheit, 290
GIGO (garbage in, garbage out), 88
Gleitman, Henry, 319
goals
   performance and learning, 405–6
   in social intelligence theory, 403–4
golden mean, of Freud, 221, 228
gratification, delay of, 31–32, 118, 121–25, 398
Gray, Jeffrey, 163–66, 166, 167, 176–77
guilt
   in Erikson's theory, 270
   Freudian explanation of, 234, 241

habit hierarchy, 364
habituation, 343–44
   and classical conditioning, 349
Hamlet, on reaction formation, 246
health, physical, and classical conditioning, 346–47
health locus of control, 372–73
hedonism, 341–42
Heidegger, Martin, 289
heritabilities, 180–87
   behaviorists' denial of, 342–43
hierarchy
   in collectivist culture, 324
   of goals, 403
   habit, 364
   of needs (Maslow), 294–95
   in neurobiological explanation, 177
Hilgard, Ernest R., on classification, v, 416
Hippocrates, 167
Hitler, Adolf, 129, 136–37
Hobbes, Thomas, 340
homosexuality
   determinants of (combination approach), 197–200
   and genes, 185–86
   in psychoanalytic approach
      and anxiety, 241
      and phallic stage, 227
      and projection, 246–47
      and reaction formation, 245, 246
hormones, 173–76, 176, 177
   and sexual-orientation explanation, 199
Horney, Karen, 264, 268–69
Hull, Clark, 350, 365
human condition, universal, 331–32
human experience, varieties of, 310–11
humanistic (phenomenological) psychology, 2, 6, 283, 285–89, 293, 411–12
   and Bandura on determinism, 379
   and chronological order of approaches, 413
   current state of, 302–4
   existential optimism (Rogers and Maslow), 294–97
   flow (Csikszentmihalyi), 301–2
   Personal Construct Theory (Kelly), 297–300, 319, 388, 402

humanistic (phenomenological) psychology
  (*continued*)
  vs. scientifically oriented psychology, 335
  and self-knowledge, 213
  see also phenomenological approach
Hume, David, 340
humor, Freudian view of, 254–56
humors, as personality determinants, 167–68
hypothalamus, 173
  lateral, 164
hypotheses, 34

id, 231–32
  and brain, 231
  and psychic conflict, 240–41
I (informant) data, 15–21
ideal-self conceptions, 296
identification, Freud on, 226–27, 233–34
identity, in Erikson's theory, 271
ideographic assessment, 319
idiocentrism, 326–27
incremental theories, 406, 407–8
Indian culture
  as collectivist, 326
  sense of self in, 316–17, 318, 324
individual differences
  measurement of, 60–61
  number of words for, 57, 73–74
  vs. pigeonholing, 6–7
  and trait approach, 59–60
individualistic cultures, 324–26, 419
  and idea of personality, 418
inferiority, in Erikson's theory, 270
inferiority complex, and Adler, 266
infidelity
  men's vs. women's view of, 191
  psychological vs. biological view of, 196
informant (I) data, 15–21
information
  chunks of, 387–88
  withholding of (research), 52n
inheritance of personality, *see* behavioral genetics;
  evolutionary theory
inhibition, as brain function, 160–62, 164–65
inner cities, subculture in, 310
inner psychology, and informant (I) data, 20
insight, and operant conditioning, 349–50
instinct(s)
  reproductive, 192–93
  in reptiles, 152
integrity tests, 94, 95, 137–38, 144
intellectualization, 247–48
intelligence, social, 401–5
internalization, by superego, 240
  see also identification, Freud on
internal locus of control, 104, 372
internal structure, and psychoanalysis, 206
interpersonal behavior or relations
  and cognitive processes, 417
  neo-Freudians' emphasis on, 265–66
interpretation
  Sontag on, v
  of T data, 30–32
intimacy, as Eriksonian stage, 271
intraclass correlation, 180n
introspection
  behaviorist view on, 337
  see also awareness
introverts, 161, 162–63, 165
  Jung on, 268

IQ, expectancy experiment on, 100
IQ tests, 80
irrational behavior
  and psychoanalysis, 204, 210
  and trait approach (Murray), 203–4

jaded people, 344
Jansen, Dan, 253
Japanese, returned from U.S., 323
Japanese culture, as collectivist, 324
jealousy, sexual, 190
  and phallic stage, 227
Johnson, Ben, 175
jokes, in Freudian view, 255–56
Jordan, David Starr, 391
judgment
  informant (I) data as, 15, 16–17
  lens model of, 114
Jung, Carl, 213, 235, 263, 264, 267–68
  on libido, 216n
  method of, 265
"Just Say No" campaign, 125, 356

Kelly, George, 297–300, 305, 383, 388, 396, 397
Kennedy, Rosemary, 157, 157n, 158
Kierkegaard, Søren, 289, 304
Kihlstrom, John, 401–5
King, Rodney, beating of, 358
knowledge
  declarative, 391–93
  procedural, 394–96
Kohler, Heinz, 349
Kramer, Peter, 173

language
  evolution of, 194–95
  and left cerebral hemisphere, 159
latency phase, 225
Law of Effect, 349–50, 351
  and cognitive approach, 382
  and defense mechanisms (Dollard and Miller),
    369–70
law of unintended consequences, 194
lay judgments of personality, 98
  accuracy of, 105–16
  by others, 99–103
  by self, 103–4 (*see also* self-judgments)
L (life) data, 13–14
L-Dopa, 168, 171
learning, 338
  and behavioristic analysis, 338
  types of
    classical conditioning, 344–49
    habituation, 343–44
    observational, 378
    operant conditioning, 349–54
lecturing
  and declarative vs. procedural knowledge, 395
  flow from, 301
  predictions on, 112
left- and right-handedness, 323
lemon juice test, 162
lens model of perception and judgment, 114
libido, 216, 218, 229, 263
  and fixation, 230
  and id, 232
  and neo-Freudians, 265
  and Rogers, 294
Liddy, G. Gordon, 285, 288
life outcomes (L) data, 13–14

life situations, for non-deceptive research, 53–54
life span development, 271
lifestyle, and Adler, 266
limbic system, 153
LIST acronym, 13, 26
Little, Brian, 331
lobotomy, 156–58
Locke, John, 339, 340
locus of control, internal and external, 104,
    372–73
Loevinger, Jane, 233, 266
long-term memory, 391–96
    movement to, 390
Lorenz, Konrad, 188
love, modern psychoanalytic research on, 275–79
Luther, Martin, 325

McClelland, David, 321–22
maladjustment, psychological, Rotter on, 374–76
many-trait approach to understanding behavior,
    119–28
Maslow, Abraham, 294–95
mass media, see media
Masson, Jeffrey, 214n, 264, 264n, 265
mathematics, and girls' self-concept, 104
mating behavior, sex differences in, 188–91, 195
maturity, Freud on, 228
meaning
    change in through classical conditioning, 345
    existentialist lack of, 290
media
    generalizations from, 393
    television violence, 343–44
medical profession, and intellectualization
    defense, 248
medical schools, Freudian psychoanalysts in,
    214n
medical training, 36, 210
memory
    and extreme behavior, 21
    long-term, 390–96
    repression of, 244
    short-term, 387–88, 390
    working, 389–90
mental energy, and psychoanalysis, 206–7
mental health
    assessment of, 96
    Freud on, 228
mentalistic concepts, behaviorist rethinking of,
    361
mental retardation, and heritability, 182
Miller, Neal, 364–70, 415
mind
    behaviorist rethinking of, 360–61
    and brain, 149, 206
    as cognitive model, 384
    in phenomenological approach, 285–86
    psychoanalytic conception of, 206
    structure of (Freud), 231–34
Minnesota Multiphasic Personality Inventory
    (MMPI), 28, 79, 80, 82, 90, 91–92, 157
minority subcultures in inner city, 310, 328
Mischel, Walter, 62–64, 66, 397–401
Mitwelt, 290
MMPI (Minnesota Multiphasic Personality
    Inventory), 28, 79, 80, 82, 90, 91–92,
    157
modeling, 377
moderator variable, 67, 67n, 106–7
modern culture, and psychoanalysis, 211–12

Moniz, Antonio, 157
morality
    and Eriksonian development, 270
    and phallic stage, 227
moral reasoning, collectivist vs. individualist, 325
motivation
    cognitive approach to, 405–8
    in Dollard and Miller theory, 364, 365–66
    and goals, 403
    as reinforcement value, 373
motivational theory, of Hull, 350
motivation variable, 138
Murray, Henry, 84, 143, 203–4, 210, 264, 413
Myers-Briggs Type Indicator (MBTI), 268

names, in Freudian slips, 252
narcissism, 25
natural T data, 26–27
nature-nurture ratio, 184
    see also behavioral genetics
Nazism, 129, 136–37
needs
    hierarchy of (Maslow), 294–95
    Hull on, 350
    testing for, 83–84
negative reinforcement, 369
NEO personality test, 79
neo-Freudians, 6, 264–66, 272
    Adler, 266
    Erikson, 269–71
    in future, 279
    Horney, 268–69
    Jung, 267–68
    see also individual neo-Freudians
neomammalian brain, 153–55, 193, 231
nervous system
    central and peripheral, 169
    difficulties in study of, 149
    and hormone function, 173
neurons, 169
neuroticism
    on Big Five list, 119, 144
    as essential trait, 143
    Eysenck on, 161
    and frontal lobes, 158
    and Gray's system, 165
    as mental energy drain, 207
    as supertrait, 177
neurotic needs, 269
neurotransmitters, 169–73, 177
    and psychoactive drugs, 168
Nietzsche, Friedrich, 289, 293, 304
nonverbal expressions, in inner-city subculture,
    310
norepinephrine, 171

obedience
    and anal stage, 223
    Milgram study on, 52–53, 72
objective tests, 82–83
    combination of methods in construction of, 93
    empirical method in construction of, 89–93
    factor analytic method in construction of,
        86–89, 93
    rational method in construction of, 83–86, 93
objectivity, as psychology goal, 335
observational learning, 378
observer (O) data, 15n
Occam's Razor, 258
occupational choice, sublimation served by, 250

OCEAN (list of traits), 144
Oedipal crisis, 226, 262, 263, 270, 274
Oedipal theory of sex-typing, 259
One Flew over the Cuckoo's Nest, 158, 158n
openness, 119
operant behavior, 351–54
operant conditioning, 349–54
    vs. classical conditioning, 354–55
operational definition, 258
Operation Desert Storm, 310
opportunities, and reputation, 99–100
opportunity costs, 299–300
opposites, doctrine or principle of, 217–18,
    220–21
"optimally adjusted person," 96
optimism
    existential, 294–97
    test for, 85–86
oral stage, 219–22
organ inferiority, 266
Origin of the Species (Darwin), 187
other-directedness, 142
outgroup bias, 313

paleomammalian brain, 152–53, 231
paradigms, 2, 299
parallel distributed processing (PDP), 274, 399
paranoids, test answer of, 90–91
parapraxes, 251–54
    vs. wit, 257
Parkinson's disease, 171
parsimony, 298
    Freudian theory lacking in, 258
Pavlov, Ivan, 344–46, 362
Pearson correlation coefficient, 48n
peer judgments, 110–11
percentages of variance explained, 48–49, 69
perception
    behaviorist rethinking of, 360–61
    individuals' interpretations of, 283
    lens model of, 114
    of personality, 73–74, 419
    and reality, 287
    and sensory/perception buffer, 384–87
    and unconscious processes, 273–74
perceptual defense
    as psychoanalytic mechanism, 273–74
    and sensory-perceptual buffer, 386
permissiveness, as parenting style, 224
perseveration, 157
Persian Gulf war
    and cross-cultural misunderstanding, 310
    intellectualization in, 248
persona, 267
Personal Construct Theory, 297–300, 319, 388
    and schemas, 402
personality, 1–2, 76–77
    Allport definition of, 195
    and behavior, 420
    computer simulation of, 417
    cross-cultural study of, 283–84
    designer, 172
    and having vs. doing, 401
    perceptions of, 73–74, 419
    and situation, 61
    as Western idea, 418
personality assessment, 76–78
    lay judgments, 98 (*see also* lay judgments of
        personality)
    tests, 79–80

as business, 78–79
objections to, 94–95
objective, 82–93
projective, 29, 80–82
purposes of, 93–96
"personality coefficients," 65, 71
personality psychologists, 1
    see also psychologists
personality psychology
    and analysis of friends or family, 208–9
    approaches to, 2–3, 4, 411–14
        choice among, 415–16
        need for awareness of, 415, 416
        and topics, xxv
        (*see also* behaviorism and behavioristic
            approach; biological approach; cross-
            cultural differences; phenomenological
            approach; psychoanalytic approach and
            theory; trait approach)
    and everyday life, xxiv
    future of, 416–19
    goal of, 1–5
    goals for course on, xxiii–xxiv
    and perception of personality, 73–74, 419
    and pigeonholing, 6–7
    as quest for mutual understanding, 420
    research methods in, 9–10 (*see also* research
        methods)
    self as assumption of, 317
    whole person as subject of, 2
    see also psychology
Personality Research Form (PRF), 93
personality system (Mischel), 398–99
personality tests, 26, 28
personality traits, 77
    and behavioral genetics, 179–80
    and classical conditioning, 347, 355
    cross-cultural generality of, 320
    factor analysis on, 89
    and Indians' conceptions, 317
    neurobiological account of, 176–77
    number of words for, 57, 73–74
    and right vs. left brain, 160
    see also trait approach
personal strivings, measurement of, 86
person perceptions, 73–74
person-situation debate, 62–64, 74
    and person perceptions, 73–74
    and predictability, 64–69
    and self-monitoring, 139
    and situationism, 69–73
pessimism, test for, 85–86
phallic stage, 225–27
    Erikson's reinterpretation of, 270
    and Oedipal crisis, 226, 262, 263, 270, 274
phenomenological approach, xxv, 2, 6, 283,
        285–86, 304–5
    and consciousness or conscious experience,
        286, 287, 305, 388
    existentialism, 286, 289–93
    humanistic psychology, 283, 285–89, 293–304
        (*see also* humanistic psychology)
    influence of, 302, 306
phenomenology, 283, 289
    as rationalism, 339
phobias, 348
    and efficacy expectations, 377
"physics envy," 34, 285, 303
pigeonholing, 6–7
pleasure principle, 232

Pledge of Allegiance, and reptilian brain, 155
political humor, 255
political orientation
    and authoritarianism, 129, 136–37
    and Q-sort, 128
politico-economic conservatism (PEC) scale,
    130
pornography
    and doctrine of opposites, 217
    and reaction formation, 245–46
Positron Emission Tomography (PET), 155
power, punishment as lesson on, 359
praise, 355
preconscious, 236–37, 383, 389
predictability, and person-situation debate, 64–69
prediction, as personality-assessment criterion,
    77
primary process thinking, 232, 234–36
    and displacement, 249
principle or doctrine of opposites, 217–18,
    220–21
procedural knowledge, 394–96
process vs. content in psychology, 330–31
projection, 246–47
projective tests, 29, 80–82
prostitute, city prosecutor's soliciting of, 203,
    205–6, 207, 217
Prozac, 168, 170, 172
pseudoconservatism, 131, 131n, 135, 136
psychic conflict, see conflict, psychic
psychic determinism, 205–6
psychic energy, 216, 218
    libido, 216, 217, 218
    and repression, 244
    Thanatos, 217–18
    vagueness of, 258
psychoanalysis, 204
    and clinical psychology, 209–10, 211
    future of, 272
    hostility toward insights of, 208–9
    and modern culture, 211–12
        and literary analysis, 214–15
psychoanalytic approach and theory, xxv, 2, 7n,
    204, 205, 257, 260, 411
    as beautiful theory, 210–11, 257, 260
    and chronological order of approaches, 413
    and consciousness, 236–37, 388
    defenses and slips in, 240–50
    and developmental stages, 218–19, 229–31
        anal, 222–25
        genital, 227–29
        oral stage, 219–22
        phallic, 225–27, 270, 274
    and internal structure, 206
    and mental energy, 206–7
    and modern cognitive research, 383
    modern psychoanalytic research, 272–79
    and modern reactions to Freud, 261–64
    and neo-Freudians, 264–66 (see also neo-
        Freudians)
    and parapraxes (slips), 251–54, 257
    vs. phenomenological approach, 287
    and primary and secondary process thinking,
        234–36
    and psychic conflict, 207
    and psychic determinism, 205–6
    and psychic energy, 216, 218
        libido, 216 (see also libido)
        Thanatos, 217–18
    and psychology departments, 214

    and self-knowledge, 213
    shortcomings of, 257–59, 416
    and structure of mind, 231
        ego, 231, 232–33, 240–41
        id, 231–32, 240–41
        superego, 231, 233–34, 240–41
    and therapy, 211, 213, 237–38
    unique aspects of, 207–11
    and wit, 254–57
    see also Freud, Sigmund
psychological differences, number of words for,
    57, 73–74
psychological research, see at research
psychological situation, 373–74
psychologists
    intellectualization as occupational hazard of,
        248
    and psychology as science, 335
psychology, 1
    biology as replacing, 195–96
    and consciousness, 305
    cross-cultural, 320, 418–19 (see also cross-
        cultural differences)
    as cumulative, 413
    in future, 418–19
    "hard" vs. "soft," 35n
    self-consciousness over method in, 34–35
    unifying perspective lacking in, 414–15
    see also personality psychology
psychopathic personalities, test answer of, 90–91
psychopharmacology, cosmetic, 172
psychosurgery, 155–59
psychotherapy
    and Bandura's theory, 377
    and behavior patterns, 109
    humanistic, 296–97
    psychoanalytic, 211, 213, 237–38
    psychosurgery as, 156–59
    Rotterian, 376
psychoticism, 143, 161–62, 165, 166
punishment, 355–60
    actual vs. believed, 371–72
    in operant conditioning, 351
puzzle box, 349

Q-sort, 119–21
    and delay of gratification, 121–25, 126–27
    and depression, 128
    and drug abuse, 125, 128
    and political orientation, 128
questions
    Erdman on, v
    Freud's raising of, 279
    and personality-psychology approaches, xxv, 3,
        412, 416

racial differences, and ethics of research, 51
random influences, 38
rational control, as Freudian aim, 213, 237, 268
rationalism, 339
rationalization, 247
rational method, of test construction, 83–86, 93
reaction formation, 245–46
reality principle, 232
reciprocal determinism, 379–80
reductionism
    biological, 149, 196
    as research strategy, 341
regression, 230–31
rehearsal, 390

reinforcement
  in classical conditioning, 346, 364
  in Dollard-Miller theory, 365
  and expectancies, 372, 377
  negative, 369
  in operant conditioning, 351 (see also Law of
    Effect)
reinforcement value, 373
relative constructs, 108
relativism, 329
  dangers of, 330
  of phenomenological view, 289
reliability, of data, 36–39
representative design, 43–44
repression, 243–45
  as negative reinforcement, 369
  research on, 274
  and self-judgments, 24
reproduction, and genital stage, 228
reproductive instinct, 192–93
Rep Test, 297, 299
reptilian brain, 151–52, 231
reputation
  effects of, 99
  peer judgments, 110–11
research, on personality
  cross-cultural, 311–14
  gender bias in, 41–42
  improvement advocated in, 66–68
  modern psychoanalytic, 272–79
  and psychoanalytic approach, 209
  in trait approach, 59
research funding, in psychology, 23–24
research methods, 9–10
  correlational and experimental designs, 44–46
  and data, 11–13
    informant (I data), 15–21
    life outcomes (L data), 13–14
    self-judgments (S data), 21–25, 103–4 (see
      also self-judgments)
    test (T) data, 25 32, 64, 80, 81
  and effect sizes, 46–51
  ethics of, 51–54
  method emphasized, 34–35
  and quality of data, 36–44
  and scientific education, 35–36
research psychologists
  Freud and psychoanalysis shunned by, 215, 272
  and objective science, 335
respondent conditioning, 351
responses
  conditioned, 345
  generalizability across, 44
  unconditioned, 345
reward
  actual vs. believed, 371–72
  and attitude change, 72
  vs. punishment, 355–56, 357, 360
Richards, Ann, 318, 318n
right- and left-handedness, 323
rigorous humanism, 303
Rodgers Condensed CPI-MMPI Test, 92
Rogers, Carl, 294, 295–97, 304
Role Construct Repertory Test (Rep Test), 297,
  299
role models, and Oedipal story, 262
roles, situations at odds with, 19–20
romantic love, modern psychoanalytic research
  on, 275–79
Rorschach, Hermann, 80

Rorschach ink blot test, 29, 80–81
rote repetition technique, 390
Rotter, Julian, 370–76, 382, 383
Rychlak, Joseph, 302–4

Sartre, Jean-Paul, 289, 291, 293, 302, 304, 331
schemas, 388, 402–3
Schindler's List, 329–30
schizophrenics
  and lobotomies, 158
  and MMPI question, 28–29
school, see education
science
  and consciousness, 305
  and criticism of Freudian theory, 207–8
  as search, 35
scientific education, vs. technical training, 35–36
scientific understanding, trait approach for
    118–19
  essential-trait approach, 143–46
  many-trait approach, 119–28
  single-trait approach, 129–43
scripts, 392, 393
S data, see self-judgments
secondary process thinking, 234–36
second-order conditioning, 346
secure children, 276
self, 103
  as cultural artifact, 317–19
  and efficacy expectation, 377
  Indian sense of, 316–17, 318, 324
  transparent, 110
  Western notion of, 316
self-actualization, 294
self-concept, 103, 104
self-control, and anal stage, 223
self-esteem
  importance of, 103
  and testing, 95
self-fulfilling prophecies, 100–101, 102, 376
self-judgments (S data), 21–25, 103–4
  accuracy of, 107–9
  and behavioral genetics, 179n
  of entity/incremental theorists, 406–7
  in personality tests, 80
    faking of, 91
    objective tests, 84
  and T data, 28, 29
self-knowledge, in psychoanalytic and humanistic
    approach, 213
self-monitoring, 138–43, 144–45, 401
self-regulatory systems and plans, 398
self-schema, 392, 402
self system, Bandura on, 379–80, 398
Sellers, Peter, 254
semiotic subject, 316
sensory/perceptual buffer, 384–87
septo-hippocampus, 164
serotonin, 168, 170, 171–73, 176
sex differences
  in delay of gratification, 121–24, 126–27
  and ethics of research, 51
  in mating behavior, 188–91, 195
  see also women
sexism, in psychoanalytic theory, 259
  of Freud, 229n
sexist jokes, 256
sexual abuse
  effects of, 96
  Freud's view of, 214, 214n

sexual arousal, Dollard and Miller on, 365–66
sexuality
    and amygdala, 159
    in Freud's theory, 207, 265, 279
        and genital stage, 228
        and libido, 216 (see also libido)
        and phallic stage, 225–26, 227
    and mating behavior, 188–91, 195
    and neo-Freudians, 265
    and steroids, 175
    and testosterone, 174, 175
sexual orientation
    determinants of (integrative approach),
        197–200
    see also homosexuality
shaping of behaviors, 352–53
Shoda, Yuichi, 398
short-term memory, 387–88
    and movement to long-term memory, 390
Shweder, Richard, 316, 320
shyness, 99
    and self-schema, 402
sibling rivalry, 246
significance, of data result, 46–47
Singapore, U.S. teenager punished in, 309–10,
    323
single-parent family, and phallic stage, 226n
single-trait approach to understanding of
    behavior, 129
    and authoritarianism, 129–37, 144
    and conscientiousness, 137–38
    and self-monitoring, 138–43
situation, influence of, 61–64, 74
    and person perceptions, 73–74
    and predictability, 64–69
    and self-monitoring, 139
    and situationism, 69–73
Sixteen Personality Factor Questionnaire (16PF),
    79
Skinner, B. F., 6, 286, 337, 342, 351–54, 362
Skinner box, 351, 363, 364
slips, Freudian, 236, 237, 251, 252–54
Snyder, Mark, 138–39
social-cognitive theory, 279
social constructions, 105
social intelligence, 401–5
social interest, and Adler, 266
social issues
    and personality assessments, 96
    and uses of research, 51–52
    see also political orientation
sociality corollary, 298
social learning approach, 2–3, 412
    and cognitive approaches, 3n, 335–36, 382
social learning theory, 6
    of Bandura, 376–80
    and behaviorism, 3n, 336, 363
    cognitive, 396–401
    of Dollard and Miller, 363–70, 415
    of Rotter, 370–76
social psychology, xxv
    and perception of personality, 419
    and situationism, 70–71
sociobiology, 187–95
sociosexuality, judgment of, 111
Sontag, Susan, on interpretation, v
Spearman-Brown formula, 38
sports
    accidents in, 253
    coaches in, 253–54, 395

stages of psychological development
    Eriksonian, 269–71
    Freudian, 219–31
    see also developmental psychology
Stalin, Joseph, 136
statistics
    Binomial Effect Size Display, 49–51, 69
    correlation coefficient, 47–49, 65, 71
    heritability coefficient, 181
    percentages of variance explained, 48–49,
        69
stereotypes, 393
steroids, anabolic, 175
stimuli
    conditioned, 345
    generalizability across, 44
    unconditioned, 345
stimulus generalization, 346
strange situation experiments, 276
strategies, in social intelligence theory, 404–5
stress, and Freudian stages, 229
strivings, measurement of, 86
Strong Vocational Interest Blank (SVIB), 79, 90,
    91
students, college, see college students
studying, as thinking vs. rote, 390
subjective representations, 76–77
subjects, generalizability over, 40–43
sublimation, 250
    and aggression, 367
    wit as, 254
Sullivan, Harry Stack, 264
superego, 233–34
    and brain, 231
    and psychic conflict, 240–41
superstitious behaviors, 351–52
supertraits, 177
SVIB (Strong Vocational Interest Blank), 79, 90,
    91
symbols
    Freudian grammar of, 235
    and Jungian archetypes, 267
systematic desensitization, 348

tabula rasa, 339, 342
tachistoscope experiments, 385, 386
Tahiti, ecology and personality in, 328
talking cure, 213
Talmud, on perception, 287
Target Stores, 92
TAT (Thematic Apperception Test), 29, 81–82,
    143
T data, see test data
teaching
    expectancy in, 100
    see also education, lecturing
technical training, vs. scientific education, 35–36
teleological analysis, 303
teleological fallacy, 194–95
temperaments, 197, 400
"terrible twos," 223
test(s), personality, 79–80
    business of, 78–79
    objections to, 94–95
    objective, 82–93
    projective, 29, 80–82
    purpose of, 93–96
testability, and Freudian theory, 259
test (T) data, 25–32
    in Mischel's analysis, 64

test (T) data *(continued)*
  from personality tests, 28–29, 80
    projective tests, 81
testosterone, 168, 173–75, 177
Thanatos, 217–18
therapy, *see* psychotherapy
thinking
  behaviorist rethinking of, 360–61
  and chunks, 388
  courses on, 394
  in ego, 233
  Jung's classification of, 268
  and long-term memory, 390
  primary process, 234–36
  secondary process, 234
Thorndike, Edward, 349–50, 362
thrown-ness, 290
tightness, as cultural trait, 322–23, 326–27
toilet jokes, 255
toilet training, and anal stage, 223
Tomlin, Lily, 285n
tough cultures, 321
trait approach, xxv, 2, 7n, 57, 59–60, 411, 416
  and chronological order of approaches, 413
  and cognitive approach, 399–401, 408
  and cross-cultural issues, 315
  individual differences as focus of, 59–60, 180
  irregular behavior ignored by (Murray), 203–6
  measurement of individual differences in,
    60–61
  and personality assessment, 76–96
    lay judgments, 98–116 (*see also* self-
      judgments)
  vs. phenomenological approach, 287
  and scientific understanding, 118–19
    essential-trait approach, 143–46
    many-trait approach, 119–28
    single-trait approach, 129–43
  self-knowledge avoided in, 214
  and situation, 61–64, 74
    and person perception, 73–74
    and predictability, 64–69
    and situationism, 69–73
  see also personality traits
transference, 237–38, 274
transparent self, 110
Triandis, Harry, 309, 320–21, 419
Truk island, ecology and personality in, 328
truthfulness, in research, 52
t-test, 48n
twin studies, 180
Type A personality, 80
Type C personality, 80

Umwelt, 289–90
unconditional positive regard, 295
unconditioned response (UCR), 345
unconditioned stimulus (UCS), 345

unconscious processes, 206, 206n, 236–37
  behaviorist approach neglects, 3
  and cognitive psychology, 279, 383
  cognitive unconscious, 264
  collective (Jung), 267
  and perception, 273–74
  research on, 273–74
  symbolic grammar of, 235
  trait approach's neglect of, 204, 413
unexamined life, bad faith as, 291–92
unintended consequences
  law of, 194
  of punishment, 356–57
universality of human condition, 331–32
unpredictability, in conditioning, 347
untestability, of Freud's theory, 259
utilitarianism, 342–43

validity
  and accuracy of personality judgment, 106, 116
  of data, 39–40
  of personality tests or judgments, 77
values
  collectivist vs. individualist, 325
  vs. culture, 329–30
vocational guidance, and Myers-Briggs Type
    Indicator, 268
vocational interest tests, 94
  Strong Vocational Interest Blank, 79, 90, 91
Vonnegut, Kurt, Jr., 3–4, 292

Walden II (Skinner), 342
war, intellectualization in, 248
Watson, John, 6, 337, 342
Weinberger, Dan, 264
Westen, Drew, 264, 273
Whole Earth Catalog, aphorism from, 22–23
wit, Freudian view of, 254–57
women
  careers plus families for, 228–29
  as collectivist, 324
  and Freud, 228–29, 229n, 259, 269
  and gender bias, 41–42
  genital mutilation of, 329
  Horney on, 269
  and mathematics, 104
  and testosterone, 174–75
  see also sex differences
Woodward, Bob, 218
Woodworth Personality Data Sheet (WPDS),
    84–85
workaholics, 229
working memory, 389–90

Yankelovich, Daniel, on measurement, v
Yuppies, 271

Zuckerman, Marvin, 166–67, 176–77